DATE DUE

			PRINTED IN U.S.A.

Children's Literature Review

Guide to Gale Literary Criticism Series

For criticism on	Consult these Gale series
Authors now living or who died after December 31, 1959	*CONTEMPORARY LITERARY CRITICISM (CLC)*
Authors who died between 1900 and 1959	*TWENTIETH-CENTURY LITERARY CRITICISM (TCLC)*
Authors who died between 1800 and 1899	*NINETEENTH-CENTURY LITERATURE CRITICISM (NCLC)*
Authors who died between 1400 and 1799	*LITERATURE CRITICISM FROM 1400 TO 1800 (LC)* *SHAKESPEAREAN CRITICISM (SC)*
Authors who died before 1400	*CLASSICAL AND MEDIEVAL LITERATURE CRITICISM (CMLC)*
Authors of books for children and young adults	*CHILDREN'S LITERATURE REVIEW (CLR)*
Black writers of the past two hundred years	*BLACK LITERATURE CRITICISM (BLC)*
Short story writers	*SHORT STORY CRITICISM (SSC)*
Poets	*POETRY CRITICISM (PC)*
Dramatists	*DRAMA CRITICISM (DC)*
Major authors from the Renaissance to the present	*WORLD LITERATURE CRITICISM, 1500 TO THE PRESENT (WLC)*

For criticism on visual artists since 1850, see
MODERN ARTS CRITICISM (MAC)

volume 32

Children's Literature Review

Excerpts from Reviews,
Criticism, and Commentary
on Books for Children
and Young People

Gerard J. Senick
Editor

Sharon R. Gunton
Alan Hedblad
Associate Editors

 **Gale Research Inc.** • *DETROIT* • *WASHINGTON, D.C.* • *LONDON*

STAFF

Gerard J. Senick, *Editor*

Sharon R. Gunton, Alan Hedblad, *Associate Editors*

Kathryn Horste, Michael Magoulias, Anna J. Sheets, Brian J. St. Germain, *Assistant Editors*

Jeanne A. Gough, *Permissions & Production Manager*
Linda M. Pugliese, *Production Supervisor*
Donna Craft, Paul Lewon, Maureen Puhl, Camille P. Robinson, Sheila Walencewicz, *Editorial Associates*
Jill Johnson, Elizabeth Anne Valliere, *Editorial Assistants*

Sandra C. Davis, *Permissions Supervisor (Text)*
Maria L. Franklin, Josephine M. Keene, Michele M. Lonoconus, Shalice Shah, Kimberly F. Smilay,
Permissions Associates
Jennifer A. Arnold, Brandy C. Merritt, *Permissions Assistants*

Margaret A. Chamberlain, *Permissions Supervisor (Pictures)*
Pamela A. Hayes, Keith Reed, *Permissions Associates*
Susan Brohman, Arlene Johnson, Barbara A. Wallace, *Permissions Assistants*

Victoria B. Cariappa, *Research Manager*
Maureen Richards, *Research Supervisor*
Robert S. Lazich, Mary Beth McElmeel, Donna Melnychenko, Tamara C. Nott, *Editorial Associates*
Karen Farrelly, Kelly Hill, Julie Leonard, Stefanie Scarlett, *Editorial Assistants*

Mary Beth Trimper, *Production Director*
Catherine Kemp, *Production Assistant*

Cynthia Baldwin, *Art Director*
Barbara J. Yarrow, *Graphic Services Supervisor*
C. J. Jonik, *Desktop Publisher*
Willie Mathis, *Camera Operator*

Library of Congress Catalog Card Number 86-645085
ISBN 0-8103-8471-X
ISSN 0362-4145

Printed in the United States of America
Published simultaneously in the United Kingdom
by Gale Research International Limited
(An affiliated company of Gale Research Inc.)
10 9 8 7 6 5 4 3 2 1

The trademark **ITP** is used under license.

Contents

Preface   vii

Acknowledgments   xi

Preface

L iterature for children and young adults has evolved into both a respected branch of creative writing and a successful industry. Currently, books for young readers are considered the most popular segment of publishing, while criticism of juvenile literature is instrumental in recording the literary or artistic development of the creators of children's books as well as the trends and controversies that result from changing values or attitudes about young people and their literature. Designed to provide a permanent, accessible record of this ongoing scholarship, *Children's Literature Review (CLR)* presents parents, teachers, and librarians—those responsible for bringing together children and books—with the opportunity to make informed choices when selecting reading materials for the young. In addition, *CLR* provides researchers of children's literature with easy access to a wide variety of critical information from English-language sources in the field. Users will find balanced overviews of the careers of the authors and illustrators of the books that children and young adults are reading; these entries, which contain excerpts from published criticism in books and periodicals, assist users by sparking ideas for papers and assignments and suggesting supplementary and classroom reading. Ann L. Kalkhoff, president and editor of *Children's Book Review Service Inc.,* writes that "*CLR* has filled a gap in the field of children's books, and it is one series that will never lose its validity or importance."

Scope of the Series

Each volume of *CLR* profiles the careers of a selection of authors and illustrators of books for children and young adults from preschool through high school. Author lists in each volume reflect these elements:

- an international scope.

- representation of authors of all eras.

- the variety of genres covered by children's and/or YA literature: picture books, fiction, nonfiction, poetry, folklore, and drama.

Although earlier volumes of *CLR* emphasized critical material published after 1960, successive volumes have expanded their coverage to encompass important criticism written before 1960. Since many of the authors included in *CLR* are living and continue to write, their entries are updated periodically. Future volumes will supplement the entries of selected authors covered in earlier volumes and will include criticism on the works of authors new to the series.

Organization of This Book

An author section consists of the following elements: author heading, author portrait, author introduction, excerpts of criticism (each followed by a bibliographical citation), and illustrations, when available.

- The **Author Heading** consists of the author's name followed by birth and death dates. The portion of the name outside the parentheses denotes the form under which the author is most frequently published. If the majority of the author's works for children were written under a pseudonym, the pseudonym will be listed in the author heading and the real name given on the first line of the author introduction. Also located at the beginning of the introduction are any other pseudonyms used by the author in writing for children and any name variations, including transliterated forms for authors whose languages use nonroman alphabets. Uncertainty as to a birth or death date is indicated by question marks.

- An **Author Portrait** is included when available.

- The **Author Introduction** contains information designed to introduce an author to *CLR* users by presenting an overview of the author's themes and styles, biographical facts that relate to the author's literary career or critical responses to the author's works, and information about major awards and prizes the author has received. The introduction begins by identifying the nationality of the author and by listing the genres in which s/he has written for chidren and young adults. Introductions also list a group of representative titles for which the author or illustrator being profiled is best known; this section, which begins with the words "major works include," follows the genre line of the introduction. The centered heading "Introduction" follows the major works section and announces the body of the text. Where applicable, introductions conclude with references to additional entries in biographical and critical reference series published by Gale Research Inc. These sources include past volumes of *CLR* as well as *Authors & Artists for Young Adults, Classical and Medieval Literature Criticism, Contemporary Authors, Contemporary Authors Autobiography Series, Contemporary Authors Bibliographical Series, Contemporary Literary Criticism, Dictionary of Literary Biography, Drama Criticism, Nineteenth-Century Literature Criticism, Poetry Criticism, Short Story Criticism, Something about the Author, Something about the Author Autobiography Series, Twentieth-Century Literary Criticism,* and *Yesterday's Authors of Books for Children.*

- **Criticism** is located in three sections: **Author's Commentary** (when available), **General Commentary** (when available), and **Title Commentary** (in which commentary on specific titles appears). Centered headings introduce each section, in which criticism is arranged chronologically. Titles by authors being profiled are highlighted in boldface type within the text for easier access by readers.

- The **Author's Commentary** presents background material written by the author or by an interviewer. This commentary may cover a specific work or several works. Author's commentary on more than one work appears after the author introduction, while commentary on an individual book follows the title entry heading.

- The **General Commentary** consists of critical excerpts that consider more than one work by the author or illustrator being profiled. General commentary is preceded by the critic's name in boldface type or, in the case of unsigned criticism, by the title of the journal. *CLR* also features entries that emphasize general criticism on the oeuvre of an author or illustrator. When appropriate, a selection of reviews is included to supplement the general commentary.

- The **Title Commentary** begins with the title entry headings, which precede the criticism on a title and cite publication information on the work being reviewed. Title headings list the title of the work as it appeared in its first English-language edition. The first English-language publication date of each work is listed in parentheses following the title. Differing U. S. and British titles follow the publication date within the parentheses.

Entries in each title commentary section consist of critical excerpts on the author's individual works, arranged chronologically by publication date. The entries generally contain two to six reviews per title, depending on the stature of the book and the amount of criticism it has generated. The editors select titles that reflect the entire scope of the author's literary contribution, covering each genre and subject. An effort is made to reprint criticism that represents the full range of each title's reception, from the year of its initial publication to current assessments. Thus, the reader is provided with a record of the author's critical history. Publication information (such as publisher names and book prices) and parenthetical numerical references (such as footnotes or page and line references to specific editions of works) have been deleted at the editor's discretion to provide smoother reading of the text.

- Selected excerpts are preceded by **Explanatory Notes,** which provide information on the critic or work of criticism to enhance the reader's understanding of the excerpt.

- A complete **Bibliographical Citation** designed to facilitate the location of the original book or article follows each piece of criticism.

- Numerous **Illustrations** are featured in *CLR*. For entries on illustrators, an effort has been made to include illustrations that reflect the characteristics discussed in the criticism. Entries on authors who do not illustrate their own works may also include photographs and other illustrative material pertinent to their careers.

Special Features

Entries on authors who are also illustrators will occasionally feature commentary on selected works illustrated but not written by the author being profiled. These works are strongly associated with the illustrator and have received critical acclaim for their art. By including critical comment on works of this type, the editors wish to provide a more complete representation of the author's total career. Criticism on these works has been chosen to stress artistic, rather than literary, contributions. Title entry headings for works illustrated by the author being profiled are arranged chronologically within the entry by date of publication and include notes identifying the author of the illustrated work. In order to provide easier access for users, all titles illustrated by the subject of the entry are boldfaced.

CLR also includes entries on prominent illustrators who have contributed to the field of children's literature. These entries are designed to represent the development of the illustrator as an artist rather than as a literary stylist. The illustrator's section is organized like that of an author, with two exceptions: the introduction presents an overview of the illustrator's styles and techniques rather than outlining his or her literary background, and the commentary written by the illustrator on his or her works is called "illustrator's commentary" rather than "author's commentary." Title entry headings are followed by explanatory notes identifying the author of the illustrated work. All titles of books containing illustrations by the artist being profiled as well as individual illustrations from these books are highlighted in boldface type.

Other Features

- The **Acknowledgments,** which immediately follow the preface, list the sources from which material has been reprinted in the volume. It does not, however, list every book or periodical consulted for the volume.

- The **Cumulative Index to Authors** lists all of the authors who have appeared in *CLR* with cross-references to the various literary criticism series and the biographical and autobiographical series published by Gale Research Inc. A full listing of the series titles appears before the first page of the indexes of this volume.

- The **Cumulative Nationality Index** lists authors alphabetically under their respective nationalities. Author names are followed by the volume number(s) in which they appear. Authors who have changed citizenship or whose current citizenship is not reflected in biographical sources appear under both their original nationality and that of their current residence.

- The **Cumulative Title Index** lists titles covered in *CLR* followed by the volume and page number where criticism begins.

A Note to the Reader

CLR is one of several critical references sources in the Literature Criticism Series published by Gale Research Inc. When writing papers, students who quote directly from any volume in the Literature Criticism Series may use the following general forms to footnote reprinted criticism. The first example pertains to material drawn from periodicals, the second to material reprinted from books.

[1]T. S. Eliot, "John Donne," *The Nation and the Athenaeum,* 33 (9 June 1923), 321-32; excerpted and reprinted in *Literature Criticism from 1400 to 1800,* Vol. 10, ed. James E. Person, Jr. (Detroit: Gale Research, 1989), pp. 28-9.

[1]Henry Brooke, *Leslie Brooke and Johnny Crow* (Frederick Warne, 1982); excerpted and reprinted in *Children's Literature Review,* Vol. 20, ed. Gerard J. Senick (Detroit: Gale Research, 1990), p. 47.

Suggestions Are Welcome

In response to various suggestions, several features have been added to *CLR* since the beginning of the series, including author entries on retellers of traditional literature as well as those who have been the first to record oral tales and other folklore; entries on prominent illustrators featuring commentary on their styles and techniques; entries on authors whose works are considered controversial; occasional entries devoted to criticism on a single work or a series of works; sections in author introductions that list major works by the author or illustrator being profiled; explanatory notes that provide information on the critic or work of criticism to enhance the usefulness of the excerpt; more extensive illustrative material, such as holographs of manuscript pages and photographs of people and places pertinent to the authors' careers; a cumulative nationality index for easy access to authors by nationality; and occasional guest essays written specifically for *CLR* by prominent critics on subjects of their choice.

Readers who wish to suggest authors to appear in future volumes, or who have other suggestions, are cordially invited to write the editor.

Acknowledgments

The editors wish to thank the copyright holders of the excerpted criticism included in this volume, the permissions managers of many book and magazine publishing companies for assisting us in securing reprint rights, and Anthony Bogucki for assistance with copyright research. We are also grateful to the staffs of the Detroit Public Library, the Library of Congress, the University of Detroit Library, Wayne State University Purdy/Kresge Library Complex, and the University of Michigan Libraries for making their resources available to us. Following is a list of the copyright holders who have granted us permission to reprint material in this volume of *CLR*. Every effort has been made to trace copyright, but if omissions have been made, please let us know.

COPYRIGHTED EXCERPTS IN *CLR*, VOLUME 32, WERE REPRINTED FROM THE FOLLOWING PERIODICALS:

The ALAN Review, v. 10, Fall, 1982. Reprinted by permission of the publisher.—*American Reference Books Annual 1982,* v. 13, 1982. Copyright © 1982 Libraries Unlimited, Inc. All rights reserved. Reprinted by permission of the publisher.—*Appraisal: Children's Science Books,* v. 3, Winter, 1970; v. 4, Winter, 1971; v. 5, Fall, 1972; v. 6, Winter, 1973; v. 7, Winter, 1974; v. 8, Winter, 1975; v. 9, Winter, 1976; v. 10, Spring, 1977; v. 12, Winter, 1979; v. 14, Fall, 1981; v. 15, Spring-Summer, 1982; v. 16, Spring, 1983; v. 17, Winter, 1984; v. 17, Spring-Summer, 1984; v. 18, Spring, 1985; v. 19, Spring, 1986; v. 19, Summer, 1986; v. 19, Fall, 1986; v. 20, Spring, 1987; v. 22, Summer, 1989; v. 22, Winter-Spring, 1989; v. 23, Winter, 1990; v. 23, Summer, 1990; v. 23, Autumn, 1990; v. 25, Winter, 1992. Copyright © 1970, 1971, 1972, 1973, 1974, 1975, 1976, 1977, 1979, 1981, 1982, 1983, 1984, 1985, 1986, 1987, 1989, 1990, 1992 by the Children's Science Book Review Committee. All reprinted by permission of the publisher.—*The Atlantic Monthly,* v. 265, January, 1990 for "Grey Owl" by Kenneth Brower. Copyright 1990 by The Atlantic Monthly Company, Boston, MA. Reprinted by permission of the author.—*Best Sellers,* v. 36, June, 1976; v. 38, March, 1979; v. 42, June, 1982; v. 44, June, 1984. Copyright © 1976, 1979, 1982, 1984 Helen Dwight Reid Educational Foundation. All reprinted by permission of the publisher.—*Booklist,* v. 73, December 15, 1976; v. 73, May 15, 1977; v. 74, September 1, 1977; v. 74, May 15, 1978; v. 75, October 15, 1978; v. 76, May 1, 1980; v. 79, March 15, 1983; v. 79, June 1, 1983; v. 81, September 1, 1984; v. 82, November 1, 1985; v. 83, December 15, 1986; v. 83, April 1, 1987; v. 83, July, 1987; v. 84, October 15, 1987; v. 84, February 1, 1988; v. 85, October 1, 1988; v. 85, February 1, 1989; v. 85, April 15, 1989; v. 86, November 15, 1989; v. 87, September 1, 1990; v. 87, October 1, 1990; v. 87, January 1, 1991; v. 88, September 15, 1991; v. 88, October 15, 1991; v. 88, June 1, 1992. Copyright © 1976, 1977, 1978, 1980, 1983, 1984, 1985, 1986, 1987, 1988, 1989, 1990, 1991, 1992 by the American Library Association. All reprinted by permission of the publisher.—*The Booklist,* v. 66, June 15, 1970; v. 72, February 15, 1976; v. 72, April 1, 1976. Copyright © 1970, 1976 by the American Library Association. All reprinted by permission of the publisher.—*The Book Report,* v. 2, November-December, 1983. © copyright 1983 by Linworth Publishing Co. Reprinted by permission of the publisher.—*Books and Bookmen,* n. 339, December, 1983 for "Travelling Artist" by Carolyn Hart. © copyright the author 1983. Reprinted by permission of the author.—*Books for Keeps,* n. 38, May, 1986; n. 40, September, 1986; n. 55, March, 1989; n. 62, May, 1990; n. 65, November, 1990; n. 77, November, 1992. © School Bookshop Association 1986, 1989, 1990, 1992. All reprinted by permission of the publisher.—*Books for Your Children,* v. 10, May, 1975; v. 14, Winter, 1978; v. 20, Spring, 1985; v. 23, Summer, 1988. © *Books for Your Children* 1975, 1978, 1985, 1988. All reprinted by permission of the publisher.—*Book World—The Washington Post,* September 11, 1988. © 1988, *The Washington Post.* Reprinted with permission of the publisher.—*British Book News,* Children's Supplement, Autumn, 1981. © *British Book News,* 1981. Courtesy of British Book News.—*Bulletin of the Center for Children's Books,* v. 21, November, 1967; v. 25, July-August, 1972; v. 27, February, 1974; v. 27, April, 1974; v. 28, November, 1974; v. 28, February, 1975; v. 29, July-August, 1976; v. 31, June, 1978; v. 32, October, 1978; v. 32, March, 1979; v. 34, May, 1981; v. 35, September, 1981; v. 36, May, 1983; v. 36, July-August, 1983; v. 37, May, 1984; v. 39, May, 1986; v. 42, September, 1988;

Company. Reprinted by permission of the publisher.

COPYRIGHTED EXCERPTS IN *CLR*, VOLUME 32, WERE REPRINTED FROM THE FOLLOWING BOOKS:

PERMISSION TO REPRODUCE ILLUSTRATIONS APPEARING IN *CLR*, VOLUME 32, WAS RECEIVED FROM THE FOLLOWING SOURCES:

Wilhelm Grimm. Newly translated by Brian Alderson. Copyright ©1978 by Brian Alderson. Illustrations copyright ©1978 by Michael Foreman. Reprinted by permission of Doubleday, a division of Bantam Doubleday Dell Publishing Group, Inc./ Illustration by Michael Foreman from *Sleeping Beauty & Other Favourite Fairy Tales*, chosen and translated by Angela Carter. Illustrations copyright ©1982 by Michael Foreman. Reprinted by permission of Schocken Books, Inc./ Illustrations by Michael Foreman from *Long Neck and Thunder Foot*, by Helen Piers. Illustrations copyright ©1982 by Michael Foreman. Reprinted by permission of Penguin Books Ltd./ Illustrations by Michael Foreman from his *Michael Foreman's World of Fairy Tales*. Illustrations copyright ©1990 by Michael Foreman. Reprinted by permission of Pavilion Books./ Illustration by Grey Owl from his *Pilgrims of the Wild*. Copyright © 1971 by Canada Permanent Trust Company. Copyright 1935 Charles Scribner's Sons; copyright renewed ©1963 Canada Permanent Toronto General Trust Company. Reprinted in the United States with the permission of Charles Scribner's Sons, an imprint of Macmillan Publishing Company./ Illustration by Grey Owl from his *Sajo and the Beaver People*. Charles Scribner's Sons, 1941. Copyright ©1936 by Grey Owl./ Illustrations by Maira Kalman from her *Hey Willy, See The Pyramids*. Copyright ©1988 by Maira Kalman. Used by permission of Viking Penguin, a division of Penguin Books USA Inc./ Illustrations by Maira Kalman from her *Sayonara, Mrs. Kackleman*. Copyright ©1989 by Maira Kalman. Used by permission of Viking Penguin, a division of Penguin Books USA Inc.

PERMISSION TO REPRODUCE PHOTOGRAPHS APPEARING IN *CLR*, VOLUME 32, WAS RECEIVED FROM THE FOLLOWING SOURCES:

Courtesy of Melvin Berger: **pp. 1, 40**; © by Carol Kitman 1993: **pp. 64, 71, 74**; Photograph by Alton E. Bowers: **p. 65**; Photograph by Mark Gerson: **p. 76**; Illustration by Michael Foreman from his *War Boy: A Country Childhood*. Copyright © 1989 by Michael Foreman. Reprinted by permission of Little, Brown and Company: **p. 102**; AP/Wide World Photos: **p. 108**; Archives of Ontario, Acc. 9773, S15547: **p. 122**; Archives of Ontario, Acc. 9261, S14230: **p. 126**; Archives of Ontario, Acc. 9348, S14261: **p. 137**; Estate of Carl Van Vechten, Joseph Soloman, Executor: **p. 140**; Courtesy of Viking Children's Books: **p. 176**; © Hiroshi Nagai: **p. 187**; Courtesy of Chizuko Kuratomi: **pp. 188, 191**; Reproduced by permission of Writers House Inc.: **p. 193**.

Children's
Literature
Review

Melvin Berger

1927-

American author and illustrator of nonfiction.

Major works include *The New Water Book* (1973), *Disease Detectives* (1978), *The Stereo Hi-Fi Handbook* (1979), *If You Lived on Mars* (1989), *The Science of Music* (1989).

INTRODUCTION

Berger is a popular and prolific author of informational books for children and young adults which explain aspects of science and music. Often published in series format, his books reflect a diverse range of interests, including computers, food, astronomy, the occult, and true crime. Berger is perhaps best known for his "Scientists at Work" series which deals with pollution, cancer, crime detection, oceanography, weather, and medical research. He is particularly concerned with exploring environmental issues, and in *The New Water Book* and *The New Earth Book: Our Changing Planet* (1980) Berger demonstrates the impact of technological advances on nature. Berger has additionally written many books on music, which he describes as attempts to "relate the art of music to the social, political, and scientific ideas of the time." Writing some of his books with his wife Gilda, who is also a children's author, Berger frequently employs a relaxed prose style, his own photographs, and numerous anecdotes to give his work a humorous and humane quality. Writing for readers in the early primary grades through high school, Berger has been lauded for his ability to simplify his subjects without trivializing them and to make scientific processes intelligible by providing concrete examples and details. Although some commentators maintain that Berger's explanations lack precision, most critics praise him for relating technical and abstract issues in relevant and engaging terms.

Born and raised in Brooklyn, New York, Berger was passionately interested as a child in both science and music. After two years studying electrical engineering at City College, he left to play viola for the New Orleans Symphony and the Pittsburgh Symphony. Returning to university, Berger received degrees from the University of Rochester's Eastman School of Music and Columbia University; he then taught music at the latter and at City College as well as in the Long Island school system. Berger embarked on a writing career in the early 1960s, in response to a request from McGraw–Hill for literature on science topics for young people. His first book, *Science and Music* (1961), was written with Frank Clark and explains the relationships between the two fields, including such topics as how each instrument makes its distinctive sound as well as the history of recording techniqes. Berger returned to the latter theme in 1979 with *The Stereo Hi-Fi Handbook*, a detailed survey of how sound is reproduced and a guide to the installation and maintenance of stereo systems.

Critics considered this work a valuable presentation of both general and practical information for young students. Among Berger's earliest scientific books are those written for the series "Science Is What and Why." These include such titles as *Atoms* (1968), *Stars* (1971), and *Computers* (1972), and are written in a style simple enough to be understood by second graders. Berger also wrote a series of books for young musicians, consisting of such titles as *The Violin Book* (1972), *The Flute Book* (1973), and *The Clarinet and Saxophone Book* (1975). These works illustrate the history of individual instruments, explain how they are made, and provide information about prominent musicians. As the editor of the "Industry at Work" series aimed at middle-grade readers, Berger wrote several books charting the course of various industrial processes from raw material to finished product. These titles include *Automobile Factory* (1977), *Food Processing* (1977), and *Printing Plant* (1978). In the "Scientists at Work" series, Berger uses his first-hand experience of visiting scientists and observing their work to illuminate the applications of science to such fields as medical research, veterinary medicine, and law enforcement. *Disease Detectives,* for example, focuses on the story of Legionnaire's disease to depict the ways in which scientists, doctors, and paramedics work together to discover the causes of illness. Berger has additionally written many highly praised books on ecological issues. Prominent among these is *The New Water Book* which contains information on the water cycle and the importance of water to living beings while providing a comprehensive discussion of water pollution. Both alone and in collaboration with Gilda, he has written several dictionaries, such as *The Photo Dictionary of the Orchestra* (1981) and *Drug Abuse A-Z* (1990), which explains related terms in text and pictures; he is also the creator of pop-up books on prehistoric subjects and adult nonfiction on music.

Berger's books have achieved international recognition and have been translated into sixteen languages. Moreover, *The New Water Book*, *Disease Detectives*, and *The Stereo Hi-Fi Handbook* were named Outstanding Science Trade Books for Children by the Joint Committee of the National Science Teachers Association and the Children's Book Council in 1973, 1978, and 1979 respectively. *Consumer Protection Labs* was named a Notable Trade Book in the Field of Social Studies in 1974 and *Quasars, Pulsars, and Black Holes* was named a Library of Congress Best Children's Book, 1964-1978. In addition, several of Berger's works have been named Children's Books of the Year by the Child Study Association in their respective years of publication.

(See also *Contemporary Literary Criticism*, Vol. 12; *Something about the Author*, Vol. 5; *Something about the Author Autobiography Series*, Vol. 2; *Contemporary Authors New Revision Series*, Vol. 4; *Contemporary Authors*, Vols. 5-8.)

TITLE COMMENTARY

Science and Music: From Tom-Tom to Hi-Fi (with Frank Clark, 1961)

It is a poor month that cannot bring forth at least one book that is not on a glamor-science but on one of those interesting sections of human knowledge too often taken for granted and too seldom really understood. Consider *Science and Music* by Melvin Berger and Frank Clark. This doesn't explain Bach, or Fabian either; but it does explain how sounds are made by strings and tubes and why the sounds can be produced at different pitches and, for that matter, what pitch is. Musical instruments provide a subject of wide interest, and the simplicity of the book is such that even a musical lowbrow and scientific illiterate can learn a great deal.

> *Isaac Asimov, in a review of "Science and Music," in* The Horn Book Magazine, *Vol. XXXVII, No. 5, October, 1961, p. 455.*

This brief textbook discusses the physical background of musical sounds in all-too-basic English. Example: "At the opposite end of the brass family from the trumpet is the tuba. Tuba in Latin though means trumpet! Trumpet notes can go very high. The tuba's notes are always low. The sound of the trumpet is clear and brilliant. The tuba is deep and mellow." Explanations and [Gustav Schrotter's] drawings describe with exceptional clarity how a voice or another instrument produces the peculiar sound

it does. Included are some of those home-made instruments familiar to the public school music teacher: the garden hose bugle, the tuned pop bottles, the yardstick-and-string monochord which demonstrates overtone vibrations, etc. A capsule history of the phonograph, an explanation of modern recording and playback techniques, and a discussion of some electronic instruments occupy the last half of the book.

Certainly the book can be useful in training the young in musical things they should know, but not even the very young need to be addressed in language quite so simple.

> *John Haskins, in a review of "Science and Music: From Tom-Tom to Hi-Fi," in* Notes, *Vol. XIX, No. 1, December, 1961, p. 75.*

An interesting approach to the subject of musical sounds, in a book that has clearly given information but is weakened by a carelessness in the writing and occasionally in the illustrations. These are in neither case inaccuracies, but consist of such errors as, "We say the boy's voice is cracking. When they are fifteen . . ." or irrelevant comments, or diagrams that seem inadequately labelled. After a first chapter that gives some background in the nature of sound, the authors discuss the human voice, groups of musical instruments, and various recording devices. A brief glossary and an index are appended.

> *Zena Sutherland, in a review of "Science and Music," in* Bulletin of the Center for Children's Books, *Vol. XVI, No. 1, September, 1962, p. 2.*

Triumphs of Modern Science (1964)

In eleven short essays, the author employs an easy, story-telling approach to scientific breakthroughs of the 20th century. Penicillin and the anti-biotic drugs: chemical germ killers and chemical curatives; virology; vitamins; atomic theory into energy; and radio-astronomy receive excellent coverage that emphasizes who discovered what and how along with the immediate effects of the discoveries and what new knowledge was built upon them. The essay on Einstein's theory of relativity takes time out for fun with the limericks developed by students to keep its essentials in mind. In dealing with Freud's Theory of the unconscious, there is an excellent, simple presentation of the standard interpretations of dream-symbols. Each essay ends with suggestions for further reading drawn from general available titles.

> *A review of "Triumphs of Modern Science," in* Virginia Kirkus' Service, *Vol. XXXII, No. 6, March 15, 1964, p. 303.*

[In *Triumphs of Modern Science*] there is emphasis on the individual's participation in scientific discoveries. (Actually, I would like to know what prompted some of the inclusions as part of modern science, unless by "modern" the author means anything between 1900 and 1960.)

Each chapter is a biography of the scientist identified with a particular discovery, and includes the histories of penicillin, viruses, antibiotics, X-rays, DNA, radioactivity, and relativity. I like the human element in this type of reporting, because I think that young readers can relate to it and see the possibilities that exist for their own achievements in science studies. However, I wish the author had emphasized somewhere that many discoveries are not made suddenly, but usually have, as a foundation, years of work carried out by many people and leading to one individual's spectacular "breakthrough."

The writing is clear and expository, and there are suggested lists for further reading at the end of each chapter.

> *Evelyn Shaw, in a review of "Triumphs of Modern Science," in* Natural History, *Vol. 74, No. 9, November, 1965, p. 17.*

Famous Men of Modern Biology   (1968)

A science book with the humanities reader in mind, **Famous Men** investigates the work of fourteen biologists from Pasteur to the *Double Helix* duo. Brevity precludes elaborate biographical data and necessitates condensation of the scientific method but each chapter does develop some personality through anecdotes, such as the preoccupied Salk assuring his neglected wife. "My dear, I'm giving you my *undevoted* attention." Mr. Berger does for biology what Bernard Jaffe did for chemistry in *Crucibles;* the two are similar in style of presentation, selection of known names, and the ability to relate the technical in relevant, stimulating terms for the youngster with some background in the science.

> *A review of "Famous Men of Modern Biology," in* Kirkus Service, *Vol. XXXVI, No. 8, April 15, 1968, p. 468.*

In this short collection of biographies the author presents the story of the remarkable accomplishments and discoveries of 14 researchers in the biological sciences. The book's first section describes the achievements of Pasteur, Koch, Ehrlich, Banting, and Fleming, who brought new methods and understanding to the cure and prevention of disease. Following this, the author describes the contributions made to the disciplines of genetics and heredity by Darwin, Mendel, Morgan and Muller under the heading, "The thread of life." In the final section, "New directions," author Berger vividly presents how various sciences and disciplines were brought to bear on old and new biological problems by Stanley, Salk, Calvin, Crick, and Watson. The biographies tend to be superficial, as would be expected in a collection of this sort. The book might be useful for introducing younger readers to more detailed biographies of the scientists. For this reason, it is especially unfortunate that the author included no bibliographies. (pp. 118-19)

> *A review of "Famous Men of Modern Biology," in* Science Books & Films, *Vol. IV, No. 2, September, 1968, pp. 118-19.*

Smacking of the literary style of Paul de Kruif, Mr. Berger's stories of the achievements of fourteen selected modern biologists run smoothly, holding the reader's interest remarkably well. In an age when books simulate picture

galleries, it is unusual to pick up a book and read it just for the prose.

> *Douglas B. Sands, in a review of "Famous Men of Modern Biology," in* Appraisal: Children's Science Books, *Vol. 3, No. 1, Winter, 1970, p. 8.*

Atoms   (1968)

In comparison with the many books on the topic, this offers nothing new, being neither innovative in the use of analogy, exciting in the method of illustration [by Arthur Schaffert], or more up-to-date. What we have is a rather simple presentation, acceptably handled and nicely pictured. Among the nearly twenty others on approximately the same level, some are poorer, many are of similar quality, several are considerably better. Among the latter are the Freemans' *Story of the Atom* and Landin's *Atoms for Junior,* either of which would be a first choice.

> *A review of "Atoms," in* Kirkus Service, *Vol. XXXVI, No. 21, November 1, 1968, p. 1221.*

In a generously illustrated but uncluttered format, the author introduces with only partial success the complex world of the atom to elementary students. He describes where atoms are found, their states, similarities and differences among them, how they combine, and how man has learned to get power from them. Oversimplifications and erroneous statements occasionally mar the text, e.g., "Atoms are everywhere. Atoms are everything. And everything is atoms . . . Everything is either a solid, a liquid, or a gas." In both cases, other forms of energy—for example, light, heat, electricity—are ignored. The vocabulary is within the grasp of very young readers and the black, white, blue, and orange illustrations help to elucidate the abstract topic, but false impressions and confusion will result from some of the inaccuracies and generalizations, making this a less desirable title than the Adlers' *Atoms and Molecules* (John Day, 1966) or Lewellen's *The Mighty Atom* (Knopf, 1955).

> *Harold F. Desmond, Jr., in a review of "Atoms," in* School Library Journal, *Vol. 15, No. 7, March, 1969, p. 141.*

For Good Measure: The Story of Modern Measurement (1969)

This book more clearly belongs on the science bookshelf than do most which deal with measurement, a reflection not of its relative quality—although it is a fine book—but of the fact that others get so involved with numbers and scales and the rationale for standardized measures that little time is left to explore the scientific uses of measurement. Here the organization is around areas such as sound, electricity and magnetism, light and radiation, though there are chapters on such standard topics as mass, length and time. Each unit is treated historically, length moving from the Biblical cubit through establishing the wavelength of Krypton 86 emission as a standard and on to today's use of laser interference to set unit lengths. Thus a great deal of scientific development in the fields is covered in exploring the changing nature of measuring. In contrast, a more common approach such as Carona's (in *Things That Measure*) offers simply a historical outline of devices.

> *A review of "For Good Measure," in* Kirkus Reviews, *Vol. XXXVII, No. 5, March 15, 1969, p. 318.*

Standardized weights and measures are commonplace and enter into all phases of human life, activity, and interaction. Because of their universal use, few laymen know the history of the development of standardized weights and measures, and for them Mr. Berger has supplied a complete, readable and not-too-technical little book. The introductory portion traces the genesis of measurement as a long historical process, first by describing the concepts of magnitude or dimension conveyed by man's natural senses—touch, vision, hearing, biological clocks—with an elementary discussion of their physiology. The need for some extension of man's senses led to the development of measures of length, mass, and volume which were at first crude and variable in accordance with local innovations and customs. Gradually as civilization developed the need for uniformity of units of measure came about, and as history shows these were more and more precisely defined and standardized. The book goes on step by step beyond the internationally accepted and adopted basic standards of length, weight and mass, to discuss some of the modern concepts and methods in metrology, as applied also to energy, electricity, temperature, time, sound pitch and intensity, photometry, colorimetry, radiation, and other entities. An appreciation is developed for the fact that absolute accuracy in measurement has not been and may never be achieved. Innovations and refinements are continually improving the reliability of the approximations. Here and there interesting experiments are suggested which should interest many young people—would that there were more. Additional illustrations [by Adolph E. Brotman] would have enriched a factually correct but occasionally dry text. The author has had the advice of officers of the National Bureau of Standards and of various research laboratories and manufacturers of scientific equipment. The book, lamentably, lacks a bibliography or reading list, but it has a good index. It is good collateral study material as well as for general reading.

> *A review of "For Good Measure: The Story of Modern Measurement," in* Science Books: A Quarterly Review, *Vol. 5, No. 2, September, 1969, p. 104.*

An excellent, well-written account of problems and techniques in the field of measurement. The historical information is lively and well-integrated into the whole, the technical sections are lucid and imaginative. This is a very fine account suitable for a wide variety of readers of a very complex and difficult field.

> *Richard H. Weller, in a review of "For Good Measure," in* Appraisal: Children's Science Books, *Vol. 4, No. 1, Winter, 1971, p. 4.*

Tools of Modern Biology (1970)

The author of *Famous men of modern biology* here describes simply and clearly some of the techniques employed in modern biological research. After explaining the scientific method and discussing general research methods such as observation, classification, and the use of measurements and statistics he tells how individual scientists have developed and used many specialized instruments and processes, including the light microscope, electron microscope, centrifuge, chromatography, X rays, radioactive tracers, and radiation. An introductory treatment for junior high and younger high school readers. Selected bibliography appended.

> *Helen E. Kinser, in a review of "Tools of Modern Biology," in* The Booklist, *Vol. 66, No. 20, June 15, 1970, p. 1270.*

The first part, "Methods of modern biology," is a good exposition of the evolution of scientific method which began with Francis Bacon's instruction to define the problem, obtain information, find an explanation, and engage in experimentation. These steps are all involved in problem solving, and as examples the author describes Redi's study of the theory of spontaneous generation, and Claude Bernard's investigation of the process of carbon dioxide poisoning. The section continues with discussions of the role of observation, the use of classification, the importance of discussion and bibliographic research, and the use of statistics in biological research. The second part of the book is devoted to scientific instruments and their use in various types of research situations: simple, compound, and electron microscopes; centrifuges; chromatography; x-rays; radioactive tracers and radiation; and computers. The book concludes with a selected bibliography and an index. It is not too difficult, especially the first part, for junior high students; senior high students can use the entire book as collateral reading in a biology course to give them a better understanding of scientific research in which, hopefully, they will receive elementary indoctrination through their laboratory exercises. (pp. 132-33)

> *A review of "Tools of Modern Biology," in* Science Books, *Vol. 6, No. 2, September, 1970, pp. 132-33.*

An understandable and interesting book on the methods and instruments of modern biology. The author's frequent use of anecdotes and examples makes the explanations clearer and provides much fascinating information about natural phenomena. Such pertinent topics as the uses of radiation on living tissues, cryobiology, the electrocardiograph and electroencephalograph are covered; the chapters on biometrics and computers are especially useful. Diagrams [by Robert Smith] help explain the "how" of the operations described. This would be useful outside reading material for all science enthusiasts.

> *Harold F. Desmond, Jr., in a review of "Tools of Modern Biology," in* School Library Journal, *Vol. 18, No. 1, September, 1971, p. 183.*

Masters of Modern Music (1970)

Little benefit derives from the collective treatment of four-teen composers where no sense of interchange, no corpo-rate forum is created to advance or compare their respec-tive Great Ideas—to use Percy Young's 1967 title [*Great Ideas in Music*], which better serves Schoenberg's 12-tone revolution and better projects the very notion of innova-tion. These are separate biographies, accurate and ade-quate perhaps to introduce the lesser-knowns, though the promise of entries like John Cage and Vladimir Uss-achevsky—contemporary pioneers in electronic music and synthesis—isn't fulfilled by the too-brief, too-abstract discussions. As to the more familiar names: Stravinsky and Copland have both been excellently studied by Arnold Dobrin, and there is no shortage of basic material on Sibe-lius, Prokofiev, Richard Strauss, Gershwin, or Bartok. Ticklish aspects of the various lives, political or more often amorous, are discreetly side-stepped in a word or two: more importantly, patterns of musical thought need substantive amplification. At least, however, no musical literacy is required for easy assimilation, and there are lists of recordings and readings appended that will expand on the unimaginative competency of the sketches. (pp. 965-66)

> *A review of "Masters of Modern Music," in* Kirkus Reviews, *Vol. XXXVIII, No. 17, September 1, 1970, pp. 965-96.*

Melvin Berger has presented his readers with the story of fourteen leading composers of the century. He has selected Stravinsky, Schoenberg, and Bartók to represent "Musical Explorers"; Richard Strauss, Sibelius, Hindemith, Pro-kofiev, Copland, and Britten, "Music in the Main Stream"; Gershwin, Richard Rodgers, and Menotti, "Music for the Many"; and John Cage and Vladimir Uss-achevsky, "The New Music." All fourteen were born be-fore the outbreak of World War I, and there is not a French, Yankee, or black composer among them. Within these limitations his list has been well chosen, despite a few possible objections. Surely, for instance, Webern should be added to the first three men, as one of the "com-posers who have pointed out the new directions of modern music." Young composers virtually stampeded in his di-rection in the 1950s, just as earlier they had turned in the direction of Hindemith. The author, however, has fol-lowed the present trend of placing Hindemith only among those "composers who have carried forward the musical traditions of the past." In addition, certain statements in the text raise the question of whether Richard Strauss and Sibelius are modern enough to be included at all. The reader is told that many were shocked to read of Strauss's death in 1949: "Since his outstanding works were all writ-ten before 1911, they were sure that he had died nearly half a century earlier." As for Sibelius, the reader learns that he "did no more composing for the final 30 years of his life."

In any case, the composers chosen are attractively pres-ented. Each is introduced by a striking incident or charac-terization, which brings him close to the reader at the out-set. The style is readable and especially appealing to the young person looking for a guide. One result of this format is that it makes the work suitable as a novel but not as a source book for specific data. Although the text is accurate in giving the general sense of things, the very cursive style that makes it move sometimes blurs particular points and allows years to slip into each other. Thus, in the Hinde-mith chapter, the reader finds that "the German Republic was being taken over by the Nazis." Several sentences later, the statement is made that "Then, in 1929, he wrote his controversial opera, *Neues von* [*vom*] *Tage (News of the Day),* which became the target for open attack in the Nazi-controlled newspapers." From this, the reader could not gather that in 1929 Hitler was for the moment all but for-gotten and that it was in 1934, five years after the first per-formance of the opera, that Nazi control enabled Goebbels to make his famous attack on it.

At another point, the assertion that there is "no tonality at all in Schoenberg's Second Quartet" is contradicted al-most at once by the statement that it is "in the last move-ment of the Quartet that Schoenberg wrote this first exam-ple of atonal music." Actually, this work, which is usually called Schoenberg's *F# Minor Quartet,* takes leave of to-nality only in the last movement when that voice is heard breathing "the air from a distant planet."

The last paragraph of the book raises a dated question: "Will the growth of electronic music mean the end of con-certs and live performers?" When young Stockhausen swept the country with his tapes back in 1958, it was al-ready apparent that the days of pure electronic music were numbered. Today, it is generally recognized that no mat-ter how avant-garde a composition is, there has to be at least one live body on the stage along with the appliances.

The text contains no musical examples. Berger has provid-ed a very short bibliography and discography, which are to be praised for their selectivity. The portraits of The Fourteen are fine if formal. The recommendation for *Mas-ters of Modern Music* is read it, but don't lean on it. (pp. 70-1)

> *Henry Leland Clarke, in a review of "Masters of Modern Music," in* Music Educators Jour-nal, *Vol. 58, No. 4, December, 1971, pp. 70-1.*

Storms (1970)

A simple, nicely illustrated [by Joseph Cellini] explanation of rain, lightning, and thunder with a more limited treat-ment of hail, sleet, and snow. The rising of warm air is clearly explained on a kinetic-molecular basis. The same basis could have been used in explaining evaporation and condensation but was not. Household examples illustrate the movement of hot and cold air, condensation, creation of an electric charge by friction, and the noise accompany-ing the rapid expansion of air. The information on light-ning, thunder, and the appropriate precautions to be taken in an electrical storm is similar to that found in Branley's *Flash, Crackle, Rumble and Roll* (1964). Most of the ma-terial is also covered in Zim's *Lightning and Thunder* (1952), but the format of Berger's book is more appealing.

> *A review of "Storms," in* Kirkus Reviews, *Vol.*

XXXVIII, No. 18, September 15, 1970, p. 1039.

Thunder and lightning, hail, rain, snow and windstorms are adequately investigated at the second grade reading level. Simple observations of familiar phenomena are used to illustrate basic scientific principles: e.g., making a wind by opening the door to a heated bathroom. Safety precautions during a storm are included but not overly stressed. The illustrations are more decorative than useful. If additional material on this level is needed, this could supplement Branley's superior *Flash, Crash, Rumble, and Roll* (1964) and *Rain and Hail* (1963, both Crowell).

Frankie C. Miller, in a review of "Storms," in School Library Journal, *Vol. 17, No. 5, January, 1971, p. 64.*

Berger has developed a logical sequence readable during the latter half of the second grade. This evaluation is based on the word-recognition curve developed by Fry of Rutgers University. *Storms* is an addition to the "Science is What and Why" series. The author is a public school teacher and has also contributed two other books in the series: *Atoms* and *Gravity*. A storm denotes a different phenomenon to children living in varied sections of our country. Referring only once to a hurricane and a tornado without further explanation leaves much to be desired, especially for children from the southeast and midwest. This is a serious shortcoming of the text. Berger makes several questionable statements such as, "If lightning strikes the building or the car, the metal frame carries the electricity safely into the ground." Actually a car's tires create a Faraday cage and the electricity is not grounded through them. Airplanes have been damaged during flight by lightning, but the damage is external and the current seems to dissipate outward. Another quote is, "More of the sun's heat bounces up into the air from land than from water." This is misleading, for the color of the surface and the angle of the sun's rays create a large variation in reflection. A child's interest in reading a book is developed through activities. The child is shown how to make a wind through differential air masses, how to cause condensation, and how to develop a spark through static electricity. Safety-conscious teachers will be pleased with the presentation, as storm-precaution procedures are thoughtfully presented. This is a well-written book for second grade and is recommended except for students in central and southeastern U.S.

A review of "Storms," in Science Books: A Quarterly Review, *Vol. 6, No. 4, March, 1971, p. 306.*

Stars   (1971)

The size of the stars, their distance from the earth, how they make heat and light, why they seem to twinkle, and how they occur in galaxies are clearly explained in a book that reads at a late second or third grade level and can be understood by a first grader. The Milky Way spinning in space is compared to a gigantic pinwheel (but not *called* a pinwheel), the atmospheric distortions that cause the twinkling appearance is described in terms of a child look-ing at his foot under water, and the relative distance from the earth to the sun and other stars is presented as a walk in space with each step covering 93,000,000 miles: "with one giant step you would reach the sun," but it would take a whole day of walking to reach any of the other stars. A beginning book, then, younger and less inclusive than Branley's *A Book of Stars for You,* that relates difficult concepts to a child's experience.

A review of "Stars," in Kirkus Reviews, *Vol. XXXIX, No. 8, April 15, 1971, p. 437.*

Enzymes in Action   (1971)

Less technical and of course more up to date re applied research than Asimov's *Chemicals of Life* (1954), this is a clear and comprehensive introduction to the nature and roles of enzymes from their discovery and analysis to their functions in the processing of cheese and fermenting of wine, in the causing and curing of diseases (phenylketonuria, albinism, cancer, hemophilia), in the shock of the electric eel, in natural clocks, in digestion. The description of Beaumont's observations of digestion through the permanent hole created by a stomach wound makes for perhaps the most engrossing reading, also interesting are the stories of early chance discoveries of foods, and also noteworthy is the reporting of signal experiments—past and current—and the projection of problems for future investigation. Mr. Berger proffers a good deal of correlative information on subjects as diverse as leather tanning, detergents, and famous medical histories, and winds up with a balanced, topical bibliography. Accessible . . . and accessible-looking besides.

A review of "Enzymes in Action," in Kirkus Reviews, *Vol. XXXIX, No. 11, June 1, 1971, p. 594.*

This is a short up-to-date review of enzymology and its practical application in industry. Berger covers adequately such topics as the role of enzymes in digestion, food production, and preparation of beverages; enzymes as drugs; enzymes and diseases; and enzymes at work. He describes historic and salient discoveries including the latest achievements in enzymology. The book is written in a highly simplified style. Because the vocabulary is simple, the book can be read easily by a layman. The text can be used with great profit as a collateral reading by a freshman student of biochemistry, biology, agronomy, agriculture, or medicine. Although the author uses no chemical formulas, such classical effects on enzyme activity as those of pH, temperature, and concentrations of enzyme and substrate should have been mentioned.

A Review of "Enzymes in Action," in Science Books: A Quarterly Review, *Vol. 8, No. 1, May, 1972, p. 46.*

In a captivating blend of scientific data and anecdotes, the reader is introduced to enzymes, their structure, their function and their importance in the human body. Curious accidents are related, such as the one that permitted, over many years, the observation of digestion through a hole in the stomach of a person who, nevertheless, man-

Berger at the age of four, with his parents Ben and Esther.

rometer, even (at some length) the inter-station teletype machine. The attention to office routine is sometimes excessive: "As each message is finished, the weatherman tears it off. He hangs many of them from hooks or clipboards on the wall. Some he slips into folders. A few, of little interest to the local weathermen, he throws away." Procedures in making weather maps are closely followed (how blank maps are inserted into a data plotter where a metal arm with a pen attached draws lines on them; how photographs of the maps are then sent over wires on electric machines called facsimiles), but those wavy lines (isobars) that appear on the pictured maps are never mentioned. The black and white photographs, in like manner, show a lot of screens and instruments and men turning dials. In short, this easy once-over provides a clear picture of what the various weathermen do (at a younger level than Bixby's *Skywatchers*), but only a foggy notion of what it's all about.

A review of "The National Weather Service," in Kirkus Reviews, *Vol. XXXIX, No. 4, June 1, 1971, p. 590.*

In providing an interesting, informative, and up-to-date account of the weather service's activities, the author explains the work of technicians and forecasters, and describes instruments and equipment used—weather balloons, radar, teletype, facsimile machines, and computers. The work of tornado, flood, and (the newest) air pollution forecasters, climatologists, hurricane hunters, and space-flight meteorologists are covered. Research into weather control (cloud seeding) is touched upon. The many varied black-and-white photographs add interest to the straightforward text. There is no glossary, but a short index is appended.

A review of "The National Weather Service," in Science Books: A Quarterly Review, *Vol. 7, No. 3, December, 1971, p. 228.*

---

aged to have 17 children and live to the age of 83. We learn strange details about the lack of enzymes in the British Royal family and its consequences. These are some of the many particulars that are interspersed throughout the solid text, which describes clearly and efficiently the discovery, the isolating and understanding, and, ultimately, the artificial creation of, enzymes. We learn of their uses in industry, medicine, food production, and of their ubiquity in all living things; of their extraordinary function and of the possible dangers created by their presence. This is a very readable and informative book.

Laura Musto, in a review of "Enzymes in Action," in Appraisal: Children's Science Books, *Vol. 6, No. 1, Winter, 1973, p. 6.*

The National Weather Service   (1971)

Everyday tasks of the weather observer, radar operator, forecaster, "hurricane hunter," and other meteorological technicians are surveyed to convey an appreciation of "what goes into preparing those simple sounding weather reports." Covered in the process are the functions and handling of such tools as the weather balloon, satellite, ba-

South Pole Station   (1971)

An NSF scientist beginning his one-year stay at the U.S. South Pole base tours the underground complex of living quarters, stores and laboratories at an outpost where the average temperature is 57 below zero, where all water is obtained by melting snow, where cosmic rays provide a "spectacular light show" for those who brave the surface cold to watch it. In the sleeping, mess, and recreation halls we learn that the men take turns being "house mouse" (cleaning the quarters), can see a different movie every night, and have even developed their own folklore. Visits to the weather, gravity, earthquake, and other labs point out some of the station's discoveries (such as the steady northwest movement of the magnetic pole) and many of the intriguing questions still to be answered. The Antarctic voyage concludes with a transverse, a challanging one-to-three-month trek across the ice in a caterpillar "camper" called a Sno-Cat. Narrower in coverage than Maggie Scarf's *Antarctica* (1970), which includes the history and ecology of the continent, this is a congenial guide that leaves the reader with an informed appreciation of life and work at the station and a desire to explore the subject further.

> *A review of "South Pole Station," in* Kirkus Reviews, *Vol. XXXIX, No. 11, June 1, 1971, p. 590.*

Mr. Berger has presented almost a travelog of a trip to the South Pole Station. There are numerous black-and-white photographs of scientists at work. His style is pleasant and rather low key, however he manages to inject an amazingly large amount of factual material without bogging down in detail. He presents the day-to-day life of the South Polar scientist at work and play. He includes the adventure of a trip across the ice in Sno-Cats. The major emphasis is on the scientific program and how the various individuals and their investigations contribute to an overall study of the South Pole. This book is generally restricted to the pole station and its inhabitants rather than a broader view of the South Pole. In this context, as an introduction to a particular scientific environment, rather than as one of the many already available books about Antarctica, the book is well worth reading. There is a brief list of suggested further reading and an index.

> *A review of "South Pole Station," in* Science Books: A Quarterly Review, *Vol. 7, No. 2, September, 1971, p. 131.*

This survey of scientific activities at the South Pole deals for the most part with the environment and the activities of the scientists, and not much with the science as such. This is not said in complaint, though, as these matters are quite interesting in their own right. The style is pleasant and the form, sort of a narrative Cook's tour of the station, is nice, although rather superficial. One error: the aurora are *not* caused by cosmic rays but by particulate matter emitted from the sun. Many good photographs—it *is* bleak there. (pp. 8-9)

> *John D. Stackpole, in a review of "South Pole Station," in* Appraisal: Children's Science Books, *Vol. 5, No. 3, Fall, 1972, pp. 8-9.*

Computers (1972)

Beginning off target with the borrowed gee-wow of a rocket blast-off, Berger goes on to list the space program functions performed by computers, then some of the more down-to-earth uses made of the machine by the weather bureau, post office, and bus company. The problem of finding the number of children at school with a certain birthday is followed through the input, control, processing, and output units, but with no hint of the principles behind their workings. From the first look at the control panel with "its many electronic on-off switches" it's definitely an outside view; for a somewhat clearer glimpse of the subject see [*Computers,* (1972) by Jane Jonas Srivastava].

> *A review of "Computers," in* Kirkus Reviews, *Vol. XL, No. 5, March 1, 1972, p. 260.*

In Melvin Berger's *Computers* I [found] a straight description, for the very young, of the things which can be and are being done by computers, and—to a smaller extent—

how such things are done. I don't mean that Mr. Berger tries to explain to third graders how the computer works internally; but he does give a good picture of the steps it follows in its work and makes clear how very specific computer instructions must be. This explanation should forestall some of the worry about the mechanical brains taking over the world—which seems to lurk in the minds of the uninformed.

> *Harry C. Stubbs, in a review of "Computers," in* The Horn Book Magazine, *Vol. XLIX, No. 1, February, 1973, p. 72.*

Computers contains the essential facts and provides correct and appropriate illustrations to introduce the grade school child to computer processing. In 46 pages, with a minimum of words, the author has shown some of the most important current uses of computers. The space program, data processing, weather predicting, postal sorting, and traffic control are mentioned. Some simple notions of computer operation and programming are given, and there is an (almost) accurate flow chart of a search program whose output is later displayed. (The flow chart does not quite correspond to the output, but that is a *very* minor quibble.) The author points out the sources of computer errors and makes clear the human activities which are necessary before the computer can do anything at all.

> *A review of "Computers," in* Science Books: A Quarterly Review, *Vol. 8, No. 4, March, 1973, p. 288.*

The Violin Book (1972)

Variously entertaining and inspiring background material for young performers—ranging from anecdotes about stolen Strads and Paganini's virtuosity to the construction and acoustics of modern instruments. Berger also gives some hints about repertoire and advice on career possibilities, but since he still believes in the efficacy of the self-organized New York debut ("You hope that the newspaper critics who usually attend these concerts will write rave reviews") it's hard to place much faith in the practicality of his recommendations.

> *A review of "The Violin Book," in* Kirkus Reviews, *Vol. XL, No. 7, April 1, 1972, p. 411.*

Not in any sense a how-to-do-it book, this is a text that covers the history of the instrument itself, describes major violin makers and goes into almost too much detail about construction of the instrument, discusses the numbers of people who are students and performers today (with no mention of the Suzuki method that is making such an impact on the teaching of violin) and describes briefly some outstanding concert violinists, omitting Nathan Milstein. There is some mention of the music written for violin, and a brief list of recordings are appended, as is an index. Despite the imbalance of treatment, this is a capably written book that should be useful both to students and prospective students of the instrument.

> *Zena Sutherland, in a review of "The Violin Book," in* Bulletin of the Center for Children's Books, *Vol. 25, No. 11, July-August, 1972, p. 165.*

Animal Hospital (1973)

In the relaxed, friendly manner of his *National Weather Service* and others in the series, Berger tours the examination room, treatment room, lab, x-ray room and operating room of an animal hospital, filling us in along the way on animal care, diseases, and use in research as well as the veterinarian's various tasks and kinds of employment. (Most vets go into private practice, treating either pets or livestock; their biggest employer is not surprisingly the USDA; others work in medical research testing drugs or investigating such mysteries as the aging process.) It's a pleasant enough introduction (though it's unfortunate that the only woman photographed is a "handler" or vet's assistant) and informative as far as it goes, but when they are ready to get serious would-be *Animal Doctors* will get more realistic career advice from the Whitneys [in their *Animal Doctor: The History and Practice of Veterinary Medicine* (1973).]

> *A review of "Animal Hospital," in* Kirkus Reviews, *Vol. XLI, No. 6, March 15, 1973, p. 319.*

Caring for a fallen sparrow or starving stray has started many a youngster thinking about being an animal doctor. Yet, few youngsters realize how much is involved in caring for animals or that it is a profession more demanding and more exclusive than the profession of human medicine. Berger discusses the training of the animal doctor and the way the animal hospital functions. He explains how animals are examined and treated and the various tests and laboratory procedures that must be followed to find out what ails them. The young reader will learn that, in addition to sick cats and dogs, many veterinarians are involved in the care of farm animals and the inspection, to insure high standards, of animals raised for food. The research laboratory and the importance of animals in the study of diseases in man are also explored as another area where the veterinarian plays an important role. Good illustrations are numerous and appropriate to this explanation of the work of the veterinarian.

> *A review of "Animal Hospital," in* Science Books: A Quarterly Review, *Vol. IX, No. 2, September, 1973, p. 174.*

Sixty black-and-white photographs accompany Mr. Berger's highly informative text which explains the variety of functions a veterinarian may perform in his daily duties. The writing style is simple and the subject matter is clearly presented for students in grades 2 to 6. The list of suggested readings is well chosen for youngsters in this age group, as is Mr. Berger's subject. Readers with pets will learn much about the busy schedule of the animal doctor. Those more seriously interested in veterinary medicine will become more aware of the technology, problems and rewards involved in that field of science. (pp. 7-8)

> *Robert J. Stein, in a review of "Animal Hospital," in* Appraisal: Children's Science Books, *Vol. 7, No. 1, Winter, 1974, pp. 7-8.*

The Funny Side of Science (with J.B. Handelsman, 1973)

Though Berger's collection of 50 or so jokes and cartoons has its share of clunkers, its unifying theme not only gives kids the ego boosting chance to catch on (sign in a bacteriology lab: staph only) and know better (an archaeologist dug up a vase that was marked 400 B.C.) but also offers the satisfaction of laughing at an august and erudite grownup brotherhood. There's the zoologist who complained that his mouse had died just after he had trained it to live on no food, the lab rats who had their experimenter conditioned to feed them after they ran the maze, and the definition of a statistician as "someone who believes that if your head is in a furnace and your feet in a bucket of ice water, on the average you are comfortable." On the average these are mildly amusing, which is more than we would say about all the electric radishes and ballpoint bananas that have been swamping us of late.

> *A review of "The Funny Side of Science," in* Kirkus Reviews, *Vol. XLI, No. 8, April 15, 1973, p. 458.*

A collection of more than 50 jokes and riddles plus 23 cartoons which relate, though at times vaguely, to science. Not all of the jokes are new, and some are farfetched—e.g., " 'What do you get when you cross a white birch and a red maple?' 'A barber pole.' " Readers will find many more jokes, puns, and riddles in the familiar Hoke collections (*Jokes, Jokes, Jokes,* 1954; *More Jokes, Jokes, Jokes,* 1960, both Watts); however, this book may prove useful as a humorous introduction to science, and Handelsman's cartoons are well drawn and original. (pp. 45-6)

> *Everett C. Sanborn, in a review of "The Funny Side of Science," in* School Library Journal, *Vol. 20, No. 3, November, 1973, pp. 45-6.*

The Flute Book (1973)

Though none of it is essential to their music making, young flutists will enjoy meeting their famous predecessors from Frederick the Great to Jean-Pierre Rampal, tracing the innovations that led to the standard flute designed by Theobald Boehm in 1847, seeing how modern instruments are made, and learning a little about the physics of the flute's sound and a little more about the highlights of the concert repertoire. And, given the instrument's resurgent 20th century popularity, those with a sense of humor will appreciate the 19th century image of the flutist: "He always has a pointed nose, marries a nearsighted woman and dies run over by a bus." Grace notes all, but pleasantly orchestrated.

> *A review of "The Flute Book," in* Kirkus Reviews, *Vol. XLI, No. 10, May 15, 1973, p. 561.*

Oceanography Lab (1973)

Woods Hole Oceanographic Institution has attained world prominence for its marine research activities; therefore, it is appropriate for a "biographical sketch" of that famous research organization to be written for the children of today's environment-conscious society. This well-written book describes the laboratories, ships, instruments, and the activities of this institution both on shore and at sea. The diverse investigations underway at Woods Hole are recounted, and the interesting details and sidelights about current research projects should capture and retain a young reader's interest. For individuals at a 5th or 6th grade reading level and with interests in science or marine activities, the book will provide an excellent perspective on the scope of activities at an oceanographic institution. For instructors planning a field trip to a marine laboratory, the book will provide ideas on what to ask questions about during the visit, and it can also be useful in the follow-up review of trip activities and events. Photographs are generously interspersed throughout the text and supply added interest. The reviewer is unaware of any other authoritative introduction to WHOI's oceanographic research activities presented in any detail at this level. A few titles for further reading are given, but these may be of limited value since the elementary ones pre-date 1965. (pp. 161-62)

> *A review of "Oceanography Lab," in* Science Books: A Quarterly Review, *Vol. IX, No. 2, September, 1973, pp. 161-62.*

This is sure to be a success with the young reader. It is not only well written but also has clear and well-labeled photographs which tell the story almost as well as the text does. . . . The early chapters discuss the reasons for establishing research bases, how research projects are initiated, how developed and how financed. The succeeding chapters each discuss the work of one type of scientist: the geologist, the bacteriologist, the chemist, the biologist, etc. . . . In every way this is a most interesting account of an oceanography lab, whether on land or afloat. The book opens with an introduction by John I. Schilling of the Institution and closes with a bibliography of further reading and a good index.

> *Beryl B. Beatley, in a review of "Oceanography Lab," in* Appraisal: Children's Science Books, *Vol. 7, No. 1, Winter, 1974, p. 8.*

The study of the oceans is properly portrayed as one that is interesting as well as hard work. Woods Hole Oceanographic Institution, probably the most famed of the research and training stations, is the focal point of the book. Text and photographs show scientists at their daily tasks in the lab and at sea, collecting, recording, and analyzing data about the biological and physical factors of oceans. Many instruments are shown, such as the plankton collecting net, bottom dredge, mud corer, and water sampler. The *Alvin,* a tiny research submarine, is described in detail. . . . Books about scientists at work are not uncommon, but this reviewer finds few that are uncommonly good. This is an excellent one.

> *John R. Pancella, in a review of "Oceanography Lab," in* Appraisal: Children's Science Books, *Vol. 7, No. 1, Winter, 1974, p. 8.*

The New Water Book (1973)

The New Water Book, while short on detail and depth, is

a businesslike, readable primer in which the concepts are reinforced throughout with suggestions for simple experiments which young readers can perform without expense or undue fuss. Beginning with explanations of some of the basic and peculiar "mysteries of water" (buoyancy, natural occurrence in all three stages, capillary action, etc.), Berger reviews the importance of water to animals and men and the mechanics of the water cycle, surveys the uses of water (for power, irrigation, etc.) and current methods of purifying drinking sources and treating sewage, and ends with some causes and consequences of water pollution (he is merely platitudinous about solutions, however). In all, it's a clear and well-rounded first book, and the experiments make it suitable for classroom application.

> *A review of "The New Water Book," in* Kirkus Review, *Vol. XLI, No. 18, September 15, 1973, p. 1037.*

A treatment of the subject that is comprehensive in scope, simple in style, lucid in explanation, and given added interest by the inclusion throughout the text of home demonstrations, helpfully illustrated [by Leonard Kessler] and clearly outlined. The text discusses the composition of water, its three states (liquid, solid, and gas), and some of the unusual properties of water; it describes the need for water in plants, human beings, and other animal life; it surveys water in agriculture and industry, describes the water cycle, and discusses the water supply and water pollution. A reading list and a relative index are appended.

> *Zena Sutherland, in a review of "The New Water Book," in* Bulletin of the Center for Children's Books, *Vol. 27, No. 8, April, 1974, p. 123.*

Mr. Berger has prepared an outstanding book on the important topic of water. He introduces the reader to water through discussion and simple activities designed to show the mysteries and wonders of the properties of water. Through continued discussions and activities, readers explore water and living things, water at work, water cycles, water supply and water pollution. Approximately 35 pages are devoted to discussion and activities concerning water pollution and suggestions for antipollution activites. Included are a list of national organizations which help to support antipollution programs and legislation. These activities and investigations could be undertaken advantageously as a science or social studies class or club project. The activities are well organized and would produce a well-planned unit of study.

> *A review of "The New Water Book," in* Science Books: A Quarterly Review, *Vol. X, No. 1, May, 1974, p. 61.*

Those Amazing Computers! Uses of Modern Thinking Machines (1973)

Though the word efficiency is never used, it seems to be the key concept and unquestioned value informing this survey of the computer's contribution to government, law enforcement, air and space travel, classroom learning, biological and behavioral research, even decoding Stonehenge and solving "instant insanity." There is only one cursory example to illustrate the "dangers in government" and two on the "dangers in business" of large data banks, and they focus on mechanical errors rather than political threats; Berger is evidently more interested in throwing doubt on the Warren Commission report, which he does quite effectively in a two-page string of unanswered questions he slips into a chapter on "investigating assassinations." The book ends with a chapter on the R.E.S.I.S.T.O.R.S.—a group of teenage computer "hams" in New Jersey; potential members, we suspect, will pass this over for a more technical survey. Those who share Berger's naive amazement will find his snappy series of illustrative incidents and programs easily readable.

> *A review of "Those Amazing Computers: Uses of Modern Thinking Machines," in* Kirkus Reviews, *Vol. XLI, No. 24, December 15, 1973, p. 1365.*

This is not a book on the computer itself, although the first chapter gives background by explaining computer operation and giving, very briefly, some historical information about the development of computers. The text is divided into chapters that discuss the uses of computers in science, education, business, publishing, et cetera. The fragmented format, example on example, is repetitive, but the book certainly gives a broad picture of the manifold uses of computers and, in describing some of the errors in credit ratings or in the obtaining of information by intelligence agencies for inclusion in data banks, some of the dangers. A list of books for further reading and an index are appended.

> *Zena Sutherland, in a review of "Those Amazing Computers: Uses of Modern Thinking Machines," in* Bulletin of the Center for Children's Books, *Vol. 27, No. 6, February, 1974, p. 90.*

What a refreshing insight into our modern robot, the computer! Melvin Berger briefly explains the history of computers and how they work, enlivening the text by frequently including factual anecdotes about computers, people, and situations common to all. The reader is able to appreciate the work of the computer as the author explores the varying roles it plays in many areas: science, government, business, learning, and even in leisure. Finally, one chapter is devoted to a most interesting computer club for young people, R.E.S.I.S.T.O.R.S. (Radically Emphatic Students Interested in Science, Technology, and Other Research Studies), which meets weekly in Hopewell, New Jersey. Those intrigued by this club are given an address to write for further information. So, those who are turned on by *Those Amazing Computers* have an opportunity to follow up their interest, thanks to Melvin Berger's fine job! If I had to choose my favorite book about computers, this would be it. (pp. 12-13)

> *Roberta A. Donnelly, in a review of "Those Amazing Computers!" in* Appraisal: Children's Science Books, *Vol. 7, No. 3, Fall, 1974, pp. 12-13.*

Jobs That Save Our Environment (1973)

An important vocational development task for the individual in late childhood and early adolescence is to imagine himself or herself pursuing a variety of careers which are realistic career options. Specifically, it is important that fantasy about careers be stimulated, that the individual be encouraged to consider a range of career fields and possible competency levels. In terms of these objectives, *Jobs That Save Our Environment* makes a useful contribution to the vocational development of pre-adolescent readers. Descriptions of approximately 50 environmentally-related science careers (which vary in job level) are presented in an understandable fashion. Not only is the reading level clearly within the abilities of this age group, but anecdotal materials are used in a way which should permit the young readers to easily identify with the careers which are being presented. More than 50 black-and-white photographs of real persons at work in natural settings serve to richly illustrate the text. The only major fault in Berger's work is that the use of actual photographs of current workers necessarily introduces a heavy white male bias.

> *A review of "Jobs That Save Our Environment: Exploring Careers," in* Science Books: A Quarterly Review, *Vol. X, No. 1, May, 1974, p. 64.*

Pollution Lab (1974)

. . . or how "today's pollution scientists strive to make the world a cleaner and more healthful place for us to live." Dedicated to "the men and women of the Environmental Protection Agency," this is an establishment-oriented guided tour through field stations and laboratories involved in monitoring air and water quality, researching solid waste control and recovery of resources, operating a sewage disposal plant, gathering evidence for an EPA sewage pollution suit, or trying out the many "promising methods" for dealing with oil and other spills. (Typically Berger's one example of a spill case names no industrial or commercial polluters but concerns an anomalous Ohio citizen who, when refused permission to swim in Shawnee Lake, threw a pound and a half of deadly insecticide into the lake.) Berger does give a clearer picture of the everyday tasks of environmental scientists than does Millard [in *Careers in Environmental Protection* (1974)], though as in his other *Scientists at Work* books his sentences are often blandly unsubstantial (the obvious introductory pronouncement that as world population multiplied and technology developed, "scientists were called in to lead the fight against pollution" doesn't even pose the questions of who called them in, where the barricades are, or how scientists "lead") and in the same indifferent manner the photos of technicians at work show us what their machines and devices look like from the outside but don't reveal what they are for or how they work.

> *A review of "Pollution Lab," in* Kirkus Reviews, *Vol. XLII, No. 10, May 15, 1974, p. 537.*

Pollution Lab is an interesting, informative book on the work being done to study and control pollution. It is written in plain, simple language, it is smooth, pleasant reading, yet it packs a wealth of information. Berger shows how pollution scientists and technicians in government, universities and private industry go about their daily job in the detection, analysis and control of pollution. Their work is presented in a way that emphasizes its challenges and rewards, and the book may inspire and guide young people toward a career in pollution science. Basic field and laboratory techniques of pollution detection and control are described. The scientific content on the whole is fairly accurate except for a few minor inconsistencies. (For example, on page 24, it is stated that " . . . the water temperature is related to the amount of oxygen. . . ." Here the cause and effect are seemingly interchanged. It would be more accurate to write " . . . the water temperature controls the amount of oxygen. . . ." On page 32, a temperature of 20 degrees Centigrade (68°F) is "cool" not "cold.") Still, **Pollution Lab** is a good, concise and timely presentation for young people and the layman about ecological problems of pollution and what is being done to solve them.

A review of "Pollution Lab," in Science Books: A Quarterly Review, *Vol. X, No. 3, December, 1974, p. 246.*

Most of the many books about pollution accentuate the problems and their causes, giving some facts about pollution control; here the emphasis is on research and solutions, with enough information on problems and causes to explain the need for research and control. Although this can be used for career orientation and gives a broad picture of the work of scientists and technicians in all areas of pollution control it seldom touches on the need for legislation and enforcement (especially in the pollution of air by automobiles) but it is otherwise explicit, with good organization of material, a clear if dull writing style, and good coverage of aspects of the subject. A skimpy bibliography and index are appended.

Zena Sutherland, in a review of "Pollution Lab," in Bulletin of the Center for Children's Books, *Vol. 28, No. 6, February, 1975, p. 90.*

Jobs in Fine Arts and Humanities   (1974)

Although this gives some information about careers, it covers far too broad an area to be anything but superficial in treatment. Eight partially-filled (considering space allotted to photographs that add little) pages for all the humanities; three or four pages each for such careers as acting, teaching dance, designing, conducting, etc. Some of the art careers are behind-the-scenes jobs, others are as performers. One topic, for example, is "Painters, Sculptors, Printmakers and Craft Workers." One page is devoted to a quick sketch of one painter's career, two pages to full-page photographs, another page-and-a-half to other arts than painting, a paragraph each. Adequately written, but not very useful. An "Index to careers" is appended.

Zena Sutherland, in a review of "Jobs in Fine Arts and Humanities," in Bulletin of the Cen-

ter for Children's Books, *Vol. 28, No. 3, November, 1974, p. 38.*

The New Air Book   (1974)

In a companion to **The New Water Book,** with simple experiments worked into the text wherever possible, Berger introduces just about everything he can think of that has to do with air—breathing, atmosphere, wind, weather, flying, and pollution (this last, mostly assurances about the EPA's effectiveness and instructions for measuring different kinds of pollution). The writing is clear, the experiments relevant to the matter at hand, and the frequent small drawings [by Ginlio Maestro] help to direct and maintain attention, what is missing is a sense of overall direction.

A review of "The New Air Book," in Kirkus Reviews, *Vol. XLII, No. 23, December 1, 1974, p. 1254.*

The New Air Book goes into the nature and chemistry of air, the atmosphere, wind and weather. It proves the dependency on air of all living things. It shows the many ways man has learned to use air through the ages. There are good chapters about air pollution and what is being done about it as well as what each of us can do. Experiments all through the book clarify the text and provide interesting and sometimes startling results, as in the air pollution tests. This book will be a welcome replacement for the several good but older books about air which, we now have.

Heddie Kent, in a review of "The New Air Book," in Appraisal: Children's Science Books, *Vol. 8, No. 1, Winter, 1975, P. 6.*

Much of this book about air, the atmosphere, and weather, is excellent. The text for the most part is clear and well organized. Except for a few terrible exceptions, the figures are very good in serving their intended purpose. The many experiments described should be instructive and fun. But here and there are factual flaws and incomplete or misleading statements. Ignoring buoyancy in the balloon air-weighing experiment or saying nothing about the chemical and pressure changes in the candle, glass and water experiment are unfortunate. This potentially excellent book could have made the mark if it had been more carefully checked before being published! I recommend it in spite of the problems for its generally good quality science and the many experiments included. The last few chapters on air pollution are carefully done without overstatement.

David G. Hoag, in a review of "The New Air Book," in Appraisal: Children's Science Books, *Vol. 8, No. 1, Winter, 1975, p. 7.*

The New Air Book provides an excellent description of one of man's natural resources. The author takes a detailed look at the technical aspects of air, describing what it is physically and chemically in an easy-to-understand text. In addition, Berger discusses the importance of air, weather, flying and air pollution, and what the public can do to learn more about the problems of air quality. Included are numerous experiments which can be carried out by the student using readily available materials to demonstrate properties and effects of air. Almost every experiment is accompanied by illustrations which will help students complete the experiment successfully. A number of pedantic scientific questions could be raised concerning the complete correctness of some explanations used in the book. In an attempt to simplify complex problems, Berger has sometimes oversimplified. One hopes that the book will provide the reader with an incentive to delve further into the science of air to obtain more fundamental knowledge.

H. C. Wohlers, in a review of "The New Air Book," in Science Books & Films, *Vol. XI, No. 1, May, 1975, p. 34.*

Cancer Lab (1975)

Berger observes the everyday work of the physician, surgeon, radiotherapist, clinical lab workers, virologists and others, with the usual attention to mechanics and "instrument panel" photos but with a little more background information on what the work is all about than in other of his *Scientists at Work* series (though there is nothing like the briefing on basics provided in the Silversteins' *Cancer*). The pitch is optimistic though not breathless ("more and more cancer patients are surviving major operations" and "immunology is a bright new hope"). Routine.

A review of "Cancer Lab," in Kirkus Reviews, *Vol. XLIII, No. 3, February 1, 1975, p. 123.*

The profuse black and white photographs of patients and

doctors, scientists, and technicians, as well as of equipment and even of the excised cancer, bring the easy-to-read, rather brief, and sweeping text to life. Included among the chapters are descriptions of the work of the physician, surgeon, radiotherapist, chemotherapist, immunologist, clinical lab workers, pathologist, cancer-cause researchers, virologists, drug-screeners, and basic cancer researchers. Training necessary for each area is not clearly spelled out, but casually stated as on page 67: "Most of the workers in a clinical lab are medical technologists. A good number of them are women. Many have college degrees in medical technology. In addition, most of them have received on the job training. After training, the technologists receive a state license . . ." Good for browsing and stimulating interest in cancer research. Photos are multiracial.

Doris Ullrick, in a review of "Cancer Lab," in Appraisal: Children's Science Books, *Vol. 9, No. 1, Winter, 1976, p. 9.*

Preceded by a foreword of deep feeling, this rather comprehensive book on cancer for young people proceeds to discuss, in turn, all types of cancer therapists and researchers involved in treatment and study. These discussions account for eleven short chapters, with the functions of each worker clearly delineated and the usual educational background of each suggested. The book is profusely illustrated with photographs of good quality. In a book such as this for older children, it seems unnecessary to confine the writing to very short sentences—they become tedious. Nevertheless, the boy or girl already interested in

Berger as a music teacher, conducting the high-school orchestra at Plainview, Long Island.

science or in the medical field will find this up-to-date work rewarding. Indexed. (pp. 9-10)

> *Esther H. Read, in a review of "Cancer Lab," in* Appraisal: Children's Science Books, *Vol. 9, No. 1, Winter 1976, pp. 9-10.*

The Clarinet and Saxophone Book (1975)

As in his *Flute* and *Violin* books Berger gives beginning musicians a modest boost by introducing the history, manufacture and repertoire of their chosen instrument. His look at how reeds are made and evaluated and a rundown of the various members of the clarinet and saxophone families will be most useful here. There are several pages of discography, listing jazz as well as classical performances, but the omission of Charlie Parker from a chapter on famous players is a good indication of Berger's lack of interest in jazz. Photos.

> *A review of "The Clarinet & Saxophone Book," in* Kirkus Reviews, *Vol. XLIII, No. 21, November 1, 1975, p. 1231.*

More than a basic how-to-play book, this is a welcome and useful companion to Berger's *Flute Book* and *Violin Book*. From the first single reed instrument used as early as 2700 B.C., Berger traces the history of Johann Denner's clarinet and Adolphe Sax's saxophone to the present day. The use of ancient reed instruments in various cultural settings provides fascinating background material. The making of both instruments is explained in detail with numerous step-by-step photographs. An entire chapter is devoted to the growth, development, and treatment of the cane used to make the reeds—the most essential element of both instruments. Many of the famed clarinet and saxophone players such as Tom Brown, Sigurd Rascher, Benny Goodman, Anthony Gigliotti, and David Glazer are noted with interesting anecdotes from their musical careers. There is also an appended glossary, discography, and index which will help young performers and aspiring music students.

> *Patricia M. Brown, in a review of "The Clarinet and Saxophone Book," in* School Library Journal, *Vol. 22, No. 5, January, 1976, p. 43.*

Consumer Protection Labs (1975)

Like Berger's *Pollution Lab,* this is an unquestioning description of the way things are supposed to work, with the FDA, state research agencies, Underwriters' Laboratory, Consumers Union, Calspan auto safety lab, J. C. Penney's, Lever Brothers and even drug companies all working—with presumably equal commitment—for the common goal of ensuring consumer protection. There's no hint that unsafe products ever get through their net, and nothing as controversial as Nader's brand of consumerism is mentioned; of course if what Berger gives us here were really the whole story, Nader would be irrelevant.

> *A review of "Consumer Protection Labs," in*

Kirkus Reviews, *Vol. XLIII, No. 23, December 1, 1975, p. 1337.*

A behind-the-scenes look at how various consumer protection labs function in their efforts to maintain and raise the quality of goods being made and sold in the U.S. today. Berger describes how scientists test products by riding bicycles over wooden cleats, dropping toasters off counters, stretching elastic until it snaps, and slamming cars at 60 miles an hour into steel poles. Numerous examples of research are accompanied by on-site photographs of tests being run in industrial and agriculture laboratories and food, drug, and safety agencies, as well as in private organizations such as Consumers Union and Underwriters Laboratories. However, groups such as Nader's Raiders, who feel the buying public is getting short shrift, are not mentioned, resulting in a one-sided view of how extensive and accurate the consumer tests really are.

> *Barbara Elleman, in a review of "Consumer Protection Labs," in* The Booklist, *Vol. 72, No. 12, February 15, 1976, p. 852.*

Berger describes nine types of scientific laboratories that affect consumer products. Examples are government food labs, food processing labs, safety testing labs and agricultural labs. These laboratories are run by government, private business and nonprofit consumer organizations. In each description, there is a profile of a scientist or technician selected to be representative of sex and race and to give insight into the work they do. Berger also provides information about the necessary training for these jobs. Good quality, black-and-white photographs enhance the book. Insight into the processes of science as applied to consumer protection is an attained goal of the author. However, he does not explore controversies that arise when the results of work in a government drug lab differ from the results of work in a drug corporation lab. This book should be an excellent resource for junior and senior high school students interested in consumer affairs. (pp. 94-5)

> *D. E. Ingmanson, in a review of "Consumer Protection Labs," in* Science Books & Films, *Vol. XII, No. 2, September, 1976, pp. 94-5.*

Time after Time (1975)

We probably won't be the only ones to feel disappointment when the subject of animals "inner clocks" gives way to the rotation of the earth and moon, and a short history of measuring time from the simple shadow stick we can make ourselves to today's atomic clock. But like Berger's *Storms* and *Stars,* this presents very basic explanations in the context of some more challenging, but unanswered, observations and some mind-stretching questions ("When did time begin? . . . what is the smallest unit of time?"). A likely first step beyond telling time.

> *A review of "Time after Time," in* Kirkus Reviews, *Vol. XLIII, No. 24, December 15, 1975, p. 1381.*

This book on time for young readers attempts to cover many distinct concepts. However, it is poorly organized, and its explanations are often vague. Different aspects of time are examined: inner clocks, day and night, seasons, and time-oriented natural instincts such as migration and egg laying. Although these different topics are included or mentioned, they are not explained clearly or explored in sufficient depth. I found myself asking "Why?" after such sentences as "Many trees lose their leaves at the same time every year," and "For half of the earth the winter becomes cold; it is the winter season." This introductory book would have been more successful if it had focused on fewer concepts and explored them in more detail, and with greater clarity. This is recommended only as an additional title for young scientists.

> *Christine McDonnell, in a review of "Time after Time," in* Appraisal: Children's Science Books, *Vol. 10, No. 2, Spring, 1977, p. 13.*

I recognize the difficulty of explaining abstract and complex matters to the very young, but I have seen it better done in other books. Some of the simplification seems to be due to economy of space rather than careful simplification; the explanation of the orientation of the earth's axis in the thought-experiment starting on p. 24 is a bit dubious. The paper sundial is going to wander off time rather confusingly during the day, unless the paper is tilted perpendicular to the earth's axis—and then it won't work between late September and late March because the sun will be "below" it. All in all, not bad, but not really impressive either.

> *Herbert J. Stolze, in a review of "Time after Time," in* Appraisal: Children's Science Books, *Vol. 10, No. 2, Spring, 1977, p. 13.*

Police Lab (1976)

The increasingly important role of the police laboratory in law enforcement work is skillfully presented in this well-written and profusely illustrated book. Berger covers the entire range of the criminologists' work and explains very lucidly the scientific processes in such areas as serology, toxicology, spectrography, chromatography, and pathology. Although the text points out that laboratory tests can be used to corroborate innocence, the examples presented show mainly how these tests can be used to prove guilt. With an increasing general interest in police work, this is a very good and up-to-date addition even to collections already using Kind and Overman's *Science Against Crime* (Doubleday, 1972), Lucas' *The Laboratory Detectives: How Science Traps the Criminals* (Taplinger, 1972), or Morland's *The Criminologist* (Open Court, 1972).

> *John Dawson Boniol, Jr., in a review of "Police Lab," in* School Library Journal, *Vol. 22, No. 6, February, 1976, p. 43.*

Recounting the actual circumstances surrounding a sampling of police cases effectively captures reader interest and offers a convenient lead-in to the details of how police labs go about analyzing the physical evidence related to the crime. Readers may already be familiar with the role of fingerprinting and ballistics in building a case against a suspect, but these well-chosen investigations also show,

for example, the work a document examiner does in spotting forgeries or the shrewdness an observant medical examiner displays in deciding whether or not foul play was involved in the victim's death. As a lesson Berger distinguishes, when necessary, between circumstantial and conclusive evidence and tells the courtroom verdict. Youngsters intrigued by law enforcement work will appreciate this look behind the scenes.

> *Denise M. Wilms, in a review of "Police Lab," in* The Booklist, *Vol. 72, No. 15, April 1, 1976, p. 1108.*

Berger uses nine actual cases ("only the names have been changed") to introduce his nine chapters on how different crime detection labs and methods help nail a suspect or—in one of the nine—establish his innocence. Thus a speck of gold paint between the threads of a dead child's jacket helps track down a hit-and-run driver; handwriting analysts put the finger on a forger; and a shrewd medical examiner exposes an intern who almost got away with murdering his wife. The cases have none of the narrative interest of Blassingame's *Science Catches the Criminal* (1975), but they do focus the guided tours, and Berger's surface-oriented approach works better in the police lab than in some of the other labs he's visited.

> *A review of "Police Lab," in* Kirkus Reviews, *Vol. XLIV, No. 8, April 15, 1976, p. 474.*

"Fitting In": Animals in Their Habitats (with Gilda Berger, 1976)

A simple and lucid explanation of some of the physical attributes of various species that have ensured their longevity as species or that enable them to adapt to their environments, procure food, or evade predators. The material is divided by habitat, with a few examples of animal adaptation for each. In the section on forest dwellers the quiet and gloom of the forest is noted, and the stress is on a well-developed sense of hearing (the mouse, the mole) that can help an animal escape or signal a source of food; in the quiet, a wolf can hear its mate howl, and if it hears danger sounds, a monkey can escape by leaping away on tree branches. This is not comprehensive, nor meant to be; it concludes with a rather abrupt plea for conservation and a one-page index.

> *Zena Sutherland, in a review of " 'Fitting In': Animals in Their Habitats," in* Bulletin of the Center for Children's Books, *Vol. 29, No. 11, July-August, 1976, p. 170.*

Ways in which animals have adapted to their environment is the subject of *"Fitting In."* The authors promise in the foreword to answer many questions, such as "Why does a desert fox have large ears?" and "Why does a snake smell with its tongue?". The book is organized into short chapters which discuss a few animals from each kind of habitat: water, land, desert, forest and the air. Although there is good transition between chapters, each chapter lacks internal coherence. For example, the chapter on desert animals begins by saying that deserts are quiet places and that every sound is important. The fact that desert snakes are completely deaf leaves the reader a bit confused. James Arnosky's illustrations, which combine accuracy with imagination, are an attractive asset to the book.

> *Geraldine Winkler, in a review of " 'Fitting In': Animals in Their Habitats," in* Appraisal: Children's Science Books, *Vol. 10, No. 1, Winter, 1977, p. 6.*

Adaptation is a topic which children find enjoyable and comprehensible if written at their academic level, and the Bergers do just that. They point out some differences among the animal species and tell how these differences enable species to survive their varied environments. Most of the text is devoted to how animals adapt to environments such as water, water and land, grassland, desert, forest and air. The content is interesting, simply expressed and accurate; the illustrations are satisfactory. The vocabulary would be difficult for many children in the intermediate elementary grades, but acceptable for most children in the upper elementary grades. Some topics are covered in a very general way, and a few children may be confused. However, this possibility is always present in books for this age group and it is not a serious shortcoming. Recommended for classroom use and as a library reference.

> *Donald L. Troyer, in a review of " 'Fitting In': Animals in Their Habitats," in* Science Books & Films, *Vol. XII, No. 4, March, 1977, p. 211.*

The Story of Folk Music   (1976)

"It is not really terribly important to put a label on every single song," says Berger, in a sensible attempt to define his subject—which he goes on to illustrate with representative ballads, work songs, protest music. The many examples, reinforced by repeated suggestions that the way to know folk music is to listen, sing and, if possible, play it for yourself, bolster a quick overview of the origins of ethnomusicology, the most popular folk instruments, the use of folk melodies by "art" composers, the careers of the Lomaxes, Leadbelly, and Woody Guthrie, and modern hybrids such as folk-rock. But the ten record discography that lists Judy Collins, Tim Hardin, and Bob Dylan, and then suggests sending away for a Folkways catalog, is indicative of Berger's overall slackness. A glancing introduction at best, but one that has no competition at this level.

> *A review of "The Story of Folk Music," in* Kirkus Reviews, *Vol. XLIV, No. 19, October 1, 1976, p. 1096.*

Here is a neatly constructed, wonderfully objective work by a scholar who takes his homely subject, and his young audience, seriously. Berger includes such interesting details as the mention of flutes made from a missionary's bones, lots of drawings and photographs, a collection of basic guitar chords plus the words and music to many folk songs. The historical information on folk music is generous but not excessive. The only drawback is that the author's style (a bit stilted) suggests that his book would be more appropriate for a somewhat younger audience than he addresses.

> *A review of "The Story of Folk Music," in* Publishers Weekly, *Vol. 210, No. 16, October 18, 1976, p. 63.*

Considering the scope and brevity of the work, Berger's book is only necessarily superficial. His information on the pathways of folk music, on its relationship to formally composed music, on popular instruments, and on twentieth-century American musicians is all reputable and easy to absorb. Also included are 22 well-chosen songs, complete with melodies, harmony indications, and verses—as well as a "getting started" section that diagrams guitar chords used. One may quibble with Berger's statement that "more people than ever before are listening to, singing, and composing folk songs," especially since the appended bibliography-discography argues the reverse quite well.

> *J. G., in a review of "The Story of Folk Music," in* Booklist, *Vol. 73, No. 8, December 15, 1976, p. 603.*

Medical Center Lab   (1976)

The variety, accessibility, and inherent interest of the investigations conducted in medical centers makes this lab tour in the *Scientists at Work* series pattern more successful than many. In "Clinical Labs," the first of two sections, Berger shows how "scientists help physicians treat the patients in the medical center" by doing a number of rush tests in the emergency lab, culturing blood samples in bacteriology, putting blood through a centrifuge and an automatic analyzer in biochemistry, doing biopsies in pathology, and examining stools in parasitology. Then come "Research Labs," where a doctor penetrates a pregnant uterus with a needlescope in perinatology and others do growth research on dwarfs, monitor heart functioning with ultrasound and catheters, and study rats' brains for drug effects and aggressive behavior. As usual Berger refers repeatedly to "scientists" where more specific designations would be more instructive, and as usual the accompanying photos of external operations are unilluminating, but at least in this visit you not only meet the *Scientists* but also get a handle on their *Work.* (pp. 1222-23)

> *A review of "Medical Center Lab," in* Kirkus Reviews, *Vol. XLIV, No. 22, November 15, 1976, pp. 1222-23.*

An intensive and extensive look at the myriad activities of a modern medical research center. The work of many specialists is explained; there is a supplementary career index; and generous use of clear black-and-white photos adds immeasurably to the text's usefulness. Authoritative and a must for any library serving this age level.

> *Shirley A. Smith, in a review of "Medical Center Lab," in* School Library Journal, *Vol. 23, No. 8, April, 1977, p. 62.*

Medical Center Lab belongs on the vocational guidance shelf in school libraries. The book covers both clinical labs (emergency room, bacteriology, biochemistry, pathology and parasitology), which assist the medical staff in diagnosis, and research labs (perinatology, growth, heart and brain), which seek new knowledge and new techniques of treatment. The text is well illustrated with photographs of actual laboratories. Because of the diversity of jobs in medical center labs and the brevity of the text, no particular aspect is discussed in depth; what is presented is an overall view of the many and varied careers which come together in medical center laboratories. This is done in the context of the treatment of actual patients, which is really what work in these labs is all about. The book is well indexed, and a short reading list is included.

> *Dorothy Bickerton, in a review of "Medical Center Lab," in* Science Books & Films, *Vol. XIII, No. 3, December, 1977, p. 151.*

Energy from the Sun (1976)

It is difficult to be merely factual in writing about energy these days. Authors have trouble facing the fact that, within man's current technical and engineering skills, there is no solution to the energy problem which simultaneously avoids both starvation and pollution; and when the author does face it, the editor often can't. The temptation is to choose a preferred solution, and having done so, to slant subsequent writings in its favor. I do not exempt myself from this charge.

Melvin Berger has avoided the problem by sticking to basic facts and not offering any answers. He gives an explanation of energy itself—not at all a bad one, considering the age for which he is writing—and then points out how practically all energy sources now in use can be traced back to the sun. Solar cells, tidal energy, wind, and geothermal alternatives are mentioned without any discussion of the practical difficulties besetting each. This is not negative criticism; neither the math nor the engineering would mean much to seven-year-olds. The author leaves his young readers with a list of possibilities and, we hope, an urge to find out more about some of them.

> *Harry C. Stubbs, in a review of "Energy from the Sun," in* The Horn Book Magazine, *Vol. LII, No. 6, December, 1976, p. 648.*

The emphasis of this very simple book is on the importance of the sun as a source of energy. Heat and light energy come directly from the sun, as one can see by letting a glass of cold water warm up in the sunshine. Berger explains how the food we eat comes indirectly from the sun and stresses the dependence of all living things on energy. Devices that use electricity are mentioned, and mechanical energy is explained as being produced in engines by heat from fuels, which are mainly sun-derived; coal, gas and oil are presented in this context. The author concludes with an optimistic look at new discoveries for capturing, storing and using energy. The solar cell and the solarheated house are cited as examples of direct use of the sun's energy; the splitting of atoms is listed as a source of nuclear energy; steam trapped in the earth, the blowing wind and ocean tides are mentioned as additional energy sources.

> *Blanchard Hiatt, in a review of "Energy from*

the Sun," *in* Science Books & Films, *Vol. XII, No. 4, March, 1977, p. 215.*

An absorbing account for junior children of the many ways in which the sun's energy is used by man. The text uses simple words and short sentences to explain ideas including the food cycle, fossil fuels, solar heating and cells. Each page is illustrated [by Giulio Maestro] in a clear informative way—the diagrams of an oil well, a coal mine and a solar-heated house are particularly well done—though the diagram illustrating nuclear energy might be misleading. Most children will enjoy reading the book on their own, but some adult help might be needed with the first few pages about what energy means.

The main strength of the book is that it encourages children to think creatively about science. An experiment is suggested, albeit a simple one, to illustrate the heat energy of the sun. The reader is questioned and led to question for herself, and encouraged to think of herself as a future scientist. With more books like this, we might have more scientists. (pp. 272, 274)

> *Marion Kimberley, in a review of "Energy from the Sun," in* The School Librarian, *Vol. 28, No. 3, September, 1980, pp. 272, 274.*

Quasars, Pulsars, and Black Holes in Space (1977)

Berger's brief primer begins with a quick, general review of astronomical instruments from optical and radio telescopes to spectroscopes and satellite observatories. He introduces quasars as the first stars found to be emitting both light and radio waves and mentions different possible explanations as to what they really are; with pulsars, he describes how they emit radio waves by synchroton radiation (thus the non-optical "twinkle"); and he ends with a few pages on black holes (what happens to the matter that disappears therein?) and a descriptive overview of the expanding universe. It's all totally untaxing and will help the non-science-oriented to feel comfortable with the terms and concepts, though Branley's overlapping *Black Holes, White Dwarfs and Super Stars* (1976) offers a far more stimulating sort of orientation.

> *A review of "Quasars, Pulsars and Black Holes in Space," in* Kirkus Reviews, *Vol. XLV, No. 7, April 1, 1977, p. 354.*

Decidedly simpler than Branley's *Black Holes, White Dwarfs and Superstars,* Berger's book leaves out technical explanations and opts for generalized definitions that use easily understandable analogies to clarify certain points or principles. The described capabilities of optical and radio telescopes suffice to give an idea of how scientists found out what they know about the universe; and there's an uncomplicated explanation of the spectroscope, which separates light into color and gives an idea of a star's chemical makeup. After that, an explanatory chapter is devoted to each title subject, including reportage on scientific processes of discovery and puzzles still to be researched. A glossary pins down technical terms. Use this as an organizational stepping-stone to Branley's more complicated and substantial coverage.

Denise M. Wilms, in a review of "Quasars, Pulsars and Black Holes in Space," in Booklist, *Vol. 73, No. 18, May 15, 1977, p. 1417.*

Quasars, pulsars and black holes all represent exciting new ideas in astronomy unknown a generation ago. Making wise use of photographs, the author includes an introductory review of optical telescopes, radio telescopes and spectroscopes, the tools of astronomy. . . . In the chapter dealing with new concepts in the field of cosmology, one of the most fascinating topics is the possibility of "worm holes,"—areas connecting black holes with so-called "white holes" and possibly even other universes. The book closes with a good glossary and an accurate index. Fry's readability curve analysis shows a reading level well within the junior high school student's ability, making the book a worthwhile adjunct to the astronomy unit in earth science courses taught in the eighth or ninth grades.

Philip Kutner, in a review of "Quasars, Pulsars and Black Holes in Space," in Science Books & Films, *Vol. XIII, No. 4, March, 1978, p. 220.*

FBI (1977)

Covering the training and work of Special Agents, the operations of the Laboratory and the Identification Division but not the activities of the director and other high-level administrators, this history of the FBI is a glorification of the bureau. There is no mention of past illegal FBI maneuvers nor of the controversies that have surrounded the agency, and the inclusion of current "Ten Most-Wanted Criminals" posters is useless since these will quickly become out of date.

John D. Boniol, in a review of "FBI," in School Library Journal, *Vol. 24, No. 4, December, 1977, p. 46.*

Automobile Factory (1977)

Berger covers not only the jobs in an automobile factory but the many different steps needed to produce a car off the assembly line at the rate of one per minute. In addition to workers on the assembly line, designers, planners, testing and proving personnel, and manufacturers are also presented. A discussion of each occupation (blue and white collar) mentions its responsibilities and the training and education needed. Salary information is omitted, and the dissatisfactions of routine factory work are treated in only the most general way. As with other books in this series, however, the text has sufficient black-and-white photographs, illustrating men and women doing the same or similar jobs.

Judyth Lessee, in a review of "Automobile Factory," in School Library Journal, *Vol. 24, No. 6, February, 1978, p. 54.*

The Supernatural: From ESP to UFOs (1977)

The origins of spiritualism, witchcraft, astrology, etc. are impartially discussed in light of the public's current fascination with the supernatural. Clearly written in an anecdotal style with each chapter exploring a single phenomenon, the text adequately describes the alleged feats of such famous psychics as Uri Geller and Arthur Ford as well as the pioneering research on paranormal experience undertaken at Duke and other universities. The coverage includes the opinions of believers as well as skeptics (from both magical and scientific quarters) and recounts many incidents of trickery and deception. The book best addresses those with no background but the lack of illustrations makes it a far less engaging survey than Watson & Chaneles' *The Golden Book of the Mysterious* (Golden Pr, 1976).

Anne Raymer, in a review of "The Supernatural: From ESP to UFOs," in School Library Journal, *Vol. 24, No. 7, March, 1978, p. 135.*

My vote for the most welcome science book of the year would go to this searching, unbiased study of supernatural reports. The first chapter sets the tone: The author describes a disquieting encounter he once had with a stranger in an art gallery, who spoke of actual events in Berger's life. Was the stranger receiving mental messages? The author purposely does not give an answer. The remaining eight chapters of the book examine several categories of supernatural phenomena, including faith healing, witchcraft, parapsychology, and psychokinesis. . . . Larry Kettelkamp's *Investigating Psychics: Five Life Histories* is a weaker book than Berger's, because Kettelkamp, already convinced that the supernatural exists, seeks to convince the reader and does not include examples of frauds. Knowing that natural explanations have sometimes been found makes the reader properly cautious about accepting evidence of the existence of the supernatural. Movies and newspaper accounts as well as ubiquitous horoscopes have evoked curiosity about the supernatural in many children who might benefit from Berger's account. (pp. 308-09)

Sarah Gagné, "Supernatural Phenomena," in The Horn Book Magazine, *Vol. LIV, No. 3, June, 1978, pp. 308-09.*

This is a book that will be of little use to the serious reader of any age. Loose and inaccurate, it lumps together a smattering of scientific research in parapsychology (most of which is behind the times) with astrology, witchcraft, spiritualism and UFOs. Even the effort at being impartial comes off poorly. In hit-and-run fashion, the author selects dramatic, rather than evidential, material and then cites critics and skeptics in a way that whitewashes the initial impact. Nowhere is there a valid sifting out of the real from the spurious. Even the recommended readings leave much to be desired.

Montague Ullman, in a review of "The Supernatural: From ESP to UFOs," in Science Books & Films, *Vol. XIV, No. 3, December, 1978, p. 142.*

Jigsaw Continents (1978)

In its opening at least, another trivialization. Whereas

Weiss' misdirected *Lands Adrift* (1975) features Benjamin Franklin and compares drifting continents to a touring ship, Berger begins with trumped-up drama (an earthquake in Guatemala) and references to angry gods—and the next double-page picture, presumably illustrating a paragraph introducing plate techtonics, is of two dinosaurs facing off. Later on, this entry differs from other juveniles on the subject in that instead of summarizing arguments and tracing the process of discovery, it simply explains that the earth's surface consists of rocky plates which "jostle one another at the edges," causing earthquakes or forming mountains, and that (as "some theorize") there was once a giant super-continent which has split up and drifted apart. A reasonable approach, now that the idea is established—but Berger's presentation is neither as serious nor as basic as it could be at this level.

> *A review of "Jigsaw Continents," in* Kirkus Reviews, *Vol. XLVI, No. 3, February 1, 1978, p. 108.*

In a continuous text, amply illustrated [by Bob Totten] with drawings that show the relations between drifting continental plates and such disasters as earthquakes or volcanic eruption, Berger explains the theory of plate tectonics. Text and illustrations show clearly how the present land masses could have fitted together, and include some of the clues scientists have to corroborate the theory that the earth originally had one giant land mass. The explanation isn't comprehensive, and the material might have been better organized, but the book fills a real need; while there have been some excellent books for older readers, there has been little available on continental drift for the middle grades. A brief index is appended.

> *Zena Sutherland, in a review of "Jigsaw Continents," in* Bulletin of the Center for Children's Books, *Vol. 31, No. 10, June, 1978, p. 154.*

After capturing the attention of its readers with a dramatic description of the Guatemalan earthquake of 1976, this introductory book designed for lower elementary school children sums up the theory of plate tectonics in simple terms, and shows through concrete analogies how it may be used to explain such phenomena as volcanoes, earthquakes, and the formation of certain mountain ranges. The author is weaker in presenting the facts upon which the theory is based—no mention is made of the magnetic and fossile evidence. Nor is there any attempt to describe the evolution of the theory. . . . Choppy sentences, repetitious use of words and phrases, and careless editing are further weaknesses. Certainly there is no excuse for the statement that the Grand Canyon is in Colorado! Despite these drawbacks, the book does provide a useful summary of important elements in the theory of plate tectonics in a form comprehensible to young children. (pp. 54-5)

> *Rea Alkema, in a review of "Jigsaw Continents," in* Appraisal: Children's Science Books, *Vol. 12, No. 1, Winter, 1979, pp. 54-5.*

The Trumpet Book (1978)

As in his books on the violin, the flute, and the clarinet and saxophone, Berger reviews the trumpet's origin and history, how it works and how it's made, a few famous players (mostly jazz, for good reason, but without much sense of the music), and some classical compositions with trumpet parts. Would-be musicians are told how to care for a trumpet and what to expect at their first few lessons, as well as how to listen to others: "First and foremost, you should listen for the overall musical effect. . . . Finally, listen to the quality of the trumpet playing. How is the tone? . . . Does the player hide his or her breathing?" As a writer Berger hides his breathing, but his playing is mechanical, more concerned with getting through a routine exercise than with conveying anything in particular.

> *A review of "The Trumpet Book," in* Kirkus Reviews, *Vol. XLVI, No. 14, July 15, 1978, p. 752.*

Following the same format as Berger's **Flute Book,** the long history of the trumpet is illustrated here with black-and-white drawings and photographs of the instrument in various shapes and sizes. A scientific explanation of the way trumpet sounds are produced is followed by a tour through a trumpet factory. Another chapter is devoted to closely-related instruments in the brass family such as the cornet and the bass trumpet. Short biographies of well-known players such as Louis Armstrong, Harry James, and Doc Severinsen are also included. A discussion of the types of music that have been written for the trumpet concentrates mostly on classical pieces. However, a discography at the end of the book does include some recordings of jazz and popular music. For those thinking about which instrument to play or investigating a career in music, this will help foster a finer appreciation of the trumpet; and, it will help listeners to better appreciate the efforts of trumpet players.

> *Sheila Rezak, in a review of "The Trumpet Book," in* School Library Journal, *Vol. 25, No. 2, October, 1978, p. 142.*

Disease Detectives (1978)

Although this focuses on the massive efforts made to discover the source of the "Legionnaires' disease," it demonstrates the ways in which medical, paramedical, and cooperating scientists and engineers work together to find the causes of epidemic or rare diseases. The work is coordinated by personnel at the federal Disease Control Center in Atlanta, but local agencies and specialists also contribute to the detective process. The book has some of the suspense of a detective thriller, it's informative and accurate, and it can give readers an excellent overview of the scientific method and attitude. A brief bibliography is included.

> *Zena Sutherland, in a review of "Disease Detectives," in* Bulletin of the Center for Children's Books, *Vol. 32, No. 2, October, 1978, p. 23.*

Berger has used the search for the cause of Legionnaires' disease as a framework for his description of how epidemiologists (specifically those at the Center for Disease Con-

While Gilda takes notes, Berger photographs a subject for a book in the "Scientists at Work" series.

trol in Atlanta) work. The writing style is clear and concise; technical terms are kept to a minimum and are explained in the text. *Epidemic!* by Jules Archer (HBJ, 1977) offers broader coverage of epidemiology. Still, Berger's concentration on Legionnaires' disease results in an exciting detective story as well as a book that imparts a great deal of information about how the CDC works.

> *Kathryn M. Weisman, in a review of "Disease Detective," in* School Library Journal, *Vol. 25, No. 2, October, 1978, p. 142.*

Unlike Berger's other entries in the *Scientists at Work* series, this sticks to one story—the Legionnaires' Disease mystery—to demonstrate the workings of the federal Center for Disease Control in Atlanta. The search for a bacterial, viral, or other cause takes readers into the labs where virologists painstakingly test samples with antibodies and examine them with electron microscopes, toxicologists subject them to gas chromatology, and so on—until a later, longer look at the slides turns up the previously overlooked bacteria. As usual for the series, the photos (courtesy of the CDC) are of the P.R., console variety, and Berger's text also tends to overemphasize routines and devices—but the Legionnaire's Disease case gives the book focus and continuity. (pp. 67-8)

> *A review of "Disease Detectives," in* Kirkus

Reviews, *Vol. XLVII, No. 2, January 15, 1979, pp. 67-8.*

This innately fascinating story is somewhat marred by some bias toward the CDC, picturing the CDC as the good guy while in reality there could have been faster action at the start of the epidemic and more cooperation with the state health department. While not as objective as it should be, the book is suspenseful and has clear exposition. The explanation of the differences between microbes, bacteria and viruses is somewhat confusing as are the definitions of different kinds of scientists. Descriptions of laboratory procedures are not always clear and are sometimes misleading, especially in the illustrations. A serious deficiency is the use of the illustrations and the relevance of the accompanying captions to the story. It looks as if the author tried to make general pictures of laboratory personnel fit the story. A curious juvenile would ask more questions than could be answered in the text.

> *Judith Pachciarz, in a review of "Disease Detectives," in* Science Books & Films, *Vol. XV, No. 3, December, 1979, p. 169.*

The New Food Book: Nutrition, Diet, Consumer Tips, and Foods of the Future **(with Gilda Berger, 1978)**

The book is comprehensive and readable; it ties together

several timely topics: nutrients, additives, consumer information, starvation, and the Green Revolution. The first section, on the six nutrients, is commendable for the experiments it suggests in assaying food and for being objective rather than preaching in describing the merits of good food. The second section covers digestion, balanced diet, food shopping, and overeating. It is a serious omission, I feel, not to caution children about junk food and empty calories or to explain, at least, what the terms mean. The last section admirably covers food preservation, additives, and the Food and Drug Administration GRAS list and takes a concerned look at the twelve per cent of the world's population which is chronically hungry. The authors feel it would be inhumane not to share our food with starving people, however many there might be, and they conclude with hope for the outcome of the Green Revolution. . . . With a bibliography and an index.

> *Sarah Gagné, in a review of "The New Food Book," in* The Horn Book Magazine, *Vol. LV, No. 5, October, 1978, p. 544.*

The Bergers have produced a low-key but highly informational book which should fill in a blank spot in most children's collections. . . . The book strikes a good balance between the traditional and health food viewpoints, avoiding both textbook dullness and overenthusiastic proselytising. The authors don't hesitate to give the claims on both sides of an argument and leave the conclusion to further investigation by scientists, and (one might hope) the reader. Very simple experiments illustrating a number of "food facts" are scattered throughout the book, smoothly merging into the text; they might provide some different science fair projects. Broader based than most books on this subject, this readable, well-organized, and informative introduction deserves a larger readership than it will probably get.

> *Daphne Ann Hamilton, in a review of "The New Food Book: Nutrition, Diet, Consumer Tips, and Foods of the Future," in* Appraisal: Children's Science Books, *Vol. 12, No. 1, Winter, 1979, p. 5.*

In today's world of soaring consumer prices, health foods and diets, it is increasingly important that young people develop sensible eating and purchasing habits. It is generally accepted that many of our daily eating habits develop out of what we are taught and shown as children: this is largely why children in Asia crave food that is salty or spicy, while children in the United States have a predilection for sweets. This book was written to help disseminate basic nutritional information to young people, and the Bergers have put together a well-organized discussion of nutrition, diet and consumer tips. The well-written book is nicely interspersed with easy but thought-provoking experiments that one can try at home. There are also a few fascinating recipes. (Have you ever tasted seaweed bread?) Believing that young people should also be aware of the problem of global hunger, the authors include a section on the important and fascinating work presently going on to increase food production and nutritional content. Although not sufficiently detailed to be considered a reference, this book would be very useful as collateral source material or as a teaching aid at about the sixth grade level. (pp. 43-4)

> *David M. Drucker, in a review of "The New Food Book: Nutrition, Diet, Consumer Tips, and Foods of the Future," in* Science Books & Films, *Vol. XV, No. 1, May, 1979, pp. 43-4.*

Building Construction (1978)

A clear picture of the largest industry in the U.S. emerges as Berger discusses the various work involved in building homes, factories, and skyscrapers. In logistical progression, the jobs of the planners (architects, engineers), structural workers (excavators, carpenters), finishing crews (roofers, masons), and mechanical workers (plumbers, electricians) are described and related to one another with attention given to the skills necessary for these jobs. The photographs are too few, often dark, fuzzy, and without focus on aspects of building children would not normally see, such as blueprints, ductwork, piping, and cooling towers; however, the text is presented with care and accuracy, offering a good source for career and industry-at-work units.

> *Barbara Elleman in a review of "Building Construction," in* Booklist, *Vol. 75, No. 4, October 15, 1978, p. 371.*

Bionics (1978)

Formally described in 1960 as "the study of the systems and structures of living animals and plants, and the application of these principles to devising machines and artificial systems for the benefit of humans," bionics today fits most comfortably into the realm of biomedical engineering. Berger explores this designated science's "bringing together" nature to show how medical, biological, and engineering technologies merge to provide the information researchers rely on to produce lifelike artificial systems, whether they be body parts or specialized machines such as computers or robots. The main emphasis here, though, is on body parts; and existing systems—a variety of artificial limbs, organs, induced senses—plus a quick look at computers and experimental robots demonstrate theories in practice. A simplified, smooth-reading introduction to a media-popularized topic, with occasional black-and-white photographs. (p. 1490)

> *Denise M. Wilms, in a review of "Bionics," in* Booklist, *Vol. 74, No. 18, May 15, 1978, pp. 1489-90.*

It is not customary to think of grandpa, with his dentures, spectacles and arch supports, as a bionic man, but from this humble instance of prosthesis to the amplified power replacements of folk heroes in the superman class there is a continuum. This good-humoured monograph on the subject will doubtless be devoured by young enthusiasts. It goes from the abortive attempts of Daedalus and Icarus to full robotics.

> *H. M. Thomas, in a review of "Bionics," in*

The School Librarian, *Vol. 26, No. 4, December, 1978, p. 362.*

The World of Dance (1978)

Early circle dances are probably related to the shapes of the earliest dwellings; people who dance in rows or lines often live in square or rectangular huts. . . . All peoples who go in for convulsive dancing have witch-doctor or medicine-man cultures. . . . Leap dancers usually live in mountainous or hilly regions and are herders with patriarchal societies. Such ideas are interesting but, except for Alan Lomax' association of types of arm movements with the sophistication of a society's means of production, Berger gives no hint as to where they come from or to what extent his generalizations represent speculation, accepted theory, or (as his manner suggests) recognized fact. At any rate this approach is not carried through the more routine history of dance from ancient Egypt through the Middle Ages and Renaissance to the present, although he does try, in a more conventional way, to relate developments in dance to those in other arts and to the general climate of the times—until modern times where the history degenerates to a roundup of names (of dancers, dances, choreographers, companies) with just a few tag characterizations. (Even at that, do "liveliness" and "energy" give the most accurate impression of Twyla Tharp's style?) Overall, an odd mixture of textbookish survey with ideas that demand more sophisticated treatment.

> *A review of "The World of Dance," in* Kirkus Reviews, *Vol. XLVII, No. 1, January 1, 1979, p. 13.*

A history of dance begins with an introductory chapter marred by generalizations such as "Ballet was created during the Renaissance as an expression of the new belief in an ordered, logical world." . . . The book provides a great deal of information, but it gives superficial coverage to contemporary dance (ballet or modern) especially to contemporary dancers and choreographers (no Tudor, no Fonteyn or Markova) and it omits such stars as Pavlova. Useful, but not comprehensive, the book is written in a dry style. A divided bibliography and index are appended. (pp. 110-11)

> *Zena Sutherland, in a review of "The World of Dance," in* Bulletin of the Center for Children's Books, *Vol. 32, No. 7, March, 1979, pp. 110-11.*

A mundane presentation of the history of dance, overextended and under-researched . . . . There is no mention of dance notation, provocative generalizations are unsupported, regional folk dancing is given a cursory treatment. Illustrated with mediocre photographs, drawings, and prints, Berger's survey is an acceptable updating of Haskell's *Wonderful World of Dance* (Doubleday, 1960), but libraries seeking more extensive material on the ballet should get Lawson's *The Story of Ballet* (Taplinger, 1977).

> *Jane Bickel, in a review of "The World of Dance," in* School Library Journal, *Vol. 25, No. 7, March, 1979, p. 135.*

Planets, Stars, and Galaxies (1978)

Following a brief introduction designed to impress the young reader with the wonder of the universe, Berger describes "The Earth and the Other Planets," "The Sun and the Other Stars" and "The Milky Way and Other Galaxies." By and large, his factual accounts are accurate and clear although there are a few errors and erroneous concepts. The worst of the latter is a passage implying that the earth is made up almost entirely of a molten iron core. Another section incorrectly implies that the surface composition of the planets can be accurately determined by spectroscopic analysis. The book is up to date and, in a few areas, conveys the excitement of current discoveries. One analogy, comparing stars to light bulbs, is particularly well done. On the negative side, the description of energy generation by atomic fusion is a bit complex for the readership intended, and significant areas such as stellar variability, stellar duplicity and quasars are omitted. The book is recommended as an introduction to the fast-changing science of astronomy. It should be supplemented with current information from newspapers or general astronomical or scientific periodicals.

> *Arthur A. Hoag, in a review of "Planets, Stars and Galaxies," in* Science Books & Films, *Vol. XV, No. 4, March, 1980, p. 225.*

The Stereo Hi-Fi Handbook (1979)

A large quantity of highly technical information for serious stereo students. The techniques of sound reproduction and the various components of a stereo system are discussed. Practical advice on the selection of a system is given, as well as info on installation and care of the system. No particular brands are endorsed, but specifications are recommended for each component, with suggested price ranges. Though clearly and concisely written, understanding this material will require some background in stereo reproduction.

> *Marcia L. Perry, in a review of "The Stereo Hi-Fi Handbook," in* School Library Journal, *Vol. 26, No. 1, September, 1979, p. 152.*

This is the kind of handbook often wished for by junior hi librarians: has all the facts, neatly arranged, and you can read it. Each term is well defined, the sequence of material is logical, and the illustrations [by Lloyd Birmingham] appropriate. Includes radio receivers, cassette recorders, and making your own, as well as the usual chapters on turntables, amplifiers and speakers. Best of all, Berger tells you how to read the specs and exactly what to look for in purchasing each piece of equipment. It's even useful for younger or older readers.

> *Jerry Grim, in a review of "Stereo Hi-Fi Handbook," in* Voice of Youth Advocates, *Vol. 3, No. 2, June, 1980, p. 33.*

Putting on a Show (1980)

Children thinking about play production or theater as a

career will find Berger's straightforward discussion informative, if not stimulating. Careful planning, emphasized throughout as necessary to a successful production, is integrated into the descriptions of the responsibilities of the director and actor, and duties of the individual crews involved in scenery and props, light and sound, costume and makeup, as well as tickets and advertising. Terms are defined and elaborated on with enough detail to be practical, and the supplemental diagrams are good. Unfortunately the black-and-white photographs are dark and grainy and add little to the text. Despite this negative point, beginning thespians with off- and on-stage interests will find the guidance helpful. (pp. 1287-88)

> *Barbara Elleman, in a review of "Putting on a Show," in* Booklist, *Vol. 76, No. 17, May 1, 1980, pp. 1287-88.*

The Photo Dictionary of Football (1980)

If, in order to enjoy the game, one needs to understand it, everything needed is included here. Perhaps you've wondered about the difference between a halfback and a fullback. This and other questions are satisfactorily answered, aided by many action shots. If you have the impression that football is an exclusively male pursuit—not so. But, you won't be disabused of that notion in this book. Nevertheless, it is a useful, enlightening reference tool.

> *Jean F. Hammond, in a review of "Photo Dictionary of Football," in* Childhood Education, *Vol. 57, No. 3, January-February, 1981, p. 174.*

The New Earth Book: Our Changing Planet (1980)

Illustrated with pedestrian drawings [by George DeGrazio], this is an adequate introduction to a broad spectrum of topics, described with accuracy but not described comprehensively; the water cycle is covered in just over a page, for example, geothermal energy in less than two pages. The writing style is clear and direct, marred slightly by Berger's tendency to repeat information: page 38. "Scientists believe that the rocks in these places contain large amounts of thorium and uranium, which are radioactive elements," and two pages later, discussing radioactivity in rocks in the earth's interior, "These rocks contain elements, such as thorium and uranium, which are always emitting particles and rays, and producing heat." Most of the material is not new, although Berger gives some new facts about such topics as earth tides and gravity waves. The book covers many subjects, the material is well organized, and a bibliography and an index are included, as are many suggested home experiments.

> *Zena Sutherland, in a review of "The New Earth Book: Our Changing Planet," in* Bulletin of the Center for Children's Books, *Vol. 34, No. 9, May, 1981, p. 166.*

Berger has assembled a potpourri of geologic information, but it is difficult to gauge the audience level. His staccato style can be disturbing, particularly in those instances where the circumstance introduced may not relate directly to its antecedent. At the same time, the context may call for prior knowledge that the reader may not have. The scientific method of investigation is not particularly emphasized, and little effort is made to distinguish between hypothesis, theory and fact. At times, precision seems to be replaced by generalization (e.g., placing the age of the oceans at 500 million years). Some of the illustrations might be reinforced, for clarity, with photographs. The index is moderately helpful but could have been complemented by the addition of a glossary, particularly for the precocious reader. The experiments suggested have merit, although I have some reservations about the use of moth balls and the deliberate breaking of glass in the family refrigerator. The work does not compare favorably with competing editions covering similar material. It is probably best read in groups with active teacher or parental guidance so that qualifying or reinforcing information can be supplied and questions answered as learning takes place.

> *Daniel B. Sass, in a review of "The New Earth Book: Our Changing Planet," in* Science Books & Films, *Vol. 16, No. 5, May-June, 1981, p. 275.*

I am sorry to say that I found this book very disappointing. I realize that Mr. Berger was trying to write for a very young audience and was limited, or limited himself, to a small vocabulary and concrete concepts, but even allowing for this, there was much that bothered me. Using the words "heavier" and "lighter" instead of "denser" and "less dense" has been unacceptable to science teachers for many years. Many of the statements of fact are badly dated—it is now believed that life began on Earth much sooner than two billion years after the planet's formation. Many are simply wrong; there were mammals on the planet in the Triassic period, much more than 30 to 40 million years ago. Some are true only by rather strained definitions of terms; there are in fact more solar eclipses than lunar ones per year unless one includes penumbral lunar ones and there are at least two total or annular solar eclipses every year.

Some of the experiments are good, but others decidedly not. The old candle-in-an-inverted-glass one gives no meaningful quantitative results—most of the volume drop is due to cooling of the air, but the candle goes out long before all the oxygen is gone. These compensating variables may produce an answer somewhere near twenty percent, but nothing is being proved.

> *Harry C. Stubbs, in a review of "The New Earth Book: Our Changing Planet," in* Appraisal: Science Books for Young People, *Vol. 14, No. 3, Fall, 1981, p. 11.*

Robots in Fact and Fiction (1980)

Berger has not only chosen a subject of great appeal but has presented it with a sense of excitement. A history of automata is given, current uses of robots in industry, medicine and space research touched upon and future applications surmised, all with a liberal dose of black-and-white photographs. The real fun of **Robots in Fact and Fiction** lies in the fiction part: the author examines robots in movies (from *Bride of Frankenstein* to *Star Wars*), on television (*Lost in Space* and *Star Trek*) and in comics (*Flash Gordon*). Young readers will enjoy browsing through the many wonderful movie stills that are included. Indeed, as Berger describes movie plots or episodes of television dramas, one senses the author's real interest is in film, not robots, although he does claim that fictional robots stimulate inventions of actual robots and vice versa. Suggested readings and an index are appended.

> *Connie Tyrell, in a review of "Robots in Fact and Fiction," in* School Library Journal, *Vol. 27, No. 9, May, 1981, p. 62.*

Computers in Your Life   (1981)

Not how computers work but the work computers do and presumably will do in a vacuum-packed electronics future. As in his 1972 introduction to **Computers,** Berger first takes readers on a gadget-level tour of a computer's input, storage, control, processing, and output units. The rest surveys some of its more dramatic or close-to-home functions—in hospitals, schools, homes, business, and government. We learn that libraries are switching to "zebra stripe" circulation control, that pilots are confronted with simulated collisions during training sessions, that a machine might soon beat the world champion chess player, that a combination telephone-printout system can facilitate long-distance communication, and that Japan's horrendous auto traffic is computer-controlled. Characteristically, Berger doesn't deal with the implications of these systems for workers, consumers, and society in general, or with the science of computers. What we do have is a slide show on the wonders of computers—some of which may elicit the called-for wonderment.

> *A review of "Computers in Your Life," in* Kirkus Reviews, *Vol. XLIX, No. 13, July 1, 1981, p. 802.*

This is not intended as an introduction to computers and how they function, although it gives some pertinent facts about computer programming and capabilities, but as an overview of the present diversity and the future potential of computers. Berger shows how the use of computers in offices, public services, transportation, medicine, and other fields has already changed the speed and precision of problem solving, and he shows how new applications of computer technology are beginning to be within the grasp of individuals for home use, a function that will undoubtedly increase in the future. The material is interesting, although most of it is available in other books for children; the writing style is rather flat, with occasional fictionalized passages that have an air of contrivance. A bibliography and an index are provided.

> *Zena Sutherland, in a review of "Computers in Your Life," in* Bulletin of the Center for Children's Books, *Vol. 35, No. 1, September, 1981, p. 5.*

After a short description of how computers work, the book examines the many applications of computers in medicine, communication, engineering, business, schools, helping the disabled, homes, fighting crime, and running our government. The language is clear, and the photographs are often helpful. However helpful it is to know something about these applications of the computer, this knowledge alone is not enough to really understand the role of these magnificent machines in our lives. It would seem that there are no problems we must solve in using computers wisely. The brief statement that "some workers are losing their jobs to the machine" is almost in the nature of an aside. The issue of privacy is unexamined. The use of the computer in school is limited to computer assisted instruction (CAI). No mention is made of Seymour Papert's work to convert the computer's role from an electronic workbook to a tool for generating imaginative thinking in the learner. Nor is any space given to the danger of computerizing military decisions.

> *Lazer Goldberg, in a review of "Computers in Your Life," in* Appraisal: Science Books for Young People, *Vol. 15, No. 2, Spring-Summer, 1982, p. 22.*

The Photo Dictionary of the Orchestra   (1981)

Clear, candid and interesting, the 80 photographs in Berger's book show young people as musicians, which will reinforce the concept that making music is within their grasp. The writing is clear; the definitions are concise yet complete. The diagram of orchestral section positions is helpful, as is the use of both standard and metric measurements. Although this cross-referenced dictionary is a useful reference book, some further additions and clarifications would have increased the book's value: some general musical terms, defined in the introduction (e.g., "pitch"), should have been included within the body of the dictionary, while other words (e.g., "embouchure") are omitted altogether. Some words (e.g., "recital") are used within the definitions of other words (such as "concert") but are not included, even with a "see" reference in the list of terms. A pronunciation guide for at least the most difficult words (e.g., "glockenspiel") would have helped, as would have including the pitch ranges of instruments, written in musical notation. (pp. 87-8)

> *Holly Sanhuber, in a review of "The Photo Dictionary of the Orchestra," in* School Library Journal, *Vol. 28, No. 3, November, 1981, pp. 87-8.*

Young concert-goers and novices who have discovered the symphony later in life will find this collection of black-and-white photographs with accompanying definitions very informative. The author, who has also done **The Photo Dictionary of Football** . . . , includes not only musical instruments, usually with young people playing them, but some details, such as *end pin* and *mouthpiece,* and a few terms, such as *pizzicato,* arranged in one alphabet, with adequate cross-references. The clarity of both the photographs and the brief, simply written text recommends this modest little dictionary for school and public libraries. (p. 521)

Frances Neel Cheney, in a review of "The Photo Dictionary of the Orchestra," in American Reference Books Annual 1982, *Vol. 13, 1982, pp. 520-21.*

Comets, Meteors, and Asteroids (1981)

With due attention to the background of his readers the author has produced a good, concise historical summary of our knowledge of the smaller members of the solar system. The discovery, motions, and natures of these objects are covered very well. He seems to feel more certain about some statements than does the average astronomer; for instance, the satellites of asteroids mentioned are viewed with considerable doubt in the profession, although this does not, of course, mean that they don't exist. It is unfortunate that astronomical information accumulates so much faster than a book can be produced; I understand that there is now radar evidence that the nucleus of Encke's comet is about 2.5 kilometers across, an item which would have fit nicely into Mr. Berger's presentation. Even allowing for the youth of his readers, I am not convinced that he should have simplified meteor speed so greatly; the fact is that after entering atmosphere the objects are constantly losing speed, and no average is very meaningful. But the book is a worthwhile addition to home or school libraries. Glossary and index.

> *Harry C. Stubbs, in a review of "Comets, Meteors and Asteroids," in* The Horn Book Magazine, *Vol. LVII, No. 6, December, 1981, p. 687.*

Berger has once again come through with one of his sound, simple-but-not-simplified introductions to science, this one dealing with those fascinating "leftovers" from the formation of the solar system: comets, meteors, and asteroids. . . . Each type of object is covered in a separate section detailing its nature, behavior, and place in the solar scheme, as well as their relationships to Earth and human attempts to study them. I did feel that Caroline Herschel deserved some mention in the chapter on comets, and that Trojan asteroids deserved more explanation; on the whole, however, the coverage provides a good comprehensive introduction to the subjects. Although Berger's style is a bit choppy at the beginning, it quickly smooths out and combines with the crisp format and plentiful illustrations to make a very readable book. (pp. 20-1)

> *Daphne Ann Hamilton, in a review of "Comets, Meteors and Asteroids," in* Appraisal: Science Books for Young People, *Vol. 15, No. 2, Spring-Summer, 1982, pp. 20-1.*

This is a clearly written volume full of interesting historical and technical information on a subject which should hold inquisitive youngsters fascinated. The many black and white photographs and drawings are well chosen. The glossary of terms is useful. There are, however, a few problems. The current practice as we go metric of listing the metric equivalents after the American unit values gives us here the mass of micrometeorites fallen on the earth absurdly to three significant figures. The author slipped up on one of these conversions. Depending on whether you choose to recognize American or metric, you find the forest area devastated by the 1908 event in Siberia differing by a factor of five. The alert student remembering the Biblical account of the nativity and the "star in the East" may wonder where in this sacred book, "The Bible tells us that a **comet** lit up the sky when Jesus Christ was born." This same student might do the simple orbital period calculations for the distant comet nuclei orbiting beyond Pluto and wonder why she or he gets an orbital velocity several orders of magnitude greater than that stated by the author. How much should these things downgrade an otherwise excellent book?

> *David G. Hoag, in a review of "Comets, Meteors and Asteroids," in* Appraisal: Science Books for Young People, *Vol. 15, No. 2, Spring-Summer, 1982, p. 21.*

Disastrous Floods and Tidal Waves; Disastrous Volcanoes (1981)

From Vesuvius in 79 A.D. to Mount St. Helens in 1980, [*Disastrous Volcanoes*] presents an excellent description of volcanoes and their disastrous effects. After a brief but adequate discussion of the causes of volcanoes and their relation to plate tectonics, the four major types of volcanoes and the various materials they eject are explained. Berger then vividly describes the birth and death of Paricutin (1943-1952); the destruction of Pompeii and Herculaneum by Vesuvius; the most violent of all eruptions, that of Krakatoa in 1883; the cloud of death from Mont Pelée in 1902 and, finally, the recent activity of Mount St. Helens. The fine photographs and drawings add much to a well-written text. Although there is no glossary, the index makes it easy to locate definitions. Although this is considered a "First Book," it provides a summary which will interest many adults as well as the young people for whom it is designed. It should be in every junior high school and public library.

> *Edmund C. Bray, in a review of "Disastrous Volcanoes," in* Science Books & Films, *Vol. 17, No. 3, January-February, 1982, p. 161.*

Despite the interesting subject matter and numerous photographs, [*Disastrous Floods and Tidal Waves*] is poorly organized and fails to make its point. After an introduction explaining the types of floods—river floods and sea-coast floods—a brief description is given of Noah's Flood. Flood watches and flood warnings by the National Weather Service are described, and safety measures are stressed. Some major flooding events from all over the world are then presented. However, many floods are completely ignored. It seems that the scope is too large for a book of this size and type. Nevertheless, some readers might find the subject matter interesting and exciting.

> *Bonnie McCosh, in a review of "Disastrous Floods and Tidal Waves," in* Science Books & Films, *Vol. 17, No. 4, March-April, 1982, p. 214.*

These are two excellent volumes in an uneven series of books about natural catastrophes. . . . Both books boast full-color covers, handsome page layout, good quality black and white photographs, and up-to-date information. Best of all, however, both are neatly broken down into chapters which progress logically from an overview of the causes and types of the calamities at hand, to detailed descriptions of specific, noteworthy events. *Volcanoes* includes 2 chapters on Mt. St. Helens, and separate chapters on Paricutin, Vesuvius, Krakatoa, and Mount Pelee. *Floods* courses from Noah's Flood to the destruction caused by Hurricane Agnes in 1972. Both books include dark type subheads within the chapters to further guide young readers.

Both titles are easier to read and more up-to-date than Walter Brown's excellent titles in his "Historical Catastrophes" series (*Volcanoes,* 1970; *Floods,* 1975,) both published by Addison Wesley, and are highly recommended for all collections. (pp. 22-3)

> *Susanne S. Sullivan, in a review of "Disastrous Floods and Tidal Waves," in* Appraisal: Science Books for Young People, *Vol. 15, No. 2, Spring-Summer, 1982, pp. 22-3.*

Diastrous Floods and Tidal Waves is a compendium of exceedingly distressful events, generally related to high water. With an opening nod toward Noah, the author lets us know that the Weather Service does forecast floods (and other river stage information) but without telling very much at all about the scientific basis for such forecasts. He then turns to a collection of short chapters, each of which briefly details floods characteristic of major rivers, geographic areas, or major weather (or seismic) events. The collection of statistics gets a bit wearing at times, reading about how big the dam (that broke) was, how many people drowned and how much it all cost. There is but a minimum of scientific information, other than the collection of facts, included here, but the book really doesn't claim to be a science book. Still it would be nice to read just a little explanation of why and how some of the dramatic events happened.

Disastrous Volcanoes is a straightforward account of the basic causes of Volcanoes, insofar as they are understood in predictable detail—not very well, when you get down to basics—the dramatic accounts of the effects of the really big ones of the two millenia. A chapter on the geology of plate tectonics gives framework of why volcanoes are found here and not here an chapter on types outlines the morphology of the things in four m categories. The major portion of the text, though, is given ove historical accounts of particular significant events. I would have li to have seen a bit more emphasis on the difficulties and value predicting eruptions as an inducement to study by more people, there is plenty in the book to generate interest and encourage stud the future.

> *John D. Stackpole, in a review of "Disastrous Floods and Tidal Waves," in* Appraisal: Science Books for Young People, *Vol. 15, No. 2, Spring-Summer, 1982, p. 23.*

From The National Weather Service, *written and illustrated by Melvin Berger.*

Sports Medicine (1982)

Not a guide for young athletes but a profile of sports doctors and their work, this starts with Dr. Joseph S. Torg, an orthopedic surgeon and director of the University of Pennsylvania Sports Medicine Center, on a typical afternoon with a variety of male and female patients. Another orthopedic surgeon, Dr. Dinesh Patel, is shown operating on a knee using a new device, an arthroscope that allows him to see inside the joint. The physical exam given prospective Jets at New York's Lenox Hill Hospital, a tendon transplant that saved Dodger Tommy John's pitching arm, and an Olympic silver medal won on skier Phil Mahre's rebuilt ankle are presented as spectacular sports-medicine feats; and Berger also features researchers and others who have established a National Athletic Head and Neck Injury Registry, analyzed runners' motions (a boon for running-shoe manufacturers), devised a chart matching particular sports to personal traits, and studied athletes' moods and motivation. Except for a chapter on drugs, which cites findings that commonly used amphetamines and steroids do little if any good and can do harm, there is no consideration of issues; and the emphasis is on the "amazing skill [of the doctors] and the wonders of modern sports medicine." But the work is closer than that of some Berger-profiled scientists to kids' interests, and he has taken care to include female athletes and "he or she" references to sports doctors in general.

> *A review of "Sports Medicine: Scientists at Work," in* Kirkus Reviews, *Vol. L, No. 13, July 1, 1982, p. 735.*

On first going through the book I was annoyed. On page 13 the author refers to the danger to the patient of being cut by the "small, high-speed saw" used to cut off a cast. It has been forty years, or more, since casts were removed with tools that would cut. It is annoying since the description is likely to frighten young people who read the book. Too, the book seemed over-fond of doctors. Excessively laudatory. All the foregoing changed on re-reading. The bit about the cast-saw needs to be changed, but the information content, otherwise, seems good and the fact that there are physicians who administer treatments to athletes that are not merely dubious but out and out wrong is clearly made. (p. 52)

> *James H. Campbell, in a review of "Sports Medicine," in* Voice of Youth Advocates, *Vol. 5, No. 4, October, 1982, pp. 52-3.*

This text would be appropriate for general readers except for a number of shortcomings. The sections vary in quality, but the more serious problems center around the nature of the writing, which is commercially oriented and abounds with injudicious statements. As an example, Nautilus and Cybex products and a specific "fitness center" in the New York City area are cited specifically, when reference to generic equipment and facilities would equally serve to illustrate the intended concepts. This is particularly inappropriate when coupled with statements such as "choose [a certain brandname product] because it allows a person to exercise . . . safely," which suggests that some alternative would not serve as well. The author states that "sport scientists, physicians, coaches, and trainers all use [a particular procedure]"; this type of statement is at best misleading. Although a brief list of further readings is provided, footnoted references are lacking, which further reduces the text's value. In short, general readers would be clearly disadvantaged by relying on this book.

> *Harvey Ebel, in a review of "Sports Medicine: Scientists at Work," in* Science Books & Films, *Vol. 18, No. 4, March-April, 1983, p. 200.*

The Whole World of Hands　(with Gilda Berger, 1982)

Perhaps inspired by Napier's successful 1980 adult title, *Hands,* but without its authority or substance (there is nothing here on the evolution of hands, or on hand tools), this starts in typical juvenile fashion with the bones of the hand, then works out through muscles, blood vessels, and skin. Interest picks up with the sense of touch and some simple experiments ("Isn't it amazing how far apart the pressure sensors are?"), and then it's on to handedness: How much is heredity, how much learned? And how does it relate to the right and left brain? A discussion of gestures is marked by harmless but tenuous speculation (covered by phrases like "Some say . . . ") and by evasions.

(Why include the cuckold sign without so identifying it?) Also thrown in are a few words on rings and on prostheses, more to acknowledge the topics than to convey any items of interest, and there is even a section on first aid for hurt hands. With the elements of "finger math," signs from American Indian and Ameslan sign language and a finger alphabet, a few games and tricks (scissors-paper-rock; cat's cradle), a few silly rules for handwriting analysis (which "some claim shows what kind of person you are"), and a few key principals of palmistry, it's a mish-mash that may serve for idle diversion.

> *A review of "The Whole World of Hands," in* Kirkus Reviews, *Vol. L, No. 17, September 1, 1982, p. 999.*

The Bergers give us thought-provoking facts, supported by experiments / activities, all of which revolve around our hands. What causes hand dominance? What is Ameslan? Does your handwriting show what kind of person you are? Information is presented that will quite naturally lead to further discussion and investigation in the classroom, library and home. The illustrations [by True Kelley] add light humor but are sometimes confusing. A bibliography is included and resource information is found throughout the book. While not scientifically oriented or clearly illustrated, the information is presented in a straightforward, non-opinionated manner. John Napier's *Hands* (Pantheon, 1980) is a more in-depth treatment. Put **The Whole World of Hands** on your shelf as an elementary resource on hand related facts, activities and points of interest . . . but don't be surprised when your readers take it out for pleasure.

> *Laurie Bowden, in a review of "The Whole World of Hands," in* School Library Journal, *Vol. 29, No. 6, February, 1983, p. 72.*

The Whole World of Hands is a charming little book dealing with "everything you want to know about hands." Clearly written, the text runs from science to pseudoscience and therein lies its flaw. There is no clear delineation between scientific fact and metaphysical conjecture.

> *Bertrand Gary Hoyle, in a review of "The Whole World of Hands," in* Appraisal: Science Books for Young People, *Vol. 16, No. 2, Spring, 1983, p. 15.*

Censorship　(1982)

This is an extremely brief overview of some aspects of censorship as it applies to obscenity, libel, espionage, pornography and student rights. Because of the attempt to survey such a broad range in such a limited space, only a few pertinent cases are cited and there is a paucity of historical data or reference to social pressures and implications. Too much is attempted in 76 pages. Berger tries to present the latest Supreme Court decisions under which areas of censorship are now being interpreted. The *Pico v. Board of Education* case is mentioned, but the book went to press before the decision was announced. A suggested reading list of 12 citations is given—a more appropriate number for each chapter. There is an adequate index. Another weakness of the book is the erroneous identification of John Edgar Hoover as the founder of the F.B.I. (pp. 81-2)

Wanna M. Ernst, in a review of "Censorship," in School Library Journal, Vol. 29, No. 5, January, 1983, pp. 81-2.

Bizarre Murders   (with Gilda Berger, 1983)

The Bergers, prolific and reliable authors of nonfiction books for young people, turn their attention here to the circumstances of some of history's grisliest multiple murders. Their selective, chronologically organized gallery of killers begins with an account of William Burke and William Hare's corpse-supply business and closes with a description of David Berkowitz' spree as the "Son of Sam" killer, including along the way outlines of the heinous activities of the likes of Albert DeSalvo, Lizzie Borden, and Charles Manson. While the treatment is undoubtedly a heavy dose of unpleasantness, the Bergers handle it responsibly, explicating events in a noninterpretive, largely dispassionate manner that conscientiously avoids lurid details of a violent or sexual nature, and they provide young adults with sufficient facts to satisfy their curiosity about these still widely referred to crimes without exposing them to an overdose of minutiae or sensationalism. A bibliography of adult titles and an index are provided. (pp. 953-54)

Stephanie Zvirin, in a review of "Bizarre Murders," in Booklist, Vol. 79, No. 14, March 15, 1983, pp. 953-54.

These 13 true murder cases are more brutal than bizarre and it is debatable whether reading the details of cruel murders is a harmless cathartic or a dangerous stimulus. However, the problem with this collection is not whether children *should* read about these notorious cases but whether they should read the Bergers' abbreviated simplifications. Fuller and much more interesting accounts can be found in the writings of the opinionated Edmund Pearson, the popular Gerold Frank, the witty Tom Cullen and the chatty Victoria Lincoln, whose book on Lizzie Borden (*A Private Disgrace,* Putnam, 1967) is essential reading for anyone whose only view of the Fall River murders is based on the TV dramatization. The Bergers' chapter on Lizzie is full of errors in description, implication and verifiable fact. Fact: Mrs. Borden was struck from behind; Bergers: " . . . the murderer smashed in her face." Fact: Lizzie tried *unsuccessfully* to buy prussic acid the day *before* the murders; Berger: " . . . three witnesses who saw her buy the deadly poison . . . on that same morning." Added to these inexcusable mistakes are important omissions. In the Leopold / Loeb account there is no reference to lawyer Clarence Darrow's brilliant defense. The chapter on the Boston Strangler lacks all the exciting details of the investigation. Such omissions give an unexpected flatness to what are actually fascinating cases. Intrinsically less engrossing are the crimes of psychopaths because their motives are illogical and their actions capricious: Richard Speck killed eight nurses to cover a small theft; Charles Manson killed to terrorize and rule the country; Peter Sutcliffe, the Yorkshire Ripper, claimed that Jesus ordered him to kill all disreputable women and David (Son of Sam)

Berkowitz and his "demons" chose victims at random. It may be a comment on our age that killers no longer accept responsibility for their acts, but a catalog of their bloody crimes—inaccurate, incomplete and without comment—cannot be recommended.

Wendy Dellett, in a review of "Bizarre Murders," in School Library Journal, Vol. 30, No. 2, October, 1983, p. 164.

Although [this] book does have a good bibliography and index, its treatment of the subject is too sparse to be of any use other than browsing. Despite this, the authors must be applauded for tasteful handling of the violence that results from brutal and vicious behavior. Although the violence is not sketched in visceral realism, it still communicates the horror that surrounds murder.

The book is definitely geared to the junior high school reader. All in all, a plausible purchase for a high interest / low reading level addition, but it will be of little use to the student who needs challenging materials for research in the area of violent crime.

Nancy Fritz Bunnell, in a review of "Bizarre Murders," in The Book Report, Vol. 2, No. 3, November-December, 1983, p. 37.

From The Trumpet Book, *written and illustrated by Melvin Berger.*

Why I Cough, Sneeze, Shiver, Hiccup, and Yawn (1983)

Berger offers a clear, concise explanation of some familiar bodily functions. Rather than beginning with a dry recitation of facts, the book starts: "You are playing hide and seek. You've found a good hiding place. You want to be as quiet as you can. All of a sudden—KA-CHOO!" Using this sort of child-appealing example, the book goes on to explain that sneezes, shivering, hiccups, and yawns are reflexes that work through the nervous system. Diagrams of the nervous system are ultrasimple; all of the line drawings [by Holly Keller], many full page and in color, have a friendly appeal. An excellent choice for primary nonfiction shelves.

> *Ilene Cooper, in a review of "Why I Cough, Sneeze, Shiver, Hiccup, & Yawn," in* Booklist, *Vol. 79, No. 19, June 1, 1983, p. 1271.*

Inquisitive children can find clear and concise answers to their questions about reflexes in **Why I Cough Sneeze, Shiver, Hiccup, & Yawn.** The author builds the readers curiosity about those physiological actions that are uncontrollable, and then proceeds to explain the mechanism involved, pointing out why reflexes are beneficial and necessary. The lively, colorful, humorous drawings enhance the text and help make palatable to young readers information that might otherwise be dry and uninteresting. Younger children will enjoy hearing the story while older children can easily grasp the concepts because of the simple language and examples. There are numerous books for this age level on the brain and nervous system, but usually only a page or two is devoted to the reflexes. This book fulfills a real need by explaining in more detail those puzzling occurences.

> *Judith Rieke, in a review of "Why I Cough, Sneeze, Shiver, Hiccup, & Yawn," in* School Library Journal, *Vol. 30, No. 1, September, 1983, p. 102.*

This book intends to increase children's awareness and understanding of the body and some of its actions. The introductory section, which explains why we sneeze, shiver, or hiccup and cannot control these reflexes, is well done. Throughout the book the illustrations are appealing and include children and a cat. Unfortunately, the text and pictures give readers only superficial descriptions of how the nervous system functions. The example of a child burning her finger on a hot stove is a good one, but the type on the illustration to indicate reflex action is so small that many readers may miss the information. Also, how impulses are sent along nerves is not explained, and a diagram of a reflex arc in the spinal cord is not provided. Nevertheless, young readers will be intrigued with the reflex responses that they experience. The experiments on pupil dilation and foot tickling that are included should be good classroom fun.

> *Lucia Anderson, in a review of "Why I Cough, Sneeze, Shiver, Hiccup, & Yawn," in* Science Books & Films, *Vol. 19, No. 2, November-December, 1983, p. 99.*

Sports (1983)

Alphabetically arranged, a series of entries includes descriptions of sports, sports terms, outstanding players, trophies, and special sports events. While the book gives a great deal of information, it is often uneven in treatment, occasionally arbitrary about inclusions (a soccer field is shown but not an ice-hockey rink; yet half a page is devoted to a drawing of the Stanley Cup) and choice of performers seems arbitrary. It is understandable that, given production time, no hardbound book can be wholly up-to-date, but—to stay with hockey—the exclusion of Wayne Gretzky? No mention of a hat trick? No index that might, for example, pull together "bunt," "squeeze play," and "steal" for those unfamiliar with baseball terminology?

> *Zena Sutherland, in a review of "Sports," in* Bulletin of the Center for Children's Books, *Vol. 36, No. 9, May, 1983, p. 162.*

Berger has covered broad terms and famous athletes; thus, this title could be used to answer general sports questions when brief answers are acceptable. If one is dealing with more obscure sports references or if lengthy explanations are called for, look elsewhere. Arrangement is alphabetical and the definitions economic, yet clear in their language. Photographs add interest and diagrams are helpful [Illustrations are by Anne Canevari Green]. An interesting browsing item for young readers.

> *Joe McKenzie, in a review of "Sports," in* School Library Journal, *Vol. 29, No. 9, May, 1983, p. 95.*

Exploring the Mind and Brain (1983)

Research on many diseases that have been widely discussed recently is brought together in **Exploring the Mind and Brain.** Young people interested in the brain or in mental problems should acquire insight; but the book is actually intended to inform them about the many kinds of research currently being undertaken as well as the techniques used. The material is carefully written so as not to instigate nagging worries in someone who may be insecure. In fact, except for the section on bulimia (binge eating and regurgitation), most psychological difficulties brought on by the environment are avoided. Among the problems discussed are manic-depression, multiple sclerosis, mental retardation, autism, and schizophrenia. The author also examines normal psychology: shaping human behavior; common adolescent emotional changes; personality traits as determined by questions about likes and dislikes—the efficacy of which the reader can test by answering sets of true-false questions to determine if he or she is extroverted, shy, impulsive, practical, or emotional. The book is eminently readable for a general audience.

> *Sarah Gagné, in a review of "Exploring the Mind and Brain," in* The Horn Book Magazine, *Vol. LIX, No. 3, June, 1983, p. 332.*

A case study approach effectively showcases the major areas of current brain research in this fascinating, well-written book by an experienced science writer. . . . Scientific procedures and biological processes are described with admirable clarity, either directly or metaphorically. The author is sensitive to young readers' concern about pain in human and animal testing, and in general anticipates likely questions. However, one point in the chapter on the study of rat behavior does need clarification or justification: the researcher continually applies the term "superstition" to a non-human population. Some issues of scientific method are addressed, such as the use of *Aplysia* experiments in the study of human neurology. A readable book in a rapidly changing field.

> *Nancy J. Horner, in a review of "Exploring the Mind and Brain," in* School Library Journal, *Vol. 30, No. 2, October, 1983, p. 164.*

This ambitious book attempts the difficult task of describing for the young reader modern methods of research into brain function and treatment of brain disorders. . . . That the book succeeds reasonably well is a tribute to the author's writing skills. That is was unable to entirely overcome the great difficulty inherent in explaining complex technology to young readers was inevitable. When readers lack needed background, the "black box" approach must be adopted. Moreover, those intricate explanations that are included will be very tough going for the average young reader. Despite these shortcomings, there is much of value in the book for the reader willing to go slowly and carefully. The book is illustrated with good black-and-white photographs of patients and medical personnel in both research and care settings. Intended for ages ten and up, it will be most useful in the junior high and public libraries.

> *A.H. Drummond, Jr., in a review of "Exploring the Mind and Brain," in* Appraisal: Science Books for Young People, *Vol. 17, No. 1, Winter, 1984, p. 13.*

Bright Stars, Red Giants, and White Dwarfs (1983)

This survey of the best current thinking on the life cycle of stars emphasizes their internal mechanics. Berger points out areas in which the experts are still arguing. This is a companion volume to Berger's **Quasars, Pulsars and Black Holes in Space,** matching its attractive format and updating its interpretations but not repeating the sources of the data from which these interpretations are derived. Berger's prose can't match the clarity and depth of understanding of Asimov's *How Did We Find Out About Black Holes?* (Walker, 1978) but the new information he presents for this grade range, most notably his explanation of planetary nebulae, makes this a worthwhile addition to astronomy collections.

> *Margaret L. Chatham, in a review of "Bright Stars, Red Giants and White Dwarfs," in* School Library Journal, *Vol. 30, No. 1, September, 1983, p. 118.*

Although evidently authoritative on the subject of cosmology, this book in parts will be obscure or puzzling to the majority of young readers and adults. Admittedly, some of the theory on the subject is quite complicated, but this reviewer feels a better job could have been done to clarify it. The literal meaning of words, for instance, if not chosen carefully, can give a surprising meaning, such as the statement: "Astronomers have tracked the lives of stars, such as the sun, from birth until they become red giants." Other confusion such as the inconsistency between the text and the labels on the axes of the figure showing the Hertzsprung-Russell diagram is unfortunate. On the other hand, there is much good information provided not commonly available for young people. The four page glossary is excellent.

> *David G. Hoag, in a review of "Bright Stars, Red Giants, and White Dwarfs," in* Appraisal: Science Books for Young People, *Vol. 17, No. 1, Winter, 1984, p. 12.*

This slim volume recounts the life history of various stars in simple language appropriate for junior high-school students. One meets ordinary stars, such as the sun, in various stages of maturity from protostar through main sequence to red giant and white dwarf. The more flamboyant supernovae, pulsars, and black holes are also described. Unfortunately, this fascinating story is not treated with care. It goes without saying that the purpose of illustrations is to illustrate—a point, an idea, a relationship. At the very least, illustrations and text should not contradict each other. Here, that is not the case. In describing the Hertzsprung-Russell diagram, for example, the text states, "in the upper left-hand corner, stars one million times as luminous as the sun, with a surface temperature of 72,000°F (40,250°K)," but the illustration stops at 30,000°K with a luminosity about 10,000 times the sun's. At the other end of the diagram is a similar discrepancy between illustration and text. Throughout the text, quantities are rendered in English units and SI units as in the example above. At best, this practice is awkward and distracting (as with three successive conversions in as many sentences). At worst, it leads to the silliness of precise conversions of imprecise data such as the statement that the surface temperature of a protostar after "about 20 million years" rose to 10,800°F (6,250°K), when, one suspects, this "estimate" started out as "about 6,000°K" or "6,000°C." Can these be distinguished for a protostar "after about 20 million years" anyway? Several times the conversions are simply wrong ("a temperature of about 280°F (100°K)"). In the end, the gimmick betrays the theme, and what was intended as an aid to comprehension becomes, in its thoughtless execution, an impediment. The 29 black-and-white figures are mostly stock astronomical photographs, some of which are explained in the text. In the only picture that shows people, the identities are reversed. The story dealt with here is worthwhile and repeatedly fascinating to young explorers of the night sky. However, the story is told much more reliably and completely in a somewhat older book that probably inspired this one—Robert Jastrow's *Red Giants and White Dwarfs* (NY: Norton, 1979), which was revised and issued in paperback a few years ago.

> *Leo L. Baggerly, in a review of "Bright Stars, Red Giants, and White Dwarfs," in* Science Books & Films, *Vol. 19, No. 4, March-April, 1984, p. 196.*

Energy (1983)

Basically a dictionary of terms, this book covers a wide range of energy topics including fuels, energy sources, methods of production and leading figures in fields of energy discovery and methodology. Entries range from one sentence to two or three pages, depending on the complexity of the topic. Controversial topics such as nuclear power are generally given balanced treatment, with the exception of *atomic bomb* and *hydrogen bomb,* which are described in terms of how they work without noting the effects of their use. *Energy for America* (Atheneum, 1979) by Irene Kiefer is a good narrative choice for information on energy but the glossary is less complete. All in all, a good reference source in a concise, easy-to-follow format. Layout is clean with enough black-and-white photographs and diagrams to relieve monotony [illustrations are by Anne Canevari Green].

> *Anne McKeithen Goodman, in a review of "Energy," in* School Library Journal, *Vol. 30, No. 3, November, 1983, p. 73.*

A "hybrid" junior dictionary / encyclopedia on energy, this invaluable reference book covers energy sources, concepts, and theories, and the scientists who helped develop them.

Punctuated throughout by striking black-and-white photographs, the clear, incisive text includes three-line entries on beta particles, methane, and turbines, as well as two-page articles on nuclear fusion, solar cells, and coal, among other topics.

There are several other general books about energy, for approximately the same age group: Illa Podendorff's *Energy,* Mitchell Wilson's *Energy,* John Satchwell's *Future Sources,* to cite a few. But none is as comprehensive, and none has the same useful A to Z format, as Melvin Berger's slim but densely packed book.

> *L. H., in a review of "Energy," in* Appraisal: Science Books for Young People, *Vol. 17, No. 1, Winter, 1984, p. 12.*

Space Shots, Shuttles, and Satellites (1983)

Those who have been wanting (or needing) up-to-date information on the United States space program will be pleased to see this book. It is a brief history of our endeavors in space but the emphasis is on what has been happening since the termination of the moon landings. There is relatively little on unmanned probes but good coverage of satellites—military, weather and scientific—and a current look at astronaut training, which includes pictures of women trainees. Emphasis is naturally on the space shuttle, but unlike other books which stress the ship itself and typical or projected missions, this highlights the actual flights. There is a detailed "countdown" of the preparations for and conduct of the first orbital test flight of the Columbia, and accounts of the highlights of the first six shuttle flights (test and operational). While not outstanding, this is attractive and readable, and fills a definite information gap. There is a glossary and an index. (pp. 11-12)

> *Daphne Ann Hamilton, in a review of "Space Shots, Shuttles and Satellites," in* Appraisal: Science Books for Young People, *Vol. 17, No. 2, Spring-Summer, 1984, pp. 11-12.*

In *Space Shots, Shuttles and Satellites,* Berger highlights the history, purposes and main accomplishments of the three main components of the space program. While the chapters on space shots and shuttles concentrate more on the activities of the astronauts, the chapters on the satellites concentrate more on the technological advances. This book gives a clear general overview of the topic; readers wanting more specific details about the lives of the astronauts or about satellites will need books that concentrate on those topics, such as *Artificial Satellites* (Watts, 1982) by Jeanne Bendick. The full-color cover photograph of the Space Shuttle *Columbia* and the numerous black-and-white photos inside are, for the most part, from NASA archives.

> *Julia Rholes, in a review of "Space Shots, Shuttles and Satellites," in* School Library Journal, *Vol. 30, No. 9, May, 1984, p. 76.*

Berger says that the purpose of his well-written and interesting book is to describe "How we got there, what we are doing in space, and what is planned for the future . . . ", and he is largely successful. The book opens with the chapter, "Becoming an Astronaut," which briefly describes requirements and training for the job. Three short chapters follow, presenting a brief history of space flight. The next section, on the space shuttle, is particularly well done and informative; it starts with a chapter designed in the form of a countdown, from the first inception of the shuttle idea at T-12 years to the end of the first flight of *Columbia* at about T + 54 hours. The final section introduces various civilian and military uses of satellites. This book is up to date: it covers space shuttle flights up to June 1983 and mentions current developments and concerns, such as the possible future overcrowding of satellites in geosynchronous orbits. Accurate and well illustrated with black-and-white photographs, this short book covers a lot of ground in 80 pages.

> *William H. Glenn, in a review of "Space Shots, Shuttles and Satellites," in* Science Books & Films, *Vol. 20, No. 1, September-October, 1984, p. 26.*

Computer Talk (1984)

This dictionary of computer terminology presents approximately 244 entries in a concise, easy-to-follow format. Definitions vary in length from one sentence to three pages; entries are thoroughly cross referenced to synonymous terms for computer novices. Young readers may be delighted to find entries for some of the popular video games, but disappointed that others are omitted. Collections lacking sufficient quantities of material on computer terminology at the intermediate level will be well served by this title; *The Illustrated Computer Dictionary* (Bantam, 1983), is a much more comprehensive work containing 1000 definitions.

Cynthia K. Leibold, in a review of "Computer Talk," in School Library Journal, *Vol. 30, No. 10, August, 1984, p. 69.*

Computer Talk is a hybrid of some type; not exactly a dictionary and not an encyclopedia. Advertising copy on the back claims: "This easy-to-understand wordbook will make you feel more comfortable about the computers in your life." Whatever else it may be, this is not a science book, so it need not be evaluated as such, but perhaps it can usefully be compared to a dictionary of computer terms. I suggest that you pass this one up. Definitions are not particularly clear or concise, and the book is generally uninspired, offering much less than some of the better dictionaries devoted to computer terms. If you need an elementary computer dictionary, make some comparisons before you invest in this one.

Clarence C. Truesdell, in a review of "Computer Talk," in Appraisal: Science Books for Young People, *Vol. 18, No. 2, Spring, 1985, p. 12.*

This is a short glossary of computer terms for a juvenile audience. It defines about 200 objects and concepts connected with computers. The print is reasonably easy to read, but the design is not very attractive, and the illustrations [by Geri Greinke] are neither informative nor stimulating. Most of the definitions are accurate, but a few are inaccurate, and many are incomplete, out of date, misleading in their emphasis, or grammatically incorrect. In general, there are too many errors in grammar and diction to recommend the book. Even if this were not the case, the choice of terms that are defined is poor and dated; the computer terms seen most often in today's headlines—artificial intelligence, database, and electronic funds transfer, for example—are defined poorly, and definitions of expert systems, integrated software, spreadsheet, and VLSI don't appear at all. The intended audience for this book can do a lot better elsewhere.

Frederick Hoffman, in a review of "Computer Talk," in Science Books & Films, *Vol. 20, No. 5, May-June, 1985, p. 303.*

Bizarre Crimes (with Gilda Berger, 1984)

A companion to the Bergers' **Bizarre Murders,** this latest catalog of criminal acts is suitable for a younger audience than the earlier book. After leading off with a few tantalizing crime summaries, the authors get down to cases, so to speak, concentrating on 10 particularly intriguing schemes—ranging from an art fraud involving da Vinci's famous *Mona Lisa* to a bank vault looting in which the take was carried off via the sewer system of a French city. The entertainingly presented, streamlined versions of the circumstances and outcome of each crime should find a ready audience. Bibliography appended.

Stephanie Zvirin, in a review of "Bizarre Crimes," in Booklist, *Vol. 81, No. 1, September 1, 1984, p. 56.*

Space Talk (1985)

Increasing interest in our space program justifies the concept behind this book: a dictionary of words and phrases related to space travel designed to assist students with projects and reports. However, there are several flaws that will limit its usefulness as a reference resource. First, some definitions are incomplete or present no clear concept. Earth's atmosphere is described as being "thin," but to a child, so is a piece of paper. "Igloo" is defined as "A pressurized container for *Spacelab* pallet subsystems," but there is no definition for pallet subsystems. Second, there are no diagrams to help explain difficult words, such as *azimuth* or *perigee*, or to illustrate objects. This weakness is especially apparent in the many attempts to describe the space shuttle and its parts without a simple cutaway diagram. The NASA photographs add interest, but they seldom amplify or clarify a definition. Third, there are no pronunciation guides for new words or names. Fourth, there is an inconsistency in the way words with a more general usage are defined; some, such as *program*, are related specifically to space, while others, such as *component* or *data*, are defined so broadly that one wonders why they were included. This book does have appeal as a browsing item; its sharp format with wide margins and large clean print will attract students. *Space Sciences* (Watts, 1983) by Christopher Lampton is a better dictionary of general space terms, and *Space Travel* (Watts, 1982) by Jeanne Bendick is a good introduction to the subject and is useful for reports.

Allen Meyer, in a review of "Space Talk," in School Library Journal, *Vol. 31, No. 10, August, 1985, p. 60.*

This excellent book clearly, accurately, and concisely defines, alphabetically, some 250 words primarily used in conjunction with space projects. It does not explain *why* things work, but its abundant lucid, concise definitions could be the beginning of many science projects. This book is also a good, general reference space-talk dictionary that is impressively complete. Everything from the Apollo project to x-ray astronomy and Yuri Gagarin to exobiology is accurately covered. Even dates, weights, and dimensions (in English and metric units) are included. Large black-and-white photographs make this book well worth the investment. However, the continuing rapid development of space research means that it will soon need updating.

Jason R. Taylor, in a review of "Space Talk," in Science Books & Films, *Vol. 21, No. 3, January-February, 1986, p. 170.*

This is a small specialized dictionary of about 250 space and astronomy terms. The typeface is large, the definitions clear and careful. Less technical than an adult dictionary, it is still very straightforward and businesslike. Consulting it will help students struggling with jargon in adult accounts of space exploits. (Adults who are novices will have their understanding honed, too!) Beyond the bare definitions and identifications, Berger often adds a sentence or two clarifying a distinction, giving an example, or alerting to what is significant. What he does for "ALBEDO" is typical:

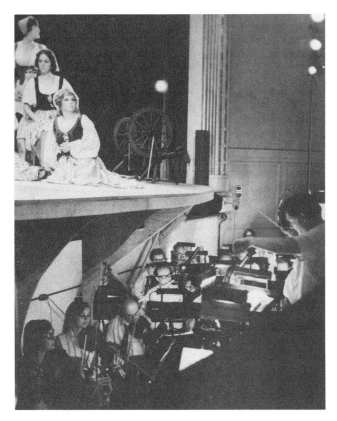

From The Photo Dictionary of the Orchestra, *written and illustrated by Melvin Berger.*

> The amount of sunlight that is reflected back in all directions (what adult dictionaries call 'incident' light) by a planet, a satellite, or an asteriod. The albedo of a body in space can be markedly influenced by clouds. That is why the cloudless Moon reflects less than one-tenth of the total sunlight it receives, while Venus, with its atmosphere of dense white cloud, reflects almost three-quarters."

Amplification like this is what helps students comprehend well enough to put what they learn into their own words.

The dictionary includes parts of space vehicles, satellites, rockets and boosters. Identifications include space centers, specific programs, various rockets, various spacecraft, about a dozen astronauts and rocket pioneers. Rarely, an entry deals with something European or Russian: U.S. space activities predominate. Many launch dates, "firsts," and noteworthy accomplishments are mentioned.

Space buffs will, of course, find omissions: a few seem surprising enough to be significant oversights: Where is mention of the first woman in space? Why do the Venus probes appear to have ended in the mid-'70s? Where is noted the goldplated message to extraterrestrials that left the Solar System on Voyager? Berger says of Skylab, that it was in orbit " . . . nearly a decade after its launch in 1973." Older readers, at least, will remember that Skylab pieces made a fiery descent into the Pacific and Australia in 1979.

Black and white photographs from NASA are the sole il-

lustrations. "Pitch," "Yaw," and many other terms need diagrams. Captions are identifying, not elucidating; even for vehicles and rockets, there are no pointers to parts. Some photographs are grainy. Less than half occur on the page with their word. There are a good number of acronyms, but none is pronounced. Is ESA, the European Space Agency, "E-S-A," "ee-sah," or "ess-ah"? The lack of pronunciations seems a missed opportunity to give students the kind of confidence in their know-how that the definitions accomplish so well.

So the book is not a model dictionary. But it can be a very helpful suporting title, and is recommended as a supplementary space choice, especially where a number of borrowers of different abilities need space materials. (pp. 16-17)

> *Arrolyn H. Vernon, in a review of "Space Talk," in* Appraisal: Science Books for Young People, *Vol. 19, No. 3, Summer, 1986, pp. 16-17.*

Germs Make Me Sick! (1985)

While nearly every child experiences at least minor illness, studies indicate that under the age of 10 very few have any real understanding of what it means. High-quality, accurate and detailed educational materials about disease are almost nonexistent. Melvin Berger's *Germs Make Me Sick!* goes far to fill the gap in this area.

Mr. Berger begins with a description of how you feel when you are sick and gets right to the point—clearly explaining *how* germs make you sick. Many 4- to 8-year-olds believe that illness is caused by such things as not washing your hands before eating, being near sick people or drinking out of someone else's glass. Mr. Berger does an excellent job of explaining that those are ways that germs get into the body, but that illness is caused by what the germs *do* once they are inside. The explanations of bacteria and viruses are especially well done. He describes how they each cause illness in different ways, which leads directly into explanations of the different methods used to treat them. The presentation of the effects of germs on the body's cells and the relation between this and the way one feels includes examples such as flu, earaches and poison ivy.

For those who have tried to explain why you should wash your hands before eating, why you should not drink out of someone else's glass, or why you have to stay in bed when you are ill, *Germs Make Me Sick!* is a splendid aide. (pp. 18-19)

> *P. Susan Gerrity, in a review of "Germs Make Me Sick," in* The New York Times Book Review, *April 21, 1985, pp. 18-19.*

To explain how bacteria and viruses cause disease in the human body and how the body responds is a difficult task; to do it in 32 pages with beginning reader vocabulary may be impossible. Berger does provide a good amount of solid information within these pages, but what he must leave out may cause some confusion or misconceptions. His description of the way bacteria and viruses grow inside the body may be alarming, especially since he does not explain that there are millions of helpful bacteria already living inside (and outside) the body that are necessary for survival. Also, the interchangeable use of *germs* with *bacteria* and *viruses* prevents the formation of a clear concept of each, and the "Rules For Good Health" need further explanation to be useful. The lack of careful organization and headings further detracts from the clarity of some concepts. The writing is uneven and dull, marred by phrases such as "and so on" and "fit as a fiddle." . . . Overall, Berger's presentation of this complex material in this limiting format does not do justice to the subject or to the intended audience. It does not compare to D. H. Patent's *Germs!* (Holiday, 1983), which is for older students.

> *Allen Meyer, in a review of "Germs Make Me Sick!" in* School Library Journal, *Vol. 31, No. 9, May, 1985, p. 68.*

Another book in the "Let's-Read-And-Find-Out Science Books" series, which may be enough of a recommendation for many libraries to acquire it without review. You can't go far wrong by buying this little book about germs, and health is certainly a most worthy topic. However, some pages of this book seem to send two different messages: the text is sometimes quite serious, yet the accompanying illustration [by Marylin Hafner] conveys a very light or even humorous attitude. This may result in a salutory effect upon the reader by preventing the "germ story" from becoming too grim. On the other hand, it might be taken too lightly. Some of the illustrations are useless or even misleading. On page 7, for example the illustrations attempt to depict the objects used by the author as analogies. The artist would have served the purposes of the text far better by providing illustrations of the viruses and bacteria which the text is trying to describe, rather than illustrating the analoguous objects. One has to wonder how this particular illustrator regards the use of illustrations to enhance text. In this instance, the illustration seems to be useless at best, and very distracting in any event.

The book ends with a few rules for good health, most of which are useful. It may be of little value, however to tell school children to brush after meals, unless the school provides appropriate opportunities. Overall, a useful book to have in the school library. (pp. 15-16)

> *Georgia L. Bartlett, in a review of "Germs Make Me Sick!" in* Appraisal: Science Books for Young People, *Vol. 19, No. 2, Spring, 1986, pp. 15-16.*

Mind Control (1985)

A fine introduction to the broad subject of *Mind Control* for the middle and junior high grades. Defining mind control as "the power to direct another person's, or one's own, thoughts, beliefs, emotions, judgments, perceptions, and behavior," he devotes a chapter each to the diverse topics of cults, brainwashing, drugs, altered states of consciousness, psychotherapy, behavior modification, hypnosis and brain manipulation through electric shock and surgery. Berger's approach is objective, dealing with the appeal and dangers involved with each area, and stressing caution. He discusses the ethics of each procedure without judgment.

A number of case histories lend variety; while presumably true, they are not documented. Berger's writing is clear and concise, presuming no prior knowledge. Margaret O. Hyde's *Brainwashing and Other Forms of Mind Control* (McGraw, 1977; o.p.) covers much of the same material, but is heavier on behavior modification and psychological therapy, including biofeedback, which Berger does not mention. Berger's book will probably appeal to young readers more because he uses the more sensational and controversial forms of mind control in the early chapters to hook their interest. *Mind Control* will not be of particular research value due to its broad scope and lack of great depth on any one topic, but it will appeal to general readers and will help in narrowing research topics. The bibliography complements this springboard function, although the books listed are aimed at adults. Books on single topics that are more suited for junior high readers include Larry Kettlekamp's *Hypnosis: the Wakeful Sleep* (Morrow, 1975); Carroll Stoner's *All God's Children: the Cult Experience—Salvation or Slavery?* (Chilton, 1977; o.p.); Robert B. Ewen's *Getting It Together: a Guide to Modern Psychological Analysis* (Watts, 1976; o.p.); Margaret O. Hyde's *Mind Drugs* (McGraw, 1981) and Neal Olshan and Julie Dreyer's *Fears and Phobias* (Watts, 1980).

> *Joyce Adams Burner, in a review of "Mind Control," in* School Library Journal, *Vol. 31, No. 10, August, 1985, p. 60.*

Berger briefly describes each type of mind control and presents a few real or fictitious cases. Because the presentations are brief, readers get an oversimplified, even simplistic, treatment of a complex subject. Many terms are defined without reference to the important issues involved or the historical antecedents of current practices. The style and vocabulary used seem intended for teenage readers. Thus, the book will probably be used for innumerable high-school essays, and the reference list at the end will be handy for this purpose. Despite the need to educate the public on this subject, a book that is hardly more than a glossary is not very useful and cannot be highly recommended.

> *Ann C. Howe, in a review of "Mind Control," in* Science Books & Films, *Vol. 21, No. 2, November-December, 1985, p. 81.*

Mind Control is a fair little book with a big built-in booby trap.

The "Introduction to Mind Control" (Chapter 1) cites some examples and makes a highly questionable declaration (unsupported by the examples) that "mind control is more effective and more widespread than ever before [and] a familiar part of almost everyone's experience." There follows an interesting and well-written chapter on cult conversions—the Moonies, Hare Krishna, and the like.

Next is "Brainwashing," still as controversial a subject as when it was sensationally overstated in the media during the Korean War. In *Mind Control* overstatement first makes brainwashing appear to have been highly effective against American prisoners of war. Later, however, the book rather quietly acknowledges the conclusions of experts that brainwashing had actually been almost totally ineffective. The book doesn't mention the infamous CIA brainwashing experiments, in which 10 years of secret "research," using techniques that caused some gruesome results, simply proved the *importance* of these supposedly brainwashing techniques.

Now comes the booby trap: In barely eight pages, Chapter 4 "covers" those "Mind Drugs" that people take themselves—hallucinogens, narcotics, alcohol, marijuana, sedatives, stimulants—and the "benefits[?] and risks" of using each.

Sandwiching drug abuse into a context of coercive mind control obscures for young minds the vast difference between coercive use for political purposes or medical use for therapy, on the one hand, and on the other, voluntary use for short-lived euphoria, "mental well-being," and other pleasant sensations, or for relief from various stresses.

It is this voluntary drug use that *is* indeed "more widespread than ever before" and familiar to almost everyone. However, this is known *not* as mind control, but as drug abuse. And its consequences are not mind control but mind *decontrol.* It is abuse of the brain and thinking, leading to intellectual disorientation and deterioration. This is not what a few people do to others coercively for control. It is what millions of people, including an enormous number of school children, are doing to themselves for "kicks."

Thus Chapter 4 is by far the most important part of *Mind Control.* It's the *only* chapter that instantly connects with the daily experiences and drug jargon of school children. Also the only chapter likely to "grab" them and become dog-eared from use. For many it will probably be the only statement they have read on drugs that was written by a reputable science writer, and therefore this chapter may affect their decisions about whether to try some drugs— "just once," of course.

Now if this were a good essay on drug abuse, some small faults present in the rest of the book would be of little consequence. But it's not a good essay. It stands out as the least carefully or currently researched part of the book, and the most casually, superficially, ambiguously, and perhaps hastily, written. It purports to both inform and warn about these drugs and their misuse; but it does neither adequately on the basis of current knowledge and experience.

The reasons people turn to drugs are presented in relatively attractive terms reminiscent of popular statements from the drug culture of the 60s, and of the drug jargon and vernacular of the "flower children" and other counterculture groups of that period.

The chapter does present caveats; some are quite strong, including warnings of bizarre and fatal outcomes. But the allure, the prospective delights, excitement, and enticement of the drugs seem to come off much stronger than the dangers and discouragement of the caveats. This may be especially true for intelligent, curious, adventurous, and overconfident young people who are "smart" enough

to "know" that they "know when to quit," and can therefore safely "try it just this once."

In this chapter of *Mind Control* alcohol rates one page, and smoking, the most widespread, readily available, and voluntary drug abuse of all, causing psychological and physiological dependence and millions of deaths, doesn't get even a sentence in this chapter, which also never mentions nicotine.

Without its wrongly conceived and too limited foray into drug abuse, *Mind Control* might be an interesting and harmless (though here and there misleading or confusing) selection for younger readers. Before putting it on the library shelf, one should first read it carefully, with special attention to Chapter 4—keeping in mind that large, vulnerable audience of very young readers and adolescents who are already far more familiar with drug abuse for kicks than they will ever be with coercive mind control techniques for political or medical purposes—youngsters who already "know all about marijuana," and many of whom are already using marijuana or other drugs or being daily bombarded with invitations, temptations, and free samples. (pp. 13-15)

> *Leon Summit, in a review of "Mind Control,"* *in* Appraisal: Science Books for Young People, *Vol. 19, No. 2, Spring, 1986, pp. 13-15.*

Computers: A Question and Answer Book   (1985)

The book for people who think *Trivial Pursuit* is an educational game. Berger has organized a group of questions and answers in broad categories including programming, uses of computers, history of computers and how computers work. There is no strong unifying principle that links the questions together. For example, in the section entitled "How Are Computers Used In Medicine and Government?" the following questions are found: "Who was the first paraplegic to walk with the help of computers? Who is the biggest user of computers in the world? What is computer matching? Is it true that New York City almost went broke over a computer error? How does FOSDIC help the Census Bureau? What is NORAD?" These are perhaps interesting questions, but on completing the book, readers are left with a collection of meaningless facts. There are neither illustrations nor a pronunciation glossary to enrich understanding.

> *Edwin F. Bokee, in a review of "Computers: A Question and Answer Book," in* School Library Journal, *Vol. 32, No. 5, January, 1986, p. 77.*

Berger has done his usual competent job here, providing an introduction to what computers do, how they work, how they are used in medicine and government, how individuals are likely to come in contact with them, where they came from, and what we can expect of them in the future. He uses a series of questions and answers organized within the above topics and occasionally elaborates on his answers in later discussions. The only illustration is a table of decimal and binary number equivalents. There is a detailed index. A similar book by Daniel Cohen—*Question* and *Answer Book: Computers* (NY: Simon & Schuster, 1983)—provides a bibliography of material for further reading and a number of black-and-white illustrations; also, Fred D'Ignazio's *Star Wars Question & Answer Book About Computers* (NY: Random House, 1983), offers large-page format and color illustrations.

> *Sarah Berman, in a review of "Computers: A Question and Answer Book," in* Science Books & Films, *Vol. 21, No. 4, March-April, 1986, p. 223.*

It is difficult to know for whom this collection of questions and answers, arranged in a half dozen categories, is intended. The beginner who needs instruction in binary numeration is likely to be mystified by the descriptions of machine and assembly language. The experienced practitioner who may want to know such things as neurometrics and interblock gaps is hardly likely to need a description of a flowchart.

The book suffers from other problems as well. It is inaccurate to say that a computer is an electronic machine because "it runs on electricity, which is a flow of electrons." My toaster, too, runs on electricity, but we do not call toasters electronic machines. It is only partially true that people buy dot matrix printers because they are cheaper than character printers. Dot matrix printers are also more flexible; you can do more things with them. Some answers, such as the ones about the assignments of numbers to the letters A-Z and to the ASCII code, are confusing. The introduction of cutesy humor does not help: LISP "is not a speech impediment," and a bug in your program does not require that you call an exterminator. This is especially true because some twenty pages later, the history of "bug" is given quite seriously. There are no illustrations. A verbal explanation of flowchart and turtle graphics is inadequate.

This introduction to computers disguised in questions and answers does not work. I suggest that the author consider a second, revised edition based on the questions that children actually ask.

> *Lazer Goldberg, in a review of "Computers: A Question & Answer Book," in* Appraisal: Science Books for Young People, *Vol. 19, No. 4, Fall, 1986, pp. 21.*

Star Gazing, Comet Tracking, and Sky Mapping (1985)

As I read this elegant and useful book about naked-eye astronomy, I kept wishing night would come so that I could try some of the suggested activities. This book features star charts for each month, which highlight the 30 constellations visible from the United States. The myths and stories connected to the constellations and their stars are told alongside excellent instructions for best viewing. How to look for comets and observe meteors is explained in detail, and this section also includes instructions for reporting observations to appropriate scientific organizations. It should have been mentioned that "professional" comet hunters often spend hundreds of hours searching and that Comet Halley will not make very good viewing in many parts of the United States. There are directions for making star charts for your exact latitude and ideas for some mapping projects. Careful directions are also included for making an astrolabe and for many other interesting naked-eye projects. A list of references, including magazines, cassettes, maps, and Comet Halley information, followed by an index, complete this fine book. Elementary and junior-high teachers often complain that astronomy units lack activities; this book is highly recommended to them. It is also recommended to anyone who wants to learn to see the skies with a minimum of equipment and a maximum of pleasure.

> *Hilary Hopkins, in a review of "Star Gazing, Comet Tracking and Sky Mapping," in* Science Books & Films, *Vol. 21, No. 3, January-February, 1986, p. 163.*

Prehistoric Mammals: A New World (1986)

Because children are so fascinated both by prehistoric animals and paper engineering, they will be drawn to this pop-up book as a display or discussion item. After a brief introduction to the Age of Mammals, the text (which is difficult for a pop-up book audience) assumes a catalog approach, describing various species, their fossil sites, characteristics, and descendants. There's nothing intrinsically informational about the third-dimensional aspects of the book [which is designed and engineered by Keith Moseley and illustrated by Robert Cremins] except in one case, where a tab pulls back and forth to demonstrate the feeding mechanism of an Amebelodon. The skeleton cutouts are striking, however, and will make this a drawing card where its companion volume, [Moseley's] *Dinosaurs: A Lost World,* has proved popular.

> *A review of "Prehistoric Mammals: A New World," in* Bulletin of the Center for Children's Books, *Vol. 39, No. 9, May, 1986, p. 161.*

Like its companion pop-up book, *Dinosaurs: a Lost World* (Putnam, 1984) by Keith Moseley, **Prehistoric Mammals: a New World** will be a big hit with prehistory fans. Alternating skillfully designed replicas of prehistoric creatures' skeletons with 3-D pop-up versions of the animals themselves, the quality of art is a cut above most pop-up books on the market today. Clear watercolor illustrations are annotated with brief descriptions of each animal, covering its habitat and the time period in which it lived. A chart at the end of the book helps locate some (but not all) of the creatures mentioned within the time span of the Cenozoic Era. Unfortunately, several of the pop-up animal skeletons are never shown in "flesh and blood," which makes it difficult to visualize the creatures. Also, the text sometimes provides tantalizing but incomplete tidbits of information. For instance, readers are told that Synthetoceras had a strange Y-shaped third horn growing out of its nose, but no explanation is provided as to what this horn was used for. Miller's *Prehistoric Mammals* (Messner, 1984) covers more animals, but is equally spotty in providing information. Berger's book is better written. Although the pop-up format may shorten its circulating lifespan in public libraries considerably, as a reserve or reference item, this book will still be well-used.

Cathryn A. Camper, in a review of "Prehistoric Mammals: A New World," in School Library Journal, *Vol. 33, No. 1, September, 1986, p. 116.*

My first-grade daughter sat still for a reading of this book, so it is of interest to children. My daughter certainly couldn't have read the book herself, as numerous scientific names and other technical terms are used. The illustrations include eight pop-ups, most of which are representations of skeletons, and I question their value. A cut-out skeleton that doesn't move is not very appealing. The skeletons are not as complex as the real ones would have been, but, even simplified, they have too many holes for little fingers; a great deal of damage could be done to the book. Hence, librarians or classroom teachers should think hard before purchasing such a book. Parents with plenty of money for books who want to encourage an interest in prehistoric life in their children might be pleased with it, but most potential readers would be better served by a less expensive, conventional volume with more pages.

Martin LaBar, in a review of "Prehistoric Mammals: A New World," in Science Books & Films, *Vol. 22, No. 5, May, 1987, p. 314.*

Atoms, Molecules, and Quarks   (1986)

Berger brings the subatomic "particle zoo" to the young adult audience in this up-to-date look at quarks, the smallest and most elementary subatomic particles to date. Quarks have a more colorful terminology than the more familiar particles, and this terminology is made clear by charts and glossary definitions in addition to explanation in the text. The text is divided equally among discussions of atoms, molecules, and quarks. The classic experiments that led to the discovery of each subatomic particle are discussed. Experiments for the student are scattered throughout and all, with the exception of one that calls for dry ice, may be performed with household articles and in safety. Black-and-white line drawings [by Greg Wenzel] add to the clarity of the text, particularly in explaining how to set up the experiments. The chapter on molecules and molecular bonding will supplement libraries' chemistry collections, which tend to be small in relation to the other sciences. The theory of the quark as an atomic building block enhances earlier 20th-Century atomic theory by adding a new foundation to each of the subatomic particles with which we are most familiar. (pp. 96-7)

Margaret M. Hagel, in a review of "Atoms, Molecules and Quarks," in School Library Journal, *Vol. 33, No. 3, November, 1986, pp. 96-7.*

In an engaging manner Berger provides information about the composition of natural materials. The writing is well suited to students in grades 7 through 11. Berger begins by introducing the notions of atoms, elements, compounds, molecules, and quarks. These notions are developed further in three chapters, on atoms, molecules, and

quarks, and the interrelationships are made clear. The chapter on atoms begins with Democritus' idea that atoms are the smallest indivisible particles of matter—a notion that was later shattered by experiments that revealed electrons, protons, and neutrons as constituent parts of atoms. Fusion and fission are also covered. The chapter on molecules describes their structures and the types of forces that hold molecules together. It provides examples of the carbonhydrogen bond and includes the products derived from petroleum. The last chapter, on quarks, begins with the idea of Murray Gell-Mann that protons and neutrons are each made up of three quarks. Subsequently, a classification of 18 quarks on the basis of three pairs of flavors and three colors is introduced along with the concept of the gluon, which holds quarks together. The book ends by introducing hadrons and leptons. The author has done a nice job of presenting these ideas clearly. Interspersed are step-by-step instructions for a few simple experiments that can be performed easily at home. The illustrations and photographs depict the text well except for the photograph on page 59; here the young reader will be unable to locate the spot where a proton and an antiproton are destroying each other. This book would be a useful addition to any school library. (pp. 168-69)

Dattatraya P. Dandekar, in a review of "Atoms, Molecules and Quarks," in Science Books & Films, *Vol. 22, No. 3, January, 1987, pp. 168-69.*

Hazardous Substances: A Reference   (1986)

This is a dictionary guide to more than 230 hazardous substances in our environment. Substances include those occurring naturally (arsenic, tobacco); produced (chlordane, asbestos, aspartame); and byproducts (PCBs, dioxins). Noise, radiation, and other environmental hazards are included. Hazardous substance disasters in modern times including Bhopal, India; Love Canal, New York; and Chernobyl, Soviet Union, are briefly presented. Sections are devoted to terms used in the field, a brief discussion of Federal Laws and agencies, where to write for more information, and references to text.

For each substance the author provides common name, acronym, formula, description, standard or legal limits for exposure, uses, and health effects. Entries are brief varying in length from six lines for "paraquat" to two pages devoted to "acid rain."

This is a very fine, current, first reference source of hazardous materials for children and teens which will have many uses in school and public libraries. (pp. 12-13)

E. K. G., in a review of "Hazardous Substances: A Reference," in Appraisal: Science Books for Young People, *Vol. 20, No. 2, Spring, 1987, pp. 12-13.*

The introduction clearly explains the purpose and organization of the handbook and can be read by students of junior high age and up. Entries are made under the common name of the substance, with cross references from alternative names, and include the acronym, if any, the chemical formula, a description of its appearance and characteristics, the legal standard for exposure, a history of its use and present applications, and the symptoms and significance of overexposure on human health. The format is open and attractive; topics are easy to locate. Technical terms are kept to a minimum, and a handy glossary at the front of the volume defines those which are used in the annotations. Information is given objectively and succinctly. Most helpful to students wanting more information on the topics are an annotated list of Federal laws and agencies responsible for controlling hazardous substances in the environment; a directory of agencies and groups to contact for further information; and a bibliography of recently published books and pamphlets.

In addition to its ready-reference value, **Hazardous Substances** suggests a wealth of topics for more extensive research. Although it contains no illustrations, it has a decided fascination for those who have made contact with such substances as smokeless tobacco and turpentine in their daily lives. (pp. 25-6)

> *J. D., in a review of "Hazardous Substances: A Reference," in* School Library Journal, *Vol. 33, No. 8, May, 1987, pp. 25-6.*

Berger fails to state in his introductory remarks the intent of the book and to whom it is directed. It is of no value to the professional and could be somewhat dangerous to the layperson because of its potential to stimulate a level of concern about certain chemicals that is totally unwarranted. Berger's credentials are not provided, and, therefore, one cannot judge his competence in this area. He does not distinguish between significant epidemiological evidence, experimental laboratory animal evidence, and speculation. He does not consider duration of exposure and dose, both of which are critical to an assessment of risk. Some of his statements and even some of his definitions are inaccurate. Critical statements are not always referenced. I do not recommend this book as a reference for the following reasons: unqualified statements could be misinterpreted by the layperson; the book has no substantive value to the professional; the information is presented in a fragmentary manner and fails to describe the whole story; and, as a reader, I got the feeling that the idea of writing a book on this subject was rapidly conceived and hastily assembled.

> *Steven W. Mann, in a review of "Hazardous Substances: A Reference," in* Science Books & Films, *Vol. 23, No. 2, November, 1987, p. 72.*

The Artificial Heart   (1987)

In his usual clear, thorough fashion, Berger explores the history and controversial aspects both of heart transplants and of artificial implants.

Since the development of the heart-lung machine at mid-century, researchers have been working toward an artificial device that is portable as well as reliable; several different models are described, though the Jarvik-7 seems to be by far the most widely used, and Berger appends a chart listing every artificial heart recipient through March 1987, with information on each patient's subsequent (usually brief) medical history. Heart transplants are not very much more common; and because donors are often hard to find (so great is the shortage that "about 1/3 of all transplant candidates die while waiting for a new heart"), artificial hearts have found a use as temporary installations, put in to buy time. Berger devotes a chapter to the ethical questions raised by this strategy, and another to the psychological trauma many heart recipients suffer.

Other books, such as Skurzynski's *Bionic Parts for People,* treat some of these topics, but this expands the discussion. Index, bibliography.

> *A review of "The Artificial Heart," in* Kirkus Reviews, *Vol. LV, No. 19, October 1, 1987, p. 1458.*

A well-written, comprehensive overview of the development of the artificial heart, with a look at current uses and bioethical dilemmas. Much space is devoted to Barney Clark's experience, as well as to examinations of several other cases. An early chapter is devoted to the anatomy of the healthy heart, emphasized by detailed black-and-white drawings and diagrams. The history of the heart transplant procedure is presented, followed by a review of the development of various artificial apparatus. The practice of using an artificial heart as a bridge to transplant is considered, including the ethical issues that are raised by the circumstance. Quality of life, research vs. therapy, costs, and informed consent are all examined. Finally, psychological considerations and legal issues are raised, questions that must be answered even as transplants are taking place. Good black-and-white photos of the pioneering doctors, patients, and devices are scattered throughout, accompanied by a couple of political cartoons. There is a great deal of information here, and much food for thought, presented in a clear, appropriate manner. Although it is similar to other recent publications on artificial organs, because this one deals specifically with the heart, it is well worth considering.

> *Denise L. Moll, in a review of "The Artificial Heart," in* School Library Journal, *Vol. 34, No. 4, December, 1987, p. 90.*

Combining technical information about biomedical engineering with consideration of ethical and psychological issues, Berger looks at the development of the artificial heart, the procedures to implant it, its main uses, and the problems it raises for patients and doctors. . . . Separate chapters deal with medical ethics (Who should receive the artificial heart implant? Who should pay? Is the implant therapeutic or experimental?); with adjustment problems of patients, relatives, and medical staff; and with legal issues (What if the patient wants to turn off the machine and end treatment?). Though Berger is sometimes melodramatic ("The doctors were desperate") and exclamatory, his chatty, well-organized text, with clear diagrams and photographs of patients and their machines, successfully integrates humaninterest stories with general information. No notes, but most quotations are attributed, and the bibliography includes journals, books, magazines, newspapers, and government reports. Glossary; index.

Hazel Rochman, in a review of "The Artificial Heart," in Booklist, *Vol. 84, No. 11, February 1, 1988, p. 921.*

Lights, Lenses, and Lasers (1987)

Clearly but simply, Berger introduces light and lenses, illuminated with a scattering of quick experiments and demonstrations that let readers participate and illustrated with useful black-and-white photos and [Greg Wenzel's] diagrams. The portion on light and lenses is welcome as so many of the old standard texts about light are no longer available. The section on laser mechanics and applications is merely run of the mill, containing (understandably) only one home experiment and (less acceptably) unnecessary generalizations and hyperbole. Careless readers could draw the conclusion that all lasers produce light of equal high intensity. Even the most careful readers will not be able to find the dividing line between what has been done once or twice under carefully controlled conditions and what can be done reliably every day. This does not make this worse than other books on lasers, just not up to the promise of Berger's sections on light and lenses. *A Look Inside Lasers* (Raintree, 1981) by Jim Johnson is a slim, colorful volume that spends more time on laser mechanics and less on applications. Both *Lasers, the Miracle Light* (Morrow, 1979) by Larry Kettlekamp and *Laser Light* (McGraw, 1978) by Herman Schneider supply more detail.

> *Margaret Chatham, in a review of "Lights, Lenses, and Lasers," in* School Library Journal, *Vol. 34, No. 7, March, 1988, p. 204.*

Berger's survey of his complex subjects is a cohesive discussion which begins with several experiments demonstrating the various properties of light. The author explains natural, artificial, and biological light, reflected light, shadows, color, how light travels, and how to measure light. In explaining how lenses work, he discusses the human eye, magnifying glasses, microscopes, and telescopes. Lasers receive a somewhat lengthier treatment with discussion of the way lasers work and some of their uses. The text is quite up-to-date with explanations of how lasers are used in compact disc technology, fiber optics, and holography. Well-chosen photographs and clear diagrams accompany the challenging but lucid narrative. Technical terms are explained in context. The informative introduction is timely, thoughtful, and in sharp contrast to the glut of shallow miscellanies published on lasers in recent years. Glossary and index.

> *Margaret A. Bush, in a review of "Lights, Lenses and Lasers," in* The Horn Book Magazine, *Vol. LXIV, No. 2, March-April, 1988, p. 220.*

Lights is a potentially outstanding book held back by imperfect editing. First, the good points. The book covers the nature of light and its everyday manifestations, the basics of optics, and the science and applications of lasers in a concise and readable fashion. It is up to date, with brief coverage of fiber optics and optical compact disks. In particular, it is notable for its inclusion of simple, cleverly de-

signed experiments illustrating the principles at work. Unfortunately, the hour I spent with the book revealed enough errata to make me uncomfortable with its reliability. Two examples: a discussion of the electromagnetic spectrum reverses high and low frequencies, and Fahrenheit is consistently spelled without its first "h". Such editorial lapses are especially disappointing in an otherwise fine volume.

> *Allan Fisher, in a review of "Lights, Lenses and Lasers," in* Appraisal: Science Books for Young People, *Vol. 22, No. 3, Summer, 1989, p. 14.*

Early Humans: A Prehistoric World (1988)

A pop-up book always has a novelty appeal and 3D skulls and mammoths hold the attention. In this case, the pop-up element has been used to assist understanding, mainly where comparisons are needed. The book shows a development from Australopithecus to Cro-Magnon man and the pictorial representation helps to show the succession of our ancestors when the time scale is difficult to understand. The greater part of the book deals with comparisons between Neanderthal and Cro-Magnon, pinpointing aspects of the latter's life which bring him nearest to modern man; buildings homes, using tools and making pictures. Whether flat or 3D, the large illustrations are good in a photographic style and the smaller diagrams are informative. [The book is engineered by John Strejan and illustrated by Michael Welply]. The text is brief but the details which have been selected are consistently interesting. This is a confusing subject, owing to the evolving state of knowledge and the difficulty children have in grasping the time scale, but this is a reasonable and enjoyable window on one area.

> *Pat Thomson, in a review of "Early Humans," in* Books for Your Children, *Vol. 23, No. 2, Summer, 1988, p. 16.*

At a time when the concept of human evolution is once again evoking some negative reaction, there is a clear need for educational materials that address the subject in an accurate yet easy-to-understand way, particularly for young children. For its format, this pop-up book is wonderful because the third dimension allows one to see difficult-to-grasp aspects of human evolution, such as skeletal changes. (This is a format that would be useful in college textbooks.) However engaging the presentation, this book reads as if the author, who does not seem particularly versed in human evolutionary theory, perused a few textbooks, then produced this distillation. A working knowledge of the theories involved is necessary to see the weaknesses, not so much of inaccuracy as of bias, and of an effort to bridge the gap between conservative and progressive interpretations of the fossil record. My point is best illustrated by the Neanderthal material. Although reference is made to the initial, scientific errors in interpretation of the fossils, this author still draws on the also inaccurate, related conceptualization of Neanderthals and attempts to blend this with a more modern interpretation. The result is confusion and contradiction. There is also a

Berger at home.

dogmatic presentation depicting the constituents of the human lineage, beginning with *Australopithicus afarensis,* but this is still a controversial interpretation. In addition, attempts are made to make the material more relevant by stressing the similarity to *Western* cultures—an unnecessary, subtle form of bias. Best to read and use this book only with additional material provided by an informed teacher. (pp. 97-8)

> *Sharon Fetter, in a review of "Early Humans: A Prehistoric World," in* Science Books & Films, *Vol. 24, No. 2, November-December, 1988, pp. 97-8.*

Books on human ancestors are susceptible to quite a few pitfalls: sexism, racism, and over-simplification to name a few. Although this book stumbles a bit, it is largely a well-done effort. The pop-up format is a terrific one for making meaningful points about early human beings. Readers can compare the size and shape of an Australopithicine skull (Lucy) to that of a Cro-Magnon and can lift a few flaps and compare the skeleton and brain case of a Cro-Magnon with that of a Neanderthal. These visual comparisons lend meaning to statements about the changing human form. They also give the young reader the opportunity to compare and contrast the differences among the various forms—and to think about the significance of the differences they observe.

The balanced coverage of hunting and of the survival behaviors with the emergence of cultural practices is commendable. The only objectionable "stumbling" by this book is under the first main heading. Although the book is entitled **Early Humans,** the first heading is "Evolution of Early Man" and describes in detail our most significant early human fossil: Lucy, a woman! Overall, gender biases are not a problem, which puts this book several steps ahead of many similar publications. The book stands out even more because the elaborate and beautiful pop-up scenes make an appealing invitation for young readers to explore and think about human prehistory. (pp. 18-19)

> *Barbara W. McKinney, in a review of "Early Humans," in* Appraisal: Science Books for Young People, *Vol. 22, Nos. 1-2, Winter-Spring, 1989, pp. 18-19.*

UFOs, ETs, and Visitors from Space   (1988)

Berger takes the role of debunker here, at least in most of the cases he discusses. He admits that while 90 percent of UFO sightings and encounters with ET-like beings are false, there are some incidents that have never been reasonably explained. Beginning with a recounting of Orson Welles' "War of the Worlds" broadcast, the author offers two fables that illustrate different ways to think about

UFOs and ETs. One suggests that even a sole unexplained sighting is proof such things exist; the other purports that these odd incidents often have simple explanations. Berger then describes a number of situations that seem to have otherworldly dimensions and concludes with this-worldly reasons. This organization affords a few problems. By the time readers get to the deductions, they may have forgotten the original situations. Still, there is much here to pique the curiosity of young readers who seem to have a natural interest in this topic. Illustrated with black-and-white photographs and several surprisingly poor line drawings.

> *Ilene Cooper, in a review of "UFOs, ETs & Visitors from Space," in* Booklist, *Vol. 85, No. 3, October 1, 1988, p. 263.*

Berger sorts through the hype surrounding reports of "flying saucers" and alien space visitors to uncover a less glamorous, but probably truer interpretation. He describes, in the style of the tabloid writer, several famous encounters with UFOs and writer Erich Von Däniken's evidence of past alien visitors. For a few pages it almost seems like UFOs and aliens are real, but then Berger turns the tables by filling in the missing details or offering a simpler explanation. To show that scientists are indeed interested in finding real extraterrestrials, Berger includes a chapter on SETI—the Search for Extraterrestrial Intelligence. The same SETI information can be found in other books, but it is the contrast between careful observation and wild speculation that drives home the point of this book. Line drawings and photographs are of varying quality. This book may not change many minds, but as long as science fiction belongs in libraries, so does this volume.

> *Alan Newman, in a review of "UFOs, ETs & Visitors from Space," in* School Library Journal, *Vol. 35, No. 3, November, 1988, p. 134.*

While UFO sightings don't receive much public attention these days, the notion of extra-terrestrial beings lingers on, if largely through the fantasies played out in popular movies and video games. Berger deals with the two phenomena separately, citing numerous examples of purported events. Nearly all cases of unidentified flying objects examined here were eventually found to result from identifiable causes—swamp gas, debris in the atmosphere, planetary appearances, etc. The author points out that scientific study has never verified any of the sightings as true though many Americans persist in believing in the existence of UFOs. He appears to allow somewhat more credibility to the possibility of ETs, examining the evidence from studies of radio signals and the physical evidence of possible extraterrestrial visitations in various countries. The discussion throughout is interesting and reasonable but falls a bit short in its coverage. Though one tantalizing unexplained episode from 1986 is included, there is very little mention of either alleged events or scientific study during the past decade. Organizations dedicated to research of UFOs and ETs (Mutual UFO Network, Center for UFO Studies, et al) are not identified. Informative photographs and diagrams are included, but the lack of a bibliography is an unfortunate oversight in regard to such an intriguing topic. Still, the book is attractive, readable, and thoughtful

and fills a gap since few children's books have appeared on these topics in recent years.

> *Margaret Bush, in a review of "UFOs, ETs, & Visitors from Space," in* Appraisal: Science Books for Young People, *Vol. 22, Nos. 1-2, Winter-Spring, 1989, p. 19.*

Switch On, Switch Off (1989)

Berger diffuses the mystery of electricity in this comprehensible presentation, a new addition to the Let's-Read-and-Find-Out Science Book series. The author explains, through a simple experiment with electrical wire, a bar magnet, and a compass, how electricity is produced and transmitted via a circuit. This concept is expanded as the function of a town's generator, which supplies electricity to individual homes, and the use of switches to turn lights on and off are demonstrated. [Carolyn] Croll's illustrations combine appealing rosy-cheeked children (and their curious cat and dog) with vivid, clear diagrams of the magical force in action. Simple and effective.

> *Phillis Wilson, in a review of "Switch On, Switch Off," in* Booklist, *Vol. 85, No. 16, April 15, 1989, p. 1462.*

An easily intelligible text printed in large type and bright, inviting pictures and diagrams combine to create an excellent introduction to the topic of electricity for second- to fourth-grade readers. After a brief definition of energy— "Energy is anything that does work. You have lots of energy"—the author focuses on the specifics of electrical energy: what it is, how it is produced, and how it flows from generator to the individual light bulb. By following this progression, the reader effortlessly learns the functions of generators, circuits, switches, and plugs. Also provided are instructions for making a simple electrical circuit with safe, easily available materials. This feature is especially useful and can be used as a springboard for an independent science project. One of the more successful books in the Let's-Read-and-Find-Out science series to have been published lately, this volume offers just enough information, presented in an appealing, uncomplicated format.

> *N. V., in a review of "Switch On, Switch Off," in* The Horn Book Magazine, *Vol. LXV, No. 3, May-June, 1989, p. 384.*

As is typical of *Let's Read-and-Find-Out Science* books, this one succeeds in making a complex subject understandable to young readers. Its information seems too simplified at times, however, and the illustrations are also quite simple and somewhat flat, though brightly colored. Overall, this book is slightly more than acceptable for its purpose and audience.

> *Barbara Roberts, in a review of "Switch On, Switch Off," in* Science Books & Films, *Vol. 25, No. 1, September-October, 1989, p. 35.*

The Science of Music (1989)

An introduction covering how sound is made is followed

by a section on the human voice and hearing, which gives way to the bulk of this book, an explanation of how musical instruments differ, produce sounds, and are made. These basic descriptions of instruments are arranged by types: percussion, strings, woodwinds, brass, and pianos, which includes other keyboard instruments. Each chapter provides a brief history of that type of instrument and explains the differences among the members of that family of instruments as well as how that family differs from or resembles others. Two final chapters cover recording music and playback devices, explaining the workings of records, tapes, compact discs, microphones, amplifiers, and speakers. The generally readable, although not compelling, text is somewhat repetitious (e.g. Grenadilla wood is mentioned in conjunction with two instruments, but the second reference reads as though this wood were not introduced two pages earlier); however, students will appreciate the organization, which makes it useful for reports. Informal line-drawings [by Yvonne Buchanan] illustrate the instruments and concepts discussed; these sketches are effective in demonstrating the physics of sound, but not as successful at showing the instruments.

> *Jeffrey A. French, in a review of "The Science of Music," in* School Library Journal, *Vol. 35, No. 13, September, 1989, p. 259.*

The Science of Music attempts to introduce primarily junior and senior high students to the field of musical acoustics. . . . Relatively free of errors, this book is also easy to read and will not stump younger readers with an abundance of technical terms. Some secondary school students may find it too limited, but it should stimulate others to read further. The list for further reading easily could have included additional works of merit, such as Rossing's *The Science of Sound* and Backus' *The Acoustical Foundations of Music.* I recommend this book as fairly accurate, well organized, and, with some reservations, fairly complete in scope.

> *Richard F. Schwartz, in a review of "The Science of Music," in* Science Books & Films, *Vol. 25, No. 1, September-October, 1989, p. 23.*

The wonderful information world that today's youngsters inhabit has been enriched yet again by Melvin Berger. . . . In **The Science of Music** Berger engages his readers in the world of musical sounds, reminding them that music is both an art and a science.

How is sound produced? What are the distinguishing elements of sound? Berger smoothly carries these two questions through each member of each family of orchestral instruments, then into recording and playback equipment, and finally into the outer limit (for the moment) of electronic synthesizers. In each case the author's well-crafted exposition of sophisticated information is generously complemented by descriptions of experiments or other hands-on involvement, none of which is costly or labor-intensive: using a balloon to see how vibrations produce a buzz in brass instruments and re-creating acoustical principles by making a set of maracas from empty pint-sized milk containers, to cite but two examples. . . .

The index provides selective and not entirely error-free ac-

cess, but the latter defect proves hardly to be a fatal flaw. A short reading list of books is provided, and the author urges young readers to use magazines to keep pace with the rapidly changing technology for sound recording and playback.

Berger not only poses the right question ("How does the science of sound join with the art of music to create the glorious sounds we hear?), he also provides a splendid answer.

> *Jean M. Bonin, in a review of "The Science of Music," in* Notes, *Vol. 47, No. 1, September, 1990, p. 71.*

Solids, Liquids, and Gases: From Superconductors to the Ozone Layer (1989)

[In the following excerpt, the critic explains why he gave Berger's book a rating of "Good" rather than a higher rating.]

[**Solids, Liquids, and Gases**] is illustrated with several dozen photographs and line drawings, the variety and quality of which are quite good. In several cases, however, there is insufficient attention to linkage of the illustrations and text; the captions are very brief, and the references in the text to the illustrations are generally terse.

Berger's prose is very lively and his choice of topics is quite reasonable (though I was surprised that his last chapter—which deals with pollution and the ozone layer—entirely omits any reference to carbon dioxide buildup and the possibility of a consequent warming trend). The author has included a number of do-it-yourself experiments, most of which appear to this reviewer to be workable and relevant.

Given the positive aspects of this book, why did it not receive a higher rating? I cite three main reasons. First, there are too many instances in which the author set himself up to give details that he did not deliver. For example, there is a drawing of a bimetallic-strip thermostat, but there is no discussion of how it works! Second, there are some technical errors, such as a reference to "nitrogen dioxide" in the discussion of acid rain, and the statement that the slightly higher boiling point of heavy water (as compared to ordinary water) is important to its role as a coolant in nuclear power plants. Third, some of Berger's "high interest" lines are likely to be confusing or misleading: "Only two liquids, water and oil, are found in nature . . . ", "you cannot touch it (air) . . . "; "the super-energy of the laser can, in a billionth of a second, fuse the two chemicals."

In summary, this is a good book, one that deserves a place in school libraries. However, with only a few changes, it could have been truly excellent. (pp. 13-14)

> *William H. Ingham, in a review of "Solids, Liquids, and Gases," in* Appraisal: Science Books for Young People, *Vol. 23, No. 1, Winter, 1990, pp. 13-14.*

Beginning with a definition of matter, Berger proceeds to discuss its three states, explaining their natures, properites and behaviors. Simple experiments, complete with safety precautions, are included throughout, helping to illustrate the concepts. The black-and-white drawings and photographs also expand the text and clarify the experiments.

In addition to the above, the discussion of solids includes crystals and plastics, while solutions are examined in the chapter on liquids, and the chemistry of air and the layers of the atmosphere are covered under gases. Berger introduces topics of current interest in connection with each state of matter. Following the overview of solids, there is a chapter on conductors, semiconductors and superconductors. The unusual liquids, like heavy water, slippery water and acid rain, have their own chapter, and time is given to plasma and nuclear fusion, air pollution and the ozone layer.

Because of the many topics covered, the book is an overview. Other sources would have to be used for further information. Explanations are limited and simple. The writing is straightforward and easily understood. The precautions given in the experiments frequently call for adult help. All of these factors make this book suitable as an introduction for children in the intermediate grades. Unfortunately, the small size of the type could lead readers to believe that the material is more difficult than it really is, daunting some who would otherwise find it interesting and informative.

The book has an index and a glossary. A misprint was found in the glossary definition of condensation, calling it the process of cooling a liquid to change it into a gas. The correct definition is found in the text. These problems are minor and, overall, the book provides a good foundation on matter and its three states. Recommended for school and public libraries.

> *Peggy Skotnicki, in a review of "Solids, Liquids, and Gases," in* Appraisal: Science Books for Young People, *Vol. 23, No. 1, Winter, 1990, p. 13.*

This book is an interesting synthesis of the kinetic molecular nature of matter and currently relevant phenomena ranging from superconductivity to ozone-layer depletion, from squeezing pieces of cake to bending glass. The illustrations are high quality, especially those included in demonstration directions, which are given as diagrams uncluttered by labels. One illustration (p. 31) could have been improved by eliminating the speckled background. Blank spaces between the water molecules would more clearly show junior readers that dissolved salt "molecules" occupy empty spaces between water molecules (speckling the water molecules themselves would also be an improvement). The only major deficiency in this volume is the poor choice of photographs. Although the cover is well chosen (a color close-up of superconductivity levitation), a photograph intended to illustrate forest fire pollution (p. 66) fills nearly half the frame with a fire truck. Most other photographs are equally poor. A minor correction should be made on page 9—the number of protons alone determines type of atom: the number of neutrons specifies differences (isotopes) within that type. Overall this book is very good for its level; however, it is unfortunate that the aging British system of measurement is used exclusively

rather than the more international (SI) metric system or at least a combination of the two. This book is recommended for use as a combination classroom demonstration manual and a general background text.

> *Ronald F. Smith, in a review of "Solids, Liquids and Gases: From Superconductors to the Ozone Layer," in* Science Books & Films, *Vol. 25, No. 3, January-February, 1990, p. 131.*

If You Lived on Mars (1989)

What will life be like for the first colonists on Mars? Berger answers this question with a broad view of an imaginary first colony, beginning each chapter with "If you lived on Mars . . . " and describing the colony in the present tense, as if it actually exists. He covers the colony's structure and layout, housing, history (linking real history from Schiaparelli and Lowell through the Viking missions with the projected colonization program), gravity, atmosphere, water, food, time measurement, weather, transportation, sightseeing, and methods of terraforming. The descriptions of the colony and related technology are not overly detailed; rather, the tone is closer to travel brochure than technical report. The overall premise works fairly well, but at times appears to be too obviously a frame for basic information. Routine photos of Mars and drawings of landing craft are included, but the colony is not represented pictorially. Students accustomed to Star Wars (not SDI) gadgetry will find this futuristic view ordinary, but its value lies in detailing Martian conditions and demonstrating how they affect the design and function of the colony.

> *Dennis Ford, in a review of "If You Lived on Mars," in* School Library Journal, *Vol. 36, No. 1, January, 1990, p. 110.*

If You Lived on Mars is a delightful book which could be as useful in an English literature program as in a science class. The text reads smoothly, and there are just enough facts and illustrations to make the book an intriguing intellectual experience as well as a visual treat.

You are in the future now, with a great deal of history behind you. " . . . the first people who lived on Mars, starting in the year 2027 . . . " With this kind of direct writing, we are soon willing to suspend our disbelief and live on the red planet. "Now, however, fifty-six years have passed. People are beginning to bring trees, plants, and animals to Mars . . . "

And so it goes. Ingeniously, the author weaves his web of science fiction based upon scientific fact, and does so in a style which leaves the reader reluctant to break off from the wonder of it all. One almost longs for the future when, perhaps, all or some of this may come true.

To be sure, we can carp about some of the "facts," but then we would be the losers. Any author audacious enough to propel us into the future must make some guesses about the manner in which science and technology will evolve, and no two of us would make the same wagers. No matter, take it as one author's chronicle of life on Mars, and enjoy it for what it is.

And what a story it is! Read it aloud to your science classes for a treat, or read it aloud to your English classes to stimulate your students' own innovative writing. Better still, use this book as the centerpiece for an interdisciplinary study in science writing. Any way you read it, your students will benefit. (pp. 13-14)

> *Clarence Truesdell, in a review of "If You Lived on Mars," in* Appraisal: Science Books for Young People, *Vol. 23, No. 3, Summer, 1990, pp. 13-14.*

Though the topics covered in this book are appropriate to the subject of living on Mars, the information is inconsistent and incongruent with the graphics, which are also poor. For example, though the story takes place 50 years after the first manned landing on Mars, it is proposed that the trip will still take from six to nine months, the amount of time such a trip would take today. Though fusion power is proposed for the colony, fusion propulsion, which could reduce the travel time to a few days and is already under development, is not considered. Nuclear energy to power a Mars base, which appears in one of the graphics and is also under development now, is not mentioned in the text. The book is appropriate for junior high school and young adult readers. The material could provide the basis for a school science curriculum for an entire year; it includes discussions of energy, space travel, biology, space medicine, chemistry, and other areas of interest. But it is recommended that the teacher supplement the book with more accurate material from NASA and other sources.

> *Marsha Freeman, in a review of "If You Lived on Mars," in* Science Books & Films, *Vol. 26, No. 1, September-October, 1990, p. 57.*

Our Atomic World (1989)

In **Our Atomic World,** atoms, elements, and physical and chemical properties are taken from the abstract to the concrete through concise explanations and simple demonstrations to be performed by the reader. The electron cloud concept is illustrated by whirling a key about on the end of a string. An experiment in chemical changes involves the oxidation of steel wool. Is there space between the atoms in a liquid? Readers can check it out by using water and salt. The author defines and emphasizes a scientific vocabulary in bold type in the text and in the glossary. There are good color photographs or diagrams on every page, but a few could have been better chosen or captioned more carefully. One photograph shows a large water detector built to monitor proton decay and used to detect neutrinos. But proton decay is never discussed, and from the information previously given readers may not be able to understand what it is or why it is important. Also mentioned are social issues involving superconductive technology, radiation, and nuclear power. Because there are a lot of ideas here, uninitiated readers may not understand everything on the first reading. But repeated readings are well worth the time. An excellent supplemental book in the classroom.

> *Cynthia A. Bradbury, in a review of "Our*

Atomic World," in Science Books & Films, *Vol. 25, No. 4, March-April, 1990, p. 208.*

Drug Abuse A-Z (with Gilda Berger, 1990)

[**Drug Abuse A-Z**] is aptly titled. The authors use a dictionary approach to describe a very thorough composite of drugs and related terms. The book is clearly written and easy to read, which makes it a good reference source for its target audience of students at the junior high and high school levels. In addition to the drug descriptors, the authors offer an interesting review of related federal legislation that regulates drugs. The book falls short in its limited offering of other references and agencies providing further information. This is unfortunate, because a comprehensive list of the wide variety of available sources in both categories would have greatly enhanced the book. By presenting such a short list of resources, the authors may give their young readers the false impression that help is not readily available.

> *Cathy J. Brown, in a review of "Drug Abuse A-Z," in* Science Books & Films, *Vol. 25, No. 5, May-June, 1990, p. 255.*

Using brief, concise definitions, the Bergers explain more than 1000 drug-related terms in dictionary fashion. There is no entry for AIDS or other physical diseases prone to addicts, or about the danger of sharing needles. An introductory section explains the broad drug categories and the major federal drug laws, and there are addresses and phone numbers of appropriate agencies. This updates Richard Lingeman's *Drugs from A to Z* (McGraw Hill, 1974) and *The Encyclopedia of Drug Abuse* (Facts on File, 1984) by Robert O'Brien and Sidney Cohen, both of which were published before the emergence of crack but which have longer entries. The Bergers' short definitions relay the substantive information in enough detail for brief reports.

> *Martha Gordon, in a review of "Drug Abuse A-Z," in* School Library Journal, *Vol. 36, No. 8, August, 1990, p. 152.*

As a quick ready reference, **Drug Abuse A-Z** does serve a purpose. It is easy to use and, although in some definitions difficult words are used, these words in turn are defined in their alphabetical position.

For those students wanting to know more about drugs and drug abuse, additional references will be needed. There are a number of titles available for youngsters from upper elementary grades through high school. This useful drug dictionary will be a good companion to those more comprehensive volumes. (pp. 11-12)

> *Tippen McDaniel, in a review of "Drug Abuse A-Z," in* Appraisal: Science Books for Young People, *Vol. 23, No. 4, Autumn, 1990, pp. 11-12.*

Seasons (1990)

Taking young readers on a journey through the year, Berger explores the mystery of the seasons by providing insight into how the tilt of the earth's orbit affects seasonal changes. Beginning with spring, he charts the changes in weather, stages of plant growth, and animal adaptation through summer, autumn, and winter. Woven among the facts is information on the customs, holidays, and legends associated with each season. [Ron] Jones' dramatic, full-color illustrations reflect the colors and wonders of each season. The stages of a caterpillar's metamorphosis, the parts of a flower, the drama of a summer storm, and the warm palette of autumn colors are among the rich backdrops for the text, which, unfortunately, is set in colored panels that visually cramp the dramatic page spreads. Despite this minor flaw, Jones' art enhances Berger's smoothly integrated and clearly written narrative, creating a volume that will satisfy the curious. (pp. 929, 933)

> *Linda Callaghan, in a review of "Seasons," in* Booklist, *Vol. 87, No. 9, January 1, 1991, pp. 929, 933.*

How Life Began (1990)

A dramatic and awe-inspiring exploration of how life began, the formation of this planet, the reign of the dinosaurs, and the development of human beings. Here is a successful blend of solid scientific theory and enticing storytelling that encourages a sense of wonder while sparking further inquiry. Readers witness the "big bang" 15 billion years ago that created the universe and are then placed in the land of the terrible lizards. The large format, text set off in boxes, and striking illustrations [by Jerry Lofaro] offer easy access to a complex subject. Pronunciation of scientific names and an adequate index are provided. This exceptional book is marred only by the overuse of exclamation points.

> *Denia Lewis Hester, in a review of "How Life Began," in* School Library Journal, *Vol. 37, No. 7, July, 1991, p. 76.*

This is a very brief beginning to evolution and natural selection studies. Terms and the names of species are in bold letters, with a pronunciation guide and the time frames listed accurately correspond with other reputable sources.

The striking illustrations add a sense of awe to an otherwise bland text which reads like a textbook listing basic facts.

For example, in the section, "To Modern Humans," very little is cited about the tools, eating habits and abilities of early man. The emphasis is placed on the physical attributes of each species, when each species lived, and when each disappeared.

The book ends with four questions: "Will life continue to develop as it has in the past? Will new forms of life appear and grow? Will humans rule wisely? What do you think?" Unfortunately, there may not be enough information in this book for young children to form hypotheses for these open ended questions. Serious students would be better advised to consult Joanna Cole's, *Evolution* (Crowell, 1987) or Kathryn Lasky's, *Traces of Life* (Morrow, 1989).

An index is included, but a glossary and bibliography are lacking. The weak binding will not hold up to many circulations. This will serve best as a browsing book for younger children interested in evolution.

> *Keven W. Booe, in a review of "How Life Began," in* Appraisal: Science Books for Young People, *Vol. 25, No. 1, Winter, 1992, p. 13.*

From the pre-biotic soup to modern man, Melvin Berger tells the story of life on Earth in **How Life Began.** Berger begins with the Big Bang Theory and subsequently launches into a discussion of the origins of life on primitive earth. A brief but thorough discussion of how the pre-biotic soup gave rise to amino acids and ultimately the first cell provides the setting for the emergence of the first multicellular organisms. Berger then systematically details the origins of life on land, including its emergence from the sea and and the evolution of fish, amphibians, reptiles and mammals. He includes an excellent section on the dinosaurs, which incorporates a treatise on the practical implications of the many structural differences found among these reptiles. I was disappointed, however, with the surprisingly brief discussion of the evolution of birds and flight. This fascinating subject deserves greater attention. The section covering the evolution of modern humans is interesting and reasonably thorough. He introduces the earliest primates and discusses the emergence of apes and other higher primates. Berger culminates with a section on the development of modern humans, beginning with australopithecine and including Homo Habilis, Homo Erectus, Neanderthal and Cro-Magnon man.

The most striking feature of this book is the phenomenal quality of the illustrations. Jerry Lofaro has created drawings which are nearly as instructional as the text. For example, a picture of the earliest ancestor of the horse is superimposed on a picture of the modern horse. This effectively conveys the similarities and differences between these two related creatures. This illustration and many others perfectly complement the text.

My major criticism of this book is exemplified by the difficulty I had assigning it an age recommendation. Although the concepts are presented in a manner simple enough for younger children, vocabulary seems appropriate for an older audience. I am concerned that children old enough to handle the vocabulary will find the text oversimplified. Despite this criticism, I strongly recommend **How Life Began.** It is an excellent introduction to the evolutionary history of life on Earth and will certainly spark an interest in young readers to learn more about this fascinating subject.

> *Shawn M. Ahern, in a review of "How Life Began," in* Appraisal: Science Books for Young People, *Vol. 25, No. 1, Winter, 1992, p. 13.*

Ouch! A Book about Cuts, Scratches, and Scrapes (1991)

Berger describes the healing process, pointing out the roles played by red or white blood cells, and by the platelets.

Clear and sequential, if minimally marred by a tendency to include exclamatory remarks ("Sometimes it is even hard to remember where you cut yourself!"), the continuous text ends with advice: wash the wound, cover it, and see a nurse or doctor if the bleeding won't stop. Illustrations [by Pat Stewart] include diagrams that show the stages in healing; these are both more attractive and more informative than the pedestrian, harshly colored pictures of children. Simply written for primary grades readers, this may be useful to read aloud to even younger children.

Zena Sutherland, in a review of "Ouch! A Book about Cuts, Scratches, and Scrapes," in Bulletin of the Center for Children's Books, *Vol. 44, No. 9, May, 1991, p. 210.*

A vibrant, interesting introduction to the skin's healing process. A group of third graders act out the many ways one can suffer a cut or scrape, and the preferred treatment, while the narrative details the functions of red cells, white cells, scabs, etc. The writing is a little overdone at times, with an excess of exclamation points. It is, however, clear and easy to follow, packing a great deal of information into minimal text. Full-color drawings show the students in various situations, with just a few diagrams. Races and genders are well represented, and all are active participants. Geared for a younger audience and more narrowly focused than Kathleen Elgin's *The Fall Down, Break a Bone, Skin Your Knee Book* (Walker, 1974; o.p.), this would be valuable both to teachers presenting human-body units and for general use. (pp. 87-8)

Denise L. Moll, in a review of "Ouch! A Book about Cuts, Scratches, and Scrapes," in School Library Journal, *Vol. 37, No. 5, May, 1991, pp. 87-8.*

M(aurice) Boutet de Monvel

1850(?)-1913

(Born Louis Maurice Boutet de Monvel) French author and illustrator of picture books and reteller.

Major works include *Good Children and Bad* (written by Eugene Plon, 1890), *Joan of Arc* (1897), *Select Fables from La Fontaine* (1901), *Old Songs and Rounds* (1912), *Our Children* (written by Anatole France, 1917).

The following entry emphasizes general criticism of Boutet de Monvel's oeuvre. It also includes a selection of reviews to supplement the general commentary.

INTRODUCTION

Esteemed as one of the greatest illustrators of children's literature as well as the first major French illustrator in the field, Boutet de Monvel is acknowledged for introducing a representation of childhood in his works that is both refined and realistic. Commentators note that his paintings and illustrations express his understanding of and sympathy with children as independent beings, free from adult mannerisms. Often compared with Walter Crane and Kate Greenaway, Boutet de Monvel depicted the exuberant and mischievious nature of children, revealing himself as a keen observer of human nature who developed an artistic style aimed at capturing the fundamental character of his subjects. He stated, "I sought in every little figure, every group, the essence, and worked for that alone." Typically, Boutet de Monvel's books reflect the daily experiences of children as well as their songs and fables, manners and relationships. Moreover, Boutet de Monvel imbues his works with a sensitivity towards French history and cultural traditions. He is perhaps best known as the creator of the biography *Joan of Arc,* the only book he both wrote and illustrated. In this work, he outlines the life and death of France's national heroine while carefully placing her within the world of the late Middle Ages. As an illustrator, Boutet de Monvel employed a variety of artistic styles and media. In working with pen, he quickly found that the lack of color necessitated a highly sensitive use of line in order to denote character. Critics often observe that his delicate lines, even in faces with simple features, convey emotion and effectively differentiate one child from another. Boutet de Monvel additionally worked in watercolor, where he demonstrated a precise use of light and shade that survived reproduction in black and white. His lithographic work further employed nuanced coloration, accented outlines, and flat tones that have elicited comparisons with Japanese woodcuts. Lauded for his exquisite evocations of everyday life and the natural world, Boutet de Monvel is often acknowledged for the accuracy of his visual representations of both urban France and elegant interiors. Praised for his imagination and technical skill, Boutet de Monvel's illustrations are celebrated for a wide

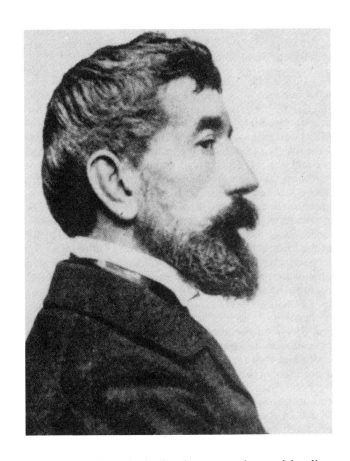

range of qualities, including humor, pathos, spirituality, drama, and aesthetic beauty.

Boutet de Monvel was born in Orleans, France, the home of Joan of Arc. The eldest in a family of numerous brothers and sisters, he later claimed that his observations of his siblings inspired much of his illustration. As a young man, he studied at the École des Beaux-Arts in Paris and began to exhibit his works in Parisian Salons at the age of twenty-four. At that time, France had no children's illustrator of note, and Boutet de Monvel entered the field as a means of supporting his family. He began his career when an acquaintance gave his name to an editor who needed someone to illustrate *La France en-zigzag* by Eudoxie Dupuis. In the early 1880s Boutet de Monvel began providing pictures for the French edition of the children's magazine *St. Nicholas,* an event which established him as a major illustrator for young people. Subsequently, he collected and illustrated children's songs and provided the pictures for *Good Children and Bad,* a tongue-in-cheek handbook of children's etiquette by Eugene Plon. Following this, he published *Our Children* which featured text by Anatole France, whose daughter's portrait he had painted. *Our Children* depicts the daily life of a peasant child in the summer and is considered one of the most engaging books illustrated by Boutet de Monvel. It features a subtle use of color lithography and employs the representation of patterned fabrics and wallpapers to highlight the decorative and two-dimensional qualities of his illustrations. Boutet de Monvel also illustrated *Select Fables from La Fontaine,* a collection of tales from the French poet and fabulist. Boutet de Monvel illustrates each fable in a series of drawings, similar to a comic strip, which combine clarity, elegance, and a sense of the tragic.

Most critics describe *Joan of Arc* as the artist's supreme achievement. With tender sympathy, Boutet de Monvel relates the life of Joan, beginning with a portrayal of her as a simple and loyal child, continuing through her triumphant leadership of the French forces in the Hundred Years War, and culminating in her betrayal and death at the stake in 1431. The book is comprised of forty-three paintings done in watercolor and ink with black line. Frequently compared with fifteenth-century French illuminated manuscripts and Pre-Raphaelite painting, *Joan of Arc* features a rich color sense and incorporates sophisticated design elements in rendering the grandeur and detail of the Middle Ages. Although critics have faulted the text, in particular for its nationalistic sentiment and wooden tone, *Joan of Arc* is widely regarded as one of the most beautiful and influential books for children. Selma G. Lanes has asserted that "Boutet de Monvel's masterpiece merits a place of honor beside the Lobels, Sendaks, and Steigs on the contemporary bookshelf." In his lifetime, Boutet de Monvel achieved popular and critical acclaim and won major French awards for his painting; as a portrait painter, he was considered the artist of choice by French society for portraits of their children. At the end of the nineteenth century and in the early years of the twentieth century, his books appeared in several translations and his art was exhibited in the United States. Currently, he is regarded as an especially original artist who helped to define the direction of the illustrated book; his work has also influenced such twentieth-century artists as Maxfield Parrish and Maurice Sendak. Michael Patrick Hearn calls Boutet de Monvel "France's most celebrated illustrator of children's books," and adds that he "was the first artist to introduce a modern image of childhood into the picture book."

(See also *Something about the Author,* Vol. 30.)

Will H. Low

[In 1882] there appeared a little book, *Vieilles Chansons et Rondes (Old Songs and Dances),* soon followed by another, *Chansons de France (Songs of France),* in which, breaking through the shell of scholastic trammels, the talent of Monvel takes its first flight. These little books, oblong quarto in form, are of fifty or sixty pages, and on each page, surrounding the words and music of the song, is a decoratively treated drawing. . . . In the charming books which the fortunate children of this generation have in such number, I know none superior to these or to their successors, *La Civilité Honnête et Puérile,* republished in this country as *Good and Bad Children,* and the *Fables of*

La Fontaine. I do not think that any critical description of them can be made better than a quotation from a letter of M. de Monvel in which, speaking of drawing with a pen, he says:

> Having at my disposition a means so limited [as the pen], I have learned that there is one all-important element which we must seek in everything which we would reproduce, and which, for want of a more definite word, we may call the soul, the spirit of the object represented. A rude stick planted in the ground has a particular character and interest of its own, and if we make of it a drawing which is commonplace, it is because we have failed to grasp its spirit. No other stick would have the character which belongs to this particular one, and this, which is true of the rude stick, applies the more as we ascend the scale of creation. This is the lesson taught me by the necessity of expressing much with the thin, encircling line of the pen, and all is there. In comparison with this sense of individual character in anything which we try to represent, all else is unimportant.

This is a brave profession of faith, which an examination of the artist's work renders convincing. Through all these little figures we find everywhere a truth of gesture, a reality of type, that are surprising; the children resemble one another only as one child is like another. They are French children, but there the resemblance ceases. And their heads, their hands, their little feet, express so much! An oval contour, two dots for eyes, a couple of delicately indicated accents for mouth and nose, and we have Mademoiselle Fifine, who turns her cheek and submits to the chaste embrace of Monsieur Paul, in pinafore. Then, in quite another vein, we have the three robbers making off with the newly shorn wool, and below, when brought to task by the owner, who, good woman, begs its return on bended knees, how fine the assumption of innocence on the part of the thieves! Again, in the fable of La Fontaine of the man who sells the bearskin before catching Bruin, how the story tells itself without the author's aid! All these are in delicate outline, filled in with flat tones of color sometimes subdued and delicate, and at others gorgeous in wealth of strong primary tones, and with the precision and daring of a Japanese. And throughout the work, though the little figures may not be more than two inches in height, the manner in which they are drawn, the indication of the turn of a wrist, the way that they stand on their feet, denote the masterly draftsman quick to seize and strong to express with accuracy and ease the movement and character of his figures. A later book, *Nos Enfants,* with text, by that charming writer, Anatole France, shows the same qualities on a larger page, and is replete with tenderness, half amused, and yet thoroughly in sympathy with child life. Here we have the grave little doctor visiting the indisposed doll, while the little mother, gravely resting her chin on the headboard of the bed, awaits the result of the diagnosis. Very charming, also from this book, are the glimpses of country life—the good old peasant grandmother, the children gathering fagots, or the little becapped girl who submits with a mingling of terror and joy to the amicable caress of a great Newfoundland dog. Of more import to Monvel than Salon honors was the reception accorded these works. Their popular success was great, and grave critics, turning aside from the consideration of large official painting, treated these delicately traced pages with becoming seriousness. (pp. 256-58)

[In] the next important work which Monvel undertook, the illustration of *Xavière,* by Ferdinand Fabre, we have a series of thirty-six drawings which for originality both in method and conception place him not only in the front rank of art, but give him a place by himself. Here we feel that he literally knows himself, that with a congenial subject he is completely master of the situation. The original drawings were executed in water-color . . . The reproductions are in black and white, but so thorough is the work of the artist, so delicately adjusted is the scale of light and shade, that the loss of color is hardly felt. The characters of the story, a village priest, his old woman-servant, and two children, a boy and a girl, and the simple rustic surroundings both in and out of doors, make up the subjects of the pictures. The atmosphere of the story surrounding these characters is felt through all the work; the good priest in his close-fitting robe, like a legacy from medieval times, moves quietly through it all, with his homely, saintly face; the shrewd goodness of the old servant gives a touch of strong reality; and the young girl Xavière, with her sweetheart Landry, adds an idyllic note. It is difficult

for me to write of these drawings in aught but a superlative way, for with this strong accentuation the means employed are the simplest. The beauty of ordinary daylight and lamplight effects in an interior simple almost to the point of barrenness is so well expressed that one almost forgets that simplicity is of all qualities the most difficult to obtain. The sureness of hand which in slighter works we have remarked in Monvel's drawings seems greater here where the scheme of light and shade is carried so much further, and the luminosity and the color quality of some of the drawings is surprising. How exact in the sense of truth and character, in the "soul of the object represented," are the scenes where the priest and his little household are seated before the fire, the effect of lamplight where the priest searches the pages of St. Jerome, or that of the dappled sunlight as the children dance around the tree to the sound of Landry's flute! The enumeration of these various subjects at the risk of being tiresome must include at least that of the closing drawings where poor Xavière dies, all of which are treated with a sympathetic touch, especially that of the last communion. . . . (pp. 259-61)

The future of M. de Monvel will be interesting to watch, but the present of his artistic career is no less interesting. He stands by himself, and in the midst of the painters of

From Chansons de France, *written and illustrated by M. Boutet de Monvel.*

his time and country, given up for the most part to the exemplification of a pictorial dexterity almost without parallel in the history of art, he is one of the very few who has found the emotional quality. Gifted with a capacity which has been carefully trained, so that technically he is armed with knowledge equal to that which the same severe training has given his *confrères,* he uses it instead of allowing it to use him. In the truest sense he is an impressionist, in as much as his view of nature is an outcome of his own temperament; for in the painting of the future, impressionism must mean more than a wilful subordination of aught else than the visual faculty applied to external objects, and he who sees with the eyes of the soul, and, without faltering technically, translates this inner vision, will be the true impressionist. There are men—their names come to me as I write—who are gifted with the rare qualities which make the complete artist, and who, from a sense of the overwhelming difficulty of adequate technical achievement, from uncertainty of purpose, or from a mean desire to be "in the swim" of a realistic age (or moment, as ages are counted), content themselves with showing how a work of art should be made instead of making it. Therefore, we may be grateful to M. de Monvel that, having through devious ways found what he has to say, and having acquired the means of saying it, he is not ashamed of his honest emotion, and from the gay note to the grave, from the miller and his sons to where the life of Xavière fairly fades from our sight—for what he has to say, and for his manner of saying it—he is a welcome arrival on the field of modern art. (pp. 268-70)

Will H. Low, "Maurice Boutet de Monvel," in The Century Illustrated Monthly Magazine, *Vol. XLVIII, No. 2, June, 1894, pp. 253-70.*

The Dial, Chicago

The Juvenile book of the year, one of the most original and beautiful of many years, is that in which M. Boutet de Monvel, in a series of colored pictures, gives his conception of the personality of *Joan of Arc.* The text is a brief and simple story of the life of this "humble peasant girl who is the Patroness of France, who is the Saint of her country as she was its Martyr." It is told without flourishes, which could only injure its exalted beauty. But the pictures are eloquent of the child's simplicity, her singleness of purpose, her self-sacrificing devotion and loyalty, and the purity of her exaltation. With all these qualities the artist shows the most exquisite and tender sympathy. From the first drawing, where she is merely the simple, ignorant, industrious peasant-girl, to that one where she stands, clear-sighted and ennobled, the accuser of her worldly judges, he understands her and he makes us understand her. The simplicity and spirituality of this slender little creature, as we see her in these pictures, are never open to question. Around her, the color and movement are shown with rare and wonderful art. Every line, every harmony of tint, is made to help in the expression of the emotion of the moment. The color reaches its climax of brilliancy in the sumptuous scene of the coronation, and darkens into sombreness as the tragedy advances. There is fine decorative feeling in the arrangement of line and color, and the characterization is admirable. It would be

difficult to say too much in praise of these beautiful drawings. . . .

A review of "Joan of Arc," in The Dial, *Chicago, Vol. XXIII, No. 275, December 1, 1897, p. 342.*

Norman Hapgood

Even in great art the originality which suggests a new way of seeing the world is rare. It is the possession of this one quality, above all others, which makes Maurice Boutet de Monvel stand out, with a few of his contemporaries, from the army of artists, more or less slaves of tradition following in the footsteps of their masters. It is this quality which makes the work of De Monvel appreciated wherever he is known. Here is a man who belongs to no school, who does not exploit his tools, who speaks for the people because he picks out things to represent that are not obvious, and yet which, when seen, are of interest alike to the simple and the philosopher, to the most civilized man as to the child.

Another attainment even more rare in the history of art is the successful rendering of child life. The adult usually draws children indiscriminately, seeing them as a mass of little creatures much alike, or else noticing them for the light they throw on our lives. Philosophers would say that our attitude towards them was subjective. We call them sweet, or cunning, or something else that describes the way they make us feel, not the way they themselves feel and think. Yet a child is an independent being, and the effect it has on us is an unimportant element in its own life. The artists, whether poets, novelists, painters, or sculptors, who have given the life of a child from the inside could almost be counted on one hand. These prevailing external views grow naturally out of the two facts that we cannot remember what the world was to us, and that the audience for which we speak is grown. In the fable the lion explains the victories of men over beasts in literature by the statement that the men write all the books. Perhaps Robert Louis Stevenson thought of this fable when he wrote *A Child's Garden of Verses,* in which the mind of the child has at least an equal expression with the mind of his older and sophisticated observer. The mingling of the two points of view promises to be the modern spirit.

Boutet de Monvel, although he is in part a man of age and experience, the head of a household, with a place in the world which he sustains with dignity and takes to heart seriously, amusing himself with the child's ingenuousness, is also one who understands and whose talent is particularly fit to depict the child as an independent creature with a life of its own. His children are genuinely childish, with no admixture of adult quality. The earlier artists gave often the physical attributes of babyhood, but they put in the baby body the soul of a man, or no soul at all. In the old religious pictures the child may show divinity, spirituality, in his face, but he does not show infantile thoughts. He was not treated psychologically. Della Robbia boys might walk, their forms are so real. We also know their personalities; each one of them is an individual child, and Della Robbia is an exception among the masters. But it is more than pitiful, it is irritating, to see in all the galleries of Italy those little forms with the heads of clever, knowing old people, with eyes full of wisdom and worldliness.

So the hearty baby bodies in the pictures of Rubens have no sign of as many different natures as there are in the distinct men and women of the same paintings. Most great dramatic artists, realizing instinctively that men do not see children from the inside, have kept them out of their works. In all of Shakespeare's plays there is no child who counts for much; and in all great drama, perhaps, the one child who is famous is the Joas of Racine.

In a sense, at least, as the artist himself thinks, it was accident that led De Monvel to a field so far removed from the interests of strong artists; but when hazard led him there, little time was needed to show him how to fill it. If he was to draw children, he must draw them with the reality with which he had always seen their elders. He must give us not only the charm of their fragility and innocence, but, if not the revelation, at least a clear suggestion, of what they feel. Whether or not chance influenced his choice of subjects, the world is the gainer. Young persons are usually bored by the child; they meet him and pass him by; but old people notice him. The more experience a man gains and digests the simpler his interest becomes; complexities in the end appear trivial, and the elementary things are seen as the elemental and important ones. De Monvel reached such a spirit younger than most men do. He always had a marked element of sane and serious reality in him, and nature allowed him to begin where most of us are landed when love and sorrow, suffering and change, have taught us to see the big, significant outlines. His fortune from the beginning was to see fundamentals, and experience taught him to depict what he saw with means as simple and choice as his vision. A few lines, a few dots, make a face. There is no smartness of presentation, there is only a meaning, and nothing to obscure the meaning. As in all true art, his technical processes are not obtruded, and will be seen only by those who look for them; while the things represented are patent to all. For such a nature there could be no better subject than the child, for all the elements of human life are in him, and only the elements, out of which later the sifting, expanding, and crushing experience will make the human drama.

Boutet de Monvel, choosing without hesitation art as a career, entered the studio of Cabanel when he was a little over twenty. He joined the army after Sedan, and came out of his war experiences with a sadness which still overpowers him when speaking of *nos malheurs.* After some work in the less conventional studio of Julian, dissatisfied with its restrictions, he entered, in 1875, the studio of Carolus Duran. Almost immediately the need of money forced him into illustration, the field in which we know him best and in which his originality took such striking form. M. de Monvel himself thus describes the change, in conversation: "At first I painted pictures like the rest of the painters, and perhaps I should be doing that still if I had not been driven to illustration. When I took that up, having only the pen with which to work, I was obliged always to study the difficulties of reproduction, to do something that would come out well when printed. Of course, I found out directly that I could not put in the mass of little things which I had elaborated on my canvases. Gradually, through a process of elimination and selection, I came to put in only what was necessary to give the character. I

sought in every little figure, every group, the essence, and worked for that alone."

The secret taught him by the difficulties in reproduction has helped him in all that he has done. There is no unnecessary detail in the old couple on the beach, one of his early pictures . . . , or in the gay pictures of the gracefully grotesque and amusing side of childhood. His books have ranged over rather a wide field. *Old Songs for Little Children (Vieilles Chansons et Rondes pour les petits enfants)* appeared first. In it De Monvel's humor is apparent, bordering now on caricature and now on comedy. *French Songs for Little Frenchmen (Chansons de France pour les petits Français)* followed, with the same gaiety, but with freer expression. A mock treatise on politeness, *La Civilité puérile et honnête,* brings a daintier, more varied atmosphere, for the study is becoming deeper and the understanding clearer. The individuals differ much more; each has more distinctness, more reality, more charm, the old men and the women as well as the children. The *La Fontaine* is a new development, not only because it brings animals to the front, but because it shows the artist making his effects with simpler touches and with the exact meaning still more free and more telling also. In stories by Anatole France, with his studied simplicity, De Monvel found some of his best inspiration; and his masterly little creations stand not simply as a graphic comment on the text, but as a revelation of a subject which the writer has treated only in a fragmentary and superficial manner. Before speaking of his later work, his *Xavière* and his *Joan of Arc,* we might try to find out the secret which De Monvel has learned, and which enables him to give us children in a fashion so direct and complete, and with such charm and freshness of presentation. We might speak of the expressiveness which lurks in a little hand clutching a dress, in the angular folds of a Sunday frock, in a slow and stolid walk, in a foot seeking the ground, but it would explain nothing. The one attitude, the one expression, is chosen which has a special meaning and a special charm, and that is all there is to it. In looking at these drawings artists' only advantage over people ignorant of art is that they know how wonderful the thing is, how difficult it is to do it; but they are not able to feel or enjoy the result any better. To draw well, to color well, to have solved the problem of lithography in color, is simply to have the tools. It is the freshness, the alertness of the eye, the truth and eagerness of the mind, which makes De Monvel an artist original from the start, who has worked out the best freedom,—freedom from everything irrelevant. His simplicity is adequate to express not only the personalities of the children, with their own solemnity, and the tender amusement which they inspire, but also to deal with the most serious, dramatic, even tragic subjects, as shown in his two later works, *Xavière* and *Joan of Arc.* Probably, of all his work, these two books contain his most ardent feelings. The opening picture of the "Joan of Arc" strikes a note held throughout. Jeanne rides at the head of an army, her eyes fixed on a vision, a sword in her outstretched hand; behind her rush the living soldiers, with an onward motion that shows what it means to be a great draughtsman; and as the living soldiers press on, the very dead, fallen in battle, break from the ground to follow; their faces struggle up, their open mouths salute the Maid, they wave their swords, and, although they cannot free their bodies, their spirits help her on to victory. There are few such noble pictures as *Xavière* offers, wonderful revelations of the French country people, sympathetic transcripts of the simple life of humble folk; admirable pages, where one feels that everything is true to the best and the most serious in life.

When De Monvel first gave us these colored illustrated books, the surprise was great in the success with which a technical difficulty had been so competently conquered that the famous colored prints of England seemed antiquated and the effects which the Japanese reached by a different method had been equaled. But that surprise is now giving way to admiration for the qualities of the man who inspires the workman. Sentiment is the largest ingredient of true art, as it is of life; and the sentiment of De Monvel in *Joan of Arc* and *Xavière* reaches its highest purity. In this last he addresses himself to an older audience. In *Joan of Arc* he meets the interests of the childish reader, but he expresses himself as genuinely in each book. They seem ideal and beautiful dreams, forceful in drawing, with a psychology which makes every face individual in a more complete, but no less simple, sense than the faces in his lighter works are real. Noticing that an artist is making funny children or grotesque animals, we are inclined to take him lightly, as if we measured genius by solemnity or by acres of paint; but if we turn back to the more amusing books, after being excited by *Xavière* and *Joan of Arc,* we see them with a new eye. It is the same artist looking into the hearts of many things and recording with a sure hand.

M. de Monvel is now making frescos for the church which is building at Domremy, the birthplace of the Maid whose story he is to tell again; but his studio is full of portraits of children and of sketches for illustrations. One series, just finished, dealing with the little peasants of the country, is to be followed by the street boys of Paris. There is little danger that with his eagerness of mind De Monvel runs any risk of working one vein to death; neither will he abandon for his larger work the line in which he has been a pioneer. His future activities promise to be as full of variety and development as his past, and it is hoped that he may devote more and more of his time to what, in the mind of the best judges, is his greatest field. The painting of portraits is probably the highest as well as the lowest and most common achievement of art. There have been many great portrait painters; but outside of Velasquez and a very few great masters, it is hard to think of any truly good portraits of children. An increasing demand for De Monvel's portraits of children has been the natural result of the popularity of his illustrated books. Of course, he had always been making portraits in his illustrations; he has told himself how hard it is to make each little figure in a group a separate person; and all these constant efforts of many years made the step to portrait painting an easy one. His portraits have been as successful as his own fanciful children. Not only has he been able to give the appearance of his sitter with the certainty and vividness which was to be expected of him, but he has proved his high artistic judgment in the way which all accessories are subordinated and yet used to strengthen the central effect. . . . [In] his portraits, backgrounds and the arrangement of acces-

sories show exquisite tact, and while serving their purpose of putting the face and figure into relief, add, one might say, some side explanations to the type. It is marvelous how all parts of the canvas belong to the portrait; how typical accessories and background are so subtly and intelligently handled that one does not realize they are there at all. (pp. 197-204)

> *Norman Hapgood, "A Painter of Children—Boutet de Monvel," in* McClure's Magazine, *Vol. X, No. 3, January, 1898, pp. 197-204.*

Marie L. Van Vorst

Children are everywhere a part of the indoor and outdoor world; they are on the door-steps, on the thresholds, at the windows. They come from school, they dance, they sing, they play, they laugh, they weep. They are good, naughty, stupid, delightful. They have their codes, their manners, as class and as individual unit. It requires more than a shibboleth to penetrate their charmed ring. The big people, staring through windows which the world has stupidly transformed into a kind of ground glass, see these little people scarcely at all. Occasionally, however, comes some one who has remained always a child at heart. Through a more transparent medium than the rest, he looks out at the laughing throng. Among certain poets and painters who turn from the window and tell the world what they see is Boutet de Monvel. To him the children wave and nod, smile and beckon. They tell him their games; best of all, he remembers his own. "My memory," he says, "is extraordinary; from 'way back in my littlest childhood, from time to time, come vivid pictures. I have always keenly observed my surroundings, and I never forget." (pp. 572-73)

He began early in life with serious determination, and he works to-day with an ardor no less fervent than that of his youth, when he knew hardship, and, like the majority of those who finally succeed, was as familiar with discouragement as with hope. "No, no," he said almost irritably; "the painting of children is not my serious work; my dreams, my ambitions, were far different. I wished to do large canvases and decorations, but necessity forced me into another field."

In order to gain one's daily bread, one must give to the public what it demands. De Monvel was a husband and a father, and that he might supply the needs of his family he put aside for the time his larger ambition. "I went," he says, "from publisher to publisher in search of orders for illustration—in vain. I was thoroughly discouraged and disheartened, when at last a publisher gave me a child's history of France to illustrate; then came some work on a French edition of 'St. Nicholas.' I had never before painted children, but I did then."

As soon as he began to draw and paint children (which he did with an originality of scheme, a beauty of color, that make the little pictures works of art), a world of memories came to his aid. His resources appeared to be inexhaustible. His clever schemes, his skilful execution, his variety of subjects, fill one with wonder at his intimate relation with child life. He explains it in a measure, very charmingly: "I had a houseful of little brothers and sisters. I was the eldest of them all, and they made a great impression

"MADMOISELLE, NOW IT IS MY TURN," SAID ONE.

"NO, MADMOISELLE, I DON'T WANT TO GIVE IT TO YOU," SAID THE OTHER, "BECAUSE YOU WERE NAUGHTY."

"NOT AT ALL, MADMOISELLE, IT IS YOU WHO STARTED IT."

IN A MINUTE THEY ARE FIGHTING WITH THEIR NAILS LIKE BAD ALLEY CATS. THEIR BROTHERS ARE OBLIGED TO SEPARATE THEM, AND THEIR MOTHERS ARE DESOLATED TO HAVE SUCH LOW CHILDREN.

From Good Children and Bad, *written by Eugene Plon. Illustrated by M. Boutet de Monvel.*

upon me. I used to watch them at their games and plays, their funny little figures flying about; they were always with me; and, for the most part, my own little people, as I remember them in our home in Orléans, exist again to-day, in countless poses, as my picture-children. Of course I observe them constantly in the Bois and on the avenues, these little children of Paris, but I like to think that it is that influence from the past that has inspired a great deal of my pictured child life."

After his début appeared his delightful books, *Chansons et rondes* (1883), *Chansons de France* (1884), *Nos enfants* (1886), *La civilité puérile* (1887) *Fables de La Fontaine* (1888), *Xavière* (1890), *Jeanne d'Arc* (1897), until all that his publishers and his public asked of him was that he should draw children, children indefinitely. Thus was he forced into a field of art in which he has no rival. In *Chansons et rondes* and *Chansons de France,* he has illustrated the old songs and dances, some of which correspond to our nursery rhymes, and some of which are folk-songs; for example, "Sur le pont d'Avignon" and "Malbrouck s'en va t'en guerre."

The children all through these books are distinctively French, of course. They belong only to the land of green-boled, slender trees, red-roofed villages, broad white roads, and gay boulevards. Their drolleries, their trickeries, their humor, are national; they are infectious and delightful. But in *Nos enfants* there is a lovely spirit of childhood which is universal, and the book is a poem from beginning to end. The text is that of Anatole France, who gives, in a few words, the summer-day life of a little peasant child, besides several other pastels of child life.

De Monvel's illustrations are full of atmosphere and an exquisite feeling for the out-of-door world. The fine effects of light and shade, the tone and composition of these pictures, place them far beyond any others of their class, and proclaim them the work of a consummate artist. Boutet de Monvel spoke to the children of France as they had never been spoken to before. Bending over the bewitching pictures, they exclaimed, "Ah, *he* understands!" And the fathers and mothers, looking from the little ones who read and enjoyed to the pages over which they bent, saw at once that here was a painter with a new and rare faculty for comprehending childhood. They sought Boutet de Monvel to paint their sons and daughters, till he became, one might say, "painter in ordinary" to the children. (pp. 575-77)

His illustrations of Ferdinand Fabre's *Xavière* placed Boutet de Monvel in the first rank of illustrators. In the pictures which he made for this touching romance he showed a deep knowledge of human nature in general, breadth, and a complete mastery of his subject. They are full of pathos, very realistic, and tender. In studying these, as well as becoming familiar with his portraits of children, and, above all, when we consider his decorations, we get the proper conception of the man and painter, devotedly, conscientiously working for the highest things in art. Interesting as is the sphere we have been considering, it is not his most serious work; nor does his armful of books for children fully represent his art.

Boutet de Monvel was born in 1850. He studied in Paris under De Rudder and Cabanel in the Julien School, and with Carolus Duran. For the development of his peculiar talent, however, he found no school. Its genre was unknown; indeed, he scarcely knew it then himself: but his ardent studies, instead of leading him to adopt the more academic form of expression, became his tools; his strongly individual talent declared itself, and demanded expression in its own peculiar form; and finally he broke completely away from the schools and followed his bent.

In his illustrations for *Jeanne d'Arc* De Monvel has struck his highest note. This work is the result of pure inspiration. It is spiritual and beautiful, and must invariably call forth, in response, the best feelings, and through his interest in this subject the painter will eventually attain his most important success.

"The idea came to me like a flash—like an inspiration," he said when questioned. "My publishers asked me for another book for children; I had nothing in mind. One day, as I was crossing the Tuileries Gardens, I came suddenly upon the little statue by Frémiet, at the entrance of the Rue des Pyramides, and when I looked up at Jeanne d'Arc, I had my subject! Strange, isn't it, that no one had ever thought of making a book of this kind before?" *Jeanne d'Arc* is a children's book, so called; it is as well a book for all lovers of art. Interesting as are the drawing and composition, the color of the illustrations is their great charm. "It is not color really," said M. de Monvel, touching caressingly the delicate yellow robes of the priests, and indicating a slender tree; "it is the suggestion, the impression of color. The pictures do not come out as soft in tone as are the water-colors themselves. It is always a disappointment; much of the finesse of outline is lost." Indeed, beside the originals the reproductions, good as they are, seem almost crude. The book is dramatic. M. de Monvel has a gift for depicting crowds. The grouping, the live, spirited attitudes, the masses that fairly surge and sway, shout and acclaim, wave their banners and flash their spears—all this is the arrangement of a skilful stage-setter, who may well have inherited his love and understanding of artistic scenic detail from his talented ancestors, whose names are famous in the history of the French stage. (p. 577)

The words with which he prefaces the book of *Jeanne d'Arc* are stirring and full of the patriotism of the Frenchman who has himself fought for France: "Open this book with reverence, my dear children, in honor of the humble peasant girl who is the patroness of France, who is her country's saint, as well as its martyr. Her history will teach you that in order to conquer you must have faith in the victory. Remember this in the day when your country shall have need of all your courage."

Boutet de Monvel is eminently an idealist, with a fancy as brilliant as the wing of a butterfly. He says: "A photograph gives you a truthful representation of the object as the world sees it, but the painter gives you what he alone sees. It is that difference of vision, that unique conception, which is his talent. The use of the model I believe to be a mistake. I never use one myself. How can a hired subject feel or remotely express my idea? Let a manikin support the drapery, if necessary, but the movement, the expression, must go from my mind direct to the canvas without interruption." It is this which makes Boutet de Monvel's work always imaginative, if sometimes fantastic. His pictures are visible fairy-tales, in which the child, the poet, the painter, each may find a world which is his own, and which is truly instinct with delight and charm. (p. 578)

> *Marie L. Van Vorst, "The Painter de Monvel,"*
> *in* The Century Illustrated Monthly Magazine, *Vol. LVII, No. 4, February, 1899, pp. 572-78.*

Irene Sargent

It can not be too strongly insisted that art for the child should consist in common things translated into pictorial terms; the essentials of the presentation being simplicity and correctness of principle. To offer to the child's mind complexity of form is like placing before him an involved problem in mathematics, when he is barely capable of adding and subtracting. To set before his eye false drawing and badly combined color is to vitiate his perception of beauty, as surely as his musical sense would be debased, were he habitually to listen to instruments falsely pitched and discordant one with another.

To choose then expressions of art which shall at once gratify and develop the very young is a difficult task; since few masters have created from the child's point of view, the same as comparatively few writers have reached the child's heart, and appealed simply and strongly enough to the developing imagination—that first of all faculties to be awakened: stating the essential only, and leaving the detail to be supplied by the young mind, which struggles for experience, as a fledgling bird tries its wings in the inspiring air of spring. That which is simple in lesson, story, or picture, leaves, as it were, space which the childish mind can animate with dream-people and fanciful circumstance, constantly changing to suit its changeful moods; while that which is complex discourages the child from the first, repels him, and denies play to his imagination.

The masters in art able successfully to portray children, have always been and are now much less numerous than the corresponding writers; most of the portrait-artists, justly celebrated for their "fair children," having presented solely picturesque external charm; while a painter like Mlle. Breslau, capable of sounding the soul of the child, of recording its bitter griefs and its ecstatic happiness, arises scarcely once in a generation.

But these geniuses, although choosing children as their subjects, appeal to their equals in understanding and experience. They can, therefore, be understood as forming a larger class even than those who, from the child's point of view, yet with a master's power, deal with the things of art.

Among these distinguished few, the French painter and illustrator Boutet de Monvel, occupies a unique place. . . . (pp. 403-04)

Little critics, in turning the pages of a picture-book illuminated in more senses than one by the designs of this master, feel that they are playing with real children: merry, mischievous, active and wilful—in all points like themselves. They see the spirit of childhood made visible in a few lines and touches, and they respond to it, as they would, were it manifested in actual life—in the street, the school, or the nursery—instead of being confined to the printed page. In the past, the child has been robbed of adequate representation in art, and it would now seem as if the French master and several of his contemporaries—among whom may be named the portrait artists, Sargent, Mlle. Breslau and Cecilia Beaux—had arisen to right a great share of the wrong. (p. 405)

[Children] can not fail to be instructed by his faultless line, by his delicacy of execution, his vigor and grace. They will be unconsciously inspired by his accuracy and ease; interested and charmed by his indication of a turn of a head or wrist, by the way the little figures stand on their feet, march or dance. Older critics will observe, in order to discuss, the delicate outlines filled in with flat tones of color, sometimes subdued and delicate, at others, gorgeous in wealth of strong primary tones, and applied with the precision and daring of a Japanese. But these fine points will not fail of their refining influence upon children, whose artistic sense, nourished and developed by such principles, will afterward reject the false and the complex, in favor of this simplicity which is so difficult to attain, because it approaches perfection. Nor will the lessons be lost, even if they are presented in black and white; since the French illustrator adjusts his scale of light and shade so delicately that the absence of color is scarcely felt. (pp. 407-08)

[The] artistic success with which we are here concerned, grew out of pressing material needs; while certain exquisite qualities were developed under the requirements of mechanical reproduction, in allusion to which the artist . . . writes:

> I aimed at methods of drawing which should come out well when my pictures were printed. I advanced by a process of elimination and selection. I came to put in only what was necessary to give character.

In the pursuit thus described, accuracy of line, strength, and style were early possessed by the illustrator, if they were not his already at the beginning of his struggle. But the one point which long conquered him and still longer threatened his success, was his tendency to over-blacken his shadows, as was natural for a pupil of Carolus-Duran. Gradually, however, he freed himself from this, his great fault, by the use of the light tones and the unaccented sil-

houettes demanded in the printed reproductions of his drawings.

At last, he stood apart, higher than any of his compatriots in a special field of work, interesting and fertile. Yet, with true human perversity, he was not content. His aspirations were those of a portrait painter and mural decorator, in both of which capacities he has attained distinction, particularly in the latter, through his scenes from the life of Jeanne d'Arc, painted on the walls of the church at Domrémy, the Norman village which was the birthplace of the virgin martyr. But it is always true that man proposes and God disposes. The mural paintings, sympathetically conceived, finely grouped and executed, the portraits of adults, remarkable for their grace and distinction, will not be M. Boutet de Monvel's highest claim to remembrance; since that resides in his incomparable rendering of children and child-life from the point of view of the subjects represented: work executed with a simplicity, gratifying alike to the ingenuous whom elaboration does not yet attract, and to the experienced who have rejected it as useless and insignificant. (pp. 408-09)

> *Irene Sargent, "Art in the Home and in the School: A Lesson from Boutet de Monvel," in* The Craftsman, *Vol. VII, January, 1905, pp. 400-11.*

Barbara Bader

[The books of Kate Greenaway] are not new renderings of childhood classics like the *Bluebeard* of Crane or Caldecott's *John Gilpin* but books of her own devising, about children, and as such an example to others—most immediately to Maurice Boutet de Monvel. Putting their songs into pictures (***Vielles Chansons et Rondes, Chansons de France***) or making light of their manners (***La Civilité Puérile et Honnête***), he takes them as they come, good and bad; but in the illustrations for Anatole France's ***Nos Enfants*** and ***Filles et Garçons*** they are individuals, preoccupied with the business of living, and while we smile at them in recognition we respect their seriousness.

Then came ***Jeanne d'Arc***, simple and dramatic and majestic, so exactly observant that a crowd remains a congregation of persons, so astutely composed—stage-managed, really—that the eye is constantly drawn back to the still center. You are there, in the trite phrase, watching from a high doorstep, seen in turn . . . , looking now at the flaming torches, the jostling figures, the gleaming helmets, now at the cause of the agitation, calm and grave, now and again at the horseman . . . , remote and, for all that he holds the standard, detached from the scene.

When he took up illustration, Boutet de Monvel testifies, "I was obliged always to study the difficulties of reproduction, to do something that would come out well when printed. Of course, I found out directly that I could not put in the mass of little things which I had elaborated on my canvases. Gradually, through a process of elimination and selection, I came to put in only what was necessary to give the character." In his color work he allowed little shadow, and the resulting combination of unaccented outline and flat tone was called Japanese; but printing by lithography yielded thin, soft colors—"the suggestion, the impression of color," the artist called it—and the effect was different from that produced by woodblocks, whether in Evans's work or the woodcuts of the Japanese.

While Crane, Caldecott and Greenaway had immediate and lasting success in the United States, Boutet de Monvel became the rage. . . . [Exhibitions] of his work toured widely in 1899, 1906-07 and 1921, and on the first occasion he accompanied the show, lecturing (in French) and painting children's portraits at the various stops. Meanwhile his books were appearing in translation: *Good Children and Bad* in 1890; La Fontaine's *Fables* (1893), which was imported; *Joan of Arc* almost immediately, in 1897 (and again in 1907, 1912, 1916, 1918, 1923, 1926, 1931, sometimes from a different house and in a different form); and then in quick succession *Old Songs and Rounds* (1912), *Girls and Boys* (1913), *Our Children* (1917).

No sudden spurt in American picturebooks resulted any more than it had from the smaller Crane-Caldecott-Greenaway conflagration. (The one consequential American in Boutet de Monvel's debt, E. Boyd Smith, lived long in France.) Rather, the opposite occurred: the artistic European book drove the homelier American product out of favor though not, immediately, out of the hands of children. (pp. 4-6)

> *Barbara Bader, "Starting Points," in her* American Picturebooks from Noah's Ark to the Beast Within, *Macmillan Publishing Co., Inc., 1976, pp. 2-12.*

Michael Patrick Hearn

France has never boasted a great history of fine picture books for children. During the nineteenth century, when Paris was the undisputed art capital of the world, the French failed to develop a tradition of juvenile book illustration comparable to that of the English and the Germans. . . .

It was not until the last quarter of the nineteenth century that there appeared in Paris a children's book artist of the stature of Walter Crane and Kate Greenaway. In his pop-

ular albums and especially in his *Jeanne d'Arc* published in 1896, Louis Maurice Boutet de Monvel . . . created several of the finest picture books ever published for children.

His introduction to this art form was largely accidental. . . . As were most of his contemporaries, Boutet de Monvel was rigidly trained as an academic painter, and several of his early canvases were exhibited at the annual Paris Salon. Having not yet arrived at a method uniquely his own, the young artist had little success as a painter, and he soon went from publisher to publisher in search of work. "You see," he explained in later life, "when I began to illustrate, the publishers of Paris were leagued together in a sort of informal syndicate for the protection of a few artists and the repression of the younger men who wished to innovate. Newcomers, like myself, were thought intruders." Unexpectedly, an acquaintance gave the artist's name to an editor who needed someone to illustrate a child's history book, *La France en-zigzag* (1878) by Eudoxie Dupuis; and the next day the startled young man received by mail a commission for "forty little pen drawings, about three times the size of my thumbnail." He was poorly paid for this meticulous work, but it did lead to other assignments.

He infrequently contributed to the juvenile weekly *Le Journal de la jeunesse*, and one or two of his illustrations appeared in such children's books as Émile Desbeaux's *Les Pourquois de Mlle. Suzanne* (1881) and Aimé Giron's *Ces Pauvres Petits!* (1882); but these designs were generally uninspired. Wood engraving was still the most popular form of reproduction, and Boutet de Monvel never fully comprehended its possibilities. He was still working in what he called his *manière noir,* which suffered at the hands of his engravers.

Boutet de Monvel did not gain a name for himself until he became a regular contributor to *St. Nicolas.* This children's magazine was designed to be the French equivalent of the successful American periodical edited by Mary Mapes Dodge, but most of the art and writing in the Pari-

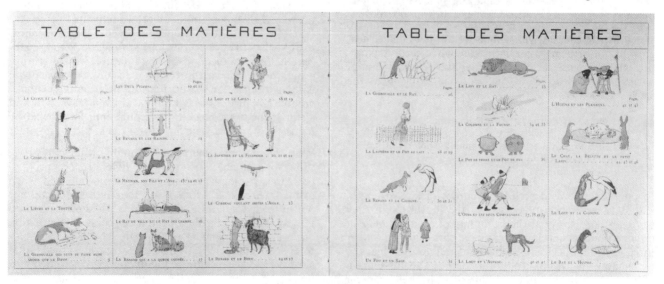

From Fables Choisies Pour Les Enfants, *by Jean La Fontaine. Illustrated by M. Boutet de Monvel.*

sian monthly originated in France; only a few pieces, including Palmer Cox's "Brownies" and some early Howard Pyle stories, were translated from the American *St. Nicholas*. Boutet de Monvel's principal responsibility was the illustration for the monthly column "Les Jeudis de St. Nicolas." His patriarch, however, was not the "jolly old elf" of American tradition but rather the benevolent sage *Père Noël*, with mitre, crook, and cowl.

Before joining *St. Nicolas*, Boutet de Monvel rarely made studies of children. . . . In his pert sketches of boys and girls he relied primarily on his extraordinary memory, on recollections of his own childhood. The eldest of nine children, young Maurice was responsible for looking after his brothers and sisters. "I had a special gift which somehow helped me to soothe them when they cried and were out of temper," he explained to an interviewer. "I used to watch them at their games and plays, their funny little figures flying about; they were always with me; and, for the most part, my own little people, as I remember them in our home in Orléans, exist again today, in countless poses, in my picture-children. Of course I observe them constantly . . . in Paris, but I like to think that it is that influence from the past that has inspired a great deal of my pictured child life."

For his delicate pen-and-ink drawings of children, the artist had to reject many of the techniques he had mastered in the art academy. Without the luxury of color he developed a manner suited to the limitations of photographic reproduction in line. In all his sketches he looked for what "we may call the soul, the spirit of the object represented. . . ." The artist took no less care in the illustrations for *St. Nicolas* than he had in his more pretentious salon paintings; for "it is one of my cardinal beliefs that it should be possible for the sincere artist to find pleasure in everything he undertakes. I have always done with zest what has been given me to do, and I am not conscious of a positive preference for one form of art expression over another." His delight in doing these illustrations was shared by the public, and "Les Jeudis de St. Nicolas" quickly became the most popular feature of the new magazine.

In 1883, when the magazine editors decided to sponsor a painting competition for children of all countries, a selection of the artist's designs was published with accompanying texts by Eudoxie Dupuis as a coloring book, *Les Petits Coloristes*. The elaborate volume (offered alone or with a box of paints) included a certificate to be signed by the child when the completed book was returned to the publisher; it would be judged by a jury of the journal's illustrators "truly like the pictures in the Salon!" The preface also noted that because St. Nicholas was the patron not only of the rich and happy but also of the poor and sick, the hand-colored copies would be redistributed to boys and girls in charitable institutions, and the young contestant was advised to consider their needs while coloring.

These illustrations were also known abroad, largely through unauthorized reproduction in juvenile magazines, such as the British *Little Folks* and the American *Harper's Young People, Infant's Magazine*, and *St. Nicholas*. Boutet de Monvel was soon popularly coupled with Kate Greenaway as a master of child life, but he tried to reassure his

admirers: "I had never seen one of her books when I commenced my work. Hers is the work of a great artist, and our methods are quite different." Only his early line drawings for a collection of moralistic verse, *La Comédie enfantine* (1881), by Louis Gustave Fortuné Ratisbonne, are comparable to her illustrations in *Under the Window* and in *Little Ann and Other Poems* by Ann and Jane Taylor. The French artist, however, developed his own conception of the child. Kate Greenaway depicted young people as an adult hoped them to be; Boutet de Monvel pictured boys and girls as they saw themselves. This distinction is evident not only in his *St. Nicolas* illustrations but also in his designs for Lucien Biart's *Quand j'étais petit* (1886), a novel about childhood more for adults than for children, and for the picture book *La Civilité puérile et honnête* (published in English as *Good Children and Bad*) written by "Uncle Eugène" Plon, a relative of the artist. The book, a mock treatise on manners, perhaps best displays the artist's special perception of the young. Boutet de Monvel recognized that naughtiness was as much a part of childhood as was goodness. A child may wipe his nose upon the curtains, scratch his head with a fork at the dinner table, throw a temper tantrum, stick out his tongue at a friend, and yet not have to face some dire consequence. The artist cleverly contrasts his sketches of such uncivilized creatures with elegant studies of formal interiors. "Oh, no," the artist once confessed, "I wasn't a good boy myself, by any means. They tell me I was really quite unbearable." In depicting children in all their moods, both good and bad, Boutet de Monvel was the first artist to introduce a modern image of childhood into the picture book.

Boutet de Monvel may not have been acquainted with Kate Greenaway's work, but he certainly knew Walter Crane's successful picture books. During his sojourn at *St. Nicolas*, the artist decorated two anthologies of traditional French songs—*Vieilles Chansons et rondes pour les petits français* with settings by Charles M. Widor and *Chansons de France pour les petits français* arranged by J. B. Weckerlin. These books, his first work for children printed in color, proved him to be as proficient with the brush as with the pen. Their format was obviously derived from Walter Crane's *The Baby's Opera* (1877) and *The Baby's Bouquet* (1878). Similar in design to these nursery song books, the French collections embraced all the concepts of the book as a single unified artistic statement. The same care lavished on the illustrations for the text is evident in the decoration of the title page, half-title page, and table of contents. Boutet de Monvel's approach to these drawings also suggests the influence of Crane; his flat translucent color and pure line is as free of secondary tone as are the wood engravings of the English artist's picture books. The French music books are merrier than the English. As Boutet de Monvel—unlike Crane—was less interested in elevating than in entertaining the young, his pages are not so formally constructed as those of his predecessor; yet Boutet de Monvel was no less inventive in his decorative devices.

As Crane illustrated Aesop, so Boutet de Monvel chose La Fontaine for the third of his popular picture books. Although this edition of the classic French fables published in 1888 retained the format of his previous volumes, Boutet de Monvel turned not to Crane's *The Baby's Own Aesop* (1887) but to the *Images d'Epinal,* the forerunner of the modern comic strip, for his design. This modification of form allowed him to concentrate more on characters than on decoration. He had to minimize his technique to a sequence of figures, generally without a background, whose gestures subtly and only slightly change from image to image, as in the frames of an animated cartoon. The delicate drawings possess as much individuality as do Grandville's interpretations of the same characters. Boutet de Monvel's color also had to be minimal; his tints were added much like the simple hand-coloring of the anonymous Epinal picture sheets.

The artist's reputation as an illustrator of children's books eventually led to a second lucrative career, that of a painter of children's portraits. Among his many subjects, which included the progeny of actresses, aristocrats, and American senators, was the daughter of the writer Anatole France. The author and the artist collaborated on one of the loveliest French children's books of the nineteenth century, *Nos Enfants,* which later was published in two volumes as *Nos Enfants* and *Filles et garçons.* The sensitive essays are graced by many of Boutet de Monvel's most charming studies of town and country children, exquisitely printed by lithography with soft, subtle color harmonies as fresh and delicate as those in the celebrated etchings of Mary Cassatt. Boutet de Monvel, like Mary Cassatt, borrowed freely from the flat design of Japanese wood engravings; and the patterns of his fabrics and wallpapers emphasize the decorative two-dimensionality of his compositions.

Nos Enfants was a true collaboration of author and artist. Several of the essays were apparently suggested by already completed drawings and by ideas proposed by the illustrator. Just as Boutet de Monvel painted a portrait of the author's daughter, so too did Anatole France compose verbal portraits of the painter's two sons. He shared with the artist a sympathy for his subjects. Perhaps France's clever conceits, his elegant phrasing, can only be fully comprehended by the mature reader; perhaps his studies are more about, than for, children. As for the art of *Nos Enfants,* the inserted plates are not fully integrated with the text, but this complaint is only a small criticism of such an extraordinary suite of pictures.

The success of the portraits eventually left the artist little time for illustration. His publishers pressed him for another children's book, but it was not until 1896 that he found a subject worthy of his full attention: the life of Joan of Arc. It may seem odd that an illustrator best known as an entertainer of children should have found inspiration in the tragedy of a saint, yet the Maid of Orléans has fascinated humorists from Charles Dickens and Mark Twain to George Bernard Shaw. Despite his reputation, Boutet de Monvel was no less reverential in his depiction of the martyr's passion than was Giotto in his treatment of the life of St. Francis of Assisi. (pp. 170-77)

Her story proved to be the perfect subject for this native of Orléans. Although his family had moved from the district soon after his birth, for his father was called to the University of Paris to lecture in chemistry, the boy spent many vacations in his birthplace, and he thus grew up on the local legends of the saint. "In Orléans they sell a kind of sugar candy in little boxes, on the covers of which are gay pictures of Jeanne d'Arc," he later recalled, "and whenever I had a few sous I used to buy one of these boxes of bonbons. . . . Of course every time I licked the sugar I saw the picture, which I grew to know very well indeed!" The same affection he felt for the girl in his childhood he lavished on his series of forty-five watercolors of her life.

This work when exhibited in Paris brought the artist a further commission to paint a set of six panels to decorate the basilica of her memorial chapel at Domrémy. Because of illness, Boutet de Monvel failed to complete these oil paintings in time, and they were never installed in the church. He did finally finish them just before his death; the panels are now housed in the Corcoran Gallery in Washington, D. C. The artist planned these six paintings as if they were book illustrations "to be, as one enters the Church, as though one looked at an open missal."

His picture book *Jeanne d'Arc* surely achieved this effect. The exquisite designs embrace the legend's diverse themes—the patriotic, the feminine, the religious. The tender restraint of the maid's faith counterpoises the many rhythmic pageants swarming with shouting crowds, full of pomp and ceremony. His battle scenes are so intense that even the frame cannot always contain the fierce combatants. But in all this turmoil there is no confusion in the composition, and each figure remains an individual. His skirmishes are as skillfully constructed as those of Paolo Uccello; his forms are as clearly delineated as the Arcadians in Puvis de Chavannes's frescoes. So ambitious are Boutet de Monvel's panoramas that only the double-page spread can fully express their pageantry.

In all these intricately composed dramas, the artist's line remains characteristically economical. The outlines are as delicate as those of his other work. The subdued colors of the peasants' clothes balance the dazzling patterns of the princely garb of the court. His handling of light is no less than masterful. In scenes with but limited illumination, whether it be moonlight or flaring torches, Boutet de Monvel uses only the subtlest tones. His restrained sources of light emphasize the action of his compositions. By contrast, the visionary saints and angels are ablaze with unearthly light.

Such technique was challenging to his printers. The artist feared that the lithographs did not fully retain the integrity of his watercolors. "It is not color really; it is the suggestion, the impression of color. The pictures do not come out as soft in tone as are the watercolors themselves. It is always a disappointment; much of the finesse of outline is lost." *Jeanne d'Arc* is nonetheless an exceptional example of fine French color lithography, perhaps the most beautiful picture book for children printed in the nineteenth century. Not even Walter Crane attempted so ambitious a publication, and one may conclude that no modern artist will, either.

Boutet de Monvel also provided the text, which is generally as clear and direct as the art. The narrative is as swiftly paced as the illustrations, but the prose is slightly tainted

From Joan of Arc, *written and illustrated by M. Boutet de Monvel.*

by his French chauvinism, a quality to be expected of a veteran of the Franco-Prussian War. The title page, showing the warrior leading contemporary French troops into battle, reminds the reader that the Maid of Orléans is indeed the patron saint of France.

After the turn of the century, because of poor health, the artist retired to his country home. With the exception of several articles and some watercolors of the life of St. Francis of Assisi commissioned by an American publisher, he accepted fewer and fewer requests for illustrations. His illness had affected his art, and his line lost some of its authority. His main preoccupation was the completion of the six Joan of Arc panels.

In his day, Boutet de Monvel was nearly as influential as were Walter Crane, Kate Greenaway, and Randolph Caldecott. He had many imitators but few equals. His *Jeanne d'Arc* inspired a successful series of picture books about French history, all brightly lithographed in color; however, most of the illustration lacked the conviction of his finest work. Of the work of his contemporaries, only the Swedish picture books of Carl Larsson, such as *Ett Hem* (1899) and *Andras Barn* (1913), contain studies as sympathetic as those of *Nos Enfants;* and much of the splendor of *Jeanne d'Arc* is matched by the sumptuous editions of the Pushkin *skazki* decorated by the Russian artist Ivan Bilibin.

Boutet de Monvel's most ardent disciple was the young Dutch illustrator Henriette Willebeek Le Mair. A child prodigy, at sixteen she went to Paris with her parents to meet the famous French illustrator. She hoped to study with him, but he discouraged her by insisting that she work alone to develop her own talent and personality. He did consent to meet with her once a year to discuss her progress, and he advised her on the painting of children's portraits. Consequently, her gentle picture books such as *Little Songs of Long Ago* (1912), *Old Dutch Nursery Rhymes* (1917), and Robert Louis Stevenson's *A Child's Garden of Verses* (1926, all McKay) owe much to the French artist's song books.

His acceptance by American illustrators was certainly dramatic. When he visited the United States, he was lauded in the press, and most of his books were soon available in translation. "Never have children been better observed, more intelligently studied," wrote Joseph Pennell, "nor their gestures, clumsy and graceful, more simply and directly noted. He was always decorative, and there is not a line in his drawings without meaning." The illustrator E. Boyd Smith, after a long sojourn in Paris, provided a Yankee descendant of *Jeanne d'Arc* in his *Story of Pocahontas and Captain John Smith* (1906, Houghton). Maxfield Parrish, too, was profoundly influenced by Boutet de Monvel's sense of design; the composition of King Dagobert's throne room in *Chansons de France* frequently reappears in the American's paintings and illustrations, most notably in his "Old King Cole" mural, now over the bar of New York's St. Regis Hotel. Even R. F. Outcault's Buster Brown may be partly descended from characters in the French picture books.

Boutet de Monvel's influence persists in modern book illustration. His image of the child is reflected in Hilary Knight's drawings for Kay Thompson's incomparable *Eloise*. "My mother Katharine Sturges, herself an illustrator, had collected most of his books as well as prints by his son Bernard," Knight has explained, "so that from the time I could turn a page I was involved in his work. His 'style,' his way of laying out a page, and the movement and attitude of his children, certainly were direct influences on all of my work, and on *Eloise* in particular." Maurice Sendak spoke of Boutet de Monvel's drawings for **"The Wolf and the Lamb"** in the magazine *Rolling Stone:* " 'I think of these fine, softly colored and economically conceived drawings as a musical accompaniment to the La Fontaine fable, harmonic inventions that color and give fresh meaning in much the same way that a Hugo Wolf setting illuminates a Goethe poem.' " The attitudes of many of Sendak's small figures echo the poses of Boutet de Monvel's French children. In France his spirit is kept alive by the young illustrator Satomi Ichikawa. Her work is now being published in the United States in such picture books as *A Child's Book of Seasons* and *Friends.*

Several of Boutet de Monvel's books have recently been reissued in Paris, but these garish reproductions retain little of the integrity of the artist's original color harmonies. Perhaps all the advances in modern printing technology cannot duplicate what his nineteenth-century printers achieved. Searching for the incomparable original editions is well worth the effort. (pp. 177-80)

Michael Patrick Hearn, "Maurice Boutet de Monvel: Master of the French Picture Book," in The Horn Book Magazine, *Vol. LV, No. 2, April, 1979, pp. 170-80.*

Gerald Gottlieb

Joan of Arc was a visionary—devout, energetic, stubborn, ignorant but intelligent, gifted with military genius, and aflame with her mission. She became France's national heroine. In 1896 a fellow countryman of the Maid, an artist named Louis-Maurice Boutet de Monvel, set out to celebrate her achievements in a book for children. By then, of course, Joan had been revered in France for nearly five centuries. There had been countless illustrated versions of her story, for children of every age. But Boutet de Monvel now managed to create a new masterpiece. His ***Jeanne d'Arc*** would be more admired and loved, and would influence more artists and illustrators, than any other children's book of its era.

Boutet de Monvel was born in 1850 in Orléans, a city that had been obsessed with Joan of Arc ever since the Maid delivered it from siege in 1429. As a boy in Orléans he saw the name of the young heroine everywhere—on streets and squares, on public statues, on boxes of candy. The boy became an art student, and by 1874, at the age of twenty-four, he was an academic painter, exhibiting at the Paris annual Salon. Early in his career he turned to the illustration of magazines and books for children, and here he enjoyed success both financial and artistic. (At the same time he pursued another career, with even happier financial results, becoming international society's painter of choice for portraits of children.) Among the children's books he illustrated in the 1880s was ***La Civilité puérile et honnête,*** a work on etiquette for the young in the manner of the French courtesy books, which had a history going back to the Middle Ages (though Boutet de Monvel's treatment was somewhat tongue-in-cheek). He also illustrated a selection of La Fontaine's ***Fables.*** In both works he demonstrated an ability to reconsider and reinvigorate a time-worn theme, to take a traditional subject and make something new of it.

This ability came into play again in 1896, when he took as a subject the figure that had been omnipresent in his Orléans childhood—Joan of Arc. Inspiration, he later wrote, came to him in Paris, as he stood in the Place des Pyramides before the gilded statue of the Maid, stiff and erect on her charger, brandishing her sword toward the Tuileries. The theme, even the inspiration, were hardly new. But Boutet de Monvel, with his special talent for quickening the traditional, produced a series of pictures that would be his *chef-d'oeuvre,* his own monument to the Maid.

For this new children's book he not only painted the pictures but also wrote the text. And a comment is perhaps necessary here about that text. Boutet de Monvel, it must be remembered, was a painter, not a writer. Even less was he a scholar; and consequently some of the facts in the book have been called into question. But it must also be remembered that Boutet de Monvel's ***Jeanne d'Arc*** was a work of its time. It should be judged as such. Consider the book's title page, upon which the Maid, in mediaeval armor, leads eager French riflemen dressed in the uniforms of 1896. Presumably she is leading them to a victory, one that perhaps will help the nation forget the defeat suffered by French arms in the Franco-Prussian War of 1870-71. The battles listed on the standard the riflemen bear are those of Napoleon's pre-Waterloo triumphs. Boutet de Monvel is calling for, or dreaming of, a resurgence of the military glories won by not only Joan the Maid but also the Emperor Napoleon. Nor is this title-page propaganda absent from the pages that follow, even though they are set in the Middle Ages. Boutet de Monvel's pictures may depict the fifteenth century, but his writing is infused with the nationalistic fervor of the 1890s. One can hardly expect to find in it the balance, the measured reason of an ideal historian.

So much for Boutet de Monvel the writer. Boutet de Monvel the artist is quite another matter. The text of ***Jeanne d'Arc*** may be flawed, but pictorially the book is a work of genius. It was recognized as such from the very first. "Unique," one critic called it. Indeed it was; but its images were rooted in the past. Although the flat, shadowless coloring of the pictures was reminiscent of Japanese prints (which had been much in vogue in France, witness Gauguin), or of children's paintings, many of the images had a more distant source. It was certainly a more logical source, for it was contemporaneous with the Maid herself. We know that Boutet de Monvel read mediaeval chronicles—Froissart, no doubt, and Monstrelet—from which he surely took the events, the dramatic confrontations, of his ***Jeanne d'Arc.*** But did he not perhaps also pore over the illuminations in mediaeval manuscripts? The massed groupings of men and horses, the stylized backgrounds, and above all the opulent detail of robe and wall hanging, are all to be seen in illuminated manuscripts from early fifteenth-century France, the time and place of the Maid's life. They can be seen, for example, on the vellum leaves of the *Très Riches Heures du Duc de Berry,* illuminated by the Limbourg brothers, and in work that the Boucicaut Master produced for Charles VI, the father of Joan's feckless and ungrateful Dauphin.

However one may speculate about the pictorial sources of Boutet de Monvel's greatest creation, its influence was pervasive on the children's books that followed. That is why its pictures seem so familiarly modern to us today, nearly a century after the artist produced them to transport and inspire children and to do homage to the peerless heroine of his own childhood. (pp. 9-11)

Gerald Gottlieb, in an introduction to Joan of Arc *by Maurice Boutet de Monvel, The Pierpont Morgan Library and The Viking Press, 1980, pp. 6-11.*

Maurice Sendak with Virginia Haviland

[The following excerpt is from an interview with Maurice Sendak by Virginia Haviland.]

Many of the artists who influenced me were illustrators I accidentally came upon. I knew the Grimm's *Fairy Tales* illustrated by George Cruikshank, and I just went after everything I could put my hands on that was illustrated by Cruikshank and copied his style. Quite as simply as that. I wanted to crosshatch the way he did. Then I found Wilhelm Busch and I was off again. But happily Wilhelm Busch also crosshatched, so the Cruikshank crosshatching wasn't entirely wasted. And so an artist grows. I leaned very heavily on these people. I developed taste from these illustrators. Boutet de Monvel, the French illustrator, who is still not terribly well known (which is a great surprise to me), illustrated in the twenties, or earlier perhaps—and had the most glorious sense of design and refinement of style. His pictures are so beautifully felt and they are supremely elegant as only French illustration can be. They are very clear, very transparent, extremely fine. At the same time, they can be very tragic. There are things in his drawings, which perhaps now would even seem too strong for children—although at one point, they did not. There is a perfect example of his method in one of his illustrations for the *Fables* of La Fontaine—**"The Wolf and the Lamb."** They are a series of drawings, very much like a comic strip. It's like a ballet. The little lamb moves toward the stream and begins to drink, and the ferocious wolf appears and says: "What are you doing here? This is my water!" Of course, he's rationalizing the whole thing, he's going to eat the lamb up anyway, but he's putting on this big act about it being his water. Now, the lamb knows that there's no chance for escape, and while the wolf is bristling—and in each drawing his chest gets puffier and his fangs get fangier, and his eyes are blazing, and he looks horrendous—now, in proportion to him, growing larger on the page, the lamb dwindles. It has immediately accepted its fate, it can't outrun the wolf, it doesn't even listen to the words of the wolf, this is all beside the point: it is going to die, and it prepares itself for death. And while the wolf goes through this inane harrangue, the lamb folds itself in preparation for its death. It leans down, it puts its head to one side, it curls up very gently, and its final gesture is to lay its head down on the ground. And at that moment the wolf pounces and destroys the lamb. It is one of the most beautiful sequences I've ever seen and one of the most honest in a children's book. There's no pretense of the lamb escaping, or of there being a happy ending—this is the way it is, it does happen this way sometimes, that's what de Monvel is saying. And this is what I believe children appreciate. (p. 38)

> *Maurice Sendak with Virginia Haviland, "Questions to an Artist Who Is Also an Author," in* The Openhearted Audience: Ten Authors Talk about Writing for Children, *edited by Virginia Haviland, Library of Congress, 1980, pp. 25-45.*

Gabrielle Maunder

[The following excerpt is from a review of the 1980 edi-

tion of Joan of Arc *with an introduction by Gerald Gottlieb.]*

This edition is of enormous historical interest. Gerald Gottlieb, Curator of Early Children's Books at the Pierpont Morgan Library in New York, which owns one of the few remaining copies, traces its antecedents and the influences to be seen in the artwork. Quite correctly, he stresses the superb draughtsmanship and pure, delicate colouring of the numerous plates, and a reading of his introduction is very worthwhile. I would, though, take issue with him over the association he finds between de Monvel's work and that of the hands at work in the *Très Riches Heures du Duc du Berry* (the Limbourg brothers). There, the miracle is the sharpness and edge of the drawings and the peacock brilliance of the colours; here, the line and the colours are muted and shaded, and show more clearly their kinship to the Pre-Raphaelites. Indeed, that was the relationship which immediately sprang to my mind—that this author/artist had adapted the Pre-Raphaelite aesthetic in the service of a high romantic religious document.

Text and drawings together are absorbing testaments to the fervour of religious war, not—as Christian history reveals—an Islamic monopoly. The book is undeniably French and shows in every inch of its illustrations and every sentiment of its text the characteristic of 'La Gloire', intrinsic to the French consciousness. The pictures and the text glow with fervour and there can be little doubt that God is on the side of the French against the 'godams'.

Now, there *is* an interesting connection. Shaw's play regenerated Joan the peasant, with her ignorance of social finesse at the court and her affinity with the men-at-arms. Boutet de Monvel shows Joan as a 'jeune fille bien elevée'—wearing clothes of the artless simplicity which comes from only the finest cloth, and with her hair in a demure bun at the nape of her neck. Not for nothing is the motif at the conclusion of the book two wreaths entwined, one the victor's laurel wreath and the other of thorns.

This volume does seem to me to be an invaluable document for those teachers interested in the place of historical myth in national sensibility. Additionally, and of equivalent merit, is its interest as a sample of French children's books, standing in sharp contrast to the robustness in English books for children of Caldecott, and the lyrical pastoral of Kate Greenaway. A symptomatic indicative of national differences perhaps? (pp. 75-6)

> *Gabrielle Maunder, in a review of "Joan of Arc," in* The School Librarian, *Vol. 29, No. 1, March, 1981, pp. 75-6.*

Selma G. Lanes

Two of the rarer commodities in the world and in literature today are heroism and piety. So it is a particular pleasure to welcome back *Joan of Arc*—in a handsome reprint made from a first edition in New York City's Pierpont Morgan Library—the master work of the French illustrator Louis Maurice Boutet de Monvel.

Published in Paris in 1896, the picture-history of France's national saint was, in part, a labor of love; the artist had been born in Orléans, the city liberated by Joan from the

SOON SHE PERCEIVED THAT THEY
WERE AFTER BREAD, LIKE LITTLE
BEGGARS. THEY WERE INDEED BEGGARS,
BUT THEY WERE ALSO SONGSTERS.
FANNY WAS TOO KINDHEARTED TO
REFUSE THEM BREAD WHEN THEY PAID
FOR IT WITH SONGS.

From Our Children: Scenes from the Country and the Town, *by Anatole France. Illustrated by M. Boutet de Monvel.*

English in 1429. Boutet de Monvel also had a more timely motive—to create for the children of his day a stirring picture book about a past moment of French glory. (p. 79)

An academic painter who eventually won international fame as a portraitist of children, Boutet de Monvel had already illustrated several notable juvenile works, among them two collections of songs, a popular book on etiquette, and a brilliantly designed selection of La Fontaine's fables. But nothing ever matched his *Joan of Arc,* a story with unbeatable ingredients—religious fervor, court pomp, massed armies, pitched battles, and a unique heroine. Joan's life bore many parallels to Christ's and to the lives of other Christian martyrs. Chosen by God, she struggled and briefly triumphed; she was cruelly denied by those she aided, betrayed to her enemies, and executed in 1431. She died in Rouen—burned at the stake—when she was only nineteen.

Unquestionably first among *Joan of Arc*'s enduring qualities are its forty-three serene and majestic paintings done in watercolor and ink with black line, covering the major events in her brief existence. Handsomely composed, deeply felt, and executed with a consummate sense of color and with a healthy respect for historically accurate settings and costumes, the pictures remain fresh and moving today. Boutet de Monvel's book-size illustrations have a nobility and grandeur usually associated with the great church frescoes of the Renaissance. Their pleasingly flat rendering combined with a sophisticated use of design ele-

ments—the patterns on wall coverings, floor tiles, and court dress—owe a debt to the Japanese prints so popular in the artist's day.

The intimate opening picture, dominated by tender tones of pastoral green, introduces us to the peasant child of Lorraine. Dressed in drab homespun, she winds flax while tending the family cow. What a contrast to the next illustration, a mesmerizing re-creation of Joan's initial vision at the age of thirteen! The Archangel Michael appears, golden-haired and gold-armored; he is enclosed in a silvery aura, which is itself ringed by luminous tongues of golden flame. If the book gets under way with a brilliantly lit vision of the Archangel Michael announcing Joan's mission to help the Dauphin be crowned King of France, it closes with a decidedly sepulchral apparition of two female martyrs, St. Margaret and St. Catherine, comforting a spent Joan before her burning at the stake.

Uncannily, with only the subtlest alterations in his pale backgrounds, Boutet de Monvel manages to convey the quality of light in each picture—indoor or outdoor, morning or late afternoon, dawn or dusk. Employing a palette at once muted and daring, the artist constantly surprises and delights the viewer with his unexpected color combinations: The Dauphin's palace contains a peach rug strewn with pink roses, and court costumes are aglow with sumptuous yellows, rich reds, and burnt oranges. Throughout, the artist makes brilliant use of browns, black, and white. Joan's formal battle dress is inspired: a splendid sleeveless tunic worn over her silver armor. Long and white with a delicate fleur-de-lis pattern in gold, her graceful robe has wondrously scalloped edges. It manages at once to suggest the wings of an angel, the fragility of a bird, and the vulnerable femininity of this reluctant soldier of God.

As in a passion play or tableau, each gesture is exaggerated for maximum narrative clarity. But, despite the simplicity of his figures, Boutet de Monvel manages to suggest the heroine's single-minded devotion, the nobles' arrogance, the Dauphin's vacillation. Like the old Cecil B. De Mille biblical extravaganzas with their casts of thousands, the artist's pictures are teeming with soldiers, nobles, and clerics. Yet every visual detail is deftly exploited for dramatic impact. When Joan first marches into battle, we can clearly read her banner—the names of Jesus and Mary embroidered on one side next to a winged angel kneeling before Christ. The graphic tour de force of the work is a double-page illustration depicting the English defeat at Patay. Worthy of Paulo Uccello, it is a panorama of armored soldiers, thrusting lances, and mounted horsemen at full gallop. Each of the picture's two parts is a separate framed unit. But a French steed on the right-hand page bursts through its frame, racing headlong toward the left-hand page. And the rows of poised lances and spears, although interrupted by the white space between the pages, carry across from the right side to the left. Marginal gaps add to the cinematic sense of frenzied action.

Boutet de Monvel's own text, reverent if somewhat wooden, quotes liberally from Joan, as her words were reported in accounts of her own time. Her statements are touching in their unflagging faith. Examined by a council of clerics, the untutored girl says, " 'I may not know my ABCs, but I come on behalf of the King of Heaven.' " Captured at Compiègne, she cries, " 'I have sworn and given my faith to Another . . . and I will keep my vow to Him.' " And on being tried as a heretic, she offers no defense but " 'I am sent by God. . . . Send me back to God, from whom I came.' "

Almost as remarkable as his stately pictures is the fact that the artist managed with incredible felicity to accomodate one of the longest picture-book texts ever—some five thousand words—in ink-bordered rectangular blocks incorporated into his mostly full-page illustrations. Sometimes the text floats within the picture space; other times, it is anchored to the top or the bottom margin of the page. So effectively are the words locked into each illustration that the reader or listener never suffers any loss of visual detail. No matter how long the text-block is, we somehow manage to see the picture whole—right from the start. Curiously, despite the book's elegance, this particular juxtaposition of boxed words with pictures is reminiscent of a comic strip—a regal one, to be sure.

The English text has been pared down by Gerald Gottlieb, Curator of Early Children's Books at the Morgan Library, from a translation done in 1897. Mr. Gottlieb has also provided an illuminating new introduction. The shortened text gains in clarity and grace for a contemporary American audience, and only a few gems are lost. Unfortunately, the book's overall size has been slightly reduced—just enough to diminish the luxuriousness of the original book. Although the color reproduction overall is felicitous, the present edition is printed on shinier, whiter stock than was its predecessor, resulting in some muddling of the original limpid colors: Greens are occasionally altered to blues, oranges deepened to red or bleached out to yellow, blues rendered brighter and harsher. The design modifications on the book's cloth cover and title page, however, are effective and respectful of the original.

Never before *Joan of Arc,* in the brief history of children's picture books in color, had so handsome and exalted a work appeared. On grounds of both aesthetic purity and narrative content, Boutet de Monvel's masterpiece merits a place of honor beside the Lobels, Sendaks, and Steigs on the contemporary child's bookshelf. (pp. 80-3)

Selma G. Lanes, "A Second Look," in The Horn Book Magazine, *Vol. LVIII, No. 1, February, 1982, pp. 79-83.*

Robin F(idler) Brancato

1936-

(Born as Robin Fidler) American author of fiction.

Major works include *Winning* (1977), *Blinded by the Light* (1978), *Come Alive at 505* (1980), *Sweet Bells Jangled Out of Tune* (1982).

INTRODUCTION

Brancato writes realistic, sensitive, and thought-provoking stories for young adults that center on teenagers who overcome the hardships with which they must contend while maturing from childhood to adolescence. Praised for her understanding of young people, Brancato uses methods for handling teen problems that are considered unique in young adult fiction; Louise A. DeSalvo has found that "instead of protecting kids from adversity, the implicit message in each of Brancato's novels is that we need to help them develop their resources for coping with it." In all of her writings, Brancato presents her young adult protagonists with trying situations and difficult decisions regarding such issues as paralysis, death, and alcohol and drug abuse. Brancato claims to enjoy what she calls "writing stories that raise questions for readers to think about in terms of themselves," and answers them through the exemplary actions of her teen characters, all of whom achieve some form of success through their own strength, character, and intelligence. Some critics find her books offensive due to their sexual leniency and usage of profanity. According to Brancato, who is deeply concerned about the credibility of her stories, such language and behavior is necessary because it is true to the characters she portrays. She writes, "The gradual disappearance of certain taboos today has given writers an exciting, widening choice of subject matter and language. But the pitfalls have widened, too. Along with the freedom to 'write about anything,' comes the responsibility to avoid poor taste, sensationalism, trendiness." Most commentators, however, find the underlying values of her works both moral and, in many respects, traditional, noting specifically her recurrent references to literature. A former high school English teacher, Brancato often draws from poetry, plays, and fairy tales, combining these references with her own experiences and observations to support or convey a particular principle. For example, in Brancato's best known novel *Winning*, a high school teacher draws examples from Fyodor Dostoyevsky's *Crime and Punishment* and Arthur Miller's *Death of a Salesman* to teach a paralyzed student the value of life.

Born in Reading, Pennsylvania, Brancato was profoundly affected by World War II. Her first book *Don't Sit Under the Apple Tree* (1975), which focuses on twelve-year old Ellis Carpenter's post-World War II experiences, draws heavily from Brancato's own childhood. She further cites

her family's move from her childhood home to a Pennsylvania coal-mining town at the age of fifteen as an important influence on her development; this event is accurately represented in Brancato's second book *Something Left to Lose* (1976) in which Jane Ann Morrow must move to another part of Pennsylvania, leaving behind everything she values. *Winning,* Brancato's third and most widely regarded novel, tells of a high school senior named Gary Madden who is paralyzed in a football injury. His tutor, Ann Treer, is a recently widowed English teacher whose involvement with Gary enables her to come to terms with her own loss. Critics have lauded this work for its convincing portrayal of the effect Gary's disability has on his teacher as well as his parents, friends, and girlfriend. While the book is drawn from an incident which occurred at Brancato's school when she was a teacher, much of its material was obtained through research. Prior to writing about Gary's struggle with his paralysis, Brancato visited numerous hospitals and rehabilitation centers, interviewing patients, their families, and friends. Brancato also conducted extensive research—including attending a three-day workshop given by a religious cult—before writing *Blinded by the Light,* a story about a teenage girl who attempts to save her brother from a religious cult notorious for influencing

youths through drugs and brainwashing. Despite Brancato's efforts, the book was poorly received; most critics
found her characters overly-simplified stereotypes and her
depiction of cults one-sided, sensational, and unconvincing. Conversely, *Coming Alive at 505,* which involves a
high school student who temporarily acts out his dream
of becoming a disc jockey, was praised for its handling of
teen pressure and suicide, although some have found its
numerous plots and subplots confusing. Commentators
generally agree that Brancato's best works are those that
concentrate on a character's development rather than
plot. In *Sweet Bells Jangled Out of Tune,* for example, fifteen-year-old Ellen sneaks out of her home to help her se-
nile grandmother, Eva, against her parents wishes. Central to the novel's development is Eva's transformation
from a wealthy and envied woman to a bag lady. Russell
H. Goodyear has proclaimed that "seldom does a writer
of adolescent literature provide as much insight into psychological cause and effect as Robin Brancato has." Brancato's *Winning, Come Alive at 505,* and *Sweet Bells Jangled Out of Tune* have been named Best Book for Young
Adults by the American Library Association in 1977,
1980, and 1982 respectively.

(See also *Something about the Author,* Vol. 23, *Something
about the Author Autobiography Series,* Vol. 9, *Contemporary Authors New Revision Series,* Vol. 11, and *Contemporary Authors,* Vols. 69-72.)

AUTHOR'S COMMENTARY

[*The following excerpt is from a symposium in which
several authors for young readers made statements
about censorship.*]

Fortunately, I haven't felt myself to be the victim of censorship very often. My hardback and paperback publishers have never curtailed my free expression. Though my
editor at Knopf has given me plenty of advice on my six
novels, I don't recall ever being asked to change a word
or phrase or to shrink from a subject or a reference because it was too unseemly or raw or realistic. And when
these same novels have appeared in paper, they have been
reprinted by Bantam exactly as they were in hardback.

On the few occasions when I have felt the chilly wind of
censorship, it's come from the direction of publishers of
school editions of books and magazines. I have been
asked, in the case of two of my novels, to agree to changes
in the paperback book club editions (such as Xerox or
Scholastic) and in the versions of my books that have appeared in the Scholastic magazines. These changes have
included the replacing of more colorful expletives with
blander ones and the deletion of the best part of my one
(very brief, very tasteful) sex scene. Also, when *Redbook*
printed a condensed version of one of my novels, five-
letter substitutes were found for four-letter words. In each
of these instances I had the choice, of course, of withholding permission to reprint, but I chose to give permission,
since in none of the cases was the spirit of the work affected adversely.

I haven't had a problem very often with self-censorship,

either. My choice of subjects, characters, and settings has
rarely led me into dangerous territory. I don't regard myself as timid or squeamish, but the fact is, I write mostly
about what I've experienced or observed, and my experiences and observations have been primarily inside the
bounds of what's acceptable to the reading majority. In
the matter of language, when it's appropriate to the character, I like to create the illusion of gross or profane or un-
grammatical speech with a sprinkling of examples rather
than by overkill.

I suppose the best summary statement I can make concerning my feelings on censorship is the answer I wrote
to one of the two readers who have ever criticized, in writing, *my* choice of words. Here is the letter and the response:

Dec. 1, 1978

Dear Mr. Brancato, (sic)

I am an eighth grade student at Marshfield Jr.
High School in Marshfield, Wisconsin, and recently I read your novel **Winning.** I enjoyed the
story but was offended by the bad language. I
think the story would have the same impact
without the bad language. It is my feeling that
authors today think that bad language and sex
are needed to keep the reader's interest—I dis-
agree and I know that other students feel the
same way I do. I would be very interested in
hearing your reasons for your choice of words.
If you can find the time, please write and let me
know how and why you chose the words you do.

Yours truely . . . (sic)

Jan. 5, 1979

Dear Shawn,

Your letter concerning language in Young
Adult novels is interesting and pertinent. I agree
that choice of language is often a problem for
writers of books for young people.

I suppose I don't like "bad language" any more

Brancato being read to by her father, W. Robert Fidler.

than you do. The main trouble with it from my point of view is that it is boring, unimaginative and lazy. In conversation it often fills in where original and interesting language ought to be. However, my business as a writer is not so much to pass judgment on how people speak, but to try to record their speech accurately for the sake of telling a story whose underlying values, I hope, are moral and positive.

When I employ "bad language," as you call it, and references to sex, it is not because I think these are needed to sell books or to hold the reader's interest, but because sex and body functions and the names for them, both polite and impolite, are parts of life, and I am interested in portraying life as it really is. If I fudge on details by creating an angry football player who says, "Oh, sugar!", who will trust me later, when I try to convey the important things that athletes think and feel?

I could, of course, choose to write only about people who use good language, but that would eliminate a lot of possibilities for characters. I guess what it comes down to is that even though I, too, dislike bad language, that doesn't keep me from liking or even loving a lot of people who use it. I want them in my books, too, even at the risk of offending a few readers.

I hope that you will continue your interest in reading and language. I hope that fewer people in the future will feel the need to use lazy, unimaginative language, so that it will fade away and I won't have to put it in my books. And I also hope that you will come to agree with me that what is more important in judging people in both real life and literature is not the purity of their language but the goodness of their spirits.

My best wishes,

Robin F. Brancato
(pp. 138-39)

Robin F. Brancato, "Some Thoughts on Censorship: An Author Symposium," in Top of the News, *Vol. 39, No. 2, Winter, 1983, pp. 137-53.*

GENERAL COMMENTARY

Louise A. DeSalvo

It was the summer of 1955 that marked the end of innocence for my friends and me. It wasn't that each of us hadn't suffered before. We had already discovered that the roofs of houses and the closets of basements were safe hiding places from parental rages. We had each lived through blackouts and air raid drills and years of separation from our fathers during World War II. We had survived the death of family members: Eddie's grandfather had died; so had mine (the one who sang Italian songs and gave me everything); so had Eunice's mother and three other members of her family in a fiery automobile crash that emblazoned the image of charred bodies into our brains through

the pictures on the front pages of newspapers. And we had just recently endured the suicide of a friend's mother who, as the story was told, hanged herself by tying a rope around a door knob, looping it over the top, and kicking the chair out from under herself. So far as we could tell, as a group of adolescents, we were representative.

No, it wasn't that each of us hadn't suffered before. It was that no one had yet told us that not only had we already endured; we had already prevailed. That is what we learned that summer as we sat on the curb at the corner of Banta Place and Prospect Avenue in my home town, popping bubbles of tar with our sneakers and sucking noisily on quickly melting ice pops as we talked about the books we were reading—about *The Old Man and the Sea, A Farewell to Arms* (now *that* was suffering), and *All Quiet on the Western Front*—and the heat seduced us into lethargy and comradeship. What we learned together that summer was that children and young adults are as capable as adults are of prevailing in the face of adversity and suffering. Hadn't each of us lived through the very same things as the heroes and heroines of those fictions?

What we needed literature for then was to *verify* the feelings that we had each struggled with alone in the closets of our basements and the roofs of our houses, in the solitary spaces of our own private suffering. It is a lesson desperately needed by the young people of today, a lesson which they seem not to have learned, if soaring suicide, alcohol and drug abuse rates among youngsters are any indication: that they are powerful enough and resilient enough to withstand hardship, if necessary, and to endure and to prevail, just like we did.

The novels of Robin Brancato mark signposts in the stages that children must live through in learning about adversity, and the way-stations they must pass through in coping with hardship. Her novels, and others like them teach young people about their own capacities for coping with problems without relinquishing the joys that come with living.

Ellis Carpenter, the heroine and narrator of Brancato's first novel, *Don't Sit Under the Apple Tree,* is poised somewhere between childhood and adolescence. As the novel opens having already lived through the greater part of World War II, she has developed both the scars and the special kind of resilience that come from surviving in difficult times. Her response to the war has been complicated by the fact of her German grandmother, to whom a kid named Sam incessantly refers, making her wonder whether or not she and her "Grossie" *do* have a predisposition to barbarism despite their trying to live like decent human beings and model citizens.

Even though she has grown up with war bulletins and air raids, with the keeping of a class scrapbook into which "sickening clippings" are regularly pasted, with movies like *The Purple Heart* about an American soldier who had his tongue cut out by the enemy because he wouldn't talk, with her best friend's brother, Les, being reported missing in action, Ellis clings to the belief in the sanctity of life and understands all too well its fragile and fleeting nature. The novel opens on V-E Day with the stunning juxtaposition of the report of Hitler's death with Ellis' voice: "The morning rain had washed earthworms onto the sidewalk and I walked on tiptoe so I wouldn't step on any."

But what Ellis has gone through already is nothing compared to what she must yet endure. She must pass from winning a citizenship award to understanding her ambivalent feelings about her own brother—she loses him almost deliberately when they journey into the woods in which they lose their innocence: "On one side of the rippling water lay sunny fields of tall grasses and daisies. On the other side were woods full of evergreens and pine cones, umbrella plants and jack-in-the-pulpits, rocks and moss." She must move from looking at adult love and friendship ideally, to learning that lovers are sometimes unfaithful and cruel to one another: she has treasured a picture of Les and his girlfriend Judy, sitting under a tree, bearing Judy's inscription pledging eternal fidelity, but then Ellis sees Judy in the arms of another soldier on July 4th, while Les is still missing in action. She must proceed from learning about death in the abstract from radio bulletins and newspaper clippings to facing the actual deaths of Les and her Grossie.

Ellis must also confront some primal fears and some deeply seated terrors in addition to those engendered by the outside world. What is so vital about this novel is that Brancato understands the relationship between the two. Early in the novel, while waiting to fall asleep, Ellis experiences a feeling she often has, a feeling that

> something was going to happen, and I had no control over it. When the feeling came I would try to bury my head in the pillow and imagine pleasant things, but soon I would look up in spite of myself and see shadows on the wall, the hulking clothes tree in the corner, and worst of all, the bookcase. . . . The long shelves, the dark wood and the glass doors made me think of a picture I had seen of Snow White in a glass coffin.

Ellis uses Snow White to make sense of her fears of death and nothingness, feelings that she first believes are idiosyncratic but which she validates and verifies through remembering an analogue to her experiences in the literature with which she is familiar. A fear that would otherwise remain inexplicable to her thus becomes manageable. The reference to Snow White also tells us that another of Ellis' primal fears which she will not face until later in the novel is her fear of sexuality—she must give up the safety of her easy and warm relationship with her best friend, Jules, for the complications of adolescence; she passes from sexual innocence to sexual awareness.

This passage into adolescence has been made possible by Ellis' grandmother. In a powerful and poignant scene, Ellis travels to her grandmother's house (the reference to Little Red Riding Hood is intentional) soon before the old woman's death. Ellis learns that facing the reality of the world and its hardships is as possible for her as it has been for her courageous namesake, Mary Ellis, who lived a good life despite the death of her lover during the First World War; she learns that she must "try harder to accept the good things that come to us without feeling guilty."

Her grandmother gives Ellis a volume of poems by Emily Dickinson, once owned by Mary Ellis—a volume that will later help Ellis sort out her feelings when Grossie dies, a volume that stands for the healing potential of literature. When her grandmother dies, Ellis opens the volume and reads:

> The bustle in a house
> The morning after death
> Is solemnest of industries
> Enacted upon earth,—
> The sweeping up the heart,
> And putting love away
> We shall not want to use again
> Until eternity.

Brancato's second novel, *Something Left to Lose,* deals with creating a balance between impetuosity, spontaneity and a healthy hedonism on the one hand, and reason, deliberateness, and necessary self-discipline on the other. As the novel opens, Rebbie Hellerman and Jane Ann Morrow seem to represent these poles—Rebbie skips out on responsibility as often as Jane Ann embraces it. In the novel, both of their capacities for dealing with hardship will be tested: Rebbie must face the fact of her mother's alcoholism and her father's death. Jane Ann must face a move to another part of the state that will deny her everything she has come to value.

Rebbie's defiant death-wish is juxtaposed against Jane Ann's timid and almost reluctant life-hold. But Rebbie's obsession with astrology—she won't make a move without first consulting her horoscope—and with knowing obscure details about presidents ("which three-time loser for the Presidency of the U.S. supposedly died as a result of *overeating?* William Jennings Bryan. Died in 1925.") indicated that beneath her spontaneous facade is a deperate need both to see herself as part of a larger pattern and to relinquish responsibility for what she does.

Jane Ann's anxiety attacks, where she loses her sense of identity and must repeat to herself ritualistically the facts of her identity ("I am Jane Ann Morrow. I live at 814 Oak Street, Windsor, Pennsylvania. My parents are James and Evelyn Morrow.") suggest that the control *she* exerts over feelings and emotions is life-suffocating. Jane loves the stage because it is a place where she can "look like she was doing the right thing, but how come, in everyday living, she was so often unsure of herself?"

The reasons for Rebbie's problems are obvious: she is saddled with an alcoholic mother whom she loves and an uncaring father who escapes the nightmare of his family by working obsessively at his law practice. There is one gesture of affection that remains between Rebbie and her mother:

> Jane Ann watched Rebbie measure out a small amount from the bottle on the coffee table. She wiped the glass with a paper napkin and handed it over carefully. It was the closest, most loving, she had ever seen Rebbie to her mother. . . .

The reasons for Jane Ann's problems are less obvious. She has lived out life in a good, normal home with a nurturing mother and a productive reasonable father, but she cannot escape the growing pains that afflict everyone, no matter how well taken care of they are. Brancato knows that adversity is an ordinary, everyday, and *universal* condition: we are delusional if we think that we can banish it by creating isolated paradises of peace and tranquility for our children to grow in. It simply won't work. Life has a way of messing up paradise, as Jane Ann learns.

Instead of protecting kids from adversity, the implicit message in each of Brancato's novels is that we need to help them develop their resources for coping with it. Brancato reminds us that we have made it far too easy for the weakest and most alienated of our children to choose death, or the death of the soul, over life. As Rebbie states it, we have taught kids that "The best people are dead . . . Janis Joplin . . . She's dead. Humphrey Bogart's dead. President John F. Kennedy's dead. So are thirty-five other American Presidents—a few crummy ones, but most of them good. W. C. Fields is dead, and Shakespeare." It is no wonder, then, that Rebbie has adopted Janis Joplin's litany to the troubled of her generation, that freedom is having nothing left to lose; that Jane Ann fears that Rebbie will commit suicide after her mother is hospitalized once again. Jane Ann knows that there is something paradoxical in using the corpses of literature and history to teach kids about survival and loving life, even though death is something that she must face. She thinks about her role of Emily in *Our Town:*

> Death—even in the play! *Especially* in the play, since the whole third act took place in a graveyard. She couldn't escape it. Maybe if she said

Brancato at the age of three.

the word a hundred times she'd get it out of her head. Death, death, death, death . . . Ridiculous. That didn't help. What would?

Rebbie helps. She counters that part of Jane Ann which prefers fantasies of perfection and death to the risk of raw reality. And Jane Ann helps Rebbie: she helps her learn about self-control and about both of their capacities for courage. Together they learn Mrs. Soames' lesson in *Our Town*—"My, wasn't life awful—and wonderful."

Winning and *Blinded by the Light* expand and amplify Brancato's earlier themes. In *Blinded,* Gail Brower engages in a quest for her brother Jim who has entered the Light of the World, a religious cult which demands obedience to a father figure, sexual abstinence, and self-denial. The L. O. W. is successful because it offers its adherents simplistic solutions to life's real problems: it purports to substitute a loving community for parental betrayal, bliss for hardship, happiness for suffering, certainty for chaos, paradise for the real world. One member of the cult describes its allure:

> ". . . I happened to run into a beautiful brother singing like crazy right on the street. I ran up to him, blissed out at the thought that somebody could be that happy . . . and he told me about a family that was so high on life they didn't need anything artificial . . . that's the story of a lost soul who went off to drown in darkness and found instead the Light of the World!"

Like *Antigone* (about which Gail writes a college term paper), *Blinded* deals with the conflicting claims of family love and loyalty and adherence to a higher authority; like Antigone, Gail must go underground to be reunited with her brother. She participates in a cult initiation weekend and she sees that they "want things to be perfect—by magic. They love *everybody* but no one special person." Even though she knows that the L. O. W.'s formula for recruiting new members is a skillfully concocted combination of flattery, group approval, exhaustion, and indoctrination, she herself almost succumbs, learning how seductive the group's allure can be and how vulnerable almost everyone is: "Stay. Avoid decisions. No more hassles."

She later learns that the L. O. W.'s methods include manipulating the blood-sugar levels of its adherents, making alternating states of depression and euphoria a very powerful and carefully regulated form of group control for its leaders. The Jonestown Kool-Aid, laced with cyanide and tranquilizers, is chillingly anticipated in *Blinded.* As Brancato suggests and as the Jonestown mass suicide/murder indicates, joining groups like the L. O. W. means that one will more closely resemble the inmates of concentration camps than the inhabitants of paradise.

Winning is Brancato's finest novel. It recounts the relationship between Ann Treer, a recently widowed English teacher, and Gary Madden, one of her high school students who has become permanently disabled as a result of a football injury. That Brancato calls the novel *Winning* is not only an ironic commentary on our national preoccupation with victory at almost any price, it is also a paean to the victory of the human spirit. The novel alternates between Gary's increasing awareness of the meaning of his injury, his denial, anger, depression, and near suicide, and Ann's responses to the opening up of the old wound of her husband's death, which Gary's disability represents. Although she agrees reluctantly to tutor him she begins to need Gary to reteach herself how to feel, to care passionately, and to love again. And he needs her to teach him to face the reality of his disability with courage, to take the hard and not the easy way out, to face the fact that although he will never walk again, his life is still just beginning.

Ann refuses to treat Gary in anything but a forthright and direct way. She insists upon his dictating a journal, knowing it will be an important release for him. She insists upon his grappling with the weighty and difficult issues of *Crime and Punishment*—issues such as whether or not disasters are caused or fated, that reverberate with special meaning for Gary:

> "Rashkolnikov's all of us in the sense that he feels deprived, as we all do sometimes. He deludes himself into thinking he's special. . . ." Should she, after all, force a kid who had barely escaped death, a kid who couldn't move his head or hold a book, a kid who would never walk and didn't know it yet, to finish a 510-page, often-depressing novel about a murderer?

Nor does she avoid the difficulties of *Death of a Salesman,* although, preoccupied as she is with her own response to his disability, she inadvertently almost encourages Gary to contemplate suicide.

> " . . . answer this question on *Death of a Salesman.* Why does Willy kill himself?"
>
> "Because he lost his job, right?" Gary said. "Because nobody respected him anymore. What else is there to say?"
>
> "Consider his suicide as an act of love, an act of self-sacrifice."
>
> "Act of love?"
>
> Suddenly it came clear to him, so *clear,* out of the cloud inside his head! The best way to pull off his act of love . . . Bite the thermometer, really hard. Swallow the jagged particles of glass, the dense little silver ball that would split apart inside him and split again and again until pinheads of silver filled his bloodstream.

But Ann comes back to him in time and helps him learn that he is not Willy Loman, "a worn out man who spent his whole life avoiding the truth. You're not like them, but you can learn something from them." And when Ann admits to Gary that she needs *him* to make *her* feel, his victory is ensured:

> Ann covered her eyes, put her head down, and laid her face against the sheet.
>
> "Ms. Treer? Hey, Ms. Treer . . . please." He shifted so that he touched her hair with his shoulder.

The special magic of Brancato is that she erects contemporary novels on the very same set of emotive and intellectual principles as those works to which she alludes in her fiction—the fairy tales, the poetry of Emily Dickinson, the *Antigone, Death of a Salesman,* and *Crime and Punishment*—without compromising her ability to speak in a modern voice. It is a voice that young people will profit from hearing.

A student of mine once heard Brancato relate an anecdote that summarizes what her work is all about and the toughness of the spirit behind it. While she was doing research for **Winning** at a rehabilitation center, one of the patients asked her what she was doing there. She replied that she was doing research for a novel about a young disabled football player.

"How does it end?" the patient asked. "He lives," Brancato replied. "Will he ever walk again?" "No." "Then kill him off." "I can't," she said. "The book is called **Winning.**" (pp. 16-18, 50-1)

> *Louise A. DeSalvo, "The Uses of Adversity: Robin Brancato's Novels as Patterns for Adolescent Coping,"* in Media & Methods, *Vol. 15, No. 8, April, 1979, pp. 50-1.*

TITLE COMMENTARY

Don't Sit Under the Apple Tree   (1975)

Robin Brancato has captured the somber moments of self-awareness awakening 12-year-old Ellis Carpenter throughout the turbulent summer of 1945. As World War II winds down, Ellis experiences the joy of true friendship, the enormity and pain of death and the confusions of physical maturing. The children and adults who play parts in the life of the hero are warm and human. The writing evokes a particularly troubled time in America's history with fine detail and accuracy.

> *A review of "Don't Sit under the Apple Tree,"* in Publishers Weekly, *Vol. 207, No. 11, March 17, 1975, p. 57.*

Here's another novel which looks back nostalgically to the good old 1940's, with special emphasis on the summer of '45. (How can the summer I lost my two front teeth and learned to ride a bicycle—not necessarily in that order—be nostalgia already?)

Don't Sit Under the Apple Tree is packed with all of the now-familiar 1945 trivia details, slightly glamorized by the rosy haze of memory. In her first book, Robin F. Brancato evokes memories of victory gardens, tin can collections, air raid drills, milkweed pod lifejackets, silver-colored pennies, gold star mothers, Jack Benny's radio program, food shortages and gas rationing. These and other features of that year are given to us through the eyes of the first-person narrator, a spirited girl named Ellis Carpenter.

Ellis tells us how it was in Wissining, Pa., the summer World War II was coming to an end. A few crucial things happen that affect her life. She wins a coveted Citizenship Award from her school. The brother of her best friend Jules dies in action at Iwo Jima and, in Wissining, Ellis's beloved grandmother dies. In between these important moments, the novel focuses upon the events of a slower, gentler era where children spent their time marching in Fourth of July parades and giving magic shows to raise money for the war effort.

In 1945 a girl like Ellis would have been called a tomboy, but by our current standards she has all the right feminist vibes. Her best friend is a boy. She plans to be a detective (like Nancy Drew) and then she grows up and is impressed that the new girl on the block has a mother who is a lawyer. I like Ellis. Citizenship awards notwithstanding, she is no goody-goody. Instead, along with most of us, she is a fairly good citizen wrestling to contain all of her bad citizen impulses. I find myself wishing, however, that Robin Brancato had been able to develop and bring alive some of the other characters in this book. The first-person genre does give immediacy, but it can be limiting—particularly in children's fiction. To most self-absorbed pre-adolescents—including Ellis Carpenter—the rest of the world often appears shadowy and two-dimensional.

> *Susan Terris, in a review of "Don't Sit under the Apple Tree," in* The New York Times Book Review, *March 30, 1975, p. 8.*

The historical setting is superficially developed (the war is remote enough for Ellis to say, "There was something special in the air—maybe it was the excitement of V-E Day, or maybe it was just the perfume of lilac bushes."), and there is one unresolved and disturbing incident: The Fourth of July Dance where Ellis feels, for the first time, like a "tomboy" misfit, seems to mark the end of her active and vigorous life ("I wondered what it would be like to wear cute short dresses, hold hands with a boy and comb my hair a lot like the older girls at the dance."). However, Brancato's treatment of characters is sensitive and humorous (except Ellis' one-dimensional father); and, Ellis' close relationship with her German grandmother is nicely drawn, as is her friendship with her classmate Jules.

> *Cyrisse Jaffee, in a review of "Don't Sit under the Apple Tree," in* School Library Journal, *Vol. 21, No. 9, May, 1975, p. 52.*

Something Left to Lose (1976)

Jane Ann, a ninth grader whose thoughts and actions throughout are more appropriate for a 12 year old, tries to work through the usual conflicting loyalties to her friends, her family, and herself. She is concerned with a part in the school play, her first boyfriend, her family's plans to move to another town as well as the personal problems of her best friend, Rebbie (Rebbie's mother is an alcoholic, her father is rarely home). The book is well written and is enjoyable to read, but the characterizations are stereotyped and predictable: Rebbie is from an unstable home, therefore she is the odd one; Jane Ann is from a middle-class home, therefore she is average; a third friend, Lydia, is from a home in which both parents are professionals, therefore she is the mature, poised one of the group.

> *Pamela Jajko, in a review of "Something Left to Lose," in* School Library Journal, *Vol. 22, No. 8, April, 1976, p. 84.*

Jane Ann's friend Rebbie, whose mother drinks and whose prominent father is usually away, thinks that she has nothing left to lose—and the crazy desperation that results is both what attracts her straighter friend and what makes Jane Ann's parents, guidance counsellor and even, later, her new (first) boyfriend feel that Rebbie is bad company. But Rebbie's demands, citing their friendship pledge, become something like blackmail as Jane Ann, fearful that she might try to kill herself, reluctantly agrees to cut class and play rehearsal, drink beer, and even go off in a car though at fourteen the girls are too young to get a license. Brancato can write a scene that you have to believe, her teens have more mettle than most fictional YA's, and what's more Jane Ann's conflict comes across as a real, involving dilemma and not the set-up you'd expect from such alternatives.

> *A review of "Something Left to Lose," in* Kirkus Reviews, *Vol. XLIV, No. 8, April 15, 1976, p. 481.*

This book for teens in grades seven and up is a light, fast-reading book. The plot is not deep but it does have some exciting, enjoyable, and tense incidents. . . .

Teenage girls are likely to enjoy the book since it centers around happenings similar to those in their own lives. The author is a high school English and journalism teacher, and would be well-versed in knowing teenagers and their antics, attitudes, problems, and opinions. Her portrayal of the three diverse personalities vividly shows this to be true.

> *Mary Columba, P.B.V.M. in a review of "Something Left to Lose," in* Best Sellers, *Vol. 36, No. 3, June, 1976, p. 102.*

Winning (1977)

A football accident near the beginning of his high school senior year leaves Gary Madden paralyzed from damage to his spinal column—prognosis: he will never walk again. The plot centers on Gary's experiences in the hospital, where at first he is completely immobile, and later at a rehabilitation institute, where he gains some use of his arms and hands. Concurrent with Gary's story is that of his young, recently widowed English teacher whose involvement with Gary through tutoring helps her come to terms with the loss of her husband. The main thrust of the narrative concerns Gary's struggle to accept his condition; Brancato is, perhaps, too superficial in dealing with Gary's mental anguish and gradual determination to go on with life, but her portrayal of the effect of Gary's condition on his parents, his friends, and his girl, as well as the mutually beneficial relationship between him and his English teacher, is realistic. A generally moving and involving junior novel that avoids being maudlin.

> *A review of "Winning," in* Booklist, *Vol. 74, No. 1, September 1, 1977, p. 30.*

You can't help but root for Gary, a quintessential good guy, who muscle by muscle diligently progresses from almost total paralysis to partial recovery of his arm movements. And Brancato also supplies an ultra-supportive

Brancato holding her grandson Clayton. Looking on are her husband John, son Gregory, and daughter-in-law Patrice.

supporting cast to help him through rough times: there's a true-blue girlfriend, a good buddy from his gridiron days, fussing but well-intentioned parents, and a young, recently widowed English teacher who teaches Gary to see "anagrams as the metaphor for my life—making something new out of the scrambled parts." At times the generalized insights into being handicapped come perilously close to the type of easy truths caught on reruns of *Marcus Welby*. But Brancato has a telling eye for detail—e.g., Gary's embarrassment over involuntary erections—and an uncanny ear for dialogue, especially the bluff bantering between Gary and his rehab roomies, which add heft—and heart—to this hospital story.

A review of "Winning," in Kirkus Reviews, *Vol. XLV, No. 18, September 15, 1977, p. 995.*

In an impeccably constructed and unsentimentalized story, Brancato reveals the effects of the trauma on Gary and others in his life. Among them are his stunned parents, his confused young sweetheart and friends, some of whom desert him. All these characters are realistically portrayed, thoroughly understandable. A standout is Ann Treer, Gary's English teacher. Coming to terms with her own tragedy, the accidental death of her young husband, she pulls Gary up out of suicidal despair. "Mizz Treer," as the boy calls her, convinces him that his body may be helpless but his mind is definitely not. With her encour-

agement, he finds what "winning" means and looks forward to college. Like Brancato's other novels, this is a superior work.

A review of "Winning," in Publishers Weekly, *Vol. 213, No. 1, January 2, 1978, p. 65.*

[It's hard] to write a believable and yet not totally depressing story about someone who is not going to die but who has a severe physical problem that cannot be cured. Robin Brancato succeeded in doing this in **Winning,** the story of English teacher Ann Treer and an injured high school football player, Gary Madden. When the book opens, he has not been told that he is permanently paralyzed. Ann has reluctantly agreed to tutor him at the hospital, and she is surprised when he asks her to bring him some books from the library:

"Which ones?"

"Books—that I could read—that we could read when you're here."

"O.K. What books?"

"Books about what's wrong with me. You know, about spine injuries."

She protests that surely he ought to ask his doctor who would not only know what books to recommend but could also give him whatever information he needs. But Gary doesn't want to ask the doctor; in fact, he doesn't want anyone to know that he is curious so Ann agrees:

> "I'll do what I can," she said. "You mustn't count on me, though. I don't know what books I can get."
>
> Gary smiled ironically. "Just get one that widens my view of the world."
>
> "So you do see the value of books!" Ann said.
>
> "Yeah. They tell us about ourselves."

As Ann Treer leaves, she ponders why Gary has chosen her to be his agent in confirming his suspicions and concludes that it is:

> because she wasn't as likely to judge him as the doctor was, probably. Not about to measure his manhood as his friends might. Because she hadn't borne him, with all the pain and expectations surrounding that. Because she didn't worship him and hanker for him, as Diane did.

The value of such fictional treatments . . . is that they involve the reader in the problem from many different viewpoints. A relationship is shown between physical and emotional problems. For example, one of the strong points of Brancato's book is that it shows the ripple effect of Gary's accident: how it changes his friends, his parents, his girlfriend, and his teacher. In one brief moment their definition of winning is changed forever. In the new situation, surviving—just wanting to survive—means winning, and readers cheer with Gary when he makes it through the depression that causes some of his hospital mates to commit suicide. (pp. 103-04)

> *Alleen Pace Nilsen and Kenneth L. Donelson, "The New Realism: Of Life and other Sad Songs," in* Literature for Today's Young Adults, *second edition, Scott, Foresman and Company, 1985, pp. 78-111.*

Blinded by the Light (1978)

Catchy title and timely topic aside, Brancato delivers a temperate but unilluminating look at fanatic religious cults, here the "Light of the World," which has claimed Gail Brower's older brother Jim as one of its most rabid followers. Caught somewhere in between the no-holds-barred desperation of her parents, who have hired a "rescuer" to get back their son, and the easy objectivity of her college roommate, who insists that everyone has "the right to choose *not to be free*," Gail tries to track down her brother; first at a country retreat, where she spends a weekend with a blissed-out bunch of LOWs, and finally at a mass rally at Philadelphia, where Jim proposes a trade-off—a day of Gail's at the LOW hotel for a day of his at home. Brancato's contention that just 24 hours of little sleep and less food could turn someone as level-headed as Gail into a mind-blown zombie ready to sign herself away to "Father Adam" is as hard to swallow as the see-through propaganda pounded into all the LOW acolytes. Moreover, in the absence of a convincing plot

(this culminates in Gail's melodramatic eleventh-hour rescue by her boyfriend), one at least expects an inside peek into this type of religious movement. Yet no real light is shed on the insidious seductiveness of the LOWs (they are pictured as a kind of misdirected, overaged scout troop), so that ultimately we come no closer to understanding these cults than we do by watching Moonies at work on the street. (pp. 1191-92)

> *A review of "Blinded by the Light," in* Kirkus Reviews, *Vol. XLVI, No. 21, November 1, 1978, pp. 1191-92.*

Here is one of the first in what will surely be a flood of books whose theme is religious cults and their attraction for the young adult. (p. 406)

Tension builds page by page and the author is able to create a sense of pressure as it comes down on Gail, almost sweeping her into the malestrom of cultism. Realism carries the tale as Gail's one chance to "save" Jim, after the accidental (?) death of a fellow L. O. W., is left undetermined, leaving the reader to wonder if Jim will see the truth or twist it to fit his already warped beliefs. Can Gail resolve her own problem as to how much she has the *right* to interfere with her brother's decisions? No final conclusion is reached but the no-man's land of decision making is painted in somber tones, clearly underlining the fact that few situations are all black or all white. Very casual acceptance of the Pill, co-ed bedding down, and an attitude toward academics as second-place could cause problems in some libraries, a shame because knowledge of such cultism should be offered at a young age today. (pp. 406-07)

> *Hildegarde Gray, in a review of "Blinded by the Light," in* Best Sellers, *Vol. 38, No. 12, March, 1979, pp. 406-07.*

The subject of this poorly written book is a serious one: the influence of pseudo-religious cults on American youth. In light of the cult-related events which recently took place in Guyana, it is impossible to dismiss as insignificant the psychological power that some of these organizations wield. It is disappointing, therefore, to find this novel only marginally concerned with *why* certain people are attracted to groups committed to the destruction of human individuality. Instead, its focus is the omnipotence of these groups, and the message is that most people, however critical and aware they may be, are extremely vulnerable to the methods employed by such organizations. This in itself is a highly questionable assumption, and a message of dubious value to adolescents.

At the beginning of the story the main protagonist, Gail, a college sophomore, is in mortal terror of coming involuntarily under the spell of the proselytizing young people who represent an organization modeled on "Reverend" Moon's Unification Church. Her parents share this fear and are especially concerned because Gail's brother, a highly intelligent and reasonably happy college senior, left school to join the group the previous year. The family has not heard from him since, and they assume that the group has managed to deprive him of his faculties for critical thinking and decision-making. This in fact turns out to be precisely his fate, although we never learn why. And herein lies the main problem with the book.

The tenor of the book's opening and much of what follows is that of hysteria. "They" are out to get Gail, only "they" are neither communists nor freaks of nature, but rather teenagers preaching love and peace.

The book is also sexist. Gail draws sympathy from her boyfriend Doug by saying "I'm so dumb, I'm so clumsy," to which he replies, "I love dumb, clumsy women . . . they make me feel superior." Most of the story describes Gail's attempt to reach her brother by pretending to be an initiate in the cult which he has joined. After only two days with the group, she is on the verge of signing away all of her worldly possessions to the organization's "spiritual father," a man whom she decried 48 hours earlier. But her boyfriend Doug, like the proverbial fairy-tale prince, arrives with split second timing to rescue her. For this deed she is overwhelmingly grateful and, strangely, her reasoning abilities return immediately.

The novel depicts college students as people who are generally too immature to assume responsibility for directing their own lives. All the cult members are people escaping from unhappy families, unemployment and alcoholism by yielding their self-will and decision-making power to the group's leaders. In the end we learn that Gail's brother is aware that he has repeatedly been duped and lied to by the group's leadership but inexplicably, this knowledge does not anger him or motivate him to alter his decision to remain with them and do things that run contrary to his own sense of right and wrong. This is a book which does more harm than good.

> *Maxine Fisher, in a review of "Blinded by the Light," in* Interracial Books for Children Bulletin, *Vol. 10, No. 4, 1979, p. 17.*

Come Alive at 505 (1980)

Not up to *Blinded by the Light* or to her other successes, Brancato's new novel is crammed with too many digressive plots for conviction. A senior in high school, Dan Fetzer sniffs at college and relies on the gabby tapes he makes incessantly to win him a contest opening the door to a career as a disc jockey. His other two interests are attracting Mimi—a fat girl, new to the local high school—and plotting with her, his friend Marty and a snide kid, George, to elect a nonexistent senior the class president. When Mimi confides in Dan that George had supplied her with the pep pills that had helped her lose weight and then landed her in a hospital, her remarks are accidentally (hmmm) taped. George gets hold of the tape and is up to no good. It's odd to find, incidentally, the presumably admirable young characters resorting to profanity and vulgarity to express all their reactions.

> *A review of "Come Alive at 505," in* Publishers Weekly, *Vol. 217, No. 12, March 28, 1980, p. 49.*

Danny Fetzer's obsession is radio—eclectic Talk and Tunes radio. . . . Danny has already put together hundreds of tapes of his own show, broadcast from his imagi-

nary station, WHUP 505. The show is a mix of humor, music, contests and listener call-ins. Danny wants listeners, life, his future to "come alive," so he organizes an elaborate hoax to shake up the students at Duncan High; meanwhile, he enters a local radio station's Talent Search contest.

In maneuvering the hoax, he becomes involved with mysterious Mimi Alman, whose weight problem and frosty manner can't disguise her sexy voice, dry wit and beautiful face. Add a half-dozen of the wimps, nice guys, jokers and villains whom we all recognize from high school. Throw in the terrifying anxieties of coming of age in these days of drift—too many possibilities, early disillusionment, drugs, teen-age suicide—and you have a book which the jacket copy touts as "energetic . . . sure to appeal to today's media-oriented generation."

The book does have energy: from Danny's clever radio patter (I laughed out loud at an interview with Shiv Mendoza-Smith, the imaginary lead guitarist of the British punk group Guts) to the tight, action-filled scenes that follow one another as closely as the segments of a successful radio show. Robin Brancato is a terrific DJ whose dialogue never misses: these *are* today's media-oriented kids talking.

But the jacket illustration and copy, the pop display type all seem to be shouting Now! to disguise the book's true genre, which is neither media-oriented, trendy nor Today. What Mrs. Brancato has written to follow such successes as *Winning* and *Blinded by the Light* is an old-fashioned, optimistic adventure-romance. Whatever your vintage and orientation, it will leave you smiling and all-in from rooting and caring.

> *Kathleen Leverich, in a review of "Come Alive at 505," in* The New York Times Book Review, *April 27, 1980, p. 65.*

The drug scene, complete with one-dimensional pusher, is presented rather limply. Otherwise, the characters are strong and the dilemmas believable. Dan Fetzer is likable and, while Mimi's background smacks of early afternoon soap, her personality and relationship with Dan spark our sympathy and interest.

> *Steve Matthews, in a review of "Come Alive at 505," in* School Library Journal, *Vol. 26, No. 10, August, 1980, p. 74.*

Sweet Bells Jangled Out of Tune (1982)

For years 15-year-old Ellen has been forbidden to visit her grandmother Eva, who has gradually disintegrated from mild eccentricity into being a genuine bag lady. Eva drives recklessly around town, picks through garbage, steals tips off of restaurant tables. When Ellen finally does visit her, she finds that Eva's house is a shambles, there are no utilities or food, and Eva's companion/housekeeper has died long ago. After talking with her mother and various social-service professionals, Ellen tricks Eva into signing herself into a hospital. The story, told in the present tense, moves quickly and smoothly, and Brancato demonstrates a fine hand with dialogue. One extended conversation be-

Brancato at her desk.

tween Ellen and a psychiatrist is awkwardly loaded with virtuous information about mental health care, but for the most part the message—in some cases, the end justifies the means—is exposed through action. This is not a particularly thought-provoking novel, but it will grab readers and is especially recommended to librarians looking for good high/low material. (pp. 67-8)

> *Roger D. Sutton, in a review of "Sweet Bells Jangled Out of Tune," in* School Library Journal, *Vol. 28, No. 9, May, 1982, pp. 67-8.*

This novel is about two child-women. One, into her seventies, lives a life dominated by the ghost of her father. The other, just turned fifteen, struggles to escape the bonds of childhood. . . .

This is an exciting story with a fast-moving plot. Brancato writes with an ease that is a delight to the reader's ear. I was most pleased with how well it read out loud, a trait that unfortunately is not often characteristic of many contemporary adolescent novels. (It is a shame that many junior and senior high school teachers do not read out loud to their students. How else will students learn the rhythms and nuances of oral language? Certainly not from pap and drivel like "One Day at a Time"!)

Ellen is a dynamic, well-developed character. The reader sees her grow into maturity through her relationships with her mother, her girlfriend Josie, and an intriguing boy, Ben Bernhauser, who wears an earring in one ear. What makes the plot especially compelling is the mystery of Eva's life. How did a woman, once rich and envied, end up as a bag lady? Seldom does a writer of adolescent literature provide as much insight into psychological cause and effect as Robin Brancato has.

This fine novel rates a solid "A" and should not be missed.

It's no wonder that two of Ms. Brancato's previous books have been listed in the ALA's Best Books for Young Adults.

> *Russell H. Goodyear, in a review of "Sweet Bells Jangled Out of Tune," in* Best Sellers, *Vol. 42, No. 3, June, 1982, p. 188.*

This is another Brancato winner—as well researched, fully characterized, and sensitively delivered as *Winning;* but this one has a female main character and is more useful as a class novel. . . .

Through [a] seemingly simple plot, Brancato develops dynamic characters. Readers see Ellen grow as she deals with teenage situations as well as more difficult "adult" problems such as whether to encourage her grandmother to commit herself to a psychiatric ward. We see that, because of Ellen's love, Grandmother Eva realizes she must seek help. Even Ellen's mother, a minor character, changes as she overcomes her past feelings for Eva and helps her.

The plot, growth in characters, and open ending offer much for discussion in junior high classes. Because of these and Brancato's insights, students will both identify with Ellen and better understand the gray-haired lady whose "sweet bells jangled out of tune."

> *Gerry McBroom, in a review of "Sweet Bells Jangled Out of Tune," in* The ALAN Review, *Vol. 10, No. 1, Fall, 1982, p. 21.*

Facing Up   (1984)

Jepson, Dave Jacoby's best friend, was a bit zany and always in trouble. Dave was a little in awe of him, loved him, and sometimes envied him his freedom and his girl, the beautiful Susan Scherra. When Susan began hinting that she was tired of Jep, partly because of his heavy drinking, and that she was interested in Dave, he was consumed by self-disgust for betraying his friend but fell in love with her, anyway. Finally realizing that she was a sensation seeker, Dave stopped seeing her, but Jep found out about their relationship and caused a drunken scene. Driving the unconscious Jep home, Dave had an accident; Jep was killed, and Dave, though cleared of blame, was filled with unutterable guilt. He sank into lethargy and depression and decided to leave home; but two of his friends, rightly fearing he might try to commit suicide, went after him. Dave's struggle to regain his equilibrium is told in a tight, clean narrative that clearly pictures Jep's magnetic personality, Dave's innate decency, and his loving but overprotective parents. Less observant of the social milieu than *The Outsiders* and furnished with more conventional characters than M. E. Kerr's books about high school life, the story of an adolescent friendship and its tragic outcome is nevertheless filled with vitality and interest. (pp. 199-200)

> *Ann A. Flowers, in a review of "Facing Up," in* The Horn Book Magazine, *Vol. LX, No. 2, April, 1984, pp. 199-200.*

Facing Up is the latest in a long succession of popular,

contemporary novels by the well-known young adult writer, Robin Brancato. Among her accolades are no less than three American Library Association "Best Books for Young Adults" awards. Yet to this reviewer, **Facing Up** is a rather pulpish teen-age melodrama that exudes schmaltz. It is also written in a style that certainly would not challenge an intelligent young reader. Perhaps its virtue lies in the message that despite horrible personal tragedies, one has to adjust and life must go on.

> *Aaron I. Michelson, in a review of "Facing Up," in* Best Sellers, *Vol. 44, No. 3, June, 1984, p. 115.*

Robin Brancato has a string of successful novels to her name, including two which have won the American Library Association award for the Best Book for Young Adults. **Facing up** deserves similar commendation. . . .

The differences between true feeling and physical attraction, loyalty and deception, and friendship and acquaintanceship are well dealt with. The novel will certainly introduce thirteen- to fifteen-year-old readers to a totally new conception of teenage school and social life. This, along with the strong plot and sympathetic characterisation, makes it a book worth recommending, for perhaps the more reluctant reader.

> *Robin Barlow, in a review of "Facing Up," in* The School Librarian, *Vol. 37, No. 3, August, 1989, p. 112.*

Uneasy Money (1986)

Mike Bronti thinks his troubles are over when, on his 18th birthday, he wins $2.5 million in the New Jersey lottery. With his first installment check of $94,000, he indulges himself, but Mike is too intent on extravagance to heed his father's financial advice. In trying to prove his business acumen, he loses almost all of his first year's winnings in a real estate scam. By book's end, Mike is broke again (until the next lottery check), yet considerably wiser. Brancato (**Don't Sit Under the Apple Tree,** etc.) has created an interesting situation. However, characterizations tend to lack depth. The plot is a series of crises, with the hero getting into progressively worse scrapes. The story stops at its final climax and picks up a few months later,

in a too tidy ending. Readers are deprived of learning exactly *how* Mike faced facts and resolved his problems.

> *A review of "Uneasy Money," in* Publishers Weekly, *Vol. 230, No. 22, November 28, 1986, p. 78.*

Mike's appealingly breezy and up-front first-person narrative, revealing his enthusiasms and naivete, easily involves readers in his sometimes painful and often humorous route to rediscovering himself. However, like the cartoons that Mike draws, the story is filled with caricatures of family and friends whose sole purpose seems to be to give shape and form to Mike's misadventures. Decidedly lighter than the author's other YA novels, **Uneasy Money** is easy and amusing, with all of the "right" messages." (p. 113)

> *Jack Forman, in a review of "Uneasy Money," in* School Library Journal, *Vol. 33, No. 4, December, 1986, pp. 112-13.*

This American story tells how teenager Mike Bronti wins $2.5m on the state lottery and starts to spend, spend, spend. His Parents warn of the dangers, but since their practical advice is limited to suggesting Mike consults an accountant some time, the lad naturally takes no notice. After an orgy of silliness, he rediscovers what's really worth having in life, etc. It's all as predictable as a Victorian tract.

Not a bad read: just trivial but unexpected interest emerges from author Robin Brancato's implicit assumptions about women. Mike's girlfriend is a prim but gorgeous airhead trying to snare him into conventional matrimony via sex. His pal Lynne comes second to his male friends, is apparently asexual and seems to want no more than the chance to support Mike through thick and thin. His mum adores him and makes him food and his granny does the same, only more so. Very likely the poor guy will end up married to sexless Lynne. This is life? Perhaps it is, in a way.

> *Jenny Woolf, in a review of "Uneasy Money," in* Punch, *Vol. 295, No. 7695, July 1, 1988, p. 50.*

Michael Foreman

1938-

English author and illustrator of picture books, fiction, and nonfiction.

Major works include *All the King's Horses* (1976), *Panda's Puzzle, and His Voyage of Discovery* (1977), *Long Neck and Thunder Foot* (written by Helen Piers, 1982), *Sleeping Beauty and Other Favourite Fairy Tales* (translated by Angela Carter, 1982), *War Boy: A Country Childhood* (1989).

INTRODUCTION

Considered among the most talented creators of contemporary children's literature as well as a brilliant artist, Foreman characteristically writes and illustrates fantasies that deal with serious, topical subjects while remaining appealing and accessible to children. Called a protest writer by some critics for tackling such issues as arms control, conflict resolution, feminism, war, and pollution, he is praised for his success in translating his messages into metaphor and allegory; his tongue-in-cheek humor also lends whimsy to Foreman's mature, thoughtful themes. The merging of his qualities of earnestness, imagination, and humor has made his books highly popular and has qualified certain of his creations as classics of their genre. Foreman's stories are considered unusual as children's books because they commonly leave the reader pondering an ambiguity; it is part of Foreman's approach to storytelling that he has a resistance to fully resolved narrative endings. Often using his own travels as inspiration, he frequently sets his stories in strange and eerie landscapes or in settings suggestive of exotic countries. As preparation for his paintings in *The Saga of Erik the Viking* (written with Terry Jones, 1983), for example, he visited Scandinavia to see the remains of the long ships and studied the paintings of India at first hand for *Seasons of Splendour: Tales, Myths, and Legends of India* (written by Madhur Jaffrey, 1985).

Although his texts are acknowledged as both clever and sensitive, Foreman is best known as an illustrator. He works primarily in pencil and watercolor with the occasional application of elements of collage, such as tissue paper. His use of the watercolor medium is unconventional in his preference for bold, vibrant, saturated color, especially in the blues and golds. Celebrated for the "grainy" watercolor effect he creates, in part by the texture of the handmade paper he uses, Foreman heightens it by mixing in sugar, gravel, and even boot polish to build up three-dimensionality. Often lauded for his design sense, he frequently uses full-page color illustrations in his works which commonly include small, funny touches and crowded detail. Critics have pointed to the spectacular foreshortening and deeply plunging distant views that Foreman uses to create drama in his illustrations. This dis-

torted perspective gives his cityscapes and landscapes dreamlike qualities that are reinforced by his colors, reminiscent of dawn or dusk, glimmering moonlight or luminous ocean. The atmosphere of the exotic and of infinite detail created by these means reveals one of Foreman's artistic objectives: "The thing I like to try in a picture book is to use a large subject and put in as much as possible visually so that children can keep going back to the book and finding new things."

Foreman was inspired to become an artist by the illustrated magazines and comic books he saw in his mother's village shop in Pakefield, Suffolk. Although he had access to few books as a child, Foreman notes that having Kenneth Grahame's *The Wind in the Willows* read to him at the age of fifteen was a turning point in his life. A local teacher recognized the boy's talent for drawing and arranged for him to attend the nearby Lowestoft Art School, where he earned a National Diploma in Design in Painting. During the academic year 1958-59 Foreman studied commercial art at St. Martin's School of Art in London, where he later returned as a lecturer in graphic arts; he has also lectured at the Royal College of Art, the London School of Painting, and the Central School of Art, London. Foreman's inclination toward themes of political significance showed itself early in his first illustrated book, *The General* (1961), with its pacifist and antinuclear moral. Written by his first wife, Janet Charters, the book was, in the words of Douglas Martin, "hailed by art students as a breakthrough by a contemporary." Foreman spent 1960-63 at the Royal College of Art in London, years when David Hockney, Allen Jones, and Zandra Rhodes were on the painting faculty. During a trip to America in 1965, he served briefly as art director for *Playboy* magazine and later, after returning to Britain, for several English publications.

Foreman marks 1967 as the real beginning of his professional career as an illustrator. In that year he wrote and illustrated *The Two Giants,* a lighthearted tale that satirizes the foolishness of conflict. The two giants, Boris and Sam, are friends who begin quarrelling with each other over a seashell. They hurl rocks at each other until each notices that the other is wearing one of his opponent's socks. The mismatched socks remind them of their former friendship for each other, and they are reconciled. The simple tale represents Foreman's ability to take a weighty, antiwar theme and communicate it through a humorous allegory. Another antiwar allegory, *War and Peas* (1974), deals with the theme of famine and uses outlandish and laughable characters to alleviate the seriousness of the subjects. The ruler of an impoverished kingdom, King Lion, travels by bicycle to the realm of his neighbor, Fat King, to petition aid for his people, but Fat King shows his greedy nature and chases away King Lion. After friendly birds sow seeds to reduce the grain shortages, the Fat King refuses reconciliation with King Lion and ends up wallowing in the masses of his own food stuffs. The illustrations in *War and Peas* are designed to convey the ideas of excess and gluttony—the Fat King is shown as a pudgy equivalent of the mounds of puddings, pies, and tarts in which he revels—and Foreman turns to a hyperreal color style in the manner of food advertisements to enhance the lusciousness of the confections. Another of his books from the 1970s with a definite moral, *All the King's Horses,* garnered a great deal of attention when it appeared. Considered one of the first books for children to put a modern spin on the fairy tale, this witty and anti-traditional tale that features an unconventional princess has been called a feminist interpolation into children's fiction. The heroine is an Amazon-like princess, not delicate and golden-haired, the narrator tells us, but "a BIG girl. And *dark.*" Any man who would win her hand must wrestle with her and win. The traditional ending of this type of tale is subverted when the princess overthrows her last challenger and rides away with the horses her father has won from all her defeated rivals. Making up a quite different sort of children's book are the autobiographical reminiscences of *War Boy: A Country Childhood,* a highly acclaimed book that tells of Foreman's life in a Suffolk village during World War II. Rather than using a standard linear narrative, the book is put together from anecdotes, piecemeal recollections, overheard conversations, and nostalgia, rather in the manner of a collaborative family album. In delving into the means by which children adjust to war and danger, it includes excitement and humor, as well as the terror of German incendiary bombs. In his review of *War Boy,* Marcus Crouch observes, "The draw-

ings and paintings that crowd [Foreman's] pages might have been done on the spot, so convincing are all the details" and he singles out the landscapes of war for their vividness: "barrage of balloons over a cold grey sea, water-meadow and marsh lying empty under a summer sky . . . done with all his mastery of tone and design."

In addition to the illustrations he created for his own picture books, Foreman has provided pictures for the books of many other prominent authors for children and adults. These books include juvenile classics by such writers as Hans Christian Andersen, the Brothers Grimm, Rudyard Kipling, Sir James M. Barrie, and Robert Louis Stevenson, as well as more current writers, such as Alan Garner, Roald Dahl, Jane Yolen, and Terry Jones. His pictures have also graced the works of Charles Dickens, Ernest Hemingway, Daphne du Maurier, and Aldous Huxley, as well as Leon Garfield's prose adaptations of the plays of Shakespeare and Peter Dickinson's retellings of Old Testament stories. In addition, he has published his own collections of Mother Goose rhymes and fairy tales, the latter illustrated with scenes from the variety of cultures he has visited in his travels. An award-winning collection of Foreman's pictures in the category of children's classics is *Sleeping Beauty and Other Favourite Fairy Tales,* a translation by Angela Carter of seventeenth-century stories by Charles Perrault and Madame de Beaumont. Imaginative and dreamlike motifs, such as a castle entrance represented as a face with open mouth, heighten the eerie and sinister elements of the stories, while the pictures for other tales such as "Puss in Boots" maintain the satire of the French originals. Foreman's illustrations, both for his own books and those of other writers, have been awarded many prizes. He won two Greenaway Medals in 1982, for *Long Neck and Thunder Foot* and for *Sleeping Beauty and Other Favourite Fairy Tales,* and a third Greenaway in 1990 for *War Boy.* His *City of Gold and Other Stories from the Old Testament* was highly commended for the Greenaway Medal in 1980 and two of his other books have been commended for the medal, *The Brothers Grimm: Popular Folk Tales* in 1978 and *Seasons of Splendour: Tales, Myths, and Legends of India,* in 1985. He has been awarded the Kurt Maschler Award twice, in 1982 for *Sleeping Beauty and Other Favourite Fairy Tales* and in 1986 for *Early in the Morning: A Collection of New Poems* and was runner-up for the Maschler Award in 1985 for *Shakespeare Stories.* He also won the Francis Williams Illustration Award in 1977 for *Monkey and the Three Wizards.* In addition, Foreman was named a Royal Designer for Industry and has received several awards for his painting.

(See also *Something about the Author,* Vol. 12; *Contemporary Authors New Revision Series,* Vol. 10; and *Contemporary Authors,* Vols. 21-24, rev. ed.).

AUTHOR'S COMMENTARY

[*The following excerpt is from an interview by Michael Boyd.*]

Boyd: What made you first turn to the field of children's books?

Foreman: Children's books are the only ones which consist mainly of pictures in four colour. I do books which are picture stories and because there aren't picture books for adults, they tend to be classed as children's books.

Boyd: So ideally you would like them read as avidly by adults as well as children?

Foreman: I don't know how avidly they are read by anybody. Some books tend to take off with different age groups. Some books work very well with very young children. I can only base this really on letters that I get from them. . . . I have several ideas for books at any one time and they will lay around for some months. And the reason for selecting one rather than the others is because one seems to be more important at that point in time to do. This depends very much upon what is happening in the world: what people seem to be talking about and there seems to be a right time to do a particular thing.

Boyd: Michael I don't want to use the word "message" as that sometimes has unfortunate overtones but are you trying to get across something like this as well as telling a story?

Foreman: It is not as well as telling a story. It's the whole reason for telling the story. Not to put across exactly but to communicate in some way things that are a part of my life at that time. It is very much a way of life . . . I don't think in terms of doing a book for children or I have to do a story for a particular age group. If the thing has the message; the message is the reason for doing that story.

Boyd: Could your books be in any way construed as your personal protest about things you find in the world?

Foreman: It is not necessarily a protest. It could be a celebration of things that are going on in the world or things that are being ignored.

Boyd: Bearing all these factors in mind did your latest book *War and Peas* have a long gestation period?

Foreman: It took about two years from the conception of the idea to finishing the book. The drawings took longer than usual. They are much more complicated than any drawings I have done before. And the story was difficult to pare down to a few lines because it was a big subject. As the title implies it is about war and peace. It is an epic but it is an epic in about two hundred words and twenty pictures. The thing that I like to try in a picture book is to use a large subject and put in as much as possible visually so that children can keep going back to the book and finding new things.

Boyd: Michael when you get an idea that operates on various levels do you try it out on children before getting down to the nitty-gritty of drawing the pictures?

Foreman: Yes, I try it out on children of different ages. I don't show them the pictures. I just describe the plot. You can tell from their eyes how they react. Some of them tend to be rather polite and say, 'Oh yes, it is very nice.' But you get quite a good indication of where the thing falls down.

Boyd: Once you have settled on the story line do the subsequent illustrations make you want to change it in any way?

Foreman: The illustrations tend to tell as far as possible the whole story but the text can change over the months during which I am doing the drawings. It is only when the drawings are more or less finished can you see which bits are mystifying to other people. Very often a thing will make obvious sense to me because I have visualised the whole thing and I understand what I am trying to do but where there is a lack of communication you need words to bridge the gaps in time and place.

Boyd: Do you want ultimately to produce a story book without words?

Foreman: I have done two or three in the past. It all depends on how difficult is the story that you are trying to tell. You can tell a very cosy simple story without words but the problem is when you attempt something which is more complicated. For instance, you could tell a very simple story in film like "The Red Balloon" which has very little dialogue, but the films I like are films that throw everything in. My favourite director is Ken Russell. Everybody says that he goes over the top and I think thats what people should do—put it all in and let people take out what they can.

Boyd: If you don't really regard your books as children's books per se, how do you regard them?

Foreman: I think they have much more in common with a popular song. Somebody like Bob Dylan or John Lennon can write about a topic or a subject and they don't consider age groups. A song reflects their attitude to life and can communicate with anybody who has experienced the same thing or hopes for the same thing.

Boyd: Going back into time when you were a child were you an avid reader of children's books?

Foreman: No I had no children's books at all. No books in the house. The nearest thing we had to a book was The Radio Times. I would like my books to be as direct and as simple and strong as comics, comic strips and also as relevant as the newspapers and tv.

Michael Foreman and Michael Boyd, in an interview in Books for Your Children, *Vol. 10, No. 3, May, 1975, p. 2.*

GENERAL COMMENTARY

Derek Birdsall

After a decade which has seen an unprecedented boom in the quantity of graphic design, it is perhaps worth stopping for a moment to see where we have got to in terms of quality. It seems to be a truism that a quantitative increase in anything does not usually lead to a proportionate increase in quality; this seems to hold good in graphics, and particularly in photography and drawn illustration.

There are many illustrators (and for that matter photographers) who are industriously producing thousands of images without making a single observation. It is difficult to know how this has come about. Copyists and critics are obsessed with the apparent 'style' of the image and fail to divorce form from content, to take into account the nature of the catalyst, the artist. Young artists labour under the difficulty of having very few opinions which seem worth communicating; or more exactly, little experience which seems worth sharing.

Whilst this may be more a lack of confidence than of experience, the final result is the same; the learning / doing process gets out of step, and a reliance on mere technique gets in the way of simple observations, simply presented.

Furthermore, the very acceptance of the 'business' of graphic design has led to an increase in the number of artists and designers accepting a functional role as opposed to a conceptual or personal one. This in turn leads to a diminution in the responsibility, if not the ability, that the artist—and particularly the graphic artist—really needs to effect the choice of images available to us, and to bring about the restoration of the increasingly unfashionable—because increasingly inconvenient—role of the individual.

Michael Foreman has to a large degree opted out of the routine role. Whilst he achieved an early success with his children's books, he became aware that this success was already turning sour: increasing commissions from the advertising and commercial world gave him less freedom, not more, and in any case tied him down, and left him less time to travel when the opportunity arose. Yet travel was vital in giving him, quite literally, more experience to draw on.

During the last three or four years he has almost circumnavigated the world; indeed, he has followed the route of Marco Polo from Venice to Peking and travelled the length of the legendary Trans-Siberian railway, which he discovered was still functioning between London's Liverpool Street Station and Vladivostock.

His travels have also included Nigeria, Japan, Indonesia, Fiji and New Mexico; he is currently planning a trip down the Nile. Many of these journeys have been undertaken as a roving reporter for *Pegasus,* the international magazine of Mobil Oil Corporation, many of them at his own suggestion; and it is in this sense, as an entrepreneurial artist; that his role is significant.

He is one of those quiet people whose spaces between their remarks are as meaningful as the remarks themselves; but whose remarks nonetheless have a simplicity and clarity that exactly reflect the nature and quality of their work.

Though speech seems curiously superfluous to Michael, words are certainly significant; his children's stories are as carefully written as they are drawn. Some of the notes in his sketchbooks are as exquisite as the drawings they annotate: 'frequently flooded by the Adriatic and constantly by tourists' (Venice); 'the few high buildings that are being constructed are very Soviet in character and look as strangely obsolete and remote as the heads of Easter Island' (Peking); 'warm orange from the early morning sun spreads slowly across the landscape like a water-colour, seeping into the bones of the earth and frozen limbs of trees' (China); 'it no longer matters if the train is fast or

stopped, we are all suspended, lost in this long long bedroom, with real flowers for wallpaper' (Trans-Siberian Railway).

His own notes reveal the integrity behind his drawings. The drawings themselves show him to be a romantic *animator:* he draws animals better than people, and people better than things. His world, like that of all romantics, is not peopled by people: one suspects his ideal world would consist only of Eve and all the animals: animals for whom he has invented a mythology of his own.

If he has a style, it is elegance, but it is as an observer and to no mean extent as a draughtsman that he makes his work utterly convincing. As George Bernard Shaw said, 'Artists do not prove things. They do not need to. They know them.' (p. 446)

> *Derek Birdsall, "Michael Foreman," in* Graphics, *Vol. 32, No. 187, 1976-77, pp. 446-51.*

Carolyn Hart

One of Michael Foreman's best known illustrated stories is the hilarious tale of a Mongolian Princess ("a big girl and *dark*") who decides that her future husband must be able to beat her at wrestling—if he fails he must give her father, the King, 100 horses. The Princess is an unruly character and while her suitors don't stand a chance, the King winds up with a lot of horses. At last a large and handsome woodcutter arrives (the King is beside himself with pleasure; "It will serve my daughter right to get lumbered with a lumberjack") but while the Princess is sizing up his large and handsome muscles she hears the whinney of horses and the clink of hooves and without hesitation chucks the gorgeous woodcutter over the heads of the watching crowd and rides off into the Mongolian sunset, complete with all the King's horses.

"I wrote it for a small girl who was mad about horses" says Michael Foreman, disarmingly "but she thought it was terrible—what she *really* wanted was the handsome Prince, not the horses at all." *All the Kings' Horses* was hailed as the precursor of women's lib in children's fiction. Its author says he's not too sure about the women's lib content but admits that out of all his earlier books it's the one that received the most attention. In fact, it's only one title in a large and widely acclaimed output: part of a career which began when he sold his first book at the age of 21 to Routledge and which, apart from a brief sojourn at *Playboy* and its English equivalent, *King* ("I used to draw all the cartoons for *King* and sign different names to them"), has been continuing, increasingly successfully, ever since.

Foreman himself seems a far cry from the cigar-smoking image of most *Playboy* entrepreneurs. He is a quietly spoken, shy man of devastating handsomeness—he looks at least ten years younger than he is (but he has a son of 20, a friend of his assured me)—who divides his time between trips abroad (mostly with a sketchbook and rucksack), a house in St Ives, Cornwall and a studio in London where he lives with his wife and (second) small son.

He was born in Suffolk where his parents had a newsa-

The rocket ship made stops all along the way. The helicopters darted out, and the robbers slid down chimney after chimney.

But now a surprising thing began to happen. All of the children's angry shouts turned to cheers. The robbers were amazed. They began to grin behind their beards. It was a lot more fun than stealing.

From The Great Sleigh Robbery, *written and illustrated by Michael Foreman.*

gents shop (a drawing of the shop and the room in which he was born appears on the end papers of **Christmas Carol**) and spent much of his youth delivering newspapers. "We didn't have any books at all when I was a child, so I was never saturated with book illustrations, although I did read all the magazines we used to get in". The major influences on his work have been, therefore, not the pictures of established children's artists like Dulac and Rackham, but the Old Masters and an assortment of comic-strip characters and cartoons, which may explain the often quirky drawings and odd animals and children that adorn the pages of his books.

Apart from his own books, which include **War and Peas, The Panda and the Odd Lion, All the King's Horses** and **Land of Dreams,** Foreman has also illustrated the work of Hans Christian Andersen, Dickens, Robert McCrum (**The Brontosaurus Birthday Cake**), David Garner and Terry Jones, whose acclaimed **Fairy Tales,** is a marvellously eccentric collection of thirty new fairy stories. His pictures are full of strange and eerie landscapes, seen mostly at dawn or dusk; moons glimmer through mist, and seas are full of luminous fish while the shores team with exotic animals and birds. Much of his work is the result of his travels abroad. He goes on at least one major trip a year, sometimes for specific books, sometimes not.

His first venture was across Russia on the Trans-Siberian express ("It was like being in a trance, you would spend three days in the same forest"). Last year it was Japan. Next year it will be Australia and India for a collection of Indian fairy tales he is illustrating with Madhur Jaffrey.

"I do a lot of research when I'm travelling—I find it thrilling to discover the particular 'art' of different landscapes and work them into a book. But I find I have to travel by myself, otherwise I'm constantly getting involved in other people's impressions of a place. When I was in China I had to be terribly rude and completely ignore the people I was with. I try to be invisible when I'm travelling, so I tend to listen in on conversations rather than participate in them—I just want to look and draw". The result is a marvellous conglomeration of one man's impressions of foreign landscapes, customs and characters firmly based in the familiar context of a child's world, so that old Chinese gentlemen rub shoulders with angelic European children; exotic butterflies and English frogs are mixed up with Dutch windmills and Byzantine bridges.

His books are unlike any other children's books I have seen in the last few years: they are, far removed from the pop-up, push-up and pull-out books that are all the rage at the moment, relying far more on atmosphere, imagination and a sense of humour. Of current children's illustrators he most admires Quentin Blake—"Blake draws directly from childhood, and I think he is very underrated." Michael Foreman himself has been writing and illustrating children's books for almost two decades, and seems entirely satisfied with his lot. "I enjoy the work I do enormously. It allows me complete freedom of expression and I can make a living out of it at the same time—there's really nothing else I would rather be doing."

> *Carolyn Hart, "Travelling Artist," in* Books and Bookmen, *No. 339, December, 1983, p. 29.*

Elaine Moss

Michael Foreman's picture books, direct descendants of the pre-war comics like *Rainbow,* have a limitless visual appeal, but young children are obviously put out by the lack of concrete answers (in their terms) to the questions Foreman poses. To them it is most unsatisfactory that, in *Panda's Puzzle,* they follow the bear on his long quest to find out whether he is a black bear with white patches or a white bear with black patches, only to discover that it doesn't really matter. Older readers understand the deeper philosophical content of this book. They read *Moose* as a political commentary on the sabre-rattling that goes on between Russia (Bear in the story) and the United States (a fierce Eagle); and they are intrigued by the idea of dinosaurs finding modern Earth too disgusting to live on—an idea Michael Foreman explores in *Dinosaurs and All that Rubbish.* His *All the King's Horses* is the only funny book I know about woman power and therefore wields more clout (it is about an Amazonian princess who wrestles all her suitors out of the ring) than all the deadly serious tomes on Women's Lib put together. (pp. 127-28)

> *Elaine Moss, " 'Signal' Contributions: 1970-1980," in her* Part of the Pattern: A Personal Journey through the World of Children's Books, 1960-1985, *Greenwill Books, 1986, pp. 45-160.*

Douglas Martin

[In the late 1950s, Foreman] sought entry to the Royal College of Art, but had to consider how to make the best use of the year that would elapse between applying and getting in. The freelance market had to be explored; outlets for commercial drawings for the press in his Camden Town locality were readily established, but he was conscious that the fine art bias of his portfolio was ill-calculated to achieve a breakthrough at a wider and more viable level.

To remedy this, he worked on a tentative story-line and began to produce sample drawings for a picture book. These were submitted to Routledge & Kegan Paul. They were not at the time active publishers of children's books, but Sir Herbert Read, then a director of the company, was actively committed to the Campaign for Nuclear Disarmament, and so the book came to be published as *The General* with a text by Janet Charters, Michael Foreman's first wife.

The book had quite an impact; it was recognisable as a pacifist tract for the times (that made it 'communist-inspired' in the United States), but it was also hailed by art students as a breakthrough by a contemporary. It remains remarkably fresh and immediate, despite a well-discharged debt to André François in the handling of certain passages. Routledge offered him a couple of other titles to illustrate in this same year, but apart from that he was destined to be absent from the book publishing scene for almost six working years. (p. 294)

Michael Foreman's return to book illustration in 1967 was signalled by the publication of two new picture books to his own texts, *The Perfect Present* and *The Two Giants.* He did these largely because he recognised that he was no longer known in the field and therefore people simply weren't offering him books to illustrate. *The Two Giants* makes brilliant use of torn-paper technique, which suggested itself as an answer to some of the technical problems to be encountered in subsequent adaptation to film animation:

> I was approached by some young people in Denmark for permission to make an animated film of *The General.* They had no money, but they liked it, and so I said 'Sure', and went over to do extra drawings and we became very friendly, but I saw how difficult it was to animate pictures of that kind. So I thought of torn-up paper shapes for *The Two Giants* as these could be easily manipulated in order to overcome many of these problems.

Technical problems of this sort have apparently always held a fascination for Michael Foreman. He evinces similar concern for print quality, and visits colour printers whenever possible to discover how far the artist's presence or intervention can influence the final result. There is a preoccupation with transcribing the quality, tone and texture of the paper which the artist has used to that on which the book is to be printed. Reproduction houses are quite used to capturing the colour image from the sheet, whilst suppressing most of the effect from this substrate; but Foreman builds up his effects with a reliance on the integrity of the paper surface to the extent that he must start again if things go wrong. His celebrated 'grainy' watercolour effect depends not only on the printer's facsimile reproduction of the texture of rough handmade paper, but on his own skill in causing and controlling the precipitation of watercolour pigment particles from the wash. Foreman claims that he sometimes mixes-in sugar, gravel or even boot polish to build up these luminous washes and reticulated textures. He uses concentrated watercolour in preference to the traditional 'cakes' for the added brilliance they confer, combining the best properties of watercolour with those of coloured inks. But at the end of the day he recognises that it is the objective printed result which has to count, and admits that the grainy effect often becomes more pronounced along the way.

In taking 1967 as the year in which it becomes possible to identify book illustration as the clear path that Michael Foreman has chosen for the future, it is interesting to observe that the approximate total of books illustrated in the decade 1967-76 (27) is doubled by that for 1977-86 (54). The rate of output for his own picture books however remains steady (8 and 7 respectively), and this is perhaps to be explained by the fact that as entrepreneur he was taking his own book output to his publisher on a package proposal basis, whereas publishers were slower to commission him to illustrate other kinds of book and to identify those fields in which he would excel. [He had remarked] that at first he could not afford to do more book illustration . . . , [but this comment] should not be taken simply at its economic face-value—for then all illustrators could say the same; rather it has to do with his whole working approach, above all with his need to travel to specific locations, which under-powered commissions could not hope to fund even in part.

At this point it may be more rewarding to discuss this obsession with travel, and to try to map out some other underlying features which characterise his individual approach, although this entails disregarding the chronology of the books he has illustrated.

It was for his work as a *travel* illustrator that he was honoured with the designation 'Royal Designer for Industry', and travel and its converse—staying at home—provide a key to his visual inspiration. In over-simplified terms, he believes that ersatz experience or the second-hand image can never suffice, for children least of all. And so Alan Garner leads inexorably to Alderley Edge, Madhur Jaffrey to a four-week journey through India. **Panda and the Bushfire** required a seven-week trip to Australia, and he revisited the southern hemisphere recently to gain background for some retellings of Maori legends. These are merely a few episodes taken at random from the log of a prodigious traveller, who heads for Heathrow rather than to the reference library in search of authenticity. There are few countries he hasn't visited by now, at times following up a given assignment, at others pursuing a momentary impulse that may relate to some as yet undefined project.

Sometimes a chance synthesis of some of this material seems within reach, as when a publisher found him uniquely placed to illustrate an anthology of universal prayer drawn from cultures all round the world. However, the corpus of unpublished sketchbooks and finished works resulting from his travels constitute Foreman's visual autobiography, which will surely start to find its way into print in due course.

If travel brings back a cargo which adds something to the text for children unable to make the voyage for themselves, then this is rationale enough for his work as an illustrator; but staying at home can be equally special. In the way in which Stanley Spencer saw biblical events taking place in his native Cookham, if to a lesser degree, Michael Foreman draws family, friends and places, in Fulham or at St Ives, Cornwall. They appear unexpectly in his illustrations for a wide range of authors. This is a coinage not to be debased: it belongs to a personal vision and to literary affinities freshly discovered:

> As a child we had no books in the house at all. I didn't really have that habit. But now I tend to come to read books for the first time, that's to say classics, when I'm asked to illustrate them. To some extent I think that's a little bit

fortunate, because I haven't had other artists' pictures in my brain before . . .

Foreman speaks quietly and economically, personally and through his work, although one never underestimates the power which is held in reserve. There are superficial characteristics which make his style instantly recognisable from book to book, and yet each is very different. Many of the gentler watercolours and line drawings rest on the page, sharing a common reading plane with the typography, and in this way the poetry of the illustrations unfolds in pace with the text. In practice it is rare for words and pictures to be brought together so naturally, and illustrators frequently lack this technical ability to *accompany* a text, depending on others to find the best compromise between their drawings and what is possible in terms of typography and book production. Foreman attributes many insights in this area to his long friendship and numerous collaborations with the distinguished book typographer, Derek Birdsall.

Technical mastery of the whole picture surface is fundamental to his skill in resolving three dimensions into two, whatever the depth of field; that is to say, there are no 'throw-away' areas, weak passages or ill-considered edges. Unless the intention is contrary, this induces an initial effect of calm which is qualified into a precise mood after a few moments of the observer's attention. Calm resolves into childhood recall or dreamland, isolation or engrossment. Sentimentality is absent, and the sharp factual recapture of a childhood activity precludes nostalgia. This can perhaps be seen at its best in **A Child's Garden of Verses**—a wonderfully illustrated book.

Foreman believes that every manuscript or text should set the artist off on a new line of enquiry, and yet it suits his working method to have two or more projects in concurrent progress, since he likes to be able to dodge from one to another should a temporary block develop. Each published title works on its own terms for the reader, but the range and variety of handling and style only really become apparent when a collection of his books are studied comparatively. The selection of favourites becomes a subjective matter where standards and output are are so uniformly high, as has been the case throughout the past decade; but my personal short-list would have to include his two early picture books, **The General** and **The Two Giants,** for their verve, directness and staying power. **Moose** and **Dinosaurs and all that Rubbish** are fine examples of his middle-period picture books for Hamish Hamilton. Alan Garner's **The Stone Book Quartet** is a splendid achievement. . . . (pp. 302-07)

Michael Foreman's work for children's books has been widely honoured, but the popularity ratings accorded by children themselves must count for even more. He is greatly sought after these days, and has to turn away more titles than some equally professional colleagues possessed of a more catholic range. He has always had the integrity to do that whenever confronted by a project for which he felt insufficient commitment, and which might have yielded a result below his consistent personal best. (p. 307)

Douglas Martin, "Michael Foreman," in his
The Telling Line: Essays on Fifteen Contem-

porary Book Illustrators, Julia MacRae Books, 1989, pp. 291-311.

Donnarae MacCann and Olga Richard

Michael Foreman's picture books are a profile of an era. Born in 1938, Foreman has been unavoidably influenced by the trauma of the cold war, the trashing of the planet, and the many confusions about identity that take form in estrangements and self-doubt. If all this seems a bit heavy for children's books, we are simply forgetting the dynamics of the creative process. As an artist, Foreman expresses himself and his surroundings; his metaphoric statements are not necessarily limited to particular age groups. The struggles over international peace, an undefiled planet, and an inner-directed personality—these have been an integral part of Foreman's generation. Their expression is traceable in every art form.

As we take a retrospective look at some of his major works, we discern these public and personal themes. Additionally, Foreman alludes to parenting in books about "Ben" and to his own childhood in *War Boy.* Unlike the picture books, *War Boy* is not for the very young, but it is one of the important literary events of 1990. This chronicle of war-torn England is one of the rare autobiographies by a major figure in contemporary children's literature, and it is a moving memoir of wartime and its unique madness in the life of a child.

Foreman has designated one of his antiwar picture books—*War and Peas*—as a work that will perhaps survive the test of time. He has produced, however, a small but significant body of works that focus on conflict resolution. *The Two Giants* is one of the best. The characters go to battle over a seashell, but soon discover that they are wearing mismatched socks. This revelation helps the giants regain their sense of perspective and humor. And, perhaps, the sock pairs also provide a hint of interdependence. In any case, amicability is restored, and mismatched socks become the order of the day as a reminder and a precaution.

The foolishness of conflict has rarely been presented with such spontaneous symbolism and visual audacity. Foreman emphasizes the intrinsic shapes of things. He makes them large enough to command attention, minimizes their few embellishments, and leaves ample space for inventive arrangements. The book is bold and colorful as the result of Foreman's intuitive design sense and the rich color-over-color masses that he constructs with tissue paper and watercolor.

Moose is a more explicit antiwar fable. Here Foreman allows no ambiguity as to the identity of the principal contenders, nor does he avoid proposing a role for a neutral country. This neutral player is a peace-loving animal who builds a shelter from the sticks and stones being hurled back and forth by an eagle and a bear. In time, the allies of the antagonists become more fascinated with the shelter than with the battle. This leaves Eagle and Bear to grumble and rumble by themselves, while the other creatures join Moose in building a Mooseum and an Amoosement Park.

In this book, Foreman's text is more impressive than his illustrations. The narrative is clever, well constructed, and plausible in its treatment of characterization.

> Moose was just an ordinary Moose. He worked a little too hard, got cross in hot weather, and was poor. What he liked best was to sit outside in the cool of the evening and sing quietly to himself.

This passage sounds as if the author might be describing his perception of himself, and it is the specifics of that selfhood that make the portrait convincing. The drawings, however, reflect a cartoonish influence that makes them all too predictable. They lack that strong personal touch that characterizes Foreman's best work. Moose's shelter is not persuasive as architecture or as abstraction. Like the churlish bad folks and the innocent good folks, the shelter is little more than a conventional cartoon. Still, this book has some rare moments: the scenes with the neurotic Eagle bellowing at Moose, the portraits of Bear's cronies, the utopian setting and its magical patterns on the last page.

War and Peas adds famine to the war theme. An emaciated King Lion bicycles to a neighboring realm to seek foreign aid. This neighbor, Fat King, chases him off and ends up wallowing in the sugary desserts spilling from his army's supply trucks. His tanks, meanwhile, become mired in their own tracks, and this opens the way for friendly birds to sow seeds in the tire ruts—a plan that will ultimately reduce the chronic shortages. But offers of peace from King Lion only confuse the greedy potentate: " 'Never heard of it,' said the Fat King. 'What's the recipe?' "

Watercolors (usually reserved for more conservative ideas) are used here to create a frenzy of color, shape, and movement. Puddings and pies surround the war machines, and the result is as ludicrous as it sounds. Foreman designs the desserts in the super-real manner of food commercials, and he characterizes the overindulgent monarch in such a way that he resembles a pudgy confection. King Lion, on the other hand, is a lean Don Quixote-type. This set of contrasts controls the narrative line, while the setting becomes increasingly playful in a design sense. It moves from richly textured cakes and tarts to an outrageous culinary climax.

Besides these antiwar tales, several antipollution stories were created early in Foreman's career. In *Dinosaurs and All That Rubbish* an industrialist fancies a distant star and plans a journey to the new land. His rocket-building factories spew smoke and rubbish until not a shrub or tree remains on earth. The protagonist soon abandons his new planet, finding that there is nothing there, and heads for *another* star. Meanwhile, dinosaurs break through the earth's crust and vow to clean up the mess. When the industrialist reaches his new star, he discovers it is Earth, a green and lovely Earth. "At last," he says, "I have found my star." But he is in for a good tongue-lashing: "If you had been ruled by your heart instead of your head," says a dinosaur, "you would not have ruined this beautiful place when you lived here before."

In his illustrations, Foreman devises a funny little man

who is quiet and unassuming. He does not yearn for bigger factories; he merely longs for a star because it is a thing of beauty. But when this small wish becomes a large environmental problem, the artist has some difficulty in translating such an essentially cerebral concept into colors and shapes. The brooding, toxic, urban landscapes do not combine successfully with cutesy, lime-colored dinosaurs. The former are serious and painterly, the latter are greeting cardlike and trivial by comparison. In short, the wasteland and all its contaminants are more impressive than the agents of restoration! Yet, Foreman does establish and sustain his premise, and his compelling images of a poisoned planet are an integral part of the parable.

Another allegory about conservation, *Trick a Tracker,* is less focused on a social theme. Animals in the story outfox our cave-dwelling ancestors by inventing skateboards and swooping down upon the unsuspecting hunters. This reduces the success of the trackers, who ultimately begin chasing each other as "truck drivers, coach drivers, car drivers, motorcyclists, speed cops, road hogs." The folks have tricked themselves, and the animals return to their old ways and wild habitats.

Pictorially the animals range from modeled to linear shapes. Some have textured edges, and some are slick like the scary wigglies that kids carry to school in their pockets. Using ingenious perspective devices, Foreman enhances interest in his skateboarding beasts, but he really excels in this book in his portrayals of people. They are snappy, low-keyed figures who race about in a suitably crazed condition, but minus the kitsch that occasionally infects Foreman's other creatures.

Most of Foreman's other writings divide into two additional thematic groups. In one he performs as a philosopher, and in the other, as a father. In the inspirational stories, his emphasis is upon the need for inner-direction and self-determination. *The Travels of Horatio* features some all-too-believable hippo-parents. Father advises son: "Mud was good enough for my father and his father and his father's father. It's good enough for me, and for your mother, and it should be good enough for you." But Horatio must go his own way, and there is a nice logic in making a young hippo a member of a moving van crew. Pushing pianos is no sweat, but then one gets stuck in Horatio's mouth, and the pianist must perch on his tooth as he concertizes. Foreman is good at mixing a dab of logic with volumes of imagination and then finding a thoroughly satisfying finale.

This television film (which later became a book) combines various visual techniques. Foreman's hippos are bulky masses of wet color or scratchy line, his birds are flatly decorative, and his urban architecture is softened with washes over the buildings. Each page is different, but they all share the artist's courageous and inventive design sense, as well as his humor.

Horatio's quest is mild compared to the introspective struggle in *Panda's Puzzle, and His Voyage of Discovery.* A bear is plagued with the worry "Am I a white bear with black bits or a black bear with white bits?" The individuals he encounters in his journey supply no clear answer, but their diversity suggests to Panda an alternative focus and identity. He is content when he finally labels himself "a traveller who plays tunes." That ends the quest, but for the reader the journey has been rich in allusions to values, perspectives, and the many ambiguities that unsettle us.

Some unevenness is not surprising in such an ambitious work. The discrepancy here rests in the fascinating existential difficulties versus their rather bland visualization. Pictures lack the tension and cohesive design that such a provocative narrative deserves. There is, however a big sense of loneliness and emptiness that underscores the worldwide dimensions of the setting. And, as in all of Foreman's work, individual objects are conceived with great sensitivity.

The pictorial cohesiveness that is missing in *Panda's Puzzle* is fully realized in another philosophical story: *Land of Dreams.* This poetic work blends its uplifting text with a subtle color technique. Its leading characters are retrievers of lost dreams, which they repair and return to the world of mortals. Foreman paints their fanciful, icy realm so as to maximize the illusion of space, and he designs color accents in their patchwork clothing. The lively costumes do not disturb the basic style, the unobtrusive merging of sculpted objects with a vast environment.

With similar harmony and stylistic consistency, Foreman developed books on domesticity, as in *Ben's Baby*—an homage to mothers. He started his second family after 1980 (he had already fathered one child in the 1960s) and showed the same enthusiasm for family chronicles as for books about hard, existential problems. *Ben's Baby* is a simple, fact-based account of family outings and hospital visits at the time that Foreman's third child was born. Visually, the book transcends the limited scope of its subject. The artist's graphic technique accommodates an unmistakably affirmative response to life. Consider the rooms full of new mothers or the folks on the playground. Foreman's mood-building methods can be discerned in characterizations, color accents, subtle shadings, and sympathetic groupings.

We turn, finally, to just one example of Foreman's collaboration with a separate author, although this is an important and distinguished aspect of his professional life. Ann Turnbull's *The Sand Horse* (1989) was an ideal test for him—a fantasy about a horse carved in sand and longing to join the ocean waves that we typically personify as "white horses." The carver and his neighbors are designed as small figures against a spacious sea and sky, and they share with the sculpted horse a feeling of wistful, fleeting impermanence. The pale colors, elusive edges, and arrangements of small shapes add a hint of tragedy as well as peace to these shadowy, well-drawn forms. Then the mood changes, and we watch the drama of the ephemeral horse breaking free of his sandy constraints and roaring into the smashing waves. Foreman makes the contrast vivid. Waves, gulls, and horses are white-touched, ice-blue shapes against a brilliant blue-green sea. The sand horse, alone in the scene after the beachgoers leave, is a haunting image.

War Boy, as we mentioned at the outset, is an autobiogra-

The Dragon King changed into a whirlwind and, whisking down to the cauldron, snatched up the chilly dragon and bore him off to the Northern Ocean. Presently the Wizard was slithering about in the boiling oil trying desperately to get out, but alas! before long his skin was cooked, his flesh was stewed and his bones had been boiled apart.

From Monkey and the Three Wizards, *written by Michael Foreman and Peter Harris. Illustrated by Michael Foreman.*

phy, not a "picture book" as we usually use the term. But the book is full of pictures and provides a compendium of Foreman's most effective styles. The artist's strong, honest aesthetics works to imbue everything with feelings suitable to the times and events. Whether he draws the tensions of war or the restfulness of the English countryside, he dazzles us with his beautiful line work, atmospheric watercolors, and explicit architectural designs.

Interviewers have, of course, queried Foreman in an effort to explain his talent. Responding to these probes, he lists some major influences in his life: Kenneth Grahame's *Wind in the Willows* (which he encountered at the age of fifteen), his many travels, and the politically inspired songs of Bob Dylan and John Lennon. Certainly Foreman is a romantic like Grahame, and, in the manner of Dylan and Lennon, he lets his art and his social conscience freely connect. But there is more to Foreman than pastoral charm and political activism. One suspects that his immersion in difficult subjects is accompanied by a vision of youthful explorers, readers with untold promise. That respect for the young makes all the difference. It leads in the direction of persistent experimentation—creative solutions on behalf of an eager, impressionable audience. (pp. 107-09)

> *Donnarae MacCann and Olga Richard, "Picture Books for Children," in* Wilson Library Bulletin, *Vol. 65, No. 7, March, 1991, pp. 107-09.*

TITLE COMMENTARY

The Perfect Present (1967)

An oversize picture book in which Santa Claus, appealed to by an unhappy double-decker bus in London, takes the bus on a ride through the sky. The bus suggests that the rest of the traffic would enjoy the same treat, so Santa shouts, "Come on!" to two milk carts and a policeman on a bicycle; eventually the parade in the sky has a seafood stall, some burglars, a flock of priests, grannies in wheelchairs, children in hospital beds, a truckload of unsold Christmas trees, and so on. Landing in Trafalgar Square, the people have a party and the vehicles honk horns and wink headlights. Only the bus hears Santa's sleighbells as he takes off, but all the rest of the year the vehicles smile to themselves as they remember their perfect present— free flight. The illustrations are very handsome: bold, bright paintings of night skies filled with the strange entourage and of London scenes. The story has an element of the ludicrous that has some appeal, but the style is so stiff and the plot so contrived that the situation seems bizarre rather than funny.

> *Zena Sutherland, in a review of "The Perfect Present," in* Bulletin of the Center for Children's Books, *Vol. 21, No. 3, November, 1967, p. 41.*

Michael Foreman has brought off a good double. His story

for *The Perfect Present* is original, lively and pointed. His illustrations match precisely the down-to-earth—if up in the sky—fantasy of his text. Father Christmas gives an abandoned London bus a treat and takes it for a ride over London, and they are joined by all sorts of people and things, burglars, a flock of cycling priests, a fire-engine, children in hospital beds, a circus, in an exhilarating and seasonable flight. The views of London are quite lovely, and so is the dead-pan seriousness of it all.

> *A review of "The Perfect Present," in* The Junior Bookshelf, *Vol. 31, No. 6, December, 1967, p. 371.*

The Two Giants (1967)

Michael Foreman's illustrations for his original fable are bright and imaginative, but his story offers little to warrant that careful treatment. Two giants, Sam and Boris, live together in perfect harmony until the day they quarrel over a sea shell. Enemies now, a flood nearly overtakes them and they seek refuge on two mountaintops and take turns hurling stones at one another. Just as destruction is imminent, their startled glances reveal that each is wearing one of the other's socks. The fight is ended by this reminder of former friendship, and they promise always to exchange socks—"just in case." Moral suasion for peace, but the children won't be impressed.

> *Barbara S. Miller, in a review of "The Two Giants," in* School Library Journal, *Vol. 14, No. 4, December, 1967, p. 60.*

This is a grand story told with fine economy, and with appropriately enormous pictures, so crude as to conceal the art which has gone into making them. The artist makes interesting use of textures. This is one of those books which the children like much better than their parents do, and even the nasty ones will hardly quarrel with the admirable moral.

> *A review of "The Two Giants," in* The Junior Bookshelf, *Vol. 32, No. 1, February, 1968, pp. 27-8.*

The anti-war moral attached to this folk-tale puts no brake on the comedy in the pictures, which show the giants falling out, contesting with rocks and making friends again when the sight of their odd socks dissolves anger in laughter. The illustrations play on the idea of size. The giants are shown in close-up and at a distance and at points between the two, and this effectively compensates for a story which is virtually one simple statement.

> *Margery Fisher, in a review of "The Two Giants," in* Growing Point, *Vol. 6, No. 8, March, 1968, p. 1079.*

The Great Sleigh Robbery (1968)

Michael Foreman produced a topical book last Christmas, the best really Christmassy book of the season. He does it again this year. *The Great Sleigh Robbery* tells the exciting story of how the most successful robbers in the world kidnapped Santa Claus. They brought off the coup brilliantly in mid-air, but they had not allowed for the reaction of children all over the world. Wherever they came down to land they were met by hordes of furious infants. At last they had to do a deal with Santa Claus and to help him in his now delayed operation. Some, but not all of the villains were converted by this experience. Mr. Foreman adopts an appropriately serious air in the telling of the story. His pictures are cruder than we expect from him and some of the colour is psychedelic in its garishness. Where he excels is in minute humorous detail. There are innumerable delightful and hilarious touches.

> *A review of "The Great Sleigh Robbery," in* The Junior Bookshelf, *Vol. 32, No. 6, December, 1968, p. 357.*

Everybody from the Eskimos to the Pacific Islanders believes in Santa Claus in this whackabout but if you can go that far with Mr. Foreman, the rest is easy to take. Almost as easy as it was for Triggerfinger Joe and his band of robbers to intercept Santa by helicopter and carry him off in their rocket. The hard part is trying to land: witnesses to the kidnapping have spread word around the world so that wherever the rocket goes, angry children appear (massed blacks with white eyes in the jungle, climbers strung out around "the mountains of the East"). At last, low on fuel, the robbers would let Santa go—but he's late and insists they help with deliveries (a hilarious scene: Santa-clothed robbers descending chimneys from helicopter ladders). The next morning, though Triggerfinger Joe and two of his men steal Santa's silver, the others remain to help invent new toys (some of them weapons) and generally keep up the holiday spirit. As audaciously colored and conceived as Tomi Ungerer if not as cutting, and a relief, at least, from the usual Christmas goody-goodies.

> *A review of "The Great Sleigh Robbery," in* Kirkus Reviews, *Vol. XXXVII, No. 16, August 15, 1969, p. 849.*

The full page illustrations in this 8" × 10¾" book are lushly colored and drawn with skill, but their content is often aimed at adults—the Mona Lisa is hanging in Triggerfinger Joe's office. Also, the story reads like a political satire, especially the ending with the takeover of Santa by organized crime. It's too grimly possible to be comic. (p. 169)

> *Marilyn R. Singer, "Inside the Vacuum of Reverence," in* School Library Journal, *Vol. 16, No. 2, October, 1969, pp. 168-71.*

Horatio (1970; U.S. edition as The Travels of Horatio)

There is a magic that only writers of children's books can perform: they know the trick of turning an animal, fearful or repulsive in real life, into a lovable or funny character. It's magic that only good writers know. And Michael Foreman is a good writer with a wild, free imagination. (You remember his *The Great Sleigh Robbery* and *The Two Giants*.) In *The Travels of Horatio* he transforms one of the most repulsive of animals, the hippopotamus, into a beguiling dreamer who leaves home and mother to see the wonders of the world. What he finds and what he does about it make for a wonderfully wise and funny book.

> *A review of "The Travels of Horatio," in* Publishers Weekly, *Vol. 198, No. 23, December 7, 1970, p. 50.*

Not content to wallow in the mud for the rest of his days like all the other hippos, Horatio wanted to dance, to fly kites. He wanted to see the world. A favourite theme no doubt, but endowed here with a striking freshness. Horatio arrives in the big city, becomes a furniture remover and then by accident and subsequent ingenuity sees his dream come true: instant fame as one half of a concert duo. Michael Foreman has done some excellent books in the past, marked by a ceaseless flow of original ideas, but this is quite his best achievement. His crowds are marvellously funny spectacles, his jungle scenes ablaze with colour. Yet the most remarkable picture of all is that of the hippo, alone and far above the city, flying his kite and dwarfed by the massive wall of sky-scrapers. A splendid book with pages whose texture and appearance are a joy to behold.

> *Jeff Jackson, in a review of "Horatio," in* Children's Book Review, *Vol. I, No. 1, February, 1971, p. 14.*

Horatio, the hippo, thinks there must be more to life than mud, so he sets off to see the world. The culmination of his adventures occurs when a grand piano he is moving to the concert hall opens up and gets stuck in his mouth. The concert is played then and there, and Horatio irresistibly begins to dance to the music. At the end of the piece, "unable to contain all the music in his heart," Horatio lets go a great whistle, thereby spewing both Maestro Pizzetti and the piano from his mouth. Instant fame, in the form of a TV contract and a world tour, greets this foolish freak show. Some of the vivid watercolor illustrations are imaginative and effective (e.g., palm trees with pink, yellow and orange trunks and varicolored fronds); but they can't redeem the vacuuous tale.

> *Melinda Schroeder, in a review of "The Travels of Horatio," in* School Library Journal, *Vol. 17, No. 7, March, 1971, pp. 118-19.*

Moose (1971)

Michael Foreman made a reputation with sparkling humour and bold draughtsmanship. His new book marks an advance—or possibly a retreat. He enters the world of satire, which is doubtful territory for someone speaking to children. Moose is a homely soul whose peace is disturbed by the cold and later the warm war between the bear and the bald-headed eagle. He builds himself a fascinating structure out of the debris of the war, and this interests all the animals so much that they leave the warmongers to get on with it alone. The message is underlined with some naive symbolism—the eagle's eyrie is among mountains which look like skyscrapers and he smokes fat cigars, and Moose's pleasure-garden develops into a heart-shape. The drawing is mostly crude.

> *M. Crouch, in a review of "Moose," in* The Ju-

nior Bookshelf, *Vol. 36, No. 1, February, 1972, p. 22.*

A political satire about an innocent moose caught in the middle of a battle between Eagle (America) and Bear (Russia). Moose attempts to reason with them, but when they won't listen he begins to build a beautiful utopia with the sticks and stones they have been hurling at each other. As the war continues, Eagle drafts monkeys in hard hats and Bear orders the other animals to come to his aid. The illustration of Bear's army shows strong elephants and hippos on the front lines with the smaller, frightened and confused animals behind them. Soon the armies leave their leaders to help Moose build his shelter and join him in song, and Bear and Eagle are left alone with no weapons. Young children probably won't grasp the Bear-Eagle symbolism, but will definitely feel the strongly conveyed anti-war theme. Except for two spreads where the text suggests evening and the pictures are of daylight, the action-filled color illustrations help to bring across the book's message.

> *Linda Johnson, in a review of "Moose," in* School Library Journal, *Vol. 19, No. 6, February, 1973, p. 58.*

Dinosaurs and All That Rubbish (1972)

[The] strident advocacy of Michael Foreman in ***Dinosaurs and all that Rubbish*** is frankly embarrassing. Mr. Foreman's bowler-hatted hero pollutes his planet in order to build a rocket to reach a star, but on landing there he finds it to be a desolate place and he sets off again for a more attractive one. This, when he arrives, turns out to be Earth—but Earth turned paradise, through the kindly intercession of a group of dinosaurs who have burned all the rubbish in volcanoes and allowed forests 'like a smile around the world' to replace telegraph poles and pylons.

In addition to the crude sentimentalism of this episode, there follows a moment when the brontosaurus ('our heads are the same size, but my heart is much bigger than yours') informs Mr. Bowler Hat: 'This time the earth belongs to everyone, not parts of it to certain people but all of it to everyone, to be enjoyed and cared for'—and the story closes on a grand chorus from all living things: 'EVERYONE! EVERYONE!'.

Messianic fervour of this kind may be unexceptionable in a public meeting, but it is quite out of place in a picture book, and particularly in one like this where it is at odds with such engagingly jolly drawings. Solemn palaeontologists may disapprove of the anthropomorphic dinosaurs and mastodons, but their cavortings among the rubbish and flowers have a puppyish enthusiasm which speaks far louder than the prosy prose. Mr. Foreman showed in ***Moose*** that he could let the pictures do the work; what a pity that he forgot his own lesson here.

> *Brian W. Alderson, in a review of "Dinosaurs and All That Rubbish," in* Children's Book Review, *Vol. II, No. 6, December, 1972, p. 179.*

Michael Foreman's ***Dinosaurs and all that Rubbish*** [is] a more successful modern fable than his earlier *Moose*, which seemed too closely linked to a specific political confrontation. This new story is about pollution, and makes the very valid point that pursuit of a dream is not a particularly worthwhile activity if we ignore the possibly disastrous side-effects of our obsession. Mr. Foreman's story starts with a man whose eyes are so steadfastly fixed on a distant star that he cannot see the terrestrial beauties he is devastating when he orders the building of a rocket to take him there. The heat generated by all the debris from his project awakens a horde of dinosaurs and other prehistoric beasts, and they tidy up the mess, creating a paradise that the man is glad to come home to after his fruitless journey. The message is clear and will bear frequent repetition, and the author's illustrations, whether of endless slagheaps and factory chimneys, or of improbable and exotic flora and fauna, are impressive.

> *"Whispers Down the Wastepipe, Fables for Our Times," in* The Times Literary Supplement, *No. 3692, December 8, 1972, p. 1494.*

Foreman's oddly superreal paintings effectively contrast the dinosaur's tropical paradise with man's dismal world of factory smoke and rubbish, but this fable is just as heavyhanded and muddleheaded about pollution as **Moose** and **The Two Giants** were about war. . . . A creature most children associate with maladaptation and ferocity makes a strange sort of savior for anyone inclined to think about it, but the dinosaur does get off one amusing (if patently senseless) line—"As a matter of fact our heads are almost the same size, but my heart is much bigger than yours"—and maybe we should be content that Foreman's heart is in the right place.

> *A review of "Dinosaurs and All That Rubbish," in* Kirkus Reviews, *Vol. XLI, No. 8, April 15, 1973, p. 452.*

War and Peas (1974)

The opening of Michael Foreman's **War and Peas** looks promising: a crowned and skinny lion in steel-blue armor—a kind of Don Quixote on wheels—bicycles through a dusty yellow landscape. He is the king of a drought-stricken country, en route to a rich neighbor in search of foreign aid. Next door an obese ruler sits on a throne set among layer-cake mountains and skyscrapers of ice cream parfait—presumably a realm of high nutrition though there doesn't seem to be a protein in the place. In any case, the fat king's going to keep it all. The skinny ruler pedals home empty-handed and pursued, for some reason, by tanks, trucks, the Light Brigade and a bloated army in mottled fatigues mounting a fullscale invasion. But virtue triumphs, fat fighters being none too good at their trade. The army is disposed of in eight pages and the drought in two sentences: "Just look at those fields. Your army trucks have dug up our land and now the seeds will grow." (In case you're wondering about the title: the fat king greedy to the end, mistakes peace for *peas*. Seems he's never heard of the former.) Good intentions, unfortunately, are not enough to sustain Foreman's tale. His point is weakened by an undistinguished text and his often sensitive art ill served by his heavy-handed attempt at allegory.

> *Ann Sperber, in a review of "War and Peas," in* The New York Times Book Review, *January 12, 1975, p. 8.*

The heavy-handed contrast drawn between a nation of hard-working needy animals in human dress and a greedy kingdom of overfed people overshadows the humor in this attractive picture book.

> *Judith S. Kronick, in a review of "War and Peas," in* School Library Journal, *Vol. 21, No. 7, March, 1975, p. 87.*

Michael Foreman's parable is, supposedly, a plea for peace but it doesn't come off. At the story's conclusion, the Lion says "Peace" to the Fat King, who replies: "Never heard of it. . . . What's the recipe?" Is this book really a request for peace and sharing or merely a vehicle for Mr. Foreman to demonstrate his brilliant graphic art talents? The book *is* beautiful: muted watercolor scenes contrast with huge collages of cakes, cookies, malteds and luscious desserts. All the world loves "pretty" pictures, but whether the content of this book can stand on its own merit is a real question.

> *EdCelina Marcus Snowden, in a review of "War and Peas," in* Interracial Books for Children Bulletin, *Vol. 6, No. 1, 1975, pp. 4-5.*

All the King's Horses (1976)

This witty and elegant picture book is less pretentious than some other works by Michael Foreman but nevertheless it conveys its moral—this time it is women's lib. A princess in Asia is 'a BIG girl. And *dark*'. Her father wants to marry her off, but she wants a man she can respect, one who can wrestle with her. Any man who fails has to give the king a hundred horses. The princess mangles all her suitors including the statutory huge and handsome young woodcutter and prefers her freedom riding the wide plains with the thousands of horses her father has gained. The design and colouring, the spaciousness of the landscape are continually pleasing. The humour would probably attract older children than the usual picture book age group. While the moral is obvious, the wittiness carries it off. (pp. 7-8)

> *Gillian A. Leary, in a review of "All the King's Horses," in* Children's Book Review, *Vol. VI, October, 1976, pp. 7-8.*

Taking a cue from the Williams/Henstra turnabout fairytales, Foreman has a princess refuse to marry any man she can beat at wrestling. Crowds assemble for the matches at which one rich and powerful contender after another is "twisted and turned, mangled and mauled, and thrown out of the ring." Then a poor but handsome woodcutter's son takes his turn: Foreman as good as rolls the drums, turns up the volume, stops the action—and the handsome youth meets the same fate as the others. At that the princess jumps onto a horse and rides off, followed by "all the king's horses" ("thousands upon thousands"), whom, it is said, she continues to lead—rushing back and forth across Asia in a ghostly something-or-other. Stylish, but senseless—with thin pastel watercolors (of slant-eyed spectators, a brawny Nordic non-hero) which secure the tongue in the cheek but don't engage on their own.

> *A review of "All the King's Horses," in* Kirkus Reviews, *Vol. XLV, No. 13, July 1, 1977, p. 666.*

There are no bones made about the militant feminist message in this harsh tale of a big, strong Asian princess who dumps her despotic father's choice of rich suitors, demanding a man who can match her in the wrestling arena. . . . Foreman's watercolors make skillful and haunting use of surrealistic space and perspective but the evil potentate and the spectators at the public mashings look more and more bestial as the story goes on. Readers find little relief from leering faces in sulphurous highlights, claw-like fingers, and limbs grotesquely bent out of shape.

> *Laura Geringer, in a review of "All the King's Horses," in* School Library Journal, *Vol. 24, No. 1, September, 1977, p. 127.*

Monkey and the Three Wizards (1976)

[Monkey and the Three Wizards *was originally written in Chinese by Ch'eng-en Wu; the English-language version is by Peter Harris.*]

From The Brothers Grimm: Popular Folk Tales, *illustrated by Michael Foreman. Translated by Brian Alderson.*

Monkey and the three Wizards concentrates on one episode in the immensely long traditional tale of the Chinese animal-god, the conflict with the three Asiatic wizards in which Monkey wins passports for himself and his companions to travel to India to obtain Buddhist writings for the monk Tripitaka. The translator explains the legend as a whole and offers conjectures about author and date. He notes that Monkey had acquired magic powers before the contest in which he makes rain, guesses riddles and endures beheading in a way that reveals the King's wizards as animals possessed by evil spirits. Michael Foreman's smooth, diffuse water-colours alternate with line and grey wash on pages tinted blue or grey, in a sumptuous book which, for its elaborate pictures and long, complex text, suggests a readership of seven or so upwards. On the other hand the book could be read aloud to younger children as a way of introducing Monkey, a mythical character fascinating in his alien make-up whose adventures are available for older children to read in Alison Waley's *Dear Monkey* (Blackie 1973; Collins, Lions, 1975), an abridgement of her husband's definitive translation.

> *Margery Fisher, in a review of "Monkey and the Three Wizards," in* Growing Point, *Vol. 15, No. 5, November, 1976, p. 2994.*

[In this book, the] text seems to be just an excuse for delicate chinoiserie from the illustrator, Michael Foreman. Peter Harris in his introduction says that the original which he has translated from the Chinese is probably the work of a 'second-rate poet,' Wu Cheng-en. That being admitted, it might have been better to go all out for what the seventeenth century meant by paraphrase and have a poet re-tell the story. Peter Harris has no doubt been faithful but the result is a wooden prose which has aimed at sounding idiomatic and missed. Monkey himself never emerges as the charming trickster he should be and the end, squeamish parents be warned, is a saga of decapitation, blood and guts without the magical quality of Grimm or Andersen. (p. 22)

> *Maureen Duffy, "The Innocent Eye," in* The Spectator, *Vol. 237, No. 7746, December 11, 1976, pp. 22-3.*

Harris' introduction explains that this was taken from the old Chinese adventure *Journey to the West,* which in turn was based on even older material about a Buddhist monk who traveled to India to collect scriptures for the Emperor; somehow a wonder-working monkey got into the story, and here he gets involved in a series of life-or-death contests with three wizards who turn out to be wild animals possessed by evil spirits. Though their magic is strong, Monkey's is supreme; he starts out by making it rain, thinks nothing of being decapitated (he simply calls back his head as it rolls away), and changes himself with equal ease into a gnat an iron nail. All of this helps get the monk's expedition on its holy way and proves to the local king the superiority of Buddhist magic to that of his false wizards. The source notes could help put this over in the classroom, though out of context Monkey's performance won't strike American children as all that special, and Foreman's theatrical watercolor dreamscapes make him all the more remote. (pp. 280-81)

A review of "Monkey and the Three Wizards," in Kirkus Reviews, *Vol. XLV, No. 6, March 15, 1977, pp. 280-81.*

Monkey's exploits, more fantastic than edifying, make entertaining reading in the great Oriental epic, *Journey to the West.* However, the retelling of a single episode from that novel in which Monkey bests three wizards is pedestrian. Foreman's watercolor illustrations are fanciful but cold, and the long blocks of small type are off-putting.(pp. 47-8)

Allene Stuart Phy, in a review of "Monkey and the Three Wizards," in School Library Journal, *Vol. 24, No. 3, November, 1977, pp. 47-8.*

Panda's Puzzle, and His Voyage of Discovery (1977)

[Michael Foreman] goes from strength to strength, always exploring, through his picture books, fresh ways of expanding the readers' visual and philosophical perception. *Panda's Puzzle,* a delicate Chinese-inspired picture book, is quite the most beautiful Michael Foreman has yet painted. Panda sets out from his mountain on a voyage of discovery in order to decide whether he is "a white bear with black bits or a black bear with white bits". For, says the Buddhist priest, "If you don't know what you are how can you decide anything?" After world-wide adventures Panda returns to the Buddhist monastery:

"Have you discovered what you are?"
"Yes," said Panda, "I'm a traveller who plays tunes."
"So is the wind," said the old man. "But are you a black bear or a white bear?"
"I don't care," laughed Panda,
The old man smiled.
"A great discovery!" he said.

Michael Foreman's mystical book works on the consciousness at many levels like folklore. . . .

Elaine Moss, "Back to Basics," in The Times Literary Supplement, *No. 3949, December 2, 1977, p. 1411.*

Panda's self-conscious quest is self-consciously handled in Foreman's latest message-heavy, picture-pretty artifact. Happy in his forest innocence, Panda suffers an identity crisis when he sees his reflection in the lid, and two bears (one black, one white) on the label, of an empty can "left behind by untidy travelers." "Am I a white bear with black bits or a black bear with white bits?" then becomes Panda's consuming problem, and in his search for the answer he meets various people and animals, each of whom has his own guiding adage. (The flippest: " 'It's all a matter of background,' said the chameleon.") In the end Panda realizes that he too must make his own definition— "I'm a traveler who plays tunes." And as for whether he's black or white, "I don't care!" But, in contrast to the existential conclusion, essence clearly precedes existence in Foreman's abstract presentation, where every encounter is set up to make a point: for example, a lizard positions himself to look down on the proud cockerel, who doesn't mind because the tower cock looks down on the lizard; this prompts Panda to muse that "There must be more to

life than how high up you are"—a line, incidentally, which recalls the more provocative refrain of Sendak's Jennie, just as the tin can image dimly reflects Hoban's "last visible dog." So much for striking out on your own.

A review of "Panda's Puzzle," in Kirkus Reviews, *Vol. XLVI, No. 7, April 1, 1978, p. 367.*

Mr. Foreman's Panda wishes to know whether he is a white bear with black bits or a black bear with white bits, and to find the answer, he travels all around the world, through tender watercolor pictures of everything from the Sphinx to the New York Public Library. . . .

Panda, though it has hints of profundity, has a problem with both text and pictures: They are unable, like their hero, to decide what they are, cartoon or impressionism. Panda decides it doesn't matter what he is, but the book itself leaves its question unresolved.

Natalie Babbitt, in a review of "Panda's Puzzle," in The New York Times Book Review, *April 23, 1978, p. 32.*

The Brothers Grimm: Popular Folk Tales (1978)

[The Brothers Grimm: Popular Folk Tales *is translated by Brian Alderson.*]

This newly translated, beautifully illustrated collection of Grimms' tales reminds me of a strange but telling remark made to me some time ago by an English friend who, apropos the German national characteristic of cruelty, included German fairy tales among the examples of his thesis. Cruelty, undoubtedly, is a marked feature of these extraordinary folktales which, to my mind, are unmatched in narrative imagination, symbolic richness and varied atmosphere. Yet this characteristic—certainly not a prerogative of the Grimm collection, but an integral part of the original—is only offensive to those readers who censure their children's readings according to moral standards which assume that fantasies of aggression or violence are alien to the dear little things. Modern psychology teaches us otherwise. In fact, the appeal of fairytales, not least the Grimms' in their undiluted, pre-Disney form, lies precisely in this free-ranging fantasy aspect: this straight route into the heart of the unconscious is a route which all ages of men can travel, as experience of life is not necessary for the traveller.

Brian Alderson's selection and translation of, not the best perhaps, but of some of the most stunning and bold tales in the Grimm collection, and Michael Foreman's subtly suggestive illustrations, capture their quintessential spirit, thus transforming apparently well-known classics of the nursery into freshly experienced, not at all comfortable or predictable, laconic tales of cosmic adventure, global misfortune and well-deserved happiness. Even such favourites as "Hansel and Gretel", "Snow White" and "Rumpelstiltskin" appear in a new light. Shorn of all moralistic or sentimental accretions, the primitive emotions and primal imagery are clearly focused; there is suddenly a terrible beauty and startling strangeness. I found I reexperienced the intense childhood emotions which I had had on first reading (and then on repeated rereading) of what spellbinding witches inflicted on innocent children or briefly, careless lovers, how wicked stepmothers inexorably pursued their helpless charges, what happened to arrogant princesses and thoughtless fathers, shrewd little tailors and retired soldiers. The unpredictability of encounter and action, the ritual repetition, the timelessness and speed of the plot and the final satisfying resolving formula now produce a déjà vu effect, the fear and the delight are repeated.

What is new, in this collection, is the surreal detail, the bold inventiveness, the stark contrasts. Michael Foreman's illustrations, which are suffused by the eerie blue or brown lighting of the dream, full of the elongations and curvatures of symbolist stylization, or the spikiness of nightmares, catch the dramatic, the grotesque, and the unreal aspects as well as the lyricism of the German fairy tales. Nothing quite matches David Hockney's illustrations of the tales, those fine line drawings which captured the terror and the evil, the bleak scenery and the captive, lost, and haunted figures, moonlit castles, crystal glass mountains and fearful apparitions. Yet Hockney elucidated the adult, the archetypal aspects of the fairytale. Michael Foreman and Brian Alderson aim to capture the child's imagination, too.

> *Gertrud Mander, "The Pleasures of Fear," in* The Times Literary Supplement, *No. 3966, April 7, 1978, p. 387.*

The ideal storyteller has many voices and Brian Alderson has had a ready ear for them. Michael Foreman's interpretation of the tales is a good deal more limited, for his colour plates and drawings make their effects again and again by setting weird, grotesque or sinister people and objects (a bony Death, spindly soldiers hurled into the air by magic, the witch's house in "Hansel and Gretel", the fish who brought about the downfall of the fisherman's wife, the egg of "Fitcher's Bird", the rapunzel plants in the witch's garden) against landscapes which would seem ordinary enough except in relation to what has been posed in them. The illustrations point to the doubts and fears which lie behind the tales rather than to their robust and often well-balanced humour.

> *Margery Fisher, in a review of "The Brothers Grimm: Popular Folk Tales," in* Growing Point, *Vol. 17, No. 2, July, 1978, p. 3358.*

Winter's Tales (1979)

Six curious little episodes—barely tales—in a large (8 ½ × 11½) picture-book format with sleek, theatrical illustrations [by Freire Wright]. In the first and most mundane, a scarecrow laments his plight ("I'm out in all kinds of weather. My clothes are a mess. It's lonely too"), then rejoices when the birds unexpectedly (and inexplicably) gather on his snow-covered form. The second finds Mrs. Claus playing the discontented housewife one year ("Let me help you deliver the presents It's time I saw something of the world"); and then, the next year, taking over Santa's delivery route—after chiding him for his inadequacy. The outcome? The hitherto-unseen Christmas turkey bolts out the window, bent on "seeing something of the world" too. Elsewhere a beetle ("Want! Want! Want!") happens on a

chocolate log; Santa, mistaking an ogre's ear for a chimney, somehow clambers down to his heart and, festooning it with ribbons, somehow transmits "the spirit of Christmas"; some mice are saved from a predatory cat by the sudden appearance of "a most ferocious and fearless mouse in shining armor"—whose wind-up key unlocks, for a mouse couple, "warm memories of their first Christmas together." Only one, involving the adornment of forest trees (instead of the town's perfect specimen), grows from the experience and emotions of Christmas; virtually all the rest are contrivances that turn on word-play and one-liners.

> *A review of "Winter's Tales," in* Kirkus Reviews, *Vol. XLVII, No. 24, December 15, 1979, p. 1428.*

Michael Foreman is better known as an illustrator, but the texts of his picture books have always been distinguished by economy and mastery of words and here he appears accompanying another artist. *Winter's Tales* is in effect a set of six mini picture books, each of about five pages and all associated with winter and Christmas. Freire Wright's drawings are strong and original in both technique and idea, but the credits really go to Mr. Foreman for his sharply individual tales and for the superb economy with which he presents and controls them. Good sense and discreet wit abound.

> *M. Crouch, in a review of "Winter's Tales," in* The Junior Bookshelf, *Vol. 44, No. 2, April, 1980, p. 62.*

City of Gold and Other Stories from the Old Testament (1980)

[City of Gold and Other Stories from the Old Testament *is written by Peter Dickinson.*]

It would be nice to say that *City of Gold* is a tour de force and leave it at that. Unfortunately it doesn't, quite, come off. Ambitious and innovative it certainly is. Peter Dickinson is a master storyteller and the Old Testament stories themselves are indestructible. That only leaves the audience, or the writer's relationship to it to go wrong.

Each of the 33 episodes, from the Fall in the garden to the fall of Jerusalem, is, technically, told by a different voice, as part of the oral tradition from which the written Bible grew. One or two are songs, set out as poems. But for the most part we are eavesdropping on the reminiscences of an old priest, or a shepherd, or a persecuted Jew. Most were onlookers, like the veteran soldier who watched Absalom die, or inheritors of a tradition, like the fisherman whose great-grandfather saw the Red Sea overwhelm Pharaoh's army. But some were participants in a larger drama, even if they had only bit-parts, like the boy Elijah raised from the dead, now grown up to be a philosophical sea-pilot.

The trouble is they are not *really* different voices, as the blurb claims. They are not the anonymous Jewish historians of the Authorised version, nor the commonplace people-in-the-desert out of which all that history was built.

They are all Peter Dickinson. It is the voice of an author, which is what these stories resist.

Here and there is a total success, as when the David and Goliath story is given as a cautionary tale by a sergeant lecturing his Babylonian recruits on slingshot avoidance. This is as surefooted as David Jones, a little bit of military knowhow that nicely pleats the centuries. But the more serious and lyrical moments often do not find so happy a convention.

The hopping from one register to another makes for bumpy reading; perhaps Peter Dickinson intended us to skip? But there is a momentum to the stories and, of course, a cycle through the building and destruction of the City, so that they cannot really be absorbed piecemeal. It is a handsome book, with subtle and dramatic paintings by Michael Foreman, who often comes closer to depicting the invisible than Peter Dickinson does to describing the ineffable. And it is so nearly brilliant, if only with reflected glory.

> *Mary Hoffman, "Reflected Glory," in* The Times Educational Supplement, *No. 3361, November 21, 1980, p. 30.*

The notes appended to Peter Dickinson's retellings of Old Testament stories emphasise the variety of sources—from early oral tradition ('folk tales, songs, legends, treaties, proverbs and so on') to the work of recorders and scholars determined to keep tradition alive during the Exile and the later collation of around 200 BC. The use of the term 'stories' in the sub-title is apt, for he evokes oral tradition deliberately in his narrative method, but the pieces are linked by a theme at once historical and doctrinal. These 'stories' relate to the history of a nation and a faith: the title *'City of Gold'* indicates that Jerusalem, the goal for centuries of wandering and dispersal, is the true centre of the book. The last piece, 'The Fall of the City', is put in the mouth of an exiled Jew speaking to 'an informal class of boys' in Babylon: they are to 'remember Jerusalem, the city you have never seen' so that future generations may rebuild it. The relevance to the present day is part of the broad historical theme.

History takes more than one form in the book. Facts and dates, with comments on the author's interpretation of his sources, are given succinctly in appended notes. Formal history is also served by the order of the pieces, corresponding to that of the Bible; they are grouped in sections which serve to distinguish the legendary and figurative material (Fall and Flood, for example) and the centuries during which a nation was slowly and painfully created, from the intricate, changeable years of Kings and Judges and the final collapse of the Israelite kingdoms. The idea of God, the establishment of monotheism, lies behind each event and its political significance. This is narrative rather than theology, but behind the most rational interpretations (of the crossing of the Red Sea, for example) there is always a fundamental meaning.

A third, indirect historical element comes from the selection of narrators for the various stories. Often these throw unexpected light on them. For instance, the contest of David and Goliath is described by 'a sergeant in the Baby-

lonian army, training recruits in weapon drill' during the Exile, particularly in the proper use of the Shield; Saul's mental state is analysed in a lecture on demonic possession given at a Jewish medical school in Alexandria some two centuries after the King's death; there is an acid undercurrent in the story of Joseph as told by a professional storyteller at a wedding feast in North Canaan, since the guests belong to a district in rivalry with the Southern tribes of the house of Joseph.

With this device, Peter Dickinson reflects the stylistic variety of the Old Testament in his own way. The homely voice of a shepherd suits his retelling, to his son, of the near-sacrifice of Isaac; the death of Absalom is described in practical but feeling tones by a veteran soldier of David's army; a Hebrew entertainer compares notes with a Babylonian rival on the details of the Flood legend; there is a stark relevance in the way a father hiding with his family during the rebellion of Antiochus explains the parallel with the Twelfth Plague of Egypt and the Exodus. Events which often seem puzzling and obscure to the young can be illuminated by a particular approach. Elijah's defeat of the worshippers of Baal, for instance, is described by a priest of one Israelite kingdom to a colleague from another, at a time when beliefs were obscured or forgotten. He speaks with longing of older, simpler times than his own. . . . Continuity, pictorial drama, meaning, human feelings combine in Peter Dickinson's striking text. They combine also in the water-colours and black and white decorations with which Michael Foreman confirms the essential mood of each piece—in the frozen action of David and Goliath, the desert colours and space of the scene where Cain hides his face from a huge pointing hand of cloud, the starlit battlements of the City, the mysterious light of the Burning Bush. From this fruitful partnership has come a version which should stir a wide readership to look again at the Old Testament, as history, myth and a record of human thought. (pp. 3802-03)

> *Margery Fisher, in a review of "City of Gold and Other Stories from the Old Testament," in* Growing Point, *Vol. 19, No. 5, January, 1981, pp. 3802-03.*

The trouble with nearly all 'versions' of the Bible, even De la Mare's, is that the modern words, be they never so comprehensible, are infinitely inadequate when compared with A.V. How wise therefore of Peter Dickinson—and what a brilliant brainwave!—to avoid comparisons. His *City of Gold* selects stories from the Old Testament from Eden to the Babylonian Exile, and narrates them in a variety of voices, some contemporary, or nearly contemporary, some looking back from some specified point in remote time. For example, the tale of David and Goliath is told by a Babylonian drill-sergeant who analyses the fatal errors committed by the gigantic Philistine; his voice is that of drill-sergeants throughout all the centuries. The death of Absalom is described by an eye-witness, now very old and beyond fear of the consequences of telling a truth to the disrepute of the ruling House. And so on. Every reader will identify his own favourite, grim or funny, poetic or spiritual. Folk-tale addicts will note how, in this kind of retelling, the primitive tale out of which the Biblical story evolved shows up clearly, as in the story of Joseph and his brethren, or in that of Samson, which Mr. Dickinson turns into a kind of Border ballad.

We are in Mr. Dickinson's debt already for many and varied experiences. Now he adds to our debt with this remarkable book, a tour de force, brilliantly executed, and a revelation to Bible-readers and others alike. How wise of him to stop where he does, before written history comes to shine a light on the Bible narrative which extinguishes its mysteries.

As in the Gollanez Andersen and Grimm, which are uniform with this book, *City of Gold* is illustrated by one of the most intelligent of modern book-artists, Michael Foreman. There is no doubt at all about his vision, or his feeling for atmosphere. These are both, perhaps, at odds with his technique and with the limitations of print. The book is printed throughout on a light coated paper, on which the vignettes which introduce each story lose some of their strength. This is the price to pay for the full-page colour plates. These have a curiously old-fashioned air, as if they were done by a disciple of Nielsen or Rackham. The broad frame around each adds to the artifice. Brilliantly drawn, it is true, but not, for the most part, contributing to the mood set by Mr. Dickinson's prose. A most memorable book, nevertheless.

> *M. Crouch, in a review of "City of Gold and Other Stories from the Old Testament," in The Junior Bookshelf, Vol. 45, No. 1, February, 1981, p. 27.*

Trick a Tracker (1981)

How, aeons ago, the hunted animals invented skateboards to trick their human trackers—and then, through the ages, the trackers "built trucks and wagons of every description, each one bigger and faster than the last . . . so they could all rush shouting through the world once more." But now, "the old animals say, 'The trackers have tricked themselves. . . . They're too busy chasing each other to bother chasing us.' " Given Foreman's flair as an illustrator of outrageous fancies, the scenes of the animals skateboarding through the air, across deserts, and down the sides of pyramids have a verve that kids can appreciate; but the hackneyed message—man-the-despoiler yet again—reduces the whole affair, finally, to a tract. Some exuberant, inventive silliness offset by some pretty silly moralizing.

> *A review of "Trick a Tracker," in Kirkus Reviews, Vol. XLIX, No. 18, September 15, 1981, p. 1156.*

Trick a Tracker has . . . originality, not to say whimsicality, and would appeal very much to some in the four-to-six age group. When man first begins to hunt, the animals fight back, disguising their tracks and finally developing skateboards to avoid their predators. These skateboarding pages are the core of the book; with verve and imagination the rampant animals are shown leaping over obstacles and shooting down mountains. The admiring human audience then build their own wheeled machines and are so delighted that they forget to chase the animals. The pictures, in

From Sleeping Beauty and Other Favourite Tales, *written and illustrated by Michael Foreman.*

lovely shades of blue and green, contribute enormously to the enjoyment of the fantasy.

> *Celia Gibbs, in a review of "Trick a Tracker," in British Book News, Children's Supplement, Autumn, 1981, p. 14.*

With tongue firmly in cheek, Foreman rewrites the history of the wheel and presents humans ("trackers") as thinking they are much smarter than they really are. . . . Foreman's text, which reads well aloud, is tight and humorous, with a logic all its own. His full-color illustrations in dazzling watercolor are threaded together by movement and match the story's wit. Pages alternate between double spreads and ingeniously designed pages with panels that visually move the story along. One does wonder if most children can grasp the historical puns; will they find the humor in its satirical approach to man's development? Still, the book is too interesting to pass by.

> *George Shannon, in a review of "Trick a Tracker," in School Library Journal, Vol. 28, No. 3, November, 1981, p. 91.*

Panda and the Odd Lion (1981)

Michael Foreman's story is a bit conventional in essentials, that of the misfit animal who goes on a quest to establish his identity. The interpretation, as one might expect from this highly individual artist, is by no means conventional. The odd lion, who grows wings, travels with his panda friend through many countries until he finds his prototype in St. Mark's Square in Venice. Mr. Foreman, using a soft palette in which blues and pinks predominate, gives us a rare treat. It is not so much that he draws better than others, but a strong intelligence lies behind everything he does.

> M. Crouch, in a review of "Panda and the Odd Lion," in The Junior Bookshelf, Vol. 46, No. 1, February, 1982, p. 14.

In this sequel to *Panda's puzzle,* Panda helps a misshapen lion, driven from home by his brothers, to come to terms with his oddness. They travel the world together until with his new found self-respect Lion returns to his homeland, where he is loved and accepted by everyone. Panda's final comment: 'If you can't join them—beat them' is the essence of the tale. Just looking at Michael Foreman's beautiful skyscapes, it is not difficult to agree with Lion that: 'It seems to be people's ambition to have wings.' The fluidity of colour heightens the desire for and feeling of flight. A book which has a lot to offer readers at the top end of the primary school, and beyond. (pp. 119-20)

> Jill Bennett, in a review of "Panda and the Odd Lion," in The School Librarian, Vol. 30, No. 2, June, 1982, pp. 119-20.

Sleeping Beauty and Other Favourite Fairy Tales (1982)

[Sleeping Beauty and Other Favourite Fairy Tales *is selected and translated by Angela Carter.*]

[*The following excerpt is from an essay in which Idris Parry compares Foreman's illustrations with W. Heath Robinson's illustrations for* Perrault's Complete Fairy Tales, *translated by A.E. Johnson and others.*]

Angela Carter's new translation of Perrault is beautifully done, colloquial, bound to please, though some young readers may stumble over "ingenuous" and "debility". Ten of her tales are from Perrault, the other two from Mme de Beaumont, including the irresistible "Beauty and the Beast", surely one of the most fascinating tales in all literature and, in its psychological subtlety, way beyond anything told by Perrault.

Michael Foreman's illustrations in colour and black and white are imaginative. But where, in the full-page picture of Cinderella's coach, is the sixth footman? The fairy godmother transformed six lizards into footmen "who stepped up behind the carriage in their laced uniforms and hung on as if they had done nothing else all their lives"; Michael Foreman gives us only five footmen on the step behind the magic coach. Children are as pernickety as professors when it comes to accuracy. They can believe the impossible but usually jib at the improbable.

Both Foreman and Heath Robinson depict the incident when the father in "Beauty and the Beast" rides at night through driving snow towards the Beast's castle. Foreman's picture is a scene from toy theatre, a cardboard figure on a cardboard horse, no doubt fun for children, as toy theatre always is. In Heath Robinson's drawing both man and horse seem to shiver in a biting wind, and a huge black sky signifies the terror to come. It is easy to see which artist accepts the incident as real.

> Idris Parry, "Romantically Real," in The Times Literary Supplement, No. 4156, November 26, 1982, p. 1306.

In 1979 Angela Carter published a series of acidly brilliant variations on classic fairy tales, *The Bloody Chamber.* The originals she so chillingly explored are translated in **Sleeping Beauty and Other Favourite Fairy Tales** in a coolly ironic, brisk edgy prose which resonates to those darker fictions, while at the same time remaining faithful to her often maltreated originals. Ten of the tales are by Charles Perrault; Angela Carter's translations have already appeared as *The Fairy Tales of Charles Perrault* (Gollancz, 1977), with eerie, haunting etchings by Martin Ware. The two tales added in this edition are by a later writer influenced by Perrault, Madame Leprince de Beaumont.

It is her "Beauty and the Beast" which forms the basis of most later retellings, and the subtext of Carter's "The Courtship of Mr Lyon" and "The Tiger's Bride". In an afterword, Angela Carter notes the introduction in Mme de Beaumont's work of a novelistic element foreign to Perrault, whose tales, despite their rhymed moral endings and seventeenth century court trappings, retain the simplicity of their oral ancestry. That simplicity was to be betrayed by later writers, displaced by the empty, ornate verbosity of the *Cabinet des Fés.* But the literary elements provided by Mme de Beaumont for her beast-marriage tale are, as Carter notes, subtle teasings out of the implicit emotions of the story rather than mere embellishments. If any translation can persuade us to read "Beauty and the Beast" afresh as a short story, forgetting both the more earthy appeal of beast-marriage folktales such as the English "The Small-Tooth Dog" (in Addy's *Household Tales*) and the artificial curlicues of later retellers, it is Angela Carter's.

The same is true of her crisp, perfectly balanced Perrault translations. There is real wit, to be relished at each re-reading, in lines such as this, when Puss-in-Boots reaches the ogre's castle: "The ogre made him as welcome as an ogre can." The words are concise but treacherous: leading us up to predictable paths then dropping us into unseen pits. Ware's etchings perfectly caught this aspect of the translations, making *The Fairy Tales of Charles Perrault,* perhaps, an adult book. Michael Foreman's illustrations in this edition, some in black and white, but mostly in his familiar brightly-coloured air-brush style, are less concerned to dig beneath the surface. There are subtleties—Sleeping Beauty as a landscape across which the Prince rides; a castle entrance as a threatening face, with the portcullis its bared teeth—but they are of a different order to Ware's image of disquiet. The result is very fine in its way, and a fitting companion to Foreman's Andersen, Grimm and Old Testament illustrations.

> Neil Philip, "Beauty and Beast," in The Times

Educational Supplement, No. 3472, January 14, 1983, p. 30.

Miss Carter keeps close to the text, even to the morals. In a concluding note she shows a penetrating critical understanding of Perrault's and Madame de Beaumont's very different approaches to comparable tales. She is especially illuminating in her comments on that masterly short-story, 'Beauty and the Beast'. In colour and monochrome alike Michael Foreman's illustrations are full of life and humour, but in spirit they are far from the mannered elegance of the text. Good as they are, they prevent this from becoming the definitive collection of classical French fairy tales for this present generation. A desirable book nevertheless.

M. Crouch, in a review of "Sleeping Beauty and Other Favourite Fairy Tales," in The Junior Bookshelf, *Vol. 47, No. 1, February, 1983, p. 26.*

Angela Carter has chosen to retell the Perrault tales, together with two by Madame Leprince de Beaumont usually associated with them, in a compromise style which reflects their courtly origin but also brings them forward to our own times by the use of neologisms. The guards in one tale 'dozed off after a spree' while anxious royal parents 'visited all the clinics' for consultation. The unexpected intrusion of phrases like these into a formal style is intriguing, though it does sometimes interrupt the lucid flow of stories whose mood and atmosphere can never really be anything but mannered. This is a true re-telling rather than an edited translation, and the book should suit children around eight or so who will be comfortable with the stories but not necessarily with editorial comment. Michael Foreman's water-colour pictures and the ancillary drawings emphasise the strange and sinister elements in the tales, with spindly human figures and towering buildings they present enough details of costume, gesture and behaviour to evoke something of the original tone of the collection and, at least in 'Puss in Boots', the underlying touches of satire which justified the offering of fairy—tales to a blasé adult audience and which are, or should surely be, inseparable from the magic and adventure element. (pp. 4036-37)

Margery Fisher, in a review of "Sleeping Beauty and Other Favourite Fairy Tales," in Growing Point, *Vol. 21, No. 6, March, 1983, pp. 4036-37.*

Carter's translation is elegant and contemporary (the childless king and queen visit "clinics" and "specialists") but faithful to the internal and external structure of the originals (Little Red Riding Hood and her grandmother, for example, are "gobbled up," and there is no rescuing woodsman; the "morals" at the end of most stories are retained). The vocabulary is sophisticated (*ingenuous, intimidated, improvised, precariously, clambered* and *ingenuity* all appear in the brief tale of "Puss in Boots") and so is the epilogue giving some historical background. Foreman alternates water-colors with black-and-white illustrations, combining romantic and lyrical elements (and allusions, such as one to Botticelli's *Venus and Primavera*) with droll caricatured faces. Carter and Foreman's work makes for a volume considerably more attractive than *Perrault's Fairy Tales* (Dover, 1969), illustrated by Doré, but not much behind in sophistication.

Patricia Dooley, in a review of "Sleeping Beauty & Other Favourite Fairytales," in School Library Journal, *Vol. 30, No. 3, November, 1983, p. 74.*

Land of Dreams (1982)

Michael Foreman is at the height of his powers now. He must surely be the most intelligent of British masters of the picture-book. This does not make him easy to follow. In **Land of Dreams** an old man and a boy, vaguely Tibetan, stand on the mountains, seeing blown on the wind the fragments of their dreams. Some of these fall into the snow, and the two gather them and assemble them, then launch them back into the world. There is a sudden conventional, but quite unexpected, twist on the last page. Beautiful, brilliant, but is it accessible to the young?

M. Crouch, in a review of "Land of Dreams," in The Junior Bookshelf, *Vol. 46, No. 6, December, 1982, p. 220.*

Michael Foreman's illustrations are some of the most interesting in books for children. He has the courage and the ability to present children with illusory and elusive pictures which command the eye and challenge the intelligence. In any book with which he is involved, the illustrations make as strong a statement as the text, which is why he works best when partnered by a distinctive author—Terry Jones, for example, in **Fairy tales.** Here he is both author and artist, and though I welcome this, I do hope he will not abandon illustration. We can't afford to lose him as there are few enough about with his interpretative skills; and whilst this short and surrealistic story is appealing, the book is remarkable for its mysterious and delicate drawings. (pp. 128-29)

Gabrielle Maunder, in a review of "Land of Dreams," in The School Librarian, *Vol. 31, No. 2, June, 1983, pp. 128-29.*

Michael Foreman has used delicate shades of blues, pinks and white to create a truly dreamlike quality in the pictures of this beautiful book. . . .

When I first read this book, although my reaction to both pictures and text was positive, the book did not provoke the strong feelings which subsequent readings have done. It was when I introduced it to my class by reading it aloud that I began to appreciate the strengths of the story. Its tone, for me, is reminiscent of Oscar Wilde's 'Selfish Giant' and matches the illustrations in dreamlike intensity. It is the fusion of picture and text, with their ethereal quality and power, that makes this such an unusual book.

Jill Bennett, in a review of "Land of Dreams," in The Signal Review of Children's Books, *Vol. 1, 1983, p. 12.*

Long Neck and Thunder Foot   (1982)

[Long Neck and Thunder Foot *is written by Helen Piers.*]

Long Neck and Thunderfoot adopts the fashionable trend of *unterrifying* monsters. Each of these creatures is frightened of the other. A fine idea for the many children obsessed by dinosaurs, its washcolour pictures are witty in spite of the murky blues and greens that predominate. But the text is not especially defined; it tends to lose direction.

> Peter Fanning, "Sweet and Sour," *in* The Times Educational Supplement, *No. 3472, January 14, 1983, p. 34.*

When two dinosaurs meet they are terrified of each other. So each takes steps to improve its armament. When this leads to no decisive result they try different tactics, but these only bring pain to both parties. Their last crafty idea is successful; they throw a party for all the beasts of the forest. Parents reading this delectable tale to their young will be uplifted by the obvious political parallels; the children will be satisfied with a good story exceedingly well told and illustrated by Michael Foreman who manages to combine beauty and high humour. An outstandingly good picture-book.

> M. Crouch, in a review of "Long Neck and Thunder Foot," *in* The Junior Bookshelf, *Vol. 47, No. 1, February, 1983, p. 17.*

[A] parable of our own world, in the tale of two dinosaurs who pursue an entirely unnecessary arms race until an accident forces them to realise that they can live just as well as friends. The pictures are smooth and relaxed and the dinosaurs themselves make the point about the dangers of aggression very sharply through attitudes and nicely contrived facial expressions. Michael Foreman has made good use of conjectures about the shape and the natural habitat of the extinct species to give body as well as humour to his scenes. (pp. 4047-48)

> Margery Fisher, in a review of "Long Neck and Thunder Foot," *in* Growing Point, *Vol. 21, No. 6, March, 1983, pp. 4047-48.*

The Saga of Erik the Viking   (1983)

[The Saga of Erik the Viking *is written by Terry Jones.*]

The Saga of Erik the Viking follows Erik and his band of men as they sail west in search of "the land where the sun goes at night", a journey reminiscent of that made by Erik the Red who colonized first Iceland and then Greenland in the late tenth century before his son, Leif Eiriksson reached the east coast of America. Erik and his men are caught up in a series of hair-raising adventures: encounters with the Enchantress of the Fjord and Sea Dragon, bloodcurdling battles with the Dogfighters, a journey under the lip of the Edge of the World, and a meeting with the chess-playing Death (shades of *The Seventh Seal).*

For characterization, I give Terry Jones a zero rating: few of his human characters (as opposed to his rogues' gallery of mermaids and monsters) are sharply defined. For his-

torical sense, he gets much the same—the book may be set in the Viking Age but, apart from gathering that it was robust and stoic, we learn next to nothing about it. For dialogue, qualified approval. The book is nothing if not racy but the mock-heroic diction is unsettlingly uneven in tone. For narrative thrust, imaginative resourcefulness and wit, however, unqualified admiration. And for unobtrusive Right Thinking, a special cheer! This is a perceptive and fundamentally moral book that portrays self-doubt as an evil and predatory bird, stresses the importance of quest not goal ("our true goal lies within ourselves"), and asserts that there is no justification whatsoever for depriving others, however monstrous their behaviour, of lives or land.

Michael Foreman goes from strength to strength. He is a master of the varying viewpoint: we look *down* on a boatland of Vikings threatened by viper rain, *up* into the cruel fangs of the Dogfighters, *across* a sweeping icescape to the pendant moon. His images are often on eyes—scared eyes, blazing eyes, eyes of light, sockets where eyes should be. And here, maybe, one does come face to face with the compellingly exuberant lives yet haunted imaginations of the Vikings.

> Kevin Crossley-Holland, "Star Saga," *in* The Times Educational Supplement, *No. 3514, November 4, 1983, p. 24.*

[In **The Saga of Erik the Viking** there] is a minimum of description and much action. Characterization becomes clear through deeds. Originally invented as bedtime stories for the author's son, the short, episodic chapters make the book appropriate to read aloud to primary grade children. The language is a humorous mixture of mock-heroic and colloquial, recalling the Nordic Sagas, the Odyssey and the Arabian Nights, yet adding its own humorous twists. The characters take themselves so seriously while stating the outrageous, and keep straight faces while solving problems by unlikely means that one can almost hear Jones' Monty Python compatriots reading the parts. The story is beautifully enhanced by 45 black-and-white pen-and-ink illustrations, and 39 in brilliant color washes, some fanciful and some frightening. With its large size, wide margins and short chapters, the book will be attractive to reluctant readers and may even lead them on to other epics.

> Annette Curtis Klause, in a review of "The Saga of Erik the Viking," *in* School Library Journal, *Vol. 30, No. 2, January, 1984, p. 78.*

Terry Jones has given an unmistakeably riotous, penetrating personal touch to Scandinavian saga and fable in **The Saga of Erik the Viking,** adding a firm moral to a series of events in which Erik and his band, venturing in the 'Golden Dragon' to find the fabled land where the sun goes down, learn that their quest has been its own justification in teaching them the value of courage, loyalty and persistance. . . . The whole book crackles with life with the racy, concrete, energetic prose and with Michael Foreman's stunning illustrations, alternately black and white and in full colour, which provide a second, highly dramatic narrative. One picture in particular, showing Death engaged in a chess game with human pieces, underlines the point and purpose of this striking book. (pp. 4248-49)

Margery Fisher, in a review of "The Saga of Erik the Viking," in Growing Point, *Vol. 23, No. 1, May, 1984, pp. 4248-49.*

Cat and Canary (1984)

Left alone by his master ("Oh, you are lucky. You just lie around the house all day, lazy cat."), our hero shakes off all feline passivity; freeing the canary and fixing breakfast before taking to the roof. The rather cutely drawn cat has pacifist / vegetarian tendencies—"He never chased birds. After all his best friend was a canary."—though the message, previously the *raison d'être* of Michael Foreman's books, is muted here. Once airborne, however, Cat becomes almost disembodied, soaring above the city blown by winds and seen from dizzying perspectives. The New York City background, with the GE, Chrysler and Empire State buildings all recognizable if topographically misplaced, forms a dramatic backcloth to Cat's uncontrollable flight in washes of violet evening light and falling snow. Finally, in the manner of more traditional animal tales, Cat is rescued by Canary and a flock of friendly birds.

The slight but resonant story of brief freedom and return to safety is given the full Foreman treatment. The city's most photogenic aspects are selected for a technique which involves vibrant colour, light and shade, busy detail—anything which might add to the drama. Full colour pages contain spectacular foreshortenings and long-distance views. The result is unharmonious but undoubtedly exciting.

Peter Blake, in a review of "Cat and Canary," in The Times Literary Supplement, *No. 4261, November 30, 1984, p. 1379.*

Foreman's oversized, luminous watercolors exactly suit the flight of fantasy, from glowing sunrise to glittering, snowy evening. The double-page spreads are filled with wonderful perspective and drama as Cat flies over the city. Although the text and one of the illustrations do not synchronize, the pictures will carry the story, and they are large enough for group sharing. A charming fantasy, beautifully composed, with a fresh approach to a well-loved theme.

Susan H. Patron, in a review of "Cat & Canary," in School Library Journal, *Vol. 31, No. 7, March, 1985, p. 150.*

What do all those city cats do while we go about our daily lives? Many children, trudging off to the rigors of after-school enrichment classes must wonder. And how to reconcile that awful fact of life: that those marvelous bright-eyed feliness so often like to gobble up the equally wondrous creature, the bird? **Cat & Canary,** with its panoramic illustrations of New York, answers both questions with charm and excitement.

"You are lucky," laments the master of our cat hero before leaving for work. "You just lie around the house all day, lazy cat." Not true. Our friend promptly opens the cage of the apartment's other occupant, the canary, and, instead of eating him, goes to the roof to watch him fly

and, not unlike many a child, dream of joining him in a glorious ascent above the city's immense buildings.

One lucky day on the roof Cat finds a kite—another wondrously unshackled item in a child's universe—and, while trying to untie it, is caught up himself and pulled into the air. This frees Cat and us and, best of all, the author-illustrator Michael Foreman, to allow Cat wing—in bold full-color paintings—from rooftop to midtown skyscraper, from bird's-eye-view to pedestrian-eye-view, capturing the beauty and wonder of Manhattan Island in a perfect visual love affair with New York.

Lest this adventure disappoint the fierce-hearted youngster used to sterner stuff on Saturday morning television, Cat's early ecstasies turn to fear when a storm catches him above the midtown landscape. The city for him, as it so often does for all of us, briefly darkens. Just when things might give us all a terrible fright, Canary, allied with other birds, rescues Cat, flying him home just in time for the Master's return. "What a lazy cat!" says this tedious man. "I bet you haven't moved all day." One can hear the laughter of children enjoying this irony, and perhaps later dreaming of Michael Foreman's New York, knowing now what all those city cats have been doing.

Margaret Joskow, in a review of "Cat & Canary," in The New York Times Book Review, *April 28, 1985, p. 26.*

Panda and the Bunyips (1984)

Panda and his friend the winged Lion leave their African home to see the world, and usually food and drink are plentiful. But they are thirsty and hungry as they fly over a red, barren landscape. Eventually they find a place to sleep, and a Bunyip (a mythical Australian beast) climbs out of the water to greet them. He has his own journey to make, to the ocean, where all the legendary creatures meet every thousand years—sea serpents and silver flying fishes among them. They "sport" and gossip for six days, and on the seventh, head home. In the tonal gradations of dusky skies, Foreman's watercolors, on textured paper, are more intrinsically interesting than the banal storyline. He creates wide-open vistas, with startling perspectives, and gives some of the murkier scenes at night an other-worldly quality. (pp. 92-3)

A review of "Panda and the Bunyips," in Publishers Weekly, *Vol. 233, No. 14, April 8, 1988, pp. 92-3.*

Shakespeare Stories (1985)

[Shakespeare Stories *is written by Leon Garfield.*]

A collection of stories based on plays may seem an essentially untheatrical enterprise, a translation from the public, first-person enactment of events by a whole company of players to a private, third-person recounting of them by a single voice: a movement away from the stage to the study. That is how Mary and Charles Lamb presented their selection of twenty *Tales from Shakespeare.* It was

From Long Neck and Thunder Foot, *written by Helen Piers. Illustrated by Michael Foreman.*

"an introduction to the study of Shakespeare" for young persons, and especially for "young ladies", on the grounds that boys, having access to "their fathers' libraries at a much earlier age than girls", frequently had a good knowledge of Shakespeare's plays well before their sisters were allowed "to look into this manly book". The Lambs' preface does not mention the theatre.

Leon Garfield and his illustrator, Michael Foreman, make no statement of intent, but the dedication of their book to the Royal Shakespeare Company points to an essential difference between Garfield's method and the Lambs'. Whereas the Lambs provide a simplified reading experience as a preparation for a more complex and difficult experience of the same kind, Leon Garfield seeks to convey in prose narrative the experience, not of reading the twelve plays that he includes, but of seeing them performed. . . .

Though the presentation of the volume suggests that it is intended primarily for young readers, Leon Garfield's uncondescending tone gives the stories a wider appeal: they are not pale reflections of the plays, not introductions to the study of Shakespeare, but fresh creations with a life of their own. Michael Foreman's illustrations provide a somewhat uneven accompaniment to the text. Some, striking enough in themselves, are at odds with the story: Malvolio cowers in a great avenue of trees that threateningly suggest human faces when he should be at his most bumptious, whereas Garfield's witches, like Shakespeare's, are earthbound old women, Foreman's—in an admirably designed painting—materalize from the sky, weirdly supernatural figures that dwarf Macbeth and Banquo. Faces, frequently pop-eyed, are generalized, but Foreman's liking for splashes of wash gives Othello a superbly bright yellow cloak, the battlements of Elsinore are rendered with atomospheric power, and the black-and-white line drawings have both charm and wit.

Stanley Wells, "The Theatre of the Page," in

The Times Literary Supplement, *No. 4282, April 26, 1985, p. 478.*

Now and then an artistic alliance is formed which seems so inevitable as to be heaven-sent. Leon Garfield's recasting of Shakespeare's plays as stories appears in prospect to be a natural of this kind. If there is one contemporary writer for children who seems likely to be capable of appropriating Shakespeare for his own purposes, with all the confidence and ability to handle the full spectrum of emotions, the heady love of language and underlying tact which that implies, it is he. . . .

What is one to say about Michael Foreman's pictures? His talent is quite naturally dramatic, he's a fine draughtsman and a lovely colourist, but isn't it time he gave himself (and us) a rest—a chance to dig deeper? His besetting sin is his facility, and he is probably not helped by being besieged by publishers.

Kevin Crossley-Holland, "Masters," in The Times Educational Supplement, *No. 3597, June 7, 1985, p. 49.*

How about this then? Two of the leading creative artists of our day combining to grapple with the greatest writer of all time?

The result is not at all bad, either. Leon Garfield is not so much overawed by his task as driven to excess by it. In other words he sometimes overwrites like mad in order to match his original, and the contrast between his purple patches and Shakespeare's dialogue, faithfully reproduced, is too sharp for comfort. It is not all like that. Quite often Mr. Garfield is content to tell his story straight, and when he is in the mood no one tells a story better than he. (p. 185)

There can be few reservations about Michael Foreman's contribution to the book. He is at his best, both in the many monochrome pictures in the text and in the big colour-plates. (Isn't it strange, by the way, that with all our technological advances we still can't integrate colour-plates with the text; they still have to stand out like glossy aliens.) He does much by suggestion, not showing too much but creating an atmosphere, leaving the reader to supply his own interpretation. He uses space brilliantly, Malvolio tiny among the clipped yews, mad Lear filling the page and riding right out of it at the reader, Shylock and the Ghost of Hamlet's father, each caught in a pool of moonlight among shadows. Mr. Foreman ranges through the gamut of the emotions with complete assurance. (pp. 185-86)

> *M. Crouch, in a review of "Shakespeare's Stories," in* The Junior Bookshelf, *Vol. 49, No. 4, August, 1985, pp. 185-86.*

Seasons of Splendour: Tales, Myths, and Legends of India (1985)

[Seasons of Splendour: Tales, Myths, and Legends of India *is written by Madhur Jaffrey.*]

The magic of Indian mythology and of an Indian childhood have been captured by Madhur Jaffrey in a cycle of stories meant to correspond with the seasons. Much of life in the country is shaped by annual events, festivals, anniversaries and each has an appropriate celebration. There is a deity to be worshipped for every occasion, and the best part is that they are human—they get angry and make mistakes and set them right—and it is that which endears them to children.

Written (in the best Indian tradition) so that they can be read aloud, the author has used anecdotes from her own childhood to explain the significance of festivals and customs. Episodes from the epic Ramayana and tales of the miraculous exploits of the young god Krishna form a substantial part of the book. These, like the Greek myths, have the popular elements of wicked kings and queens, demons and noble heroes. The fables become more relevant when the author says, "all of India worships the blue god Krishna. My feelings for him have always been a bit more personal. Not only was I raised on the banks of the Yamuna River, as he was, but I was born on the feast day of his birth".

What distinguishes Madhur Jaffrey's stories is that they do not belong to the parents-versus-naughty-child genre. They are set in proper families, with husbands and wives, daughters, sisters and mothers in law. They speak of relationships in the family as a whole, not a truncated nuclear unit, emphasized by her own accounts of growing up in the midst of a host of storytelling aunts and a battery of cousins. This explains why certain stories are recounted on the day when wives fast for their husbands, or why on the spring festival of Holi, "all Indians, of all ages, have the licence to rub or throw colours—water-based, oil-based or powder form—on the victims of their choice. No one is considered worthy of exemption, dignified grandmothers included."

Cultural synthesis (as in the games played by the author where Robin Hood encounters Prince Rama) is totally alien to the English child. Madhur Jaffrey's memories of an "English convent" education combined with an intensely Indian (yet westernized) family are deadly accurate and evoke great nostalgia in me, for I had a similar upbringing.

This synthesis is not apparent in Michael Foreman's illustrations (he travelled to India especially for the book). They are jewel-like and accurate in physical detail but they are in the "Arabian Nights" style, evocative of magic lamps and flying carpets. Greater use of the miniature tradition or the folk element would have given his work a stronger Indian flavour.

> *Uma Ram Nath, "Sugar and Spice," in* The Times Educational Supplement, *No. 3597, June 7, 1985, p. 52.*

Madhur Jaffrey has devised a scheme for **Seasons of Splendour** which helps to give full value to the dramatic qualities of Indian legends and tales. Each section represents a festival or some commemorative event, from the religious celebrations of Divali to more simple domestic occasions; we see how her family life was arranged round these festivals and her easy, pleasing prose carries us through tales of gods and monsters, sad maidens and triumphant warriors, making each tale accessible to children for whom the details of landscape and people must seem alien. In contrast, Michael Foreman has stressed in his dark-toned, dramatic scenes the exotic flavour of the tales. His human and animal forms are subtly exaggerated, his backgrounds rich in swirling colour, his monsters hugely menacing. The very different style of words and pictures adds to the exciting, surprising quality of this strikingly elegant volume.

> *Margery Fisher, in a review of "Seasons of Splendour," in* Growing Point, *Vol. 24, No. 3, September, 1985, p. 4489.*

In **Seasons of Splendour** [Jaffrey] sets her myths and folk-tales firmly within the cycle of an Indian year, with appropriate narratives for the different seasons and festivals—Khrishna's birthday during the monsoon rains, Divali, Holi and so on: a charming device in itself, and one which allows her to preface each set of stories with a page or two of childhood reminiscence, recalling the setting in which she first heard them.

These introductions are the best thing in the book. The background is at once exotic and cosy, and Mrs Jaffrey describes it well: the huge household headed by a formidable grandfather, "Barrister Sahib", beneath whose rolltop desk the children stage theatricals; plump, fragrant aunts, fresh from the bath in well-starched saris, settling down on the sofa to tell stories. . . .

[But] the author's sureness of touch deserts her when it comes to the stories themselves. These include fragments of Indian myth and epos as well as somewhat moralistic folk-tales; and it is to Jaffrey's credit that she gives a fairly full version of the Ramayana story. But when she first presents the Princess Sita, the talent for description she shows in her autobiographical anecdotes lures her on to destruction:. . . . As with description, so with dialogue. Several stories are marred by the brightly naturalistic tone of the exchanges between kings and princesses, fabulous beasts and gods. They talk, in fact, rather like Barrister Sahib's grandchildren are reported to do; and, in stories of this kind, it rings false. It may also account for a slight, pervasive sense that Jaffrey is somehow patronizing her readers, condescending to their limited ideas of how such personages might speak. This is not present in all the stories; but it recurs too often for comfort.

Mrs Jaffrey has been ill served, too, by her illustrator. Michael Foreman does not seem at ease in the mode he has chosen for the full-page pictures, that of a parody of Moghul miniatures. A good parody requires intimate understanding, as well as affection for the convention used as its point of departure; if Foreman has either, he has been unable to express it. Some of the pictures are tuppence-coloured mawkish, others at once garish and frightening. This is attributable, in part, to his use of colour; but the drawing—and it applies to the abundant black-and-white illustrations also—is often deliberately crude. There are one or two exceptions; but the total effect is cheapening and—once again, though in a different way from Mrs Jaffrey's—patronizing. This is a period piece in more senses than one, illustrating one of the odder byways of English cultural fashion in the 1980s.

> *Eva Gillies, "High Days and Holi Dyes," in The Times Literary Supplement, No. 4302, September 13, 1985, p. 1014.*

Seasons of Splendour is enriched immeasurably by the watercolors of Michael Foreman, whose illustrations echo the traditional painting of India without being bound by them. They are vivid and magical and somehow archetypal: the monsters are horrible without being frightening; the princes and princesses could be any child who wanted to find himself in them. The colors are as brilliant as a sari shop, but subaqueous, like a dream. The resonances of this magical and profound storybook will sing on in the heart and mind long after the hundredth bedtime. (p. 51)

> *Barbara Thompson, "Within the Timeless Gates," in The New York Times Book Review, November 10, 1985, pp. 33, 51.*

Panda and the Bushfire (1986)

By now, Panda and his winged-lion chum are pretty familiar too. So prolific is Michael Foreman that every new book threatens to devalue his currency—yet ends up confirming a talent impervious to the normal mechanisms of the market-place. Here his odd, curiously resonant, duo bolster their epic status with koalas, firefighters, and spread-after-spread of the Great Yonder, blue and otherwise. Makes most picturebooks seem stay-at-home.

> *Chris Powling, in a review of "Panda and the Bushfire," in Books for Keeps, No. 38, May, 1986, p. 29.*

An eminent, award-winning British illustrator, Foreman was apparently fascinated with the challenge of representing the fire, with its trees becoming torches; the billowing smoke, sparks; the effect of water, the twilight aftermath. From that point of view, his dramatic watercolors effec-

tively evoke the experience and have considerable visual appeal. The story, however, is slight, no more than a basic escape-and-rescue incident; and the pictures of Panda and his friends trapped by fire could easily provoke nightmares in the too young or over-susceptible.

Interesting, though, for the art, the artist, and the setting.

> *A review of "Panda and the Bushfire," in Kirkus Reviews, Vol. LIV, No. 22, November 15, 1986, p. 1721.*

Early in the Morning: A Collection of New Poems (1986)

[Early in the Morning: A Collection of New Poems *is written by Charles Causley.*]

Early in the Morning is a triumph of collaborative creation, between poet, composer, illustrator and (uncredited) book designer. The long wait for a new volume of Causley's matchless children's poems has proved fully worthwhile. His writing here is full of joy and exuberance, as well as the familiar plangent note of loss and longing. Some of them really are as the blurb describes them, new nursery rhymes, telling stories of hectic compression which are entirely dependent on the logic of rhythm and rhyme. Others strike a more personal note, while never straying far from the demands of narrative. "John, John the Baptist", "One for the Man", "Stone in the Water", "Tell, Tell the Bees": the emphatic simplicity of the titles prepares us for something special.

Causley's words themselves draw wonderful pictures in the head: of Tommy Hyde, for instance, writing a love letter on the strand, and "watching for the water to rub it off the shore / And take it to my true love in Baltimore."

The illustrator, Michael Foreman, has had to exercise perfect discretion to prevent *his* pictures standing, as it were, between the poet and the reader. He has succeeded in this much more fully on the black-and-white pages than on the colour ones. Some of the pen-and-ink drawings are so perfect it is hard to imagine the poems—for instance "Janny Jim Jan" and "I Love My Darling Tractor"—without them. The colour work seems to be trying too hard.

> *Neil Philip, "Picture Poems," in The Times Educational Supplement, No. 3685, February 13, 1987, p. 46.*

If anyone is qualified to write *new* nursery rhymes it is Charles Causley. He can hit off the jaunty, the bizarre, the inconsequent, the mysterious notes to perfection—'Mistletoe, mistletoe old, Cut it down with a knife of gold' or 'My cat Plum Duff when feeling gruff Was terribly fond of taking snuff'—what could be simpler or more authentic sounding? Twelve of the poems have been set to music in a series of melodies whose rhythms and dynamics range from the bouncy and jolly to the sad, meditative or gentle. The pictures are happy and unfussy, often with rich colour precisely defining a bird's plumage or the petals of a flower, just as often adding their own jaunty humour to a fanciful domestic incident.

> *Margery Fisher, in a review of "Early in the*

Morning," in Growing Point, *Vol. 25, No. 6, March, 1987, p. 4775.*

The rhymes sound a little like Dennis Lee's, but are somewhat more subdued, perhaps because they are for a younger audience. The layout of the pages, the rhythm and tone of the poems, and the choice of words, are all very British. Some readers may find this makes the book less accessible, but many librarians will find good material for their programs for younger children. Foreman has had fun doing a combination of full-color and black-and-white illustrations. His sprightly vignettes pick up the tone of the various verses and keep the book from appearing too heavy.

> *A review of "Early in the Morning: A Collection of New Poems," in* Kirkus Reviews, *Vol. LV, No. 7, April 1, 1987, p. 551.*

British poet and anthologist Causley offers 40 new poems that hint at the lively sounds of nursery rhymes and give an occasional dollop of their nonsense as well. . . . [Small] ink drawings and watercolor paintings interpret the poetry in a beguiling way. The lyricism generally associated with Foreman's illustrations is a bit restrained, but he brings fresh delight to the more rollicking verses.

> *Carolyn Phelan, in a review of "Early in the Morning: A Collection of New Poems," in* Booklist, *Vol. 83, No. 21, July, 1987, p. 1676.*

Ben's Box (1986)

What is never in doubt is Michael Foreman's skill as an artist: conception and colours, techniques and treatment show the signs of talent we expect from this distinguished illustrator. The story of Ben's empty box that in imagination and play serves as a castle to be defended against dragons, a boat swamped by an octopus, a submarine attacked by a shark, a space ship defying hostile enemies, is told in a simple, brief text, half-a-dozen full page illustrations and elaborate pop-ups. Considerable ingenuity and masses of bright colours certainly create an illusion of monsters and mayhem, fantasy and fun. But, after the initial impact of these bursting extravaganzas, how long will delight and interest last?

> *G. Bott, in a review of "Ben's Box," in* The Junior Bookshelf, *Vol. 51, No. 2, April, 1987, p. 77.*

Ben's Baby (1987)

Michael Foreman, as he should by now, knows just what he's up to. **Ben's Baby,** his attractive account of a little boy waiting for a new baby, leaves out all the harsher possibilities, the sickness and the sibling rivalry. But it gains its richness from the delicate symbolism of the pictures—anxiety shown in a broken kitestring, happiness in the newly extended family walking under the glowing arch of the trees—and from its cinematic cutting through the dark time of winter to the coloured promise of summer. **Ben's Baby** works by its acceptance of limits, its new enactment of the old paradox that stories can be most realis-

tic at their most artfully fictional. For a five-year-old it could have as much to say about books as about babies; that there's a two-way door between literature and life.

> *Tom Deveson, "Shared Anxieties," in* The Times Educational Supplement, *No. 3753, June 3, 1988, p. 46.*

This reassuring British book reflects pregnancy from the child's point of view. During a fall hike in a park, Ben's father asks him what he wants for his next birthday, and he answers, "A baby." Foreman follows the family through the seasons, and the following summer, on the day after Ben's birthday, a new brother is born. Text is minimal; most pages have only one or two sentences. The attractive watercolor illustrations range from pastel pink and blue on the cover to brilliant oranges, greens, and blues inside. Each picture has an interesting composition: the museum contains life sized dinosaurs; and the park shows ducks, rowers, runners, flags, buildings, foliage, and groups of people. Most interesting is a realistic looking ultrasound picture, of which Ben asks, "Is that my baby? Is it waving?" A good choice for children awaiting a new baby.

> *Jean Gaffney, in a review of "Ben's Baby," in* School Library Journal, *Vol. 34, No. 11, August, 1988, p. 80.*

If the death of a beautiful woman is the most poetic of subjects, then the birth of a baby must be the most dangerously sentimental. Yet illustrator Michael Foreman, whose soft washes of watercolor skirt that abyss of mawkishness into which other children's artists skip with careless abandon, reveals again a perfect balance of prose and picture.

While his parents search for chestnuts in a grove along the river, four-year-old Ben rides his new birthday bike. "What do you want for your next birthday, Ben?" asks his mom. "A baby," answers Ben. His "dad laughed and stopped looking for chestnuts". Somehow Foreman manages to charge that last phrase—"and stopped looking for chestnuts"—with a quiet but distinct sexual edge, one that's reinforced by his picture of the father glancing up toward the mother, both of them frozen in mid-motion.

The rest of the book, naturally enough, takes us through the months as we await the birth of "Ben's Baby." . . .

As in such restful classics as *Goodnight Moon* or *The Story of Ferdinand,* simple sentences and comforting images make this familiar story ideal for a 3- or 4-year-old a bit anxious about the prospect of a younger brother or sister. Its lullaby prose also makes it a perfect bed-time story even after the baby is born.

> *Michael Dirda, in a review of "Ben's Baby," in* Book World—The Washington Post, *September 11, 1988, p. 9.*

The Angel and the Wild Animal (1988)

Sometimes there is an angel in the house and at other times a wild animal. This is a vivid portrayal of a young boy's changes of mood from a sunny, angelic child into an unruly, wild animal who succeeds in making all the adults around him very angry indeed. The antics of the child such as flooding the house, crashing into things on his toy car, and racing around the supermarket with a shopping trolley all show situations which I am sure will be familiar to many parents. The language is simple and concise and reads well. The illustrations are full of emotion and life and superbly capture the changes in the child's moods. An unusual book which will be enjoyed by child and parent alike.

> *Margaret Hunt, in a review of "The Angel and the Wild Animal," in* The School Librarian, *Vol. 37, No. 1, February, 1989, p. 15.*

With intuitiveness and creativity, Foreman has written a story about a child who is sometimes an angel, sometimes a wild man, but most often just a little boy. . . . Foreman's playful illustrations probe both the good and bad aspects of a highly imaginative child with a good dose of humor and much finesse. The colors are bright, offset by dark, bold type. Readers familiar with last year's *Half Wild and Half Child* by Lizi Boyd will enjoy this treatment of a similar theme.

> *A review of "The Angel and the Wild Man," in* Publishers Weekly, *Vol. 235, No. 6, February 10, 1989, p. 69.*

Foreman's spare text and softly colored pencil sketches make a definitive statement about the various moods of a child. One disconcerting picture shows a sharp-toothed, angry child. It is effective but may be somewhat startling. Overall the gentle, comforting quality of the text and pictures tempers its realistic depiction of the behavior of a particularly active child. Parents will recognize these difficult moments, and may appreciate the opportunity the book brings to talk about feelings and behavior. Children reading on their own may find the text confusing; this is a story best suited to sharing. Some may see it as a springboard for discussion; others as a reassuring sketch of life with a mercurial child. (pp. 87-8)

> *Gail C. Ross, in a review of "The Angel and the Wild Animal," in* School Library Journal, *Vol. 35, No. 10, June, 1989, pp. 87-8.*

War Boy: A Country Childhood   (1989)

Michael Foreman's pictorial war memoirs of a Suffolk childhood in the Home-front-line are tuppence-coloured and well worth both pennies. He was born three years ahead of me in 1938, so I have to take it on trust that when the Americans arrived a four-year-old would have

People gave up carrying masks after a few months. We were taught to spit on the inside of the mica window to prevent it misting up. Gas masks were good for rude noises and fogged up anyway.

Hitler will send no warning — so always carry your gas mask

Illustration by Michael Foreman from his War Boy: A Country Childhood *(1990), published by Arcade.*

dreamed that if he ran along behind enough of the trucks he would be spotted as the new Mickey Rooney and packed off with his family to Hollywood. A little later, aged seven, I was Dick Barton, but that's another man's story.

War Boy is dedicated to Foreman's older brothers and to his mother, who died in 1982, and the anecdotes, statistics and piecemeal recollections which accompany a delightful spread of atmospheric illustrations come across as a curious mixture of memory, and gap-filling hindsight—a kind of collaborative family album in which the small boy who was keeps peeping out from behind the material he has subsequently collected from conversation, careful reading and other people's nostalgia. The book is none the worse for this, but it does tend to isolate those occasional marvellous moments of total accuracy (grabbed from his bedroom when the house was hit by an incendiary bomb "the sky bounced as my mother ran") from the more familiar, well-worn Dad's Army scenarios and from the adult-glossed memories such as the one where, aged three and a half, Michael is being carried off to bed on Christmas night and looks back from his mother's arms at "other boys' fathers sitting round our table wishing it was their little boy they had just kissed goodnight". Foreman's own father had died a month before his youngest son was born which gives the incident a moving poignancy at the same time as it highlights the Nomansland *War Boy* inhabits between the child's-eye view and adult experience.

I suppose what this amounts to is that the book will interest its younger readers while bringing a lump to the throat of many of Foreman's contemporaries. The pictures are at their best where vivid particulars are isolated by an explosion of colour set against a gentle wash, such as when one of the motor-cyclists training as despatch riders on Hill Green careers out of control, bouncing down the slope and bursting into flames. Or, more domestically, in the infant school classroom when Miss West's drawers flash a startling periwinkle blue. Elsewhere Foreman occasionally strays into a more Ovaltine-y version of Gordon Beningfield territory, but not for long and never disastrously.

John Mole, "From the Home Front," in The Times Educational Supplement, *No. 3824, October 13, 1989, p. 28.*

Michael Foreman grows in stature all the time, and this fragment of autobiography displays at once his versatility and his strength. His memories of what it was like to grow up in a Suffolk village in wartime reminded me just a little of *The Young Ardizzone*, an impression strengthened by one page where the similarity in line technique is quite startling. But Mr. Foreman has been better served by his publisher. His book is presented beautifully.

The artist was just past his third birthday when a German incendiary bomb dropped through the bedroom roof, missed his bed, bounced and, after a second impact, landed conveniently in the hearth. It is not surprising that an early memory of this kind has been retained vividly. But, on the evidence of this book, Foreman has a phenomenal memory and, as befits an artist, a visual one. The drawings and paintings that crowd his pages might have been done

on the spot, so convincing are all the details. As a child would, he records the excitement and the humour as at least equal in the memory with the terror. Among the action drawings are a few full-scale studies of a landscape in war—barrage balloons over a cold grey sea, watermeadow and marsh lying empty under a summer sky—done with all his mastery of tone and design.

With so much vitality and action in the pictures, it would be easy to overlook the text. This is in its way just as successful. The artist treats words with the same respect he accords to his colours. He is a lively writer, and a discreet one too, knowing how much to leave unsaid as well as how to bring an episode sharply into focus. Altogether as delightful a book as it is impressive. Apart from the concern with childhood it is not specially a book for children, although they will find it a good guide to history. Parents and grandparents will find it absorbing and authentic. (pp. 10-11)

M. Crouch, in a review of "War Boy: A Country Childhood," in The Junior Bookshelf, *Vol. 54, No. 1, February, 1990, pp. 10-11.*

A collection of memories of the artist's childhood during World War II is presented as if seen through the eyes of a child for whom all the world is unquestionably natural and right. . . . The sense of comradeship, frequently tinged with bawdiness, among the people is almost palpable. The illustrations of scruffy little boys playing games, people racing to shelters in the light of searchlights and gunfire, and soldiers enjoying a crowded, smoky, cheerful Christmas party seem to illuminate all aspects of life as it must have been. These vignettes are scattered about in no particular order, apparently as they came to mind, and often leave the reader wishing for more detail and explanation. But the juxtaposition of war with the everyday life of a child carries total conviction and the true stamp of experience undergone. (pp. 347-48)

Ann A. Flowers, in a review of "War Boy: A Country Childhood," in The Horn Book Magazine, *Vol. LXVI, No. 3, May-June, 1990, pp. 347-48.*

One World **(1990)**

AUTHOR'S COMMENTARY

Sometimes a book demands to be born. You wake up and there it is, slipping out like a baby dolphin, ready-formed and heading for the surface.

But others aren't so smooth. They start as a smidgeon of something with an idea beating inside. You pick it up, tickle it and breathe on it, then tuck it away, kangaroo like, until it needs attention again. Other adventures become more demanding, but all the time the smidgeon clings on, close to your heart. Incubating, tugging at you.

Land of Dreams took 14 years before it saw the light of day. My new book, *One World,* took seven years from conception to finished book, and in the beginning it was quite a different creature.

Several years ago I realised that children were much better

informed and more concerned about what was happening in the world than many adults.

For the first time ever, through their access to television, children were able to see what was going on, and know about it directly, as it happened, not the edited text book version or through the filtering process of parents. And not just from excellent children's programmes, like "Newsround," but also the regular news and current affairs programmes which are part of the home environment.

I see our young sons laying on the floor amid lego and crayons when an item on the six o'clock news suddenly catches their attention, and sometimes their imagination.

> 'What's that, Dad?'
> 'What does that mean?'
> 'Why are they doing that?'

I remember as a teenager in Suffolk painting 'Ban the Bomb' on the police station. The mother of a friend of mine told me I'd 'grow out of it' and that as I got older I'd understand the ways of the world.

Today's parents are different. The teenage Aldermaston marchers are today's middle-aged. The flower children and young anti-Vietnam protestors are today's parents. They don't tell their children to grow out of it. Many adults have kept faith with their youthful ideals.

It seemed to me that there was a small group of very old people making decisions on behalf of a vast number of other old people which would affect the lives of very young people for a very long time. The short term plans to comfort the demise of these old dinosaurs would put a blight on the lives of those too young for a voice and with most to lose. Now that children had access to the news, I hoped they'd find a voice.

I decided to do a book which would raise issues children could in turn raise with adults, at home and in the classroom.

During the summer of 1983 I began the first draft of a story that was eventually to become *One World.* The first draft had the working title of 'Hey! I am Me'. It contained a brief history of the world and the growth of the industrial revolution and the industrial / military complex, plus a quick tour of the planet and its journey through space—all in 32 pages. Needless to say it was confusing and didn't work.

The book was peopled by the old leaders. Only one still holds office, and she needs no introduction. Multitudes of children swarmed through the pages of the book proclaiming 'Hey! I am Me', and demanding answers to their questions about their inheritance—the world, and the threat of its destruction.

The book contained scenes of mediaeval war machines and huge industrial machines consuming vast amounts of energy. Armies of men, women and children toiled in appalling conditions, and generations of children asked 'Why?'

They were told, 'Sshssh! It's always done that way. Wait till you're grown up. You'll understand.'

I did many versions over the next four or five years but just couldn't get the balance right. It was either too didactic and angry, or too diffuse and the point was lost. There were too many points, I was hitting out in all directions. Publishers ducked. It contained everything I wanted to say, but was too difficult to grasp. All spouts and no handle.

Then came the Reykjavik Summit. A world leader did what General Jodhpur had done in my first book, *The General* (published 1961). He turned his back on the arms race. The other leaders (who'd been leaning on him) had to step back or fall over. They had to step back and rethink. The bogie man wanted to boogie.

History went into overdrive. Parts of the book that had given me such problems were suddenly out of date.

Sometimes a book comes out ahead of its time. It comes out and nothing much happens. The already converted notice, and everybody else ignores it. Then something happens in the world which prompts similar books and forms a minor genre in which the earlier book can find a place.

While visiting a school in Germany earlier this year, I was told that *Dinosaurs and all that Rubbish* is more important now than when it was first published in 1972. Wrong. It just gets more attention now.

And much of that additional attention came after Chernobyl.

At 1pm on the day of Chernobyl, I brought the family in from the garden. I didn't fancy eating our picnic while the clouds went over.

At 3pm three-year-old Ben said 'Let's play. Daddy you be the bad cloud and I'll be the picnic.' During the course of an afternoon a catastrophe had become part of a child's imaginative play.

The threat from the arms race faded beside the accelerating spread of pollution. Even the old leaders made green noises. But only noises.

I started again, and this time I determined to keep the book simple.

I always write the first draft of a story in whichever notebook I'm carrying around at the time. When travelling I never take anything to read to fill the long hours of enforced idleness. Train journeys are great for daydreaming. Delayed flights are good times for people-watching, and the long limbo hours of night flight, when all you love are a thousand miles away, and you feel weightless, stateless and probably legless after a few airline drinks, are rare opportunities for the brain to float, unfettered and de-ranged, into the soup of ideas.

Anyone with a young family will know how rare such moments of real self-indulgence are.

When I'm back home and I feel the story is getting somewhere, I make a little dummy book of folded paper, usually 32 pages in length. I write the story through the pages to see how well it fits, leaving space for pictures, and seeing where the breaks come in the text.

When the text is broken up by the act of page turning it reads differently. Turning the page becomes an extra bit of punctuation. Writing several sentences on a page is like several quick cuts in a movie. Turning the page acts as a kind of dissolve. Like the end of a stanza in a poem. So I find it necessary to work and re-work the idea through a series of blank books rather than sheets of flat paper.

Of course, I'm visualising the pictures all the time and deciding how much of the idea can be told visually.

At this point I know if it's going to work smoothly or become a case for lengthy incubation. However, even if I think it works well, I'm always in the middle of another book which has to be finished first. So there's always a delay, maybe of months, before I can begin pictures for the new idea. This enforced delay gives time to re-think, and often when I pick up the idea again I find it has lost something—maybe even its life.

So then the initial idea, the spark, lies buried in its notebook. Another spark, another journey, might make a connection, like Frankenstein's monster and the lightning, and the idea begins to twitch again.

This time it wasn't lightning, but a Cornish beach. During the summer of 1989 my sons spent a lot of time exploring rock pools. Suddenly, there it was. A rock pool. A microcosm of the world. Its beauty, its life and its fragility. The simple approach.

'Hey! I am Me' became *One World.*

One World with one child and one small part of the planet. Several versions later I realised it needed a touch of dialogue and introduced a second child.

Of course, there are echoes of the wider world, and beyond. I wanted to keep a sense of the enormity of space and time, and the right of every living thing to its own little bit of that space and time.

It's not the book I set out to write seven years ago, but it's close to what I wanted to say! (pp. 4-5)

> Michael Foreman, "The Birth of a Book," in
> Books for Keeps, No. 62, May, 1990, pp. 4-5.

Michael Foreman's contribution to the 'green' debate is characteristically unconventional and sincere. This is a picture book, superficially for small children (and perhaps welcomed by them) but with implications for all. For those youngest readers an adult interpreter will be needed. Two children are messing about on the beach. As they dip into pools and chase shrimps they look beyond the miniature environment and make their own world. They hold 'their world in their hands', and see in it an image of a world rapidly being poisoned and destroyed. At night they look at the moon and stars and think of 'all the other children who lived under the sky'. The brief text has the refinement of a poem. The author's pictures, with the typical Foreman blues and golds, hint at inner meanings. A diffi-

cult book and an important one. It deserves to be supported.

> Marcus Crouch, in a review of "One World,"
> in The School Librarian, Vol. 38, No. 4, November, 1990, p. 142.

This book looks and reads like a picture book, and is by a well-known and respected picture-book creator. However, its theme of the parallels between the microenvironment at our feet and that of the entire planet seem well beyond the grasp of that readership. The story is slight. . . . The illustrations are in Foreman's familiar style—his distinctive watercolors shine from each page, and the blues and yellows are particularly eye-catching. His depiction of the children and the life of the seashore is accurate yet lyrical, with several interesting shifts in perspective. The little girl, refreshingly, is definitely the leader. The cause is worthwhile—royalties are being donated to Friends of the Earth. However, young children are unlikely to understand Foreman's point—how many of them will understand a connection between a depleted rock pool and the destruction of rain forests? A final line—"And that world, too, they held in their hands"—imposes an unfair burden of guilt on young shoulders. While adults want to encourage an interest and (eventually) an involvement in the environment, this is not necessarily the way to do it. The book may be useful as a discussion starter with older children, if they are not put off by its format. (pp. 94-5)

> Barbara Hutcheson, in a review of "One World," in School Library Journal, Vol. 37, No. 11, November, 1991, pp. 94-5.

The link between the tiny and the vast is the core of this simple story. The minute denizens of the pool generate images of great whales; the smear of oil on its surface is a reminder of a poisoned world; the children's decision to restore the ransacked habitat promises hope for the earth.

This book is a sermon, but one so economical with words and profuse with beautiful illustrations that its message is conveyed as lucidly as birdsong.

> G. H., in a review of "One World," in Books for Keeps, No. 77, November, 1992, p. 17.

Michael Foreman's World of Fairy Tales (1990)

[This] is a highly personal selection of fairy tales from all around the world. *Michael Foreman's World of Fairy Tales* has a spectacular title page map of the world, rich in vivid colours and bearing the dedication 'For the children of the world'. The stories do come from all of the world—Australia, the Arctic, Cornwall, Ireland, Russia, New Zealand, Arabia, France, Japan, China, Mexico . . .

The titles are magical: 'How the Raven Brought Light to the World', 'The Fool of the World and the Flying Ship', and 'The Four Dragons' from China. This is no mere token poly-ethnic collection—Michael Foreman has imbued all of the pictures with the characteristics of each distinctive culture, but brings his own interpretation to what he saw as he travelled thousands of miles, often in the company of the actual storyteller. The attendant contrasts are striking.

Fiona Waters, in a review of "Michael Foreman's World of Fairy Tales," in Books for Keeps, *No. 65, November, 1990, p. 26.*

Michael Foreman's Mother Goose   (1991)

Using subtle tones of color washes and pencil, Foreman's delicate illustrations provide a visual tour of the world of nursery rhymes. Each double-page spread presents a landscape of related verses, with visual links often provided from one spread to the next, creating a dynamic, fun-filled pace. "Little Tommy Tucker" sings to the bakers of "The Pasty," which is being eaten in bed by John of "Diddle, Diddle, Dumpling" fame. As the reader turns the page, the pasty's mice run by "Robin the Bobbin," "Little Jack Horner," Jacky of "Cakes and Custard," and Mr. and Mrs. Jack Sprat. With old favorites joined by less common rhymes as well as riddles, tongue twisters, and nursery game rhymes, families can enjoy repeated journeys through Foreman's linear landscape.

Linda Callaghan, in a review of "Michael

Foreman's Mother Goose," in Booklist, *Vol. 88, No. 2, September 15, 1991, p. 153.*

A book that encourages readers to take a fresh look at traditional nursery rhymes, most of which are included here along with a few surprises such as *Robinson Crusoe* and "The Twelve Days of Christmas." The size and shape is perfect for lap-time sharing with one or two youngsters, and delicate yet detailed illustrations, usually several to a page, will give pleasure to both children and adults. When there is a single illustration sweeping across a double-paged spread, it emphasizes the drama and movement also evident in smaller drawings. Repeated viewings reveal facial expressions and humorous details not noticed on first observation. Shades of blue dominate in sea and sky backgrounds and also in the foreground of many pictures, giving a soothing quality to this collection, even amidst the giggles. The humorously witchlike Mother Goose on the dustjacket seems to be soaring into the pages strewing stars and leaving a lone tailfeather in her wake. That feather floats through the frontispieces pursued by a child who, appropriately, catches it at the end of the foreword by Iona Opie. This invitation to follow an image continues throughout the book. Young viewers may not see the visual playfulness of the carefully considered juxtaposition of images immediately; but, as soon as it is noticed, they will

From Michael Foreman's World of Fairy Tales, *written and illustrated by Michael Foreman.*

delight in discovering the many different ways of connecting pages. Often a character from one rhyme jaunts on into the next vignette. Sometimes a necessary part of one illustration actually slips around the corner onto the next page. All result in a unified work that flows from page to page. One can enjoy individual rhymes, with their soft, muted but clear colors, delicate lines, humor and quiet liveliness; but, oh the loss, if readers don't follow these pages from beginning to end.

> *Kay E. Vandergrift, in a review of "Michael Foreman's Mother Goose," in* School Library Journal, *Vol. 37, No. 10, October, 1991, p. 111.*

The Boy Who Sailed with Columbus (with Richard Seaver, 1992)

The New and Old Worlds exchange captives in a tale of a ship's boy who is left behind by Columbus and grows up to be a respected sage and healer. Young Leif is thrilled to be on the adventure of a lifetime, but disturbed when he sees natives kidnapped to display back in Spain. Then Leif himself is captured and taken to the mainland, where he becomes "Morning Star," the "eyes" of a blind old wise man. Years later, seeing European ships off his adopted coast and having forebodings of what is to come, he flees westward with his family. Small details and vignettes accent the spacious, oblong blocks of text and also link Foreman's full-page watercolors—all lit by explosions of reds and blues and livened up by occasional comic touches. Human figures are generally small (and frequently naked), but always the focus of action. Columbus's accomplishments and attitudes are getting plenty of scrutiny; though Foreman's story is only loosely based on the historical record, and has more action than analysis, it should set readers thinking.

> *A review of "The Boy Who Sailed with Columbus," in* Kirkus Reviews, *Vol. LX, No. 6, March 15, 1992, p. 393.*

This beautifully illustrated and imaginative story combines factual information with a sensitive treatment of Native Americans. . . .

Foreman's luminous watercolors, many of which are full page, are competently executed and are perfect accompaniments to the text. The cover art and picture-book format will attract readers to this moving and thought-provoking fictional account.

> *Jean H. Zimmerman, in a review of "The Boy Who Sailed with Columbus," in* School Library Journal, *Vol. 38, No. 15, May, 1992, p. 112.*

Foreman's story recalls various narrative traditions, from the cowboy-and-Indians dichotomy of good and evil (make that evil and good) to the European ideal of the noble savage. Yet, there's little conflict here and little character development, so the literary result is rather bland. The artwork, however, is unusually lavish and ap-

pealing for a book of children's fiction. Foreman's watercolor illustrations appear on nearly every page, reproduced in full color and varying in size from small vignettes to full-page paintings. Looking like a picture book in format, though much longer and more sophisticated, this will draw readers with its wealth of evocative illustrations; it may be chosen as a classroom read-aloud for that reason, as well. Conrad's *Pedro's Journal* remains the best fictional treatment in the "ship's boy with Columbus" subgenre, but Foreman's splendid watercolors are well nigh irresistible.

> *Carolyn Phelan, in a review of "The Boy Who Sailed with Columbus," in* Booklist, *Vol. 88, No. 19, June 1, 1992, p. 1762.*

Jack's Fantastic Voyage (1992)

Jack loves his grandfather—his old wooden house by the sea which resembles an old boat, his paintings of wild seas and shipwrecks, and his stories. It comes as a shock when he hears the local children sneer and make fun. Mud has been thrown and some of it sticks to Jack's illusions about the old man, only to be washed away when one night Grandfather tells the wildest story of them all. As he tells it, the house breaks away from its moorings and sails into a sea-green, sea-blue world of storms and schooners, seals, stars and ice. The text is engaging, Michael Foreman's pictures entrancing. A lovely book to share with a small child, cuddled up.

> *Michael Kirby, in a review of "Jack's Fantastic Voyage," in* The School Librarian, *Vol. 40, No. 3, August, 1992, p. 94.*

Michael Foreman's luminous watercolours beautifully capture the love between Jack and his grandfather, and the sheen on ice, the grace of a humpback whale breaching, and the glare of sun on the seashore. Particularly breathtaking are the double-page spreads showing the ships, the ice, and the various animals playing around the ships.

I would be hesitant in giving this book to a young child, however, I feel that the slightly lengthy text would better suit children 6 years or older.

> *Lynne Roberts, in a review of "Jack's Fantastic Voyage," in* Reading Time, *Vol. XXXVI, No. IV, November, 1992, p. 16.*

Foreman's watercolor illustrations produce an ethereal quality with their soft hues and visions of the sea. His love of the water and its creatures is evident. We are such stuff as dreams are made on . . . , and this author / illustrator has given readers the right stuff.

> *Joyce Richards, in a review of "Jack's Fantastic Voyage," in* School Library Journal, *Vol. 38, No. 11, November, 1992, p. 69.*

Grey Owl

1888-1938

(Pseudonym of Archibald Stansfeld Belaney; also wrote as Wa-sha-quon-asin) English-born Canadian author and illustrator of fiction and nonfiction.

Major works include *The Men of the Last Frontier* (1931), *Pilgrims of the Wild* (1934), *The Adventures of Sajo and Her Beaver People* (1935; U. S. edition as *Sajo and the Beaver People*), *Tales of an Empty Cabin* (1936).

The following entry presents general criticism of Grey Owl's oeuvre. It also includes a selection of reviews to supplement the general commentary.

INTRODUCTION

A keen and insightful observer of nature determined to "bring before the Canadian people the beauty and soul of their own country," Grey Owl wrote fictional and biographical works based on his experiences in the Canadian wilderness that have been praised for arousing the environmental consciousness of children and young adults. Although he consciously directed only one of his works to young people, he is considered with such authors as Ernest Thompson Seton and Charles G. D. Roberts as a prominent nature writer for this audience. His writings, which include and often interweave personal reminiscences, adventure stories, and legends with vivid descriptions of wildlife and the Canadian landscape, were immensely popular in his day and are still considered relevant to contemporary readers concerned about preserving the natural world. *The Men of the Last Frontier, Pilgrims of the Wild, The Adventures of Sajo and Her Beaver People,* and *Tales of an Empty Cabin,* acclaimed for their authentic and humorous depictions of animal life and behavior, especially that of the beaver, colorfully express Grey Owl's affection and respect for wildlife. These works also evoke moving pathos in their descriptions of an animal's fight for survival against predators—including man—and the harshness of the elements; for this reason the conservationist Grey Owl has been called a subtle propagandist. Nevertheless, Dorothy D. Sikes has noted that Grey Owl "provided some vivid portraits of the men who inhabit these wilderness areas; courageous, honest, tale-telling, respecting each other for what they do, not for who they are, and keeping to a strict code of conduct in their work." Although his writings have been denigrated as trite and amateurish by commentators who consider them excessively sentimental, and too subjective by some who note that his fondness for beavers led him to depict their predators unfavorably, Grey Owl is largely regarded as an engaging author whose works reflect what *In Review* maintains was "the remarkable perception of a man years ahead of his time."

By his own testimony Grey Owl was a "half-breed" Indian born on the Rio Grande in Mexico, his mother an Apache and his father a Scottish frontiersman and friend of Buffalo Bill Cody. Although fictional, this background enhanced the intrigue and romance surrounding Grey Owl's public persona, as the biographical facts of his existence were not discovered during his lifetime. In truth, Grey Owl was born Archibald Stansfeld Belaney in Hastings, England. Raised by his grandmother and two aunts after his father's forced exile from that country, he developed a kinship with a variety of local animals and became obsessed with North American Indian lore. He traveled to Canada at the age of sixteen, where he became a fur trapper and was adopted as blood-brother by the Ojibwa Indians, who called him Wa-sha-quon-asin (He Who Flies by Night, or Grey Owl). In 1926 Grey Owl made an Iroquois woman named Anahareo his common-law wife and, despite her aversion to his livelihood, continued trapping with untempered zeal. At Anahareo's insistence, however, two beaver kittens were adopted into the couple's home as pets after Grey Owl had killed their mother. Dubbed McGinnis and McGinty, these animals—along with their successors Jelly Roll and Rawhide—prompted the sentiment and affection which are vividly imbued in Grey

Owl's animal stories and in three educational films for which he served as both actor and director. "To kill such creatures seemed monstrous," he asserted. "I would do no more of it. Instead of persecuting them further I would study them, see just what there really was to them. I perhaps could start a colony of my own; these animals could not be permitted to pass completely from the face of this wilderness."

Grey Owl started his first beaver colony in the winter of 1928-1929. In order to earn a living and spread his philosophy, he began writing essays and submitting them for publication. The English journal *Country Life* published one such piece and commissioned another. Two years later, the commercial success of Grey Owl's first book, a collection of adventures and observations called *The Men of the Last Frontier,* prompted him to write an autobiography detailing his and Anahareo's life in the wilderness. *Pilgrims of the Wild* increased Grey Owl's fame in Canada and throughout the British Isles, making him a romantic figure whose image was enhanced by a series of lectures that he delivered in full Indian regalia. These discourses were received enthusiastically by audiences including the royal family and young Princesses Margaret and Elizabeth at Buckingham Palace. Children who heard his addresses were especially intrigued by Grey Owl's description of the habits and antics of beavers, which he related in the same affectionate, sentimental, and understatedly humorous manner which informs his writings. He wrote one book especially for children, illustrating it himself with pencil sketches in the same manner he employed for his other works. *The Adventures of Sajo and Her Beaver People* relates the story of two Indian children whose family sells one of their two beaver kittens. The young people and their remaining pet are engaged in a host of adventures and difficulties as they attempt to recover their little friend, with whom they are reunited at the end of the tale.

During his lifetime Grey Owl was revered as a self-taught Indian who had amazingly mastered the white man's literary style. After his death, when the truth about his heritage was revealed, he was considered a fraud, an opinion that caused his books to fall into some disfavor. More recent critics recognize him as an influential naturalist, comparable to Henry David Thoreau, whose campaign regarding the beaver helped to save that animal from extinction. Kenneth Brower writes of Grey Owl, "No man was more important to Canadian environmental consciousness, or to the environmental consciousness of the entire British Commonwealth, for that matter. . . . His fictive gift . . . laced his readers and listeners into buckskins, strapped them into his snowshoes with him. His unmasking . . . has only made him larger, deepening his mystery."

(See also *Something about the Author,* Vol. 24; *Contemporary Authors,* Vol. 114; and *Dictionary of Literary Biography,* Vol. 22.)

AUTHOR'S COMMENTARY

[*The following excerpt is from the preface to* Sajo and the Beaver People.]

While the events recorded in this modest tale did not, in all instances, occur in the chronological order here appointed them, all of them have taken place within my knowledge. Indeed, most of them are recorded from personal experience and from first-hand narrations by the participators themselves.

Save for a few of the details connected with the two children's visit to the city (regarding which I had only the impressions of two bewildered youngsters to work on, and further obscured by the passage of over a quarter of a century), no circumstances have been brought in that are not actual fact.

Any Indian words used are correctly rendered from the Ojibway language, in the regional dialect of the area involved, and are spelled phonetically so as to simplify pronunciation. The words are simple, and their meanings are made to appear in an easy and natural manner.

In the illustrations I have made no attempt at artistry, confining myself strictly to clear outlines, in the interests of accuracy—not that my efforts in this direction were at all endangered by any vigorous attacks of artistic ability. My two sole departures into the, to me, treacherous field of poetic license occur, firstly, in the figure of the moose who stands guard at the heading of Chapter Two. Although the scene is laid in the month of May, I have given him a full set of antlers, as he would appear later in the season, thus offering a more interesting educational exhibit than would the somewhat mule-like creature he would appear without them. Secondly, the owl that is represented at the head of Chapter Four is not of the variety known as the Laughing Owl, who, in spite of his vocal capabilities, is rather a commonplace, uninteresting-looking specimen of his genus. I have therefore supplanted him by the more representative type, known as the Great Horned Owl. So, like all good transgressors whose misdeeds are about to be exposed, I make this timely confession.

The delineations of animal character are to be taken as authentic, and the mental and physical reactions ascribed to the animals are as nearly correct as a lifetime of intimate association with wild life, in its own environment, can make them. These portrayals, as well as all other descriptions, have been very carefully drawn, so that the young reader will not be transported into a world that is altogether make-believe, but may gain new and pleasing impressions that need not later be discarded as mere phantasy. My intention was to write a child's story that could be read, without loss of dignity, by grown-ups. (pp. xi-xii)

It is my hope that, besides providing an hour or two of entertainment, this simple story of two Indian children and their well-loved animal friends may awaken in some eager, inquiring young minds a clearer and more intimate understanding of the joys and the sorrows, the work, the pastimes and the daily lives of the humble little People of the forest, who can experience feelings so very like their own. And the writer even ventures, at the risk of being considered presumptuous, to allow himself the thought that perhaps, too, it may invoke in the hearts of even those of more mature years a greater tolerance and sympathy for those who are weaker or less gifted than themselves.

Above all, may it be my privilege to carry with me, as fellow-voyagers on this short, imaginary journey to the Northland, a small but happy company of those who, for so short a time, dwell in that Enchanted Vale of Golden Dreams that we call Childhood. (pp. xiii-xiv)

> *Grey Owl, in his* Sajo and the Beaver People, *Charles Scribner's Sons, 1936, 187 p.*

Punch

From all points of view **The Men of the Last Frontier** is a delightful book. "Grey Owl" ("the English equivalent of the author's name among the Ojibway Indians, in which tribe he is a 'blood-brother' ") writes with real distinction, and the tale he has to tell of his life as a trapper and so forth in a Canada that, to his sorrow, is all too rapidly disappearing, is as inspiring as it is informing. And the reason is that "Grey Owl" has an innate love for nature and a deep sympathy with animal life. It is impossible, for instance, to read his chapters on beavers, "The Tale of the Beaver People" and "The House of McGinnis," without an increasing affection for animals in general and for beavers in particular. I can confidently recommend this book—which is admirably illustrated—to everyone interested in natural history, for here are great adventure and keen observation recorded by one who has learnt wisdom while spending years of his life in the solitary places of the world.

> *"The Silent Places," in* Punch, *Vol. CLXXXI, December 16, 1931, p. 672.*

The Times Literary Supplement

As preserver of the last families of beaver and as fire ranger "Grey Owl" writes with knowledge and authority [in **The Men of the Last Frontier**]; but to anyone unacquainted with the political aspect of this subject, what haunts the memory are his unforgettable vignettes of frost-bound valleys and their aching winter nights, of the Indian—a shadow among shadows—stalking game, and above all, of the charm and pathos of the beaver, whether watched at its interminable industry, or sitting before the fire as the author's solitary comrade. The publisher offers an apology for "Grey Owl's" elusive grasp of the English tongue. This takes one a little aback, as it is difficult to recall any record of the great North-West so brilliantly and lovingly handled.

> *A review of "The Men of the Last Frontier," in* The Times Literary Supplement, *No. 1571, March 10, 1932, p. 163.*

R. L. Duffus

The United States lost its last frontier when Oklahoma was opened to settlement forty years ago, but Canada, as Grey Owl testifies in a book full of love for the wilderness and intimate acquaintance with it [**The Men of the Last Frontier**] still has one. Grey Owl is the son of a Scotch father and an Apache mother. As a young man he went to Canada, was adopted into the tribe of the Ojibways, and became a trapper. Somewhere along the route he acquired enough education—and it must have been a pretty good one if, as his publishers say, his manuscript has been changed only enough to clear away ambiguities and phrases which "would have read too strangely"—to write his book. The result is that one's chief criticism is that Grey Owl is too literary. He is no frontier Jim Tully. He gives us, on the whole, not the vernacular of the trail but a translation of that vernacular into language city people can grasp. Perhaps he has had to explain things to too many tenderfeet.

But Grey Owl is no stuffed Indian. He is real and honest and he lets his readers behind the scenes of a life comparable for glamour and heroism with that which was lived in the American Rockies during the golden decades of the beaver trade nearly a century ago. The difference is that the wilderness men are fewer than they used to be, that game is getting scarcer and civilization pressing onward, and that the line of stark conflict and kinship with nature has been thrust far into the stern Northern lands. The Canadian borderman may spend his Summer cruising in "the Strong Woods," or beyond, in search of hunting grounds. His real work is done in the Winter, after the first big freeze. In the depths of the wilderness he has built himself a log cabin and stocked it with the necessary provisions for a long siege. Then he lays out his lines of traps, over which he must plod on snowshoes at regular intervals, often by night, usually in bitter cold. He may be alone for months at a time. Obviously this is no life for a man who likes crowds and motion pictures. But it is a life that seems to have its attractions, if only in the sense of ability to endure and conquer. . . .

Perhaps few woodsmen have Grey Owl's poetry of expression, though many of them must have felt the emotions which he describes in his chapters on "The Land of Shadows" and "The Fall of the Leaf." Few, perhaps, have his profound sympathy with the Indian which his own Indian blood and his tribal membership have given him. The chapter on "The Trail of Two Sunsets" is worth reading by anybody who has gone too far in his reaction against Cooper's or Longfellow's portrayal of the red man. The Indian, certainly, is not at his best when he comes down to the "rails." In the forest he is a different and, probably, better creature; at any rate he is a more competent and appealing one. Grey Owl's description of the life of the Ojibways is more sympathetic than Parkman's of the life of the Ogillallah, and probably just as accurate.

Though Grey Owl was for many years a trapper and, later, as a member of the Canadian Expeditionary Forces, shot at nobler game than could be found in the northern forests, he has turned in recent years against the unnecessary shedding of blood. Some of his comments on the destruction of Canada's natural resources, and especially those touching upon the ravages wrought by the "Bohunk" or "Bolshie," are far from poetic. He has anything but tolerance for the South European immigrant. But his own repentence for his years of bloodshed takes pleasant form in his attempt to keep the beaver from extinction, and in the happy chapter on "The House of McGinnis," in which he elaborates upon the advantages and disadvantages of beavers as pets. "Ahmik, the Beaver People," were sacred to the Indians; they are now sacred to Grey Owl.

The Canadian wilderness cannot be conquered as that of

the United States was, for it runs up to the Arctic Ocean. Much of the game, however, can be and has been killed off, and the life of Indian and frontiersman has thus been deprived of its means of support. The frontier retreats northward, with just a touch of Hollywood in its final gesture: "Northward, northward, ever northward, back into the days that are long forgotten, slipping away over the hills into the purple distance, beyond the Land of Shadows, into the sunset."

Grey Owl, it will be obvious, is a sentimentalist. Perhaps one has to be in Northern Canada if one is to keep alive and sane. But his is a worthy sentimentalism about a worthy subject. His book should outlast its season and many another season.

> *R. L. Duffus, in a review of "The Men of the Last Frontier," in* The New York Times Book Review, *May 22, 1932, p. 4.*

The Saturday Review of Literature

[*The Men of the Last Frontier*] tells of the life north of civilization in the forest belt that crosses Canada. Grey Owl calls it the Land of Shadows. His chapters on the trail, the still hunt, and the fall of the leaf stab the memories of us who have been in his country. There is first hand power in "On Being Lost." His main study, however, is the beaver. It is they who have adopted Grey Owl. They are his dog and cat, and he is possibly the first man to reveal their friendliness and childlikeness.

When you consider how much of this author's time has been spent in the bush and away from everything a modern writer thinks he needs, the high level of his writing is amazing. To observe is one thing, to communicate is quite another, and to feel is still another. Grey Owl does not always skirt the muskegs of sentimentality lying in wait for the nature writer. But if he is as sound as his pages seem, he will not be carried away by easiness and popularity.

> *"A Nature Writer," in* The Saturday Review of Literature, *Vol. VIII, No. 45, May 28, 1932, p. 757.*

The New Statesman & Nation

This delightful study of the wild [*Pilgrims of the Wild*] does exactly what it sets out to do; which is to convey to the reader the author's intense and intimate communion with Nature. In this autobiography, "Grey Owl" tells us how, inspired by his wife, he practically gave up his livelihood as a trapper to protect the beaver, the trapper's most valuable prey. The rescue of two beaver kittens, whose mother had been trapped and killed, and their subsequent rearing, is described so vivaciously and graphically that we share the author's delight in the companionship of these mischievous, intelligent, tidy, affectionate and talkative animals. There is matter in the book for the animal-psychologist, and, thanks to "Grey Owl's" pertinacity, a colony for observation is now under his care and the protection of the Canadian Government.

> *A review of "Pilgrims of the Wild," in* The New Statesman & Nation, *Vol. IX, No. 204, January 19, 1935, p. 84.*

The Times Literary Supplement

Readers of Grey Owl's delightful book *The Men of the Last Frontier* will recall a chapter entitled "The Tale of the Beaver People." In his new volume [*Pilgrims of the Wild*] Grey Owl has elaborated the theme in a sympathetic and intimate study of those highly intelligent and affectionate little animals. He reveals without sentimentality the personality of the beaver with all its domestic virtues and an unexpected assemblage of engaging eccentricities as well. Rarely have naturalist and humanist been so amiably blended. The beaver is, as a companion, not simply scrupulously clean and gentle but determined to become part of the household, and with its indefatigable energy and genius for construction constantly creating new embarrassments. Fortunate are the creatures who are under Grey Owl's official guardianship as "Protector of Wild Life" in Canada. The ancient alliance between the Beaver People and the Red Indian has once more returned, and this fascinating chronicle affords a moving reflection upon the shameless waste and revolting cruelty of the white trapper.

> *"Natural History," in* The Times Literary Supplement, *No. 1724, February 14, 1935, p. 95.*

Anita Moffett

[*Pilgrims of the Wild*], like its predecessor, *Men of the Last Frontier,* is a book of rare quality. . . .

The Indian. . . . did not seek to dominate nature, but took his part in it, "holding to the unity of life in all things," and this feeling is shared by those of other races who have known for any length of time the life of the wilderness. For the most part they have not put their feeling and perception into words. In this book the wilderness, with its values, is made articulate. Told with utter authenticity and fidelity to the truth of the life its describes, it is imbued as well with deeply poetic feeling. *Pilgrims of the Wild* is a record of a twofold achievement—a victorious struggle against heavy odds in behalf of the wilderness and its inhabitants, and the interpretation of that wilderness to those able to appreciate its significance.

> *Anita Moffett, "Rare Forest Lives," in* The New York Times Book Review, *April 7, 1935, p. 19.*

The Times Literary Supplement

[Grey Owl conceived *Sajo and Her Beaver People*] as "a child's story that could be read without loss of dignity by grown-ups." The opening scene is set in Northern Canada, in the country of the Ojibway Indians. We are invited to inspect the water home of a beaver family. Suddenly a raiding otter breaks the protecting dam with the result that two kitten beavers are washed down stream. A kindly Indian saves them and takes them home as pets for his children, Sajo, a girl, and her brother Shapian, who delight in their engaging ways. But times are bad for the four playfellows. To stave off starvation the Indian has to sell to a trader one of the kittens. It eventually reaches the Zoo of a Big City. Sajo has a dream in which she is bidden by the Great Spirit to bring the beaver back. She and her brother thereupon set off down the river to the Big City on a quest that is successful.

The story is primarily one for children, both in the simplicity of the planning and characterization and in the tact with which the author, while reckoning with the terrors of "the Wild," refrains from insisting on their more painful aspects. But he makes no sacrifice to sentimentality in contriving, as he does, a happy ending for his beavers; and we can assure grown-ups solicitous for their dignity that he spares no pains to convince them of his knowledge of animal habits and the incidents of river travel in Northern Canada. He supplements his narrative of what befell his two pairs of youthful adventurers with drawings—among them "A Plan of a Beaver Pond"—as to which, he tells us, that he has subordinated artistry to accuracy, and with many notes in which he explains Canadian terms and usages. Outstanding among the incidents is the escape of the children, together with terrified animals of all kinds, from a forest fire. The interpretative gift claimed for him is to be found in his description of it:—

> Animals that seldom wetted their feet were swimming in the pool—squirrels, rabbits, woodchucks, and even porcupine. Deer leaped through or over the underbush, their white tails flashing, eyes wide with terror. A bear lumbered by at a swift, clumsy gallop, and a pair of wolves ran, easily and gracefully, beside a deer—their natural prey; but they never even looked at him. For none were enemies now; no one was hungry, or fierce, or afraid of another . . .

"Beaver People," in The Times Literary Supplement, *No. 1755, September 19, 1935, p. 577.*

The Times Literary Supplement

From time to time there emerges into human cognizance a man or woman whose personality, without any conscious bid for publicity, makes an instant and immense appeal to the English-speaking peoples. The response to that appeal has little in common with the acclamation accorded to a popular jockey or a famous film star, since it is evoked not by worldly success but by a force of character which is without thought of self. Such a one is Grey Owl. In his autobiography, *Pilgrims of the Wild,* published early in the year, this child of a Scots father and an Indian mother has related how he abandoned his trade of professional trapper in Canada because he saw that, owing to the depredations of such as he, the wild life of his country was rapidly becoming extinct, and set himself to impress public opinion with the necessity of preserving the creatures of the wild. In that book he told, too, how he came to study and tame the beaver, and now he has cast the results of his experience and his knowledge into fiction form. It is not so much a children's book as one of those rare books which have so catholic an appeal that children and grown-ups read them with equal pleasure—perhaps the secret of every children's classic. Whether *The Adventures of Sajo and her Beaver People* will become a classic it is too soon to say; but it is quite certain that this season one of the most popular presents for children will be this story of Sajo and her brother Shapian and the beaver kit-

tens which their father, Big Feather, brought home to them. Grey Owl has a natural gift for narrative and, more than that, the gift of communicating to others his love of living things. Here is the very spirit of the wild shining from the printed page, and tenderness linked with observation in a realization of the kinship and glory of life. Those who read of Grey Owl's country and of the things he cares for will share with him the rustle of the trees in the Moon of Falling Leaves, the call of Talking Waters and the voices of his Forest People who dwell in the Land of the North-West Wind.

"Grey Owl and More Beavers," in The Times Literary Supplement, *No. 1765, November 30, 1935, p. 807.*

Eric F. Gaskell

Far away in the great West Country, in the Land of the North West Wind, a solitary cabin stands beside a lonely lake. Miles on miles of virgin forest surround it; and the solemn stillness of the great lone land consecrates it forever. There, far removed from the impatient surge of cities, beyond the last outposts of civilization, one of the most significant experiments ever undertaken in the interests of Canadian wild life is being conducted today. The Beaver People—symbolic of our nationhood from earliest times—have entered into their inheritance in that remote Utopia.

A tall, lean woodsman, his features betraying a lineage as venerable as his native forests, is the dominating personality in a drama of unique interest. Of his work among the Beaver People there is no need to write. The press and the radio have carried the amazing story of his success to every corner of the Dominion, and even beyond the seas. But there is another aspect of his life, of even greater significance for those Canadians whose first concern is the cultural development of their native land. For in this strange, romantic figure they recognize an authentic creative artist, a man possessing rare gifts of expression, who has already made several noteworthy contributions to contemporary literature. His books have a special message for Canadians; they are, in the very truest sense, redolent of the soil of Canada.

I refer, of course, to Wa-Sha-Quon-Asin, better known to many thousands of English-speaking readers as Grey Owl—the Indian ex-trapper who is devoting his best years to the problems of wild life conservation in this country. A vast experience, gleaned from many seasons spent in lonely bush camps and on the trail, enables him to interpret the true spirit of the silent places for those who have not been privileged to know them at first hand. In vivid prose he has recaptured the romance of an era that is passing—the day of the frontiersman, with its inevitable suggestion of adventure. Scarcely more than five years ago he made an obscure beginning as a writer; today he enjoys an enviable reputation and a distinguished career is indicated. This remarkable achievement is not without a deeper significance; for to many his writings have come as a strong voice crying in the wilderness, urging Canadians to take a more intelligent and far-seeing interest in their great heritage.

The Voice of the Indian, long silent in the land of his fa-

Grey Owl at the age of thirteen, Hastings, England.

thers, is at last raised in an impassioned plea for a better understanding of the red man's philosophy. With the passing of the old order of frontiersmen—men who have retreated steadily into the Land of Shadows before the onward march of civilization—much of the romance and color of pioneer days is in danger of becoming lost to the present and oncoming generations of Canadians. Now a spokesman has arisen whose solemn duty it is to interpret for us the saga of the Northland—"to convey to the White Man, before it is too late, something of the spirit of a vanishing race." Three charming books bear witness to the zeal with which he has pursued his mission; and their reception indicates just how admirably the author has achieved his purpose.

Those who hold that romance is dead in the twentieth century have only to read Grey Owl's life story to be convinced of the instability of their argument. Contemporary literature affords no more revealing instance of human idealism triumphant even in adversity.

Grey Owl, heir of the ancient aristocracy of woodsmen, has in his lifetime beheld the slow encroachment of the white man's civilization (doubtful blessing!) where once the beauty of an unspoiled land stretched without blemish from the Great Lakes to the rim of the Arctic. In the inex-

orable advance of the new order the Indian, slow to concede defeat, acknowledges the ultimate doom of his race. But the last tragic chapter in the history of the red man is not without a ray of hope for the future; and all because an Indian trapper, more gifted than his fellows, has caught a splendid vision.

Born less than fifty years ago on the banks of the fabled Rio Grande, Grey Owl came to Canada at an early age. The Ojibway Indians of Ontario adopted him into their tribe, and he has never ceased to regard them as his people. With them he has followed the trap-line and the trail, hunting over a vast wilderness where few "outsiders" penetrate in quest of game. Varied experiences as fire ranger and guide have brought him into intimate contact with many types of men—trappers and sportsmen—and he has had ample opportunity to study their different reactions to the forest life. His love of the silent places is sincere and all-embracing; to him the vast hinterland, the Land of Keewaydin, is home. A long apprenticeship in the arts of the woodsman has taught him to discern the "beauty at the goal of life." He has learned to love the cathedral-stillness of the northern forests, the awesome majesty of white-fanged rivers, the mystic beauty of the changing seasons, the moods of a storm, and those silent companions of the trail—the Little People of the Forest. For all these things, as for his adopted brothers, the Ojibways, he cherishes a deep affection. They are to him a solemn legacy, sustaining him in the vital things of the spirit, and in the more immediate demands of the flesh. "Without them I am nothing," he has written; and the tribute is as sincere as it is simple. He is one of that fortunate brotherhood.

> Who have builded fires where Nature
> Wears no make-up on her skin.

The wilderness has never failed him. His fine physique pays tribute to the nomad life—a life deliberately chosen, and followed with increasing enthusiasm through eventful years. There may have been times when the game did not seem worth the candle; but the indomitable spirit of a stoic race has survived any such periods of mild depression. When, in recent years, he married, the wisdom of his choice was at once evident. His wife, Anahareo, elected to follow the trail with her husband; and together they have gone on pilgrimage, fulfilling a gallant purpose in their determination to pursue the quest to the end.

Anahareo was largely instrumental in changing the whole course of Grey Owl's career. From a chance incident one morning, when her intervention saved the lives of two beaver kittens, helpless little creatures whose parents had fallen by the hunter's gun, came inspiration and the germ of a broad vision for the future. Grey Owl was led to reconsider his choice of trapping as a profession; and the grim tragedy of the Little People of the Forest, threatened with extinction by ruthless hunters, came to him as a challenge. He gave up beaver trapping, and resolved to devote his time and talents to the conservation of the species. The immediate problem was to locate a colony of beaver suitable for experimental purposes. With this in view the pilgrimage commenced; and the journey thus undertaken reads like a modern odyssey. From heartbreaking days spent in the district of Touladi, in Quebec, the trail led ever westward across half a continent to a triumphant ending on the pleasant shores of Ajawaan Lake, in Prince Albert National Park. (pp. 1-3)

During lonely days spent in his bush camp in eastern Quebec he had tried his hand at writing articles on Canadian wild life, and these had been accepted by an English publisher. Their success brought the logical suggestion that he should write a book, to be based on his experiences as trapper and guide. That was in 1929. Two years later *Men of the Last Frontier* appeared.

This book is a significant landmark in contemporary Canadian literature. As the title suggests, it is a chronicle of life in the northern wilderness of Canada—the last remaining frontier on this continent. It is the record of a trapper's life, told with unusual charm and dignity, and almost poetic in its appeal. The sympathies of the reader are at once enlisted; and no one can fail to be moved by the sheer beauty of Grey Owl's descriptive passages. Stories of the trail and vignettes of camp life crowd the pages. The comradeship of simple men, attuned to the forest life, receives a graceful tribute from one who cherishes a long and intimate association with that splendid fraternity. The author interprets the mysterious beauty of the silences with a touch that has almost a lyric quality. The immortal saga of the Beaver People (almost the story of Grey Owl himself, so closely has he identified himself with them) is first touched upon in these pages. There is a powerful appeal for the preservation of our vast forests, a plea for conservation of wild life, and a scathing indictment of the vandalism of ignorant trespassers in the silent places.

There are memorable passages in the book, some of them unsurpassed in our literature. For instance, there is that passionate scene where the author, in the solemn, elegiac words of Neganikabo, Stands First, symbolizes the passing of the Indian. The effect is essentially dramatic. And there is a moving epiloque in which two symbolic figures, a White Man and an Indian, standing on the borders of the wilderness, contemplate the inexorable advance of that civilization which carries with it the seeds of their destruction. In all this, of course, there is a lesson. It is the business of Canadians to strive, by every means in their power, for a better understanding of the problems confronting those who are intimately concerned with the conservation of our splendid national resources. Grey Owl is a subtle propagandist; he makes an irresistible appeal to the hearts and minds of men. If we do not heed his warning now a future generation may have reason to recall his prophetic words when the subject of the vanishing wilderness is raised. The last lines of the epilogue envisage such a time:

> And with them went all of the wild that had life, following the last fading line of the Vanishing Frontier, Northward, Northward, ever Northward, back into the days that are long forgotten, slipping away over the hills into the purple distance, beyond the Land of Shadows, into the sunset.

Grey Owl's life is now irrevocably bound up with the fortunes of the Beaver People, and in his later books he pays graceful tribute to his Little Brothers. *Pilgrims of the Wild,* his second book, is the record of that gallant pil-

grimmage begun in distant Touladi; it is the autobiography of a remarkable personality. Published late in 1934, it achieved immediate popularity; nothing quite like it had ever been done before. It is the work of one who is at heart a poet, with a poet's genius for interpreting the fundamental values of life. Emotional reactions are to Grey Owl the sum and substance of the human drama. No one can read *Pilgrims of the Wild* and fail to be convinced of this fact. It is a simple story, simply told; but with the precision of an artist, who, unaware of his own power, creates a masterpiece, Grey Owl has recorded an actual saga of human experience in which the twin virtues of loyalty and nobility of purpose achieve a triumph in the face of many difficulties. From this amazing document, a classic of self-revelation, the author emerges as a great humanitarian. His love for his friends, the Beaver People, is the motivating influence in a life devoted to their interests. They are his charges, and for their welfare he is proud to accept responsibility. A desire to share this enthusiasm is manifested in all his writings.

Grey Owl has published a third book, *The Adventures of Sajo and Her Beaver People,* one of the most delightful tales for children ever to appear in this or any other country. Briefly, it is the story of two Indian children whose home is at the Place of Talking Waters in the far away Land of Keewaydin, home of the North West Wind. Gitche Meegwon, their father, is a renowned hunter. On one of his trips he rescues two tiny beaver kittens whose home has been destroyed by a roving otter; these he presents to Sajo, his daughter, as a birthday gift. Adventures in the great north woods, and in the city, form the basis for an enchanting narrative. Poignant moments of near tragedy are relieved by thrilling instances of youthful heroism, and the tale moves to a triumphant ending. Best of all, the story is substantially true. The descriptions of wild life are as authentic as a lifetime of association with such things can make them. Quaint sketches by the author add greatly to the charm of the book.

The fabled Northland, whence have come heroic tales of the early voyageurs and stout-hearted coureurs-des-bois, has at last produced a classic for children. I justify my profession of faith in the enduring qualities of Grey Owl's delightful story by endorsing the author's own contention that an adult can read the book without loss of dignity. That, after all, is the supreme test of excellence in the juvenile field. If an award similar to the John Newbery medal were available in Canada it would go without question to Grey Owl.

In the summer of 1930, when I was vacationing at Metis, in Quebec, one afternoon, while fishing a familiar trout stream in the hills south of the village, I came upon a strange camp occupied by an Indian. Attracted by the novelty of the situation (no Indian tepee having been seen in that precise spot within living memory) I approached for a closer inspection. The strange visitor, engaged in preparing a meal at that moment, acknowledged my present with a casual nod. I have since regretted that I did not pause at least long enough to make his acquaintance at that time; but it was growing late, and I passed on to my fishing, never guessing that one of the most notable experiments in the annals of Canadian literature was to have its real beginning in that unlikely place. In his humble camp, beside that pleasant stream, Grey Owl prepared his first public lecture; and there a new vision came to him, the fulfilment of which has made him famous.

Grey Owl's message for Canadian readers is a pertinent one. He is, above all else, a patriot. In a letter to the present writer he describes his mission as an attempt "to bring before the Canadian people the beauty and soul of their own country." In this he has succeeded. Canadians owe it to themselves to heed him.

Lastly, what is Grey Owl's status in the ranks of Canadian writers today? Within the space of five short years he has become a legend. To the mere mention of his name attaches all the spontaneous admiration that is the just due of one who has rendered valiant service in the cause to which he stands committed. He stands apart as the spokesman for a race of men who have almost ceased to be articulate. And he is the divinely gifted interpreter of the Northland, mystic and beautiful; the stalwart champion of the Little People of the Forest, who have found in him a friend. Because of that splendid bond of friendship, inspired and sustained by the whispered wisdom of the silent places, Grey Owl has won an abiding place in our literature.

The mysterious beauty of the deep woods has inspired him; and the silent places are to him a testimony of all that is most enduring in a changing world. There, when dusk falls, the clear, sweet voice of the whitethroat sparrow pierces the impending stillness in a calm assurance of faith. It is Grey Owl's reward, and answer. Mino-ta-kiyah—it is well! (pp. 3-5)

> *Eric F. Gaskell, "Grey Owl: Pathfinder and Artist," in* The Canadian Bookman, *Vol. XVIII, No. 6, June, 1936, pp. 1-5.*

The Times Literary Supplement

In [*Tales of an Empty Cabin*] Grey Owl uses the device of the "Empty Cabin," in which he listens to ancestral and other ghostly voices, to provide a frame for reflections on the natural resources of Canada, the history of the Indians, the proper treatment of wild animals, the legend of Hiawatha, the tall tales of the voyageurs and such other themes as are suggested to him by the forest life he knows so well.

There are two styles displayed in this book—a clear humorous narrative style that says what it has to say simply and clearly, and a reflective eloquent style that will be appreciated chiefly by those who like a highly rhetorical and embroidered method of asserting not very recondite truths. Most readers will prefer the first style, in which we learn a great deal about the vast wilderness, in whose boundless contiguity of shade Grey Owl and his beaver friends have their dwelling. We learn why forest travellers do without butter. We learn how much can be carried at a portage and what manner of men perform these feats. (The most remarkable story of this type concerns two Indian boys whose filial piety would have earned Roman approval.) We hear some of the stories told in the forest of the *loupgarou*, feared in the Canadian woods as much as

in his native France, and of the two famous rulers of the Carolinas who here appear as kings, not as mere governors. We hear, too, echoes of great events in Indian history, of the successful military prowess of the *Métis* in the second Riel Rebellion and of the defeat and destruction of Custer at the Little Bighorn. There is a very interesting discussion of Fenimore Cooper and of Longfellow; and Grey Owl defends both old masters against some cheap modern denigration with, perhaps, an insufficient allowance for those critics who think that, no matter how faithfully Longfellow reproduced Indian sounds, he could write very bald verse all the same. But Grey Owl has a ready answer for most critics and is able to turn the tables very effectively, even if that involves a degree of contempt for the swordsmanship of the knights who murdered Becket that does not make sufficient allowance for their religious emotions. On religion in general Grey Owl has something to say.

Readers of earlier books by Grey Owl will be pleased to encounter once again the beavers whose industry, ingenuity and idiosyncratic characters should delight young and old who have a taste for the animals of fables—only they are real ones this time. The human characters too—Indians, half-breeds, whites—have their own attractiveness, whether it is because of their physical prowess and endurance or because of the enterprise exemplified in the careers of men like Dan O'Connor. But even Dan could have his leg pulled at times, as when he had his own dogs sold to him. Despite the shadow of cruelty to animals and the ugly memories of massacre and betrayal of the Indians, this is in the main a cheerful book; and the friendly beavers and bears are creatures one would willingly go a long way to meet. The illustrations are, with one exception, admirable.

> *"A Listener in the Wilds," in* The Times Literary Supplement, *No. 1812, October 24, 1936, p. 850.*

Constance Lindsay Skinner

Grey Owl is a welcome addition to the company of nature writers for children. Boys in the teens are becoming acquainted with his two other books, written for adults, *Pilgrims of the Wild* and *Men of the Last Frontier,* and are enjoying his fresh, vigorous descriptions of the wilderness and its creatures. Half Indian in blood, Grey Owl is all Indian in the woods. He writes about the four-footed people as Indians have always felt about them, even when they killed them for their own food and clothing.

In the old days, when the Northern tribes lived off the hunt, it was customary to placate the spirit of the slain animal by a brief song of thanks, in which the hunter explained that he had killed out of necessity and not in wanton cruelty. The Indian's belief in the secretness of life included all animal life. If Grey Owl can exemplify this ancient racial faith today with a more humane spirit, as protector and not hunter, it is because the trader has brought blankets and oatmeal into the North. Employed as a game warden in Prince Albert National Park, Saskatchewan, Grey Owl can give his Indian feeling for the Little Brothers full scope.

His favorites evidently are the beavers, a nation always respected by Indians for their wisdom, gentleness and industry. He told us a lot about beavers in *Pilgrims of the Wild.* In [*Sajo and The Beaver People*] he introduces us to two adorable beaver kittens and a lovable little Indian girl named Sajo.

The story begins dramatically. Sajo's father, canoeing homeward, sees the wreckage of a beaver house tossing down stream. He knows by certain signs that an otter, the beaver's relentless foe, has attacked a home where there are young ones, in order to feed on tender flesh. He makes all speed to the spot, rescues the helpless beaver babies and takes them home to his little daughter. A simple plot runs through the book, but I think young readers will care less for it than for the details of a young beaver's daily life as it grows from babyhood to maturity in a world of clear waters, "singing leaves," birds and deer, with the vivid light of an Indian's vision upon the whole. It is a book for family reading, with something for all ages above six years.

> Constance Lindsay Skinner, "Beavers and Palaces," in New York Herald Tribune Books, *November 15, 1936, p. 28.*

The New York Times Book Review

The beavers are most consistently the heroes of this book of wilderness experience and woodland lore [*Tales of an Empty Cabin*]: Jelly Roll, the Queen Beaver, "jovial, wayward and full of whims;" Rawhide, her consort, "calm, silent and inscrutable;" their children and an occasional "aboriginal" that strays in from the wild and becomes an inmate of the beaver colony. Yet this book is not solely about beavers, or even solely about animals. Grey Owl, whose writing about the beasts of the North Woods is already familiar, writes here of many features of the wilderness. But the beavers run in and out through his pages, and the last of the volume's three sections is almost wholly devoted to the animals. It is the most engaging section in an always interesting book.

Grey Owl decided some time ago to give up hunting and trapping and shooting and to study the animals as their friend. He started a beaver colony in which the Canadian Government became interested. The government offered him, therefore, a home for himself and his beavers, and a place for a real animal and bird sanctuary, in the wilds of the Prince Albert National Park in Saskatchewan. He settled down by a lakeside, and as soon as he had got his lodge in that vast wilderness the beavers were all over the place.

They built a mud hut in his living room; they roofed their own house with his shingles; they even stole a workman's paint brush. They loved him and strove to protect him, and lived their lives by his side, just as dogs do. And they were absorbingly interesting. So were the bears. So were the loons and other birds. So, even, were the muskrats. Almost every animal, in almost every species, has its own individuality, Grey Owl tells us, just as we know dogs and cats and horses do.

But in his Beaver Lodge Grey Owl looks back rather wistfully to the free days of his wilderness roving. He remembers the legends and the adventures of Indians and trappers and rivermen in that wide Northland which is still utterly "primitive." The entire northern section of Canada—the largest part of the Dominion—is practically untouched by modern progress, a virgin wilderness still. "A traveler may leave London and be in Winnipeg in the time that it takes some trappers to cover the vast reaches of lake and forest that lie between their hunting grounds and civilization." That is Grey Owl's world, from which he brings us a varied collection of stories.

There is a visit to one of the "hidden villages" of the Indians; there is a letter from an Indian soldier in the World War. Indian legends are collected under the title of "The Mission of Hiawatha," and there is an allegory of the white man's conquest in the centuries-long life of a pine tree. Dissertations of relative standards, both of comfort and of hardship, are pleasantly provocative. All the pictures of the wilderness and of the river life have a distinct fascination of their own. Grey Owl writes with a grave beauty of expression for all his mastery of modern vernacular. He has a woodsman's deep love of his woods and of their wild creatures. He brings the woodland very close. And his animals are very much alive. (pp. 12, 33)

> "Indian Lore," in The New York Times Book Review, *December 13, 1936, pp. 12, 33.*

Time, New York

Grey Owl's account [of life with Jelly Roll and Rawhide in *Tales of an Empty Cabin*] makes these kittens sound like something out of a Walt Disney cartoon. . . .

Grey Owl's account of his life with the beavers takes up about one-third of *Tales of an Empty Cabin.* The remainder is stories of the North woods, Indian legends, personal reminiscences, a tribute to the remote Mississauga River of Ontario, descriptions of wilderness heroism, appeals for the preservation of wild life. In part an amateurish piece of work, it is nevertheless lighted with many passages of extremely keen observation and made engaging by Grey Owl's sincerity and humor. Grey Owl did not intend to be a writer and when he started did not know what he was letting himself in for. Now, with his fourth book, he says, "I fully realize that all this while I have been sauntering around on holy ground, improperly dressed and with my boots on."

> "Beaver Man," in Time, New York, *Vol. XXVIII, No. 25, December 21, 1936, p. 63.*

Lovat Dickson

[*An author and critic who was Grey Owl's English publisher, Dickson arranged the lecture tour of England that helped to bring Grey Owl international fame.*]

To many young people the passing of Grey Owl was felt as a very personal loss. Many thousands had read his books, and more had seen and heard him on the lecture platform. Many had shaken hands with him and heard his cheery greeting. No wonder he will be missed! Everyone who met him felt that he was a very uncommon type of man. But beyond this was his record of useful work, his wonderful gift as a speaker, which combined humour with eloquence, and, of course, his books. Who can forget the experience of dipping into *Pilgrims of the Wild* for the first time, or the thrill of reading *The Adventures of Sajo?*

Grey Owl was, by nature and training, rather remote from human feelings. It was as though he sought to teach the lesson of kindness and sympathy to animals by withholding what he had himself of those qualities from human attachments, and devoting them to all the beasts of the forest. Yet his heart was quick to respond to anyone whom he thought was ill-treated, or oppressed, or held in contempt. Thus, he deliberately in England made friends of people in the more humble walks of life, and was often taciturn to those whose standards of comfort he thought protected them from some of the harshness of the world. A little incident comes to my mind which is typical of Grey Owl. He gave up the only free day he had during his last lecture tour in England to go to a zoo near Birmingham—a journey of over two hundred miles from where he was—because he heard that a beaver was not properly housed there. He spent the day at the zoo talking to the little animal, whose proper home was in the forests five thousand miles from there.

Grey Owl's grave is on a little wooded knoll overlooking Lake Ajawaan, where Jelly Roll, the Queen of the Beaver People, and Rawhide and their large family now live their lives in peace. Grey Owl's work, I have been assured, will be carried on, and the lives of the beaver colony at Ajawaan will always be protected.

> Lovat Dickson, *"Grey Owl," in* The Junior
> Bookshelf, *Vol. 2, No. 3, May, 1938, p. 119.*

Lovat Dickson

Grey Owl's brush with *Country Life* over their quite reasonable attempts to correct certain shortcomings in his style, and their perhaps not so justifiable change of the title of his [first book from *The Vanishing Frontier* to **The Men of the Last Frontier**], ought to have been forgotten long before. But in the woods things are not forgotten so easily. Grey Owl, having thought much about it, made up his mind that this book [*Pilgrims of the Wild*] should not suffer what he thought of as the dire fate of his first. It should be published without a comma altered, by someone who would give a solemn undertaking to respect his will in that matter. He set about finding a new publisher and turned for advice to the only man he felt he could trust in the literary world, his Canadian publisher, Hugh Eayrs of the Macmillan Company.

To him he put the question whether there was any publisher in England who knew anything about Canada; and who could further be bound contractually in advance not to alter a single detail of his book.

It required on the face of it an easy-going individual with a Canadian background, and whether I merited the first description or not, I could certainly claim the second. My publishing company had been in existence for only two years, and after a somewhat meteoric start, due more to good luck than management, had entered upon a period of expansion. Like Grey Owl, though I did not know it then, I felt, as I still feel, that I owe all the good fortune that has attended my life to my Canadian experiences, and

Grey Owl (right) with friends at Biscotasing, Ontario, Canada, in 1913.

flushed with the insolence of success I decided that part at least of the expansion I intended my company should undergo should be in the direction of Canadian books. (pp. 298-99)

I determined to corner Canadian literature and make myself a patron of it. I had the modesty and wit to know that I must have an ally, and the perspicacity or luck to find someone whose knowledge of the field was greater than mine, and whose warm-hearted sympathy and encouragement has made him one of the best-loved men in Canadian letters.

Fate, which times these things, arranged the rest. For just as I was approaching Hugh Eayrs with my ambitious plan for making Canadian literature known in London, Grey Owl was approaching him from three thousand miles the other side to find someone amenable to orders to produce his book in London.

So within a month the manuscript of *Pilgrims of the Wild* reached me, accompanied by a staccato little note from Grey Owl commending it to my attention and begging the favour of my decision. Not for me the friendly wordy letters that had come *Country Life's* way; not until I had proved myself capable of submitting to orders, and had shown that I could restrain myself from correcting a split infinitive, and look tolerantly upon the use of the verb "lay" when what he meant was "lie," without dashing in to repair the error.

My emotional reaction on reading *Pilgrims of the Wild* was not hypocritical. Grey Owl and Anahareo entered into my heart as I read the manuscript, and when I wrote him about it I did so with an enthusiasm that broke down his reserve but not his modesty. And, being only thirty-two, and but a fledgling in the publishing world, with more enthusiasm than experience to guide me, I swore to him that I would sell fifty thousand copies of the book. Eventually I did, but not before I had almost killed Grey Owl and myself in the process.

It was a pleasure to report the sales to him week by week. As the critics continued to acclaim *Pilgrims of the Wild,* the demand for it rose until it was selling no less than eight hundred copies a week. With what pride I wrote him to announce these figures; with what enthusiasm and congratulation on my prowess he answered me. We swore to each other that we were buddies who would see this thing through; that out of our endeavours we should make the Beaver People safe throughout Canada for all time. For I had become an enthusiastic adherent to Grey Owl's cause. Who would not, who corresponded with him as I did, who read his letters and saw revealed there the modesty and sincerity of the man? I knew that I was in touch with something I had not met before in life, a quality of absolute and selfless truth, and I thrilled to it, as later thousands were to thrill to it here.

Grey Owl had finished writing *Pilgrims of the Wild* in the spring of 1934, but the book was not published in London until January 1935. The delay arose from two causes. The first was the search for a submissive publisher which ended with his discovery of me in September 1934. The second was the astuteness of the editor of the *Illustrated London News,* Mr. Bruce Ingram. *Pilgrims of the Wild,* good book though it was, seemed hardly fitting material to be serialized in such an august journal, but Mr. Ingram had seen *Men of the Last Frontier,* had recognized the vital human story this Wilderness man had to tell, and had stolen a march on *Country Life,* who were anyhow at this juncture in disgrace in one corner of the Wilderness; and, in short, had arranged to serialize parts of *Pilgrims.* That process occupied the months up to Christmas, while I possessed my soul in patience, waiting to launch the book itself. That I did in January, as soon as the serial was completed.

But meanwhile, nearly a year having elapsed since he had finished the manuscript of *Pilgrims of the Wild,* Grey Owl had taken again to his pen; and in that year, unknown to me (for I was not yet on intimate terms with him) had nearly finished yet another book. That was *The Adventures of Sajo and Her Beaver People,* perhaps the greatest of his literary achievements.

The book was written for [his daughter] Dawn. It was autobiographical in a strange way. Two different periods of his life were welded into one story, for Sajo was a little girl he had known and loved when he was living with the Ojibways, and who had died of tuberculosis before she had reached womanhood; and Big Small and Little Small were McGinnis and McGinty, of the old Birch Lake days.

When the manuscript reached me it was entitled "The Story of Chilawee and Chikanee"; and for a moment I almost fell into the trap in which *Country Life* had foundered. I cabled him that this title was not good enough, and suggested "The Adventures of Sajo." He cabled back that it must be "The Story of Chilawee and Chikanee," or nothing at all. The cable companies prospered while we conducted a wordy debate along their lines of communication, until finally we compromised on *The Adventures of Sajo and Her Beaver People.*

With the publication of this book, the success of *Pilgrims of the Wild* was repeated, and then surpassed. We were selling one thousand copies each week of *Sajo,* and there seemed no end to what the books might do. *Sajo* was a book for children, and through it Grey Owl came into contact with many thousands of young admirers all over the world.

The illustrations he drew for the book somehow set the key for it. They were illustrations that a child could understand, and that an adult could admire. He had never had a lesson in drawing, and anything other than the things he loved he could never depict. But men in the buckskin clothes of the Wilderness, or wild animals in their natural state, he could capture with his pencil and show as though they were living, breathing things. They gave movement and an added poignancy to the scenes through which Sajo, Shapion and their two little beaver passed. (pp. 300-03)

> *Lovat Dickson, in his* Half-Breed: The Story of Grey Owl (Wa-Sha-Quon-Asin), *Peter Davies, 1939, 345 p.*

Robert Cantwell

What [Grey Owl] had accomplished was the individualizing of wild animals, and while there were astounding false notes and flat passages in his work—astounding because the level was generally so high—they seemed appropriate and rather touching as the revelations of a self-taught Indian striving for the white man's poetic and emotional effect. All of Grey Owl's writing, if considered as a single work, was a bold and original creation. He had built a kind of lonely homespun epic in which the shattered survivors of two vanishing species, the Indian and the beaver, came together and made their peace.

Grey Owl had no scientific training and did not claim to make a scientific contribution, but there is little in today's standard works on the beaver that is not incorporated, in living terms, in Grey Owl's books. (pp. 119-20)

Whatever else was questionable about Grey Owl, one fact was plain. He wanted his life to begin when his work in conservation began. . . . [His] mystical feeling of kinship with nature and of the abiding value of life, human and animal, was not false, and he became an Indian, not from a desire to perpetrate a fraud but to signalize a break forever with a past that meant nothing to him. (p. 126)

> *Robert Cantwell, "Grey Owl: Mysterious Genius of Nature Lore," in* Sports Illustrated, *Vol. 18, No. 14, April 8, 1963, pp. 112-26.*

Science Books: A Quarterly Review

Pilgrims of the Wild is a simple, warm personal tale. . . . A story of the author and his Indian wife, Anahareo, and how four beavers, McGinnis, McGinty, Rawhide, and Jellyroll wrought drastic changes in their lives. . . . The ways of beavers intimately observed during the period they inhabited the same house, their antics, and their almost-human actions are shared with the reader. Comparable to the Ernest Seton Thompson stories; this is excellent reading for young ecologists which is valuable for its humane aspects rather than for its scientific data. . . . Especially recommended for public library collections, but good for any conservation student.

> *A review of "Pilgrim of the Wild," in* Science Books: A Quarterly Review, *Vol. 7, No. 2, September, 1971, p. 139.*

Judith Janc

This story of the adventures and misadventures in the 1920's of two Canadian Indian children and their two pet beavers [*Sajo and the Beaver People*] was first published in 1936. It's unfortunate that it didn't die an honorable out-of-print death, for what may have been considered an acceptable animal story in 1936 is really over-sentimental pap totally unsuitable for 1971. The characters, both Indian and Anglo, and especially the boy and girl protagonists, are one-dimensional stereotypes. The style the preface labels "quaint" is trite almost beyond endurance. And, the extremely simple, uninteresting sketches, except for the one of the beaver pond, do nothing but parrot the text both in what they depict and in their captions. (pp. 114-15)

> *Judith Janc, in a review of "Sajo and the Beaver People," in* School Library Journal, *Vol. 18, No. 3, November, 1971, pp. 114–15.*

Victor B. Scheffer

By modern standards, Grey Owl's writing was over-picturesque, devious, and sentimental. He was largely self-educated, and most of his studying, except for a period of early schooling, was done relatively late in life. He himself admits to using a "precise and somewhat stilted English . . . like a stiff and ceremonious suit of Sunday best." He can hardly be blamed for imitating the style of certain popular outdoor writers of his time. Gene Stratton Porter had her hero, Freckles, kneel on the trail to kiss the footprint of the dream-girl. Ernest Thompson Seton had a wild mother coyote bring a poisoned bait to her captive pup to release him from the cruel world of man. Zane Grey, and Jack London, and even Kipling were fired with more imagination than is perhaps good for a reporter of natural history.

Yet Grey Owl continues to be read, for several very good reasons. First, he had what he called in others "angularity of character." He was an oddball, and the odd-balls of the world are attractive, especially the ones that break away from the crowd and achieve fame; this is particularly true in the overorganized modern world. The reader shares Grey Owl's excitement when, after writing his first animal story in longhand, he walked forty miles to a mailbox, sent the manuscript to England, and weeks later received a

check. We are drawn to a man who confesses a moral conversion in the midst of a somewhat vacant and even destructive life. And we respect a man who proves to be a minor prophet. Grey Owl knew the meaning of what is now called "environmental sensitivity," though he did not use that term. He cautioned that man should not dominate nature but take his place in it. He deplored the way men of his time looked upon wild animals, first at their commercial value and only later at their useful role in maintaining a rich and varied environment. He felt that "good business" alone was a poor objective of wildlife management. Today his philosophy has finally come into style. (pp. xiii-xiv)

Perhaps the greatest attraction of Grey Owl's writing is the insight it gives into the character of a man who had an unusual way with animals. This quality appears between the lines; Grey Owl did not recognize it in himself. When he let his pet beavers run loose, they chose to spend some of their days in the wild and some in the artificial habitat of his cabin. They even slept with him on occasion, and a man who will make room for a wet beaver in the middle of the night is a sympathetic man indeed. (p. xiv)

> *Victor B. Scheffer, in an introduction to* Pilgrims of the Wild *by Grey Owl, Charles Scribner's Sons, 1971, pp. xi-xvii.*

Diana Thompson

Grey Owl's [*Tales of an Empty Cabin*] are partly legend, partly personal experience and partly a plea for the preservation of the wild life and the forest. In his youth, Grey Owl earned his living by trapping and shooting animals in the vast, unopened Canadian north. The first two thirds of his book deal with survival in the woods, and here the reader begins to appreciate the beauty and magnificence of our north as it was in 1936.

In the last third of the book, Grey Owl gives up hunting forest creatures and turns to protecting them instead. This section particularly will appeal to conservationists for it is here that he makes a strangely contemporary plea to all mankind to begin protecting the forest and its animals. His concern reflects the remarkable perception of a man years ahead of his time.

Unfortunately Grey Owl has for the most part a lofty style of writing and a fondness for long and difficult words which even an older child would have trouble understanding. When he occasionally abandons this style, as he does in one story entitled "Cry Wolves," the result is an exciting tale that any child would understand and enjoy. Whether the child would be able to wade through the first part of the book to reach this story is another matter.

> *Diana Thompson, in a review of "Tales of an Empty Cabin," in* In Review: Canadian Books for Children, *Vol. 6, No. 3, Summer, 1972, p. 24.*

Lovat Dickson

Grey Owl was to show an unusual expertise in the process of what he called "putting himself across," as I was to find out . . . when publishing *Pilgrims of the Wild.* "This is a book written by an Indian," he continually insists to

Country Life. "Refer to me as an Indian writer." He . . . gives his father's name as MacNeill, and his own birthplace as Hermosillo in Mexico. The illusion is complete. He has said goodbye to Hastings, and has assumed the Indian identity. From now on there could be no retreat from this position. Belaney belonged to the past. He signed all letters Grey Owl, and even had his bank account in that name.

The happiest winter of [the lives of Grey Owl and Anahareo] followed. Archie started to write a second book. This was *Tales of an Empty Cabin,* which is very much the same kind of book as *The Men of the Last Frontier:* a series of essays celebrating the things dearest to his memory. *The Men of the Last Frontier* sprang from his recollections of the early days on Bear Island, and at Bisco just before the war. *Tales of an Empty Cabin* springs largely from his later experiences as a riverman and forest ranger, and deals more closely with the coming of McGinnis and McGinty into their lives. The book, I think, was laid aside before it was completed, because he was moved by sadness to write *Pilgrims of the Wild.* This, his masterpiece, was written in the winter of 1933-4. But this first winter at Ajawaan was 1931-2, and the scratch-scratch of the pen which Anahareo heard all day was at work on memories which are recaptured in the early chapters of *Tales of an Empty Cabin:* on getting lost in the woods, on a day in a hidden Indian town like the one at Bear Island, and on drawing portraits like the unforgettable one of Red Landreville, the riverman and the Sage of Pelican Lake. These were stories of the past that he could tell to Anahareo. But *Pilgrims of the Wild* had to be written alone. . . . (pp. 225-26)

The manuscript was finished at Christmas-time in 1933, and without waiting to hear from his publishers what they thought of it, he immediately started to write a children's story which was completed by the autumn of 1934, some months before *Pilgrims of the Wild* was published. This children's book he called *The Adventures of Chilawee and Chickanee,* but when it was published in the summer of 1935 it was called *The Adventures of Sajo and Her Beaver People.* This time the change of title met with his approval.

It was when he had the manuscripts of these two books in his hand that Grey Owl's next English publisher [Editor's note: Dickson himself], a restless and ambitious man, gave a twist, quite unconsciously, to the fate of all these actors, calling Anahareo home from her wandering, and Grey Owl to the theatre halls of England.

It was to be the death of Grey Owl. But it gave a remarkable flowering to his last years. If, like Henry Thoreau, he had remained in the woods, he might have been remembered as no more than what Henry James called Thoreau: "a sylvan personage [with a] remarkable genius for the observation of the phenomena of woods and streams, of plants and trees, and beasts and fishes, and for flinging a kind of spiritual interest over these things." But Grey Owl is remembered for something much deeper and more lasting.

The urge to escape from the constrictions of our workaday lives is constantly nagging at us, and Thoreau reawakened in men a longing for mysteries that their forefathers had known, when men desired to live, as Henry James puts it in analysing the "slim and crooked" nature of Thoreau's genius, "for the ages and not for Saturday and Sunday; for the universe, and not for Concord." Grey Owl was reminding them of a world they had lost—the world of Nature patiently waiting our return—as *Walden, or Life in the Woods* reminded New England society in 1854 of the simplicity and rural purity of a world being lost to them by the onrush of commercialism and the harsh imperatives of Puritanism. (p. 229)

One does not have to be an expert to pick out a great book; it is the not-so-great that demand judgement. Important books have their own authority; something masterful is apparent as soon as one begins to read. *Pilgrims of the Wild* is to life in the Canadian wilderness what *Robinson Crusoe* is to life on a desert island. What holds us in Defoe's work is the courage of man in surviving the fate of being abandoned in an empty world. It is a story of moral courage, and the powerful interest it arouses comes from the thousand details of how Robinson Crusoe "made do". In *Pilgrims of the Wild,* moral courage is also what the characters exhibit, and the interest again is provided by the details of what it is like to live in the woods, to live cheek by jowl with animals, to find a plateau on which existence can be shared and enjoyed with the living things that share the world with us. That Grey Owl had been a cruel trapper once was not important. The past ends with the opening page of the narrative. Grey Owl is in flight from the social order in which we also live, to another into which he leads us imaginatively, and from which, at the end of the story, we withdraw with regret and longing.

When I started to correspond with the author I found him as simple and genuine as I imagine Henry Thoreau to have been. Everyone knows the story of Walden Pond. Thoreau built his hut on the shores of the pond with his own hands, cultivated his vegetable patch, made his own clothes, and lived for several years on the expenditure of a few dollars. The charm of the story comes from showing how happily a man can exist without the aids and comforts men spend their lives in toil to acquire. In reading Thoreau we get an image of a sweet and wholesome man, although we know that in fact he was difficult and uncommunicative, turned his back on society, and was a rebel against the state by refusing to pay his taxes.

There is enough in Grey Owl's story to show that he must have been a trial to local authority. He certainly contributed nothing to peace and order in Biscotasing, and he had to take to his heels to escape a warrant for disturbing the peace. He was continually in trouble in the army for infractions of discipline, and only a very perceptive platoon officer saw that he could flourish best when left alone, and made him a sniper. And yet there was an essential honesty and simplicity in him which came over very strongly in his letters to me, and made me anxious to convert others to share my wonder at the discovery of this unusual man.

But it was an undertaking of a rather large order to bring an unknown Métis from the Saskatchewan bush and hope to put him over in London in the mid-thirties as an unspoilt man. The temper of the English at that time was distinctly iconoclastic, and it was an inauspicious moment for promoting prophets. Times were hard economically, and a sombre pessimism about the future was the prevailing mood.

But I was not so much worried by the cost, which I hoped would be recovered from the extra sales generated by the publicity, as by the effect on so holy and dedicated a man if the crowds were small and the response lacklustre. I was daunted by the prospect of having on my hands for three months a man with a mission, who might regard every minute not spent in advancing the cause as a sinful waste of time. I doubted whether I could fill up a lecture schedule. The English are constitutionally allergic to this form of entertainment. It would mean winkling out schools and women's luncheon clubs and church groups. The prospect was far from encouraging.

What spurred me on was the way in which, after some hesitation, having accepted my invitation, he threw himself into the preparation and planning of the venture. He shamed my brand of professional optimism but practical lack of experience.

He became the leader as we planned the project in an exchange of lengthy letters, and we—I use the plural to include the four or five members of my staff who were involved with me in preparing plans—became the followers. He exhibited a good deal of managerial capacity in instructing us on how to present him to the public, and in this he showed a judgement better than ours. It was hard for us, for instance, to resist the temptation of striking the humanitarian note. But on this point he was adamant: he was not an animal evangelist but a man of action. He was not a St. Francis of Assisi; on the contrary, where he came from he was "considered a pretty tough egg." What he was coming to tell the British about was the Beaver People, the Indians, the North—harsh, savage, yet beautiful.

In this he read the English mind better than we did. He reached unerringly to the instinctive longing felt by nearly everybody at a time of crisis for a way of life uncomplicated by progress, unthreatened by war and poverty and hunger. The world depression of the thirties was at its worst. No ray of hope showed on the gloomy horizon. There seemed no reason why unemployment, the dole, hunger and fear, and a bad conscience among people who did not suffer these things to the same degree, should not become a permanent feature of modern life. *Pilgrims of the Wild* told of the same economic forces desecrating a noble prospect elsewhere, and driving not only people but animals to hunger and flight. It also showed how a man of moral courage turned and stood against these harsh pressures. As our plans developed under his energetic prompting, we saw this really was not stuff for schools, Boy Scout troops, and church groups, but for every man jack struggling for survival in a shifting world. This book and its author offered no cure, but they offered hope. Grey Owl grasped it all in a single phrase when he told his audiences: "You are tired with years of civilization. I come to offer you—what? A single green leaf." Once that message got across, we were to have no trouble filling his schedule. We were near-

ly swamped in the flood of public enthusiasm that acclaimed him.

I speak of his simplicity and genuineness, although I am now aware of what I was ignorant of then, that his claim to be of mixed parentage, Indian and white, was false. It did not really matter. Long years had passed since his birth and schooldays in England, and he had truly assimilated himself to the Indian way of life. He had willed himself into believing the fantasy about his birth. He had never known his father, and he had seen the woman who claimed to be his mother only infrequently. The tight-lipped, disapproving silence about his father preserved by his grandmother and aunts, and the attitude not very far above contempt his Belaney relatives had for his disorganized mother, combined to form in his imagination the idea that something was being kept from him. From that it was an easy step to imagine a more romantic origin for himself. His schoolfellows had believed his story, and from the age of seventeen on he had lived the life that he had dreamed of and longed for since he had first been able to read for himself. To be an Indian! What he laid claim to, some at least of his English audiences also longed for imaginatively. Through him they could live that existence momentarily. If his love for that life had not been so genuine and wholehearted, he could never have inspired them. The secret of his success was his genuineness and his simplicity. These terms are the right ones. (pp. 231-34)

There could be no doubt about the genuineness of his feelings for nature. I could think of no writer in Canada who had caught so truly the essential boom-note of this huge, rocky, monolithic land. He made pure Canada, the Canada outside the concrete urban enclosures, come alive. We saw it as we had first learnt about it in story and legend; the illimitable forests, the rushing rivers vigorous still after a million years of biting their way through the antedeluvian rock, gushing finally into the great sea-going tideways of the mighty St. Lawrence, or the Mackenzie, or the Columbia. He showed us the men who challenged these great forces of nature to wrest a living from them, and the animals who had their place in that unsullied, still primitive world. (p. 239)

I do not believe that anyone else could at that time have put into words just what Grey Owl's appeal was. But everybody had felt themselves ennobled by supporting it. It was, in fact, a spectacular precursor of the protest demonstrations that were to be such a feature of life thirty years later. The first intimations of what unregulated progress could do to the environment in which we lived were being uncomfortably felt by the public, who had been satisfied, up to that time, to enjoy the benefits of progress without asking what the cost of it might be. The sprouting factory chimneys belching smoke, the receding countryside as cities spread out, the concrete like a lava flow from some threatening volcano pouring over the land, grander shops and meaner dwelling houses, the choking city air, the growing sense of claustrophobia, all helped to lend enchantment to the view of distant forests, blue lakes, green hills, and clear skies, where animals roamed free and men did not fear for their jobs; the Grey Owl country.

But Grey Owl came to tell them that even the forests were

Grey Owl and Anahareo holding McGinnis and McGinty, near Dovcet, Quebec, c. 1927.

being tainted, and the animals were in flight from the creeping, poisoning, destructive tide of civilization. He did not ask them directly to help to hold back that tide by gestures and sacrifices, by refusing to wear furs; or urge them to press for enactment of legislation to protect the environment by imposing stiffer regulations for licensing the use of the land, by setting up National Parks, by declaring closed seasons on the trapping of animals. When he strayed into these issues in his talks he was always plainly uncomfortable, speaking by the book rather than from his mind.

No, he was a poet, recreating for us dreams of innocence. His lectures sang the glories of the past when the earth was untrammelled by the yokes by which men in search of wealth enslave their weaker kind and hold them captive to their jobs in cities. All his books are laments for the old days, thirty years before, when he had been young. There were giants in those days, and he sings their glory as Homer did the primitive heroes of early man. And to such effect that his readers and his listeners were caught by his vision. They longed to turn aside from the things that plagued them—the threat of war, unemployment, everlasting penury in the midst of plenty—and find such an Arcadia as he described. They knew it wasn't possible; they were helpless as though in a nightmare. He had broken free. He took no more life, lived simply with the animal world in a green glade far away. And because this man had shown it was possible, they could keep their dream.

No one believed more ardently in the vision he created than the creator himself. He knew that life was not really that simple, for beneath the surface as he enticingly pictured it, there were a thousand worries. Anahareo was leaving him, he found it more and more difficult to write, drink plagued him from time to time, women bothered him but he could not live without them and his affairs were endlessly complicated. But once it had been like his description, simple, strong, clean, and happy. He took refuge in the past when he had been young and innocent and keen, and had first come to this Northern country. . . .

> when I roamed at will through the rock-bound Ontario wilderness, all my worldly goods loaded into one small, swift, well-beloved canoe or, in Winter, contained within the four walls of a none too spacious log cabin, hastily erected on the shores of some frozen, or soon to be frozen lake.

Men were men then. He exaggerated their glory only because he saw it again with the imagination of a youth of seventeen. (pp. 240-42)

I had published *Tales of an Empty Cabin* in October 1936. In some respects it is the most delightful of Grey Owl's books, for it deals exclusively with the characters, both human and animal, who were always the subjects of his best anecdotes, calling forth that warm, ironic humour which his literary style needed as an anchor against the tug of his rhetoric. The mighty Mississagi River is at the heart of the book, and Beaver Lodge and its inhabitants, "all things both great and small", are at the end of it. (p. 247)

[He] did not use the word conservationist about himself in its modern sense; hardly anybody did at that time. He had a set of simple ideas, that the beaver should be protected in every province in Canada, that all wildlife deserved some degree of protection from wholesale slaughter, and that the Indians were the people best fitted by nature and tradition to be the custodians of the wilderness, and should be trained to act as caretakers of the nation's wild heritage. He could only state these principles; he could not organize them into being. He knew that only the government could introduce these measures and force them into being. (p. 252)

When the truth had been established, and it was no longer possible to doubt that the boy born in Hastings as Archie Belaney had been buried in Saskatchewan as Grey Owl, it was possible to see that an eccentric of an unusual kind had passed across the scene. England has long been a breeding-place for this rare species, which seems often to require several generations of inclination towards the unusual to produce at last the notable specimen which, by chance mutation, seems to have in just the right proportions unusual intelligence, a quickened sympathy with life in whatever form, an instinct towards self-dramatization, and a suppressed energy, all of which when released produce results often of a salvationist nature. Some cause, some oppressed people, some persecuted species, has to be rescued. The names of Sir Richard Burton and Lawrence of Arabia spring automatically to the mind, partly because they adopted other beliefs and dress to achieve their goals. But we are reminded too that Darwin, when he set out to voyage in the *Beagle*, was prompted by the same need to escape the oppressions of mid-Victorian society before proceeding by sympathetic observation to discover in the world of nature the origin and meaning of life.

Grey Owl, to use the name by which he will always be remembered, came to Canada at a time when the natural world was beginning to show the scars inflicted on it by the unregulated pursuit of wealth. At first he was only uneasily aware that the bright, romantic image he had treasured for so long was not altogether there in reality: animals writhed in their death-throes in traps, some Indians wore European clothes, got drunk, could be wastrels. Timber-fellers were infiltrating the big woods, and the detritus of the sawmills and the prospectors' dynamite was beginning to foul the rivers. Life was not perfect. Yet to be alive in this setting was paradise. His writings about those early days all sing the joys of the great forests, the mighty rivers, and the men and animals who live along them.

It was the First World War that changed him utterly. He came back to the woods to find that destruction had left desolation even here. High fur prices had brought in men evading military service who had had to live by trapping. They had introduced wholesale methods of slaughter, and the animals had retreated to remoter places. The timber cruisers and the prospectors had scarred and blackened the woods. The Indians' old hunting grounds had been taken over, and fights for prized territory were not uncommon amongst rival factions. Prohibition had come in, and with it the moonshiners and the stills. Men, Indians and white alike, had been degraded.

Sickened by these things, the tough *hombre* in him, which had always been part of the romantic image, took over from the poet and dreamer. Part of Belaney's trouble was, in the opinion of Factor Woodsworth, that he never grew up. Mr. Woodsworth was right. But it was also the quality of Belaney's particular condition that he did not submit to the repressions which we accept as we grow to conform to society. Saint or sinner, he could be either. But never the good, grey, steady hue that Mr. Woodsworth liked to see in a man.

For those few years from 1918 to 1925 there is no trace in his record of that close and sympathetic observation of and accord with animals which everyone had noted in him from the time he was a little boy. His mother, on one of her two widely separated visits to the Belaney household in his childhood, was told of the "menagerie" which he had been allowed to have in one of the rooms on the top floor.

"He kept all kinds of things in that room," she wrote to me in that breathless unpunctuated style in which all her reminiscences, verbal or written, were conveyed. "I or others seldom ventured without his protection, but they were all quite tame and would come to him even the reptiles."

She remembered on the occasion of this visit the trouble he had given over St. Helen's Woods:

> He would knot his sheets to get to the ground from his window and it was high—One morning I went into his room early and behold a rope was tied to the bedpost and out of the window he had climbed hours before

It was on that visit also that

> going upstairs to bed a snake was lying along the stair I was to tread upon—I was of course terrified—his only worry was in case I had wounded the little beast.

The same thing was remarked by [his friend] Bill Guppy in Temagami, and by [Grey Owl's first wife] Angele and the Bear Island band when he first came among them. And [his landlady] Mrs. Sawyer noticed it too, in the early days in Bisco, because it was so unusual. People took it for granted that boys should go after birds and squirrels with catapults and that dogs should be tied up, sometimes without water. It attracted attention when a man was kind to animals.

But after the war he was a changed character; a ruthless trapper, a hard drinker, quick to draw his knife. No longer does he amaze them with his skill on the piano; he never touches it, and he consorts much more with Indians than with white men.

"He took a fancy to the Indian people, I think," says Mrs. Sawyer, "and let his hair grow and then he coloured it, dyed it black, and then he used this alum in the water. He bathed his face and arms, and it gave him a real, real brown tan. Then he used to braid his hair and tie it with little buckskins. That was just the way he was, you know. He took a fancy to them and he liked their ways."

At first a kind of self-abasement seems to prompt all this. He takes upon himself the humiliation he sees the white man as having thrust upon the Indians. In towns he will not use the sidewalk but walks in the gutter instead. He eats with his hands, professing disdain of cutlery. He likes his meat fly-covered. But when he is with the Indians he is like St. Paul among the early Christians; arousing them to a self-awareness of their proud history, of the wrongs that have been done them, of the old customs and religious rites with which their ancestors had marked the passage of their lives. Once, long ago in his English boyhood, he had invented the romantic tale of his half-Indian parentage, and of his birth in an Indian encampment in Mexico. Now he asserts the truth of this, and of his upbringing by Indians and his training in their ways.

There is just enough truth in this for it to be half-believed. He had married an Indian, although this he did not openly admit in Bisco. He had lived for some years with the Bear Island band, and all his woodcraft had been learnt from the Indians with whom he had hunted and worked. As much later, in 1936, he was to write in reply to a letter from Chief To-To-Sis, "the Indians taught me the very things that are now making me famous." And he reminds him that what he is doing for them is not done for any reward, "but because I love you—because Indians were my very first friends, because the Indians took me and made a man of me."

Confronting the white man, he is for the underdog, as symbolized both by Indians and by animals. What he comes in time to say to white audiences is, in effect, "I can prove to you that these people—and these beavers—are articulate in their own right," and he does it by showing them in their natural environment, behaving as moral creatures leading purposeful and useful lives, until the white man's itch for domination and possession persecutes and scatters them. To the Indians he is not the defender but the catalyst, the stirrer-up of pride, the evangelist pointing out their only road to salvation. Get education, he urges them, *but do not forget that you are Indians.* Do not become just poor imitations of white men. *Be proud to be Indian.*

The metamorphosis, the Indianization of Archie Belaney, was gradual but steady. By 1925 he was in appearance and behaviour what he claimed to be, a man of mixed blood, who earned his living by trapping, lived rough, and behaved toughly, and was a constant thorn in the side of authority; a bad man to get mixed up with in a drinking bout or a fight.

He might have ended as George Belaney had done, and been killed in a drunken brawl, but for the accident of circumstances. He fell in love with Anahareo, carried her off to the woods with him, and found in her revulsion against the cruelty of a trapper's work the key that opened again the locked doors on his lost childhood, now over thirty years away. It had been screened behind the horrible years

of war, and the struggle since for a living in these desolate woods. The two beaver kittens he rescued at Anahareo's plea appeared to him as emissaries from a hunted band suing for mercy, appealing to him as the dreaded hunter.

From that time on his life changed, although . . . the change was not sudden and dramatic. Surrender to his own true self came only slowly. But when it did it was complete. And, because of the intensity with which he always felt things that touched him closely and the genuinely great gift he had for observing and describing the behaviour of animals, this surrender made him, the outcast Métis without training but with what were thought to be inherited primitive skills, the most famous and certainly the most admired field naturalist of his day.

He seemed to be quite unaware of what he had achieved. "Nothing to it," he wrote to Lloyd Acheson, his old fire-ranging boss on the Mississauga, "but a little kindness and patience." (pp. 257-61)

> *Lovat Dickson, in his* Wilderness Man: The Strange Story of Grey Owl, *Atheneum, 1973, 283 p.*

Sheila Egoff

After spending some years as a trapper and hunter in Ontario, [Grey Owl] became repelled by the cruelty and senseless killing and turned to conservation instead. His dream was of a time when all animals in the wilderness would have sanctuaries set aside for them. While trying to establish his own beaver sanctuary, he began to write stories in order to support his family. They were first published in England and it was in that country that his books had their greatest success. His one children's book, *The Adventures of Sajo and Her Beaver People,* was published in 1935, the year after his autobiography, *Pilgrims of the Wild,* appeared. *Sajo* falls into the category of the realistic animal story, since it deals with a year in the lives of two beaver kittens, Chilawee and Chikanee. In the preface Grey Owl maintains that all events, 'although they might not have occurred in the chronological order as presented', were recorded either from first-hand experience or from 'first-hand narrations'. The story tells how the two beaver kittens were rescued by an Indian, who took them home as a birthday present for his daughter Sajo. Both Sajo and her brother Shapian become attached to the helpless, lovable little animals, and Sajo in particular lavishes upon them the love she herself has lacked since the death of her mother. Much of the first part of the book is concerned with the play and learning habits of the kittens and particularly with the emergence of their different temperaments. Chikanee is the quieter, more helpless one and has a special love for Sajo; Chilawee 'had a rather jolly way about him, and was more of a roisterer, one of the "all for fun and fun for all" kind of lads to whom life is just one big joke.' As there was no doubt about their affection for, and their dependence upon, the children, so there was no doubt about their love for one another. They had never been separated for a minute of their young lives.

Hard times come and the father is forced to sell one of the kittens to pay part of his debt at a company store and then to go off on a trip to make up the rest. With true Indian stoicism Sajo and Shapian stand by as the company trader picks the more delicate and gentle Chikanee to be sold to a city zoo. Sajo begins to pine, Chilawee mopes, and in a dream Sajo understands that she must go to the city to rescue Chikanee. Sajo and Shapian go off together, and on the way Shapian saves his sister's life in a forest fire—a vivid and realistic bit of writing. The children eventually come in contact with white people who help and speed them on their mission. Towards the end of the book this becomes a 'hanky' story, but it is saved by Sajo's dignity and because the animals are pathetic even without the attempt to humanize them. Chilawee is put down in the cage with Chikanee: 'Then, the truth slowly dawning in the little twilight minds, they crept to one another, eyes almost starting out of their heads, ears wide open, listening, sniffing. . . . ' The story ends with the return of the two beavers to their home pond—a realistic note—and with Grey Owl's views on conservation triumphant. As an animal story for children, *The Adventures of Sajo and Her Beaver People* is significant because it is the only one written in Canada that preserves realism and still shows a highly emotional link between children and animals. (pp. 138-40)

> *Sheila Egoff, "The Realistic Animal Story," in her* The Republic of Childhood: A Critical Guide to Canadian Children's Literature in English, *second edition, Oxford University Press, Canadian Branch, 1975, pp. 131-52.*

Joan McGrath

[*The following excerpt is from a review of the Laurentian Library Edition of* Sajo and the Beaver People *published in 1977.*]

Grey Owl (otherwise Archie Belany) was a story-teller in both senses of the word. Perhaps, in time, even HE began to wonder who or what he really was. Born in England, he had no valid claim to Indian heritage; but his stories evince a deep and abiding love for the northern Indian lands and their small wild inhabitants.

The 'high spots' of *Sajo and the Beaver People;* the forest fire; little Sajo's pathetic offer to give her beloved beaver kitten to the zoo to save his brother from pining with loneliness in his concrete prison; and the glorious reunion of Sajo and her beavers after their struggles and heartbreak, still pack a powerful wallop. This handsome new edition of the beloved story, complete with Grey Owl's idiosyncratic sketches, is very welcome; but some of the attitudes expressed will not be to modern taste. Today's reader will be less than amused by the inclusion of a stock-figure Irish cop who calls himself "a Mick," confusing the children whose Ojibway word for beaver is "a-mik." His contrived and unconvincing brogue is likely to offend where surely no offense was intended. Derogatory remarks about "halfbreeds" will be equally unwelcome.

The author's partisan viewpoint is another source of difficulty. He describes the beaver-hunting otter as an "evil," "cruel," "sly" monster. Love for one species of wild life should not preclude fair treatment of another; happily, writers of modern animal stories no longer attribute base human motivation to wild creatures who merely obey natural instincts. Child readers may need adult guidance to bring this piece of special pleading into a more acceptable perspective.

Though there are undoubtedly points deserving of criticism, *Sajo* is a very special book, whose good qualities far outweigh the bad. Grey Owl's best-loved book, his only book written for children, has a strong claim to classic status. (pp. 50-1)

> *Joan McGrath, in a review of "Sajo and the Beaver People," in* In Review: Canadian Books for Children, *Vol. 12, No. 1, Winter, 1978, pp. 50-1.*

Celeste A. van Vloten

Grey Owl shed his identity as Englishman Archie Belaney soon after he reached the Canadian wilds in the early 1900s and adopted the lifestyle of frontiersman and trapper. However, that lifestyle slowly evolved into one which was an anomaly of anomalies, a life of a *non-hunting* Indian living in the bush, as he came to respect and love those he called his brethren, the Little People of the Wilderness. Grey Owl discovered within himself the ability to write passionately about his life and his brethren, and the ready market he found for his works and his lecture tours not only supported his family but enabled him to further his mission of preservation of the wild. His strong feelings for wild animals of the Canadian North are manifestly revealed in two recent reprints of his works, *Sajo and the Beaver People* and *A book of Grey Owl.*

Originally titled *The Adventures of Sajo and her Beaver People,* this book, first published in 1935, is the tale of two beaver kittens rescued by an Indian father who gives them to his two children, Sajo and Shapian. The four young creatures learn quickly to care for each other as the author erases the line separating human from animal, for the two beavers show the same kind of behavior their human friends do, and for the same reasons. Unfortunately, the father is forced to surrender one of the kittens to the local trader, and the two children, disconsolate at the loss, eventually decide to retrieve their zoo-bound little friend. They endure ordeals as they travel from their home in the Wilderness to the city; and city life presents a world as alien to them as the forest is to city dwellers. The lost kitten suffers as well, in his concrete and steel pen, with a concrete puddle-sized pool for a pond. Suffice it to say all five are reunited. But Grey Owl does not end the story at this obvious point; instead, after the celebrations are over, the father tells his children the baby beavers are old enough to return to where they belong. With a strong sense of loss, they take the two kittens back to the beaver pond.

The book is funny, sad, thought-provoking, and satisfying. It contains sketches done by Grey Owl that are a little fuzzy but still attractive. The story does verge on the sentimental in parts, but it does so much in the same way as the works of the British veterinarian and writer James Herriot do, for Grey Owl shares Herriot's style of affectionate description of his animals' acts and appearances. If Herriot inspires the reader to become a veterinarian, Grey Owl creates a longing to become an inhabitant of the Canadian wilderness.

Grey Owl holding Jelly Roll at Metis, Quebec, 1929.

tales, not in any didactic moral pronouncements. Hence both *A book of Grey Owl* and *Sajo and the Beaver People* are books that are more than worth reading for anyone, at any age. (pp. 90-2)

> Celeste A. van Vloten, "Grey Owl: Wilderness Man's Words," in Canadian Children's Literature, No. 50, 1988, pp. 90-2.

Hugh A. Cook

Originally published in 1938 and reprinted eleven times, [*The Book of Grey Owl: Selected Wildlife Stories*] contains selections from four of Grey Owl's works: *The Men of the Last Frontier, Sajo and the Beaver People, Pilgrims of the Wild,* and *Tales of an Empty Cabin.*

The volume begins with a preface by Lovat Dickson, who gives the reader some biographical information about Grey Owl. This sets the mood for the remainder of the book. If a teacher or librarian is considering reading some of this work to a class, the reader should ensure that the audience knows who Grey Owl was and what he was attempting to achieve with his writing.

Well over half the stories deal with tales about the beaver. This is probably because Grey Owl allowed them to live with him in his cabin and thus came to know and understand them best. He also relates stories about the moose and the smaller animals of the forest around his cabin who followed him in hopes of a hand-out.

This book is still needed and should be read to our youth by our adults so that all will come to understand the need we have for preserving some of our environment in its more natural state.

There is a four-page glossary of terms commonly used by the travellers of the far north at the time, and the last section of the book deals with the ways of the North American Indians as Grey Owl knew them.

This is definitely a book a teacher should consider reading to a Junior class. (pp. 186-87)

> Hugh A. Cook, in a review of "The Book of Grey Owl: Selected Wildlife Stories," in CM: Canadian Materials for Schools and Libraries, Vol. XVII, No. 4, July, 1989, pp. 186-87.

Kenneth Brower

The trail to Grey Owl's cabin began among aspen under a big prairie sky. In late September, when I set off in pursuit of the old Indian, the aspen—poplar, he would have called them—were nearly leafless, all their green turned yellow-gold, all the gold fallen to the ground. The beaked hazel had dropped its leaves too. The rose hips and high-bush cranberries displayed themselves on naked branches. Puddles in the trail were covered with half-inch panes of ice. On the 1,200-foot escarpment of Riding Mountain, summer is abbreviated, ending a few days before its conclusion on the Manitoba plains below.

An elk had crossed the trail in one spot, and in several places moose. They had left deep tracks, which last night's freeze had set as hard as fossil hoofprints in stone. The

That longing is not abated after reading *A book of Grey Owl.* Although not a cohesive story like *Sajo and the Beaver People,* it evokes the same response, with, however, an added note of wonder and awe. A selection of stories from Grey Owl's major works, it contains actual, if a little dark, photos of Grey Owl with some of his animal friends. It begins with exciting and moving excerpts from *Adventures of Sajo and her Beaver People* and continues with excerpts judiciously grouped from other works: *Men of the Last Frontier, Pilgrims of the Wild,* and *Tales of an Empty Cabin.* Successive sections focus on the habits of beavers, the wilderness trail, wild animals other than beavers, and on North American Indians. Each chapter is a coherent, integral unit, and there is no sense of abruptness or discontinuity in the flow of the stories except where the editor has noted unobtrusively the source of the excerpt. Grey Owl has written with the graceful ease suited to one so passionately intimate with his subject. His style matches his tales, as heroic deeds are told with heroic words, and serene scenes depicted smoothly and softly. In both books, his humor relies on understatement and a light irony that never descends to bitterness, and his messages of respect for the wilderness, the animals who inhabit it, and the men who survive in it, are only revealed in the telling of the moose tracks were the larger and more pointed. They were a day or two old, yet each time I passed a set I took a nervous, reflexive look into the forest around.

Here and there pocket gophers had pushed mounds of black tailings from their burrows onto the trail. In passing I nudged a mound with the toe of my boot. It had no give. It had lost the fine, airy lightness the mounds have in warm weather. Now and again my boots detoured for the pocket-gopher mounds. They did so because of the same powerful obligation that caused them to veer occasionally and tramp on those first panes of autumn ice. I dutifully kicked a few mounds apart. They were black with moisture on the outside, gray on the inside. The wet black exteriors gave the impression that this prairie soil was even richer than it was.

My trip to Grey Owl's cabin was part hike and part pilgrimage. I went in curiosity and a certain embarrassment. Americans know so much less of Canadian history than Canadians know of American. I had grown up in a California household where environmentalism and its poets and heroes made most of the table talk, yet before coming to Manitoba I had never heard of Grey Owl. No man was more important to Canadian environmental consciousness, or to the environmental consciousness of the entire British Commonwealth, for that matter. If his deeds had been done at a slightly lower latitude, we all would have heard of him. In the pantheon Grey Owl belongs with Henry David Thoreau, John Muir, Aldo Leopold, and Rachel Carson—or perhaps with Lewis Mumford and Joseph Wood Krutch, on the level just below.

I was curious about Grey Owl because he is doubly now a fossil. He has been dead in a personal way for half a century, and he is said to be dead as a type.

In the environmental movement of the 1970s and 1980s bureaucratization has been the trend. Those old clarion voices in the wilderness and *from* the wilderness—Thoreau's, Muir's, Leopold's, Grey Owl's—have done their job in alerting mankind to the environmental threat, according to the new wisdom. The day now belongs to pragmatic, reasonable men who know the art of compromise and can work effectively with Congress and Parliament. The era of the "stars," those seminal, charismatic, flawed, larger-than-life characters whose eloquence and example brought the natural world back into the world, is finished—or so the bureaucrats themselves assure us.

The trail to Grey Owl's cabin, in more than one sense, was cold.

. . . . .

By his own testimony, Grey Owl was born in Hermosillo, Mexico, in 1888. His mother was Katherine Cochise, of the Jacarilla Apaches, his father George MacNeil, a Scot who had served as a scout in the Southwestern Indian wars. MacNeil was a good friend of another old Indian fighter, Buffalo Bill Cody, who in 1887 invited the MacNeils to join the Wild West Show that he was taking to England for Queen Victoria's Jubilee. Grey Owl's gestation, curiously enough, was in England. Their son's birth imminent, the MacNeils returned to the New World.

From Mexico the family moved north. At the age of fifteen, the boy parted company with his parents and set off on his own into Ontario. He learned woodcraft from the Ojibways, who adopted him, and he became a trapper and a river guide. The Ojibways called him *Wa-Sha-Quon-Asin,* He-Who-Flies-by-Night, or Grey Owl. The Ojibways appear to have been shrewd judges of character. He-Who-Flies-by-Night would prove the perfect name for Grey Owl.

As the years passed in the north woods, Grey Owl saw less and less of whites and more of Indians. At times he refused to speak anything but Ojibway. He was a man given to dark moods, and occasionally to violence—from time to time he was in trouble with the law—but for the most part his backwoods friends, both Indian and white, found him a humorous man and a good companion. In 1915, when he was twenty-six, he enlisted in the Canadian Army, and he fought as an infantryman in France. Temperamentally unsuited to military life, he made an indifferent soldier until his platoon commander realized that his solitary nature, his obsession with field craft, his gift for immobility, and his skill with a rifle were all the makings of a good sniper. Grey Owl spent the remainder of the war attempting to shoot enemy soldiers one by one. He was wounded in the wrist and in the foot—one toe had to be amputated—and his lungs were scarred by mustard gas. By all accounts of the backwoodsmen who knew him, he returned to Canada a more melancholy man.

He was not cheered by what was happening to the north woods. The forests of his youth were fast becoming overlogged and overhunted, and he had trouble making a living as a trapper. By 1925, at the age of thirty-seven, he was on the run from the law, pursued by a nemesis, one Inspector Jordan. His crime was not very serious—he had punched a station agent—but Grey Owl was not the sort of man who wanted to spend any time at all in jail.

Traveling with him was the love of his life, an Iroquois girl named Anahareo. Anahareo, a partly acculturated Indian, disliked the cruelty of trapping. It was a sensibility new to Grey Owl, and one that slowly began to tell on him. One day, near the lodge of an adult beaver he had trapped, Grey Owl rescued two beaver kittens he had just orphaned. He took them to his cabin—"two funny-looking furry creatures with little scaly tails and exaggerated hind feet," he would later write. It was the beginning of the end for the trapper in him. He and Anahareo named the kittens McGinnis and McGinty and learned how to care for them.

"They seemed to be almost like little folk from some other planet, whose language we could not yet quite understand," he would write. "To kill such creatures seemed monstrous. I would do no more of it. Instead of persecuting them further I would study them, see just what there really was to them. I perhaps could start a colony of my own; these animals could not be permitted to pass completely from the face of this wilderness."

In the winter of 1928-1929 he started his first colony. The country he chose for it proved to be poor in game, and to make ends meet he had to write. One northwoods article was accepted by *Country Life,* which liked it enough to commission another. His beaver-colony scheme had a temporary setback when McGinnis and McGinty returned to the wild, but from an Indian friend Grey Owl acquired a new female beaver kitten, whom he named Jelly Roll, and later he rescued a male, Rawhide, from an otter trap he had set. He travelled to Métis-sur-Mer, a resort town on the Gulf of St. Lawrence, in the hopes of earning some money lecturing, and was eventually invited to speak to the Ladies' Club. He began that talk, he would later admit, "like a snake that has swallowed an icicle, chilled from one end to the other," but by the middle he had found his stride, and the ladies of Métis-sur-Mer loved him. A collection was taken at the end, and it earned Grey Owl $700, more than he and Anahareo had made in that whole season of trapping. His reputation grew. He continued to write articles. In September of 1930 the National Parks of Canada made a film of his work with beaver.

In April of 1931 Grey Owl boarded the train in Quebec with Jelly Roll and Rawhide—Anahareo had left him, as she would often in their life together, to go prospecting—and he and his beaver traveled west to Riding Mountain National Park, where they were to start a new career. The government had decided to support Grey Owl and his beaver colony: he would be working at Riding Mountain on salary. The park superintendent tried to direct him to Lake Audy, a large body of water near the southern boundary of the park. The lake had plenty of aspen and balsam poplar of the right size for beaver, and a history of beaver habitation, but Grey Owl rejected it. Lake Audy was too close to the park boundary, he said. The streams flowed directly out. In springtime the young male beaver would migrate away from the park's safety and would be shot or trapped. Grey Owl chose Beaver Lodge Lake instead. In the vicinity of that smaller lake the creeks ran north, tributaries to no waterway flowing out of the park until they joined the Ochre River. Grey Owl liked the smaller lake's isolation and the shape of its shoreline. The superintendent surrendered, and a cabin was built for Grey Owl on the shore of Beaver Lodge Lake.

"I once spent a season in the great high oasis of Riding Mountain," Grey Owl later wrote, "with its poplar forest and rolling downs carpeted with myriad flowers, that stands like an immense island of green above the hot, dry sameness of the wheat-stricken Manitoba prairie that surrounds it."

There is no better summary description of Riding Mountain. One of the mysteries of Grey Owl is that a half-breed boy raised by Ojibways could have composed it. How, in the backwoods of Ontario and Quebec, could the author of a phrase like "the hot, dry sameness of the wheat-stricken Manitoba prairie" have developed his style?

Grey Owl's fondness for the great high oasis of Riding Mountain quickly soured. He did not like the park's waterways, which did not permit the free canoe travel he loved. He concluded that the encircledness of Riding Mountain was wrong. The hot, dry sameness of the beaver-hostile country surrounding the national park was inimical to his rebeavering scheme. He requested a transfer, which was granted. In October of 1931, six months after arriving at Riding Mountain, he took his beaver and their new kittens and moved to Ajawaan Lake, in Prince Albert National Park, Saskatchewan.

Grey Owl was gone, but his influence persisted. The authorities at Riding Mountain National Park liked his beaver reintroduction plan and they stuck with it. Beaver, decimated in the eighteenth century by Assiniboine, Cree, and Saulteaux trappers, began to multiply in the park.

In November 1931, the month after he came down from Riding Mountain, Grey Owl's first book, *Men of the Last Frontier,* was published in London; the next year it came out in Toronto and New York. At his new cabin at Ajawaan Lake he wrote a second book, *Pilgrims of the Wild.* The Canadian government produced more films on his beaver. His fame spread on both sides of the Atlantic. In 1935 his English publisher arranged a tour in Britain. Grey Owl arrived at Southampton, wearing a blue serge suit, moccasins, and a gray sombrero, his face lean and ascetic, his black hair braided in two plaits. He lectured and showed his beaver films, first to small audiences but soon to packed houses, with policemen controlling the queues. He was a sensation.

"Europe had not heard such a voice as his since the eighteenth century and the beginning of the industrial revolution," his publisher, Lovat Dickson, wrote years afterward, attempting to explain Grey Owl's impact on the England of 1935. "Suddenly here was this romantic figure telling them with his deep and thrilling voice that somewhere there was a land where life could begin again, a place which the screams of demented dictators could not reach." The tour was extended to four months, in the course of which Grey Owl gave two hundred lectures to more than a quarter million people. *Pilgrims of the Wild,* which had already been reprinted five times in the nine months since publication, was reprinted again every month of his tour. He had come to England with his belongings in a knapsack; he left with eight large pieces of luggage full of gifts for himself and his family. He was presented, as he embarked on the ship home to Canada, with the check representing his earnings from the tour. Grey Owl seems to have been a man genuinely uninterested in money, and never once in England had he asked how the tour was profiting. He was returning to his beaver a rich man.

As a writer, Grey Owl had many voices—too many voices, some might argue.

"And it is reflections such as these," Grey Owl wrote, in the preface to his *Tales of an Empty Cabin,*

> that finally aroused in me a distaste for killing, and brought a growing feeling of kinship with those inoffensive and interesting beasts that were co-dwellers with me in this Land of Shadows and of Silence. So that ultimately I laid aside my rifle and my traps and like Paul, worked for the betterment of those whom I had so assiduously persecuted.

And yet just pages later, in a chapter called "Cry Wolves!" this same Paul of the wilderness wrote,

> The tall snow-covered trees along the shore

seemed to stare down on me kind of dour and grim, like I had butted in where I wasn't wanted. And man! she was cold. . . . Anyway I picked off up the lake and saw a wolf alright enough, out of shot, and screeching blue murder. I sneaked up onto a point and saw the rest of the lake and say, it looked to be just covered with wolves.

Later still, in a chapter called "A Letter," Grey Owl gave us a note we are to believe he wrote in 1918, from the Canadian woods, in his semiliterate days, to the nurse who had tended him when he was recovering from war wounds in an English hospital. "Dear Miss Nurse," he began.

> Nearly four months now the Canada geese flew south and the snow is very deep. It is long time-since I wrot to you, but I have gone a long ways and folled some hard trails since that time. The little wee sorryful animals I tol you about sit around me tonight, and so they dont get tired and go away I write to you now. I guess they like to see me workin.

Grey Owl was in chronic violation of the seventh rule of the nineteen that, according to Mark Twain, govern literary art. In his essay "Fenimore Cooper's Literary Offenses," Twain, after noting that Cooper, in the space of two thirds of a page of *The Deerslayer,* committed 114 offenses against literary art out of a possible 115—a record—proceeded to state those rules. Rule 7 requires "that when a personage talks like an illustrated, gilt-edged, tree-calf, hand-tooled, seven-dollar Friendship's Offering in the beginning of a paragraph, he shall not talk like a negro minstrel in the end of it."

Grey Owl himself would have shrugged off any attempts to defend his style. Internal evidence suggests that he owed something to Twain—his rhythms are more Huck Finn than Ojibway—but otherwise he and Twain had different tastes. Grey Owl *liked* James Fenimore Cooper, though he misspelled his name, and he was also an admirer of Longfellow. In his essay **"The Mission of Hiawatha,"** Grey Owl wrote, "It has become a pose of modern ultra-sophistication to scoff at those works of Fennimore Cooper and Longfellow that portray the life of the North American Indian. Those who do so are, not infrequently, equipped with little or no knowledge of the subject."

Of the literary rules on Twain's list, Grey Owl periodically violated the eighth as well. Rule 8 requires "that crass stupidities shall not be played upon the reader as 'the craft of the woodsman, the delicate art of the forest.' " Grey Owl habitually violated rule 9, which requires "that the personages of a tale shall confine themselves to possibilities and let miracles alone; or, if they venture a miracle, the author must so plausibly set it forth as to make it look possible and reasonable."

In the "Cry Wolves!" chapter, Grey Owl violated rule 9 in a miraculous encounter with wolves on thin ice:

> I got a whiff of the strong musky smell these animals make when they mean business, and I saw right away I was up against it; no fooling this time. The wolves came towards me, spreading out, and commenced to snap and snarl and

worry at the air, for all the world like a bunch of dogs baiting a cow. I was right out on the weak spot, and as they crept up on me, the ice commenced to groan and crack with the extra weight, and I could see myself being soon measured for a harp and a pair of wings unless things took a change. This time I had the thirty-two special, and felt right at home. I didn't stop to do any figuring, but let go a few with the old artillery. The light was poor, and although I pass for being pretty handy with the hardware, I saw only two of the lobos fall. The rest backed off into the dark and commenced to howl, but it wasn't long before they came back for more. They fanned out like troops under fire. . . .

These suicidal maneuverings, in an animal as intelligent and man-wary as the wolf, may not be technically miraculous but they are certainly preternatural. They are in violation of the spirit of rule 9, if not the letter.

Fifty-eight wolves, at the latest count, reside in Riding Mountain National Park, and for several years a scientist named Paul Paquet has been studying them. When I described Grey Owl's account to Paquet, and later to Ludwig Carbyn, the Canadian Wildlife Service research scientist who was overseeing Paquet's work, the two men just laughed. Wolf scientists everywhere, I have found, are accustomed to this sort of exaggeration and are surprisingly charitable toward its perpetrators. Many grew up reading Ernest Thompson Seton and will admit to a fondness for that whole school of wolf writing. Grey Owl certainly was not the last popular Canadian nature writer to invent adventures with wolves.

Grey Owl's best book, ***Pilgrims of the Wild,*** is an account of the transformation at the heart of his life's drama—the story of his flight with Anahareo through the slash and burn of ruined country, his realization that the day of the trapper was in twilight, his rescue of the beaver kittens, his metamorphosis from trapper to advocate of animals. In ***Pilgrims*** he finds a single voice, one that seems to be his own. There is a nice symmetry to his cast of characters: two human beings and two beaver. Grey Owl is at his best when writing about the beaver. For page after page his beaver observations are sharp, humorous, and entirely believable.

> Their hands—one can call them nothing else—were nearly as effective as our own more perfect members would be, in the uses they were put to. They could pick up very small objects with them, manipulate sticks and stones, strike, push, and heave with them and they had a very firm grasp which it was difficult to disengage.

> Each had a special liking for one of us, and continued faithful to his choice. . . . They would generally lie on our bodies, one on each of us, the favoured position being a rather inconvenient one across the throat.

> At three months of age they ceased to be of any further trouble to us save for the daily feed of porridge, an insatiable and very active curiosity regarding the contents of provision bags and boxes, the frequent desire for petting that seemed to fill some great want in their lives, and

From Pilgrims of the Wild, *written and illustrated by Grey Owl.*

the habit they had of coming into our beds, soaking wet, at all hours of the night.

They were hostile to anything they deemed to be an intruder and became very angry at the continued visits to the tent of a weasel, one of them eventually making a pass at him, the agile weasel, of course being in two or three other places by the time the blow landed.

They were . . . gentle and good natured, they gave out no odour whatever, and were altogether the best conducted pair of little people one could wish to live with.

. . . . .

The trail to Grey Owl's cabin descended from the negligible elevations to which it had climbed, and now its lowest stretches were flooded, owing to beaver dams. I was able to pick my way around most of the wet spots, but finally, halfway to the cabin, the path dipped to a swampy place where all detours were under water. Most beaver ponds in autumn are tea-colored. Here the volume of the flow was such that the tea had clarified. The path became a clear, cold stream flowing shallowly over a bottom of golden leaves. The margins of the stream, in all directions, for as far as I could see, were marshland under a half inch of ice. There was nothing to do but ford.

Grey Owl's beaver-seeding scheme succeeded better than

he ever dreamed. The topographic maps for Riding Mountain National Park are all a little off, because surveyors have trouble traveling far in any direction without running into a beaver pond or marsh. Beaver are doing so well in the park that population pressures continually force excess animals to move out. In summertime beaver are a principal food of the park's wolves, but the wolves can't eat enough of them. The expatriate beaver invade the wheat farmland around the park's periphery, just as Grey Owl predicted they would. They dam streams on private land, irritating the farmers, who trap and shoot them—just as Grey Owl predicted—and they present park authorities with a big public-relations problem. Park wardens are not supposed to interfere with beaver, but occasionally they do blow a beaver dam, just so human visitors can keep their heads above water. Grey Owl's "little people," if left to their own devices, would turn the escarpment of Riding Mountain into a high reservoir in the middle of the Manitoba plains.

The aspen forest opened up into sedgy meadows and a connected system of beaver ponds. I passed a dry pond. Sedges and willows were taking it over from the outside in, and the remnants of the old lodge made a mound in what was now meadow. The lodge was the slightest of swellings, but it was artifice, and that caught the eye, just as the artifice of Indian middens does. I saw the cabin ahead. It stood on a slight prominence above what had to be Beaver Lodge Lake. When I crossed the marshy outlet to the lake, the long grasses there were still in shadow. It was nearly noon, but the tussocks lay this way and that under the weight of frost, as if by scythe. The frost-mown grasses were crunchy underfoot.

A few yards from the cabin I came into the light. The sun was warm on Grey Owl's porch. I pulled off my daypack and set it against the logs of the cabin wall. The signs said GREY OWL'S CABIN. PLEASE RESPECT THIS NATIONAL HERITAGE and CABANE DE GREY OWL. AIDEZ-NOUS A CONSERVER CE PATRIMOINE NATIONAL. For the most part visitors had done as the signs asked, carving few initials on the logs, inside or out. I searched the walls for some mark of Grey Owl's, and found none.

. . . .

The climax of Grey Owl's second tour of England, in 1937, was a command performance at Buckingham Palace. The original plan for his palace lecture had Grey Owl and the other guests waiting in the reception hall. The footmen would throw open the doors, and the King and his family would enter. Grey Owl and the other guests would stand, and Grey Owl would begin his lecture.

Grey Owl, democrat and showman, insisted that the protocol be reversed. King George VI, good-humored, agreed to be seated first. The footmen threw open the doors, and there, in his buckskins, stood Grey Owl.

He saluted the King and said, *"How Kola,"* and a few more words in Ojibway. "Which, being interpreted, means 'I come in peace, brother,' " he explained to the King. The King smiled and acknowledged the greeting. Grey Owl began his lecture. The Queen, the Queen's parents—the Earl and Countess of Strathmore—and much of the palace staff were in attendance that day, but the true Grey Owl fans at Buckingham Palace were Princesses Elizabeth and Margaret. The command performance had been arranged mostly for them. Grey Owl, the canny performer, was quick to understand this. After the first minutes, he directed his speech exclusively to the smallest but most enthusiastic members of his audience. He gave what Lovat Dickson, who was on hand, considered one of his most inspired performances. At the conclusion Princess Elizabeth jumped up. "Oh, do go on!" she cried. For the future queen Grey Owl did a ten-minute encore.

Afterward, the King came up to Grey Owl, Elizabeth on one arm and Margaret on the other. Troubled by what he had just learned about the possible extinction of beaver, King George asked questions about the beaver situation, and Grey Owl answered. Lovat Dickson watched his author proudly. "I was admiring Grey Owl's attitude," Dickson has written.

> He was more than ever the Indian, proud, fierce, inscrutable. Those fringed buckskins, the wampum belt, the knife in its sheath at his side, the moccasins on those polished floors, the long dark hair surmounted by a single feather, were all in such contrast with the trim, neat figure of the King, with the fair, reddish hair characteristic of the House of Windsor.

When the time came to go, Grey Owl extended his right hand to the King. He touched a royal shoulder lightly with his beaded buckskin gloves. "Goodbye, brother," the Indian said. "I'll be seeing you."

Grey Owl spoke truer, and falser, than anyone in the gathering could have guessed. Grey Owl was brother indeed to the King—or, rather, subject and countryman. Grey Owl's real name was Archibald Belaney, and he had been born in Hastings, England, forty-nine years before. He had never been to Hermosillo, and his mother was not Katherine Cochise or any other Apache. "More than ever the Indian," Dickson had mused. Never, in truth, the Indian at all.

Immediately upon Grey Owl's death in Saskatchewan, on April 13, 1938, the truth hit the papers. "GREY OWL HAD COCKNEY ACCENT AND FOUR WIVES," one British headline read. "GREY OWL ENGLISH BOY," read another.

Archie Belaney's father was not George MacNeil, Indian scout, but George Belaney, scoundrel and rotter. George Belaney was a scam artist, bigamist, pedophile, drunk, and lecher. His one real talent was in shaking down his widowed mother. At the age of twenty he succeeded in getting her to set him up in a tea and coffee business, which he quickly brought to the verge of ruin by leaving for half a year of big-game hunting in Africa, and then finished off by departing again for a month of hunting in Suffolk. At twenty-one, George impregnated the fifteen-year-old daughter of a tavern owner, secretly married her, and then, on the birth of their child—a daughter—abandoned them both. With a girlfriend, Elizabeth Cox, he traveled to Florida and spent two years hunting and practicing amateur taxidermy. At Key West, Elizabeth was delivered of their child, a daughter, Gertrude. The three were forced to return to England, Elizabeth having become violently ill from arsenic poisoning.

Arsenic is used in taxidermy, and Elizabeth's exposure could have been accidental. George Belaney may have had nothing to do with it. It is worthy of note, however, that George's great uncle, James Belaney, himself an avid hunter, the famous author of *A Treatise on Falconry,* and a bachelor until middle age, was arrested and tried for killing his young wife with prussic acid. The *Times* and other journals were certain of his guilt, but James had an excuse for possession of the poison—in his case not taxidermy but indigestion, which prussic acid was used to treat—and he was acquitted.

Elizabeth Cox recovered, at any rate. George Belaney talked his mother into setting him up as an orange planter in Florida, and he and Elizabeth returned to that state, this time taking along her twelve-year-old sister, Kitty. Elizabeth died within a year, even as their orange plantation was going under. George fell into drunkenness and delirium tremens, and then pulled himself together sufficiently to marry Elizabeth's sister, now thirteen. It was this child bride, Kitty—Katherine Cox—who in Grey Owl's revisionist history of himself became Katherine Cochise of the Jacarilla Apaches. George sold his orange grove, left his three-year-old daughter, Gertrude, with a Florida neighbor, and returned with the pregnant Kitty to

England. On September 18, 1888, Kitty gave birth to Archibald Stansfeld Belaney.

George Belaney was unable to keep a job or mend his ways. When Archie Belaney was four, the family solicitor persuaded George to sign a document agreeing to voluntary exile. On the condition that he never set foot in England again, he was to receive a small income for life. He and his son parted in tears. George Belaney would die twelve years later, somewhere in Mexico.

Archie Belaney was brought up in Hastings by his grandmother and his maiden aunts. He was a loner, a reader of weekly serials on Indians, an animal lover who kept a menagerie in the attic. He had frogs, mice, a snake he called Rajah, and later a defanged adder that he liked to bring to school in his pocket or shirt. He was a good actor, with a talent for parody. His trademark was hooting like an owl. He spent his free time wandering the sea cliffs at Hastings or in St. Helen's Woods, a preserve north of the Belaney house, and in the wan English summertime he grew almost swarthy. (Later, as a grown man in the long summer days of the Canadian north, he would tan even darker. Unsatisfied, he would be driven to dye his skin darker still. One of his biographers has speculated that this habit may have begun in his English boyhood, his pocket money in Hastings going to cheap dyes.)

"A third eccentric joined the School," his grammar school's history noted of his arrival in September, 1899.

> This was Archie Belaney. He did not conceal firearms in his pockets, but just as likely might produce from them a snake or a fieldmouse. Born eleven years before, and living at 36 St. Mary's Terrace, he was a delicate boy but full of devilment; and fascinated by woods and wild animals. . . . What with his camping out, his tracking of all and sundry, and wild hooting, he was more like a Red Indian than a respectable Grammar School boy.

In his teens Archie grew more and more like an Indian. His dream was to go to Canada and live among Indians, study them, maybe write an anthropological text. His aunts tried to dissuade him, but he persisted. In 1906, when he was eighteen, his way was paid to Toronto, with the understanding on the part of his family (if not himself) that he would study farming. No one knows what happened to him next. He would return several times to England, but in Canada he had already begun to disappear into the myth of his own making.

That Grey Owl's secret could have gone undetected by his English and American audiences seems, in hindsight, odd. It required of those audiences a willing suspension of belief in the laws of genetics. Dark eyes are a dominant trait. A blue-eyed Scot and a black-eyed Apache are unlikely to produce a blue-eyed son. It required a romantic ignorance of how American Indians dress in the twentieth century. Buckskins, wampum belts, braided hair, and feathers still had some ceremonial use in the 1920s and 1930s, as they have now, but Grey Owl, in the photo sections of his books, is shown *hunting* dressed like that. The acceptance of Grey Owl as an Indian required, as well, considerable naiveé about the nature of literary art. A small boy taught

his three R's by an Apache aunt in dusty Indian encampments on the Mexican desert—with the first R subsequently polished, over long winter nights in boreal forests, by reading descriptions of bear traps and shotguns in mailorder catalogues—does not learn to write in the several mannered styles of Grey Owl.

Grey Owl's frontispieces alone should have tipped off the public. Nearly every one of them is a scowling portrait of the author in braids and buckskins, his brows knit darkly, the corners of his mouth turned down. Some scowling Indians can be seen in the old daguerrotypes, but most nineteenth-century Indians—most nineteenth-century Europeans, for that matter—stared into the new machine with a stony absence of expression. Grey Owl overdid it.

From the very beginning, in fact, some people saw through Grey Owl. The Ojibway knew he was not Indian or part-Indian. Many of the white people of the Canadian backwoods knew Indians well enough to know that Grey Owl wasn't one of them—not the way he played classical music. "If you're an Indian, I'm a Chinaman," a Quebec man once told him. The rivermen of the Mississagi River took him for a white man with maybe a streak of Indian blood. Grey Owl demonstrated his knife-throwing talent for them—this was supposed to be an Indian skill—but he also recited Shakespeare. Rumor was that he was a McGill man, the prodigal son of a rich Montreal family.

Not even all the English were fooled. On Grey Owl's first English tour, one of the stops on his lecture circuit was Hastings, Archie Belaney's home town. Grey Owl spoke to a packed theater at the White Rock Pavilion, not far from St. Helen's Wood—his first hunting grounds. Among the listeners was Mary McCormick, one of twelve children who had lived in the house next door to the Belaney place. Mary's younger brother George had been Archie Belaney's friend and classmate. It had been Archie's habit to signal George and her other brothers by hooting like an owl. Occasionally he would climb the roof and appear at the boys' window before dawn, awakening the brothers with his owl call, and once he had built a wigwam on the McCormick's lawn. Mary McCormick was middleaged, like the tall Indian in buckskins at the podium. Thirty years had passed since Archie Belaney's departure from England. At the conclusion of the lecture, as she left the theater, McCormick turned to a friend. "That's Belaney, or I'll eat my hat," she said.

For the first days after Grey Owl's death, the English press had fun with him. People love a hoax, and the Archie Belaney in Grey Owl had been uncovered. Within a week or so the press began to have second thoughts about him. On April 22, 1938, nine days after Grey Owl died in Saskatchewan, an editorialist for *The Times* arrived at what for me is the correct view of him: "Tu-whit tu-whoo-hoo-Who was he really, this mysterious Grey Owl? . . . The strange bird seems to be acquiring as many birthplaces as Homer, as many wives as Solomon. . . . Was he Grey Owl at all, or another gentleman of the same name, like the author of Shakespeare's plays?

"He . . . gave his extraordinary genius, his passionate

sympathy, his bodily strength, his magnetic personal influence, even his very earnings to the service of animals."

Grey Owl did give those things, and that is what does matter.

In the initial gusto with which the English press went after Grey Owl, there was surely some envy. For all he was not, Grey Owl was in fact a competent trapper. He was a good shot with rifle and shotgun. He could throw knives accurately—a useless talent of the sort that no boy grows old enough not to admire. Grey Owl really did have troubles with the law, and spent part of his life as a fugitive. It's hard not to look up to him secretly for that.

In Hastings the twelve-year-old Archie Belaney had amazed his aunt Ada with his knowledge of Canadian Indians. He showed her a map on which he had marked in the linguistic groups of aboriginal Canada, the Athabascan-speakers in the northwest, the Iroquois in the south, the Algonkian in the east. He showed her how the Algonkian-speakers, the group that interested him most, were divided into tribes: Ojibway, Cree, Naskapi, Penobscot, Micmac, Algonquin, Têtes de Boules, and Montagnais. His penny novels on Indians were illustrated in the margins with drawings he had done of Indians fighting white men.

It happens that my own illustrations at that age were of Indians fighting white men. They were drawings full of carnage, the Indians always winning, the cavalrymen riddled by arrows and spears. I was a twelve-year-old expert on Indians myself. My specialty was the Western tribes, and of those, I liked best the Apaches—Grey Owl's putative maternal line. I know, for example, that his "Jacarilla" Apaches should be spelled "Jicarilla." I can still tell you the date Geronimo surrendered: September 4, 1886, just two years before Grey Owl's birth to Katherine Cochise in Hermosillo, Mexico—or, if you prefer, just two years before Archie Belaney's birth to Katherine Cox in Hastings. At ages nine to twelve I dreamed of being an Indian. Little Archie Belaney had actually gone and done it.

Margaret McCormick, another sister in the clan that had lived next door to the Belaneys, put an interesting twist on the Grey Owl question when she was interviewed after his death. Had Archie Belaney become Grey Owl, she wondered, or had Grey Owl become Belaney? The real wonder of his life, she suggested, was that the physique, the proclivities, the temperament—the soul—of an Ojibway had found its way into an English schoolboy.

It is a truism that fiction is often truer than truth. Grey Owl was a walking, talking fiction who made real to his urban audiences, as a less false man could not, the plight of beaver and bear and lynx. His fictive gift, his fictive impulse, laced his readers and listeners into his buckskins, strapped them into his snowshoes with him. His unmasking—his defeathering—did not diminish him but over time has only made him larger, deepening his mystery.

Grey Owl was full of imperfections, yet was one of those Thoreau called "men with the seeds of life in them." Today's environmental bureaucrats seem to be correct that Grey Owl's type is in eclipse, their own type in ascen-

dancy. It is also true that tropical forests are vanishing at an accelerated rate, toxic wastes are multiplying, the oceans are dying, holes are appearing in the ozone layer, the Ontario lakes that Grey Owl paddled are going dead and fishless under acid rain. Reasonable, politically astute men and women are fine. They make good soldiers in any movement. They are useful for chores and follow-up. But what we need more than ever are men and women who capture our imaginations. (pp. 74-84)

> *Kenneth Brower, "Grey Owl," in* The Atlantic Monthly, *Vol. 265, No. 1, January, 1990, pp. 74-84.*

George Woodcock

Like T. E. Lawrence, Archie Belaney—alias Grey Owl—is one of those literary figures who survive more by the drama and oddity of their lives than by the quality of their writing. But Grey Owl was something more than a consummate and convincing fraud; the egotism of acting out his chosen Red Man role often shaded into a genuine altruism. The self-destroying zeal with which, in his last years, he propagated his double cause—the salvation of the wilderness and its inhabitants, and justice for the native peoples—is something to be admired even if the pursuit of his obsessive goals led to a great deal of unhappiness for other people. His treatment of women was execrable, and I have often wondered that feminists have not made him one of their special targets; perhaps it is his undoubted standing as a pioneer environmentalist (before even Aldous Huxley and B.C. writer Roderick Haig-Brown seriously attacked the issue) that has protected him from their anger.

But as a writer, popular though he was in his time, Grey Owl has not really stood up. His prose was rhetorical in a very Edwardian way, and his rhapsodic descriptions of the wilderness pall on modern readers, while his arguments seem too simplistic. In spite of his pretensions, he knew too little about the Indians of Canada to speak effectively for them, and today we prefer to listen to the voices of the real native people. At the same time, environmental issues are more complex and far-reaching than he realized, and nobody these days would make the same impact as he did in the 1930s with repetitive tales of the taming of wild beavers.

> *George Woodcock, "Archie's Great Wilderness Adventure," in* Quill and Quire, *Vol. 56, No. 4, April, 1990, p. 26.*

Heather Kirk

Saint, sinner, sick! While alive he was worshipped as one of the greatest spokespersons for Canada's Native people and nature. Since his death in 1938, when the Indian Grey Owl was revealed to be Englishman Archibald Stansfeld Belaney, he has been called a fraud, an imposter, and a liar. And now a new biography [Donald B. Smith, *From the Land of the Shadows: The Making of Grey Owl,* 1990] portrays him as a pathetic, emotionally-disturbed alcoholic. Are any of these assessments just? I would say, no. They are too extreme. They reveal an uneasy relationship with the kind of intuited but nevertheless valuable perceptions that can be revealed through myth. Furthermore,

From Sajo and the Beaver People, *written and illustrated by Grey Owl.*

they reveal a lack of appreciation for the mysterious processes involved in creating outstanding art.

Yes, like that other famous Canadian literary dissembler, Frederick Philip Grove (born Felix Paul Greve in Radomno, Prussia), Grey Owl (born Belaney in Hastings, England) took a new identity in a new land. Yes, like that spectacularly popular American writer, Ernest Hemingway, Grey Owl drank too much and had a number of wives. Yes, Grey Owl seems to have had serious emotional problems. Nevertheless, Grey Owl was also a gifted writer who conveyed an urgent message effectively. The message, that we must conserve our natural resources as the Native people did—"Remember you belong to nature, and it to you"—was not a mere slogan but a vital prophesy with religious implications. Half a century after Grey Owl's death, we recognize the truth of this only too well. What's more, the prophesy is contained in at least one literary work of sufficient distinction that it can still profitably be read and taught today, both for the message and the means of expression: myth.

Grey Owl's best and best-known book, the autobiography *Pilgrims of the wild* (1935), rewards close study with insight into the complexity and skill of its author. Theatrical public image, hidden psychological pressures, storyteller's instincts, and moral indignation can be seen to work together to form an indivisible whole greater than the parts. Exactly how the parts work together is exceedingly difficult to understand much less describe. Still, there can be seen a sort of chain-reaction mechanism wherein acceptance by an authority of the public image (an image

which subtly dramatizes otherwise hidden, inexplicable, even forbidden inner tensions and convictions) frees the artist to tap the deepest wellsprings of his psyche and allows a controlled but vital flow of information to be released, thereby relieving his inner tensions in a constructive way where others (who may or may not have undergone similar experiences) may also benefit. The skilful use of myth by this outstanding artist universalizes his inner life, allowing many (young and old) to share the insights of one. Difficult, deeply-felt meaning is thereby conveyed effectively with seeming simplicity.

In *Pilgrims of the wild* there are at least four "parts" or levels of meaning, levels which might be called (1) realistic, (2) psychological, (3) romantic, and (4) apocalyptic (the latter two terms borrowed cavalierly from Northrop Frye). The creative "chain-reaction" probably moves in a 1, 2, 3, 4 progression through the parts or levels.

(1) On the realistic level, corresponding perhaps to the narrator's outer or projected self, or public image, Grey Owl explains how he came to be a nature writer and found a beaver sanctuary in a national park. A period of about four years is covered in considerable detail, much of the detail verifiable by other witnesses such as his helpmate, the Iroquois woman "Anahareo." Allusions are also made to earlier periods, such as his fifteen years in Bisco, his war service years, and his childhood; the very few concrete details here are likewise verifiable. The realistic level of the text is its ostensible purpose, an objective report submitted to intelligent adults. At this level, the writer is proving the truth of his message by proving that he is an authority.

(2) On the psychological level, corresponding perhaps to the narrator's unconscious self or id, Grey Owl relives traumatic events that took place when he was about four years old, events that were crucial in forming his identity. No verifiable details about these events are given in the text; for such details one must turn to an outside text such as Lovat Dickson's biography of Grey Owl, *Wilderness man*. The psychological level of the text lends it a sense of emotional urgency: for both the narrator and the reader who identifies with him, the text is cathartic. At this level, the writer is healing himself (the child within).

(3) On the romantic level, corresponding perhaps to the narrator's conscious self or ego, Grey Owl tells a kind of bed-time story to his own child. The tale is a pleasant, soothing fiction that explains how he himself created the world as the child knows it, making a place for the child in this world and keeping the world safe for the child so that it will grow and flourish. The romantic level of the text, the level of wish fulfillment, gives the text great appeal, drawing the reader into the world created and ultimately reassuring him of its existence in perpetuity. At this level, the writer is healing and guiding (other) children (and the child within other adults). He is also making himself a hero.

(4) On the apocalyptic level, corresponding perhaps to the narrator's will or superego, Grey Owl is writing a funny, new New Testament. He is a bumbling pilgrim-turned-preacher subverting the story of Christ through humour; the beavers, McGinnis and McGinty, Jelly Roll and Rawhide, are parodies of Christ. The apocalyptic level, like the romantic level, increases the appeal of the text by mocking its author, veiling its seriousness, and by disarming the reader. This level can be interpreted as a joke on the overly strict adults of his childhood, but its ultimate effect is to persuade morally. At this level, the writer is gently admonishing and guiding adults.

All four parts or levels exist in the narrative more or less simultaneously, creating a fugue-like effect. Progress in the narrative is through time to change on all four levels. The measurable time of Grey Owl's life, sandwiched between the mythic times of his ancestors and descendants, is highly stylized, with spring and fall presumably juxtaposed to heighten their symbolic associations (i.e., birth and death, Easter resurrection and Harvest plenitude). Table 1 shows how time and events are manipulated in *Pilgrims of the wild*:

Table 1: Time and events in *Pilgrims of the wild*

Book 1 "Touladi"

Prologue:	**PRESENT**	
	-Rdg. Mtn. Pk.	-beavers flourishing;
Ch.1:	**INFINITE TIME**	
	-"North"	-mythic time of ancestors;
	17 YEARS	
	-Bisco	-15 years; leaves in spring;
		-wanders two years;
	-Abitibi	-marries Anahareo in fall;

		-finds M&M beavers in spring;
Chs. 2-9	**ONE YEAR**	
	-Touladi	-arrives in fall;
		-writes in winter;
		-loses M&M beavers in spring;

Book 11 "Queen of the Beaver People"

Chs. 10-16	**TWO YEARS**	
	-Touladi	-gets Jelly Roll in spring;
		-writes in winter;
		-gets Rawhide in spring;
	-Rdg. Mtn. Pk.	-goes to Park in spring;
	PRESENT	
		-family flourishing in fall;

Epilogue		
	INFINITE TIME	
	-new North	-mythic time of descendants.

Progress through time on the four levels is as follows: (1) on the realistic level, from irresponsible destroyer to responsible conserver of nature; (2) on the psychological level, from unloved child to loved child; (3) on the romantic level, from sterility to fruitfulness; (4) on the apocalyptic level, from birth through death to resurrection.

Now let us look closely at the four levels of meaning.

1. Realistic Level

Like the relic imbedded in the altar of a Catholic Church, imbedded in the Prologue of *Pilgrims of the wild* is the observable, objectively-recorded, verifiable reality of the beaver family, Jelly Roll, Rawhide, and offspring, living at home in the wild, yet in harmony with their human friend, Grey Owl. In the prologue, movie cameras record the beavers coming up from the lake, adding sticks to the earthwork structure in Grey Owl's cabin, begging an apple from "the man," and then returning to their natural habitat. Nor is this evidence of Frye's "peaceable kingdom" false, for the author assures us: "It has all been very casual, in a way. No rehearsing has been done, no commands given; the actors have done just about as they like." What's more, the man behind the camera eye ("alert, silent, watchful") is not from that American tinseltown, Hollywood, but from the staid, Canadian National Parks Service: he is a reliable witness. The filming passage in the Prologue anticipates the book's climax in the penultimate chapter when an official of the National Parks Service, convinced that Grey Owl's tale bears "the stamp of authenticity," oversees the filming of the "first beaver film of any account" and offers him a government position at a "regular salary" to continue his work preserving the beaver. Grey Owl begins and ends *Pilgrims of the wild* with evidence of the truth of its message objectively attested to by certified authority.

But throughout the text, wildlife, which also attests to the truth of the message and the authority of its bringer, is described in painstaking detail with consummate skill. On the one hand, for example, his fifteen years among the people of Bisco pass in the book's four opening paragraphs without a specific, identifying detail about a single person, but rather with a few sketchy, subjective, emotion-charged statements about enemies and his reasons for leaving. For example, "Certain hints dropped by the Hudson's Bay Manager, who was also Chief of Police . . . made it seem advisable to cross [the first portage] immediately." On the other hand, in the final five-or-so paragraphs of the first chapter of *Pilgrims,* time slows over a period of three days until finally for a few moments it comes to a standstill as Grey Owl describes, with much specific detail, how the beavers McGinnis and McGinty came to be saved. While the text does contain some elements of fiction (suspense, dialogue), for the most part, it is a careful, objective report of his own actions and those of the wildlife and his wife, Anahareo. Furthermore, he is cognizant of his own biases and emotions, and signals them painstakingly. While he is, for instance, indifferent toward the beavers, he uses cool, Latin words like *discover* and *female* instead of the warmer Anglo-Saxon *find* and *mother.* As his attitude warms, so does his diction: thus, when the muskrat-like "creature" (cool, Latin) suddenly gives a "low (warm, Anglo Saxon) cry (Latin)," he lowers his gun.

Even when he is fully engaged emotionally with animals, Grey Owl never anthropomorphizes them. For example, by the final paragraph of the first chapter, in Saul-becoming-Paul moments, the beaver kittens have evolved from something that looked like something else (a muskrat), to readily identifiable individuals:

> . . . two funny-looking furry creatures with little scaly tails and exaggerated hind feet, that weighed less than half a pound apiece, and that tramped sedately up and down the bottom of the canoe with that steady, persistent, purposeful walk that we were later to know so well.

The adjectives "furry," "little," and "exaggerated" have only the faintest hint of non-objective, emotional overtones. The adjectival "funny-looking" does reflect the author's warm attitude and influences the reader to feel likewise warmly. The adverb "sedately" and adjectives "steady, persistent, purposeful" definitely imply that the animals exhibit some of the most abstract and admirable of human qualities (not always exhibited by humans, of course): dignity, trust and courage. Still, the animals do not wear clothes or speak English. They do nothing that animals do not do. Many witnesses—virtually any dog owner, for example—have testified that animals can be dignified, trusting, and courageous. Thus, while Grey Owl is moved to write about wildlife vividly, he does so without transgressing the bounds of verifiable animal behaviour, without jeopardizing his reputation as a reliable authority on wildlife.

2. Psychological Level

On the psychological level of the text are Grey Owl's deepest motives for pretending to be an Indian and espousing the cause of Native people and nature, as well as his motives for writing the autobiography, *Pilgrims of the wild.*

Grey Owl's principal biographers, Lovat Dickson and Donald Smith, together give what appears to be a consistent, reliable account of a deeply-troubled, alcoholic adult trying to come to terms with having been abandoned by his parents at a very young age and raised by aunts and a grandmother in a rather unhappy household. Dickson argues that Grey Owl's mythifying his origins, his making blatantly untrue statements about his parents even while still a child, is sound evidence of "an unusual state of mind." And Smith's evidence supports this argument. I would argue that, at the psychological level, *Pilgrims of the wild* challenges the world of Bisco and replaces it because Grey Owl is challenging his father and replacing him. In this reworking of the Oedipus myth, Grey Owl is now old enough and strong enough to allow himself deep probing of his psyche, a kind of self-directed psychotherapy, to allow healing. (Dickson tells us he was about thirty-six when he began to live with Anahareo; when he began writing *Pilgrims,* he was already a civil servant with a fixed income, as well as the successful author of magazine articles and *Men of the last frontier,* arguably an expanded version of the Bisco world sketched at the beginning of *Pilgrims*). The healing process involves, according to current psychiatric practice, returning to and reliving the incidents in early childhood that have caused emotional trauma. This is what Grey Owl does in *Pilgrims.*

One may suppose that, in childhood, Grey Owl (then, of course, Archie Belaney) refused to see his father as an irresponsible failure, the view held by the women who raised George's boy Archie. Rather, for the sake of his own sense of self-worth, the boy idealized his father, and when he himself came to chronological manhood he was determined to be just like the friend of Buffalo Bill, the "doughty fighter in the pacification of the West": determined to live the dream. In terms of his biography, as we know it from Dickson and Smith, Grey Owl left England (and his aunts) at eighteen and went to live in Canada. In northern Ontario, he apprenticed himself to trapper Bill Guppy (referred to in *Pilgrims* as "the king of woodsmen"). Then he attached himself to an Ojibway band and took a wife from among the band. Then he abandoned the wife (who had already borne him a child) and struck out on his own in the Biscotasing area. All this took place within about three years, so that he was probably about twenty-one when the Bisco period began. The "North" from which he has come to Bisco in *Pilgrims,* then, represents in terms of Grey Owl's psyche, his private, Oedipal myth, a very particular state of innocence: it is his frozen childhood. During this emotionally-starved period, he has created himself in his own image: the child being father to the man in the sense that, not having been properly parented, the boy had himself to construct an image of the adult person he wanted to be, then trained himself up to be that person—a lonely, exacting task.

In *Pilgrims of the wild,* when Grey Owl leaves Bisco behind, he is leaving behind an inadequate image of manhood: he is disillusioned not only with other men but also, unconsciously at first, with himself and with his artificial manhood-construct. What repels him about the construct is that it is death-producing, not life-producing. And all along he has known this unconsciously, for his father's

Inside "Beaver Lodge," Grey Owl's cabin on Lake Ajawaan, Prince Albert National Park, Saskatchewan, 1936.

abandoning of him as a child, his father's refusal to stay and nurture him, threatened *him* with death, leaving him to the mercy of the world. Psychologically, then, when Grey Owl leaves Bisco and "marries" Anahareo, he is being his wandering father marrying the "Apache" wife. It also means he is being himself as a child again and acquiring a mother. Notice that as soon as they are married, Anahareo begins to refashion Grey Owl. First his dress code, then his eating habits, then his work change under her influence. Then, too, in the course of the autobiography, Grey Owl undergoes a kind of regression-and-regrowth cycle in which initially he becomes less and less sure of himself, more dependent upon Anahareo and others like David White Stone, and helpless to protect his loved ones (the beavers). However, following the deaths of his first beavers and the desertion by Anahareo, he begins to become more and more sure of himself, more independent, effectively protecting his subsequent beavers, Jelly Roll and Rawhide, writing his first book, obtaining permanent employment, and winning back Anahareo.

At the level of the text in which he is a child and Anahareo is his mother, all the male figures in the text are father figures. Thus the Algonquin, David White Stone, who unwittingly kills the wild beaver with which Grey Owl is planning to found his colony, and who, after McGinnis and McGinty too are lost, goes with Anahareo to find some new wild beaver (Grey Owl, reminiscent of the impotent Jake in *The sun also rises,* is prevented from doing so by a war wound which is acting up), and finally who goes with Anahareo to seek his fortune in the gold mines of northern Ontario, leaving Grey Owl behind to mind the beaver kittens—is also a father figure, seeming progressively benevolent, threatening, then pathetic. Significantly, after Dave and Anahareo leave, while Grey Owl attempts again to found a beaver colony by ensuring the survival of Jelly Roll and Rawhide and writing his first book, as Grey Owl's situation improves, Dave's worsens. Upon Dave's death, Anahareo is restored to Grey Owl, Grey Owl's first book is published, and money begins finally to flow into their bank account: in terms of Grey Owl's private Oedipus myth, he has slain his father and wedded his mother, and this has brought not grief and retribution but joy and reward. The damage done to him psychologically as a child is repaired as he writes about these events in his autobiography.

Paradoxically, to win Anahareo back, Grey Owl must act out a role traditionally regarded as more feminine than masculine: nurturing the young. In babysitting the beavers so that they can miraculously become man and woman from brief childhood, Grey Owl is nurturing himself, being the father *and mother* he did not have. Thus, the story of Jelly Roll and Rawhide is also the story of Grey

Owl regrowing to manhood under his own care. Grey Owl comes to a more mature concept of manhood close to the concept of "husbandry" in the context of farming: "stewardship" or "conservation" are today's popular words. He is also reshaping his past.

3. Romantic Level

If at the psychological level, Grey Owl is a child telling a story to himself as a child, then at the romantic level, he is an adult father figure telling a story to children. The story—far more interesting, by the way, than *Sajo and her Beaver People,* the story he subsequently wrote, the one of his four books officially catalogued by librarians as a children's book—is an Origin-of-the-world tale which explains to children how things came to be as they are and reassures them of their own rightful place among these things. The hero of the tale is, of course, Grey Owl himself, the bumbling and unlikely prince, and his true love is, of course, Anahareo, the princess. In a slight variation of the classic pattern, the hero marries the girl at the *outset* of the tale; yet they do not live happily, nor are children immediately born to them, for the hero has not proven himself worthy of his true love. To really win the girl, the hero must perform a great deed. There is a dragon to be slain, a huge and fearsome one: commercialism, alias get-rich-quick schemes, alias thoughtless, selfish exploitation of nature for short-term gain. First he must slay the dragon in himself, then in other people. His weapon is the pen.

When, ultimately, the deed has been done and the true love won, the world becomes a pleasant, teeming, loving eternity, and the child of Grey Owl and Anahareo is finally born. Significantly named "Dawn," this child is, presumably, the one (representing all) to whom the tale is addressed. At the romantic level, then, the beavers are fertility symbols. "It is now Fall," begins the final chapter, "the time of Harvest, and the Queen and her little band are busy gathering in supplies against the long Winter, as are the more responsible and useful members of society everywhere." Nature itself has been saved. Following the romance pattern of works like *Sir Gawain and the Green Knight* or the *Tempest,* in *Pilgrims of the wild* the hero—both a brave knight errant and a magician-like father figure—ensures that the world which was sterile and infertile, unable to renew itself, is freed from the threat of death and flourishes.

4. Apocalyptic Level

Grey Owl not only reasons with, convinces, and seduces his readers, he frightens them, convincing them that God is on *his* side. To do this, he promotes the beavers to Christ and himself to a *Pilgrim's progress* Christian, and a biblical Joseph, John the Baptist, and Peter. The way of the wilderness trail becomes, thus, the path of righteousness. As this pilgrim-turned-prophet lays the foundations of the new church-of-the-wild, he reverses the tide of the missionaries, fur traders, gold seekers, and colonizers and leads a conquest of Europe by Canada's Native people and wildlife. (The beaver that roared?) The message of Christ is love, yet representatives of Christendom have wrought the destruction of nature. The message of the Canadians is better love, because the Beaver People are dedicated to preserving nature.

But how can such a message, even if true, be taken seriously? It cannot, unless the audience be disarmed. Disarmament is the function of the book's pervasive funniness, wherein the Christian world is turned upside down. Whereas in *Pilgrim's progress,* John Bunyan evokes sympathy to make the pilgrim, Christian, more human and appealing; in *Pilgrims of the wild,* Grey Owl evokes laughter. Bunyan's hero is pitifully earnest. He is described in the opening paragraphs of *Pilgrims progress* as "a man clothed in rags, standing in a certain place, with his face from his own house, a book in his hand, and a great burden on his back," weeping and trembling in great "distress." By contrast, Grey Owl's hero is arrogant. Not introspective but harshly judgmental, not frail but powerful, an adept canoeist and trapper, a rogue, a loner on the lam from man's law yet a law unto himself condemning those who break nature's laws, this force from the "North" can himself found a new "Frontier." Even the name of the town he leaves behind, "Bisco," rhyming with [San Fran] 'Cisco,'"—the full name is Biscotasing—gleams with the American Old West machismo that provides the glow to all his perceptions. Phallic is the "light, fast canoe" which, in the opening sentence, he is "driving . . . steadily Northward to the Height of the Land," as the town of Bisco is "dropping fast astern." At the outset of *Pilgrims of the wild,* then, the hero is being set up for a fall: not a tragic fall, but a comic fall, a slip on the banana peel of his male pride.

Cockily, Grey Owl sends "the lady a railroad ticket" and marries her when she appears. Then start the "complications." Delightful but subversive humour is suddenly introduced as, through the eyes of the new young wife, he begins to see himself as full of "woeful shortcomings." Soon the macho image is being mocked slyly, as Grey Owl is forced to review his ideas of good taste in outer wear: "My idea of looking my best was to wear my hair long, have plenty of fringes on my buckskins . . . and to have the front of my shirt decorated with an oblique row of safety pins on each side." Then the importance of the entire pilgrimage to Touladi, the land of the new "colony" which he is supposed to found, is gently subverted. The first Evangelist, who urges them to try their hand at finding gold in northern Ontario, an Algonquin Indian called David White Stone, is characterized in terms which certainly call into question his qualifications as a spiritual guide: "When in his cups he could sing Mass very passably." The second Evangelist, who points the way to Touladi, a Micmac Indian called "Joe Isaac" (note the "biblical appellation"), is characterized as "by far the most accomplished" of the "numbers of pretty fair liars, artistic and otherwise" whom Grey Owl has met in his "wanderings." The pilgrim himself, Grey Owl, is portrayed during the disastrous, picaresque train trip to Temiscouata Lake in south-eastern Quebec, as a gullible fool: they are already south of the St. Lawrence and heading "more and more South and East" before the "hypnotic effect of Joe Isaac's oracular utterances" wears off.

In *Pilgrims of the wild,* the pilgrims' crossing of the Bunyan-echoing "Slough of Despond," eight miles of "dreary ruination of stumps and slash," is lightened by the mischievous antics of the beavers: they pull the stove over, hide the dishes, and trample bannock. Then, too, the Indian-style Christmas celebrations that follow Grey Owl's terribly serious, Lear-like walk through the storm where a "feeling of kinship for all the wild" reaches "its culmination," are a parody of the traditional, humble Joseph-and-Mary, babes-and-beasts, Bethlehem scene as well as of the standard family scene on a modern December 24th or 25th. The beavers stand on their hind legs, grab at their presents, eat them, and then pull down the Christmas tree. Grey Owl and Anahareo, at a kind of home-made midnight mass, open a bottle of red wine to celebrate and drink toasts to the wild and tame beavers, the muskrats and other "birds and beasts" whom they have befriended, and "to the good Frenchman who had supplied the wine."

There is nothing funny about the seven poignant paragraphs beginning with a Biblical "And" which record the pilgrims' reaction to the deaths the following spring of McGinnis and McGinty, due to their guardians' negligence. Grey Owl's and Anahareo's grief, and their forlorn hope, humbly echo the emotions felt by Christian as he crosses Bunyan's "River of Death" to the "Celestial City," or even the emotions of sincere churchgoers contemplating the Crucifixion: Grey Owl and Anahareo are truly brought to the "Depths." Yet the resurrection which occurs in the second "Book" is a rather silly affair where the Spirit is one of quite unholy glee. The Beaver that emerges from the tomb is a survivor rather than a saviour, a tough comedienne: "And in the slack water [at the mouth of the creek where McGinnis and McGinty had had their last adventure] Jelly Roll disported herself, made tiny bank dens and queer erections of sticks, what time she was not engaged in galloping up and down the path to the tents." The new life represented by this Jelly Roll who is to become a "screen star, public pet Number One, proprietor of Beaver Lodge, and a personage, more-

over, with something to say at the seat of Government in Ottawa," is life of what are commonly called "high" or "animal" spirits.

Thus Grey Owl's evangelizing Beaver People do not take *themselves* too seriously—they have no grandiose delusions. Only their *message* is serious. "Death falls, as at times it must," Grey Owl says in the Epilogue, "and Life springs in its place. Nature lives and journeys on. . . . " The creed is an affirmation of life. The message is about rebirth.

And rebirth is what the public, private, and universal myths of Grey Owl are all about. A troubled young man matures into an effective spokesperson for the causes of Native people and nature (realistic level), when he is reborn through a private psychodrama (psychological level). He universalises his personal experience by relating it in terms of the archetypal literary motifs of human biological cycles (romantic level) transcended by a linear, quasi-religious journey of spiritual discovery and regeneration (apocalyptic level). Fact and fiction are welded skillfully into a literary invention—an art that life might do well to imitate (and perhaps Grey Owl himself confusedly tried to do this). Gifted literary writer, Grey Owl, felt that his message needed to be in mythic form to be conveyed effectively. Whether myth or message came first is impossible to determine, but if one accepts that myth can be necessary, then the Amerindian identity "Grey Owl," adopted by the Englishman Belaney, becomes a necessary means to a good end. It is part of a complex creative process. It is a medium, an image, and an artifact. It does not so much conceal as reveal. (pp. 44-53)

Heather Kirk, "Grey Owl as Necessary Myth: A Reading of 'Pilgrims of the Wild'," in Canadian Children's Literature, *No. 61, 1991, pp. 44-56.*

James Weldon Johnson

1871-1938

African-American author of fiction, nonfiction, and poetry; journalist and editor.

Major works include *The Autobiography of an Ex-Colored Man* (1912; also published as *The Autobiography of an Ex-Coloured Man*), *The Book of American Negro Poetry* (1922; enlarged edition, 1931), *The Book of American Negro Spirituals* (1925), *God's Trombones: Seven Negro Poems in Verse* (1927), *Along This Way: The Autobiography of James Weldon Johnson* (1933), *Lift Every Voice and Sing* (1970).

INTRODUCTION

A distinguished political leader, lecturer, diplomat, civil rights worker, and university professor as well as a man of letters, Johnson has been hailed as one of the most prominent figures in African-American history for his efforts to preserve that culture's rich and varied literary and musical heritage for future generations. Johnson's multifaceted career—which ranged from positions as a renowned Latin American diplomat to a Tin Pan Alley songwriter—testifies to his intellectual breadth, self-confidence, and deep-rooted belief that the future held unlimited opportunities for African-Americans, especially for their children. Regarded as a talented poet and novelist, Johnson is credited with bringing a new standard of artistry and realism to black literature through his works, which, although few in number, are considered impressive contributions to their genres. His pioneering studies of African-American poetry, music, and theater also helped introduce many Americans to the genuine African creative spirit, hitherto known chiefly through the distortions of the minstrel show and dialect poetry. Acknowledged as the principal forerunner of the Harlem Renaissance, Johnson also influenced such modern black authors as Ralph Ellison and Richard Wright. Sterling Brown writes, "By his interpretation of Negro poetry and music, by occasional essays on the problems of Negro writers, and by his own creative work, Johnson succeeded more than any other predecessor in furthering the cause of the Negro artist."

Born in Jacksonville, Florida, Johnson was raised in a home that valued education and the embracing of American middle-class ideals as a means to racial equality. As a student at Jacksonville's Stanton Grammar School, he showed early virtuosity in both music and literature, but because secondary education was not available to black students, he was sent to a preparatory school at Atlanta University in Georgia. During his undergraduate years, Johnson began to compose what he called "rather ardent love poems," and though he had received a scholarship to Harvard University medical school, he opted to return to Stanton as its high school principal. Johnson continued to

teach for several years while simultaneously pursuing other careers, becoming the first black lawyer admitted to the Florida bar; a founder of the *Daily American,* one of the first black daily newspapers in the country; and a lyricist for Cole and Johnson Brothers songwriters. With his younger brother Rosamond and his song-and-dance partner Bob Cole, Johnson wrote successful popular songs and later acted as road manager of the group when it toured the United States and Europe. Their most acclaimed collaboration, "Lift Every Voice and Sing" (1900)—a song penned in celebration of Abraham Lincoln's birthday and as a tribute to black endurance, hope, and religious faith—achieved widespread popularity and in time became known as "The Negro National Anthem." As Johnson has recounted in his autobiography *Along This Way,* "Nothing that I have done has paid me back so fully in satisfaction as being the part creator of this song." In 1906 Rosamond Johnson and Cole decided to produce their own musical, but Johnson, apprehensive about prospects for the group's future, abandoned show business to accept a position with the U.S. Consular Service at Venezuela, which he was offered in recognition of his work with the Colored Republican Club during Theodore Roosevelt's successful presidential campaign. During his three-year diplomatic tenure, Johnson continued to write poetry and completed his only novel, *The Autobiography of an Ex-Colored Man,* a frank and realistic examination of African-American society and race relations. The book describes how the narrator, a light-skinned black man ignorant of his real identity until it is imposed on him, tries to pass for white. In 1913, when a new Democratic administration refused to send him to a more desirable location, Johnson resigned his post and concentrated on writing.

When "Fifty Years," a poem commemorating the Emancipation Proclamation, appeared in the *New York Times* in January 1913, Johnson's literary reputation soared and he was hired as an editorial writer by the publishers of *New York Age* in 1914. Now an eminent newspaper columnist, Johnson felt that the black press should serve as an instrument of propaganda and used his influence to attack Jim Crow laws at home and American policies abroad in such occupied lands as Haiti. In 1916 he joined the National Association for the Advancement of Colored People (NAACP), serving as that organization's executive secretary from 1920 to 1930, a time when the NAACP gained enormous influence among blacks and wielded power on Capitol Hill. As head of the NAACP during the 1920s, Johnson led several civil rights campaigns in an effort to remove the legal, political, and social obstacles hindering African-American achievement. During these years he edited the works of little-known black poets in a seminal anthology entitled *The Book of American Negro Poetry.* Johnson's critical introduction provided new insights into an often ignored or denigrated genre and is now considered a classic analysis of early black contributions to American literature. Johnson went on to compile and interpret outstanding examples of black religious song form in his pioneering *Book of American Negro Spirituals* and *Second Book of American Negro Spirituals.* These renditions of black voices formed the background for *God's Trombones,* a set of verse versions of rural black folk sermons that many commentators regard as Johnson's finest poetic work. Creating a more flexible and dignified medium for expressing the black religious spirit, Johnson eschewed rhyme and the dialect style's buffoonish misspellings and mispronunciations to successfully render the musical rhythms, word structure, and vocabulary of the unschooled black orator in standard English. Critics also credited the poet with capturing the skilled preacher's oratorical tricks and flourishes, including hyperbole, repetition, and the ability to translate biblical imagery into the colorful, concrete terms of everyday life. As noted African-American educator R. R. Moton has stated, *God's Trombones* "contains as much beauty as I have ever read in verse. The glowing imagery, the vivid realism are a faithful record of the native genius of the Negro preacher." Five years prior to his tragic death in an automobile accident in 1938, Johnson published *Along This Way,* a memoir that Walter White has described as "one of the great biographies of our time." Commended as an inspiring personal success story of a distinguished citizen, *Along This Way* has likewise been praised by historians for its valuable insight into the larger social, political, and cultural movements of twentieth-century America. After his death, Johnson was lauded for his contributions to both literature and society; the *Christian Science Monitor*

wrote, "No Negro since Booker T. Washington has more lovingly labored on behalf of this people than has James Weldon Johnson."

Although Johnson is not a traditional writer of juvenile literature, he is considered an author whose poetry, anthologies, and autobiography are appropriate for young people. In addition, his status as a seminal figure in black history makes him a popular subject for student research. Johnson's name is especially kept alive among the young through "Lift Every Voice and Sing," a lyric that is recognized as a classic and has prompted a picture book adaptation for primary graders; he is also the subject of several biographies for this audience. During his lifetime, Johnson received the Harmon Award for *God's Trombones* and the Spingarn Award from the NAACP for "the highest and noblest achievement" by an African-American, and was presented with honorary doctorates in literature by Talledega College and Howard University.

(See also *Black Literature Criticism,* Vol. 2; *Twentieth-Century Literary Criticism,* Vols. 3, 19; *Something about the Author,* Vol. 31; *Contemporary Authors,* Vols. 104, 125; *Dictionary of Literary Biography,* Vol. 51; and *Major 20th Century Writers.*)

AUTHOR'S COMMENTARY

I find that looking backward over three-score years does not lessen my enthusiasm in looking forward. What I have done appears as very little when I consider all that the will to do set me as a task, and what I have written quite dwarfed alongside my aspirations; but life has been a stirring enterprise with me, and still is; for the willingness is not yet over and the dreams are not yet dead.

I am sometimes questioned concerning my glance forward. I am questioned by people who want to know my views about the future of the Negro in the United States:— Will the race continue to advance? Is the national attitude toward the Negro changing; and if so, is it for the better? Will the Negro turn to Communism? My answer always is that the race will continue to advance. In giving that answer, I assume no prophetic attributes; I base it on the fact that the race has given a three-hundred-year demonstration of its ability to survive and advance under conditions and in the face of obstacles that will not, by any discernible probabilities, ever again be so hard. That, I think, gives a definite earnest for the future. His "past performances" give the Negro increasing self-confidence to undertake what is before him. And, today, his self-confidence may be increased by only looking around him and noting what a mess the white race has made of civilization. By looking around, he can only conclude that, while no other race would probably have done any better, no other race could hardly have done any worse. He can at any time negatively increase his own racial self-esteem by taking an objective observation of the brutality, meanness, lawlessness, graft, crowd hysteria and stupidity of which the white race is capable.

Despite the many contrary appearances and all the numerous actual inequalities and wrongs that persist, I feel certain that in the continuous flux of the factors in the race problem the national attitude toward the Negro is steadily changing for the better. When it is borne in mind that the race problem in America is not the problem of twelve million moribund people intent upon sinking into a slough of ignorance, poverty, and decay in the midst of our civilization, in spite of all efforts to save them—*that would indeed be a problem*—but is, instead, the question of opening new doors of opportunity at which these millions are constantly knocking, the crux shifts to a more favorable position, and gives a view that makes it possible to observe that faster and faster the problem is becoming a question of mental attitudes toward the Negro rather than of his actual condition. The new doors of opportunity have been slowly but gradually opening and I believe that changing mental attitudes will cause them to be opened more and more rapidly. I see some signs of these changes in the South; and I think it among the probabilities that a gradual revolution will be worked out there by enlightened white youth, moved consciously by a sense of fair play and decency, and unconsciously by a compulsion to atone for the deeds of their fathers.

I believe that economic factors will work toward the abolishment of many of the inequalities and discriminations in the South. That section, the poorest of the country, must yield to pressure against the policy of maintaining a dual educational system, a dual railroad system, dual public park systems, and draining duplications in many another economic and civic enterprise. The absurdity of a man going into business and at the start barring the patronage of one-third to one-half of the community must eventually counterbalance all the prejudices that bolster up such an unsound practice. This process will be hastened by the growth of the economic strength of Negroes themselves. I here stress the South not under any misapprehension that it is the only section of prejudice and discrimination against Negroes, but because it is *in the South* that the race problem must be solved; because it will not be completely solved in any other section of the country until it is solved there; because essentially the status of the Negro in all other sections will depend upon what it is in the South.

Will the Negro turn to Communism? I do not think so. A restless fringe in the larger cities may go over, but the race shows practically no inclination to do so, either among the intellectuals or the masses. No group is more in need or more desirous of a social change than the Negro, but in his attitude toward Communism he is displaying common sense. There are no indications that the United States will ever adopt Communism, and it is more than probable that in this country it will, in its present form, continue to be an outlawed political and economic creed; then, for the Negro to take on the antagonisms that center against it, in addition to those he already carries, would from any point of view, except that of fanaticism, be sheer idiocy. I feel that the Negro should not hesitate at revolution that would bring in an era which fully included him in the general good, but, despite the enticing gestures being made, I see absolutely no guarantees that Communism, even if it could win, would usher in such an era. Indeed, I do not see that political and economic revolutions ever change the hearts of men; they simply change the bounds within which the same human traits and passions operate. If any such change should tomorrow take place in the United States, the Negro would not find himself miraculously lifted up, but still at the lower end of the social scale, and still called upon to work and fight persistently to rise in that scale. The only kind of revolution that would have an immediately significant effect on the American Negro's status would be a moral revolution—an upward push given to the level of ethical ideas and practices. And that, probably, is the sole revolution that the whole world stands in need of.

Often I am asked if I think the Negro will remain a racial entity or merge; and if I am in favor of amalgamation. I answer that, if I could have my wish, the Negro would retain his racial identity, with unhampered freedom to develop his own qualities—the best of those qualities American civilization is much in need of as a complement to its other qualities—and finally stand upon a plane with other American citizens. To convince America and the world that he was capable of doing this would be the greatest triumph he could wish and work for. But what I may wish and what others may not wish can have no effect on the elemental forces at work; and it appears to me that the result of those forces will, in time, be the blending of the Negro into the American race of the future. It seems probable that, instead of developing them independently to the utmost, the Negro will fuse his qualities with those of the other groups in the making of the ultimate American people; and that he will add a tint to America's complexion and put a perceptible permanent wave in America's hair. It may be that nature plans to work out on the North American continent a geographical color scheme similar to that of Europe, with the Gulf of Mexico as our Mediterranean. My hope is that in the process the Negro will be not merely sucked up but, through his own advancement and development, will go in on a basis of equal partnership.

If I am wrong in these opinions and conclusions, if the Negro is always to be given a heavy handicap back of the common scratch, or if the antagonistic forces are destined to dominate and bar all forward movement, there will be only one way of salvation for the race that I can see, and that will be through the making of its isolation into a religion and the cultivation of a hard, keen, relentless hatred for everything white. Such a hatred would burn up all that is best in the Negro, but it would also offer the sole means that could enable him to maintain a saving degree of self-respect in the midst of his abasement.

But the damage of such a course would not be limited to the Negro. If the Negro is made to fail, America fails with him. If America wishes to make democratic institutions secure, she must deal with this question right and righteously. For it is in the nature of a truism to say that this country can actually have no more democracy than it accords and guarantees to the humblest and weakest citizen.

It is both a necessity and to the advantage of America that she deal with this question right and righteously; for the well-being of the nation as well as that of the Negro depends upon taking that course. And she must bear in mind that it is a question which can be neither avoided nor postponed; it is not distant in position or time; it is immediately at hand and imminent; it must be squarely met and answered. And it cannot be so met and answered by the mere mouthings of the worn platitudes of humanitarianism, of formal religion, or of abstract democracy. For the Negroes directly concerned are not in a far-off Africa; they are in and within our midst. (pp. 409-13)

> *James Weldon Johnson, in his* Along This Way: The Autobiography of James Weldon Johnson, *The Viking Press, 1933, 418 p.*

GENERAL COMMENTARY

W. E. B. Du Bois

[*Du Bois was a leading twentieth-century black author who wrote novels, poetry, and sociological studies. The following is the full text of the address delivered by Du Bois at a dinner honoring Johnson on 14 May 1931.*]

James Weldon Johnson, in whose honor we are here tonight, was born in Jacksonville, Florida, June 17, 1871. He received his training at Atlanta University in Georgia and then became a high school teacher. In 1897, he was admitted to the bar and for four years practiced law. Then, in 1901, he came to New York City and for five years collaborated with his brother in producing music and light opera. From 1906 to 1912, he represented the United States as Consular Officer in Venezuela and Nicaragua. In 1917, he became Field Secretary of the National Association for the Advancement of Colored People, and in 1920 its Executive Secretary.

This year he resigned his Secretaryship to devote himself to literature and to serve as Spence Professor at Fisk University.

I repeat these dates and details as an interpretative background for Mr. Johnson's spiritual development. He is characterized by a sort of genial humor which escapes cynicism, on the one hand, and on the other, is never *mere* light-heartedness. Indeed, his very charm of character rises from this union of philosophical humor with stern experience, within the American veil of color, as his career indicates.

Mr. Johnson, for instance, was once nearly lynched in Florida; and quite naturally lynching to him, despite all obvious excuses and mitigating circumstances, can never be less than terribly real. He may smile over aspects of it but it can never be a mere joke.

His practice of law in the South gave him infinite opportunity to laugh at the plight of the Negro but he could never stop *simply* with laughing.

Coming to New York as a young man of 30, he had unusual opportunity to escape provincialism, both of race and of section. He met men and women of all walks of life and knew the metropolitan scene on a broad and tempting scale. He developed here that characteristic ability to meet and know and please all manner of men; and yet withal the straitness of the gates before him, the limitations of everyday life, the curious and recurrent difficulties of a

Negro's artistic career never allowed him to mistake Life for the *enjoyment* of life.

In South America Mr. Johnson touched in some respects an even wider world of nations, customs and languages. He escaped for the moment the hitherto *unescapable* sense of the color bar and he acquired that poise and individuality, that breadth and culture which his friends especially appreciate and admire. And yet, even in this career, he could not altogether lose himself in the larger world because the Department of State too peremptorily refused him merited promotion for *less* than a reason, and Mr. Johnson suddenly found himself at 40 back in New York and at the end of an era.

There was a certain incongruity in having a man with such training join the executive staff of the N.A.A.C.P. Ours was an unpopular and disturbing fanaticism. One does not usually train a teacher, lawyer, poet and diplomat and set him to propaganda and social agitation. And yet here there were singular compensations. It was, for instance, easy for Mr. Johnson to converse genially with professional Southerners and admit the difficulties of the Negro problem, the humors of the color situation, and the eternal triumphs of character. But with all this, *no one* could more easily prove than James Weldon Johnson that the color line was no *mere myth* nor wild phantasmagoria of bitter souls. Mr. Johnson, therefore, easily created a role of interpretation and sympathetic contact, both with his fellow workers and with the outer world, while *at the same time* he pushed a furious anti-lynching campaign and beseiged the courts with cases of color discrimination which could not easily be dismissed.

This, then, has been James Weldon Johnson's life and work, and for this we honor him tonight. And yet, I have no doubt but that the majority of his friends are much less stirred and motivated in their praise by these facts, than by the real and delightful comradeship which they have been privileged to enjoy with a broad and catholic soul. Mr. Johnson is one of the few men who can invade my office at 11 o'clock in the morning and receive a welcoming smile.

And finally, the friends here are especially pleased tonight to mark with applause the fact, that in the early evening of life when the sun still lingers in color on the horizon, and when creative Beauty still beckons, James Weldon Johnson is going to have some leisure to loaf and invite his soul to those pastures which he *is* so fittingly trained to enjoy. (pp. 225-27)

> *W. E. B. Du Bois, in an address delivered in 1931 and reprinted in* The Journal of Negro History, *Vol. LII, No. 3, July, 1967, pp. 224-27.*

Charlayne Hunter

[*In the following excerpt, Johnson's widow, Grace Nail Johnson, discusses her late husband as a role model for African-American children.*]

"Mr. Johnson is more alive than you could ever believe," James Weldon Johnson's 85-year-old widow observed the

Johnson as a small child.

other day, while speaking about the current centennial birthday celebration of her husband. . . .

"The excitement of every morning is the awakening to something new that comes in the mail," Grace Nail Johnson said by telephone from her apartment in Harlem's Lenox Terrace. . . .

Mrs. Johnson is the daughter of John B. Nail, who was one of the first Negro investors in Harlem real estate and who was also certified by Dun & Bradstreet. She was married to the writer in 1910.

"One reason Mr. Johnson flows so easily through conciousness," she said, "is that he wrote in so many areas that we were not thinking of. Not revolution. But a consistency of hope and the way through legal processes. Not like all these spasms of protest today."

Mrs. Johnson was alluding to, among other things, her husband's militant civil rights activities from 1916 to 1930 as field secretary and later executive secretary of the National Association for the Advancement of Colored People.

In June, the month of his birth, the N.A.A.C.P. publication *Crisis* devoted its entire issue to James Weldon John-

son's life and work. It included the hymn composed by his brother, **"Lift Ev'ry Voice and Sing,"** which became the official song of the N.A.A.C.P. and is today regarded as the **"Black National Anthem."**

Mrs. Johnson is pleased by this reawakening of interest in her husband—most of all, she said, "because his works can open the eyes of children to a good life.

"It gives them a hero to worship and it puts books about us in our homes."

> Charlayne Hunter, "Widow Says Reawakening of Interest in Work Can Inspire Negro Children," in The New York Times, October 12, 1971, p. 48.

The Crisis

[James Weldon Johnson used his talents] effectively to enrich the culture of the nation, enhance the image of a downtrodden people, and to lead them in the struggle to reclaim their stolen rights and to restore their subverted manhood.

James Weldon Johnson was a breed always rare in American life and now practically extinct. He was an exceptionally intelligent, sophisticated and elegant gentleman of unfailing courtesy. He was also a man of ideals, of courage, of commitment, of compassion. A gifted poet and writer, an astute diplomat, a militant civil rights leader, he moved with ease, grace and complete self-assurance in all levels of society—the ivied halls of academe, the glittering mansions of statecraft, the dingy resorts of the ghetto, or the plantation cabins of the black peons. He was one who could rap with the man in the street, with the restive younger generation, and with the radicals without losing his cool. And he could, in Kipling's words, "walk with kings—nor lose the common touch."

In all his fighting for the rights of his people he remained the composed gentleman, expressing himself with eloquence and without compromise and never succumbing to corrosive racial hatred or stultifying bitterness. In this he was a truly civilized person and a heroic character. . . .

[His achievements should be brought] to the attention of the generation of young black men and women who knew him not and who are the poorer for not having known him. His was a career well worth emulating 100 years after his birth and 33 years since his tragic death in an automobile accident.

> "James Weldon Johnson," in The Crisis, Vol. 78, No. 4, June, 1971, p. 112.

Buell G. Gallagher

Because he was much more than a writer, he was a great writer. And because he wrote about life, the life he knew through experience, he wrote with convincing power and moving effect; but without affectation. And because he was what he was, his writings speak the truth. (p. 119)

He was a realist first, and a poet second. He saw life steadily and saw it whole; but he was saved from the bottomless depths of cynical bitterness by his own inner resources, his "ever-ready rainbow," which added lustre and meaning to life without distorting it. (pp. 119-20)

Integrity comes in many forms, but it is easily recognized when it is present. Dearly bought, and maintained with great difficulty, it is the virtue which separates the men from the boys. James Weldon Johnson was a man of integrity: his writings reveal it.

Usually, writing was hard labor for him. . . . It was as though he were guided by the admonition of W. B. Yeats:

> Hands, do what you're bid
> Bring the balloon of the mind
> That bellies and bags in the wind
> Into its narrow shed.

But on at least three occasions, the muse hovered over him and the restless creative fire burned fiercely. One of these moments was that day in Jacksonville when he strode the front porch composing the lines of a song intended for a Lincoln's Birthday performance by five hundred Negro children. After the first stanza had been handed through the window to his brother, Rosamond, who sat at the piano composing the music, he discarded pen and paper, composing in a great rush of poet's ecstasy, unashamed tears streaming down his cheeks. "Feverish ecstasy was followed by that contentment—that sense of serene joy—which makes artistic creation the most complete of all human experiences." And when the children's chorus lifted that song, they sent it down the reverberating corridors of the generations, to move deeply the soul of man. I do not marvel that, in common usage, only the first stanza is sung. The sweet-and-bitter exulting anguish of the complete song brings the unsummoned tear and catches at the singing throat. It's all there, in the stanzas of *Lift ev'ry voice:* the suffering, the bitterness, the storms, the rod, the weary years, the silent tears, the sacrifice of our fathers in order that we may stand—oh yes! stand in soaring hope, valiant for the right. The "ever-ready rainbow" does not distort the truth it conveys.

Also, the overriding need to be delivered from feckless fame is there. It stood Johnson in good stead, later, when adulation and wealth had come to him along his way, this time as co-writer with his brother Rosamond and their friend, Bob Cole, in broadway successes and popular songs. "When success with me has seemed brightest," he was later to write reflectively, "there has never failed to lurk somewhere the shadow of doubt." That honest and saving self-doubt was the answer to the prayer he taught us all to sing:

> Lest our hearts, drunk with the wine of the
>   world,
> We forget Thee.

(p.121)

It is in the limpid prose of his autobiography that he lets out the leash of mature, well-trained talent. With what clarity he speaks of common things. (pp. 121-22)

One other time, notably, he was to know the sweet ecstasy of the "fine frenzy" of creative inspiration. In his years as American consul in Venezuela, he woke one still, tropical

night from deep sleep—completely awoke. Taking paper, he penned a sonnet and went back to untroubled sleep. In the morning, he made a couple of minor revisions and sent the sonnet off to *The Century,* where **"Mother Night"** duly appeared, unedited. The concluding sextet reveals the deeply rooted subconscious self of the man whose conscious life was an unremitting, bold and strenuous struggle for human decency and human dignity, against all the evils of bigotry and prejudice and hatred and exploitation and whatever makes man mean. . . .

He still speaks. Particularly and especially he speaks to the younger generation who never knew him as we did—through his books he speaks. Read them. . . . Get to know James Weldon Johnson. You'll never be the same. (p. 122)

> *Buell G. Gallagher, "James Weldon Johnson: Man of Letters," in* The Crisis, *Vol. 78, No. 4, June, 1971, pp. 119-22.*

William Pickens

[*The following excerpt by the former Director of Branches for the NAACP is from a collection of tributes to Johnson that were broadcast over radio station WNYC on July 14, 1938.*]

The life of James Weldon Johnson . . . is itself an answer to most of the questions posed in America about the colored people. . . .

In his songwriting days he wrote words which have become a national song for his race and which is more widely known among the common people of color than anything else he has done. Its words begin: "Lift every voice and sing." It is a song of triumph over obstacles which would serve as a national hymn for all of his fellow countrymen, irrespective of their racial connections. The song itself mentions no race, although it was written out of the experiences of the Negro race in America. It is more of a universal song than any of our national songs. Perhaps in the future men will forget that it was written by an American Negro and all Americans will sing it as a hymn of their racial history.

> *William Pickens, in a radio broadcast on July 14, 1938, published in* The Crisis, *Vol. 78, No. 4, June, 1971, p. 139.*

Jean Wagner

[Johnson's poems] suffer from a major blemish, their impersonal character. . . . Only rarely did he show himself capable of the limitless abandon without which there can be no real poetic emotion. His verses reveal nothing or almost nothing of his own intimate depths, and may even seek to hide them from us. Johnson can hardly be classed as a lyric poet, since he is too often satisfied with a borrowed or purely conventional lyricism. Compared with [Claude] McKay's earliest American poems, those making up Johnson's first collection, which came out that same year, resemble less the work of a forerunner than of a man trailing behind his time.

His chief contribution to the poetic harvest of the Renaissance was *God's Trombones,* Negro sermons in verse in which, availing himself of the example of his contemporary John Millington Synge, he tried to carry over, into a more respectable idiom than the rough Negro dialect, the essentials of the naïve, clumsy religious lyricism of the old-time Negro preacher. (pp. 351-52)

Under the collective title of "Jingles and Croons," the dialect poems make up one-third of [*Fifty Years and Other Poems*], some of them previously having been popular hits. . . . [They] are all basically commercial pieces, put together with every necessary precaution to ensure monetary success. (p. 356)

In most of these poems Johnson rather unimaginatively follows [Paul Laurence] Dunbar's themes and manner; he does not always even bother to change the title of the imitated poems or the names of the characters. Here to be found once again are all the types of song that had been in circulation twenty-five years earlier: the naïve, sugary love song, the cradle song with which the black mammy lulls her picaninny to sleep, the story of the rival rural swains, the fable that pays homage to Brer Rabbit, and even, on occasion, a discreet hymning of the good old days and of good oldtime Georgia. Johnson's portrait of the Negro, in its main lines, still adheres to the minstrel tradition. He is carefree and optimistic, plays the banjo, eats watermelon and 'possum, and steals chickens and turkeys—all traits necessary to arouse an easy sense of superiority in the white public. (p. 357)

In the domain of dialect poetry, it was hard to do better than, or even as well as, Dunbar, and in "Jingles and Croons" Johnson never attains the spontaneity of expression, the vivacious rhythm, or the melodiousness of his distinguished forerunner. (p. 358)

[Johnson] does not seem to have thought that the hostility dividing black and whites disproved the fact that they were destined to be brothers—quarreling brothers, perhaps, but brothers all the same. How else could he have given the title **"Brothers"** to a poem on lynching which, according to Sterling Brown, is "the most vigorous poem of protest from any Negro poet up to his time"? How else could he have put these last words in the mouth of the Negro, as he dies at the hands of his lynchers:

> Brothers in spirit, brothers in deed are we?

To behold the poet thus unflinchingly manifesting his faith in racial brotherhood leaves one divided between admiration for his idealism and awareness of a certain incoherence in the sequence of episodes that make up this "American drama." The most authentic and gripping part of the poem is the forceful, realistic description of the lynching—which is the first of its kind in American poetry. With greater audacity than Dunbar in "The Haunted Oak," Johnson piles up the macabre details, depicts the flesh of the victim blistering in the flames and falling away in strips, and stresses the sadism of the killers who, when it threatens to end all too rapidly, throw water on the fire to slow it down, so that they may still revel in this ghastly spectacle. We may also admire the poet's notion of having the victim's last words arouse anguish in the minds of the lynchers. He does not, however, anticipate Cullen by suggesting to us that there is a parallel between this burning

and the death of Christ on the cross, though he does eloquently suggest the victim's spiritual triumph and the moral defeat or triumphant brute force.

But how clumsily this powerful scene is introduced! It follows immediately, without the least psychological motivation, upon a no less implausible dialogue between the mob and the Negro they have seized. Doubtless it was Johnson's intention to demonstrate by concrete example that many lynchings had not a shadow of justification, and three lines before the end there is some mention of a "fiendish crime" the victim is said to have committed. But this does not eliminate the incoherence, which actually is doubled—for lynching scene, to which is grafted the idea of brotherhood heralded by the title, has no organic connection with the first forty lines or so, which could have been utilized in a separate poem. (pp. 367-68)

Johnson presents [the theme of brotherhood] much more satisfactorily in another poem, **"The Black Mammy."** Frankly departing from the sentimentality the plantation tradition had attached to every mention of this figure, who often received a somewhat hypocritical veneration in the great families of the South, the poet is interested in and illuminates only the tragic aspect of the black nurse's situation. She must lavish the same generosity on her own child and on the other, who may one day crush him. . . . (p. 369)

If Johnson rang so many changes on the theme of the hostile brothers, the reason is that this concept's internal contradiction, with its elements suggesting both fraternal love and the opposite, no doubt provided him with a fitting symbol for that other contradiction falsifying relations between blacks and whites who, though the children of the same fatherland and proclaiming the same ideal of liberty, nevertheless are divided by history and by descent.

Johnson hits upon the same contradiction once more, in different form, when he takes up the theme of interracial love in **"The White Witch."** This is probably the best poem in the volume, as it assuredly is the most "modern."

Yet, a first glance, the symbolism here may seem bewildering. (pp. 369-70)

The white witch stands, in the first place, for the eternal feminine. As early as the second stanza the poet forthrightly declares that this is no old, toothless creature who terrifies little children; quite the contrary, she is adorned with all the charms of youth. Yet she is as old as the world. Thus, her bewitching nature is principally that of love.

This portrait is rendered more complex by the racial context into which it is introduced, for the white witch is also the incarnation of the Aryan racial type with blue eyes, fair hair, and lily-white skin. At the same time she symbolizes the white purity which racist America is intent on defending against any admixture of black blood. Such, at all events, is the official doctrine, for in reality the attraction she possesses for the Negro is equaled only by the attraction she feels for him. Since she sees the Negro as closer to the state of nature than the white man, because he is still in close contact with the earth from which, like Antaeus, he derives his strength, the white woman rightly or wrongly attributes to him a greater sexual potency, and initially she expects him to reveal carnal delights hitherto unknown. . . .

Yet the witch of the poem is not only a passionate lover; she has also [an] undeniably maleficent character. . . . (p. 370)

It would still be necessary to specify the danger against which Johnson warns his racial brothers. This is the very point at which the poem moves to the symbolic level. There is no question of the traditional punishment meted out to the Negro whose love for a white woman has become known. The danger is bound up, rather, with another feature in the portrait of the white witch. The poet, who tells us that he has already yielded to her charms, has learned that beneath the fascinating exterior of the woman passionately in love she hides her vampire-like nature, and that in the sexual embrace she seeks to rob of his substance the prey who lets himself be entrapped by her wiles. . . .

Thus the poem's meaning reaches far beyond the theme of interracial love on which it is based, and in the last resort the white witch stands for the whole world of the white man. The reciprocal attraction between the two races is not only of the flesh; it is also felt throughout the many forms of civilization and culture, and in this lies, for the Negro, the chief risk of emasculation. By giving in to the powerful attraction the majority culture exerts on him, the Negro runs the risk of losing his own personality, together with his weapons of defense against the basic hostility of the white world. That is why Johnson advises him to seek safety only in flight. (p. 371)

At any level, consequently, at the heart of this poem—as was true also for the theme of the hostile **"Brothers"**—is the association of those two opposites, love and enmity. . . . Johnson does not more than state the terms of the antithesis. It will remain for others to raise the level of the debate and to strive for a synthesis. But the fact remains that Johnson broke truly fresh ground by endeavoring to elucidate, via this symbol, the extent of the basic contradiction keeping the races apart. Especially if one bears in mind the inadequacy of the few poems he published in [his later collection, *St. Peter Relates an Incident*], it is no exaggeration to assert that his genuinely creative poetic effort is contained in its entirety in [*Fifty Years and Other Poems*]. (pp. 371-72)

In Johnson's poem ["**St. Peter Relates an Incident of the Resurrection Day**"], which sets out to be humorous, Saint Peter tells the angels, long after time has ended, how on Resurrection Day all the American patriotic groups came in a body to witness the resurrection of the unknown soldier, and to escort him into paradise. But when the tombstone was raised the unknown soldier, amid universal consternation, turned out to be a Negro. . . . While this was an original idea, it was frittered away in this poorly structured poem. There is a shocking imbalance between the central theme, which extends over 56 lines of the fourth part, and the far too long introductory section of 68 lines, often uninteresting and in dubious taste. . . . But the poem fails above all because Johnson is simply not a humorist. (p. 372) [Johnson's] intent in writing *God's Trom-*

bones is succinctly expressed in these two sentences from the preface: "The old-time Negro preacher is rapidly passing. I have here tried sincerely to fix something of him." . . .

The conventionality of these eight poems is already apparent from the fact that they are monologues, whereas in reality a part of the sermon, at least, would have consisted of a dialogue between preacher and congregation. Here the presence of the latter is not even suggested, as it might have been by appropriate monologue technique—for example, by using the repeated question, as [others] had done. Nor is the monologue able to reproduce the oratorical gestures, always so important for the Negro preacher, who is equally actor and orator. (p. 378)

In principle, the language of *God's Trombones* is normal English, not Negro dialect, but here and there it is possible to note a few minor deviations from the norm. True, the dialect or familiar forms that creep in are for the most part American rather than specifically Negro. They include, for example, the intermittent usage of the double negation and of the gerundive preceded by the preposition "a"—except, however, in these two lines of **"Noah Built the Ark,"** in which "a-going" is not just typically Negro but directly borrowed from the first line of a spiritual. . . . But such forms are exceptional, no more than two or three dozen of them are to be noted in the more than 900 lines of *God's Trombones,* and their contribution to the effect Johnson was aiming at is but subsidiary.

Much more effective in giving these sermons their Negro character are the countless, more or less extensive echoes of actual spirituals with which they are studded. Sometimes a mere word or expression that has long been familiar crops up in the sermon and by its own power suddenly evokes in the reader's mind the whole naïve imagery that makes up the religious context of the spirituals, to which the preacher untiringly returns to find subject matter for his sermon. There are the pearly gates and golden streets of the New Jerusalem, mentioned in Revelation; the custom of calling Jesus "Mary's Baby," and the warning words to sinners and backsliders that they should repent before it is too late. (pp. 378-80)

Johnson gives a correct idea of the preacher's technique, designed to move rather than convince his audience, alternately raising the congregation's hopes and filling them with terror, and arousing their pity by presenting scenes from Holy Writ as though these were taking place before their eyes. (p. 381)

The most personal aspect of the preacher's art is what he creates out of his own fantasy with the aim of stirring the imaginations of his hearers. A ready fabulist, he constantly interpolates in order to supplement the bareness of the biblical narrative. Thus the creation of the world is unfolded before the eyes of the astounded congregation as though it were a fairy tale or a child's game. . . . His preaching ever relies on the concrete, with an anthropomorphism that brings down to the human level the Eternal Father, who is addressed as one would speak to a friendly neighbor. . . . Naïve, homely, and extravagant in turn, but always direct and forceful, these images have no compunction about blending in with those of the Bible so unexpectedly at times as to be almost grotesque. . . . (pp. 381-82)

If allowance is made for his borrowings from the Bible, from the spirituals, and from the Negro sermons he had heard, what then is the poet's share in *God's Trombones?* Johnson was certainly not the creator of these sermons but, as Synge remarked of his own indebtedness to the Irish people, every work of art results from a collaboration. In *God's Trombones,* the artist is clearly present on every page, and he gives even while he receives. The simplicity and clarity, so striking in these poems, are the fruits of his efforts. His musical sense is manifested in the choice of sonorities for the free-verse line which, in his hands, becomes docile and supple, and adjusts to the preacher's rhythm as well as to the rise and fall of his voice. Taking what were, after all, the heterogeneous elements of his raw materials, the poet has marked them with the unity and the stamp of his own genius, so that these sermons, as they come from his hands, have undeniably become his own to some degree.

If he deserves any reproach, it might be for his excessive zeal in idealizing and refining—or, in other words, for having thought it necessary to impose too much respectability on essentially popular material whose crudity is one of its charms, as it is also a voucher for its authenticity. His sermons are still folklore, perhaps, but stylized folklore. (p. 383)

> *Jean Wagner, "James Weldon Johnson," in his* Black Poets of the United States: From Paul Laurence Dunbar to Langston Hughes, *translated by Kenneth Douglas, University of Illinois Press, 1973, pp. 351-84.*

Eugene Levy

Johnson's essays, and much of his poetry, of [his early] period were keyed to the idea of maintaining good relations with the white man while encouraging the black man to better himself. Social uplift and race pride fitted into his plans for the future, but the present, with its increasing racial discrimination, looked gloomy. At times, Johnson seemed to avoid facing the difficulties of his day—perhaps deliberately, for he believed the race needed encouragement. The danger was, of course, that continual talk of the future would become a refuge from the pressures of the present.

Just such words of hope mark Johnson's best known poem, "Lift Every Voice and Sing." In February 1900, James and his brother Rosamond, who was an accomplished musician, decided to collaborate on an anthem to commemorate Lincoln's birthday. (p. 71)

The brothers quickly forgot their anthem after its performance by a chorus of five hundred of the city's black school children. But others over the nation picked it up, and within fifteen years "Lift Every Voice and Sing"— though it makes no direct reference to race—had acquired the subtitle "The Negro National Anthem." None of Johnson's personal tensions and doubts about the future of the race, none of the era's racial problems, are overtly articulated in the anthem. This undoubtedly was the se-cret of its success. For decades the aspirations of many blacks would increase much faster than the caste system would allow them to be fulfilled. "Lift Every Voice and Sing" became a kind of musical safety valve, making the vague but optimistic promise of a better future ("Facing the rising sun of our new day begun, / Let us march on until victory is won.") Yet the anthem, like the earlier spirituals, also carried a more dynamic message. Both as men and as Americans ("True to our God, / True to our native land"), blacks were duty-bound to persevere until they reached the goals promised by both their manhood and their nationhood. (pp. 72-3)

[In 1917, Johnson] published a respectable volume of poetry, which, though it summed up his poetic efforts over the previous several decades, did not lay out a clear path to follow. In 1918 Johnson established that path with his poem "The Creation," published two years later. The genesis of "The Creation" reveals much about the motives behind Johnson's literary change of direction as well as the factors which came together to produce that literary phenomenon we now know as the Harlem Renaissance.

Johnson himself later related the immediate inspiration behind "The Creation." He spent much of 1918 on the road, visiting town and city, organizing NAACP chapters. After a particularly exhausting day in Kansas City, he recalled, in which he had delivered four speeches to various groups, his sponsors called upon him to give another talk, this time after nine o'clock at night. Arriving at the meeting place, a black church, he discovered that his talk was to follow a sermon given by a famed evangelist. The evangelist, "a dark-brown man, handsome in his gigantic proportions," began by preaching an uninspired sermon from a formal text. The audience sat unmoved. Sensing he had not caught the emotions of the congregation, the preacher strode out of the pulpit and began to intone an old-fashioned sermon, beginning with the creation of the world, moving through the stories of the Old Testament, and reaching a climax in the tale of judgment day. Many in the audience responded to the preacher by jumping to their feet, screaming, whirling around, and even falling in dead faints. Johnson, it is hardly necessary to add, kept his characteristic outward calmness, but he found himself both moved and deeply impressed by the black evangelist. Even before the sermon had ended Johnson jotted down some notes for what eventually would become the poem "The Creation."

By the first of August Johnson had written an early draft of the poem. He completed the poem by the year's end and, calling it the "Sermon on the Creation," sent it off to [William Stanley] Braithwaite for his opinion. Although he offered a few corrections, which Johnson incorporated in the text, Braithwaite thought it excellent and suggested sending it to the *Yale Review.* "The Creation," subtitled "A Negro Sermon," actually appeared in *The Freeman* in 1920, and Johnson ultimately incorporated it into the collection of similar sermons published in 1927 under the title *God's Trombones.*

Beginning with the lines "And God stepped out on space, / And He looked around and said, / 'I'm lonely—/ I'll make me a world'," Johnson presented in a dozen stanzas a series of vivid images adapted from the creation sermons he had heard over the years. Anticipating a point of view more fully developed during the Harlem Renaissance a few years later, Johnson portrayed the black preacher, and the tradition within which he operated, as standing far above mockery or maudlin sympathy. The preacher had been made a favorite object of ridicule in the minstrel tradition; it was this tradition upon which white Americans drew for their picture of religion among the mass of Afro-Americans. (pp. 298-300)

In rejecting the minstrel caricature, Johnson stopped short of saying that the authentic preaching he heard in Kansas City was in and of itself a work of "high" art, but he did say it contained the essence of art. Like the protagonist of *The Autobiography,* Johnson took what he considered the raw material of folk art and transformed it into an artistic form to which readers of the era could favorably respond. "The Creation" contained nothing in either its structure or language which either offended or titillated most Americans; in this it was unlike some of the writings which appeared later in the Harlem Renaissance. Nevertheless, its vivid visual images: "He batted His eyes, and the lightenings flashed; / He clapped His hands, and the thunders rolled," emphasized a black folk who possessed a spontaneity lacking in the Victorian tradition but increasingly desirable in the 1920s.

In "The Creation," as in the bulk of his literary activity in the 1920s, Johnson used a soft-sell tactic. He wished to impress both the black and the white middle-class with the overall contribution of black Americans to American culture. He came to feel during this period that the most effective way to do this, as well as to expose the basic nature of race prejudice, was indirectly through works of art. The conviction grew on him that Ethel Waters's singing "Suppertime" more effectively reached a prejudiced person than any expressly polemical essay. Characteristically, the book that impressed him most during the 1920s was E. M. Forster's novel *A Passage to India.* Far from writing a "protest" novel, Forster subtly explored the effect on individuals of the racial conflicts endemic in Anglo-India. "This book deals with race prejudice in India in a highly artistic and sophisticated manner. I considered it," Johnson wrote enthusiastically to a friend, "a splendid example of how the thing ought to be done in this country."

"The Creation" makes no mention of prejudice, discrimination, or the grinding poverty to be found in black communities of both rural and urban America. Nor did Johnson point out that the spontaneity of black poetic rhetoric often grew out of a desperate effort to survive in a social situation which seemed to breed endless oppression. He, of course, knew the situation, and he communicated it to the American public in his role as an official of the NAACP. In "The Creation," however, Johnson followed the path he had laid out in his song writing twenty years earlier. He chose not to emphasize the expressly tragic nature of the black experience, as he had done in "O Black and Unknown Bards"; rather, he took a much ridiculed aspect of that experience and turned it into a work of art readily appreciated by his readers, both black and white. In doing this he hoped not only to reach their aesthetic sense, but in some fashion to transform their prejudiced attitude toward that black experience which was the very source of "The Creation."

The evangelist that Johnson had heard in the summer of 1918 provided the immediate inspiration for "The Creation," yet the incident alone does not explain why the poem took the particular form it did. Johnson claimed he had had the general idea of adapting the black folk sermon into an "artistic" form for a number of years. Certainly the protagonist of *The Autobiography of an Ex-Colored Man* expresses a similar idea when he journeys South to transcribe black folk music, which he later hopes to turn into a "higher" form of musical art. There was, however, another influence on Johnson's thinking: a more general interest of Europeans and Americans in using the folk form for artistic purposes.

In the spring of 1914, Ridgely Torrence, a young white poet-playwright, sent Johnson a note expressing thanks for unnamed favors and two tickets to what Torrence called his "little negro play." The one-act play, entitled *Granny Maumee,* was being produced by the Stage Society in circumstances which today would be labeled off-Broadway. When he went to the Lyceum Theater on March 30, Johnson saw an attempt by a white man to write a serious drama focusing on the black folk. There were no white characters in the play—only old Granny Maumee, her two daughters, and the spirit of her son lynched years ago by a white mob. Though Torrence's grip on dialect frequently slipped into a white man's stereotype, and the action sometimes edged into melodrama, such a frank attempt to portray the bitter hatred of a black woman for all things white had never before been seen on the American stage. It is ironic that the producers of the play would not honor Torrence's request to use black ac-

Johnson at the age of fifteen.

tors; the Stage Society cautiously followed the conventional practice of using white actors in blackface.

Johnson did not set down his feelings about the original production of *Granny Maumee,* but he reacted with enthusiasm when the play was next produced in the spring of 1917, this time on Broadway. Torrence allied *Granny Maumee* with two other one-act plays, both of which dealt with black themes. The *Rider of Dreams* again made use of the Southern folk, while *Simon the Cyrenian,* a biblical drama, centered on Simon, the black man who bore the cross of Jesus on the road to Gethsemane. The "dream" sequence in *The Rider of Dreams,* which involved the intoning of a sermonlike monologue, especially impressed Johnson and probably influenced him in devising the form of **"The Creation."** This time Torrence had his wish, and the cast was black. All in all, Johnson wrote enthusiastically, the production marked a historic moment for Afro-Americans. Most of the drama critics expressed nothing but praise for the black actors. George Jean Nathan, coeditor of *Smart Set* and one of New York's leading critics, listed two of them, Opal Cooper and Inez Clough, as among the ten best actors and actresses of the year—an evaluation in which Johnson took great pride. The Torrence plays closed after a few weeks; something that Johnson attributed as much to the entrance of America into World War I, which occurred within a few days of the opening of the plays, as to any lack of interest in serious drama based on black themes.

Johnson carefully culled the New York papers for critical response to Torrence's plays. One of the most frequent comments compared Torrence to the Irish playwright J. M. Synge, for the Irish Renaissance offered a ready comparison. Torrence hoped to build a national Negro theater on the order of the famous Irish Players, reported Robert Benchley, then drama critic for the *New York Tribune.* Given the race's "natural inclination for rhythm and grace," added Benchley, this project ought to be taken seriously. Irish playwrights such as Synge had legitimized, at least in the eyes of intellectuals, the Irish folk; why could not American writers legitimize the black folk?

Johnson himself was advised by critics to emulate Synge. Early in 1918 Floyd Dell reviewed *Fifty Years and Other Poems* for *The Liberator.* He rather patronizingly acknowledged Johnson's talents but rebuked him for failing to "catch the essential rhythm of the Negro." Dell then went on to urge Johnson and other black writers to use Synge as a model. A few years later, in 1921, Johnson responded to the challenge: "What a colored poet in the United States needs to do is something like what Synge did for the Irish; he needs to find a form that will express the racial spirit by symbols from within rather than by symbols from without, such as the mere mutilation of English spelling and pronunciation."

Although Johnson had been thinking along similar lines for a decade, it took the concatenation of events in 1917 and 1918 to provide the particular form developed in **"The Creation."** The subject of his poem he picked from among the classic subjects of the folk preacher. Following the path laid down by Synge and first followed in this country

by Torrence, Johnson became part of a significant development in the Euro-American literary tradition.

Johnson began to cast around for other projects under the stimulation of **"The Creation."** An anthology of black literature or poetry, he predicted to Braithwaite, would "be a sure moneymaker." The two men intended to collaborate on an anthology of poetry, but the Bostonian decided he already had too many projects underway, and Johnson agreed to go on alone. During the following few years, in his spare time, Johnson worked on the compilation. *The Book of American Negro Poetry* appeared in 1922, the first anthology of Negro poetry to be published by a major American publisher (in this case Harcourt, Brace and Company). A surge of interest in the Negro both in literature and on the stage, with such diverse plays as *Shuffle Along* and *Emperor Jones* as well as his own anthology, Johnson told his *New York Age* readers, clearly demonstrated the beginnings of a general trend.

In the early twenties Johnson began to think that *The Autobiography of an Ex-Colored Man,* published a decade earlier, had surely been issued out of its time. He toyed with the idea of rewriting it and even expanding it to bring the protagonist's life through World War I. That project did not materialize, but Johnson did send copies of the novel to such leading literary figures as Heywood Broun, Carl Van Doren, and Carl Van Vechten. . . . Ultimately the Knopfs, who had published a number of the younger black writers, including Langston Hughes, expressed an interest in *The Autobiography.* . . . The second edition of *The Autobiography,* which has remained in print for more than four decades, appeared in 1927.

During the same period Johnson was working on another type of publication. Rosamond, his younger brother, had continued in music and show business after the songwriting team of Cole and Johnson Brothers had split up in 1906. Building on Rosamond's experience as an arranger and James's intellectual grasp of the black folk experience, the two brothers in 1925 produced *The Book of American Negro Spirituals.* To Rosamond's arrangement of sixty-one spirituals, James furnished a forty-page preface dealing with the African and American musical roots of the spirituals as well as with the sociocultural milieu in which they were produced. A second collection followed a year later, though with a shorter preface.

In 1920, soon after the publication of **"The Creation,"** Johnson had begun two other "sermons"—**"Noah Builds the Ark"** and **"The Last Judgment"**—but had abandoned the poems when involved in the Dyer bill struggle. Collecting the spirituals brought him back to the subject, and he outlined another poem which ultimately became **"Go Down, Death,"** completed on Thanksgiving Day 1926 in a fever of excitement. The poem **"Listen, Lord"** was written soon afterwards. During the Christmas holidays Johnson isolated himself in his summer home in Great Barrington, Massachusetts, and finished the remaining poems in what became *God's Trombones: Seven Negro Sermons in Verse.*

Johnson's preface for *God's Trombones* served much the same function as the longer one he wrote for his collection of spirituals. In each, he elaborated on the view implicit in **"The Creation."** He extolled both the bards and the preachers for providing a truly indigenous American folk art—an art not only of value in itself but one which provided the basis for an even higher form of art. The spirituals and the sermons were both racial and national—both black and American. Allying himself with those folksong scholars who emphasized the African origins of black American music, Johnson argued forcefully that slaves brought to the new world an inbred musical instinct and talent, as well as a highly developed culturally derived sense of rhythm. Incredible as it might seem to some white Americans, Johnson claimed, black Americans were the sole creators of the spirituals. The early black bards took Africa's "primitive rhythms" and advanced them to "a higher melodic and an added harmonic development." Blending the music of their forefathers with the "spirit of Christianity," Afro-Americans produced a synthesis—the spirituals. The feeling for the spirituals descended from generation to generation, and it was the black man who most effectively enlarged on his own musical tradition, even though some whites, Johnson argued, were beginning to develop "a feel" for an essentially alien music.

The masses implicitly knew the value of their own music, but middle-class blacks after emancipation had revolted against the spirituals as a vocal sign of their former slavery. "This was a natural reaction, but, nevertheless, a sadly foolish one," Johnson lamented. The fact that an increasing number of educated black men and women were coming to appreciate their musical heritage represented for him a needed advance in race consciousness and racial self-acceptance. The acceptance of blacks by whites, Johnson believed, would grow directly out of the black man's acceptance of himself.

Torn from a worthwhile but essentially primitive African culture and forced into a more advanced Euro-American setting, the black man, despite massive oppression, had creatively developed artistically valuable forms of expression. In the 1920s, Johnson seemed to be saying, as the race emerged from the folk experience, young blacks were engaged in an equally creative process, blending this folk tradition into twentieth-century American culture.

Johnson saw the burgeoning interest in spirituals as but a part of the growing interest in things black. Although most white Americans were satisfied with the pandered version of black music often furnished by band leaders such as Paul Whiteman, Johnson still viewed the general interest as a sign of progress. As he made clear in the preface to his anthology of spirituals, white interest was only part of the story; the other part was the growing self-respect of young black artists and intellectuals. Johnson did not see either self-respect or artistic activity as being in any sense reborn in the 1920s. He cared little for the term "renaissance," for it implied previous years of inactivity. On the contrary, the work that was now coming to light, including his own, was just a sample of something that had been going on for a long time. Because recognition now given this work had stimulated further artistic efforts, Johnson came to feel a better term would be "flowering." With **"The Creation,"** his anthology of Afro-

American poetry, two collections of spirituals, *God's Trombones,* and the reprinting of *The Autobiography of an Ex-Colored Man,* Johnson became an active participant in the movement. Most significantly, he stood out as the one Negro of his generation consistently to support with private encouragement and public praise the literary outpourings of both black and white writers of the decade. (pp. 300-08)

Johnson had mulled over the idea of writing his autobiography for a number of years. The thought took concrete form soon after he had finished *Black Manhattan* in mid-1930, when he received an extension of his Rosenwald fellowship through the year 1931 largely on the basis of the project. He was well along with the book by the time he and his wife settled into their new cottage on the campus of Fisk. With time to write and physical isolation from the racial conflicts that had surrounded him in the NAACP, Johnson was able to complete the final draft of *Along This Way* in the spring of 1933. But he urged his publisher, Viking Press, to hold off publication until the fall, thus giving him time for last-minute revisions and allowing for improvement in the book market, which had been laid low by the Depression.

As in all autobiographies, Johnson presented in *Along This Way* the image of himself he wished others to see. Consequently, he had to clarify in his mind just who these others were to be. "Shall I address my autobiography to white people or black people or both?" he asked himself. To attempt to reach both audiences was, in his own words, a "course which had insured the wreck of many a literary boat steered by a Negro pilot," but he had little option but to take it. He had, after all, steered that very course in his own life. Though rarely explicit about it, one of the chief ways in which he avoided "wrecking" his autobiography was to detach himself from any overt emotional involvement in the recounting of his own past. The "spirit of detachment" in which he wrote *Along This Way* was, of course, that in which he had coped with many potential conflicts in his life. It was the spirit he identified with the character of the cosmopolitan gentleman, as exemplified by his boyhood friend Dr. Osmond Summers. After Johnson had finished the book, he had second thoughts about the wisdom of such detachment, lest it had blunted some of the points he wanted to make. Though his last-minute revisions helped to sharpen these passages, Johnson the writer still remained separated from Johnson the principal character of *Along This Way.*

Even the author showed surprise at the overwhelmingly favorable reception of his autobiography. The reviews, he wrote Claude McKay, "seemed to be too good to believe." (pp. 329-30)

The general enthusiasm for *Along This Way* is not hard to understand. It was, after all, in part a success story in the fashion of Booker T. Washington, although told with a great deal more subtlety than *Up from Slavery*. More significantly, it was one of the first autobiographical accounts of the rise of Jim Crow, the black man's migration north to the cities, the emergence of the NAACP, and the Harlem Renaissance. In *Along This Way* the reader found himself exposed to most aspects of black-white history since the Civil War, at least as seen through the eyes of one participant in the events. Even though published in the depths of the Depression, *Along This Way* sold well enough to remain in print until the present day. It was not from "egotism" that Johnson asked his publisher for a second printing in 1937, but rather from the conviction that his book "stands a good chance of becoming one of the standard American autobiographies." The reception of *Along This Way* over almost four decades would seem to justify Johnson's claim.

The note of assurance, even self-satisfaction, which Johnson frequently struck in the book put off a few reviewers. "His apparent concern to convey to his readers only the perfectly respectable," noted G. A. Steward, "has resulted in an autobiography dangerously near to that of a man thoroughly satisfied with his own attainments." Catching what most reviewers missed, Steward pointed out that Johnson never appeared to make a blunder, never became enraged, and never seemed to have had any doubt that his actions were always for the best. Johnson did on occasion become defensive in *Along This Way.* An example was the way he treated his relationship with Booker T. Washington. By the standards of the early 1930s the relationship was an error, for Washington was certainly out of favor among those active in the civil rights cause. In his autobiography Johnson neither justified the relationship nor did he apologize for it; he simply ignored it. In a similar vein, he ignored his youthful participation at the Chicago World's Fair, where he worked as a mere chairboy; he failed to explain that he had adopted the middle name of Weldon for purely literary reasons; and he neglected to mention his support of the American occupation of Haiti in 1915. None of these facts, of course, if revealed, could seriously damage his reputation. But to confess openly to a minor weakness or error, even to explain why it was not a weakness or an error, would seem to have been a threat to the justifiable satisfaction which Johnson did indeed feel about the course of his life. (pp. 331-32)

[Johnson served] as a "link," if a reforged rather than a new one, between the races. He took the velvet glove approach characteristic of turn-of-the-century Southern blacks, stripped it of its dissimulation, and adapted it to the ways of militancy and agitation. Above all, Johnson and his writings reflect a period when some blacks, at least, were beginning to regroup after the brutal imposition of Jim Crow, and some whites, at least, were beginning to reject an unqualified faith in Euro-American racial superiority.

Johnson fed both these currents in the decades following World War I. He helped to bring blacks together through his writings, by publicizing the race's cultural contributions and by furthering the NAACP in its aggressive struggle for full civil rights. He weakened white hegemony through the same means. He enabled some whites to see more accurately the black man's role in American culture, and he forced others to loosen their hold on the repressive legal tools of segregation. In word and deed, Johnson helped move blacks from the accommodation and defensive dissimulation of the era of Booker T. Washington closer to the forthright, widespread militancy of today.

Johnson would have preferred to see blacks emerge as a coequal ethnic group in an America which respected the life styles of all its peoples. He predicted, however, that black Americans, as the members of other ethnic groups, would blend "into the American race of the future." Either vision, America as a "nation of nations" or America as a "melting pot," was acceptable to him. But there had to be rapid progress toward either goal. If not, Johnson predicted "there will be only one way of salvation for the race that I can see, and that will be through the making of its isolation into a religion and the cultivation of a hard, keen, relentless hatred for everything white." America, Johnson declared, "must bear in mind that it is a question which can be neither avoided nor postponed; it is not distant in position or time; it is immediately at hand and imminent; it must be squarely met and answered." Four decades later, racial confrontation is no longer imminent; we are, as Johnson foresaw, in the midst of it. Whether the outcome is fusion, cooperation, "relentless hatred," or a mixture of the three, depends on the will and skill of those Americans, black and white, who have followed him. (pp. 348-49)

> *Eugene Levy, in his* James Weldon Johnson: Black Leader, Black Voice, *The University of Chicago Press, 1973, 380 p.*

Louis D. Rubin, Jr.

James Weldon Johnson . . . composed his earlier poetry very much in the two modes that Dunbar used: dialect and literary English. Like Dunbar, Johnson felt the inadequacy of stereotyped dialect very keenly, but he also recognized, without yet knowing what to do about it, the limitations of the ornate literary language of genteel poetry as well. A native of Jacksonville, Florida, Johnson was, unlike Dunbar, a highly educated and widely read man. After teaching high school and qualifying for the Florida bar, he collaborated with his brother Rosamond, a talented musician, in writing popular songs and musical comedy lyrics. Johnson's words to such songs as **"Under the Bamboo Tree," "Oh, Didn't He Ramble,"** and **"The Congo Love Song"** are still popular.

Dissatisfied with his poetry, Johnson knew that something was lacking, not only in his poems but in Dunbar's and those of all other black poets as well. (Apparently Johnson did not see the potentialities in the several free verse poems that W. E. B. DuBois was publishing at this time.) Johnson became intrigued with Walt Whitman's *Leaves of Grass:* "I was engulfed and submerged by the book, and set floundering again," he recollected many years later in his brilliant autobiography, *Along This Way.* When Dunbar came to visit Johnson in Jacksonville, he showed him poems he had written after the manner of Whitman. Dunbar "read them through and, looking at me with a queer smile, said, 'I don't like them, and I don't see what you are driving at.'" Taken aback, Johnson got out his copy of *Leaves of Grass* and read him some of the poems he most admired: "There was, at least," he wrote, "some personal consolation in the fact that his verdict was the same on Whitman himself."

Apparently Johnson acquiesced in Dunbar's verdict, for as late as 1917, when he published his own first book of verse, *Fifty Years and Other Poems,* he included in it no work that seems especially akin to the poetry of Walt Whitman. That volume did contain his memorable **"O Black and Unknown Bards,"** however, in which, writing in the formal literary English of the day, he achieved an almost classic precision and simplicity of utterance. There was also skillful dialect poetry. But Johnson was still dissatisfied. As he wrote in his introduction to *The Book of American Negro Poetry,*

> Negro dialect poetry had its origin in the minstrel traditions, and a persisting pattern was set. When the individual writer attempted to get away from that pattern, the fixed conventions allowed him only to slip over into a slough of sentimentality. These conventions were not broken for the simple reason that the individual writers wrote chiefly to entertain an outside audience, and in concord with its stereotyped ideas about the Negro.

What was needed was what Johnson discovered while in Kansas City in 1918, when he was engaged in field work for the National Association for the Advancement of Colored People. On a Sunday evening, after having already given four talks to Negro church groups, he heard a famed black evangelist give a sermon:

He was a dark brown man, handsome in his gigantic proportions. I think the presence of a 'distinguished visitor' on the platform disconcerted him a bit, for he started in to preach a formal sermon from a formal text. He was flat. The audience sat apathetic and dozing. He must have realized that he was neither impressing the 'distinguished visitor' nor giving the congregation what it expected; for, suddenly and without any warning for the transition, he slammed the Bible shut, stepped out from behind the pulpit, and began intoning the rambling Negro sermon that begins with the creation of the world, touches various high spots in the trials and tribulations of the Hebrew children, and ends with the Judgment Day. There was an instantaneous change in the preacher and in the congregation. He was free, at ease, and the complete master of himself and his hearers. The congregation responded to him as a willow to the winds. He strode the pulpit up and down, and brought into play the full gamut of a voice that excited my envy. He intoned, he moaned, he pleaded—he blared, he crashed, he thundered. A woman sprang to her feet, uttered a piercing scream, threw her handbag to the pulpit, striking the preacher full in the chest, whirled round several times, and fainted. The congregation reached a state of ecstasy. I was fascinated by this exhibition; moreover,

Bob Cole (left), Johnson, and his younger brother Rosamond, who supplied the music for "Lift Every Voice and Sing." In 1900, Cole and the Johnson brothers formed a successful songwriting team.

something primordial in me was stirred. Before the preacher finished, I took a slip of paper from my pocket and somewhat surreptitiously jotted down some ideas for my . . . poem.

Johnson saw now that he had been looking in the wrong place for his idiom. The place to find the diction and pattern of imagery and idiom for a poetry that could embody the experience of black Americans was not in the convention of dialect poetry, for that was not black experience, but a caricature of it written to fulfill the expectations of a white audience. Neither was the literary English of the poetry of idealism a suitable vehicle; its demands, expectations, and vocabulary were alien to the racial idiom. The model must instead be the folk tradition of black America itself, with its own cadences and metaphors. As he declared a few years afterward in his introduction to *The Book of American Negro Poetry:*

> What the colored poet in the United States needs to do is something like what Synge did for the Irish; he needs to find a form that will express the racial spirit by symbols from within rather than by symbols from without, such as the mere mutilation of English spelling and pronunciation. He needs a form that is freer and larger than dialect, but which will still hold the racial flavor; a form expressing the imagery, the idioms, the peculiar turns of thought, and the distinctive humor and pathos, too, of the Negro, but which will also be capable of voicing the deepest and highest emotions and aspirations, and allow of the widest range of subjects and the widest scope of treatment.

The poem that Johnson produced as the result of what he discovered that evening in Kansas City was **"The Creation,"** published in *The Freeman* for December 1, 1920, and later the basis for his book of seven black sermons, *God's Trombones* (1927). The first three stanzas authoritatively set the mood and tone:

> And God stepped out on space
> And he looked around and said:
> I'm lonely—
> I'll make me a world.
>
> As far as the eye of God could see
> Darkness covered everything.
> Blacker than a hundred midnights
> Down in a cypress swamp.
>
> Then God smiled,
> And the light broke,
> And the darkness rolled up on one side,
> And the light stood shining on the other,
> And God said: That's good!

In place of the singsong rhymings and the contrived semi-literacy of cotton-field dialect, here was the flowing, pulsating rise and fall of living speech, making its own emphases and intensifications naturally, in terms of the meaning, not as prescribed by an artificial, pre-established pattern of singsong metrics and rhyme. Here indeed was the influence of Walt Whitman, not woodenly imitated but used creatively and freely. Instead of abstract rhetorical platitudes couched in ornate literary English, there was colloquial speech—"I'll make me a world." Colloquial in

the true sense, however, because drawn from the actual language of men and women, not the self-conscious cutenesses of dialect. Nor was there any self-imposed limitation on emotion: "Blacker than a hundred midnights / Down in a cypress swamp" was language and metaphor that was at once expansive and natural. The diction, the cadence, the range of feeling permitted a freedom of metaphor and a flexibility of language and imagery that allowed him to express his meaning in a voice that could move from formal intensity to colloquial informality and then back again, without confusion or incongruity:

> And there the great God Almighty
> Who lit the sun and fixed it in the sky,
> Who flung the stars to the most far corner of the night,
> Who rounded the earth in the middle of his hand;
> This Great God,
>
> Like a mammy bending over her baby,
> Kneeled down in the dust
> Toiling over a lump of clay
> Till he shaped it in his own image . . .

To realize the potentialities and possibilities of the new form that Johnson discovered with **"The Creation,"** one need only compare such a stanza with lines from several of the poems in *Fifty Years and Other Poems.* Here are the opening lines of **"Prayer at Sunrise"**:

> O mighty, powerful, dark-dispelling sun,
> Now thou art risen, and thy day begun.
> How shrink the shrouding mists before thy face.
> As up thou spring'st to thy diurnal race!

The contrived stiffness of diction of this poem, with its ornate literary idiom, its forced imagery and sententious attitudinizing, seems artificial and lifeless by comparison with the far greater force and natural intensity of **"The Creation."** Contrast "Now thou art risen, and thy day begun" with "Who lit the sun and fixed it in the sky"; not only is the metaphor of God lighting the sun as if it were a lantern far more striking than anything in the other line, but the desired sense of power and vastness comes across far more convincingly.

Now compare the lines from **"The Creation"** to these lines of an early dialect poem by Johnson entitled **"A Plantation Bacchanal"**:

> W'en ole Mister Sun gits tiah'd a-hangin'
> High up in de sky;
> W'en der ain't no thunder and light'nin' a-bangin'
> An' de crops done all laid by . . .

The need to make the idea picturesque and quaint by referring to "ole Mister Sun" who "gets tiah'd" robs it of almost all potentiality for dramatic intensity and wonder. The fact that the speaker must express himself in folksy images designed to exhibit his unlettered, primitive status thoroughly dissipates any chance for serious commentary. The best that can be managed with such a speaker is homely philosophizing. By contrast, the language of **"The Creation"** can permit simple and authentic colloquial diction—"the most far corner of the night," "Like a mammy bending over her baby"—while also allowing for great intensity—"Who flung the stars," "Toiling over a lump of clay."

With **"The Creation,"** Johnson had indeed achieved a momentous breakthrough in the search of the black American poet for his proper language. Here at last was a way to deal with the unique particularities of black experience, while at the same time achieving the dignity and intensity of imaginative literary utterance. In his own way, Johnson had pointed the way toward a discovery for the black poet fully as useful as that which the Chicago poets and, more importantly, T. S. Eliot and Ezra Pound were making for American poetry in general: he had found the idiom for writing important poetry about the circumstances of twentieth-century American life.

Though Johnson went on, in the middle and late 1920s, to add six more sermons to **"The Creation"** and complete the book he entitled *God's Trombones,* it cannot be said that he himself chose to follow up and develop the implications of what he had been first to discover. Johnson was never a full-time poet; he wrote verse only intermittently, and by far the greater part of his energies was devoted to his work with the National Association for the Advancement of Colored People. Feeling as he clearly did that his formidable intellect and irrepressible energies could best be utilized in leading the legal and moral fight to ameliorate conditions under which the vast majority of black Americans were forced to live as second-class citizens in a nation in which Jim Crow laws still went almost unchallenged, Johnson had little time for the writing of verse. Save for the six-part poem he entitled **"St. Peter Relates an Incident,"** and a few other shorter poems, he produced no additional poetry. It would be left to other and younger men and women to create the poetry of twentieth-century black America. But it was Johnson, more than any other man, who opened the path, and the achievement that followed was in an important sense possible because of what he first demonstrated. The leading poets who came afterward—Toomer, Hughes, Tolson, Hayden, Brooks, LeRoi Jones—can truly be said to have followed along James Weldon Johnson's way. (pp. 19-26)

> *Louis D. Rubin, Jr., "The Search for a Language, 1746-1923," in* Black Poetry in America: Two Essays in Historical Interpretation *by Blyden Jackson and Louis D. Rubin, Jr., Louisiana State University Press, 1974, pp. 1-35.*

TITLE COMMENTARY

The Book of American Negro Poetry (1922)

AUTHOR'S COMMENTARY

[The following excerpt is from the preface to the first edition of The Book of American Negro Poetry.*]*

There is, perhaps, a better excuse for giving an Anthology of American Negro Poetry to the public than can be offered for many of the anthologies that have recently been issued. The public, generally speaking, does not know that there are American Negro poets—to supply this lack of information is, alone, a work worthy of somebody's effort.

Moreover, the matter of Negro poets and the production of literature by the colored people in this country involves more than supplying information that is lacking. It is a matter which has a direct bearing on the most vital of American problems.

A people may become great through many means, but there is only one measure by which its greatness is recognized and acknowledged. The final measure of the greatness of all peoples is the amount and standard of the literature and art they have produced. The world does not know that a people is great until that people produces great literature and art. No people that has produced great literature and art has ever been looked upon by the world as distinctly inferior.

The status of the Negro in the United States is more a question of national mental attitude toward the race than of actual conditions. And nothing will do more to change that mental attitude and raise his status than a demonstration of intellectual parity by the Negro through the production of literature and art.

Is there likelihood that the American Negro will be able to do this? There is, for the good reason that he possesses the innate powers. He has the emotional endowment, the originality and artistic conception, and, what is more important, the power of creating that which has universal appeal and influence.

I make here what may appear to be a more startling statement by saying that the Negro has already proved the possession of these powers by being the creator of the only things artistic that have yet sprung from American soil and been universally acknowledged as distinctive American products.

These creations by the American Negro may be summed up under four heads. The first two are the Uncle Remus stories, which were collected by Joel Chandler Harris, and the "spirituals" or slave songs, to which the Fisk Jubilee Singers made the public and the musicians of both the United States and Europe listen. The Uncle Remus stories constitute the greatest body of folk lore that America has produced, and the "spirituals" the greatest body of folk song. . . . [The spirituals] are more than folk songs, for in them the Negro sounded the depths, if he did not scale the heights, of music.

The other two creations are the cakewalk and ragtime. We do not need to go very far back to remember when cakewalking was the rage in the United States, Europe and South America. Society in this country and royalty abroad spent time in practicing the intricate steps. Paris pronounced it the "poetry of motion." The popularity of the cakewalk passed away but its influence remained. The influence can be seen today on any American stage where there is dancing. (pp. 9-10)

As for Ragtime, I go straight to the statement that it is the one artistic production by which America is known the world over. It has been all-conquering. Everywhere it is hailed as "American music." (p. 11)

The Negro in the United States has achieved or been placed in a certain artistic niche. When he is thought of artistically, it is as a happy-go-lucky, singing, shuffling, banjo-picking being or as a more or less pathetic figure. The picture of him is in a log cabin amid fields of cotton or along the levees. Negro dialect is naturally and by long association the exact instrument for voicing this phase of Negro life; and by that very exactness it is an instrument with but two full stops, humor and pathos. So even when he confines himself to purely racial themes, the Aframerican poet realizes that there are phases of Negro life in the United States which cannot be treated in the dialect either adequately or artistically. Take, for example, the phases rising out of life in Harlem, that most wonderful Negro city in the world. I do not deny that a Negro in a log cabin is more picturesque than a Negro in a Harlem flat, but the Negro in the Harlem flat is here, and he is but part of a group growing everywhere in the country, a group whose ideals are becoming increasingly more vital than those of the traditionally artistic group, even if its members are less picturesque.

What the colored poet in the United States needs to do is something like what [Irish dramatist John Millington] Synge did for the Irish; he needs to find a form that will express the racial spirit by symbols from within rather than by symbols from without, such as the mere mutilation of English spelling and pronunciation. He needs a form that is freer and larger than dialect, but which will still hold the racial flavor; a form expressing the imagery, the idioms, the peculiar turns of thought, and the distinctive humor and pathos, too, of the Negro, but which will also be capable of voicing the deepest and highest emotions and aspirations, and allow of the widest range of subjects and the widest scope of treatment.

Negro dialect is at present a medium that is not capable of giving expression to the varied conditions of Negro life in America, and much less is it capable of giving the fullest interpretation of Negro character and psychology. This is no indictment against the dialect as dialect, but against the mold of convention in which Negro dialect in the United States has been set. In time these conventions may become lost, and the colored poet in the United States may sit down to write in dialect without feeling that his first line will put the general reader in a frame of mind which demands that the poem be humorous or pathetic. In the meantime, there is no reason why these poets should not continue to do the beautiful things that can be done, and done best, in the dialect.

In stating the need for Aframerican poets in the United States to work out a new and distinctive form of expression I do not wish to be understood to hold any theory that they should limit themselves to Negro poetry, to racial themes; the sooner they are able to write *American* poetry spontaneously, the better. Nevertheless, I believe that the richest contribution the Negro poet can make to the American literature of the future will be the fusion into it of his own individual artistic gifts. (pp. 41-2)

> *James Weldon Johnson, in a preface to* The Book of American Negro Poetry, *edited by James Weldon Johnson, revised edition, Harcourt Brace Jovanovich, Inc., 1931, pp. 9-48.*

It is but natural that in the revival of poetry during the past decade in the United States the Negro, with his wealth of emotionalism, his imaginative and creative gifts, his abundance of experience, and his vividness of expression, should play his part. There is no racial group in America which has a larger share of that sense of rhythmic values from which poetry is formed; nor of that gift of imaginative creativeness, of being able to shake off mere mortal inhibitions and prohibitions and to soar into regions of pure fancy. It is of this gift that the "spirituals" or jubilee songs were born. When the oppression of slavery became too great for the slaves to bear, their only refuge was in flights of song addressed to that vividly tangible divine being who promised them rest in Heaven from earthly cares and sorrows. A second step in this development was the Negro dialect verse and story of which Paul Laurence Dunbar was the great master. These expressions of homely philosophy and of the trials and triumphs of the illiterate Negro go to make up a folk-lore that can be called distinctively American. We have now come to a third phase of development in which the Negro poet has almost entirely shaken off the limitations which dialect imposes. He is yet largely propagandist and he voices more frequently than is consistent with accepted literary standards his bitter and vehement denuciation of lynching, of the denial of opportunity, of the proscriptions of race prejudice. This is unfortunate, in a sense, yet it is a natural reaction. When Carl Sandburg or Amy Lowell or Edgar Lee Masters begin to write they have only the problems of ordinary mortals to contend with. But when an American Negro undertakes to express his emotions in verse or prose or music or sculpture or painting he has the additional burden of a prejudice which baffles and confronts him every minute of his waking hours. . . .

Mr. Johnson's [*The Book of American Negro Poetry*] has its chief value—and this is said in no disparagement of the work of the poets he quotes—in an admirable and well-written preface of some forty pages on **"The Creative Genius of the American Negro."** In this he establishes in a manner that has not been done before the rightful place which the Negro occupies in American literature, and his contributions in folk-songs, ragtime, and folk-dances. It will be surprising to many persons to know that the first woman poet in America to publish a volume of her works, except one, was a colored woman, Phillis Wheatley, born in Africa and brought to America as a slave. It will be interesting to know that more than one hundred Negro poets of more or less merit have published volumes of their verse ranging from pamphlets to substantial volumes. Equally surprising and interesting to the uninformed will seem the merit and value of much of the poetry that these colored writers have produced. Mr. Johnson has rendered a genuinely valuable service in thus presenting for the first time the work of these little known writers. Had Mr. Johnson done nothing else than introduce us to the work of Anne Spencer in her charming "Before the Feast of Shushan" and her beautiful "The Wife-Woman," or to the vigor and genuine merit of Claude McKay, he would have done well. Those who know Mr. Johnson's own verse need not be told of the high place that his work holds in this collection.

Walter F. White, in a review of "The Book of American Negro Poetry," in The Nation, *New York, Vol. CXIV, No. 2970, June 7, 1922, pp. 694-95.*

If it were possible to read Mr. Johnson's collection without knowing that all of it was written by Negroes, it is rather unlikely that one would think it remarkable in any way. One would be struck, here and there, by a certain simplicity, or technical competence, or musically flowing rhythm, or warmth of feeling, or occasional vivid phrase. Longer than any of these things, which are to be found in fairly good poetry anywhere, one would remember flashes of an aching indissoluble bitterness, a white anger stripped of all merely personal unhappiness, which, if one did not know by what oppressed it was uttered and against what oppressor, would be puzzling and disquieting.

But since it is known who wrote them, it is impossible to read these poems as one reads most poetry. There arise at once, from the auction block and cotton field and lynching post and Harlem slum, the faces of our dark stepchildren, whom we have mistreated and misunderstood, whose time of trouble is not yet over, who are struggling painfully out of darkness toward some degree of happiness in an alien land. We think of the general assumption—which has always been the master's excuse for keeping down the slave—that they are essentially inferior to us. Perhaps they are inferior in many of the things which our civilization likes to think are important—who can say so for sure? And who can say for sure that they are not our equals in some things, and in others even our betters?

They have their own fields to plough, which are not ours. The only music native to America is theirs; and in its particular quality of spontaneity, of free rhythm and rich harmonies, only possible in an uncomplicated spirit very near to the earth, there is nothing else like it in the world.

Is poetry one of their fields? Impossible to say as yet. On the strength of this collection by Negroes—nearly all now living—it is clear that they can write poetry as good as the great mass of ours, and they have produced one real poet, though by no means a great one—Mr. Claude McKay. It is an uneven collection. Too much of it is in the tradition of echoes, flowery phrase and emotion vaguely expressed which have always afflicted poetry. Too much of it is modelled after what is least worth copying. A good deal of it is in dialect, which always leaves me uneasy. Print cools and distorts phrases which, when spoken or sung, have a charming spontaneous gusto. Mr. Du Bois' "A Litany at Atlanta" is impressive, but as poetry is buttered too thick with indignation. Mr. Braithwaite's "Sandy Star" stirs pleasantly, like a light wind. Miss Spencer has great mastery over dreamy, half-mystical melodies. Mr. Fenton Johnson has a fine gift for direct observation and biting phrase in short prose poems whose reality makes him perhaps the most original contributor to the collection, though Mr. Claude McKay is by far the ablest poet.

I cannot quite agree with Mr. Max Eastman that Mr. McKay "reminds us of Burns and Villon and Catullus." I feel that a hospitality to echoes of poetry he has read has time and again obscured a direct sense of life, and made rarer those lines of singular intensity which express, as

Mr. Eastman aptly says, "the naked force of character." I am sorry he so often uses such indoor and inbred poetic phrases as "the Northland wreathed in golden smiles," "I have forgot what time the purple apples . . . ," or " 'neath the floating moon," when he is capable of the stark sincerity of "Harlem Shadows" or "Spring in New Hampshire," or the poignancy of "The Barrier."

If Mr. McKay and the other poets don't stir us unusually when they travel over poetic roads so many others have travelled before them, they make us sit up and take notice when they write about their race and ours. They strike hard, and pierce deep. It is not a merely poetic emotion that they express, but something fierce, and constant, and icy cold, and white hot. We quite believe Mr. Johnson when he says that "the Negro in the United States is consuming all of his energy in this gruelling race struggle." For it is the common thread running all through the book. It ranges from the restraint of Mr. Corrothers: "To be a Negro in a day like this demands rare patience—patience that can wait in utter darkness"; through Mr. Johnson's own bitter lines:

> Lessons in degradation, taught and learned,
> The memories of cruel sights and deeds,
> The pent-up bitterness, the unspent hate,
> Filtered through fifteen generations. . . .

to Mr. McKay's bitterness (in "To the White Fiends"), who when he writes

> Think you I could not arm me with a gun
> And shoot down ten of you for every one
> Of my black brothers murdered, burnt by you?

is only speaking for thousands of his race who feel the same hatred—hatred which boils over once in a while, as we know, but breaks in ineffectual waves on the stony white shore, and turns to something like the bottomless despair, felt by Mr. Fenton Johnson:

> I am tired of work; I am tired of building up
>   somebody else's civilization. . . .
> Throw the children into the river; civilization
>   has given us too many. It is better to die than
>   it is to grow up and find out that you are col-
>   ored.

Robert Littell, in a review of "The Book of American Negro Poetry," in The New Republic, *Vol. XXVI, No. 397, July 12, 1922, p. 196.*

[The Book of American Negro Poetry *was revised and enlarged in 1931.*]

James Weldon Johnson has edited **The Book of American Negro Poetry** . . . and we must venture a comment or two upon the job Mr. Johnson has done. Among the earlier singers we are glad to note, for one, James David Corrothers, the acquaintance of whose verse we first made in the old days of the *Century Magazine,* when his "Dream and the Song" was published in that periodical. The style of this five-stanza lament is of another day (Corrothers was born in '69), but nevertheless all must recognize the beauty in such a stanza as this:

> The rose thought, touched by words, doth turn
> Wan ashes. Still, from memory's urn,

Johnson (top right) as principal of Stanton High School, Jacksonville, Florida. Biographers Patricia and Frederick McKissack write, "Because of James Weldon's efforts, Stanton became Jacksonville's first black high school."

> The lingering blossoms tenderly
> Refute our wilding minstrelsy.
> Alas! we work but beauty's wrong!
> The dream is lovelier than the song.

Notable inclusions in this book are the poems of that most assiduous and remarkable of American anthologists, black or white, William Stanley Braithwaite. His "Onus Probandi" has always haunted us,

> No more from out the sunset,
> No more across the foam,
> No more across the windy hills
> Will Sandy Star come home. . . .

and now it is a positive delight to read such a poem of his as "Del Cascar," where his imagination flares into three entirely original and vivid quatrains.

James Weldon Johnson himself has done most notable work in his *God's Trombones,* those versified negro sermons that he published several years ago. Countée Cullen and Langston Hughes are, of course, familiar among the newer writers; but a young man of only thirty, one Sterling A. Brown, arouses our particular curiosity in this book. Somehow we have missed seeing much of anything of his work; and, as may be illustrated by the "Odyssey of Big Boy," he has the genuine folk rhythm and the genuine folk material in him:

> Done shocked de corn in Marylan',
> In Georgia done cut cane,
> Done planted rice in South Caline,
> But won't do dat again,
>   Do dat no mo' again.
>
> Been roustabout in Memphis,

> Dockhand in Baltimore,
> Done smashed up freight on Norfolk
> wharves,
> A fust class stevedore,
> A fust class stevedore. . . .

This is negro ballad poetry with the force of a work-song like "Waterboy" and yet imbued with decided individuality by the poet. Mr. Brown's poem, "Southern Road," has the very shuffle and hopeless laboring voice of the stone-cracking chain-gang:

> Double-shackled—hunh—
> Guard behin';
> Double-shackled—hunh—
> Guard behin';
> Ball an' chain, bebby,
> On my min'.

Mr. Johnson has made his selections with the taste of a true poet and a thorough knowledge of the extant poetry of his race. It is good to have so characteristically American a volume as this.

> *William Rose Benét, "Round about Parnassus," in* The Saturday Review of Literature, *Vol. VII, No. 37, April 4, 1931, p. 714.*

The Book of American Negro Poetry . . . is one of the most satisfactory, and richest, anthologies that I have encountered in a long time. Naturally, you will find more great poetry between the covers of the *Oxford Book of English Verse;* but there are not so many books the size of Johnson's in which there is more real poetry. Representing the poetic expression of a single racial group in a single country, it presents a body of literature of which that group may be sincerely and rightly proud. The line that runs from Paul Laurence Dunbar to Helene Johnson is a line of true singers, of poets who have made genuine contributions to poetry in the English tongue. That these poets are Negroes is a fact to be noted in the same spirit, and only for the same reason, as the fact that certain other poets are French, or German. There are many mansions in the land of poetry, but there are no Jim Crow cars; there are no themes so "white" that the black singer may not fitly handle them, if he is able. And the range of his ability becomes increasingly apparent. Take "Invocation," by Helene Johnson, one of the youngest of the poets represented in Mr. Johnson's book:

> Let me be buried in the rain
> In a deep, dripping wood,
> Under the warm wet breast of Earth
> Where once a gnarled tree stood,
> And paint a picture on my tomb,
> With dirt and a piece of bough,
> Of a girl and a boy beneath a round, ripe moon
> Eating of love with an eager spoon
> And vowing an eager vow.
> And do not keep my plot mowed smooth
> And clean as a spinster's bed.
> But let the weed, the flower, the tree,
> Riotous, rampant, wild and free,
> Grow high above my head.

Such a poem, I should think, would be sufficient reproof for those who speak as though Negro poetry should be judged from a special point of view, or judged with peculiar lenience. But the whole volume is such a reproof. American Negro poetry is simply, and should be read simply as, poetry. I refer you to Mr. Johnson's admirable anthology and his authoritative introduction.

> *Ben Ray Redman, in a review of "The Book of American Negro Poetry," in* New York Herald Tribune Books, *May 10, 1931, p. 13.*

Ten years ago James Weldon Johnson compiled his original anthology of American Negro poetry. In it he included examples of the work of Paul Laurence Dunbar, the first Negro poet of real stature to arise in America (if we forget the "black and unknown bards" who created spirituals), and, going on down through the years of the twentieth century, the best poetry of those who imitated either Dunbar or the standard English and American poets. Coming to the decade of the World War, Mr. Johnson found a second group of Negro poets to draw from, and he included much of their work, which was highly race-conscious and propagandistic. But since that time the movement has passed on, away from those who carried out a conscious attack on the "stereotyped humorous-pathetic" patterns of the Dunbar school. In the '20s the new mood gave rise to a younger group of Negro poets, pre-eminent among them being Countée Cullen and Lanston Hughes. These men revolted against "propaganda" to the extent that they tried to be, first of all, poets. But, as Mr. Johnson says, they have not succeeded—indeed, many of them have not sought to succeed—in forgetting "race." The best work of this group is colored by race—whether we choose to look at Countée Cullen's "Heritage" or the blues of Langston

Hughes. The new poets of the '20s are well represented in this revised issue of *The Book of American Negro Poetry.*

> *A review of "The Book of American Negro Poetry," in* The New York Times Book Review, *May 17, 1931, p. 18.*

First published [in 1922, **The Book of American Negro Poetry**] . . . now appears in an edition so thoroughly revised and so much enlarged by the inclusion of the work of the newer Negro poets that it is virtually a new book. Either the publishers of their works have been generous in granting permissions or the publisher of this volume has been lavish in his purchase of them, for no one of any importance has been omitted. The introductory and critical matter paves the way to a clear understanding of the spirit and value of the American Negro's contribution to poetry. One clear conclusion is that the best of modern Negro poetry is not in dialect and is not the poetry of the cottonfield and the cabin. Some good dialect poetry has been written by Negroes, but it followed a pattern made by white men. "Uncle Ned" was written by Stephen Foster, who, when he wrote it, had never been south of the Ohio River. The best of current Negro poetry can be judged without the allowance of any handicap. It retains some flavor of the bitter experiences of the race, but it is not the grotesque utterance of plantation pets or of simple souls seeking religious consolation for the rigors of slavery. No other single volume so deeply discloses the soul of the Negro race.

> *A review of "The Book of American Negro Poetry," in* The Christian Century, *Vol. XLVIII, No. 21, May 27, 1931, p. 716.*

The Book of American Negro Spirituals (1925)

AUTHOR'S COMMENTARY

I have termed [the Negro spiritual] noble, and I do so without any qualifications. Take, for example, *Go Down, Moses;* there is not a nobler theme in the whole musical literature of the world. If the Negro had voiced himself in only that one song, it would have been evidence of his nobility of soul. Add to this *Deep River, Stand Still Jordan, Walk Together Children, Roll Jordan Roll, Ride On King Jesus,* and you catch a spirit that is a little more than mere nobility; it is something akin to majestic grandeur. The music of these songs is always noble and their sentiment is always exalted. Never does their philosophy fall below the highest and purest motives of the heart. And this might seem stranger still.

Perhaps there will be no better point than this at which to say that all the true Spirituals possess dignity. It is, of course, pardonable to smile at the naïveté often exhibited in the words, but it should be remembered that in scarcely no instance was anything humorous intended. When it came to the use of words, the maker of the song was struggling as best he could under his limitations in language and, perhaps, also under a misconstruction or misapprehension of the facts in his source of material, generally the Bible. And often, like his more literary poetic brothers, he had to do a good many things to get his rhyme in. But almost always he was in dead earnest. There are doubtless many persons who have heard these songs sung only on the vaudeville or theatrical stage and have laughed uproariously at them because they were presented in humorous vein. Such people have no conception of the Spirituals. They probably thought of them as a new sort of ragtime or minstrel song. These Spirituals cannot be properly appreciated or understood unless they are clothed in their primitive dignity. (pp. 13-14)

Although the Spirituals have been overwhelmingly accredited to the Negro as his own, original creation, nevertheless, there have been one or two critics who have denied that they were original either with the Negro or in themselves, and a considerable number of people have eagerly accepted this view. The opinion of these critics is not sound. It is not based upon scientific or historical inquiry. Indeed, it can be traced ultimately to a prejudiced attitude of mind, to an unwillingness to concede the creation of so much pure beauty to a people they wish to feel is absolutely inferior. Once that power is conceded, the idea of absolute inferiority cannot hold. These critics point to certain similarities in structure between the Spirituals and the folk music of other peoples, ignoring the fact that there are such similarities between all folksongs. The Negro Spirituals are as distinct from the folksongs of other peoples as those songs are from each other; and, perhaps, more so. One needs to be only ordinarily familiar with the folk music of the world to see that this is so.

The statement that the Spirituals are imitations made by the Negro of other music that he heard is an absurdity. What music did American Negroes hear to imitate? They certainly had no opportunity to go to Scotland or Russia or Scandinavia and bring back echoes of songs from those lands. Some of them may have heard a few Scotch songs in this country, but it is inconceivable that this great mass of five or six hundred Negro songs could have sprung from such a source. What music then was left for them to imitate? Some have gone so far as to say that they caught snatches of airs from the French Opera at New Orleans; but the songs of the Negroes who fell most directly under that influence are of a type distinct from the Spirituals. It was in localities far removed from New Orleans that the great body of Spirituals were created and sung. There remains then the music which the American Negroes heard their masters sing; chiefly religious music. Now if ignorant Negroes evolved such music as *Deep River, Steal Away to Jesus, Somebody's Knockin' at Yo' Do', I Couldn't Hear Nobody Pray* and *Father Abraham* by listening to their masters sing gospel hymns, it does not detract from the achievement but magnifies it. (pp. 14-15)

This book is dedicated to those through whose efforts these songs have been collected, preserved and given to the world. It is a fitting, if inadequate, tribute; for it was wholly within the possibilities for these songs to be virtually lost. The people who created them were not capable of recording them, and the conditions out of which this music sprang and by which it was nourished have almost passed away. Without the direct effort on the part of those to whom I offer this slight tribute, the Spirituals would probably have fallen into disuse and finally disappeared. This

probability is increased by the fact that they passed through a period following Emancipation when the front ranks of the colored people themselves would have been willing and even glad to let them die. (p. 46)

A number of white persons aided in securing the general recognition which the Spirituals now enjoy. . . . But the present regard in which this Negro music is held is due overwhelmingly to the work of Negro composers, musicians and singers. It was through the work of these Negro artists that the colored people themselves were stirred to a realization of the true value of the Spirituals; and that result is more responsible for the new life which pulses through this music than any other single cause. I have said that these songs passed through a period when the front ranks of the Negro race would have been willing to let them die. Immediately following Emancipation those ranks revolted against everything connected with slavery, and among those things were the Spirituals. It became a sign of not being progressive or educated to sing them. This was a natural reaction, but, nevertheless, a sadly foolish one. It was left for the older generation to keep them alive by singing them at prayer meetings, class meetings, experience meetings and revivals, while the new choir with the organ and books of idiotic anthems held sway on Sundays. At this period gospel hymn-book agents reaped a harvest among colored churches in the South. Today this is all changed. There is hardly a choir among the largest and richest colored churches that does not make a specialty of singing the Spirituals. This reawakening of the Negro to the value and beauty of the Spirituals was the beginning of an entirely new phase of race consciousness. It marked a change in the attitude of the Negro himself toward his own art material; the turning of his gaze inward upon his own cultural resources. Neglect and ashamedness gave place to study and pride. All the other artistic activities of the Negro have been influenced.

There is also a change of attitude going on with regard to the Negro. The country may not yet be conscious of it, for it is only in the beginning. It is, nevertheless, momentous. America is beginning to see the Negro in a new light, or, rather, to see something new in the Negro. It is beginning to see in him the divine spark which may glow merely for the fanning. And so a colored man is soloist for the Boston Symphony Orchestra and the Philharmonic; a colored woman is soloist for the Philadelphia Symphony Orchestra and the Philharmonic; colored singers draw concert goers of the highest class; Negro poets and writers find entrée to all the most important magazines; Negro authors have their books accepted and put out by the leading publishers. And this change of attitude with regard to the Negro which is taking place is directly related to the Negro's change of attitude with regard to himself. It is new, and it is tremendously significant.

The collection here presented is not definitive, but we have striven to make it representative of this whole field of music, to give examples of every variety of Spiritual. There is still enough material new and old for another book like this, and, perhaps, even for another. (pp. 49-50)

This collection is offered with the hope that it will further endear these songs to those who love Spirituals, and will awaken an interest in many others. (p. 50)

James Weldon Johnson, in a preface to The Book of American Negro Spirituals, *edited by James Weldon Johnson, The Viking Press, 1925, pp. 11-50.*

It is worthy of note that, in face of determined opposition from the majority of their race, the spirituals have been kept alive mainly through the efforts of Negroes. The newest and best collection is entirely the work of colored men. *The Book of American Negro Spirituals* supplies a need that has long been felt; it is surprising, indeed, considering the widespread and increasing interest in these folksongs, that this need had not been supplied earlier. In compact form, bound so that it will lie flat open on the music rack, the volume includes sixty-one of these songs arranged for solo voice with piano accompaniment. These are prefaced by an analytical and historical introduction by James Weldon Johnson, of inestimable value to the singer who would attempt to render one of these numbers or to the lay reader who would inform himself authoritatively in regard to them. This volume is the most practical and at the same time the most thorough collection of arrangements that has yet been issued.

The Negro spirituals, unlike the folksongs of almost every other race, were created to be sung in harmony. They are so sung to-day when they are performed under the conditions which gave them birth. Negroes harmonize spontaneously and it is no novelty for a colored singer to improvise a tenor part one night and a baritone the next, depending on his mood. Naturally then, the harmonization of these songs, long kept alive in the memories of the singers and even now never performed from recorded examples in unsophisticated communities, differs greatly in various localities. It is, therefore, the prescribed task of the transcriber—when arranged for soloist, the piano supplies the missing choral harmonies—to see to it that his paraphrase satisfactorily combines the best features of many versions or is a replica of a single one, more particularly to keep his score free from esoteric harmonies (blemishes suggested by a knowledge of Debussy or Stravinsky), or operatic floridities or effective concert endings which are not Negro in spirit. Of too many of the arrangements made in the past it can be complained that they are not free from these faults. J. Rosamond Johnson, and Lawrence Brown, who transcribed five songs in the present collection—have been astonishingly successful in avoiding them. Here and there I might quarrel with an ornament in the accomplishment or an apparently arbitrary distortion of the rhythm, but on the whole the spirit is truly Negro. That these two men are Negroes is not a sufficient reason to account for the beneficient presence of the Negro spirit. Many of the very worst arrangements of the spirituals have been made by Negroes.

The collection contains most of the spirituals which have achieved wide popularity through the performances of the Fisk Jubilee Singers, Roland Hayes, Paul Robeson and others. Of these more familiar songs I miss only "Sometimes I feel like a motherless chil'," "I doan feel noways tired," "I want to be ready," "Weepin' Mary," "Were you there?" "Sinner, please doan let dis harvest pass," "O, didn't it rain," and "I know de Lawd laid his han's on me." The lack of these songs—all available either in other collections or in sheet-music form—is more than made up for by the inclusion of a number of hitherto neglected examples. Some of these are real finds and will undoubtedly soon make their appearances on concert programs. I especially recommend to the attention of lovers of spirituals, "Somebody's knockin' at yo' do'," "Singin' wid a sword in ma han'," and "Stan' still, Jordan." For the rest, the searcher will discover "All God's chillun got wings," "Deep River"—in a version from which the impurities which have long discolored its frame have been expunged—"Go down, Moses," "Steal away," and the other great prototypes of this species of folksong. Mr. Johnson, having already arranged the more familiar melody of "Nobody knows de trouble I see," has in this instance provided an arrangement of the alternative melody which, so far as I know, has not hitherto been published in a practical concert form.

A notable feature is that for the first time in a book of this character an attempt has been made to keep the dialect consistent. I may, perhaps, be permitted to give Mr. James Weldon Johnson the credit for this welcome innovation, as he has devoted a considerable passage in his preface to a discussion of this very point.

The preface as a whole may be described as a simple, sane, able and dignified dissertation on the subject, viewed from many angles. I do not see how it could have been made more admirable, taking into consideration the fact that Mr. Johnson has addressed himself to the general reader rather than to the technical musician. In the course of this preface he warns performers of these songs against the pitfalls into which they are likely to stumble, unless they be wary. Their successful rendering, he suggests reasonably, is almost entirely a matter of feeling, of a proper conception and assimilation of their spirit. Even white concert artists, he asserts, can sing spirituals if they feel them. What he means, of course, is if they understand their style. Alas, he admits, too many singers, both white and colored, are prone to sing them, on the one hand, as if they were German *lieder,* or, on the other, with a false Negro unctiousness.

He devotes attention to the charges of plagiarism which have been leveled against these songs, but he does not adduce the best argument in confutation of these silly charges. In no instance, so far as I am aware, has any one substantiated such a charge—and it has never been made by serious students of this body of song—by bringing forward the melodies from which these songs were allegedly stolen. Until such actual evidence is forthcoming we may continue to give the Negroes credit for their creation.

The compilers of this collection have been so successful in dealing with the manifold problems they have been compelled to face that it is earnestly to be hoped that they may feel encouraged by its reception presently to issue another volume and then another—an entire book might be devoted to Blues or work songs—until all the Negro folksongs that possess interest are assembled in this practical form.

Carl Van Vechten, "The Songs of the Negro," in New York Herald Tribune Books, October 25, 1925, pp. 1-2.

In velvety cascades there have flown within the last few years from the lips of Roland Hayes and Julius Bledsoe and Paul Robeson the hauntingly beautiful Negro spirituals. Throughout America and Europe these songs have gained a well deserved vogue and there has come to them the recognition so long denied them. Singer after singer has programmed them with songs by Bach and Schubert and Brahms and César Franck, and it is by such comparisons that they have been recognized as the great music many of them are.

It was inevitable that there should follow in the wake of this recognition collections of these songs and critical appraisals of their music and their words. . . . [Probably] the best of them all [is] *The Book of American Negro Spirituals* by James Weldon Johnson who, being a Negro, gets down beneath the surface of this music and reveals the extraordinary processes by which it came into being and grew. (pp. 490-91)

Mr. Johnson in an introductory essay of some forty pages gives us what is by far the most interesting and satisfying examination of the factors which brought this music into being and those which shaped it into its present majesty and beauty and wistful sadness. To his task Mr. Johnson brings not only a deep devotion but a superb critical sense, and a profound knowledge of the emotional wellsprings of these songs which, in all charity, a white person is incapable of gaining. The late Henry Krehbiel in his *Afro-*

Johnson as a school principal at the time he wrote "Lift Every Voice and Sing."

American Folksongs gave a technical exposition of Negro music which was sound and sympathetic, yet lacking in that deeper understanding so necessary to a full picture. Natalie Curtis Burlin did much in bringing a fuller recognition of the value and beauty and power of the spirituals, but she too suffered because she was approaching them from without. Mr. Johnson, however, knows what lies back of this music: the sorrows and joys, the wistful longing for surcease from pain and bitterness, the stalwart determination voiced with such haunting melody in songs like "I Ain't Going to Study War No Mo' ", the sublime confidence in an all-powerful God. The use of rhythm and melody, the solo and chorus arrangements, the blending of the beautiful in primitive African rites with the more spiritual and beautiful parts of the Christian religion, the variations and additions to the scanty store of songs in isolated regions brought by itinerant singers like "Singing Johnson" and "Ma White", are all told of in fascinating fashion. And for the first time Mr. Johnson gives a satisfactory explanation of a thing which many, many times caused chills of I didn't know what to run up and down my spine—"the curious turns and twists and quavers and the intentional striking of certain notes just a shade off the key".

But the essay is not all. Mr. Johnson's brother, J. Rosamond Johnson, and Lawrence Brown, who with Paul Robeson gained last spring so notable a success in New York in the rendition of programs of spirituals, have contributed the words and music to sixty one spirituals, many of them familiar, many of them never heard before, which by their beauty are indicative of the great wealth of these songs as yet undiscovered. (pp. 491-92)

Here are gorgeously interesting records of the vocal expressions of a gifted, imaginative, poetic race, dowered with the inestimably precious gift of song and ebullient resistance to material discomforts. No person can read . . . [this volume] with any degree of understanding and still feel condescension toward this music, one of the very few gifts to the realm of art and beauty which America has made to the world. If you have any bit of love for music, for poetry, for imaginative conceptions of a high order, you cannot fail to receive many years of happiness from these songs. (p. 492)

Walter White, "Negro Spirituals," in The Bookman, New York, Vol. LXII, No. 4, December, 1925, pp. 490-92.

The success of *The Book of American Negro Spirituals,* edited by James Weldon Johnson with musical arrangements by J. Rosamond Johnson and Lawrence Brown, is one of the most conspicuous signs that Negro folk music and Negro folk poetry are beginning to secure the general attention they have always deserved in America. For the book has become a bestseller, and concert halls which previously had opened only for Roland Hayes and Paul Robeson are filled these days with audiences come to hear less notable or even entirely unknown soloists. If the spirituals have come to be something of a fad among those who must seek each season for another thrill, and if many of the present devotees are bound to drop away before another winter brings its novelty, this does not matter a great deal. A new circle has been reached; the songs have settled that much more firmly into place. Not a few persons, of course, have always known and admired them, and they have by no means been neglected by musical and literary scholarship. Eleven years ago there was H. E. Krehbiel's *Afro-American Folk Songs*, and the current year has seen in *The Negro and His Songs*, by Odum and Johnson, an interesting attempt at historical and social analysis. But much still remains to be said.

For instance, there is the matter of origins. In his sensible introduction to the sixty-one songs which he has chosen Mr. Johnson touches this intricate subject in such a way as to make it merely tantalizing. Answering the not infrequent charge that the spirituals are derivative both in their music and in their words, he states as an axiom that they are original and lets it go at that. Now, neither of the two adjectives can have any meaning by itself. No excellent work of art can be wholly derivative, nor, on the other hand, can any work of art be wholly original. The problem of assessing originality is the problem of discovering where something came from and defining the qualities which it collected after it arrived. It was not Mr. Johnson's business to do this—it would take volumes, and I suspect that those volumes will some day be written; but he might have suggested the need of its being done. The research, when it comes at last to be made, will take someone over obscure and fascinating ground—Africa, Europe, and our Southern States; it will pry into more than one primitive religion; it will base itself in part upon an understanding of racial rhythms—if, indeed, they exist; and it will at least skirt the territory of comparative literature. (pp. 707-08)

> *Mark Van Doren, "First Glance," in* The Nation, *New York, Vol. CXXI, No. 3154, December 16, 1925, pp. 707-08.*

James Weldon Johnson claims for the religious music of the Negro a miracle of birth. In an estimable preface to *The Book of American Negro Spirituals* he asserts, with the emotionally persuasive conviction of a Fundamentalist, that the spiritual is of immaculate African origin. Like most believers in a miracle, he shows a minimum of tolerance toward those who ask for proof of the mystery. Doubters are referred to H. E. Krehbiel's *Afro-American Folksongs.* Mr. Johnson dismisses as unsound and prejudiced the conclusions of other critics who maintain that a leafage of European folk-song and the American revival hymn may be detected on the spiritual's genealogical tree.

Many of the songs in Mr. Johnson's collection will persuade even the sceptical that certain melodies and rhythms are of African inception. There is a melodic bend as unmistakable as a line of racial physiognomy, and in the rhythm, with its vagaries of verbal accent—the syllable which cannot wait for the stressed beat in the music—is heard a syncopated racial pulse. But where are the "bizarre" and "anarchic" harmonies which Mr. Johnson declares are as typical of Negro music as rhythmic current and melodic shape? The prevailing chords are tonic, dominant and subdominant, those staples of European harmony which are not a commodity of native African music.

The spiritual's title to miraculous birth may be briefly summarized from Mr. Johnson's argument. Music, as known to the primitive African, was only a chant or cry rhythmically emphasized by tom-tom or drum. Sold into slavery, the black man was converted to Christianity, and as he grew in grace his musical equipment increased. His barbaric wail was transformed by piety into the spiritual. Some of the songs, Mr. Johnson believes, were of communal origin, piecemeal compositions contributed by different members of a group under the influence of religious ecstasy. Others were the creation of single individuals, black troubadours whose rags of slavery were overlaid by a shining panoply of righteousness.

"Make a joyful noise unto the God of Jacob!" The congregation of believers obeys this mandate of the psalmist by a rising thrust of melody, We Am Climbin' Jacob's Ladder; the song mounts an octave and "the soldiers of the cross" ascend on rungs of praise to a peak of delirious rapture. Apart from the music, the text of the spirituals may be read with delight in many lines which are jeweled by naïve poetical paraphrase of Scriptural lore.

> Up to de walls ob Jericho
> He marched with spear in han',
> "Go blow dem ram horns," Joshua cried,
> "Kase de battle am in my han'."
>
> Den the lam' ram sheep horns begin to blow,
> Trumpets begin to soun',
> Joshua commanded de chillen to shout,
> An' de walls come tumblin' down.

Among the sixty-one spirituals, arranged for solo voice with piano accompaniment by Rosamond Johnson and Lawrence Brown, there are a few which employ a sophisticated piano idiom disagreeing with the primitive tune and poesy. One of the best songs in *The Book of American Negro Spirituals* is "Joshua Fit de Battle ob Jericho." Here the melody is supported by simple vigorous chords and an imaginative ear can easily catch the effect of the original version in unaccompanied vocal harmony. Whether or not the Negro spiritual partly derives from the banal gospel song of white revivalists is a question for musical critics. While they quibble over the seeds from which it grew, music lovers will feast upon the fruit, a unique hymnology of richly flavored beauty. (pp. 168-69)

> *Janet Ramsay, "Afro-American Concord," in* The New Republic, *Vol. XLV, No. 578, December 30, 1925, pp. 168-69.*

The Second Book of American Negro Spirituals (1926)

The bibliography of Negro lore is increasing rapidly. . . . Of the two books of spirituals [being reviewed, *The Second Book of Negro Spirituals* and *Seventy Negro Spirituals,* edited by William Arms Fisher], the first is by far the most important. It supplements *The Book of American Negro Spirituals,* issued so successfully by the Viking Press last fall. Mr. James Weldon Johnson implies in his preface to the new collection that further volumes will be published from time to time until Mr. J. Rosamond Johnson has exhausted the supply of notable Negro religious folksongs. *The Second Book of Negro Spirituals* contains in arrangements for piano and solo voice several of the most widely popular tunes, such as " 'Zekiel Saw de Wheel," "Were

You There?" "Sometimes I Feel Like a Motherless Child," "I Know de Lord's Laid His Hands on Me" and "Sinner, Please Don't Let Dis Harves' Pass," which were crowded out of the first collection for one reason or another, and it also contains a wealth of less familiar airs that should soon become equally famous now that they are available in arrangements for voice and piano. After a rapid survey of the volume I can already recommend "Same Train," a masterpiece if there ever was one; "My Lord Say He's Gwineter Rain Down Fire," "My Soul's Been Anchored in de Lord," "When I Fall on My Knees," "Rise Up Shepherd an' Foller," "Do Don't Toucha My Garment, Good Lord, I'm Gwine Home," "Po' Mourner's Got a Home At Last" and "I Want God's Heab'n to Be Mine." There are two versions, one major, one minor, of the miraculous "Death's Gwineter Lay His Cold, Icy Hands on Me." Doubtless I shall find many more gems when I have the opportunity to examine the book more carefully.

Mr. James Weldon Johnson's preface is charming, but it contains little information that is new. Indeed, his introduction to the first volume in this series was so authoritative and exhaustive that it leaves little more for anybody to say on this subject. Mr. J. Rosamond Johnson's new arrangements are simpler, and therefore even better than his arrangements of the songs in the first book. If musicians and singers would study his method of arranging and performing them (with the aid of Taylor Gordon) they could all learn a great deal about the proper (and most effective) interpretation of the spirituals. Mr. Johnson's dedications, by the way, read like a list of guests for a very good party. I predict that this new collection will be quite as popular as its predecessor, and worthily so.

> *Carl Van Vechten, "Don't Let Dis Harves' Pass," in* New York Herald Tribune Books, *October 31, 1926, p. 4.*

The success achieved last year by *The Book of American Negro Spirituals* deserves to be repeated by this new, second volume edited and arranged by the same gifted brothers who gave its predecessor to the world. It contains sixty-one spirituals that for reasons of space were omitted from the first book, all of them old favorites. James Weldon Johnson says in his interesting preface that "it would almost seem that the number of beautiful spirituals is inexhaustible," and he intimates that he and his brother are endeavoring to collect and preserve in permanent form all of these folksongs that it is now possible to save from oblivion. He fears that much of this music has already been lost beyond hope of retrieval and he adds that "the negro and the world are lucky in that so great a mass of his songs has been saved." Mr. Johnson's long preface is an illuminating discussion of the part the spirituals have played in the life of the negro and of their value and influence in his development and in the art of the nation. This leads him on to a brief statement of the contribution of the negro race to American culture, a swift survey that is restrained, keenly interesting and suggestive. Then, taking a glance at the future of the spirituals as a force in music, he sees in "this nobler music of the negro" such an unexplored mine of rich materials for serious composers as they could not find elsewhere. Mr. Johnson's preface is

well worth the reading of any one interested in either American music, the achievements of the colored race in America or the sources of American culture.

Among the songs included are: "Sometimes I Feel Like a Motherless Child," "Walk Together Children," "Zekiel Saw de Wheel," "Same Train," "Gimme Yo' Han' " and the familiar version of "Nobody Knows de Trouble I see," of which the first book contains a rare form. J. Rosamond Johnson, well known to concert goers throughout the country, has made, as before, the arrangements for voice and piano with skill and taste. The brothers Johnson are doing a work of such value in the preservation of these songs as to merit the heartiest commendation of music lovers and of all who are interested in American culture.

> *"More Negro Spirituals," in* The New York Times Book Review, *December 19, 1926, p. 24.*

After the success which attended the publication of the *First Book of Negro Spirituals,* it was inevitable that the authors should dig deeper into the wealth of material and give us another collection. On the whole, this volume is even more satisfactory than the series which preceded it, although I do not imagine that it will have the success its companion enjoyed, the vogue of the spirituals having to some extent died down since the publication of the latter.

Mr. James Weldon Johnson again gives us a Preface. He goes into the history of the "discovery" of the spirituals, and tells how many of them are lost forever. He does not feel their vogue to be a fad, yet I feel the very wide popularity they enjoyed in the last two years is undoubtedly lessening, leaving, however, I trust, a residue of important interest. He concludes with a discussion of the artistic movement of the younger group of Negroes in this country. Whether they will, as he claims, make a distinctive contribution to American art as Negroes remains to be seen. Suggestions of themes which may be used by composers in the larger musical forms are given, but why did Mr. Johnson select the hackneyed theme from the "Symphony to the New World", that of "Swing Low, Sweet Chariot", as the most prominent example?

The songs themselves are wisely chosen. They are, to me, more valuable than those in the other volumes, if only because they are heard less often. Such gems as "Gimme Yo' Han, All I Do", "De Church Keep A-Grumblin' ", and "Zekiel Saw De Wheel" would alone justify the publication of the volume. Here, as always, however, the problem of accompaniment presents itself. Mr. Rosamond Johnson, who arranged the songs, has learned a lesson from the songs published before, and has simplified his accompaniments, but they still leave much to be desired. In spite of this, there is great joy to the lover of folk-music to be had from this collection, with perhaps good measure added in the way of amusement when one considers some of the persons to whom the songs are dedicated.

> *Melville J. Herskovits, "More Spirituals," in* The New Republic, *Vol. XLIX, No. 632, January 12, 1927, p. 230.*

Sometimes one feels that perhaps even the humble old negro spiritual may pray to be delivered from its friends.

In this *Second Book of Spirituals* there are two features at which a lover of the negro religious songs may cavil, especially if his interest in them be rather more that of the folklorist than that of the musician. The very same objection would, of course, be raised against the *First Book* by the same folk-lorist. This objection will be two-fold. In the first place, there is no arrangement for part singing. Now those of us who have learned these songs, or some of them, as has the present reviewer, through hearing them across a field, as their weird and full harmonies floated from the windows of a church on Wednesday prayer-meeting nights, or on other occasions, will miss the opportunity to entice a group of friends into trying the parts, will regret the lack of facilities for learning some old rich bass whose rolling splendour lingers in memories of earlier days. So will some, probably more in this country, who have heard the Jubilee Singers in days gone by. For the harmonies were so essential a part of the religious singing of the negroes, were possibly the crowning glory of it. Even if one does recognize the fact that no given spiritual was by any means sung with the same harmonies by any two congregations, or even by any one congregation always, still the guidance of such arrangements as were to be found in the old Fisk collection, or in the old or new Hampton books of spirituals was a welcome aid to the lovers of these songs.

Perhaps the second objection is an ungenerous one, and really a partial negation of the first. The arrangements for piano of Mr. J. R. Johnson are frankly meant to take the place of the voice parts, and are probably the result of a conviction that the days of community or group singing of these, at any rate by whites, are past. One hopes not. Now the harmonizations by the negroes are undoubtedly very rich, but it seems to me that the elaborate accompaniments to many of the songs in these two collections take one a little too far away from the original feeling, from the folk feeling. In the effort to make the spirituals effective concert pieces, something has been sacrificed. This is by no means true of all the songs. The magnificent accompaniment to 'Go Down, Moses', in the *First Book,* is splendidly convincing and satisfying. The same thing is true of 'Zekiel Saw de Wheel' in the *Second Book,* and of a score or more in each of the two Books. I have merely selected two which at the moment I remember as peculiarly authentic in the appeal of their arrangements. But the criticism holds for many.

In spite of this, however, both books are of inestimable value to all who are interested in the religious song of the negro, which, certainly insofar as folk song, or religious song in general, or possibly all music, is concerned, is the finest product so far of this continent.

As is to be expected, the *Second Book* does not contain as many of the old favourites as does the *First,* but its sixty-one songs include an astonishingly large number of the choice spirituals. A book which contains such fine things as 'Zekiel Saw de Wheel', 'Nobody Knows de Trouble I see', and 'Walk in Jerusalem Jus' Like John' is by no means made up of left-overs.

"Folk Song," in The Canadian Forum, *Vol. VII, No. 79, April, 1927, p. 218.*

God's Trombones: Seven Negro Sermons in Verse (1927)

AUTHOR'S COMMENTARY

A good deal has been written on the folk creations of the American Negro: his music, sacred and secular; his plantation tales, and his dances; but that there are folk sermons, as well, is a fact that has passed unnoticed. I remember hearing in my boyhood sermons that were current, sermons that passed with only slight modifications from preacher to preacher and from locality to locality. Such sermons were, "The Valley of Dry Bones," which was based on the vision of the prophet in the 37th chapter of Ezekiel; the "Train Sermon," in which both God and the devil were pictured as running trains, one loaded with saints, that pulled up in heaven, and the other with sinners, that dumped its load in hell; the "Heavenly March," which gave in detail the journey of the faithful from earth, on up through the pearly gates to the great white throne. Then there was a stereotyped sermon which had no definite subject, and which was quite generally preached; it began with the Creation, went on to the fall of man, rambled through the trials and tribulations of the Hebrew Children, came down to the redemption by Christ, and ended with the Judgment Day and a warning and an exhortation to sinners. (pp. 1-2)

The old-time Negro preacher has not yet been given the niche in which he properly belongs. He has been portrayed only as a semi-comic figure. He had, it is true, his comic aspects, but on the whole he was an important figure, and at bottom a vital factor. It was through him that the people of diverse languages and customs who were brought here from diverse parts of Africa and thrown into slavery were given their first sense of unity and solidarity. He was the first shepherd of this bewildered flock. His power for good or ill was very great. It was the old-time preacher who for generations was the mainspring of hope and inspiration for the Negro in America. (pp. 2-3)

The old-time preacher was generally a man far above the average in intelligence; he was, not infrequently, a man of positive genius. The earliest of these preachers must have virtually committed many parts of the Bible to memory through hearing the scriptures read or preached from in the white churches which the slaves attended. They were the first of the slaves to learn to read, and their reading was confined to the Bible, and specifically to the more dramatic passages of the Old Testament. A text served mainly as a starting point and often had no relation to the development of the sermon. (p. 4)

The old-time Negro preacher of parts was above all an orator, and in good measure an actor. He knew the secret of oratory, that at bottom it is a progression of rhythmic words more than it is anything else. Indeed, I have witnessed congregations moved to ecstasy by the rhythmic intoning of sheer incoherencies. He was a master of all the modes of eloquence. He often possessed a voice that was a marvelous instrument, a voice he could modulate from a sepulchral whisper to a crashing thunder clap. His discourse was generally kept at a high pitch of fervency, but occasionally he dropped into colloquialisms and, less often, into humor. He preached a personal and anthropomorphic God, a sure-enough heaven and a red-hot hell. His imagination was bold and unfettered. He had the power to sweep his hearers before him; and so himself was often swept away. At such times his language was not prose but poetry. (p. 5)

At first thought, Negro dialect would appear to be the precise medium for these old-time sermons; however, . . . the poems [in *God's Trombones*] are not written in dialect. My reason for not using the dialect is double. First, although the dialect is the exact instrument for voicing certain traditional phases of Negro life, it is, and perhaps by that very exactness, a quite limited instrument. Indeed, it is an instrument with but two complete stops, pathos and humor. This limitation is not due to any defect of the dialect as dialect, but to the mould of convention in which Negro dialect in the United States has been set, to the fixing effects of its long association with the Negro only as a happy-go-lucky or a forlorn figure. The Aframerican poet might in time be able to break this mould of convention and write poetry in dialect without feeling that his first line will put the reader in a frame of mind which demands that the poem be either funny or sad, but I doubt that he will make the effort to do it; he does not consider it worth the while. . . . The passing of dialect as a medium for Negro poetry will be an actual loss, for in it many beautiful things can be done, and done best; however, in my opinion, *traditional* Negro dialect as a form for Aframerican poets is absolutely dead. The Negro poet in the United States, for poetry which he wishes to give a distinctively racial tone and color, needs now an instrument of greater range than dialect; that is, if he is to do more than sound the small notes of sentimentality. I said something on this point in *The Book of American Negro Poetry*, and because I cannot say it better, I quote: "What the colored poet in the United States needs to do is something like what Synge did for the Irish; he needs to find a form that will express the racial spirit by symbols from within rather than by symbols from without—such as the mere mutilation of English spelling and pronounciation. He needs a form that is freer and larger that dialect, but which will still hold the racial flavor." . . . (pp. 7-8)

The second part of my reason for not writing these poems in dialect is the weightier. The old-time Negro preachers, though they actually used dialect in their ordinary intercourse, stepped out from its narrow confines when they preached. They were all saturated with the sublime phraseology of the Hebrew prophets and steeped in the idioms of King James English, so when they preached and warmed to their work they spoke another language, a language far removed from traditional Negro dialect. It was really fusion of Negro idioms with Bible English; and in this there may have been, after all, some kinship with the innate grandiloquence of their old African tongues. To place in the mouths of the talented old-time Negro preachers a language that is a literary imitation of Mississippi cotton-field dialect is sheer burlesque.

Gross exaggeration of the use of big words by these preachers, in fact by Negroes in general, has been commonly made; the laugh being at the exhibition of igno-

rance involved. What is the basis of this fondness for big words? Is the predilection due, as is supposed, to ignorance desiring to parade itself as knowledge? Not at all. The old-time Negro preacher loved the sonorous, mouth-filling, ear-filling phrase because it gratified a highly developed sense of sound and rhythm in himself and his hearers.

I claim no more for these poems than that I have written them after the manner of the primitive sermons. (pp. 9-10)

> *James Weldon Johnson, in a preface to his* God's Trombones: Seven Negro Sermons in Verse, *1927. Reprint by The Viking Press, 1969, pp. 1-11.*

It is not easy in these days to write novel and impressive verse on the old grandiose Biblical themes of Creation and Judgment Day, the Flood and the Crucifixion, the hurling about of stars, the awful words of God and the compassionate arms of Jesus. College freshmen, drunk on the epic poets, attempt them without a qualm; but sophisticated writers know that there is less danger of appearing ridiculous if one chooses humbler subjects and writes about them in more casual vein. Educated preachers are too

The sheet music for "Lift Every Voice and Sing" autographed by Johnson at top right.

much worried over whether Noah was a myth and too much occupied with remaking Jesus for the business man to take the Bible literally as poetry and be excited by the majestic images and rhythms of the King James version.

The old Negro preacher was, fortunately, not bothered by the modern theologies that dissolve flesh and blood Bible people into dull abstractions; he was not confused and intimidated by a variety of literary models and critical standards, or afraid to seem undignified through extravagant fancy and impassioned intonation. Inability to read usually spared him the necessity of staying close to Scriptural detail; he had heard the stories simply told and was free to retell them with variations and pungent figures of his own. Certain ways of telling them and pointing the simple morals became traditional through generations of preachers. Mr. Johnson, who has done fine work in preserving the spiritual songs, has set down in [*God's Trombones*] a few of these traditional sermons, with a modest belittling of his own share in the product. One may suspect that he has contributed a great deal to heighten their dramatic force; and, in any case, he has revealed another type of Afro-American folk literature that deserves following up. **"Creation"** and **"Go Down Death"** are outstanding poems in their own right; the former has an almost Miltonic splendor, and in the other the splendor is brought down to earth with a strain of homely tenderness.

The sermons are a genuine fusion of distinct elements: the theme in each case is the Hebrew story, and the moral exhortation is sometimes reminiscent of the old Wesleyan camp-meeting evangelists, white as well as colored. As might be expected, the rhythm is the most distinctly Negro quality—irregular, syncopated and constantly varied. A line or two in stately Bible measure will fall away at once into a lifting quickstep, to be followed by others in indefinite variety and by recurrences of the first rhythm.

> Young man—
> Young man—
> Smooth and easy is the road
> That leads to hell and destruction.
> Down grade all the way,
> The further you travel, the faster you go.
> No need to trudge and sweat and toil.
> Just slip and slide and slip and slide
> Till you bang up against hell's iron gate . . .
> Young man—
> Young man—
> You're never lonesome in Babylon.

As to imagery—second-hand Bible figures ("the bread of life," "wash him with hyssop") are interspersed with fresh metaphors: "pin his ear to the wisdom-post," "Turpentine his imagination," "blacker than a hundred midnights down in a cypress swamp." High-flown sonorities are salted with homely colloquialisms, and the result is somehow vivacious rather than disturbing:

> So God stepped over to the edge of the world
> And He spat out the seven seas—
> He batted His eyes, and the lightnings flashed—
> He clapped his hands, and the thunders rolled—
> And the waters above the earth came down,
> The cooling waters came down.

An issue of some importance for Negro literature is raised by Mr. Johnson's elimination of dialect from his poems. Only a very infrequent "gittin' up," "I've done drunk," or some such phrase, remains; the rest is printed in ordinary English. The preface justifies this step on two grounds: First, that Negro dialect as an instrument is limited to pathos and humor, that convention has associated it with the funny or sad, forlorn or happy-go-lucky type of sentiment, so that a modern poet who wishes to transcend this narrow range must avoid the old language. Second, that the old Negro preachers, when inspired, abandoned the colloquial dialect for a more sublime fusion of Negro idioms with Bible English.

These are good points, but not quite enough to justify the discarding of so rich and musical a variant of English as the Negro dialect. If it is true, as Mr. Johnson says, that "practically no poetry is being written in dialect by the colored poets of to-day," the fact is to be regretted. The dignity and emotional range of the spirituals which Mr. Johnson has himself collected prove the large capacity of dialect as a medium. Why not go on to destroy its false associations, instead of giving up the battle so soon? No sensible person would want the modern colored poets to confine themselves to racial themes, or to write only in dialect; but there are cases where to abandon the dialect is to lose an appropriate and valuable element in the total effect. These sermons, purporting to come from the mouth of an old-time Negro preacher, seem to be just that sort of case. Granting that his language was a little more academic than the cottonpicker's, was it not much richer in idioms and grammatical freedom, in the soft elision of consonants, than Mr. Johnson makes it look in print? Some of these lines have almost the flat banality of a Broadway conversation:

> I imagine he brought her a present, too—
> And, if there was such a thing in those ancient
>   days,
> He brought her a looking-glass.

No doubt Mr. Johnson hears these lines with the rich intonation he remembers and describes in his preface; but the ordinary reader needs printed help in so hearing them. The art of writing down the various Negro dialects has been notably advanced in the last few years (witness "Tropic Death," "Black Cameos" and "Black April") and the young colored writer who scorns it is rejecting an instrument of great possibilities. The case of Synge, whom Mr. Johnson cites as having dispensed with dialect, is not quite parallel, for he, like any dramatist, could rely on actors to deliver his lines in something like the proper intonation. It is more to the point to imagine Robert Burns translated into "correct English."

> *Thomas Munroe, "The Grand Manner in Negro Poetry," in* New York Herald Tribune Books, *June 5, 1927, p. 3.*

[*God's Trombones*] is a beautifully made book. The remarkable drawings are by Aaron Douglas, like the author a Negro, the lettering by C. B. Falls, the well-known illustrator. The cover is a gorgeous gold and black design, the illustrations of black and blue-gray in fine special reproduction. Mr. Johnson, notable artist of his race, has here turned certain Negro sermons into free verse. His triumph lies in the fact that he has not descended to dialect, yet has managed to convey the very intoning of the originals in his striking versions. His preface sets forth ably the significance and gifts of the old Negro preacher. He has culled the material for his text from innumerable sermons heard and witnessed. No one who wishes to familiarize himself with the most artistic and native work that is coming from the literate Negroes of today can afford to neglect this slim, beautiful volume of Mr. Johnson's. It is a work of research turned into a work of re-creation. It fixes in distinguished form upon the printed page the essence of the best Negro preaching of all time. **"Go Down Death,"** a funeral sermon, is, both in text and illustration, one of the most striking of the seven unusual utterances here rendered.

> *A review of "God's Trombones," in* The Saturday Review of Literature, *Vol. 111, No. 46, June 11, 1927, p. 904.*

Besides an opening prayer, there are seven sermons in *God's Trombones,* and they are called **"The Creation," "The Prodigal Son," "Go Down Death—A Funeral Sermon," "Noah Built the Ark," "The Crucifixion," "Let My People Go,"** and **"The Judgment Day."** The very titles of these give an idea of the subject matter, but nothing less than quotation can give an adequate idea of the method in which these sermons are composed. Although Mr. Johnson may suggest that he is prodded by memories in the composition of these seven pieces, it is very evident that he is a distinguished and intelligent poet creating out of mist a series of curious approximations. There is sensitivity, artistic judgment, and a sustained emotional beauty in his work. If the old negro preachers discoursed and chanted in this fashion, they were poets indeed. Perhaps as good an example of this work as any is this passage from **"Go Down Death."**

> And Death heard the summons,
> And he leaped on his fastest
>   horse,
> Pale as a sheet in the moonlight.
> Up the golden street Death gal-
>   loped,
> And the hoofs of his horse struck
>   fire from the gold,
> But they didn't make no sound.
> Up Death rode to the Great
>   White Throne,
> And waited for God's command.
>
> And God said: Go down, Death,
>   go down.
> And out and down he rode,
> Through heaven's pearly gates,
> Past suns and moons and stars;
> On Death rode,
> And the foam from his horse was
>   like a comet in the sky;
> On Death rode,
> Leaving the lightning's flash be-
>   hind;
> Straight on down he came.

> *"Poetry and Eloquence of the Negro Preacher," in* The New York Times Book Review, *June 19, 1927, p. 11.*

For some time Mr. Johnson has been known as a leader among the American Negro poets, and as by all odds their best editor. His *Book of American Negro Poetry,* and his two books of *Spirituals,* with their prefaces, are monuments of patient and sympathetic scholarship and of devotion to his race in its highest achievements. (p. 291)

The present volume is his own highest achievement as a poet. The author says modestly in his excellent preface:

> I claim no more for these poems than that I have written them after the manner of the primitive sermons.

But it is something of an achievement to suggest, as he does, the spirit and rhythm of those sermons, and to do it without the help of dialect or of antiphonal repetitions. There may be two opinions about the tradition of dialect; at least Mr. Johnson makes a very good argument against it in his preface, and gets on very well without it.

With the old-time Negro, religion was a grand adventure. It exalted him into rapture, and his imagination lavished gymnastic figures upon it. Here, for example, are two stanzas from **"The Creation"**:

> Then God himself stepped down—
> And the sun was on his right hand,
> And the moon was on his left;
> The stars were clustered about his head,
> And the earth was under his feet,
> And God walked, and where he trod
> His footsteps hollowed the valleys out
> And bulged the mountains up.
>
> Then he stopped and looked and saw
> That the earth was hot and barren.
> So God stepped over to the edge of the world
> And he spat out the seven seas;
> He batted his eyes, and the lightning flashed;
> He clapped his hands, and the thunders rolled,
> And the waters above the earth came down,
> The cooling waters came down.

We have space for only a hint of the book's quality. Mr. Johnson does not claim to have originated the sermons; like Joel Chandler Harris he has set down what he heard—the essence of it; and he is entitled to credit of the same kind. Hardly to the same degree, however, as the authenticity is less complete, the art less perfect. I wish he could have let himself go a little more rashly; for the creation myth, as I heard Lucine Finch repeat her old mammy's version, was more powerfully poetic than Mr. Johnson's.

However, we should be grateful for this book. As the author says:

> The old-time Negro preacher is rapidly passing, and I have here tried sincerely to fix something of him.

> (pp. 291-93)

> *Harriet Monroe, "Negro Sermons," in* Poetry, *Vol. XXX, No. 5, August, 1927, pp. 291-93.*

James Weldon Johnson has blown the true spirit and the pentecostal trumpeting of the dark Joshuas of the race in *God's Trombones,* composed of seven sermon-poems and a prayer. The seven sermons are like the seven blasts blown by Joshua at Jericho. **"The Creation"**, **"The Prodigal Son"**, **"Go Down Death—A Funeral Sermon"**, **"Noah Built the Ark"**, **"The Crucifixion"**, **"Let My People Go"**, and **"The Judgment Day"**, they are all great evangelical texts. And the magnificent manner in which they are done increases our regret that Mr. Johnson was not intrigued into preaching "The Dry Bones In the Valley", the *pièce de résistance* in the repertoire of every revivalist to whom a good shout is a recommendation of salvation well received.

An experiment and an intention lie behind these poems. It will be remembered that in *The Book of American Negro Poetry* Mr. Johnson spoke of the limitations of dialect, which he compared to an organ having but two stops, one of humor and one of pathos. He felt that the Negro poet needed to discover some medium of expression with a latitude capable of embracing the Negro experience. These poems were written with that purpose in view, as well as to guarantee a measure of permanence in man's most forgetful mind to that highly romantic and fast disappearing character, the old time Negro preacher.

The poet here has admirably risen to his intentions and his needs; entombed in this bright mausoleum the Negro preacher of an older day can never pass entirely deathward. Dialect could never have been synthesized into the rich mortar necessary for these sturdy unrhymed exhortations. Mr. Johnson has captured that peculiar flavor of speech by which the black sons of Zebedee, lacking academic education, but grounded through their religious intensity in the purest marshalling of the English language (the King James' version of the Bible) must have astounded men more obviously letter-trained. This verse is simple and awful at once, the grand diapason of a musician playing on an organ with far more than two keys.

There is a universality of appeal and appreciation in these poems that raises them, despite the fact that they are labeled *Seven Negro Sermons in Verse,* and despite the persistent racial emphasis of Mr. Douglas' beautiful illustrations, far above a relegation to any particular group or people. Long ago the recital of the agonies and persecutions of the Hebrew children under Pharaoh ceased to chronicle the tribulations of one people alone. So in **"Let My People Go"** there is a world-wide cry from the oppressed against the oppressor, from the frail and puny against the arrogant in strength who hold them against their will. From Beersheba to Dan the trusting wretch, rich in nothing but his hope and faith, holds this an axiomatic solace:

> Listen!—Listen!
> All you sons of Pharaoh,
> Who do you think can hold God's people
> When the Lord himself has said,
> Let my people go?

In considering these poems one must pay unlimited respect to the voice Mr. Johnson has recorded, and to the pliable and agonyracked audience to whom those great black trombones blared their apocalyptic revelations, and their terrible condemnation of the world, the flesh, and the devil. Theirs was a poetic idiom saved, by sincerity and the

heritage of a colorful imagination, from triteness. If in "Listen, Lord", they addressed the Alpha and Omega of things in a manner less reverent than the frigidity of the Christian's universal prayer, it is not to be doubted that their familiarity was bred not of contempt, but of the heart-felt liberty of servitors on easy speaking terms with their Master. What people not so privileged could apostrophize Christ so simply and so humanly as merely "Mary's Baby"?

In like manner certain technical crudities and dissonances can be explained away. The interpolation here and there of a definitely rhymed couplet among the lines of this vigorous free and easy poetry will not jar, when one reflects that if poetry is the language of inspiration, then these black trumpeters, manna-fed and thirst-assuaged by living water from the ever flowing rock, could well be expected to fly now and then beyond their own language barriers into the realms of poetic refinements of which they knew nothing, save by intuitive inspiration. And if on occasion the preacher ascended from *you* and *your* to *thee* and *thou*, this too is in keeping with his character.

To me **"The Creation"** and **"Go Down Death"** are unqualifiedly great poems. The latter is a magnificent expatiation and interpretation of the beatitudes; it justifies Job's "I know in Whom I have believed" to all the weary, sorrowbroken vessels of earth. It is a revelation of to what extent just men shall be made perfect. The repetitions in **"The Crucifixion"** are like hammer-strokes of agony.

It is a tribute to Mr. Johnson's genius that when a friend of mine recently read **"Go Down Death"** to an audience in Mr. Johnson's own natal town, an old wizened black woman, the relic of a day of simpler faith and more unashamed emotions than ours, wept and shouted. Perhaps many a modern pastor, logically trained and multidegreed, might retrieve a scattering flock, hungry for the bread of the soul, by reading one of these poems as a Sunday service. (pp. 221-22)

> *Countee Cullen, "And the Walls Came Tumblin' Down," in* The Bookman, *New York, Vol. LXVI, No. 2, October, 1927, pp. 221-23.*

Along This Way: The Autobiography of James Weldon Johnson (1933)

With irony and intelligence Mr. Johnson moves through the whole story of his life. (p. 1)

At sixty he . . . [became] professor of Creative Literature at Fisk University. He had already done distinguished work both in verse and prose, and as editor of two classic collections of Negro spirituals had helped to bring the spirit of his people into the main stream of American culture. He has now used his leisure, after years of intense activity, to tell his story. It is a book any man might be proud to have written about a life any man might be proud to have lived.

Readers of the autobiography may sometimes find it hard to understand the struggles which Mr. Johnson says he went through at the turning points of his career. In the light of the outcome he seems always to have chosen not only the best path but the one path to which his faculties could have guided him. It is true, of course, that if he had not made these happy choices he might have had no career to write about. Autobiographers are men who have made the right choices. Yet this life unrolls with something of the sureness and direction which can scarcely be described without reference to the mysteries of genius and destiny which enter into the life of a great man.

The United States has not deserved James Weldon Johnson. Fitted to be a statesman of high rank anywhere, he has been confined by race prejudice to action within a minority. There can be no question that this has limited him. His life deals with black America, or with black America in its relations to white, not with all America during the past half century. A white man of affairs of half Mr. Johnson's gifts might have come into contact with twice as many people of first-rate importance. What it must have cost James Weldon Johnson to realize this, as he must have realized it, he does not say or hint. He seems early to have accepted the unmistakable bounds within which he would have to work, to have made the best of them, and to have saved for clear-sighted action the force which another Negro might have spent in blind rebellion. To be teacher, lawyer, poet, consul, journalist was never enough for him.

Something had to be done about the plight of his race in America, and he has done as much as any man alive. His book is almost the whole history of the New Negro in the United States.

Along This Way is civilized in temper, ironical, urbane, deft and reflective. Mr. Johnson speaks plainly when plain speech is demanded by his theme, but he knows that the facts are louder than any outcry about them. And if fate has made him seldom able to forget that he is a Negro, nature has made him always able to remember that he is a man. He has had a great deal of pleasure in his life which he is as willing to recount as his pains and frustrations. His story is full-bodied, with plenty of poetry and comedy. An exceptional man, he has had exceptional experiences, but he narrates them without self-consciousness. He is a story teller worthy of his story. (pp. 1, 7)

> Carl Van Doren, "A Citizen of Whom America Can Be Proud," in New York Herald Tribune, *October 1, 1933, pp. 1, 7.*

For all readers, but perhaps more especially for Americans, this account of a crowded life must be a record of deep moment. Something similar might be said for many autobiographies, but seldom as appropriately as of this whose author has shone in such varied fields as literature, politics, law, music, diplomacy and social service. When it is realized that this author is a Negro, unquestionably a leader among his people in his own or any land, his story takes on a new emphasis. One pauses to honor in all humility the vision, the courage, the endurance which this man's career has called into play.

It has been too commonly supposed that Mr. Johnson himself was the central figure in his book, *The Autobiography of an Ex-Colored Man.* Now we learn that the desire

to correct this false impression was one of the reasons why Mr. Johnson wrote the present book. For Mr. Johnson differs fundamentally in many ways from that fictitious character who renounced his race and "married white." Mr. Johnson has had no wish to renounce his people. He has been proud of his race always, glorying in his opportunity to serve it in the breaking down of limitations and prejudices. He is grateful for the fact that he "was reared free from undue fear of or esteem for white people as a race; otherwise, the deeper implications of American race prejudice might have become a part of my subconscious as well as of my conscious self."

We hear in interesting detail of Mr. Johnson's human heritage; of one of his maternal great-grandmothers, who was Hestor Argo, the Haitian woman, and of that other who was Sarah, the African woman, who had made part of the cargo of a slave ship bound for Brazil, which a British man-of-war captured and took into Nassau. We are told of the father, James Johnson, whose uprightness was a byword in every community where he settled; and of the mother, Helen Louise Dillet, who received her education in the schools of New York City and was herself a teacher during a good many years of her life. It was after the two had removed to Jacksonville, Fla., that their son, James Weldon, was born and there grew up.

Meticulously the author relates it all. He seems to have sought to give each least happening its precise weight and to have built up the whole patiently block by block. The writing is careful and capable, though seldom forceful or in the very least sensational. All is recorded deliberately, with a nice sense of reason and balance, and with an intense seriousness.

We read of the author's infancy and first memories, of his school and college years, of his family and his friends; finally of his adult years. With such a multitude of achievements to be considered, one can hardly do more than list them. We have, then, Mr. Johnson's brilliant adventurings with his brother Rosamond, into New York's "Tin Pan Alley;" we have his principalship of Stanton School; his dramatic success in passing the bar examinations in Florida; we have the years of his consulship, the publication of his books of prose and of verse, not forgetting the *Book of American Negro Spirituals* compiled jointly with his brother which remains supreme in its field; we have his public speaking; his efforts to bring about national legislation against lynching; we have his connection with the activities of the National Association for the Advancement of the Colored People. And at last we have his appointment to the chair of creative literature at Fisk University, a position which Mr. Johnson still holds.

James Weldon Johnson seems to have explored in person many of those wide avenues of opportunity which he covets for the Negro. The mere fact opens and points the way for his fellows. He has proved that America does not, cannot, close the door finally to any man capable of making a real contribution to the life of his country. Just because James Weldon Johnson has done all these things, no rational person can doubt that the prejudices and difficulties can, will, become nonexistent to other cultivated members of the Negro race. Mr. Johnson's own labors in behalf of

A postage stamp honoring Johnson.

Christian Science Monitor, *November 11, 1933, p. 12.*

James Weldon Johnson is without doubt in the front rank of our Negro Americans. Indeed, it may be doubted whether any other has lived so varied and successful a life. For he has been successively principal of a public school; the first Negro lawyer admitted to practice in Florida since Reconstruction days; a poet with immediate access to the leading magazines; the author of important books, and of what is known as the Negro's national hymn; an extraordinarily successful song writer in connection with his brother Rosamond, and the latter's equally remarkable stage and concert partner, Bob Cole; and a highly successful American Consul in Venezuela and Nicaragua, especially valuable because of his complete mastery of Spanish. But this is not all. He was for eleven years secretary of the invaluable National Association for the Advancement of Colored People, then an editorial writer of distinction, and now he is professor of Creative Literature at Fisk University. Surely it cannot be denied that this is a remarkable record. I shall not add, as so many do, that it is one of which any white man might be proud because it is precisely that kind of silly condescension which makes every cultivated Negro of this type feel as if he were being praised like Dr. Johnson's dog,—as James Weldon Johnson once suggests in this volume. The truth is that this Johnson is only among his peers when he is in the middle of the most interesting and worth while literary and musical set in New York—in which he is always a most welcome companion.

Mr. Johnson is personally modest, extremely quiet in manner, restrained, outwardly always calm, with his inner feelings well in hand, and making obeisance to no one, to no one inferior. His book portrays him well, for his narrative bears in general the rare stamp of these qualities. It would indubitably improve by condensation; too much space is given, for example, to the period of his childhood, which he is not great enough to warrant. If he carefully records all his successes he is surely entitled to do so, and it is not because they have been few. But there are moments when flashes of the deep feeling that burns behind every American Negro's exterior, burst through this quiet text, as when he sets forth in extraordinarily vivid, dramatic, and moving language his once facing death at the hands of a uniformed mob which would have killed him if he had turned his back—on the heinous charge that he had actually been alone in a Jacksonville park with a white woman! Nothing but his dauntless courage, and the fact that one of the militia officers remained a human being, saved him. That, and the all-important fact that the woman with whom he committed this dreadful offense was not white, but colored.

Most Southerners will not like this book. They are the ones who most need to read it, and not only because they are most of them ignorant of the existence of the ever-growing group of intellectuals of which Mr. Johnson is a shining exemplar. The South really believes that it alone knows the Negro, knows him for what he is worth, knows how to "keep him in his place." Yet at best it only knows the few laborers or others with whom the average white individual comes into contact. It refuses to take note of the

the advancement of the colored people have done much to hasten this outcome. Glowingly he pleads for means which shall put an end to the horrors of lynching and to other abuses. Thoughtful Americans will do well to heed such a plea as this:

> The common-denominator opinion in the United States about American Negroes is, I think, something like this: These people are here; they are here to be shaped and molded and made into something different and, of course, better; they are here to be helped; here to be given something; in a word, they are beggars under the nation's table waiting to be thrown the crumbs of civilization. However true this may be, it is also true that the Negro has helped to shape and mold and make America; that he has been a creator as well as a creature; that he has been a giver as well as a receiver. It is, no doubt, startling to contemplate that America would not and could not be precisely the America it is, except for the influence, often silent, but nevertheless potent, that the Negro has exercised in its making.

M. W., "Contribution of a Negro," in The

vast strides that the leaders like Johnson are making. The average Southerner even believes that he has the complete confidence of the Negro and his affection and liking. He will be undeceived if he peruses these pages of Mr. Johnson's and finds how the Negroes classify all white men as good and bad according to their attitude to the colored people. They will ascertain also that if the Southern white man thinks he knows the Negro, the Negroes certainly know him. Let us quote Mr. Johnson again:

> But one thing, they learned the white man with whom they had to deal. They learned him through and through; and without ever completely revealing themselves. Their knowledge of that white man's weaknesses as well as his strength came to be almost intuitive. And when they felt it futile to depend upon their own strength, they took advantage of his weaknesses—the blind side of arrogance and the gullibility that always goes with overbearing pride.

Most persons who have delved deep in the Negro question and spent years in pondering upon it eventually find themselves brought up against this fact whether they desire to face it or not. . . .

I must not give the impression that this book deals only with the hard and dreadful facts of the Negro's situation in America. It is full of most interesting accounts of Mr. Johnson's own rise, and his intellectual and artistic partnerships and friendships, his extraordinary service as Consul when the color line naturally broke down and he entertained the officers of our fleet from admiral to ensign. He made history in Nicaragua. In brief, Mr. Johnson has written more than a chronicle of himself. His own story is an inseparable part of the chronicle of his race, its aspirations, and its achievements. As such it will have a permanent place along with the autobiographies of Frederick Douglass, Booker Washington, Major Moton and others, and alongside the imperishable writings of W. E. B. DuBois.

> Oswald Garrison Villard, *"The Chronicle of a Successful Life," in* The Saturday Review of Literature, *Vol. X, No. 23, December 23, 1933, p. 369.*

The minute record of a human being's life, set down by himself, may be a fascinating form of literature. This is chiefly true when the human being is aware; and thus able to observe in retrospect and to interpret creatively all that has befallen him, and his relationship to events and to his fellows. It is to this creative interpretation, plus the power of almost "total recall," as Mrs. William Vaughn Moody named it, that *Along This Way* owes its singular interest. There are other factors, but it is from the stark picture of James Weldon Johnson, aware and sensitive and able to interpret, who has here written his autobiography, that the major interest of the book derives.

Born in Nassau, with a background which he paints in a few colorful pages, Mr. Johnson follows the fortunes of his family to Jacksonville, Florida, where he lived his boyhood. His picture of his parents, of his mother, Helen Louise Johnson, teacher, and his father, James Johnson, headwaiter at a great hotel—which the little boy thought that his father owned—and later a minister, (though not, as he said, "by trade")—these and the portraits of his grandparents are those of sturdy and definite personalities, with a sharp sense of righteousness, and a liking for good literature and for well-ordered surroundings. Mr. Johnson says of his later observation of his father: "This adaptation by my father of Christianity to life in good measure made a deeper impression on me than all the formal religious training I had been given."

The child's goings and comings, by "the fence of the barking dog" and to the church and the store, are built up in straight, clear narrative, on to the night when he fell asleep at the revival meeting and refused to be awakened until he had been carried home, and then, in explanation, claimed to have had a vision, describing and embellishing a picture of heaven which he had seen in a book. This vision he was obliged to repeat to others, "to my inward shame," and finally he was taken into the church as the result of it. At school he announced himself an agnostic. These experiences, he writes, led to "as nearly an emotional and intellectual a balance as I have reached."

All the Jacksonville boyhood, with its well-scaled narrative, its clear vignettes of persons, and its portrait of the city of that day, is given a thrilling interest as recorded by one retroactively conscious of his environment. Music, clothes, food, baseball, religion; the boy's jobs as brick-carrier and cart driver; love; the learning of Spanish—are all living experience. And it is so of the West Indian cobbler-tutor, the yellow fever of 1888, the time spent in the office of the cosmopolite—Dr. Summers, the early schoolteaching in the backwoods of Georgia, graduation at Atlanta University (with an oration on "The Destiny of the Human Race"); then the years as principal of Stanton School, which he made a high school; the failure of the newspaper which he started; and then, the thrilling experience of taking, without ever having attended a law school, the bar examination, given for two hours before a crowded courtroom, and by white men; and of his immediate admission to the Florida bar.

For it must be remembered that James Weldon Johnson is a Negro, and that his encounters with and his reactions to the white race form one of the spiritually invigorating phases of this story. Not, of course, the main phase—one of the values of the recital is in the autonomy of the narrator, the integrity of his individual contests and controls. But with that individual growth runs along many a social import of high value, such as his reactions to education, to religion and to race. His respect for and devotion to the Negro equals his respect for and devotion to the cause of the white, the brown or the red race—and this is a very great deal to say of a member of any race. All races are appraised by him solely with reference to their phenomenon of growth, of opportunity for growth. He says:

> If the jinnee should suddenly appear before me and say, 'Name some boon that you desire and it shall be granted,' I should reply, 'Grant me equal opportunity with other men, and the assurance of corresponding rewards for my efforts and what I may accomplish.' If, continuing, he should say, 'Name any race of which you would

like to be made a member, and it shall be done,'
I should be at a loss.

It is to be seen, from one so emancipated, so able to evaluate the human being in terms of humanity, that an estimate of the American white's problem in relation to the Negro, and of the Negro's attitude to the white majority's social interpretations in the matter, is of the very greatest moment. And that estimate, indeed, is implicit in the text, rather than in any utterance. One would say that it's suggested solution is made from the viewpoint of omniscience, as imagined by every highly-evolved religion or philosophy: *More light for every creature. And woe be unto those who withhold it.* This, the alleged slogan of civilization, is one which this autobiographer applies indifferently to all problems. If one wishes to make any exceptions whatever, it is with no instance from him. His humor is implicit in his text, too. Regarded with question in a restaurant, this Ph.D. begins to speak Spanish and at once quiets the questioning. Mr. Johnson's conclusion is that any Negro will do, save a Negro who is an American citizen. Asked to move into a "Jim Crow" car, this Phi Beta Kappa requests that the law be kept further and that two white men then sitting in the "Jim Crow" be moved into the first class car. This cannot reasonably be refused, but the men prove to be a maniac and his keeper, and the maniac's first act, in Mr. Johnson's vacated seat, is to thrust his manacled hands through the glass of the window.

The personal reaction is treated only twice, and one of the instances is Mr. Johnson's comment that in France he enjoyed the sense of being "just a human being . . . free from a sense of impending discomfort, insecurity, danger; free from the conflict with the Man-Negro dualism and the innumerable maneuvers in thought and behavior that it compels; free from the problems of the adjustments to a multitude of bans and taboos; free from special scorn, special tolerance, special condescension, special commiseration; free to be merely a man." For France has no social distinction complex which she can regard as a racial distinction.

The knowledge of the contribution which every race has to give to race culture came to James Weldon Johnson back in the 1890's. "I now began to grope toward a realization of the importance of the American Negro's cultural background and his creative folly art and to speculate on the superstructure of conscious art that might be reared upon them."

His brother, Rosamond Johnson, whose place is now unique as a composer and as a concert singer of spirituals, is his companion and sympathizer, and the story of their life in New York, writing light opera and songs, is highly interesting. Oscar Hammerstein sought them out, Smith and De Koven collaborated with them in "an attempt to bring a higher degree of artistry to Negro songs, especially with regard to the text." Amato and John McCormack sang **"Since You Went Away,"** Mr. Johnson's first published poem. His **"Sing a song full of the faith that the dark past has taught us"** is called the **"Negro National Hymn."** The Johnson Brothers and Will Marion Cook wrote two hundred songs for Broadway productions. They made a transcontinental trip and had a three-

months' European engagement. During all this New York period Mr. Johnson was also studying at Columbia.

Then the Colored Republican Club claimed him, and after Roosevelt's election Mr. Johnson was appointed United States consul at Puerto Cabello, Venezuela, and later at Carinto, Nicaragua. And it is strange to turn from these fascinating pages of colorful experience, even in Carinto, to the story of the days following his return to Jacksonville, in the American South. But from this return grew the beautiful and distinguished literary work for which James Weldon Johnson is now best known; and his sovereign service to both black and white races as secretary of the National Association for the Advancement of Colored People. His present post is that of professor of English at Fisk University.

Fine studies of Rosamond Johnson, of Grace Nail, his wife, and of innumerable interesting personalities met in his work and in his attendance at the Institute of Pacific Relations, add to the color and interest of the volume. The treatment of lynching is as restrained as a handling of that savage subject can well be. Mr. Johnson's last word is: " . . . man must continue to hope and struggle on; each day, if he would not be lost, he must with renewed courage take a fresh hold on life and face with fortitude the turns of circumstance. To do this, he needs to be able at times to touch God; let the idea of God mean to him whatever it may."

One likes to recall Carl Van Doren's wise and thrilling word about this autobiography: that "it is a book which any man might be proud to have written about a life which any man might be proud to have lived." (pp. 20-1)

> *Zona Gale, "An Autobiography of Distinction," in* The World Tomorrow, *Vol. XVII, No. 1, January 3, 1934, pp. 20-1.*

Lift Every Voice and Sing: Words and Music   (1970)

AUTHOR'S COMMENTARY

A group of young men [in Jacksonville] decided to hold on February 12 [1900] a celebration of Lincoln's birthday. I was put down for an address, which I began preparing; but I wanted to do something else also. My thoughts began buzzing round a central idea of writing a poem on Lincoln, but I couldn't net them. So I gave up the project as beyond me; at any rate, beyond me to carry out in so short a time; and my poem on Lincoln is still to be written. My central idea, however, took on another form. I talked over with my brother the thought I had in mind, and we planned to write a song to be sung as a part of the exercises. We planned, better still, to have it sung by schoolchildren—a chorus of five hundred voices.

I got my first line:—Lift ev'ry voice and sing. Not a startling line; but I worked along grinding out the next five. When, near the end of the first stanza, there came to me the lines:

> Sing a song full of the faith that the dark past has
> taught us.

> Sing a song full of the hope that the present has
> brought us

the spirit of the poem had taken hold of me. I finished the stanza and turned it over to Rosamond.

In composing the two other stanzas I did not use pen and paper. While my brother worked at his musical setting I paced back and forth on the front porch, repeating the lines over and over to myself, going through all of the agony and ecstasy of creating. As I worked through the opening and middle lines of the last stanza:

> God of our weary years,
> God of our silent tears,
> Thou who has brought us thus far on our way,
> Thou who hast by Thy might
> Let us into the light,
> Keep us forever in the path, we pray;
> Lest our feet stray from the places, our God,
>   where we met Thee,
> Lest, our hearts drunk with the wine of the
>   world, we forget Thee . . .

I could not keep back the tears, and made no effort to do so. I was experiencing the transports of the poet's ecstasy. Feverish ecstasy was followed by that contentment—that sense of serene joy—which makes artistic creation the most complete of all human experiences.

When I had put the last stanza down on paper I at once recognized the Kiplingesque touch in the two longer lines quoted above; but I knew that in the stanza the American Negro was, historically and spiritually, immanent; and I decided to let it stand as it was written.

As soon as Rosamond had finished his noble setting of the poem he sent a copy of the manuscript to our publishers in New York, requesting them to have a sufficient number of mimeographed copies made for the use of the chorus. The song was taught to the children and sung very effectively at the celebration; and my brother and I went on with other work. After we had permanently moved away from Jacksonville, both the song and the occasion passed out of our minds. But the schoolchildren of Jacksonville kept singing the song; some of them went off to other schools and kept singing it; some of them became schoolteachers and taught it to their pupils. Within twenty years the song was being sung in schools and churches and on special occasions throughout the South and in some other parts of the country. Within that time the publishers had recopyrighted it and issued it in several arrangements. Later it was adopted by the National Association for the Advancement of Colored People, and is now quite generally used throughout the country as the **"Negro National Hymn."** The publishers consider it a valuable piece of property; however, in traveling round I have commonly found printed or typewritten copies of the words pasted in the backs of hymnals and the songbooks used in Sunday schools, Y.M.C.A.'s, and similar institutions; and I think that is the method by which it gets its widest circulation. Recently I spoke for the summer labor school at Bryn Mawr College and was surprised to hear it fervently sung by the white students there and to see it in their mimeographed folio of songs.

Nothing that I have done has paid me back so fully in satisfaction as being the part creator of this song. I am always thrilled deeply when I hear it sung by Negro children. I am lifted up on their voices, and I am also carried back and enabled to live through again the exquisite emotions I felt at the birth of the song. My brother and I, in talking, have often marveled at the results that have followed what we considered an incidental effort, an effort made under stress and with no intention other than to meet the needs of a particular moment. The only comment we can make is that we wrote better than we knew. (pp. 154-56)

> *James Weldon Johnson, in his* Along This Way: The Autobiography of James Weldon Johnson, *The Viking Press, 1933, 418 p.*

———————

Mozelle Thompson's drawings make *Lift Every Voice and Sing: Words and Music* a powerful book. They suggest emotions rather than portray detail. But his more literal drawing of three exuberant leaping boys that accompanies the lines "Let our rejoicing rise /High as the list'ning skies, /Let it resound loud as the rolling sea" is a splendid example of the fulfillment of the illustrator's function.

> *Pamela Marsh, in a review of "Lift Every Voice and Sing: Words and Music," in* The Christian Science Monitor, *November 12, 1970, p. B2.*

Lift ev'ry voice and sing
Till earth and heaven ring,
Ring with the harmonies of Liberty;

Written originally by the two Johnson brothers for a school celebration of Lincoln's Birthday, on February 12, 1900, this famous song is often called the **"Negro National Anthem."** In her introduction, Augusta Baker quotes James Johnson as saying that nothing he had ever done paid him back so fully as being part creator of this song.

The words are given their full measure of dignity in the powerful illustrations of Mozelle Thompson.

> *Rose H. Agree, in a review of "Lift Every Voice and Sing: Words and Music," in* Instructor, *Vol. LXXX, No. 4, December, 1970, p. 98.*

Lift Every Voice. . . . is a hymn known in every African-American community as the national anthem. Written originally by the famous poet James Weldon Johnson and his brother, it is but another aspect of black cultural life virtually unknown in the rest of America. For this reason alone, this book is important, but it is also compelling for its excellent charcoal illustrations which trace with dignity and drama the history of the African American. These drawings (which depict the K.K.K., voter registration, the congregation of a black southern church, a chain gang, children playing), coupled with the strong words of the song, result in a memorable and important book which deserves a place on the children's shelf.

> *Lynne Stewart, in a review of "Lift Every Voice and Sing: Words and Music," in* School Library Journal, *Vol. 17, No. 4, December, 1970, p. 36.*

[The follówning excerpt is from the introduction to Lift Every Voice and Sing: Words and Music.]

Of all the songs the [Johnson] brothers wrote together **"Lift Every Voice and Sing"** became the one which made the most lasting contribution to the musical world and to black culture.

The depth and power of **"Lift Every Voice"** has spanned the generations. Popular entertainers record it; choral groups include it in their concerts; it has been reprinted in many song books; a black radio station signs off with it every night. But most important, *people* sing it. Wherever people, young and old, black and white, gather together in fellowship, sooner or later they are sure to lift their voices and sing this song of faith and courage, hope and joy. (p. 5)

> *Augusta Baker, "About the Song and the Brothers Who Wrote It: James Weldon Johnson 1871-1938, J. Rosamond Johnson 1873-1954," in* Lift Every Voice and Sing: Words and Music *by James Weldon Johnson and J. Rosamond Johnson, Hawthorn Books, Inc., Publishers, 1970, pp. 4-5.*

Maira Kalman

1949(?)-

American author and illustrator of picture books.

Major works include *Stay Up Late* (written by David Byrne, 1987), *Hey Willy, See the Pyramids* (1988), *Sayonara, Mrs. Kackleman* (1989), *Max Makes a Million* (1990), *Max in Hollywood, Baby* (1992).

INTRODUCTION

Described by critic Kurt Andersen as a "hopped-up late-night Dr. Seuss," Kalman is a highly regarded author and illustrator whose books are known for their humorous and energetic verbal style and vibrant illustrations reminiscent of much twentieth-century art. Considered an especially inventive creator of picture books noted for their hipness and esotenc quality, she is credited with introducing young people to aspects of contemporary culture through humor. Her books typically feature the dreamlike adventures of children and animals in urban and exotic settings, and are particularly noted for their use of irony and allusion. Critics have praised Kalman's prose, maintaining that while it contains complicated words and is occasionally beyond the grasp of young children, its quickly paced lyricism and humorous qualities elicit a positive response from readers. Commentators have additionally lauded Kalman as an illustrator, drawing attention to echoes and parodies in her work of a wide range of painters and styles, including Chagall, Matisse, Picasso, "bad" art, folk art, and Chicago imagism. Many of her drawings feature extravagant coloration, geometric shapes, and the precise representation of detail to convey a chaotic sense of movement in her subject matter as well as an ironic commentary on the adult world.

Kalman was born in Israel and grew up in Riverdale, New York. Early in her life, she felt the vocation to be a writer and, after studying piano at the High School of Music and Art in New York City, went to New York University to study literature. Upon graduating, Kalman turned to drawing and collaborated with her husband on a number of graphic design projects; her own work as a designer includes fabrics, textiles, and album covers. Her first children's book illustrations were for David Byrne's *Stay Up Late,* in which a boy and a girl prevent their baby brother from sleeping while the adults remain oblivious to their antics. The pictures for *Stay Up Late,* a work taken from a song on the album *Little Creatures* by Byrne's rock group Talking Heads, possesses the exuberant, modern style that appears in her self-composed books. In *Hey Willy, See the Pyramids,* Lulu tells her brother Alexander a series of bizarre bedtime stories. Kalman, who named the protagonists of *Hey Willy* after her two children, presents the conversation between sister and brother in the darkness, while the stories Lulu narrates are vividly and

ironically represented in a deliberately childlike manner which some critics found borders on surrealism. Lulu and Alexander are also featured in Kalman's second book, *Sayonara, Mrs. Kackleman,* in which the pair travel alone to Japan. Employing a stream-of-consciousness style, this work is lauded for its frenetic assemblage of both concrete and fantastic images, reflecting the way in which children might actually remember a visit to a foreign country. One of Lulu's stories in *Hey Willy, See the Pyramids* concerns Max Stravinsky, a dog who is also a poet and the protagonist of three of Kalman's later works: *Max Makes a Million, Ooh-La-La (Max in Love)* (1991), and *Max in Hollywood, Baby.* In these books Max successively explores New York while dreaming of moving to Paris; actually travels to Paris, where he meets other artists and falls in love with a dalmatian called Crêpes Suzette; and goes to Hollywood to make a film. Critics assert that the Max books display the height of Kalman's inventiveness, noting that the visual texture of these stories is enhanced by such effects as a typeface face that changes size and position to suit the mood of the story and the witty parodies of famous painters and filmmakers. In addition to her books for children, Kalman is the author of the text for a museum catalog on the work of sculptor Alexander Calder.

AUTHOR'S COMMENTARY

If you're not too literal-minded—and this gifted author/artist's fans are not—you can trace the history of Maira Kalman's burgeoning artistic career in the life story of her latest picture book hero, Max the poet dog.

Max Stravinsky, first introduced via a cameo appearance in Kalman's *Hey Willy, See the Pyramids* as the Manhattan-bound dog with an unleashed imagination, is the star of *Max Makes a Million,* a work best described by narrator Max himself, who says, midway through, "If I didn't mention it before, I should mention now. This book is about dreamers. Wishful thinkers. Dreamy blinkers. Crazy nuts." (p. 32)

Like Max, Kalman is a firm believer in following one's own visions. "I think the greatest skill is to find the thing that's most you, and to be able to express it most naturally. The more instinctual the work is, the more successful it is," she says, speaking from her studio in New York City's Greenwich Village. Her search for self-expression has resulted in exotic picture books animated by an antic energy. Her vibrant color and word play are matched by a wit at once laconic and exuberant.

Max spent his formative years longing for escape; Kalman spent hers pursuing various art forms. Born in Israel and raised in Riverdale, N.Y., Kalman began her training early. "My mother decided that we had to have culture—all good girls have to have culture—and so I started taking piano lessons with this very serious piano teacher, and dance lessons with a children's ballet theater. She took us to a million concerts and a million museums. My sister went to the High School of Music and Art for art, and I followed in her footsteps, going there for music—piano."

"Music and Art was very eclectic and stimulating," she continues. "There were no limits. Of course, I stopped piano lessons the minute I graduated."

Almost as if it goes without saying, Kalman throws in, "Well, I always was writing. That, I thought, was my true voice, being a writer. I felt confident about that, from a young age. And then I wrote in college. I went to NYU for literature, of course, like all good cultured girls. The minute I graduated I stopped writing, and I started drawing. I decided that my writing was horrible, and that drawing would be a wonderful way of expressing nonverbally the imagery I had in my head. And it would be funnier."

The drawing led her to editorial illustration and design. (She collaborates with her husband, Tibor, who owns M & Co., a graphic design firm; her projects at the firm range from album covers to movie titles to textiles.) As her career developed, she kept on writing for herself, "until it seemed like the wise thing to do was to combine the two. It was a brainstorm: 'Oh, you can do both together. It's called a book!'"

Her first book project was illustrating *Stay Up Late,* which takes as its text her friend David Byrne's song of the same name on the Talking Heads album *Little Creatures.* The choice reflected not only Kalman's interest in music but her attitude toward books. "It was an important choice to say, 'The books I am going to do are going to be for adults *and* for children.' The Talking Heads song was a very definitive way to begin because it spoke to both audiences at the same time."

Placing the book was fairly easy. One publisher turned it down—"I don't even remember who it was," Kalman says, "but they thought it was about child abuse." (Describing a baby's arrival in a household, the lyrics include lines like "Sister, sister, he's just a plaything. / We want to make him stay up all night.") "They didn't see the humor in it at all," she recalls, "the love, the playfulness that goes on in the family."

Kalman and Byrne then went to Penguin USA, which had published Byrne's *True Stories,* and were directed to Nancy Paulsen, now publisher of the Puffin Books imprint. "They liked it immediately," Kalman says. "And the relationship with Nancy has developed since, so that her faith in me and the writing have grown."

After *Stay Up Late,* Kalman turned in her first solo book, *Hey Willy, See the Pyramids,* which featured two children named Lulu and Alexander who tell each other fantastic stories. (Another Kalman title bears a jacket that says, "The fact that [the author] has two children named Lulu and Alexander is pure coincidence"; Lulu is now nine and Alexander is six.) If *Stay Up Late's* "zesty artwork" and text channeled "wild and wooly excitement," as a *Booklist* reviewer wrote, *Hey Willy* went further yet: the art broke out of contained panels to fill spreads completely, and the text was even less linear, more impressionistic.

The fictional Lulu and Alexander went on a voyage to Japan in Kalman's next outing, *Sayonara, Mrs. Kackleman.* After that, says Kalman, "I left my children behind, because they were getting too much attention. They'd have to pay a lot of money to psychiatrists or something if I put them in too many books. But they may reappear."

In Max, however, Kalman seems to have found a perfect fit. "The first glimmer of him was in *Hey Willy.* There was something in his story. I wanted to travel, and I wanted to take people to other places, so somewhere I realized that this dog, this poet who desperately wanted to leave, would be the means."

Max's departures are more than geographical. "Good writing," Kalman suggests, "liberates you, it takes you out of the mundane and to an extremely inspiring and creative level. It's like good music, good art, good anything—it inspires you rather than depresses you."

Why a dog? "It's more a metaphor than an actual animal: 'you treat me like a dog'; 'it's a dog's life,' etc. I think of this miserable dog whom nobody understands. It's the Russian-misery gene in me."

The Max titles in particular are studded with playful visual and verbal references to art and literature. "Architecture and music and painting have always been fascinating to me, an organic part of our lives. I make references to all the things that I see, including paintings. I have my favorites, of course . . . Matisse and Chagall are probably the two that are the strongest."

Allusions to these painters are prominent in her work. "I choose things that are interesting and funny for me, and I think they would be funny for children too. At the same time they're laughing, they're finding out about, say, this guy named Marcel Duchamp."

The language, too, is rich. Kalman relies on context to explain difficult vocabulary and, she adds, "the words will have music. When you read William Steig, the vocabulary is clearly way beyond children, but it's so lyrical and so poetic that it doesn't matter at all.

"I get letters from adults and from children," she continues. "They all have the same reaction: 'It's really funny' and 'You made us laugh.' The adults can see the different ideas and avenues of discussion that you can pursue with a child about the references, visual and literary, and the kids just look at all the characters and think that they'd like to do the same things.

"A relationship with a child is the most unlimited one you can have, creatively, and to put rigid constrictions on that is sort of scary, which tells you about most books for children. To me, 99% don't inspire you at any level. They're comforting, and they're nice, but they aren't books that take you over the top in some way. I don't know what the motivation is in publishing—look at *Eloise,* how would that fare today? Would that get published today? Would that sell well today?"

Her books' extravagant imagery gets an added fillip from their design—by M & Co., of course. Kalman says she gets "obsessive" about design, typography, paper. "It's all to create books that aren't 'product,' that are, in the best sense, books, literature," she states.

Kalman's creative urge is leading in new directions. This November, to coincide with its "Celebrating Calder" exhibit, the Whitney Museum in New York City will publish *Roarr: Calder's Circus,* with text by Kalman and photographs of the Alexander Calder work taken by Donatella Brun. Doris Palca, head of the Whitney's publications and sales, says Kalman and Calder are a serendipitous match, "grownups who love to play." For now, distribution is limited to museum stores, but Kalman says "We're hoping somebody will pick it up and distribute it all over the country. If not, we'll cry."

Given her fertile imagination, it's not surprising to hear that Kalman has a lot on the boards. "I wish Max would go to Africa. I'm also working on stories my mother told me about her childhood in Russia. My mother's life is a springboard for a lot of things that I think about.

"I'm also thinking about a math book—*my* version of math, which I think might be interesting—an emotional math book, with stories about addition and multiplication, like '14 very, very angry women ran after 14 screaming children.' " Whatever Kalman's next equations might be, you can be sure that they'll add up to something wonderful. (pp. 32-3)

Elizabeth Devereaux, "Maira Kalman's Many Muses," in Publishers Weekly, *Vol. 238, No. 43, September 27, 1991, pp. 32-3.*

GENERAL COMMENTARY

Jennet Conant

Maira Kalman has a motto: "Better a city calf than a country cow." The sentiment colors everything she does, from her hip and hilarious children's books to the bright, fanciful images she creates for an eclectic assortment of clients. Her witty, sophisticated style has won a devoted following, especially among young urban professionals whose tastes run to Alessi teapots and the Talking Heads.

Maira's literary career was, in fact, launched by David Byrne, the lead singer and lyricist for the Talking Heads. Noting that Talking Heads fans were having children, and that Mother Goose sing-alongs just weren't cutting it, in 1986, the two collaborated on a children's book called *Stay Up Late.* It was based on Byrne's song of the same name brought to life by Maira's wild and wacky creatures.

"It was and still is a good time to do children's books because the baby-boom generation is interested in new forms of art," says Maira, mother of Lulu, age six, and nine-year-old Alex. "And our generation has had such a prolonged adolescence that our taste is much closer to our kids' than our parents' was. I still feel like a child sometimes," quips the 42-year-old author, laughing. "It's the way I look at the world."

Maira's youthful sensibility is evident in the four books she has done on her own since *Stay Up Late,* her mischievous prose dancing around colorful, funny pictures that make you want to put crayon on paper. Her books take children around the world, to Egypt and other faraway places in *Hey, Willy, See the Pyramids,* and to Japan in *Sayonara, Mrs. Kackleman,* winking at cultural differences along the way: "You eat raw fish / a crazy dish. The way you bow / is really wow." In *Max Makes a Million* and her most recent book, *Ooh-la-la (Max In Love),* chronicling the adventures of an endearing poet dog, the text is packed with amusing allusions that appeal to all ages, leaving everyone in a "froufrou of delight," as Max himself might say.

According to the book jacket, Maira is a writer who lives in New York and "eats bon-bons by the barrel."

But really, she is much more than that. Together with her husband, Tibor Kalman, who has his own graphic design firm, M & Co., she has been writing, painting and illustrating for more than 12 years. The two met at New York University in 1968, and the meeting of minds was instant and complete, marking the beginning of an "instinctive collaboration."

In the early '70s, Tibor became the creative director of Barnes & Noble, and she helped with many of the advertising campaigns, graphics and store displays. "He's the practical one, I'm much more dreamy," says Maira of their partnership. "He's always telling me, 'Let your mind go. Just come up with an idea and we'll worry about how to do it later.' " Today, she's the in-house idea person at M & Co. "Projects just pop up," she says citing an advertising campaign for a shopping mall in Osaka and T-shirts and invitations for the visiting Cirque du Soleil. (pp. 171, 191-92)

At present, Maira is immersed in the next installment of her Max book series, tentatively entitled **Max in Hollywood.** She traveled to Los Angeles to research the book— "I suffer for my art," she jokes—and would like to visit China and Africa next. "Now everything that happens in my life has a reason, it goes into the books," she says, "It never ends."

Meanwhile, she is fielding movie and theatrical offers on behalf of her painterly pooch, but they haven't cut any deals yet. "Max is talking big deals to big producers," she explains, "but he's very nervous." (p. 192)

> *Jennet Conant, "Dream Weaver," in* Harper's Bazaar, *No. 3363, March, 1992, pp. 179, 191-92.*

TITLE COMMENTARY

Stay Up Late (1987)

[*Stay Up Late is written by David Byrne.*]

Kalman's paintings accompany the words to "Stay Up Late," the Talking Heads song. The action in this book is all in the pictures. A girl and boy somewhat cruelly entertain themselves by preventing their baby brother from sleeping—yanking and tossing him, pulling his hair, blasting him with music: "He's just a little plaything / Why not wake him up?" Meanwhile, adults are shown drinking, dancing, day-dreaming or napping, but not paying much attention to the children. Kalman uses a pseudochildish composition and style—imaginative and energetic, with lots of inventive asides—but her art has a mean-spirited edge that takes its cue from the lyrics: "We want to make him stay up all night." This book has a definite appeal for hip adults, but it's not for the literal-minded child.

> *A review of "Stay Up Late," in* Publishers Weekly, *Vol. 232, No. 11, September 11, 1987, p. 89.*

Strictly for the hippest of families, this outlandish interpretation of Talking Heads David Byrne's song captures the wild and woolly excitement when a new baby comes on the scene. The older sister who is describing the pandemonium thinks that baby's cute all right, but "Why not wake him up?" Once awake, everyone wants to hold him, feed him, and play with him. Sister, with sibling surety, thinks playing means pulling him by his hair or just dancing him around the room. The zesty artwork is totally New Wave: geometric shapes, bright colors, and far-out images (baby has green hair, which he wears sticking straight up, à la Ed Grimley). Similar in style to Henrik Drescher's art, these two-page spreads with squared-off

From Hey Willy, see the Pyramids, *written and illustrated by Maria Kalman.*

pictures are filled with humorous asides that parents and kids will find amusing, each on their own level. Offbeat to the max. (pp. 390-91)

Ilene Cooper, in a review of "Stay Up Late,"
in Booklist, *Vol. 84, No. 4, October 15, 1987,*
pp. 390-91.

[Editor's Note: The following excerpt was revised by the critic for this edition.] If all the eccentricities characteristic of contemporary life were to be laid end to end, they'd possibly end up pointing directly to this zizzy star of a picture book that burst onto the children's book scene in 1987. On the surface, this *New York Times* Best Illustrated Picture Book delightfully addresses a simple event: a family celebrating the arrival at home of a new baby with friends, dancing, food, and merriment "all night long." Closer analysis, however, reveals an internal intricacy in textual and visual elements that may well place this book squarely within a postmodernist reference.

Textually, **Stay Up Late** takes its fundamental idea, structure, vocabulary, and even title from the rock song "Stay Up Late," by David Byrne, from the Talking Heads' album *Little Creatures*. It begins in a sing-song way:

> Mommy had
> a little baby.
> There he is
> fast asleep.
> He's just
> a little plaything.
> Why not
> wake him up?
> Cute, cute
> little baby.
> Little pee pee
> little toes.
> Now he's
> coming to me.
> Crawl across
> the floor.
> Baby, baby
> please let me hold him.
> I want to make him
> stay up all night.

These lyrics—with their hip-hop connections. jump-cut perspectives, and alternating arrangement of simple sentences and partial phrases linked together in a kind of loosely sprung verse—immediately situate readers in quirky time. This quirkiness is heightened by the element of uncertainty since all the characters in the book remain unnamed, from the baby who occupies center stage to the surrounding family members and friends. This lack of any personal identification flattens the narrative out and, on a different level, offers readers little meaningful entrance into the story beyond a superficial level. But this should come as no surprise since such language and vocabulary are characteristic of most rock artwork anyway, a form in both music and video that Dick Hebdige tellingly identifies in his analysis of a later Talking Heads' production, "Road to Nowhere," as primarily "designed to 'tell an image' rather than to 'tell a story.' " While there is nothing inherently "wrong" with such structurings, Hebdige's distinction is an intriguing one to think about when looking

at Kalman's book and its application of the fey, ironic lyrics of the Talking Heads to the picture book format.

Visually, Kalman's colorful, off-kilter pictures are a criss-cross collection that skips across an amazing set of artistic boundaries: "bad" art, punk/funk, folk art, 1950s hip, New Wave, and Chicago imagist styles are mixed zip-zap in her work. For example, one of the three double-paged pictures in the book shows an eccentric assembly of funkily attired family members as ever gathered toasting the new baby at some remote point east of midnight in a dining room that seems to have come right out of a set for a Xavier Cugat movie. Situated as it is at the book's exact midpoint, it symbolically suggests the very heart of the story and commands our attention and commentary. Two family members or friends drink fiery bombas; other individuals, seated around a table with a lime-colored tablecloth, stare blankly at the reader. Still others, apparently not associated with the celebration, animate the deperspectivized, child- and folk-art picture plane with their own quirky grins and gesticulations, all of which veer off in angular directions. The entire celebration is set against a peach and lemon chiffon background color that calls to mind the sunny, pastel beaches of Florida. Other illustrations suggest affinities with the eccentric, stick-style paintings of Chicago artists Hollis Sigler and Phyllis Bramson, painters whom many critics consider to be working with a postmodernist aesthetic vocabulary.

Is there an end to all this visual and textual pandemonium in **Stay Up Late,** or does it go on forever? Who knows? Maybe the party ends on the final story page, but it could just as easily continue on the back cover of the book, where the family members are depicted seemingly floating in space, above it all, being carried far away from us in their wild exuberance. We look at them and they appear to be still dancing way up in a yellow sky surrounded by dozens of green, disconnected, story-related words that hang in free space like stars. Beneath their feet, this extended, crazy stanza twinkles with its own edgy light:

> Here's a funny chair. And a funny dog.
> A man has really long arms. Nice shoes!
> What are these people having for dinner?
> Here's a baby. Green hair. Dancing. The
> baby is hungry. Stars. Cars. Turn
> the page now?

So are we at the end or what? The imperative / interrogative statement "Turn the page now?" clearly gives us no clue and leaves us on ambivalent narrative terrain: there are no more pages to turn.

The postmodernist affection for pure discontinuity, thematic ambiguity, and chaos theory may have never found a more resonant structure at the primary level than **Stay Up Late.** This is a picture book that zooms around in its own orbit, leaving a collection of question marks and exclamation points scattered in its quirky path. (pp. 152-54)

Nicholas Paley, "Postmodernist Impulses and
the Contemporary Picture Book: Are There
Any Stories to These Meanings?" in Journal of
Youth Services in Libraries, *Vol. 5, No. 2,*
Winter, 1992, pp. 151-61.

Hey Willy, See the Pyramids (1988)

The pyramids? Well, sort of. This is a new-wave cornucopia of narrative and visual fragments that comprise the various bedtime stories Lulu tells her little brother Alexander. Here, for example, is the "tiny story": "Four very tiny people walked right by me on the way to school. No one knew where they were going, but they were walking very fast and carrying little instruments." The accompanying illustration features, along with the very tiny people, a flying bunny, some children with lunch boxes, a palm tree, a dog on a unicycle, and a teepee or two, one of which may be a sailboat. Deliberately naive in perspective and color, the pictures combine a self-consciously childlikeness with a free-floating irony. Although YA's may enjoy the feeling of being in on a joke, younger readers won't appreciate the hipper-than-thou tone that permeates both pictures and text, and it is doubtful as well that they will appreciate the absurdity for its own sake, untouched as it is by wit, narrative sense, or genuine playfulness. (p. 12)

> *Roger Sutton, in a review of "Hey Willy, See the Pyramids," in* Bulletin of the Center for Children's Books, *Vol. 42, No. 1, September, 1988, pp. 11-12.*

This one is far, far out, but has a heart of gold: its premise is a sister who patiently tells stories to the little brother who wakes her in the middle of the night—not a million stories, but more than the five he originally bargains for.

The stories are very brief, contain characters from the children's family, and make sense in the way that images sliding across the mind as you fall asleep make sense. (One entire story—"green face": "My cousin Ervin has a green face and orange hair. He is a scientist and he told me about germs and about something that is called nothing. His mother has very small ears but she hears everything.") The illustrations are childlike, imaginative, and surreal; their swell, bright colors contrast with the white text on black pages where the kids talk and finally "both sink in / and see flying chairs / and green hats / and pink things / and sink some and / slowly sink / into sleep." Outlandish, but born of genuine creativity and understanding. Try it. (pp. 1528-29)

> *A review of "Hey Willy, See the Pyramids," in* Kirkus Reviews, *Vol. LVI, No. 20, October 15, 1988, pp. 1528-29.*

Lovers of the offbeat, this one's for you. It's night (white print on black pages). A boy asks for a story from his sister, Lulu, and oh, what stories she tells. There's one about the very big woman walking down the street with three cross-eyed dogs, and another about the three cross-eyed dogs going to a fancy restaurant and getting a good table. The odd story poems, only paragraphs long, are matched by far-out artwork that mixes murky and bright colors and matches elongated shapes with miniature figures. Children will probably respond more to the book's wild feel than to the actual content. In any case, for the right child, this could be a mind-stretcher.

> *Ilene Cooper, in a review of "Hey Willy, See the Pyramids," in* Booklist, *Vol. 85, No. 11, February 1, 1989, p. 939.*

Sayanara, Mrs. Kackleman (1989)

With so many picture books, the question is whether or not children will understand them. With this book, the question is refreshingly reversed; that is, can adults possibly appreciate this child's-eye view of Japan as much as children will?

Kalman presents Lulu and Alexander's trip to Japan through their own vivid recollections. Some of their experiences are very down to earth, others have a wonderful Chagall-like quality of dreaminess, while still others are downright silly. This surrealistic travelogue is actually very close to how a real child might record his or her experiences when visiting a foreign country. The illustrations capture the simplicity of children's artwork, while at the same time providing lots of the imaginative intricacies that children find fascinating. Adults may be somewhat unnerved by the hopscotch skips and jumps from realism to ridiculousness, but children probably won't even notice.

While Kalman's book is by no means a reference source on Japan, it makes up for it by recounting what is truly memorable about a trip abroad—not the guidebook statistics, but the personal experiences that stick in one's memory long after the details have been forgotten.

> *Cathryn A. Camper, in a review of "Sayanora, Mrs. Kackleman," in* The Five Owls, *Vol. IV, No. 1, September-October, 1989, p. 8.*

With the same visual verve she brought to the daring but ill-conceived **Hey Willy, Look at the Pyramids,** Kalman here disciplines her considerable talent to the demands of a story. . . . Surrealistic twinges are everywhere in both pictures and text: a haiku-recruiting frog, shoes for dinner, "a beautiful movie star named Fujiko" who throws a party for an intriguing collection of clowns and clones. The visual whimsy is consistently amusing, but several of the compositions lack strong focus. This is post-modern with a vengeance, yet it's grounded by a sensible (but funny) story, and the bond between Lulu and Alexander is a loving core. Dreams and reality collide in witty ways, and underneath all the zaniness is a true and affectionate portrait of Japan.

> *Roger Sutton, in a review of "Sayonara, Mrs. Kackleman," in* Bulletin of the Center for Children's Books, *Vol. 43, No. 3, November, 1989, p. 63.*

In **Sayonara, Mrs. Kackleman,** Maira Kalman has captured perfectly the child's sense of wonder and has created a funny, exuberant and inventive introduction to Japan for people of all ages. Like her previous picture book, **Hey Willy, See the Pyramids,** this is a travelogue that follows Lulu and her little brother Alexander on their journey to a distant, foreign place. Lulu is our guide on this wondrous adventure, recounting in her own breathless way whatever seems to come to her mind, whether it be observations about the way the Japanese look or eat or bathe, or simply one of the little poems that Alexander is constantly composing.

Here is Lulu on the Tokyo subway: "The subway was shining and quiet. The workers stood in crisp uniforms.

The train smoothed into the station and was full of people. We were like marshmallows all stuffed together in a bag bouncing along, but nobody stuck their elbow in my ear." And here is the illustration: the train packed like a cattle car, the dull-suited men and women entering and exiting in polite, orderly lines, looking every bit like candy moving along the conveyor belt in Willy Wonka's factory.

We read the word "smoothed" here and know immediately that we are in the hands of the right guide; it is a child's word, and dead-on. Lulu and Alexander, in turn, have their own guide, a lovely, kimono-clad woman named Hiroko, who seems capable of taking anything in stride—including Alexander's salutory poem:

> Hey Hiroko,
> are you loco?
> Would you like
> a cup of cocoa?

It is Hiroko who takes Lulu and Alexander on the subway, to a Japanese school, to a noodle shop (where they are "served oodles and poodles of noodles" and where they learn to slurp them down with gusto, "which is a perfectly perfectly fine thing to do in Japan"). Strolling by a rock garden, they watch the gardener use a long, needle-pointed pole to pick up each leaf as it falls on the naked gravel. A rather tedious job, no doubt, but one made markedly less so by the presence of a frog who recites haiku.

In every scene, Ms. Kalman (who also illustrated David Byrne's *Stay Up Late*) fills the page—and our minds—with a wild assortment of colorful images, some based on the facts of the story and place, others a product of Lulu's and Alexander's vivid imaginations. For dinner, Hiroko takes the children to a restaurant, where they are required to surrender their shoes. While seated at the low table, Lulu tells us, "Alexander was sure they were cooking our shoes. Shoe soup? Shoe sandwiches? Shoe pie? But really it was rice and vegetables tied with tiny seaweed bows." Throughout the book, the illustrations correspond to this sort of fantasizing, with some pretty hilarious and expansive results.

Tireless, Hiroko leads the two children to a Godzilla movie, a fish market, a temple, an outdoor bath and a Noh play, where Alexander falls soundly asleep (I must admit to having done the same). She takes them for a ride on the bullet train.

And then, with a last good-bye poem from Alexander to their new friends, Lulu takes him home again—to rest up, no doubt, for yet another adventure.

In both word and image, Maira Kalman has created a picture book that is in perfect harmony with the way children think, speak and fantasize. She draws no limits here, but instead presents the world as an open book.

I am already looking forward to reading it again. (pp. 25, 49)

> *John Burnham Schwartz, in a review of "Sayonara, Mrs. Kackleman," in* The New York Times Book Review, *November 12, 1989, pp. 25, 49.*

Max Makes a Million (1990)

Every now and then, a character in literature exerts a kind of magnetic field on the reader. The force of his or her personality, speaking in a fully individualized, first-person voice, grabs us like a carnival barker and just won't let go. Holden Caulfield had that effect on a generation; Augie March came close; there have been a few others as well, but their voices aren't necessarily limited to "grown-up" books. Especially now that Max—dreamer, dog, and poet—has had his say.

Anyone who remembers *Stay Up Late,* in which Maira Kalman supplied suitably wild illustrations to the lyrics of a David Byrne song, knows to expect the unexpected from this delightfully unbuttoned writer and artist. But even familiarity with Kalman's other books can't quite prepare you for the new-wave frenzy of *Max Makes a Million.* It's a simple story—a poet, who happens to be a dog, dreams of selling his poems and moving from New York to Paris—but what matters here is texture, not story. And *Max* is loaded with texture. In a perfect blending of words and pictures, Kalman creates pages that jump with the syncopated rhythms and Day-Glo colors of city life. Max dreams of moving to Paris—"I want to say, before anything, that dreams are very important"—but, in the meantime, he finds plenty to inspire him in New York: "That crazy quivering wondering wild city. A city like an enormous orchestra. A bebop city . . . " The thing that gets Max's heart pounding about New York is that there's just so much stuff—stuff to see, like Mrs. Hoogenschmidt wearing a fish on her head; stuff to hear, like Mr. Van Tiegham playing his drumsticks on garbage cans, lampposts, metal doors, and building walls; stuff to taste, like lemon drops from Baby Henry's Candy Shop; and, of course, stuff to feel, like love for his best friend and fellow artist, Bruno, who paints invisible paintings.

Kalman is a very different kind of artist than Bruno. Anything but invisible, her wonderfully witty, remarkably detailed paintings, a battleground of competing colors, provide the perfect visual metaphor for the avalanche of sensory delights that awaits Max on the sidewalks of New York. It is narrative voice that makes Max such a forceful character, but it is perfectly integrated artwork that allows the voice to sing.

One can almost hear the opposition marshalling its arguments: Yes, it's textured; yes, it's wonderful in a weird sort of way, but it's not for children. They won't understand it. They won't recognize that when Max talks about going to Paris, the words on the page are in the shape of the Eiffel Tower, or that when he describes New York, his sentences swing to the rhythm of a Thelonious Monk piano solo. So what if they don't recognize any of that. *Max* isn't about cultural literacy; it's about energy. Adults may need books or music to rekindle their energy, but kids have plenty of the real stuff. And they're sure to recognize that Max does, too. The story of Max and his dreams is finally a celebration of eccentricity in all its forms. There are no value judgments here, no morals, no pigeonholes. The world shows its stuff, and Max laps it up, treasuring each element for its own particularity and responding with a satisfied "Ha!" Kids react to life that way naturally, at least until adults teach them about principles. No, this is definitely a book for children—and for adults with enough courage and energy left to look at life the way Max does. Ha!

> *Bill Ott, "Max Makes a Million, by Maira Kalman," in* Booklist, *Vol. 87, No. 3, October 1, 1990, p. 343.*

In this bohemian celebration, Max the dog, the poet, the dreamer, is back. His struggle for acceptance since *Hey Willy, See the Pyramids* has not been easy—Max has had to post his poems on a wall at the corner of Pastrami and Salami Streets for his fellow New Yorkers to see. Even as he pines for Paris, Max admits that New York City is fine by him: ". . . a jumping, jazzy city, a shimmering, stimmering triple-decker sandwich kind of city." In this unique blend of reality and fantasy, intermingled words and images seem influenced by such strange sources as Mamie Eisenhower's wardrobe, the Jazz Age and the Theatre of the Absurd. Banter that rings with sophistication is well matched by the esoteric illustrative approach readers have come to expect from Kalman. Although there is much to glean from an unhurried single reading, this fanciful creation yields its greatest treasures through repeated visits.

> *A review of "Max Makes a Million," in* Publishers Weekly, *Vol. 237, No. 41, October 12, 1990, p. 60.*

First introduced in *Hey Willy, See the Pyramids,* Max, the poet dog who wants to live in Paris, is trying to make his dream come true while living in "that crazy quivering wondering wild city"—New York. His friends include Bruno, an artist who paints invisible paintings; the mysterious twins Otto and Otto; and Marcello, a waiter / architect who designs upsidedown houses. Kalman introduces readers to Max' world with a text that jumps around the pages and forms itself into shapes such as the Eiffel Tower, the Guggenheim Museum, curves, or zigzags. The words themselves have the exuberant rhythm of nonsense verse and are best appreciated when read aloud. With references to pompadours, the theory of gravity, soirees, and canapes, it's clear that few young children will be able to read and understand this picture book by themselves. Kalman's wit will be best appreciated by adults, who may or may not be able to explain it to their kids. The illustrations feature wild, brightly colored modern art full of elongated fantasy figures. Chagall and Picasso have influenced her use of unexpected colors (green faces, blue hair) and method of outlining the features of her characters. The style is similar to her earlier works, but is more sophisticated and inventive. The book's strangeness will not appeal to everyone, but its message about following one's dreams at all costs is thoughtfully and imaginatively presented. (pp. 80-1)

> *Lucinda Snyder Whitehurst, in a review of "Max Makes a Million," in* School Library Journal, *Vol. 36, No. 12, December, 1990, pp. 80-1.*

Ooh-La-La (Max in Love) (1991)

Sometimes dreams aren't enough. In *Max Makes a Million,* that irrepressible poet pooch Max dreamed of making a million and moving from New York to Paris. He did both, but when we pick up his story in Gay Paree, Max is tres bleu. In the city of love, Max is alone. But not for long—not after he meets Crepes Suzette, a dazzling dalmation and the pianist at Crazy Wolf, where tout Paris goes to be seen. ("You played the legato, / my heart went staccato"). The dizzying spectacle of Kalman in full cry—mixing wildly surrealistic, pun-filled prose with the busiest, splashiest palette this side of Jackson Pollock—is on display at its most unbridled here. Each two-page spread is a smorgasbord of shapes, sounds, and colors that leave us reeling with vertiginous delight. If the life-embracing energy that drove *Max Makes a Million* seems just a bit too diffuse this time, a mish-mash soup with one too many ingredients, that is not to say that the individual flavors aren't wondrously rich. Whether Max is in New York, Paris, or Hollywood (where he's apparently bound for next), he will always find his audience—eccentrics of all ages who can't stop giggling at the gloriously silly side of life.

> *Bill Ott, in a review of "Ooh-La-La: (Max in Love)," in* Booklist, *Vol. 88, No. 4, October 15, 1991, p. 449.*

Ooh-la-la, c'est formidable! Or maybe weird and wonderful would be a better way to describe Kalman's latest book about Max, the dog poet. Busy, surreal illustrations combine with a sophisticated, witty text to create a fast-moving, hip-hopping Parisian adventure of canine amour. . . . Kalman's creativity and inventive use of language show as much in the page design as in the story itself. While children will surely enjoy listening to the rhythms and rhymes of her poetic prose and may get a giggle out of the idea of a talking dog with a talent for creative writing, the book is most likely to appeal to adults with a taste for the offbeat. Even adult readers, however, will have to pay close attention to wring every bit of fun and meaning out of Kalman's sly wordplay and visual allusions. Consequently, while not necessarily a good storytime choice, the book will surely stand up to repeat read-alouds in small group or family settings. Brilliant, bold, funny and obscure, this is definitely one of Kalman's best efforts to date. Not every reader will be in tune with the jazzy style, but most large libraries will want this tour de force in their collections. (pp. 98, 100)

> *Lisa Dennis, in a review of "Ooh-La-La (Max in Love)," in* School Library Journal, *Vol. 37, No. 11, November, 1991, pp. 98, 100.*

Max Stravinsky, "the dog poet from New York," is in Paris. From Maira Kalman's earlier book, *Max Makes a Million,* we know that Max is rich, and when he arrives he is the toast of Paris, the coolest cat or rather the hottest dog to hit town.

His adventures are described in rapid-fire English that has the flavor of fractured French, and the illustrations include witty parodies of famous French paintings, especially Picassos from a number of periods. Max wears a little

"Lulu, I want to go there."
My little brother Alexander
whispered that to me
while we were watching
a funny opera called
The Mikado.
"Where?" I asked.
"To that place where they
are singing. Pajan."
"Not Pajan, it's Japan."
"Yes, that's where I want
to go. Now. Please."

From Sayonara, Mrs. Kackleman, *written and illustrated by Maira Kalman.*

pointed cap as Picasso did, and Max's eyes, and everyone else's in the story too, often slip sideways. Max checks into a small hotel on the Left Bank, decorated in the blue period. "My room was the Blue Suite or as the French say, 'Bleu.'" So he labels the room's "Bleu bed. Bleu walls. Bleu chair."

He goes on: "I was beat. I was bushed. I lay down for a nap. I dreamt that a bleu horse was playing checkers with a bleu woman in a garden of bleu trees. The sky was pink. Go figure."

Max takes a short French lesson from "a woman, walking a leopard," in which he is instructed to put a clothespin on his nose, make his mouth into a bonbon shape, put his hands on his hips, stamp his foot and say, "Non. Non. Non. Non. Non. Non." He also learns "ooh-la-la." That is sufficient French for Max, according to his teacher, who is lovesick and "cannot concentrate."

With his limited vocabulary, Max noshes his way across Paris nibbling on baguettes, napoleons and soup du jour while he encounters a veritable menu of Parisians. They have names like Madame Camembert, Charlotte Russe and Federico de Potatoes. There is Peach Melba, who runs a world-famous glamour school, and "that divine dalmation," Crêpes Suzette, who wins Max's lovesick heart.

Crêpes Suzette performs at the Crazy Wolf nightclub, and when a blue spotlight at "the Crazy" bathes her sitting at her piano, Max is in love. She is, as Max puts it, "the dog

I had been looking for my whole life." Playing "a smattering of Smetana, a medley of Mozart," Suzette so dazzles Max that he leaps onstage to declare himself. "Oh my hootchie kootchie poochie," Max rhapsodizes, venturing into French for a final couplet; "I have found my raison d'être. / It is you, my Crêpes Suzette."

The bare bones of the plot cannot do justice to the nuttiness of *Ooh-la-la.* The text wanders around on the pictures, typefaces change for emphasis. Part of the charm of the illustrations is that although the vision is skewed and sketchy, it captures a real sense of Paris. There is a view of Notre-Dame seen through an open, shuttered hotel window, with a tray of coffee and croissants in the foreground, that resembles a Matisse painting, except there is a hunchback rather like Charles Laughton's Quasimodo perched on the cathedral roof. And although French is spoken here, it is mostly affected foolishness or right out of restaurants—about the amount most Americans in Paris speak.

As an adult who reads aloud for a living, I find the best of Maira Kalman's work is not in the art but in her tongue-twisting text. The waiter delivering the morning coffee introduces himself as "Fritz from the Ritz which I quit in a snit when the chef in a fit threw escargot on my chapeau and hit my head with a stale French bread." Try it.

Tout Paris keeps track of Max's progress through a series

of telephone calls, passing the word on the bohemian beagle beginning with Mimi: "Oui. Oui. Mimi I just got off the phone with Kiki. Oh Jacques, not Fifi, Kiki. Listen. Zouzou called Loulou, Loulou called Coco, Coco called Kiki, and Kiki called me me."

It's not quite Dr. Seuss (what is?) but it's clever and it's silly and seems loony enough to attract children, if not to all the nonsense, at least to the sound of the words. It was fun to read, and I also suspect a child familiar with Max's adventures in Paris would recognize the city, should she visit.

> *Linda Wertheimer, "An American Dog in Paris," in* The New York Times Book Review, *November 10, 1991, p. 31.*

Max in Hollywood, Baby (1992)

In a third romp, the debonair dog who fell in love in with a Parisienne Dalmatian is making a film, allowing his creator to sport with Hollywood imagery in every detail. From chauffeur-director Ferrnando Extra Debonnaire and a bellhop who sings his greeting ("no excess that can vex us . . . as long as you're a winnah / But if your flick's a flop you'll be whistling for your dinnah") to Max's assigned yesman and his yesman's yesman (Diddo), wittily caricatured types engage in satirically exaggerated film-world excesses. The sophisticated wordplay and allusions suggest adult readership; but children will also be tickled by the bantering tone, ebullient style, deftly playful art, innovative typography, and special effects ("Silent partners and laundered money provided by Viking"). For those who like this kind of thing, the quintessence of what they like.

> *A review of "Max in Hollywood, Baby," in* Kirkus Reviews, *Vol. LX, No. 20, October 15, 1992, p. 1310.*

When readers last saw that debonair dog Max, he had met his true love in Paris and was off to seek fame and fortune in Tinseltown. This book recounts his Hollywood adventures with the same irreverence, eccentricities, and sardonic wit that make Kalman's other books so unique and so memorable. Once again, the vivid, surreal illustrations punctuate the zany text, but may also stand alone in their offbeat and on-target commentaries. If possible, Max's cinematic antics meet and surpass his earlier escapades as an outlandish exposé on human behavior. Children will be caught up in the frenetic rhythms and rhymes of the text, but the allusions to the mocking of the Golden Age of Hollywood, as well as filmdom's contemporary gurus, will be lost on them. Hopefully, this creative masterpiece will find its way into the hands of sophisticated older children and those adults who will appreciate its ingenuity. (pp. 71-2)

> *Heide Piehler, in a review of "Max in Hollywood, Baby," in* School Library Journal, *Vol. 38, No. 11, November, 1992, pp. 71-2.*

Pets don't buy pet food, and I don't expect that it is children who dote on Maira Kalman's books for them. Rather, it's parents of a certain caste—youngish, well-to-do, well-educated bohemians and former bohemians—who

rush to buy her slender hard covers. It's parents whose sense of cool is tweaked by owning *Stay Up Late* (with text by David Byrne). *Hey Willy, See the Pyramids* and the rest. If the kids seem to enjoy them, well, that's nice, too.

Happily, Ms. Kalman's books—*Max in Hollywood, Baby* is her sixth—are not merely chic. They are smart and funny and high-spirited, dense with irony and strangeness in the manner of some hopped-up late-night Dr. Seuss. The milieus are refreshingly unwholesome: Ms. Kalman's recent stories take place in a goofy between-the-wars dreamland swarming with artistes and cocktails, venality and ennui.

For this one Ms. Kalman's fourth-grade Expressionist style (imagine Roz Chast imitating Paul Klee and George Grosz) seems just right. On the other hand, in the text of *Max in Hollywood, Baby* she has abandoned most of the *faux* childishness that was sometimes annoying in her earlier work. The story moves along cogently, and the language is, if anything, too grown-up.

Max Stravinsky—a dog who made his debut, briefly, in *Hey Willy, See the Pyramids*—has in the course of four books gone from miserable aspiring poet to successful expat writer to genteel Manhattan swell. Now Max gets a Marx Brothers-meets-Abbott & Costello telegram ("STOP SHILLYSHALLYING AROUND STOP STOP WASTING TIME STOP START PACKING STOP PULLING OUT ALL THE STOPS STOP") imploring him to come west and direct a movie. "Were these the ravings of a madman or an agent?" Max asks, then answers, "BOTH!"

In Los Angeles, Max is assigned a studio driver, Ferrnando Extra Debonnaire, who boasts of having "studied at the Royal Academy of Driving Directors." The story proceeds along the lines of classic caricature—Max lolls around the hotel pool waiting to be paged—with bursts of the loopy dream logic in which Ms. Kalman specializes: the studio bigwig's office is a canoe floating inside a giant blue carp. Max takes the go-Hollywood advice of a psychic ("In this town all you need is confidence, thick skin, a cold heart and a big head") and begins shooting his movie, which promptly becomes a manic nightmare of profligacy and vanity (he is particularly incensed when a script typo renders "dog" as "door") only a bit more vividly drawn than real life.

Maira Kalman's books are pieced together by M & Co, the design firm belonging to her husband, Tibor Kalman, and each has been typographically trickier than the one before. *Max in Hollywood, Baby* may represent the useful limit of that evolution, with different type sizes and fonts in a single sentence, and blocks of text teased into zany, occasionally confusing shapes. It is, at least for grown-ups, her funniest and most satisfying work. There are giddy Seussian set pieces—a jaded bellhop's soliloquy ("You used to be a nebbish, a noodle, a fool / And now you're Mr. Big Time with your own private pool"), a mogul's secretary working 10 phones at once ("HELLO. He will. HELLO. He won't. HELLO. He's mad. HELLO. He's livid. HELLO. He says the sky's the limit"). But actual children, as opposed to middle-aged hipsters entertaining the child within, will be frequently baffled.

At one point Max sings an ode to Federico Fellini, film noir, Mel Blanc and Cinemascope. What is an 8-year-old to make of the reference to Schopenhauer's "World as Will and Representation"? As Ms. Kalman writes, "If at the end of this book, once you have looked up all the words in the dictionary, you are not completely unsatisfied, I, the author, will personally send at my own expense a large pickled herring or blue carp (your choice) to your first cousins if they live in Miami." In other words, *let* the kids be a little jolted and mystified and, one hopes, intrigued; it's good for them, just as Looney Tunes' comparatively arcane references (the National Recovery Administration? Bette Davis?) have enlightened children since the 1940's.

On "Sesame Street," the particular satire inherent in the smarmy quiz master Guy Smiley may be lost on toddlers, but they laugh anyway. So when the hero of *Max in Hollywood, Baby* has a nightmare premonition of a headline—"POOCH'S PIC P.U."—and realizes that he has, as his wife, Crêpes Suzette, says, "become ze insufferable show-business schmendrick," children will get the joke, more or less, even if they've never read Variety or heard Yiddish.

On the other hand, only children who do follow the show-business trades will appreciate the irony of Maira Kalman's latest good fortune: *Max in Hollywood Baby* has already been optioned for television.

> *Kurt Andersen, in a review of "Max in Hollywood, Baby," in* The New York Times Book Review, *December 6, 1992, p. 90.*

Chizuko Kuratomi

1934-

Japanese author of picture books and poet.

Major works include *Helpful Mr. Bear* (1968), *Mr. Bear Goes to Sea* (1978), *Mr. Bear and the Robbers* (1974), *Mr. Bear's Christmas* (1974), *Mr. Bear, Postman* (1979).

INTRODUCTION

Kuratomi is best known as the creator of the "Mr. Bear" series of picture books, sixteen stories that feature a large, bumbling but well-meaning bear and his adventures with a community of rabbits. The works revolve around Mr. Bear's attempts to help his small friends. Consistently thwarted by his large size and naivete, Mr. Bear, whose mistakes are often prompted by his misunderstanding of protocol, is redeemed when his errors turn out to his advantage. For example, the first book in the series, *Helpful Mr. Bear,* describes how Mr. Bear comes to Rabbit Town from his house on the mountain to make friends; trying to assist the rabbits, he ends up accidentally smashing everything. The rabbits, who recognize his kindness and good intentions, honor him with a statue and an annual celebration. Subsequent volumes describe Mr. Bear's escapades on land, sea, and air and highlight his attempts to master such activities as acting, painting, and playing the trumpet. Called one "of the most benevolent and easily recognized characters in animal picture books" by critic Margery Fisher, Mr. Bear is considered a particularly lovable figure with whom children can easily identify. Kuratomi is also praised for the originality, simplicity, and enjoyable quality of her books about the amiable bruin.

The "Mr. Bear" books are illustrated by the well-known artist Kozo Kakimoto, who has said "I consider the Mr. Bear series my life's work." Kakimoto's paintings—impressionistic, glowing oils and color washes that are noted for their charm, texture, technical skill, and successful capturing of expression—are credited with contributing greatly to the overall success of the books. In addition to her "Mr. Bear" series, Kuratomi, who edits a poetry magazine for Japanese children and is a children's book editor in Tokyo, is the author of several picture books that have been translated into English and feature both human and animal characters as well as juvenile fiction and a collection of parables from the Bible that have yet to be translated. She received the Sankei Press Prize for *Mr. Bear Goes to Sea* in 1968.

(See also *Something about the Author,* Vol. 12, *Contemporary Authors New Revision Series,* Vol. 10, and *Contemporary Authors,* Vols. 21-24.)

GENERAL COMMENTARY

Publishers Weekly

The characters in [two books by Kuratomi and illustrator

Kozo Kakimoto] form an odd combination: a crew of rabbits and a bear in *Mr. Bear Goes to Sea,* and a circus of rabbits and the same bear in *Mr. Bear's Trumpet.* But these are odd books, for they combine some of the most poetic illustrations (I defy you to look at the picture that illustrates "over a sea as calm as a mirror" and not feel an intimation of eternity) with texts that are pleasant enough but don't quite jell. Look at them, though, or you'll miss some very unusual art work.

A review of "Mr. Bear's Trumpet" and "Mr. Bear Goes to Sea," in Publishers Weekly, *Vol. 198, No. 23, December 7, 1970, p. 50.*

TITLE COMMENTARY

Helpful Mr. Bear (1968)

Burly Mr. Bear is a bull in a china shop in Rabbit Town where his efforts to help end in smashed cars and chairs and a broken watermain. He returns to his house on the mountain but the rabbits, remembering his good intentions, honor him with a statue and an annual celebration. Appealing illustrations [by Kozo Kakimoto], accidental story.

A review of "Helpful Mr. Bear," in Kirkus Reviews, *Vol. XXXVI, No. 5, March 1, 1968, p. 255.*

Lonely Mr. Bear decides to visit Rabbit Town where his size and strength are distinctly out of place. Although he genuinely wishes to be helpful, his every attempt brings disastrous results. He finally decides he is better suited for mountain life—much to the relief of the rabbits. Originally published in Japan, this picture book features a banal story told in stilted prose which is not redeemed by the brightly colored, humorous illustrations.

Martha L. Gardin, in a review of "Helpful Mr. Bear," in School Library Journal, *Vol. 14, No. 8, April, 1968, p. 118.*

Mr. Bear Goes to Sea; Runaway James and the Night Owl (1968)

[Two] books printed in Japan soon attract the eye: **Runaway James and the Night Owl,** and **Mr. Bear Goes to Sea.** James deserts his pretty garden for the deep, dark forest, where he meets an ostrich, a leopard, a hippopotamus,

Kuratomi at the age of three.

some bees and an owl. The story is slight, but the artist [Yutaka Sugita] is the same as for last year's popular **Barnabas Ball at the Circus,** and the huge animals stare out from the pages with a stained-glass glow that stands comparison with Brian Wildsmith. [In **Mr. Bear Goes to Sea,** illustrated by Kozo Kakimoto,] Mr. Bear goes to sea with Captain Rabbit and his rabbit crew, but the bear's enormous size makes him an awkward passenger. When a fearful storm blows up Mr. Bear redeems himself, gallantly holding on to the cargo until the winds abate. Mr. Bear is always shown wearing a vast rubber ring; most endearing.

A review of "Runaway James and the Night Owl" and "Mr. Bear Goes to Sea," in The Times Literary Supplement, *No. 3475, October 3, 1968, p. 1116.*

There is no real story [in **Runaway James and the Night Owl**], merely a series of movements as a small boy looking for a playmate leaves behind him ostrich, leopard, hippo and rhino and learns that the owl can only play with him at night; back he goes to the garden and finds it now has added charms for him after the dark forest. For children who enjoy the impact of colour the exotic washes and swatches on thick embossed pages will lead them through this dream-tale; if they want more story, the attendant grown up will have to supply it somehow. The illustrations in **Mr. Bear goes to sea,** also Japanese, carry a challenge in their semi-abstract style, which sometimes leaves some doubt about what you are really looking at, though in the storm scene at sea, where Mr. Bear saves the rabbits' cargo, it adds a useful element of drama. The joke in the book is one of size, Mr. Bear being once again at a loss to adapt himself to the needs of his friends the rabbits; again it is the child who likes to spend time over picture books who is likely to appreciate this one.

Margery Fisher, in a review of "Runaway James and the Night Owl" and "Mr. Bear Goes to Sea," in Growing Point, *Vol. 7, No. 5, November, 1968, p. 1207.*

Both of these Japanese picture-books are printed on heavily textured paper which is mildly unpleasant to the touch but which is presumably required for these richly oiled colours.

Runaway James is a conventional story about the boy who is bored by home, runs away into the world and, after many adventures, decides that home is best. The point of it is contained in the strong pictures by Yutaka Sugita. These are large and splashy, also rather more frightening than children's artists are usually allowed to be. Children will probably not mind this, but they may resent being offered pictures which look so much like those they paint for themselves.

Kozo Kakimoto's drawing for **Mr. Bear,** on the other hand, is extremely professional. The story is rather heavily funny, but the interpretation is lively and occasionally quite beautiful. There is a marked difference between the drawings which advance the action, which are heavy and not too well composed, and those which set the scene or the mood, which are soft and exquisitely laid on the page.

No prizes for guessing which the artist most enjoyed doing.

> *A review of "Runaway James and the Night Owl" and "Mr. Bear Goes to Sea," in* The Junior Bookshelf, *Vol. 32, No. 6, December, 1968, p. 358.*

Mr. Bear in the Air (1969)

Mr. Bear in the Air is this particular bear's third adventure, and should win him new friends and please those already committed. Chizuko Kuratomi's ungainly hero is an adventurous chap; his earlier buffetings at sea have obviously acted as a spur to his latest ambition, to build and fly his own plane. Mr. Bear does fly his ramshackle machine, and the artist [Kozo Kakimoto] misses no opportunity provided by the words; the shadow of Mr. Bear's little plane, moving across the fields, is only one of the visual pleasures.

> *A review of "Mr. Bear in the Air," in* The Times Literary Supplement, *No. 3536, December 12, 1969, p. 1397.*

A slight story with attractive illustrations. Mr. Bear experiences frustration because he cannot "water ALL the flowers" in the world. He first builds an airplane along the lines of a grasshopper he has seen "fly"—apparently he is ignorant of true grasshopper locomotion—from flower to flower. That plane is a total flop so he constructs a more traditional model. It goes up, but Mr. Bear goes "down . . . and down . . . and down" through a rain cloud to the ground. The grasshopper convinces him that he must have succeeded since it now is raining on all the flowers. Mr. Bear's plane is still flying around up there—hence, "if you see it anywhere, please let him know." The bright, bold double-page paintings done on handsome, stippled paper have an engaging child-like quality; however, as in the other Mr. Bear books by this team (*Mister Bear Goes to Sea* and *Mr. Bear's Trumpet*), the illustrations are not sufficient to compensate for the pallid prose and foolish story.

> *Marjorie Lewis, in a review of "Mr. Bear in the Air," in* School Library Journal, *Vol. 18, No. 2, October, 1971, p. 104.*

Mr. Bear's Trumpet (1970)

In this illustrated incident, the rabbits follow the circus band in procession and Mr. Bear, who has no money to go in, is allowed to sweep up afterwards; it is now that he finds a trumpet and realises that he will have to practise if he is ever to play in the circus. Rich colour [the illustrations are by Kozo Kakimoto], heavily embossed paper, agreeable naïveté don't quite reconcile me to the inconsequence of the plot.

> *Margery Fisher, in a review of "Mr. Bear's Trumpet," in* Growing Point, *Vol. 9, No. 6, December, 1970, p. 1644.*

[The] adventures of this bumbling bear are fun indeed. In this one Mr. Bear tries to learn to play a trumpet and joins a circus. After some discouragement, he retires to his cave for the winter to practice. Think of the racket on the mountain during the snowy months! Delightful. (pp. 44-5)

> *Marian J. Poindexter, in a review of "Mr. Bear's Trumpet," in* Spectrum, *Vol. 47, No. 2, March-April, 1971, pp. 44-5.*

A pallid story with brilliant illustrations. A bored bear wonders how he will amuse himself during the long winter days underground. Hearing the sounds of a parade in Rabbit Town, he follows the Rabbit children to the sound of a trumpet. It is a Rabbit Circus! With no money for a ticket, he listens outside the tent. When night comes, he is invited inside to sleep and dreams of playing the trumpet himself. The next morning, to keep him out of trouble (he is so big and clumsy, after all, and the rabbits are so small), the Circus Master allows him to play the trumpet at a performance. When the show folds, bear takes the trumpet into hibernation to practice for the spring season. The text is childish rather than child-like, and the transitions between story sequences are awkward and confusing. But the pictures are wonderful: glowing washes in charming compositions done on very effective stipled paper. The artwork alone, however, cannot justify the addition of this book to any discriminating collection. (pp. 59-60)

> *Marjorie Lewis, in a review of "Mr. Bear's Trumpet," in* School Library Journal, *Vol. 17, No. 9, May, 1971, pp. 59-60.*

Mr. Bear and the Robbers (1971)

First of all it is the pictures [by Kozo Kakimoto] which attract one to this delightful book; the Japanese poetic vision shows its influence in the misty scenery on the second page, in the great spreads of paint indicating the enormous bulk of Mr. Bear confronting the rabbits. What is particularly attractive about these large double spreads is that alongside the blurred backgrounds there is plenty of fascinating detail, and children will like to examine each chair and bed in the house, each fork and cup on the festive table. As if the pictures were not enough, the reader finds an additional bonus in the story which is both simple and original. Innocent and naive Mr. Bear helps the robbers to take away the little rabbits' furniture and in equal trust and good faith repairs it and takes it back again. The story finishes with a nice twist: Bear and robbers are invited to the party celebrating the new furniture and it is the latters' bad consciences alone which prevent them enjoying themselves. Something fundamental here for small minds to ponder over.

> *C. Martin, in a review of "Mr. Bear and the Robbers," in* The Junior Bookshelf, *Vol. 35, No. 5, October, 1971, p. 298.*

This is the fifth of Mr Bear's adventures but there is nothing tired about it. With a pleasant, easy brand of irony that should not be above the head of the young reader (who is all too ready to suppose that he is the one being laughed at), it tells how the incredibly nice and helpful Mr Bear first abets and then foils a gang of robbers, under the impression that he is assisting a firm of furniture restorers.

> *"East Meets West," in* The Times Literary Supplement, *No. 3634, October 22, 1971, p. 1325.*

Mr. Bear, Station-Master (1972)

Children who have enjoyed the earlier adventures of Chizuko Kuratomi's simple, ponderous hero, Mr Bear, will be pleased with *Mr Bear, Station-Master,* in which Mr Bear, amid flying bunting and the music of the band, welcomes the first train to arrive at his very own railway station. True, he narrowly escapes being run down by it, but, as in all the Mr Bear books, the ending is cheerful. Kozo Kakimoto's snow-clad landscapes and massive, complicated steam engines are marvellous.

> *A review of "Mr. Bear, Station-Master," in* The Times Literary Supplement, *No. 3692, December 8, 1972, p. 1495.*

The hero of *Mr. Bear, Station-Master* wears clothes—in this case, a uniform to suit his new job at the new station of Sleepy Valley, where he is helped by his rabbit friends to get the line clear of snow and be ready for "that first, magnificent salute" to the distinguished opener. The artist has certainly established Mr. Bear by now as one of the most benevolent and easily recognised characters in animal picture books and the combination of an almost Victorian exactness in interiors and a pointilliste technique for outdoors is as effective as ever here.

> *Margery Fisher, in a review of "Mr. Bear, Station-Master," in* Growing Point, *Vol. 11, No. 7, January, 1973, p. 2084.*

Mr. Bear and Apple Jam (1973)

Chizuko Kuratomi's great, hulking hero is a lovable fellow whose mistakes and misunderstandings often land him—if only temporarily—in trouble. In this story he almost deprives Mrs Rabbit of one of her means of livelihood, and all with the best intentions, but the kindness of their friends and neighbours brings about the usual happy ending. Kozo Kakimoto's illustrations anthropomorphize the animals in a way that has charm because it is so different from cute western methods. Mr. Kakimoto is always a gifted creator of atmosphere, and one double-page spread in this book he very nearly achieves the impossible feat of conveying visually the pervasive aroma and stickiness of hot apple jam.

> *A review of "Mr. Bear and Apple Jam," in* The Times Literary Supplement, *No. 3742, November 23, 1973, p. 1441.*

There is nothing insipid or fragile about this story or the bold vibrant colours on the beautifully textured linen paper that calls out to be touched and explored by tiny fingers. Perhaps tactile exploration will not be enough, for I could well imagine some three-year-old licking the delicious page "where everything smelled like apple jam, and

was as sticky as apple jam and even looked like apple jam".

> *J. Russell, in a review of "Mr. Bear and Apple Jam," in* The Junior Bookshelf, *Vol. 37, No. 6, December, 1973, p. 382.*

Mr. Bear's Christmas (1974)

There are some who will object on religious grounds to seeing Mr. Bear playing the part of the Infant Jesus in the rabbits' Nativity play; equally, one must feel ill at ease at the sheer absurdity of scale, especially as the pictures [by Kozo Kakimoto] hardly suggest that the scene is intended to be funny. The smooth, glossy colour is as attractive as ever but the story and its treatment seem strained compared with earlier stories about the amiable bear and his rodent chums.

> *Margery Fisher, in a review of "Mr. Bear's Christmas," in* Growing Point, *Vol. 13, No. 6, December, 1974, p. 2541.*

Mr. Bear knew it was time for him to take his winter sleep but he had to say goodbye to all the rabbits first. He found them busily preparing their Christmas play and soon he became involved in trying to learn a part. He could not remember the words so he went to dig up a Christmas tree, and ended up fetching dozens. Finally he was given the part of the Infant Jesus, and so was able to go to sleep, tired but happy. This is a straightforward tale illustrated with simple but vividly coloured pictures. Mr. Bear has a different, human, expression on his face on every page, and his smile of contentment at the end of the story really radiates comfort, happiness and security. The text is written for the very youngest reader and yet the urge to read on is there. Every page brings a new surprise, a new emotion and a new happiness. This is a book which any child would love to find in his Christmas stocking, and which he will enjoy the whole year round.

> *G. L. Hughes, in a review of "Mr. Bear's Christmas," in* The Junior Bookshelf, *Vol. 38, No. 6, December, 1974, p. 337.*

Mr. Bear's Drawing (1975)

When Mr. Bear finds the rabbit school having an art lesson out of doors, he is asked to pose for them, and later to produce his own wax-crayon drawing for their exhibition. He in turn asks a flattered ant to pose for him, and his unexpectedly life-like representation wins great acclaim. In this Japanese study in greens—delicately shaded washes on an interesting matt surface with splashes of bright colour [the illustrations are by Kozo Kakimoto], over which for the most part the text is superimposed—the delightful frog-like Mr. Bear blunders through his friends' Lilliputian world, very happily demonstrating the child's view of an adult's great bulk. It also mirrors a familiar situation: the adult called upon to appreciate small children's achievements. (pp. 16-17)

> *M. Hobbs, in a review of "Mr. Bear's Draw-*

Kuratomi with Kozo Kakimoto, the illustrator of the "Mr. Bear" books, 1967.

ing," in The Junior Bookshelf, *Vol. 40, No. 1, February, 1976, pp. 16-17.*

Mr. Bear's Meal (1978)

Another very successful story about huge Mr. Bear and the rabbits. Mr. Bear is the ideal fall guy. He never quite understands the proper way to do things. In this story he eats a meal without realising he is in a restaurant. He does not pay the bill so is put in prison but the outcome once proper communication is established is, as usual, a happy one. Lots of other Mr. Bear books available well worth looking out for, both for their story content and high quality production. . . .

> *A review of "Mr. Bear's Meal," in* Books for Your Children, *Vol. 14, No. 2, Winter, 1978, p. 5.*

Mr. Bear, Postman (1979)

When Mr. Bear discovers that an elderly rabbit of his acquaintance never has any mail, he writes a letter to him each day, masquerading as an unknown granddaughter, but the stratagem fails for lack of stamps. The amiable bear works his way through yet another role through the

familiar medium of swirling colour and thick, glossy paint [of Kozo Kakimoto's illustrations], and the quiet humour is carried on posture and expression as much as on the human appurtenances Mr. Bear has borrowed.

> *Margery Fisher, in a review of "Mr. Bear, Postman," in* Growing Point, *Vol. 18, No. 4, November, 1979, p. 3611.*

Mr. Bear the Postman is another vehicle for the artist Kozo Kakimoto's palette. He paints wallpapery collages of stripey bears and baby bunnies. The first of the dozen "Mr. Bear" books I have come across, this one shows an illustrator of great originality, whose pictures provide so much to discuss and sometimes demand a good deal more than young readers may be capable of. All the same, it is a most stimulating challenge and well worth taking on.

> *Peter Fanning, in a review of "Mr. Bear the Postman," in* The Times Educational Supplement, *No. 3333, April 25, 1980, p. 25.*

Mr. Bear's Winter Sleep (1982)

Mr. Bear finds it has been worth his while to wake for long enough to take in a family of rabbits benighted in the snow, for they tend his bruised leg and bring in enough provisions to set him up for his interrupted sleep. As in previous books, Mr. Bear's benevolence is amply suggested in the rich swirls of oil paint [of Kozo Kakimoto's illustrations] which in impressionistic style follow out one more simple incident in the life of the huge animal and his ill-assorted but devoted small friends.

> *Margery Fisher, in a review of "Mr. Bear's Winter Sleep," in* Growing Point, *Vol. 21, No. 6, March, 1983, p. 4047.*

Ann M(atthews) Martin

1955-

(Also writes as Ann Matthews) American author of fiction.

Major works include *Bummer Summer* (1983), *Inside Out* (1984), *With You and Without You* (1986), *Kristy's Great Idea* (1986).

INTRODUCTION

Martin is best known as the creator of the "Baby-Sitters Club" series of stories for middle graders, works that also include the spinoff "Baby-Sitters Little Sister" series for primary graders. A prolific writer who is extremely popular with her audience, comprised mainly of preteen girls, she is also the author of several novels for middle graders and young adults that feature more sophisticated subjects and themes than her series. Praised for her understanding of children and young people as well as for the realism, excitement, and humor of her books, Martin is also commended for her skill in addressing both difficult topics—such as autism, dyslexia, kidnapping, divorce, teen suicide, and the death of a parent—and such familiar subjects as sibling rivalry, peer pressure, and self-acceptance. The "Baby-Sitters Club" books are often thought to transcend their formula status through the strength of Martin's writing: set in the mythical suburb of Stoneybrook, Connecticut, the series revolves around a group of twelve-year-old girls who form a babysitting cooperative. Led by popular and resourceful Kristy Thomas, the club is originally composed of four members: Kristy, who is modeled on Martin's best childhood friend; Claudia, an Asian-American who has her own phone and helps to get bookings for the girls; Stacey, who finds out that she is diabetic; and Mary Anne, the shyest of the group who is the author's representation of herself. In later volumes, Martin expands the club to seven members. Each book in the series describes events that take place during a short period of time, such as how Claudia learns to cope with her older sister and the death of their grandmother or how Kristy babysits for an autistic savant. By the end of each story, the challenges faced by each character are met and the lighthearted exuberance of the club is underscored. Narrated by their protagonists, the books—written in a smooth style that depends greatly on dialogue and published in a numbered format—also include notations from the club notebooks that appear in typeface simulating the handwriting of each girl. The "Little Sisters" books depart from the formula of its parent series by focusing on the feelings and experiences of younger children, such as wanting to get a pet or having a fight with a friend, and by having Kristy as the sole narrator.

"I don't feel any different now than I did at seven," Martin has said, adding that she "turned to writing as an outlet

for both my emotions and humor." To create her books, Martin draws on her background in psychology and early childhood development, her experience as an elementary school teacher of children with special needs and an editor of children's literature, and on her memory, imagination, and observation. She began her literary career with works that strongly reflect her background and experience: for example, *Inside Out* details a child's reaction to an autistic sibling in what is considered an accurate and sympathetic handling of its subject, and *Stage Fright* (1984), which Martin calls the most autobiographical of her books, describes how an introverted girl discovers that she is capable of performing in front of people while remaining a shy person. Recruited for the "Baby-Sitters Club" books by Jean Feiwel, the Scholastic editor who suggested the idea, Martin initiated the series to entertain young readers with the adventures of a group of friends who run a successful business. Originally intended to be closed-ended, the books became enormously successful among children, whom Martin feels relate to her characters and topics and respond to the humor of her works. Martin eschews references to sex, drugs, swearing, and child abuse in her "Baby-Sitters Club" books, since children as young as six are reading the series, although she claims that the most popular books in the series are those dealing with more serious issues. Though some adults object to the formulaic nature of the books and note that the series projects a white suburban ethos despite its multiculturalism, young peoople have responded so favorably to the "Baby-Sitters Club" books that they consistently reach best-seller status. In addition, the series has prompted the formation of fan clubs—Martin receives as many as twelve thousand letters per year—and such marketing spinoffs as a baby-sitter's kit, videos, and calendars with maps of Stoneybrook. Sam Leaton Sebesta and James L. Neeley write of Martin, "Not since Cecil B. DeMille has anyone managed such a large cast so ably," and Margaret Mackey adds that "Kristy, Mary Anne, and the others seem assured of a place in the minds and hearts of at least one generation of little girls and may even be remembered fifty years from now, long after their readers have outgrown the immediate reading lessons which the 'Baby-sitters' may have to offer." In addition to the books she has written under her own name, Martin has written several books as Ann Matthews that are based on movies and the television series "Punky Brewster." *Kristy and the Secret of Susan* won the Phantom's Choice Award for Middle Grade Series Books in 1990, and Martin was nominated in 1992 for a Lifetime Achievement Award from the Phantom's Choice for her significant contribution to a children's literature series. Four of her books were chosen as Children's Books of the Year by the Child Study Association of America: *Inside Out* in 1986, and *Stage Fright, With You or Without You,* and *Missing Since Monday* in 1987. Martin is also the founder of the Ann M. Martin Foundation, which benefits children, the homeless and programs for education and literacy.

(See also *Authors and Artists for Young Adults,* Vol. 6; *Something about the Author,* Vols. 41, 44; *Contemporary Authors New Revision Series,* Vol. 32; and *Contemporary Authors,* Vol. 11.)

GENERAL COMMENTARY

Sam Leaton Sebesta and James L. Neeley

Ann M. Martin's cast of main characters is so long that it would take a whole chapter to describe them, and she does. Then, systematically, the characters interact around a problem which, to an adult, seems trivial: how to coach a small child to win a personality contest in *Little Miss Stoneybrook . . . and Dawn;* how to have a good time on a Bahamas cruise in *Baby-sitters on Board!;* how to convince Mom to change her mind in *Ten Kids, No Pets.*

Not since Cecil B. DeMille has anyone managed such a large cast so ably. Crowds surge in and out of homes, malls, planes, and boats. Everyone has a good time. Exuberance is the tone of each book. Now and then there's a small crisis but it's quickly set aside amid the choreography of happy interaction: Kids are important and the world is a pleasant place for them to be.

As I write this, Ann M. Martin's paperbacks place first, second, and third on the *Publishers Weekly* list of bestsellers for middle readers. Bookstore people tell me that chil-

dren, not adults, buy these books. They read them all—the 19 **"Baby-sitters Club"** books at the time of this writing—and they ask for more.

I dozed off while reading one outside on a nice day. A playful wind riffled through the pages so that when I woke up I'd missed 3 chapters, and I didn't notice. But children do. They seem to notice every single thing in this series and other currently popular here-and-now exuberant series. They don't seem bothered by the lack of weighty themes. They read and read and read and, for what it's worth, the experience is wonderful. (p. 536)

> *Sam Leaton Sebesta and James L. Neeley, "Literature for Children," in* The Reading Teacher, *Vol. 42, No. 7, March, 1989, pp. 536-41.*

N. R. Kleinfield

The absolute best book for Nicole Zajack was the one in which Dawn moved into her new house and she and the other baby sitters became convinced there was a ghost rattling around. It turned out to be a playful mouse. "That was great," said Nicole, who's 13. "Dawn's really neat. She's just like me. She's on the quiet side, but she's definitely mature. A very neat person." After she read the fifth book, Nicole began to phone her local bookstore every day to see if the next one had come in yet. "I mean, I couldn't wait," she said. "Who could?"

"I sit glued to the books," said Kathy Ames, who's 12. "They're not out-of-the-ordinary stories, like a space creature lands in the yard. I like books that are realistic."

Nicole and Kathy, along with just about every 8- to 13-year-old American girl alive, are rabid fans of the **"Baby-Sitters Club"** books. Among the fundamental principles for their age seem to be that they must giggle at the mention of boys, learn to play the piano and have read *Logan Likes Mary Anne!, Karen's Roller Skates, Claudia and the Phantom Phone Calls* and the 18 other books in the series. Otherwise, they're just out of it.

The books, which are currently the most successful paperback juvenile series in the country, trace the adventures of a group of spunky eighth-grade girls who run a baby-sitting cooperative in the fictional town of Stoneybrook, Conn. Kristy is the club's president. Three times a week, the girls get together after school at Claudia's house. They go there because she is the only one with her own phone, which they can use to get their bookings.

Each novel details the escapades of one of the members, often a taxing baby-sitting assignment. There was the time, for instance, that Jessi baby-sat for a deaf boy and hastily had to learn some sign language. In another book, Kristy's mother remarried and the new family moved into a neighborhood where the kids mocked the Baby-Sitters Club and, worst of all, teased Louie, Kristy's aged pet collie. On yet another occasion, Jessi baby-sat for a week in a house overrun with animals and got terribly agitated when the hamster ceased walking around. She took it to the veterinarian. He was able to figure out it was pregnant.

By now, there are more than 11 million copies in print of

the 21 books in the series, all published by Scholastic Inc. New titles appear monthly, whereupon they routinely shoot to the top of children's best-seller lists. . . .

The books are uncommonly well written for a paperback children's series. They sometimes incline toward soap-opera–style plots, but the twists and turns are less formulaic than the genre usually offers.

Ann M. Martin, a slight, blond-haired 33-year-old who lives in Manhattan with a cat named Mouse, writes the series. Most children's series are the product of a stable of authors, but Ms. Martin goes it solo. . . .

The series came about because of a hunch. In 1983, Jean Feiwel, a Scholastic editor, noticed that a book about a young girl's baby-sitting job had sold well for the company, and she thought there might be something in a series revolving around a group of baby sitters. This was about the time that Bantam's "Sweet Valley High" titles had captivated young hearts and books about groups of girls were selling briskly. "There was something resonant about the idea," Ms. Feiwel said. "It just struck a chord with me."

She recruited Ms. Martin, an author of several books for children who had had a truncated career as a schoolteacher before becoming a children's book editor. She was about to leave Bantam to write full time. She was never actually part of any babysitting cooperative, though she watched her share of children growing up and baby-sits even now. . . .

Ms. Feiwel and Ms. Martin thrashed out plots. Part of the concept for the series was that each girl was to have some sort of distinctive trait or problem. Some early notions didn't get too far. For instance, Ms. Martin had suggested that it might be interesting if Stacey's parents were in jail for embezzlement, but Ms. Feiwel felt that it would not be all that appropriate. So she got the adults out of prison and made Stacey a diabetic. Originally there were four girls, though the club has swelled to seven.

Ms. Martin derives some of the plots from her own life, like the time the baby sitters use Brillo pads to wash a car and the paint comes off. "Sometimes they're things I overhear on the bus or things that people tell me," she said. "Somebody told me recently that their dog got a credit card at Brooks Brothers. I'm going to use that as a plot."

The first book was published in August 1986, with a printing of about 30,000. "There were really no high hopes or great expectations," Ms. Feiwel said. Not until the sixth book, *Kristy's Big Day,* did the series truly click. That title shot to the top of bestseller lists. Each book now goes out with a first printing of 250,000.

The baby-sitting angle seems to be what really grabs readers. "I like baby-sitting and I love reading about baby sitters and what they do," said Anna Qualset, a 14-year-old who lives in Central City, Neb., and has been hooked since fifth grade. She said she expects to read the books "forever" and then pass them on to her kids. Kathy Ames gave her lowdown: "Something always happens. It's not one thing after another, like something boring."

"We have a number of kids who have read every one and know which five are coming up," said Dudley Carlson, the manager of children's services at the Princeton (N.J.) Public Library. "It's like the old movie serials in the 30's." . . .

Paperback series of this sort tend to have relatively short existences, continuing for a few years and then fading into oblivion. No signs have appeared yet of diminished interest in the **"Baby-Sitters Club"** books.

Ann Martin said she doesn't feel close to being burned out.

"Scholastic hopes for eternity," Ms. Feiwel said. "I hope for eternity."

"I would never tire of them," said Nicole Zajack. "Never. Never. Never."

> *N. R. Kleinfield, "Children's Books: Inside the Baby-Sitters Club," in* The New York Times Book Review, *April 30, 1989, p. 42.*

Kristin McMurran

[Ann] Martin spends five hours a day, five days a week inventing adventures in the imaginary hamlet of Stoneybrook, Conn., where moms say 'drat,' kids never grow up, and family feuds are patched up before bedtime. The series centers on a clique of seven babysitters. Kristy, the leader, is modeled on Martin's best childhood friend, Beth Perkins; Mary Anne, the shy one, is a mirror image of the author.

Martin writes as if she has a passkey to the prewonder years. "There is a lot of Ann in her books," says Perkins. "She really cares about the words she writes and who she writes them for. She listens to kids and understands their sensitivity, like how it feels to wear the wrong-colored sneakers or be snubbed in the lunch line." (pp. 55-6)

> *Kristin McMurran, "Ann Martin Stirs Up a Tiny Tempest in Preteen Land with Her Best-Selling 'Baby-Sitters Club'," in* People Weekly, *Vol. 32, No. 8, August 21, 1989, pp. 55-6.*

Margaret Mackey

Anyone involved in encouraging children to read would have found our neighborhood a cheering sight over the past months. Both in school and at home, there has been a ferment over the gradual acquisition of a particular collection of books. Neighboring children have rushed breathlessly to our door, waving a new purchase under the envious noses of our daughters. There have been excited phone calls: "It's in—I saw it at Greenwood's! Are you going to get it? You can borrow mine, but you'll have to wait till I've finished—and my sister."

Two girls aged eight and ten live in our house. To the cognoscenti, that should be clue enough. All this enthusiasm and book-oriented social activity revolves round one series: the **"Baby-sitters Club"** books by Ann M. Martin. At the time of this writing, Book 35 (they come numbered) has just hit the stands.

The excitement is not confined to our neighborhood. The journal *Emergency Librarian* regularly runs a survey of children's bestsellers in the United States and Canada. In the May–June 1989 issue, the ten titles listed under American mass market paperbacks were all titles from the **"Baby-sitters Club"** series. (Is this a record?) Although this 100% tally has not been maintained, all the lists in the nine months following showed between five and seven out of ten from this series. The Canadian lists do not contain any of the titles (and indeed seem to be collected on a somewhat different basis), but there is no question that Ann M. Martin is a winner north of the border as well. The **"Baby-sitters Club"** arrived later in the United Kingdom, and it remains to be seen if it will take off there in the same way.

What is this series? What is its appeal to young readers? What should teachers, librarians, and parents make of children's enormous enthusiasm for these books? As the emphasis on teaching reading by using "real" books continues to grow, does a series like this have anything to offer in the classrooms of new readers? Or is it just one way for children to pass their free time?

The books themselves are certainly appealing to young girls. Many of the ingredients of the stories are sure-fire. Briefly, the Baby-sitters Club does what its name implies. A varying number of girls aged between eleven and thirteen have joined together to offer a babysitting service to the town. They meet three times a week, during which time they accept bookings for jobs (one of the group conveniently has her own telephone and private number, which makes her well-off but by no means far-fetched in North American terms). The idea is that with one phone call, the parent can be reasonably certain of procuring the services of an experienced sitter. There are club rules, records, schedules and so on. The series operates more or less in real time with the girls aging appropriately and their family circumstances altering. Each book covers a relatively short time-span and is recounted in the first person by the character named in the title (e.g., **Kristy's Great Idea,** or **Mary Anne Saves the Day,** or **Claudia and the Sad Good-bye**). Occasionally, the narrative is interrupted by an entry in the club notebook or some correspondence between club members; this is always indicated typographically by a "hand-written" typeface (a different one for each girl).

The strong points of the series are several. For the most part, the adventures of the girls are moderately plausible; the family upsets (death, divorce, remarriage) are neither glossed over nor exploited unmercifully. That well-known problem of getting the adults out of the way so the adventures can begin is solved, almost by definition, by the framework of babysitting. Likewise, the fascination of young readers with clubs and all their secrets and apparatus is catered to, with the added advantage of a club's serving a real, functioning, grown-up purpose. Mary Anne, as club secretary, keeps schedules of all the commitments of different club members so she can book sitters appropriately. Kristy, the president, insists on members keeping up the club notebook so that everyone knows of particular problems concerning one client or another, and sitters can benefit from each other's advice: almost a kind of inservice

training. For the preteen reader, bursting to grow up, this can look like the best of all worlds with a vengeance.

The first-person narrative plays a useful role, especially for those readers who are just getting used to reading whole books. The narrator keeps a firm grip on the reader's shoulder, as it were, with many interpolations along the lines of "Let me explain how that works" or "I'll get back to that part later." It would be difficult for even inexperienced readers to lose track of the story.

The format of one book following another allows for a great deal of natural redundancy which is also helpful to inexperienced readers. In addition, either Martin or her publisher has had the bright idea of putting the reader's powers of prediction to work by trailing each book at the end of its predecessor with a sample chapter to whet the appetite. All of these factors combine to make the opening chapters immediately gripping to the young reader.

Martin clearly expects a considerable measure of identification between her young readers and the comfortable suburban heroines of her books. This is probably one source of her great appeal. There are not many shades of grey in these books; she offers the conventional wisdom of the American middle class much as Enid Blyton, the prolific British author of children's adventure stories in the 1940's and 1950's, offered an unquestioning allegiance to the mores of the British middle classes of her time with her stories of the Famous Five, the Secret Seven, and the *Adventure* series. As with Blyton, shading, nuance, and ambiguity are not on the menu. The reader's reaction is clearly structured in advance, and the narrator does not anticipate any alternative perspectives on the story being told.

Maybe such an exclusion of ambiguity offers security to the inexperienced reader. Certainly it is a feature of many of the series books which have been so popular over the decades. In fact, Martin offers more plurality than most of these series, at least at a superficial level. Different books are narrated by different club members, and it is quite common for the narrative thread to be interrupted by a different voice in the form of the club notebook or of letters or postcards between members.

This multiplicity of narrative voices offers new readers practice in using "shifters" (those grammatical elements which change meaning according to the context in which they are used; first person pronouns fall into this category because it is impossible to identify the "I" without knowing the speaker). The rules of the series are strict: the name of the narrator is given in the title, and interruptions are clearly flagged with type-face changes. Even so, the approach calls for some reader flexibility, even sophistication, which can't do any harm and might do some good.

This way of telling the stories therefore offers some challenge to readers, but it is not an unqualified success. In fact, the multiple narration is really a bit of a fraud. No matter who is telling the story, the narrative voices are identical. Claudia is Japanese-American; Jessi is black; Stacey comes from New York; Dawn comes from California. The other three main characters grew up in Stoneybrook, Connecticut, where the stories take place. No matter. Each speaks with exactly the same voice. Furthermore, in the obligatory introduction to the club which comes at the beginning of each book, all these different girls use identical phrases and remarkably similar paragraphs.

Much contemporary fiction for older children and young adults is written in the first person, and it could be argued that the **"Baby-sitters"** books offer developing readers some useful practice in this particular form. On the other hand, much of the first-person narrative offered to young readers these days has come in for criticism. By definition, first-person narration offers a single perspective on the story; that limitation can be a source of strength, but all too often it is merely a limitation. When the narrator is young and the story is written in such a way that no alternative point of view is even considered, there is clearly the danger of what Perry Nodelman called "a doubly satisfying solipsism: the belief that our own perceptions of the way things ought to be is in fact the way they actually are, and the equally comforting belief that our own perception of the way things are is the only possible way of viewing reality. These are comfortable but dangerous delusions". With her multiple narrators, each speaking in the first person, Martin lays claim to a wider variety of perspectives. However, since her characters think and speak alike, this plurality exists in theory only and perhaps even feeds that misconception which Nodelman criticizes so vehemently—that everybody thinks alike.

Furthermore, despite the token multiculturalism, every character speaks from the perspective of the white middle class. Claudia and her grandmother indulge in a few picturesque Japanese ceremonies, but the main emphasis is on Claudia's totally cool dress sense, which is the epitome of an assimilated American. When Jessi's family moves to Stoneybrook, there is some initial unpleasantness from a few neighbors, but soon people learn that it "doesn't matter" that the Ramseys are black. When Stacey has to decide whether to live with her mother in Stoneybrook or her father in New York, one serious consideration is whether she can bring herself to give up New York's wonderful stores.

It is arguable that Martin, despite her pretense of a multiple viewpoint, is really just as monocultural and restricted as Blyton or the Stratemeyer syndicate who produced Nancy Drew and the Hardy Boys under pseudonyms. However, it is interesting to see that the charm of the series is still potent in a contemporary setting, and it is worth considering what might make it such an appealing format for young readers.

Many, many young readers devour books from one series or another. Names like the Famous Five, Nancy Drew, the Hardy Boys, and Cherry Ames have been popular, literally for generations. The series book is ubiquitous beyond the realm of the child detective as well. Laura Ingalls; Anne of Green Gables; Meg, Jo, Beth and Amy; Ramona; the Swallows and the Amazons; the Tillermans. . . . The list is formidable—and noticeably durable.

It is certainly possible to categorize such different series in terms of quality of writing. There is also a second way

of distinguishing among them, a way which may offer interested adults some insight into reading behavior. That key distinction may be summed up as the way time works in a series.

Some series books operate in a real time framework, and some constantly repeat an endless present. Even Enid Blyton's work, which is taken by many to represent the nadir of series writing, presents examples of both sides of this divide: The Famous Five live through a huge number of summer holidays but hardly grow any older. The four children who feature in her *Adventure* series at least age, even if they don't develop. When the mother of two of them remarries, the new family structure stays in place and affects later stories. In a similar way, there used to be a distinction between the ageless Nancy Drew and other girl detectives like Bolton and Beverly Gray. Though similar in many respects, these other characters progressed through life in a recognizable way, moving houses, changing jobs, acquiring husbands, and generally expecting major decisions to remain in effect through subsequent titles. It may or may not be significant that Nancy is the triumphant survivor of that group.

What are the attractions of these continuing sagas of such widely varying quality? And what may a young reader gain from pursuing a character from one book to another? "More of the same" is one obvious source of appeal, but in those books where the characters grow up, that is less clearly the case. The extended answer to the question "And then what?" is another reason for popularity but again can only be a partial answer. Series books are read and re-read to the point where every answer to the question "And then what?" must be utterly superfluous to the young reader's grasp of the stories.

What other possible reasons are there for the role played by the series book in the reading diet of so many children? One conceivable answer almost seems like a contradiction in terms: There could be a kind of intellectual satisfaction in the reading of series books which adults may often overlook. At least in those books where the heroes and heroines progress through time, there is an element of piecing together the pattern which may offer great rewards to the young reader. A very rich and methodical child, with access to a bookstore that never had problems with stock, might be able to read through each series consecutively, pursuing each heroine (or less often, hero) chronologically. Given the realistic constraints of book supply, however, most readers will approach a series on a more piecemeal basis; and it could be that in that fact lies one source of the appeal of these books. Reading any series of books out of order provides the young reader with practice and reinforcement of some valuable reading experiences and at the same time offers the satisfaction of confirming what really happened, whether the reader's deductions produced a reasonable version of incidents in the characters' past.

What happens when the child reads the books out of sequence? He or she meets a character with a past, referred to with varying degrees of skill according to the heavy-handedness of the author. The child is driven to make inferences, to compensate for gaps. Usually, when a title which fills in a missing element in the chronology becomes available, there is great excitement, and the reader pounces. Inferences can now be checked; the cross-weaving adds texture to the baldest narrative.

How many of us have read a series out of order and then later settled down to re-read every book in the correct sequence, savoring references which once baffled us and setting events in place while simultaneously recalling how we once had to piece them together out of clues scantily provided in the sequels? Even very simple books thus presented now offer pleasures of foreshadowing which might seem sophisticated in a different format. A character appears in one book; we, having already read later offerings in the series, know this person will marry/die/succeed/fail. Yet children working their way through a series in this way might still balk at flashbacks and timeshifts in a single volume. The different titles offer a key to a complicated reading process and leave the reader in greater control. Putting down one book and picking up another provides an unmistakable signpost.

It is not necessary that the writer be talented or the story challenging for some of this important practice to be possible. What probably is required is a fairly strict control of the chronology of those events which straddle a number of books; the reader making extrapolations needs some confidence that the author is not going to use the same period of time twice for different events in the way that Carolyn Keene used Nancy Drew's nineteenth summer over and over again. Given that essential competence on the part of the author, very banal and repetitive stories can acquire additional charm from being pieced together out of order. (pp. 484-87)

What are the benefits to a young reader of exposure to this kind of series? . . . [A child] might make some valuable reading discoveries, almost without noticing.

The reader sees the challenge of finding out what happened to characters both before and after the events of a particular story. This is perceived as a pleasure, the resolution of a puzzle. The reader will not consider the value of practice in prediction, extrapolation, and pattern-making, with answers supplied in the other stories to confirm or improve on the reader's inferences. The reader sees the appeal of the stories; the outsider may notice the benefits.

Nothing is gained by exaggerating the value of this kind of series book. Readers who never move on to anything more demanding miss out on a wide range of experience. It is also not helpful to dismiss such series reading with a passing sneer. The experience of making patterns, putting stories together, extrapolating, and confirming may be providing a crucial step towards more substantial reading. It is too easy to label such work as reading rubbish or as merely "better than reading nothing." But gains for young readers may be more complex than we allow for. At the very least, when they move on to those more taxing books which have sequels, they may be more at home with some of the rules. We need much more information than we have at present about how readers make use of what they have already read in order to process what they read next. Research examining these issues might produce some very interesting results.

Peter J. Rabinowitz has written an entire book about the conventions we apply to reading fiction. He lists four main rules: rules of notice (what deserves attention, what is background); rules of signification (what is important about what happens in the story, how to reach judgments about what is going on); rules of configuration (how the elements of the story fit together); and rules of coherence (how the story finally makes sense as a unit). Rabinowitz does not pay much attention to how readers actually acquire a functioning capacity to apply these rules, but it seems plausible that a series of similar books might offer useful practice. Certainly in the **"Baby-sitters"** books, the elements that could be classified under rules of notice are repeated rigidly and can therefore be assimilated and taken for granted. Thus, even a reader inexperienced in an absolute sense has the opportunity to behave like an experienced reader in this one regard at least. Temporarily, the reader is master of the conventions.

This mastery could involve a risk of restriction, of course; the young reader may insist that every book come as well flagged as the familiar series. Donald Fry (1985) raised this question in his study of twelve-year-old Karnail, a devotee of Blyton's *Secret Seven* books. "His expectations of the text are confirmed not only from book to book, but from chapter to chapter and even from sentence to sentence. But, although he may not be moving forward, he is becoming more confident as a reader, and quicker too, without being any the less attentive to what is being said.

"Yet it might be that his confidence in the *Secret Seven* series will make him prejudiced against other different books. Already there are signs that he is judging books against his expectation that they should conform to the Blyton mode." Fry suggests, "Almost certainly, Karnail's next move, from a base that is Blyton to one that is non-Blyton will be as difficult as his previous move from first base".

Even so, there is ample testimony about the importance of series books in the growth of many readers. Robert Carlsen and Anne Sherrill, in a summary of several thousand reading autobiographies accumulated by the former from his students (mainly trainee English teachers and librarians), observe, "The respondents also become momentarily addicted to both the series and comic books. Over and over the accounts describe periods where such books became their steady reading fare . . . These materials seem to be as much a part of one's literary maturation as are the children's classics". Most teachers, librarians, and parents will recognize the addiction; and many will be familiar with it from their own youth. The series book doesn't seem to show any signs of going away; we need to find out more about just what it can offer to new readers.

So the **"Baby-sitters"** books join a long line of ancestors. How honorable is their role in the development of readers? There is room for debate, but it does not seem possible to dismiss them completely. Kristy, Mary Anne, and the others seem assured of a place in the minds and hearts of at least one generation of little girls and may even be remembered fifty years from now, long after their readers have outgrown the immediate reading lessons which the **"Baby-sitters"** may have to offer. (pp. 488-89)

> *Margaret Mackey, "Filling the Gaps: 'The Baby-Sitters Club', the Series Book, and the Learning Reader," in* Language Arts, *Vol. 67, No. 5, September, 1990, pp. 484-89.*

Claudia Mills

[*The following excerpt is from an essay which was originally delivered in a different version at the Seventeenth Annual International Conference of the Children's Literature Association, May 31-June 3, 1990.*]

American youth have long been devoted readers of stories about kids who, on a grand or modest scale, set out to make their fortunes. Perhaps because work represents both money and power—and because adult control over both is a perennial frustration for children—books about children who launch their own business projects have garnered at times phenomenal audiences. . . . In recent years, Scholastic's mass-market series **"The Baby-Sitters Club"** has set industry sales records, as readers devour book after book about a group of girls who form their own baby-sitting business. What I call "entrepreneurial novels," novels about enterprising kids who go in to business for themselves, are represented on most juvenile publishers' backlists.

The popularity of such books might be seen as reinforcing the hold the American dream of rags to riches—or, for that matter, riches, period—has on our collective imagination. They might seem like capitalist manifestoes for the young, providing elementary instruction in the basic workings of a market economy, with its emphasis on innovation, risk taking, and, above all, competition. And in this way, they can seem to be encouraging the development of future Lee Iacoccas, Donald Trumps, and Leona Helmsleys: unabashed multimillionaires who proudly flaunt their financial success. Side by side with the enduring popularity of the board game Monopoly, and the emergence of new games like Trump, books about entrepreneurial youngsters can seem to fuel a culture of materialism that takes as its motto the Trumpism: "It's not whether you win or lose, but whether you win," with winning emphatically measured in dollars and cents.

But an actual look at entrepreneurial children's books, both in the nineteenth century and today, reveals that, as a body, they work instead to describe limits to the American dream understood in this way. It has been widely noted that the nineteenth-century novels present a message almost completely inverted from the cliched rags-to-riches-through-hard-work story attributed to them. While their heroes and heroines work diligently, success invariably comes to them not through their own efforts, but through the intervention of luck and chance, as some good deed brings them to the attention of a benevolent patron—who frequently turns out to be a long-lost, and conveniently wealthy, relative. And the virtues exhibited by nineteenth-century fortune seekers are conventional Christian virtues rather than any capitalist initiative, daring, or shrewdness. (pp. 189-90)

[Today's] entrepreneurial novels also undermine any stock capitalist conclusions. While they standardly present an attractive portrait of kids at work, over and over again they refuse to endorse a narrow, materialistic view of success. Whatever business success is achieved in the books, some other dimension of success is explicitly declared to be more important. And, strikingly, the central feature of a market economy—competition—is denigrated in favor of a celebration of cooperation, a more collectivist than capitalist concern. (p. 190)

In the most typical entrepreneurial novels . . . , financial success does come to the protagonists through their business and is viewed positively, but it only mirrors some deeper success that is the real focus of the novel. True success, in these books, has to do with personal growth or with the forming or strengthening of friendships among the business partners. The business provides a way for characters to test themselves and discover hidden talents; it provides a way for very different kids to work together toward a common goal. (p. 194)

Characters grow and change through their business experience. . . . [In] the launch title for the **"Baby-Sitters Club"** series [*Kristy's Great Idea*], the club is shown to help each girl in it. As the result of a baby-sitting encounter, Kristy comes to accept her stepfather-to-be; she explains, "The club has helped all of us. It helped Stacey make some friends. I think it helped give Mary Anne the courage to stand up to her father. And it showed Claudia that she can be good at something besides art." . . . The message could hardly come through more clearly: more important than any business success are self–confidence and courage, friendship and fun, cooperation and teamwork. (pp. 194-95)

> *Claudia Mills, "Capitalist Tools? Today's Entrepreneurial Novels for Children," in* Children's literature in education, *Vol. 21, No. 3, September, 1990, pp. 189-97.*

Janice C. Simpson

The Bobbsey Twins and Nancy Drew were too boring. And Trixie Belden? She was just plain dorky. But then Rebecca Langlois, a Dallas sixth-grader, discovered Kristy, Claudia, Mary Anne and Stacey. As just about every girl between eight and 12 knows, those are the founding members of the Baby-Sitters Club and the hottest fictional characters with today's preadolescent literary set. "They're funny and exciting, and the adventures they go through are stuff that can happen in real life," says Langlois, 12. She heads for the bookstore the minute the latest installment arrives.

That kind of devotion has sold more than 41 million copies of **"Baby-Sitters"** books since the series, which now runs to 40 volumes, began in August 1986. About 6 million copies of a companion series, **"Baby-Sitters Little Sister,"** for slightly younger readers, have been snatched up in just two years. . . .

Librarians give the books mixed reviews. Some find the plots predictable and the prose pedestrian, but others praise the series for attracting children who aren't always comfortable with books. "The reading level is pretty simple, and that's very important in my library, where English is a second language," says Janet Campano, who works at the Chinatown branch of the New York Public Library.

But Martin's main strength is her ability to tap into the ways young girls think and feel about life. Her stories explore the spectrum of preteen challenges from sibling rivalry and peer pressure to the death of a grandparent and the arrival of a new stepparent. Divorce is a fairly constant theme. "That's on the minds of kids a lot," Martin says. The books also touch on issues of race and ethnicity. Baby-Sitter Claudia, for example, is Asian and a talented artist, but she has trouble academically. "We wanted to defy the stereotype that every Asian is brilliant," says Feiwell.

There are still taboo subjects, however: Martin has avoided writing about drugs, sex and child abuse. "I think these topics are a little heavy for younger readers," she explains. Some kids like it that way. Such topics "would ruin the books," says Kathy Ames, 14, a Wyckoff, N.J., ninth-grader and a devoted fan. But others aren't so sure. "If these girls were real, they'd probably already be offered drugs and have to deal with it," says Langlois. Sounds like a new assignment for the Baby-Sitters.

> *Janice C. Simpson, "Adventures in Baby-Sitting," in* Time, New York, Vol. 137, No. 4, *January 28, 1991, p. 89.*

TITLE COMMENTARY

Bummer Summer (1983)

Kammy is far from enthralled when her widowed father marries Kate, and among the things she most resents are having to share her bedroom with Kate's three-year-old, having to listen to Kate's infant son scream because of his colic, and never having Dad to herself. She's unhappy and wants Dad and Kate to know it. Kammy agrees to try two weeks of camp, bitterly telling herself they just want to get rid of her, and she hates it at first. But, predictably, she makes friends at camp and decides to stay longer. Equally predictable: her acceptance of Kate and Kate's children, when they all come to camp for a visit. This is capably written for a first novel, has adequate pace, characters that are believable if not drawn with depth, and a patterned plot.

> *Zena Sutherland, in a review of "Bummer Summer," in* Bulletin of the Center for Children's Books, *Vol. 36, No. 11, July-August, 1983, p. 214.*

The camp scene comes complete with a stereotyped cast: the homesick loner, the brat, the stern-but-wise director, etc.; none of them are given more than a surface characterization. Moreover, Kammy's climactic confrontation with her nemesis, the bratty Susie, seems flat and improbable. The relationship between Kammy and her stepmother is better drawn and more plausible, while Kammy's skirmishes with stepsister Muffin will be immediately recognizable as typical of most siblings. While there are some fine moments of humor here, and the first-person narrative

is both realistic and amusing, this first novel falters in trying to handle two themes (stepfamily, first time at camp) at once. Both issues receive little more than a quick gloss.

> *Kathleen Brachmann, in a review of "Bummer Summer," in* School Library Journal, *Vol. 29, No. 1, August, 1983, p. 68.*

Inside Out (1984)

Jonno, eleven, is the narrator of a story that presents the problems that other children have in coping with a family situation in which there is an autistic sibling who creates unpleasant incidents, demands the time and attention of weary parents, and has the potential for embarrassing the other children in the family. James is four, and dominates the frazzled household; in the course of the story he starts school and begins to learn how to fend for himself (dressing, toilet-training, etc.) and how to relate to others. This is realistic: no promises are made as to James' future; as a fictionalized case history it is convincing. What the book lacks is flow and writing style and integration of the material about James and Jonno's worries about being weird or natural, being "inside out." Strong facets here, but the book doesn't quite coalesce.

> *Zena Sutherland, in a review of "Inside Out," in* Bulletin of the Center for Children's Books, *Vol. 37, No. 9, May, 1984, p. 170.*

The strength of [this] novel derives from this concurrence of thematic material: While the motive for action arises from the tensions caused by James's condition, the action itself revolves around the efforts of Jon, Lizzie, and their parents to cope with responsibilities and relationships in the outer worlds of school, work, and community. Not in any sense a case history, the book makes no effort to establish the etiology of James's illness. But once the little boy is accepted for treatment at a special school, the reader observes, along with the family, the technique used by his therapists to bring him into reciprocal contact with human beings. Considerable humor helps to neutralize the difficulties of Jon's and Lizzie's friendships at school and of their efforts to raise money for James's schooling. The author does not offer the sentimental hope that James will ever function normally. What is presented as normal, however, is the growing conviction of the whole family that even in the face of James's profound rejection of them, they can fight for his development rather than consign him to a custodial institution. (pp. 467-68)

> *Charlotte W. Draper, in a review of "Inside Out," in* The Horn Book Magazine, *Vol. LX, No. 4, August, 1984, pp. 467-68.*

Jonno, 11, wants to be accepted by the in-group, tries to earn extra spending money and must spend a lot of time caring for James, his autistic 4-year-old brother. During the course of this insightful novel, he realizes which of his concerns are truly important. Characters are well developed, especially James, whose behavior is presented with sensitivity. Reactions of schoolmates and family—father escaping to his office after James' tantrums; often overtired mother; siblings compensating for their brother's problem behavior by providing understanding and support for their mother—are also believable. Writing is awkward, relying on Jonno's first-person slangy narrative, but the subject of a child's reactions to his autistic sibling is a new one, and Martin handles it well.

> *Susan Scheps, in a review of "Inside Out," in* School Library Journal, *Vol. 31, No. 1, September, 1984, p. 120.*

Stage Fright (1984)

Dread of the spotlight rules the plot as nine-year-old Sara maneuvers to make herself inconspicuous; her innate shyness causes her trouble at parties, at school and at home. With an extroverted best friend nearly always coming to her rescue, Sara survives the dramas of daily life—until her teacher announces that *everyone* will perform in the class play. Sara is horror struck, for there is no hope of escape. Written in the first person, *Stage Fright* gives readers Sara's perspective and makes real the clutch of panic that strikes when Sara becomes the center of attention. Readers will understand, as Sara's mother cannot, that her reticence isn't the result of conscious decision; that trying to realize her mother's idea of "normal" sociability makes her miserable. Skillfully the author builds on this conflict to create a strong, appealing heroine whose affliction becomes an integral part of her personality and the story she tells. Martin does it all with touches of humor, and into a fast-paced entertaining plot introduces several well-drawn minor characters and situations. The insights into Sara's feelings and the vivid descriptions of her reactions add color and depth to a story that is light and upbeat, whose narrative seems at times even a bit *too* snappy. What may be most interesting about *Stage Fright* is that it questions the degree to which the problem of shyness can be resolved through effort when diffidence is a character trait, not a result of circumstance. Sara does prove in the end that she can face the spotlight without freezing, fainting or—as she first thought—dying, but her performance is far from shining. She does not "blossom." She is stronger in her knowledge of what she can do if she must, but she is not essentially changed by the experience. In the end it is acceptance of her nature rather than victory over it that provides resolution, and promises a growing and understanding between a mother and daughter whose temperaments are so very different. (pp. 77-8)

> *Susan Powers, in a review of "Stage Fright," in* School Library Journal, *Vol. 31, No. 5, January, 1985, pp. 77-8.*

Me and Katie (the Pest) (1985)

Ten-year-old Wendy is in competition with her sister, Katie, who is a year-and-a-half younger, and it's Katie who comes out on top every time. She is always winning prizes in music or art or for scholastic achievement. Wendy expects her sister to win the Nobel Peace Prize any day. It is not until Wendy starts taking horseback-riding lessons that she begins to shine in her own way. Unfortunately, Katie starts taking riding lessons as well, and it's

not long before the rivalry begins all over again. Martin has a keen ear for dialogue and captures the ups and downs of a sibling relationship. A quick, enjoyable read for middle-graders.

> *Ilene Cooper, in a review of "Me and Katie (the Pest)," in* Booklist, *Vol. 82, No. 5, November 1, 1985, p. 412.*

A bland story of sibling rivalry, this book has neither the humor of Blume's *Tales of a Fourth Grade Nothing* (1972) and *Superfudge* (1980, both Dutton) nor the sensitivity of Cleary's Beezus and Ramona stories. . . . The Whites live in a secure, insular world which will seem unreal to many chldren. Daddy works, mommy is a lawyer and a wonderful woman cleans, cooks and babysits while the children bounce from lesson to lesson. The characters are one dimensional, and the plot goes nowhere. The most interesting chapters are about Wendy's attachment to a horse; her love for the horse and longing for a pet of her own will strike a chord with many readers. The book will also have some appeal to children who can relate to the situation of sibling rivalry.

> *Judith L. Olson, in a review of "Me and Katie (the Pest)," in* School Library Journal, *Vol. 32, No. 4, December, 1985, p. 91.*

As told by Wendy, the tone [of *Me and Katie (the Pest)*] is consistent with the thoughts of a bright ten-year-old; the author has cleverly avoided a one-sided perspective by interjecting a sympathetic view of the younger sister through Wendy's friends and parents. The potentially more weighty elements of the situation are leavened with humor without patronizing the characters. Light fare, this satisfying dish, like a soufflé, takes considerable skill to concoct.

> *Mary M. Burns, in a review of "Me and Katie (the Pest)," in* The Horn Book Magazine, *Vol. LXII, No. 2, March-April, 1986, p. 202.*

With You and Without You (1986)

Because twelve-year-old Liza is the narrator, this has, in Martin's capable hands, no tinge of case history—but it is a fine example of an almost classic case of guilt-by-bereavement. The story begins with the family's discovery that Dad has an incurable and swiftly degenerating heart ailment. The family agrees with Dad that the last, precious months be as happy as possible. After his death they move to a smaller house and adjust to their deep loss, their new need to be frugal, and their acceptance of change. Liza is angry at the others because they seem able to have fun, while she rejects social opportunities because she feels she has no right to be happy. She refuses to visit the cemetery where Dad's ashes have been buried. She refuses to have anything to do with Christmas celebration, although she is eventually drawn into family activities. And, eventually, she faces the fact that the others are grieving in their own way and that they have simply come to see before she has that being happy is not betraying Dad. This is sensitive but not somber, convincing as the commentary of a young adolescent, and competent in characterization, pace, and structure. The dominant theme is balanced by small sub-plots involving boy and girl friends in a book that tells a family story as well as a story of adjustment to loss.

> *A review of "With You and Without You," in* Bulletin of the Center for Children's Books, *Vol. 39, No. 6, May, 1986, p. 174.*

Martin presents a sugar-coated struggle of a family enduring the terminal illness of a parent and then adjusting to his death, and the minimal amount of conflicts among family members robs a few of the characters of their credibility. Also, some of the elements fit together too neatly. However, these flaws are subdued by the author's skillful exploration of the fear, guilt and confusion that plague adolescents and young children experiencing the loss of a parent. This will be of interest to counselors and librarians, who will find it a fresh source of brief, read-aloud excerpts for group bibliotherapy, as well as to the intended audience.

> *Cynthia K. Leibold, in a review of "With You and Without You," in* School Library Journal, *Vol. 32, No. 10, August, 1986, p. 104.*

The cathartic effect of shedding tears while reading this book earns it the 5K (Kleenex) award. The O'Hara family is told in November that their father/husband has only six months to live, six months they vow will be special. Although the plot is predictable, father sickens, dies and family goes on, one is able to observe the readjustment process through the reactions of the family members. Four-year-old Hope doesn't understand the concept of death. Her father went to the hospital, her family talked of death, and yet her father came home, which proved to her that dead people come back. When Charley the cat dies, she doesn't want him buried too deep, so he will find it easy to crawl out of the grave when he comes back. Twelve-year-old Liza acts like a martyr and thinks the entire family should remain in mourning months after dad dies. Luckily, Marc Radley saves her from this self-imposed isolation.

Young readers who have lost a parent or a special person will undoubtably recognize many of their own thoughts, such as the inevitable question of the fairness of death, especially to the survivors; the difficulty of accepting the reality of death and the ultimate realization that life does go on, "with you and without you." Martin writes in a light, easy-to-read style that softens the harshness of death.

> *Pam Spencer, in a review of "With You and Without You," in* Voice of Youth Advocates, *Vol. 9, Nos. 3-4, August-October, 1986, p. 146.*

Kristy's Great Idea (1986)

Kristy's "great idea" is to form a Babysitters Club with three fellow seventh graders: Mary Anne, Claudia and newcomer Stacey. The group, organized to pool their baby-sitting assignments, seems to work well, and through the club's logbook readers can trace the girls' growing success. Meanwhile, Kristy's divorced mother announces her engagement to boyfriend Watson, much to Kristy's displeasure. Then the girl catches Stacey in a lie and con-

fronts her about it, starting a controversy that almost splits the club apart for good. But they reconcile at the end, and Kristy (through baby-sitting Watson's two children) comes to accept her mother's remarriage. Martin has written an enjoyable, light-hearted story with much appeal for middle readers. Her characters, especially the four girls, are strongly drawn, and have distinct enough personalities to carry the projected Babysitters Club series.

> *A review of "Kristy's Great Idea," in* Publishers Weekly, *Vol. 230, No. 18, October 31, 1986, p. 69.*

All of the elements of concern to preteen girls (wearing the "in" clothes, keeping friendships stable, coping with family stresses, and trying to grow up) are here, tied to the almost universal experience of baby-sitting. Characters are not drawn with great depth, but the action is on target. A pleasant offering that will find a ready audience.

> *Candy Colborn, in a review of "Kristy's Great Idea," in* School Library Journal, *Vol. 33, No. 7, March, 1987, p. 163.*

Missing Since Monday (1986)

Tenth-grade Maggie and her older brother Mike are in charge of their half-sister Courtenay while their dad and their stepmother take a long-postponed honeymoon. To their horror, four-year-old Courtenay fails to return home from preschool, and it doesn't take long for them to realize that she's the victim of kidnapping—or worse. The book chronicles what happens, including the involvement of police, other agencies, and private individuals as they assemble around the grief-stricken family to help them deal with the situation and to put into effect the mechanisms to search for the missing child. There's a great deal of information concerning how a missing child search works; in fact, occasionally the weight of the information intrudes upon the novel. Despite that, however, the suspense builds steadily throughout, as readers try to determine not only what has happened to Courtenay and at whose hands, but also who is making harassing and suggestive phone calls to Maggie. One of the solutions is fairly predictable, but the other comes as a real surprise. Middle school readers, including reluctant ones, will really care what happens to Courtenay and her family.

> *Susan F. Marcus, in a review of "Missing Since Monday," in* School Library Journal, *Vol. 33, No. 3, November, 1986, p. 105.*

Martin does a credible job with a widely discussed horror—the abduction of a child. . . . [This] is a strong, at times scary story of what happens to a family in a crisis situation. Martin also provides a decent mystery as the police and the Ellises follow all clues in an effort to find Courtenay, which eventually happens. The unusual ending, which sees Maggie and Mike's real mother as the abductor, seems a little farfetched, but readers who have been caught up in the drama should accept this denouement.

> *Ilene Cooper, in a review of "Missing Since*

Monday," in Booklist, *Vol. 83, No. 8, December 15, 1986, p. 650.*

Claudia and the Phantom Phone Calls (1986)

The four 12-year-old girls who comprise "The Baby-sitters Club" are worried about a robber whose pattern involves first calling the possible victim and then remaining silent. The girls, responsible babysitters, are at the same time gossipy girls who are variously at odds with members of their families, their schoolwork, and above all, boys. It is one of the latter who turns out to be Claudia's "Phantom caller," brave enough to dial, but too shy to ask her to the dance. Martin sometimes writes as her audience would (Claudia "goes" rather than "says," for instance). Claudia is an underachiever, but gifted in art; she has a brilliant sister she doesn't like; and she is Japanese. She should be an interesting and complex character, but she is hardly distinguishable from the other three babysitters. This contrived story is one of those ephemeral paperbacks that can easily be forgotten. (pp. 98-9)

Carolyn Jenks, in a review of "Claudia and the Phantom Phone Calls," in School Library Journal, *Vol. 33, No. 10, June-July, 1987, pp. 98-9.*

Just a Summer Romance (1987)

Fourteen-year-old Melanie summers each year on Fire Island, where her family owns a beachfront cottage. This year, with summer almost over, Melanie meets newcomer Justin Hart and knows immediately that she likes him. Justin responds in kind, and the two share the season's remaining weeks enjoying each other's company in what quickly becomes an easygoing, satisfying relationship. Both know they'll part at summer's end; Justin is especially frank on that point. Nevertheless, Mel finds a total parting of the ways difficult, and Justin promises that when his parents' pending moves are completed, he'll send her his address. When she returns home, Melanie is shocked to discover that Justin is a rising young star. Upset that he didn't reveal his background yet loath to dismiss what she felt was a genuine relationship, Melanie searches for a way to reach Justin and settle her questions. When the two finally do talk, Melanie finds that the real Justin *is* the same boy she summered with. He explains his wariness as well as his realization that he values Melanie because he's sure she likes him for himself and not for his pop-star image. In satisfying romance-story fashion, the two agree to resume seeing each other when Justin's busy schedule allows and to try to make a long-distance romance work. Martin's twist on the girl-meets-boy theme makes for a highly appealing story. Its credibility holds together because characters are believable and down to earth. There is attention to real feelings here, and thus a measure of staying power not often seen in the genre.

Denise M. Wilms, in a review of "Just a Summer Romance," in Booklist, *Vol. 83, No. 15, April 1, 1987, p. 1208.*

This is an entertaining, fast-paced, enjoyable story. The characters, particularly Melanie's family, are interesting and believable, and Melanie herself comes across as a typical teenage girl—very nice and likable. Sure to be popular.

Elizabeth Mellett, in a review of "Just a Summer Romance," in School Library Journal, *Vol. 33, No. 10, June-July, 1987, p. 110.*

Written with a humorous touch and peopled with very likable characters, this would translate well to video. It has the feel of an "After School Special." Although the situation is fanciful, the characters' dialogue and emotions are believable. Use this as a launching point to older romances and to a more mature examination of teens and fame—Kerr's *Son of Someone Famous.*

Janice Toomajian, in a review of "Just a Summer Romance," in Voice of Youth Advocates, *Vol. 10, No. 4, October, 1987, p. 204.*

Slam Book (1987)

In her "Slam Book," Anna's ninth-grade friends write comments about each other ("What a hunk . . . Gorgeous . . . Stuck up"; "She isn't playing with a full deck"; "Too perfect"). But what begins as Anna's "key to popularity" degenerates into a cruel, manipulative game and leads to tragedy.

It's cousin Peggy at a family picnic—a picnic which demonstrates what a strong, loving family Anna has—who makes the suggestion. At first the book, with its hint of forbidden danger, is fun; it does keep Anna at the center of attention. She ignores the cruelty that soon emerges, especially from rich, disturbed Paige, who disguises her handwriting and uses the book to break up Casey and Gooz. Paige's plan misfires (Gooz turns to Anna); more disguised messages tempt the butt of class wit, Cheryl, with a boyfriend. Trying to get even with Paige, Anna writes Cheryl a note that sends her to a rejection by Paige; Cheryl commits suicide, and the girls are left to face the consequences of their actions.

Martin writes smoothly, with good understanding of this age group and its concerns. Her portraits of the several families of Anna and her friends are broad but ring true and provide contrasts useful to the story—Randy, black, has the other supportive home; Jessie is surviving a bad situation; Paige may not. Anna won't suffer unduly from her thoughtlessness, but she has learned a lesson—not quite fair, perhaps, but realistic. Like Martin's other novels, this is sure to engage readers.

A review of "Slam Book," in Kirkus Reviews, *Vol. LV, No. 20, October 15, 1987, p. 1519.*

This forceful novel makes its point quite clear—slam books are not fun and games. Although the characterizations of Anna and her friends often seem to center on their psychological problems, the gritty, well-paced plot guarantees that this novel will involve readers from start to finish. (pp. 72-3)

A review of "Slam Book," in Publishers Weekly, *Vol. 232, No. 20, November 13, 1987, pp. 72-3.*

Martin has a sure grasp of the games teens play and empathy for the exultation and pain of high schoolers. Character development is rather limited, especially when adult figures are introduced. The chain of events is dramatic, yet believable. It's not difficult to fathom the message: we are responsible for our actions; our actions have consequences to others. Despite faint echos of TV's *Facts of Life*, this is a highly readable and serious title.

> *Libby K. White, in a review of "The Slam Book," in* School Library Journal, *Vol. 34, No. 4, December, 1987, p. 102.*

Ten Kids, No Pets (1988)

A rarity in this era—a jolly story about a family with lots of kids.

The ten Rossos have been named according to a system devised by their mother, using a book called *What Shall We Name the Baby?* and resulting in names like Eberhard, Gardenia, and even Dagwood. Though a benign parent, Mrs. Rosso has a system for almost everything, which keeps her family of 12 organized and functioning; but even when they move from a city apartment to the country, she is firm: ten kids are enough—there will be no pets. Nonetheless, as each child from Abigail (14) to Janthina (8) gets a chapter, a number of animals are welcomed and loved: the rabbit who arrives as the Halloween magician's prop; the Thanksgiving turkey purchased live and ultimately donated to a petting zoo; a nest of orphaned sparrows. But when Mom admits that an unexpected 11th baby is on the way, the kids have her: If she can have an extra, so can they; and, being a wise parent, Mom has to agree that fair is fair.

There are so many kids here that we don't get a chance to know any of them well; and though the chapters are tied together by the year's cycle and the pet theme, the effect is episodic. But the Rossos are a lively, enjoyable family; middle-readers should breeze happily through their experiences.

> *A review of "Ten Kids, No Pets," in* Kirkus Reviews, *Vol. LVI, No. 7, April 1, 1988, p. 542.*

The unusual Rosso family moves from New York City to the country, and each of the 10 children adapts to the change differently. They are individuals, but they have one thing in common—each wants a pet. How the family members interact with one another, how they adjust to the country, and how a pet becomes an inevitable addition to their home are the facets of this light, enjoyable book. At times there is too much telling and not enough showing of character traits, but the family as a whole is multidimensional and credible. The moods that accompany the seasons enable readers to share in the excitement, energy and caring that fills the Rosso home.

> *A review of "Ten Kids, No Pets," in* Publishers Weekly, *Vol. 233, No. 17, April 29, 1988, p. 77.*

It's refreshing to see a book in which siblings play more than a satellite role to a major character. While no one person is developed in depth, Martin does convey a good deal of information about the characters during their turn in the spotlight. The weakest character, Mr. Rosso, stays more or less in the background, while Mrs. Rosso is sketched through her children's comments. On-track dialogue and a realistic relationship among the siblings are enjoyable pluses. Great for read-alouds as well as a fine read-alone choice.

> *Kathleen Brachmann, in a review of "Ten Kids, No Pets," in* School Library Journal, *Vol. 35, No. 8, May, 1988, p. 98.*

Karen's Witch (1988)

In the first book of the **"Babysitter's Little Sister"** series, Karen is convinced that her next door neighbor, Mrs. Porter, is a witch. Mrs. Porter has frizzy gray hair, wears long black dresses, has a cat named Midnight and mumbles to herself in her herb garden. So when Karen overhears Mrs. Porter telling Midnight that a meeting is set for 12 o'clock, Karen jumps to the conclusion that it is a witches' meeting. By the time Karen realizes she is wrong, it is too late to get herself out of trouble. Writing in the first person, Martin has created a quirky heroine who is as independent as she is silly.

> *A review of "Karen's Witch," in* Publishers Weekly, *Vol. 234, No. 7, August 12, 1988, p. 460.*

Yours Turly, Shirley (1988)

Shirley Basini is dreading fourth grade—she is dyslexic and if she doesn't do well this year, she will have to stay back. Worse yet, her new teacher is strict and doesn't let her horse around. When Shirley's adopted sister Jacki arrives from Vietnam, Shirley is thrilled to help her learn English and teach her about America. But when Jacki is suddenly put in the advanced third grade class, Shirley feels jealous and threatened; she stops making an effort at school. An unexpected challenge to Jacki and Shirley's friendship, along with extra help from the school resource room, propel Shirley further ahead in her schoolwork than either she or her parents expected. Martin, the author of the recent **Ten Kids, No Pets** as well as **Bummer Summer** and other titles, tells Shirley's story in a straightforward, believable manner and creates an independent heroine who triumphs over her disability. (pp. 69-70)

> *A review of "Yours Turly, Shirley," in* Publishers Weekly, *Vol. 234, No. 14, September 30, 1988, pp. 69-70.*

The producer of **"The Babysitter's Club"** series presents a memorably lovable character: Shirley Basini, whose battle with a poor self-image is largely caused by her dyslexia.

Fourth-grader Shirley copes with her problem by being the class clown; but the classroom teacher is not impressed: he makes it clear that Shirley must either improve or be held back. Her efforts are deflected when her parents adopt an eight-year-old Vietnamese girl. At first, as Shirley mentors Jackie, she gains confidence that spills over into her schoolwork. But when Jackie turns out to be a fine, devoted reader, Shirley's resentment threatens all her hardwon progress. It takes thoughtful intervention from both her parents and a resource-center teacher to help Shirley put herself back on the right track.

Shirley has definite strengths that stand her in good stead despite her reading difficulties; her story is slickly and entertainingly written. One might quibble over the cursory attention given to Jackie's background; but the funny, positive depiction of Shirley's adventures overrides the flaws here.

> *A review of "Yours Turly, Shirley," in* Kirkus Reviews, *Vol. LVI, No. 19, October 1, 1988, p. 1473.*

This book truly defines *mediocrity*. . . . Readers do come to know and understand Shirley somewhat, but the other characters are as realistic as paper dolls. They remain completely in the background except when they come into direct contact with Shirley. The family is totally insensitive to their adoptive daughter, simply telling her what her new name will be, never asking her real name or anything about her culture. Shirley's dyslexia is treated superficially, the teacher simply stating that if she'd pay attention and try harder, she could do much better. Martin has filled the book with potentially vital, exciting, touching, and funny situations, but the story fails to deliver.

> *Nancy P. Reeder, in a review of "Yours Turly, Shirley," in* School Library Journal, *Vol. 35, No. 4, December, 1988, p. 109.*

Kristy and the Snobs   (1988)

In the sorting-out process we all have to use when we meet new people, none of the distinctions of class, income, appearance or behaviour works perfectly; social adjustment (especially perhaps for the 'teens when they are important to understandably insistent egotism) are a matter of trial and error. As the title *Kristy and the Snobs* suggests, a girl moving into a new environment in an American city sorts out the neighbours first of all by class. The impressively named Shannon Louisa Kilbourne, annoyed when the newcomer advertises a baby-sitting group with school-friends, cutting inadvertently into Shannon's well-established concern, attacks her rival with cutting criticisms and flaunts the social superiority of her family life-style, while Kristy's customers fit into various social categories, headed by the rich Delaneys whose children expect their new sitter to be a willing slave. Kristy tells her own story and through her frankly, occasionally naîve coments on the people she meets we can see how and why she adjusts her attitudes, in particular realising how much she has misread Shannon's character. Chats over the garden fence, visits and neighbourhood explorations, build up a sharp picture of an urban community in all the complexity of the present day, with a girl's problems dictating the form and tone of the book. (pp. 5423-24)

> *Margery Fisher, in a review of "Kristy and the*

Snobs," in Growing Point, *Vol. 29, No. 4, November, 1990, pp. 5423-24.*

Ma and Pa Dracula   (1989)

An interesting slant on the old "moving to a new neighborhood" plot line. When fourth-grade Jonathan Primave sneaks outside in broad daylight, he meets Tobi, a friendly girl his age who tells him that school, T.V., and telephones are real, not just madeup things in books as he's been told. When he confronts his parents, they reveal their secret— they are vampires. Jonathan convinces them to let him go to school—but it's not easy being the adopted son of vampires, especially when the blood bank is almost exhausted, your parents are very hungry, and your class is coming to your house for a Halloween party. This whimsical fantasy, full of deadpan humor and a few moments of outright slapstick, is very different from Martin's **"Babysitters Club"** series. There's a certain awkwardness in explaining something ordinary as if being viewed for the first time, but children should enjoy Jonathan's naive description of school. The contrast between courtly, old-fashioned Jonathan and modern Tobi is depicted effectively, especially in the way they speak. This is a quick read with short chapters that should capture readers right away. Jonathan's apprehension at what his parents might do is maintained well without losing the humor, and the ending, in which he puts his parents' needs above his own, is satisfying. While attracting the same audience as Angela Sommer-Bodenburg's *My Friend the Vampire* (Dial, 1984), this book has a much more defined structure.

> *Annette Curtis Klause, in a review of "Ma and Pa Dracula," in* School Library Journal, *Vol. 35, No. 13, September, 1989, p. 256.*

Jonathan Primave needs to do a lot of adjusting after he discovers that his parents are vampires. . . .

[He] offers to host the class Halloween party; his subsequent attempts to keep the family secret (e.g., by shooing his parents to the basement to nap in their coffins lest they snack on his guests) are hilarious.

This highly original story is by the popular author of the **"Babysitter's Club"** series. Though the premise is silly and undeniably macabre, the book is clever, wickedly funny, and actually has a valid message about the sacrifices people make for the ones they love.

> *A review of "Ma and Pa Dracula," in* Kirkus Reviews, *Vol. LVII, No. 16, September 1, 1989, p. 1330.*

It's a weird premise for a book, but it works just fine . . . There are plenty of juicy moments as Jonathan tries to have a regular life despite his family circumstances; any kid who has ever been embarrassed by his parents will certainly sympathize with Jonathan. Though the ending— which has the Primaves moving on once more— disappoints, this is a fresh and funny story that strikes just the right mix between the real and the outrageous.

> *Ilene Cooper, in a review of "Ma and Pa*

Dracula," in Booklist, *Vol. 86, No. 6, November 15, 1989, p. 672.*

Eleven Kids, One Summer (1991)

In this buoyant and breezy sequel to *Ten Kids, No Pets,* the Rosso family (consisting of 11 children, an admirably organized mother and an endearingly absentminded father) spends the summer on New York's Fire Island. The novel takes off in a number of diverting directions, as do the amiable Rosso offspring, who range in age from six months to 15 years. Each chapter focuses on one of the siblings: among them, Abbie, the eldest, who makes friends with a handsome teenage actor filming a movie on the island; sensitive Candy, convinced that the abandoned house next door is haunted; Hannah, who engages in some unsettling practical jokes; and Woody, an entrepreneur who paints and sells seashells. Martin, creator of the **"Baby-sitters Club,"** knows well what pleases young readers, and this novel is filled with characters, escapades and dialogue that will do just that.

> *A review of "Eleven Kids, One Summer," in* Publishers Weekly, *Vol. 238, No. 38, August 23, 1991, p. 62.*

The signs of formulaic contemporary sit-com fiction are in abundance in this sequel to *Ten Kids, No Pets*. The 11 Rosso children's summer at Fire Island is filled with so many choppy family happenings and so many people that only the surface is available to readers. Plot wins out over style, and sometimes the pace and content strain credibility. In oldest child Abigail's chapter, she sets out to meet people and literally bumps into two girls and a boy who is a movie star. "The longer they talked, the more relaxed Abbie felt, and the more Justin really did seem like just a regular guy . . . She'd been on Fire Island for just two and a half hours, and already she'd made three friends. She belonged." Martin tucks in animal-rights issues and Lyme disease, a mystery, practical jokes, and a couple of bullies to make the summer complete. In spite of all these obstacles, the caring of the children for each other comes through, as does the love and good humor of their parents. But for a much better story about a large family who spends the summer on an island, try Gilbreth's *Cheaper by the Dozen* (Crowell, 1963), a true story about a Nantucket vacation a long time ago.

> *Carolyn Jenks, in a review of "Eleven Kids, One Summer," in* School Library Journal, *Vol. 37, No. 10, October, 1991, p. 125.*

Rachel Parker, Kindergarten Show-Off (1992)

Five-year-old Olivia is excited to learn that the family moving in next door includes a girl who is just her age. But when Rachel Elizabeth joins Olivia's kindergarten class, Olivia is no longer the only one who can read and write. Not only that, but the newcomer has *two* first names, a grandfather who gives out candy, an adorable baby sister and her very own puppet theater. The competitiveness between the girls makes for some amusing exchanges: when Rachel announces that she is writing a story, Olivia counters with the fact that she is writing a book, which Rachel tops by saying that she wrote a book the previous year, "when I was four." A showdown at the playground leads to the inevitable resolution of the strife, and the two youngsters end up fast friends. Olivia's first-person narrative, chatty and comic, imparts a breath of fresh air to a common situation. (Commendably, no point is made of the fact that Olivia is African American while her eventual pal is white.)

> *A review of "Rachel Parker, Kindergarten Show-Off," in* Publishers Weekly, *Vol. 239, No. 42, September 21, 1992, p. 93.*

Olivia is African-American and Rachel is white, but first and foremost they are strong-willed, precocious kindergarteners. Young children will easily recognize either themselves or a classmate in this lively pair. It is hoped they will also learn from the gentle lesson. This is a book that's sure to find a wide readership.

> *Nancy A. Gifford, in a review of "Rachel Parker, Kindergarten Show-Off," in* School Library Journal, *Vol. 38, No. 11, November, 1992, p. 73.*

Few authors have delivered stories in which children of different races are close friends—not simply members of the same class or team, but good buddies who hang out together, just the two of them, all the time. The accomplished Rosa Guy . . . has addressed this deficit with *Billy the Great.* . . .

Rachel Parker, Kindergarten Show-Off, another tale of interracial friendship, is in some ways similar to *Billy the Great* but it is also simpler, and, I suspect, easier for children to relate to. Ann Martin sets up this situation: Olivia is the star of the kindergarten until Rachel Elizabeth Parker moves next door and into the same class. Olivia, accustomed to being the only child in the class who can read or write, is nervous. Now she has a competitor.

But Rachel is also a close friend. The girls must deal with growing friction as they try to outdo each other in the classroom while also playing together after school. Naturally, Rachel and Olivia argue, patch things up, argue again and stomp off to go their separate ways. In the end, of course, they settle their differences. Predictably, but believably, they do so in a way that conveys to young readers (and to the adults they will become) the advantages of working together—a message balanced with a healthy reminder that it is possible to compete fiercely without becoming enemies.

An important difference between Ms. Martin's story and Ms. Guy's is that the friendship between Olivia and Rachel lacks the sharp racial or class undercurrents of the friendship between Billy and Rodney. In talent, training and quality of home life, the children seem absolutely equal. Some adult readers might find this unrealistic, but for many children it is real life.

> *Stephen L. Carter, "Can't We All Just Get Along? Yes, Sometimes," in* The New York Times Book Review, *November 8, 1992, p. 44.*

Emily Rodda

1948(?)-

(Real name Jennifer Rowe) Australian author of fiction.

Major works include *Something Special* (1985), *Pigs Might Fly* (1986, U. S. edition as *The Pigs Are Flying!*), *The Best-Kept Secret* (1988), *Finders Keepers* (1990).

INTRODUCTION

Rodda is perhaps the most honored of Australia's contemporary writers for children: with only five books to her credit, she is the first author to be a four-time winner of the prestigious Australian Children's Book of the Year Award. The creator of fantasies for readers in the early and middle grades that introduce the magical and supernatural into the daily lives of their young male and female protagonists, she is lauded as an especially original writer whose books are imaginative, plausible, and insightful. Rodda is also praised as an especially fine storyteller as well as for her skillful creation of character and dialogue. Set in present-day Australia, her works characteristically use the time-travel and ghost story motifs as their basis while including elements of suspense, mystery, and humor as well as thought-provoking themes. Rodda underscores her books with explorations of personal and societal issues, often describing the latter with a lightly satiric tone. *Books for Keeps* calls Rodda an "illuminating, fresh-voiced writer," and *Magpies* adds that her "gentle fantasies are unique in this area of writing for children."

The author of adult mysteries as well as an editor of a women's magazine, Rodda began writing her juvenile fiction, which she pens under her grandmother's maiden name, to match the changing ages of her eldest daughter, who was seven when Rodda wrote her first book. This tale, the ghost story *Something Special,* revolves around a rummage sale at the primary school attended by Samantha and her friend Lizzie. The girls become involved with the spirits of the owners of the clothes that are to be contributed to the sale; the title of the book refers to the fact that the clothes were particular favorites of their owners or were part of special occasions in their lives. In her next book, *Pigs Might Fly,* Rodda involves protagonist Rachel in a fantasy world where an atmospheric storm has changed the personalities of people and animals; trapped in this strange land, she enters on a quest to return home that causes *Pigs Might Fly* to be compared to *The Wizard of Oz.* A carousel takes selected riders into the future in *The Best-Kept Secret,* a story that highlights the members of a small community at pivotal points in their lives. Rodda describes how these characters learn to accept the choices they must make; protagonist Jo, an only child who helps to rescue a small boy in the future, learns when she returns to her own time that she is to become a big sister and that the child she has rescued is really her brother.

Finder's Keepers is the first book in which Rodda features a boy protagonist and is also considered to be a departure in terms of length, plot, and level of sophistication. While watching television, middle grader Patrick receives an invitation to play "Finder's Keepers," a game show that is not on any regular channel. If he finds the missing objects described by three contestants, Patrick wins a computer. Young readers are invited to solve the clues along with Patrick, who faces a moral dilemma in addition to his other challenges. Rodda's most recent book, *Crumbs* (1990), again features a boy as its main character and includes a parody of television, this time Saturday morning cartoons. *Something Special* won the Australian Children's Book Award in 1985, a prize won by *Pigs Might Fly* in 1987, *The Best-Kept Secret* in 1989, and *Finder's Keepers* in 1991; *Something Special* was named Junior Book of the Year, while the other three won the Younger Reader's Award from the Australian Children's Book Award committee.

AUTHOR'S COMMENTARY

Which author of successful adult mysteries has written

three children's books which have all won the Children's Book of the Year: Younger Readers Award? This author also manages to hold a full-time position as editor of the *Australian Women's Weekly* and to raise a family of four children, two of whom are three year old twins. The answer is, of course, Jennifer Rowe, who writes her children's books under the pseudonym of Emily Rodda, her grandmother's maiden name.

In her amazingly full life she has to find the time late at night to do the writing which she loves. Working to her night time schedule she has now completed her newest children's novel, *Finders Keepers.*

She explains: "It's about a little boy and he's the middle child in a family. I suppose because I have a middle child myself who's a boy, I have a lot of sympathy with that particular situation. You know, you've got the old child who can do everything and has that independence and you've got the kid who is the baby and the other child is somehow stuck in the middle. Patrick, in *Finders Keepers,* is a bit like that. He's not unhappy; he's just a bit crowded by the other people in the house. And like a lot of boys that age, one of the things he's really interested in is computers and another thing is television and quiz programmes. He gets caught up in a fantasy which involves going to a very special quiz programme called *Finders Keepers* which is a kind of treasure hunt. It involves crossing over into another time stream and getting back with the objects he has to find."

How do you bring all the strands of your novels together? They are so intricate but as you reach the end every little piece falls into place?

Well, I love things like that. I love things that do all tie up and in fact I find things that don't very irritating if they're that type of book. Obviously there are books that are open ended because that's what life is like—that's a different kind of book. The kind of book that I regard as an adventure or a fantasy or whatever, I think that deserves a good, neat ending. I like murder mysteries as well and *par excellence* that's what they are like. There's no little clue that doesn't have a meaning and I suppose it's the fascination for someone who likes word games or likes doing tapesty, all of which I actually do like doing. Maybe it's a response to the general messiness of life, but I find it very satisfying.

And the kids really seem to like it. They like the way it all dove-tails and fits. I found that if you wait long enough most things do have a meaning. I mean, you can see a pattern if you stand back far enough, even if you have to wait a hundred years to see it, you'll see it. I know that from studying history. It's like when you have a whole bundle of threads, if you look at them too close up you can't see that they make a picture until you get back, and then you often can see that there is a whole picture there. I suppose that's my rationalization for something I find personally satisfying.

They are certainly very satisfying to read. Even bits you've forgotten suddenly reappear and click into place.

The thing is, I don't plan that all from the start at all. I

usually plan the bones of it. Writing is such a pleasure, but because I write at night I've only got a couple of hours really. I find if I stay up too late I just get too exhausted the next day. Usually I write from 9.00 p.m. to 11.00 p.m. Now that's not really terribly long. I could go on for much longer, especially when I'm finishing a book. And for that reason I really have to enjoy it a lot to do it, otherwise I'd make excuses. I'd think I'd rather do something else, like read, go to bed or watch TV. I found that the more I plan it out, the less I enjoy it because I like to tell myself the story as I go along. So what I do is think quite a lot about it before I start so that I've got all the themes going round in my head all the time and I know the basis of it. When I started this book for example, I knew where it was going to end up. I had the end planned but not all the little strands. Then as I'm going along and I'm telling myself the story, I think, "Oh yes, that's where that fits in."

In fact, in *Finders Keepers* I actually had an element in there that didn't seem to me to fit in as neatly as everything else. But I really liked it. I kept thinking all along there must be some reason why this is here. And it wasn't until I'd actually finished the whole thing that I thought, "Oh, that's why." It's actually a big clock which is in a shopping centre near where Patrick lives and having made this clock I really liked it. It actually does play a little part in the plot which is what I intended it to do but the clock seemed to me to become more interesting than that particular part of the plot warranted. When I got to the end and talked about it with the editor and she wanted to know something about the mechanism of the barrier, how the barrier worked, that I suddenly realized why the clock was there.

I often feel that the story is telling itself and I'm just finding it out as I go along and if a thing doesn't fit in I think about it an awful lot before I throw it out because often I find (I've found this with other authors from being an editor before) that authors will unconsciously do things that have a real meaning. They've created something and they don't quite know why it's there, but when you look at the big picture, you can see why. It's because the symbols are all there. It's because they're talking in symbols often, and somethimes they haven't quite seen it for themselves.

Mostly I find that as long as I've thought enough about it in the shower or driving to work or before I start, the things are all there in my head, but it's just a matter of finding which way they should fall. I think that probably *The Best Kept Secret* was more like that than any of the others have been. Although, obviously, *Pigs Might Fly* certainly had various strands, *The Best Kept Secret* had more opportunities for that because it was about a lot of different people. I really enjoyed that; I loved it.

It might be interesting to know that *The Best Kept Secret* when I first wrote it and regarded it as complete didn't have the strand about Simon the inventor in it at all. It didn't have the yo-ball in it. It actually ended with Jo going into the house thinking about the music, she works out about the little brother and her mother asks would she like to take piano lessons. So it ended there. I was quite happy with it; I thought it was quite good.

My husband, who is a book editor too, read it and said, "It doesn't seem as thick as your other books." I went away thinking I didn't want any more adventures. I didn't want him to get stranded and anything like that because that's so ordinary. I had to find something that actually existed already within the story. So I looked at it and I looked at it and I already had the ball with the silver strings there. I started to think about that. And then I thought about Michael and Mr Milligan, the banker, and all that. So that whole strand was written after and woven in. Because it was already there really, you see. All I was doing was operating on something that was already there and just extrapolating from it, trying to work out where it came from and why it was there.

I love telling a story so that people will say, "Ah, that's how it works. That's the reason for that." But at the same time I don't want to be pat. You know you feel as though you've read an awful lot of stories where endings were very pat. I want them to be interesting and satisfying. All the letters that I get from kids say that. They obviously seem satisfied with what they've read. My own children seem to like to read them over again. I feel that's always a good sign that someone likes to read something again.

Your first book Something Special *won the Children's Book of the Year Junior Award. What effect do the Awards have, do you think?*

They have an enormous effect on sales and for that reason they have an enormous and immediate effect on your popularity as a writer. More people read it so more children write to you because their teachers have taken the book because it's been shortlisted. I think the shortlist is what actually does it more than the winning.

What about the effect on you as a writer?

Well, certainly the first didn't have so much of an effect because I was so astounded and surprised because I hadn't held out the faintest hope of actually winning. I suppose what it did do was make me think I should write another one because it had been very much an experiment and it also meant that because *Something Special* had been published by my own company (hence the pseudonym) it made me feel more justified in having let Richard Walsh, the publisher, publish it. That embarrassment that I might have felt if it had been a bit of a flop went away. I suppose the second time that I won it, I started to feel like a writer then. As a child I had always wanted to be a writer; now maybe I really was one. Second books are much harder to pull off than first ones. For that reason I was very pleased with the award for *Pigs Might Fly.* And then when I won the third one I was absolutely overwhelmed. Then I started to get frightened. I started to feel I obviously couldn't keep this up and everything I now do will be disappointing to people. I feel more self-conscious about whether what I write is good or not. Before, I would just write to my own satisfaction and now I suppose I worry more that it's not good. You see I can't tell if it's any good or not until someone else tells me. So when I finished *Finders Keepers* I really had no idea if it was just a rattling good read, if it was good literature, if the story worked, or anything else. It sounds really stupid after all those years of being an edi-

tor, but it seems that with your own work it really is very, very difficult.

But I really do love writing. When you're in the kind of business I am in you're so much in demand by a lot of people. You're sort of giving all day. And if you've also got a young family as I have, they all want things from you, of course, which you are happy to give. But the great thing about writing, is that it is your thing. You get into this world and nobody gets in there with you. I think it probably is a real refreshment for me. That's why I miss it if I don't have it. So when I'm so called "resting", when I'm not writing anything because I've just finished something and maybe I'm taking a break, getting the house cleaned up from whatever dreadful state it's got into while I've been finishing off that last book, I tend to get a bit ratty. Then I like to do embroidery. It takes me years to complete.

You don't write in the day time?

Occasionally my husband takes the kids out on Sundays for about two hours and I sometimes have that time. I absolutely love that. In the morning you can get so much done. I don't particularly want to write at night; that's the time I have available. I don't try to do anything when the children are around. It's not fair to them, except for my daughter who's thirteen and obviously stays up later than the others. She has her own things that she does and she doesn't mind that I'm tapping away. And in fact when I was writing *Finders Keepers* I was spending a bit more time, occasionally doing it on the weekends when the babies were asleep in the afternoons. As I was finishing it the children were reading it straight off the computer. If I'd come out for a cup of tea they'd say, "Go back!" because they wanted to hear what was going to happen next. That helps to keep you going.

The hardest thing I find is the starting. I do have to push that sometimes because I know that once I get a certain way into it and get to know the characters it'll go much faster and be much more fun. So I have to make myself write that first couple of chapters. Therefore, I often have to go back and change those because they're just a bit lacklustre. I often find, in fact, that I have to go back and cut them enormously because I've been rambling on and getting to know the person or setting up the family situation in a way I don't really have to. (pp. 19-21)

Emily Rodda and Magpies, in an interview in
Magpies, *Vol. 5, No. 3, July, 1990, pp. 19-21.*

TITLE COMMENTARY

Something Special (1985)

All children seem to like a ghost story, and *Something Special* is the kind of story that really captures the imagination. Perhaps the reason for this is that the focal point is a collection of clothes awaiting to be sold at Sam's mother's stall at the school fete on Saturday. After all, most children have assembled items for a jumble sale and wondered about their previous owners. In the story the owners of the clothes turn up to shed some light on their association with the garment, but where they appeared from and whether they are part of a dream is some of the over all mystery which continues to the very end of the story when the clothes are finally sold.

This is a well written book; containing an intriguing story-line that gets to the heart of the matter without too much preamble. Its strength is perhaps its warm, embracing dialogue. In addition, there is the point that children who read the story have made; namely that although the essence is fantasy, there is still something quite believable about what happened.

> *Ron Morton, in a review of "Something Special," in* Books for Your Children, *Vol. 20, No. 1, Spring, 1985, p. 16.*

A thought-provoking and eerie tale about the preparations for a school fête. The clothes that are left at Lizzie's house take on a life of their own; two children get caught up in the lives of their owners. Rare in a book for this age group (sevens to nines), the writer has the courage *not* to explain everything.

She catches quite brilliantly the dash, excitement and movement of the preparations. Yet she slows down the action effectively when time needs to stand still (how does she do that?). Sevens will like having this read to them: it takes a skilled reading to catch the rhythms. Older readers will go it alone and be challenged and captivated. This writer's work is acclaimed in Australia, deservedly so.

> *C. M., in a review of "Something Special," in* Books for Keeps, *No. 40, September, 1986, p. 23.*

A "Redfeather Book" that is several cuts above the others in this new series—a deftly written Australian import.

Helping her mother prepare for a rummage sale, Sam(antha) falls asleep and dreams that the previous owners of four of the garments tell her that these were "something special"—the dress worn the night a young girl became engaged, a teacher's favorite standby, etc. Later, she sees each one purchased for a new life with a similar person—including a delightfully satirized, condescending old battle-ax who gets the ugly houndstooth suit, and the dear old gentleman who joyfully discovers the very robe his daughter gave away. An unusual story, beautifully structured and simply but gracefully told. Wisely, the publishers have retained the flavor of many phrases such as "All right lass, steady on"; among them, though, the unnecessary change to "Mommy" jars.

> *A review of "Something Special," in* Kirkus Reviews, *Vol. LVII, No. 21, November 1, 1989, p. 1597.*

The story is told in a light tone with lots of dialogue. Sam, her best friend, and the dream people are well developed in a short space. The adults, however, are not as realistic and tend to speak in clichés. Sam's mother is often referred to by her first name, which can be confusing. Average fare for readers not quite ready for Howe's *Bunnicula* (Atheneum, 1979) or Chew's witch stories, with enough twists to keep them wondering. (pp. 106, 108)

> *Elisabeth LeBris, in a review of "Something Special," in* School Library Journal, *Vol. 36, No. 1, January, 1990, pp. 106, 108.*

Pigs Might Fly (1986; U.S. edition as *The Pigs Are Flying!*)

Only people with a sense of the ridiculous can appreciate unlikely events. While very few adults have this capacity most children relish the ridiculous. For this reason Emily Rodda's book is bound to be a great success with young readers.

Rachael is bored and sick in bed. When Sandy drew her a picture with flying pigs it set off a string of events which took her from the Outside World to the Inside. Unlikely events in the Inside World are heralded by the pigs flying. The stronger the force of the "Grunter" the more the chance that unlikely events will occur. How Rachael gets back home and what she finds out when she does arrive back are unlikely events in themselves. This is a finely crafted book and the movement from the rational to the absurd and back again is smooth, and from the literary viewpoint, believeable. The humour used is never slapstick nor banal but on the other hand is not totally cerebral. Further, Rodda's capacity for storytelling will make this novel ideal for reading aloud as well as private reading.

A must from the primary school reader 9+ years.

> *Howard George, in a review of "Pigs Might Fly," in* Reading Time, *Vol. 31, No. 3, 1987, p. 66.*

It is hard to know what to say about a novel like this. It is a well-written, well characterised story with a lively dialogue. The plot, however, is decidedly odd.

In a time warped world outsiders are sometimes trapped due to a strange environmental condition which causes pigs to fly resulting in very weird goings on and excitements which for insiders are a trial but for outsiders, are pure delight.

Rachel becomes trapped and meets some very kind insiders who are quite normal human beings until the Pigs go up and then behave very oddly. Naturally she is homesick and wants to return to her family. Eventually she finds the key to home and on her return finds her father's best friend has also been on the inside. They have some bottled water from this strange place so that they can recapture the atmosphere whilst at home.

As you can appreciate the plot is very strange and whilst providing an enjoyable read for 9-12 year olds, the book is unlikely to prove of lasting interest.

> *L. A. S., in a review of "Pigs Might Fly," in* The Junior Bookshelf, *Vol. 52, No. 2, April, 1988, p. 94.*

Rodda has created a thoroughly imaginative tale which, while it draws upon material from classic fantasies, does so in a delightful and convincing manner. Rachel enters a magical fantasy world in which she encounters an unusual weather phenomenon—flying pigs. Sandy, an unusual family friend, provides the basic material for her to enter the fantasy world. Rodda displays her most creative material in the portrayal of the fantastic world. Flying pigs are the visual indicators of atmospheric storms, measured numerically on a "grunter" scale of 1 to 10. These storms also have the ability to alter characteristics and/or personalities of people and animals. Rodda's approach is humorous and thoroughly believable. The details of the fantastic setting are carefully etched. Readers will be amused at the little pig which emerges from a clock and says "oink-oink" rather than the traditional cuckoo. The answer to Rachel's quest for home lies (happily enough) within the local public library. In finding the answer for herself, she also solves the mystery of the *real* identity of the town librarian. An engaging fantasy for beginning fans of the genre. (pp. 185-86)

> *Karen P. Smith, in a review of "The Pigs Are Flying!" in* School Library Journal, *Vol. 35, No. 1, September, 1988, pp. 185-86.*

"Pigs is pigs," as the old saying goes. Or aren't they? In Emily Rodda's utterly delightful *The Pigs Are Flying!* fat pink porkers in great numbers fill the sky, looking uncharacteristically cloudlike, during peculiar storms called grunters. And just as these happy swine are not your run-of-the-mill pigs, the book is hardly your run-of-the-mill story. . . . A comfortable swirl of suspense, adventure, and amusing characters, the lighthearted fantasy is greatly enhanced by Noela Young's pen-and-ink illustrations, which marvelously capture the unusual little town and the elevated, contented pigs tumbling about the sky. A sort of *Wizard of Oz* for a slightly younger reading audience, the chapter book, which received the 1986 Australian Book of the Year Award, will surely garner an enthusiastic following in the northern hemisphere. As one character remarks, " 'It never pigs but it pours.' "

> *Karen Jameyson, in a review of "The Pigs Are Flying!" in* The Horn Book Magazine, *Vol. LXIV, No. 6, November-December, 1988, p. 784.*

This writer's *Something Special* is one of the best stories I know for six to eights, showing them how the numinous and the magical lie within the ordinary and the everyday. This new one has more pace and vigour, but the writer's ability to create a story 'world' is still strong, never fey.

Rachel just wishes that one day *something* (anything!) would happen—a common childhood emotion? It does— when pigs do begin to fly, and the world is turned topsy-turvy. A beautifully unfolded tale from an illuminating, fresh-voiced writer.

> *C. M., in a review of "Pigs Might Fly," in* Books for Keeps, *No. 55, March, 1989, p. 18.*

The Best-Kept Secret (1988)

Fantasy provides metaphors for human encounters and emotions as an alternative to the plain narrative in which it is often more difficult to strike any new note. An unnatural, occult or bizarre series of events and characters may intrigue and divert readers but it can easily be overdone;

here, perhaps more than in any other genre of writing for children, style and time and intellectual control are of enormous importance. This is the case even in a story as relatively simple as *The Best-Kept Secret,* which can be read as pure, enjoyable nonsense offering the kind of fanciful adventure which children around ten or so can find a welcome change from their own more predictable lives. When a visiting carousel is found equipped to convey selected people into the future, Joanna and her friend Cecilia decide to take the ride; imaginative Joanna does have a vision of the future but her friend sits tight and sees nothing. Each of their fellow riders finds a reason for the journey. Cross Mr. Brean, who repairs shoes, dropout Shark Murphy and the gloomy bank manager Milligan all return with certain reassurances about their lives and Joanna, who is not without courage, takes a hand in the fortunes of a stowaway, a small boy who gets lost in the future and is found to be surprisingly close to her. Black and white illustrations [by Noela Young] with a good deal of nostalgic charm seem to lean towards the heady excitement of the time-slip but the impulse for change felt by each character deepens the fiction and justifies the use of fanciful events as a way of approaching with fresh insight and with a certain moderation of tone some familiar problems in the people of a small community.

> *Margery Fisher, in a review of "The Best-Kept Secret," in* Growing Point, *Vol. 27, No. 5, January, 1989, p. 5088.*

As various film-makers have been quick to perceive, there is something about the relentless movement and music of the old-fashioned fairground carousel which, together with the theatricality of its paintwork, can make it a little disturbing. Emily Rodda's choice of such a machine as a device for time-travel, therefore, is well-rooted and feels exactly right. Her story is subtle and layered, and pricks at the emotions in all sorts of ways. Like all good fiction it calls for concentration and, perhaps, a second reading— in other words, here is something for the keen young reader to bite on.

> *Gerald Haigh, "Daredevils," in* The Times Educational Supplement, *No. 3790, February 17, 1989, p. B28.*

In another unusual fantasy from the Australian author of *Something Special,* a time journey via carousel marks a turning point for several characters—especially for Joanna, who discovers that she's about to become a big sister.

This deceptively simple tale includes several deftly sketched characters—notably a grocer distraught because his mother wants to go back to Italy; "The Shark," a young ne'er-do-well who finds a satisfying calling on the magic carousel; and a discouraged inventor whose imminent success is linked to Jo's observations in the future— even though memories of the journey have evaporated like a tantalizing dream. A charmingly original, neatly structured story. . . .

> *A review of "The Best-Kept Secret," in* Kirkus Reviews, *Vol. LVIII, No. 10, May 15, 1990, p. 802.*

Although Jo and her fellow passengers are not aware of

it, they all are at crossroads in their lives and are helped in coming to terms with choices they must make. This is a multi-faceted story, successful as a time-travel fantasy, as a novel about learning to accept changes in one's life, and as a commentary on human foibles. The author carefully resists tying up all the loose ends; Jo and her fellow explorers are destined to forget the details of their adventure (thus ensuring that the future remains "the best-kept secret"), but they keep the sense of peace acquired from all they have seen. Illustrated with black-and-white sketches, the story will make a thought-provoking read-aloud as well as a fascinating read-alone for young time-travel enthusiasts.

> *Kay Weisman, in a review of "The Best-Kept Secret," in* Booklist, *Vol. 87, No. 1, September 1, 1990, p. 52.*

Take a bit of *The Time Machine*, sprinkle in some *Tuck Everlasting* and a dash of the movie *Big* and the result is this fantasy approach to accepting that life is always changing. . . . The 17 short chapters spin by as quickly as the carousel due to Rodda's skill in drawing readers into the story early and keeping events building at a fast clip. The characters are uniformly warm, if quirky, and even the old town crab and Joanna's stick-in-the-mud friend are treated with understanding. Young's black-and-white drawings, with their rampant carousel horses and time travelers in glowing auras, capture the light spirit of the story. An amusing, optimistic chapter book fantasy to read alone or aloud. (pp. 79-80)

> *Joanne Aswell, in a review of "The Best-Kept Secret," in* School Library Journal, *Vol. 37, No. 1, January, 1991, pp. 79-80.*

Finders Keepers   **(1990)**

AUTHOR'S COMMENTARY

[*The following excerpt is from Rodda's acceptance speech for her Book of the Year award from the Children's Book Council of Australia.*]

Finders keepers is a fairly special book for me. It was my fourth book for children, and considering the old adage about things coming in threes I suppose I felt a bit superstitious, and wondered whether my fourth book would be as good as, and achieve the success of, its predecessors.

And then, *Finders keepers* was different in three very important ways, from the other three books I'd written. First, it was my first book with a new publisher—Omnibus Books. That situation is always nerve-wracking. What if they didn't like it? What if it was no good? How embarrassing to deliver your new publisher a dud. What if, because I was new, and had been successful before, they *didn't* like it and it *was* no good but they didn't like to *tell* me, and let me publish it anyway, warts and all?

I needn't have worried, as it turned out. There's no way Jane Covernton and Sue Williams would publish anything they didn't believe in. And *Finders keepers'* warts were ruthlessly pointed out to me to be dealt with before it reached proof stage.

Secondly, *Finders keepers* was the first book I'd written with a boy as the main character. When kids ask me about writing I always say, the best way to write well is to write about what you know well. I felt I knew girls well—I'd been one myself, after all. And very importantly I had a daughter who was seven when *Something special* was published, nine for *Pigs might fly* and eleven for *The best-kept secret.* I felt safe with girls—I thought I knew how they thought and felt,, and found it easy to imagine myself into their skins.

But boys? I grew up with two younger brothers, but I have to confess their ways were always mysteries to me. But by the time *The best-kept secret* was published I had three little boys of my own, as well as my daughter, and I was starting to learn about them too—starting to see how they felt and thought about things. It was easier than I'd thought, then, to write about Patrick in *Finders keepers.* But I wasn't altogether sure I'd done it well enough.

The third thing that made *Finders keepers* different was that it concentrated more than the others on the family relationships as a background to the fantasy. This made it longer, more challenging and a little more complicated, but very satisfying.

> *Emily Rodda, in a speech in* Reading Time, *Vol. XXXV, No. IV, 1991, p. 5.*

Emily Rodda has produced another interesting novel which could well be in contention for a future award listing. Somewhat different in subject matter to her previous plots, we are led into the fantasy world of a time-travel quiz show, in which Patrick hopes to win himself a "really great computer with lots of games".

Patrick's somewhat disorganised family form a perfect background to his appearances on a quiz show which exists in his fantasy world. He receives instructions on a television channel which doesn't exist and passes through a time barrier to play. The 'happy ending' is perhaps a little contrived but anything can happen in good fantasy.

The whole tale moves at a rapid pace, fantasy and reality interchanging so rapidly that sometimes the reader may wonder whether or not they are experiencing the real or the unreal. Although Patrick predominates the story, his sister Claire is an important foil and his parents are part of the ever changing pattern. Emily Rodda also has created quite believable characters as part of the quiz team. This fast moving story will delight many young readers as will Noela Young's splendid line drawings which support the text so well.

> *Laurie Copping, in a review of "Finders Keepers," in* Reading Time, *Vol. XXXIV, No. IV, 1990, p. 25.*

This is a book for the older newly independent reader. As with her previous books, Emily Rodda establishes and maintains the fantasy throughout. *Finders Keepers* features Rodda's first male hero, Patrick, who is a well-drawn, morally aware character. His quest in the world of lost objects on the 'other side' is convincing. The tension is sustained and the reader feels Patrick's sense of frustration when it appears that his quest will be thwarted. The clues which are given for Patrick's search are intriguing and well worked out. They demand the involvement of the reader, who, like Patrick, must solve the riddles to reach the next stage of the search. The moral dilemma with which Patrick is faced during his search is well done and adds a further dimension to the story.

Finders Keepers is a strongly plotted book which children enjoy. It is well written and has Rodda's usual sure touch with dialogue, which sounds realistic and natural as does the portrayal of family life. She has captured the way children think and feel. There are lively touches of humour which include some satirical touches for older children such as the send-up of the television games show and its hosts. It is a particularly amusing touch that the games master is a robot.

Despite its length, *Finders Keepers* is accessible to the more mature readers in [the younger readers] category, but provides a challenge and invites readers to become involved with the characters and plot.

> *The Judges of the Children's Book Council of Australia, "Younger Readers Book of the Year—Winner," in* Reading Time, *Vol. XXXV, No. III, 1991, p. 5.*

As Patrick struggles to win the computer he desperately

wants, he is forced to learn a hard truth about valuing things over people. In addition to teaching this poignant lesson, Rodda serves up at least one riotous situation per chapter and keeps her adventure moving at lightning speed—making for an uncommonly satisfying read. Young's line drawings deftly keep pace with the story's changing moods.

> *A review of "Finders Keepers," in* Publishers Weekly, *Vol. 238, No. 46, October 18, 1991, p. 64.*

Crumbs! (1990)

Emily Rodda's new book *Crumbs!* seems set to fully engage young readers, and their grown ups. Hero Pete's problem is initially seen as sibling rivalry but as the quick moving story develops we see the world of Saturday morning television and artificial additive baby biscuits combine to produce a mind boggling family problem. The language and particularly the humour is just what younger readers enjoy. . . . [This is] an excellent publication which is highly recommended.

> *Kathy Forward, in a review of "Crumbs!" in* Reading Time, *Vol. XXXV, No. II, 1991, p. 24.*

Children's
Literature
Review

How to Use This Index

The main reference

> **Baum, L(yman) Frank**
> 1856-1919.....15

list all author entries in this and previous volumes of *Children's Literature Review*.

The cross-references

> See also CA 103; 108; DLB 22; JRDA;
> MAICYA; MTCW; SATA 18; TCLC 7

list all author entries in the following Gale biographical and literary sources:

AAYA = *Authors & Artists for Young Adults*
AITN = *Authors in the News*
BLC = *Black Literature Criticism*
BW = *Black Writers*
CA = *Contemporary Authors*
CAAS = *Contemporary Authors Autobiography Series*
CABS = *Contemporary Authors Bibliographical Series*
CANR = *Contemporary Authors New Revision Series*
CAP = *Contemporary Authors Permanent Series*
CDALB = *Concise Dictionary of American Literary Biography*
CLC = *Contemporary Literary Criticism*
CLR = *Children's Literature Review*
CMLC = *Classical and Medieval Literature Criticism*
DA = *DISCovering Authors*
DC = *Drama Criticism*
DLB = *Dictionary of Literary Biography*
DLBD = *Dictionary of Literary Biography Documentary Series*
DLBY = *Dictionary of Literary Biography Yearbook*
HW = *Hispanic Writers*
JRDA = *Junior DISCovering Authors*
LC = *Literature Criticism from 1400 to 1800*
MAICYA = *Major Authors and Illustrators for Children and Young Adults*
MTCW = *Major 20th-Century Writers*
NCLC = *Nineteenth-Century Literature Criticism*
PC = *Poetry Criticism*
SAAS = *Something about the Author Autobiography Series*
SATA = *Something about the Author*
SSC = *Short Story Criticism*
TCLC = *Twentieth-Century Literary Criticism*
WLC = *World Literature Criticism, 1500 to the Present*
YABC = *Yesterday's Authors of Books for Children*

CUMULATIVE INDEX TO AUTHORS

CUMULATIVE INDEX TO NATIONALITIES

CUMULATIVE INDEX TO TITLES

231

Title Index

Title Index

Title Index

Title Index

Title Index

Title Index

Title Index

ISBN 0-8103-8471-X